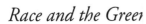

Race and the Green

environmental
history
and the
american
south

Race and the Greening of Atlanta

INEQUALITY, DEMOCRACY, AND ENVIRONMENTAL POLITICS IN AN ASCENDANT METROPOLIS

Christopher C. Sellers

The University of Georgia Press

Athens

This book was funded, in part, by generous support
from the Stony Brook History Department.

Most University of Georgia Press titles are
available from popular e-book vendors.

Printed digitally

Library of Congress Cataloging-in-Publication Data

Names: Sellers, Christopher C., author.
Title: Race and the greening of Atlanta : inequality, democracy, and environmental politics in
    an ascendant metropolis / Christopher C. Sellers.
Other titles: Environmental history and the American South.
Description: Athens : The University of Georgia Press, [2023] | Series: Environmental history
    and the American South | Includes bibliographical references and index.
Identifiers: LCCN 2022058109 | ISBN 9780820344072 (hardback) | ISBN 9780820344089
    (paperback) | ISBN 9780820364193 (epub) | ISBN 9780820364209 (pdf)
Subjects: LCSH: Civil rights movements—Georgia—Atlanta—History—20th century.
    | Environmentalism—Georgia—Atlanta—History—20th century. | Environmental
    justice—Georgia—Atlanta—History—20th century. | Atlanta (Ga.)—Environmental
    conditions—20th century. | Atlanta (Ga.)—Economic conditions—20th century. |
    Atlanta (Ga.)—History—20th century. | Atlanta (Ga.)—Race relations. | Atlanta (Ga.)—
    Politics and government—20th century.
Classification: LCC F294.A857 S45 2023 | DDC 975.8/231043—dc23/eng/20221209
LC record available at https://lccn.loc.gov/2022058109

To Julia and Phil, in reckoning with the southern history they lived

CONTENTS

FOREWORD

The epigraph Christopher Sellers chose for *Race and the Greening of Atlanta* is Langston Hughes's 1949 poem "Democracy." With the clarity and directness typical of Hughes's work, the verse serves as a five-stanza challenge, a demand for readers to face the unfulfilled promise of American ideals. African Americans "have as much right / As the other fellow," Hughes writes, and yet freedom and democracy are consistently denied to them. "I live here, too. / I want freedom just as you." Hughes calls the reader to action. "I tire so of hearing people say, / *Let things take their course*," he writes. "I do not need my freedom when I'm dead. / I cannot live on tomorrow's bread." The America that exists is not the America that could be, and it is up to not only African Americans but every citizen to make democracy real—and realistic—for all.[1]

Race and the Greening of Atlanta takes up Hughes's invocation, tracing the waxing and waning of democracy for poor and Black Atlantans from the "compromise and fear" of which Hughes writes to the civil rights activism that reaped what the poem describes as "freedom's seed." At first blush, this book is a political and civil rights history of Atlanta. Sellers details the denial of democracy to those outside the white elite in the early twentieth century under Jim Crow "rural authoritarianism." He then documents the midcentury transformation of Atlanta's governance to a truer and more inclusive democracy. Finally, he dissects the neoconservative retrenchment of the late twentieth and early twenty-first centuries that continues to permeate city affairs today. The exclusionary governance of Jim Crow is not dead, Sellers argues, and this work helps us understand why.

But *Race and Greening of Atlanta* is not just a political history rehashing civil rights–era events in the city famously "too busy to hate." Instead, Sellers uses a boundary-defying approach that reconsiders what political history should look like, resulting in a fuller, more holistic analysis of how Atlanta's culture, economics, and crucially, environment governed these swings of political history.

Sellers argues that much of Atlanta's democratic inequality was driven by economic inequality. Decades marked by a huge gap between rich and poor engendered more elitist governance; times of "compression," when the middle and lower classes had a larger share of the economy, led to more inclusive views of who deserved a political voice and who policies should benefit. While this may not come as a surprise, the joining of economic and political history is a critically underutilized tactic among historians. Sellers's work draws on the new histories of capitalism to tease out the consequential linkages between the ballot box and the pocketbook in ways that are both pathbreaking and timely.

Critically, Sellers sees the physical, urban environment of Atlanta as the fulcrum around which politics and economy moved. Political historians have largely failed to study how environmental spaces both reflected and reinforced the way that poor and Black Atlantans were systematically shut out of city governance. For their part, environmental historians often eschew political analysis, unless it applies to the environmental movement. But Sellers reminds us that politics begins where we live—and that means paying attention to the material environmental change that affects citizens' lives. He writes that racism and classism manifested themselves in infrastructure, housing, drinking water, air pollution, access to sewer lines, and more. Minority enclaves and low-income housing existed among higher levels of pollution, disease, and industrial contamination, creating a cycle in which polluted neighborhoods remained the poorest neighborhoods. The perceived "filth" of those areas solidified economic, political, and racial stigma, leading to the uneven application of such "color-blind" policies as slum removal and freeway placement that disproportionately affected people of color. In sum, the sprawling civil rights movement in Atlanta was not only concerned with ideals such as freedom and democracy but the way those ideals affected the urban landscapes that activists inhabited.

In this way, *Race and the Greening of Atlanta* also brings to mind another Langston Hughes poem: "Let America Be America Again," published in 1936. It is a stirring, hopeful piece that ends with a reflection on the central role nature plays in the experience of democracy—just as Sellers does. "From those who live like leeches on the people's lives," the poem reads, we must "redeem / The land, the mines, the plants, the rivers." True equality hinges on the very type of environmental politics that Sellers explores here. Only then, as Hughes writes, can we "make America again!"[2]

Erin Stewart Mauldin and James C. Giesen

Series Editors

Notes

1. Langston Hughes, "Democracy," in *The Collected Poems of Langston Hughes*, ed. Arnold Rampersad and David Roessel (New York: Vintage Classics, 1994), 289.

2. Langston Hughes, "Let America Be America Again," in Rampersad and Roessel, *Collected Poems of Langston Hughes*, 191.

Race and the Greening of Atlanta

"Freedom" by Langston Hughes (1949)

Freedom will not come
Today, this year
     Nor ever
Through compromise and fear.

I have as much right
As the other fellow has
     To stand
On my two feet
And own the land.

I tire so of hearing people say,
Let things take their course.
Tomorrow is another day.
I do not need my freedom when I'm dead.
I cannot live on tomorrow's bread.
     Freedom
     Is a strong seed
     Planted
     In a great need.

     I live here, too.
     I want freedom
     Just as you.

"Democracy" is the title for the 1943 original in *Jim Crow's Last Stand*.

The View from Stone Mountain

The 2020 election cliff-hanger turned much of the United States into Georgia watchers. I've been watching for much longer. My earliest memory of the state is of a granite dome flashing past the car window as my family drove down I-85 into Atlanta on a summer day in 1969. Stone Mountain, that looming, difficult-to-miss protrusion of ancient geological forces, announced our approach to one of the South's largest and most prosperous metropolises. Jutting up just thirteen miles east of downtown, acquired by Georgia in the late 1950s to convert into a state park, Stone Mountain had become an obligatory stopover for tourists coming to the big city from southern hinterlands like the small town in western North Carolina where my family lived.

We visited a year before the park's grand opening. If photos of the crowds attending Vice President Spiro Agnew's speech at that event are any indication, the faces of the visiting crowds were overwhelmingly white. That was hardly surprising, given the park's main attraction at the time. Shiny new museum buildings and lighting all directed the paths and eyes of visitors toward a carving for which the mountain had now become famous, of the heads and torsos of the Confederacy's heroes, President Jefferson Davis and his generals Robert E. Lee and Thomas J. "Stonewall" Jackson. Begun in the 1920s and restarted in 1964, it would be finished only some eight years later.[1] My fourteen-year-old eyes were curiously underwhelmed by the nearly completed carving. Those Confederate leaders just seemed puny compared to the granite face into which they had been etched.

A return visit to Stone Mountain Park in 2013 confirmed this impression from nearly half a century earlier, but the park itself had become a very different place. The parking lot and concession booths at the foot of the granite face were much like those of an amusement or water park any place in the United States. The main lawn and a front first-floor gallery still centered around the carving. In the gift shop "stars and bars" memorabilia were still sold, and the sculpture still adorned the front of many a T-shirt. But emblems of the Confederacy were now relegated to two walls of the store, and on the shirts a U.S. flag and eagle flew above the carved heads of Confederate leaders. The second floor of the museum now told a more varied story centering on the mountain itself: from its geological origins to the many groups who had lived around it and visited it—Native and African Americans as well as whites. The complexion of visitors had also changed. Gathering on the great lawn stretched out before the sculpture, in preparation for a free concert scheduled at dusk, were many couples, families, and youthful cadres whose skin was Black or Brown. The contrast with earlier times was compounded when I ventured up along the mile-long trail to the summit. There, by my own informal count, nearly 40 percent of the people belonged to minority groups, enjoying a vista that spanned from the Atlanta skyline to the north Georgia hills. Displays in the small museum at the summit featured the plant and animal life of the huge granite outcrop on which we stood, much of it now endangered or rare. Nothing I saw atop recalled what only a single tucked-away paragraph in the museum below had intimated: a century before, ceremonies on this mountaintop had catalyzed the rebirth of the Ku Klux Klan.

Atlanta's most renowned natural icon, Stone Mountain poses riddles running to the heart of this book. A mere twenty minutes' drive from downtown, this hulking reminder of the region's history bears the imprints of two starkly clashing visions of its peopled past, still squaring off uneasily against each other. Resting on a car-owning and souvenir-buying affluence achieved over the mid-twentieth century, the one now prevailing is not just Black and white but multicolored and, to tell from my stroll, much more inclusive and democratic. Looking backward, the park's curators have discovered a former racial diversity that can ground its claims on the present and, far from incidentally, a nature centered on the enduring geological and ecological features of this mountain. This window on yesteryear turns a squinting or indifferent eye on its predecessor, that other version of the past so evident here, of an Atlanta and South still haunted by the "Lost Cause" defeated in the Civil War. In that past, which southerners of a subsequent generation (including me) knew mostly from textbooks and family stories, naked racism and violence cohabited with "Southern hospitality," and would-be gentility with widespread poverty. Half a century and more after losing that war itself, the region's rulers cast a fond eye back on defenders of slavery and, in the name of "white supremacy," crafted an exclusionary, authoritarian governance. They marshaled this mountain in their service, scratching a lasting, monumental rendition of its defeated, long-dead heroes in its granite. It was a period of cruelties great and small, one that has indeed remained "with us," as William Faulkner so famously put it, through tales told by parents, grandparents, teachers, and media, as well as by this carved-up slice of mountainside.[2] Beyond this granite face, this past has done more than just linger. Its latter-day descendants have actually prevailed in U.S. politics, in the unabashedly white nationalism unleashed during the 2016 election campaign and in the presidency that followed.

Stone Mountain's strange incongruities bespeak those wrenching changes through which Atlanta and the U.S. South have passed during the twentieth century, so many of which have left tracks on the mountainside. This book makes the case for not severing practices like park making into a separate "environmental history" but, instead, treating the urban environment as a central thread for a more encompassing account of Atlanta's and the South's transformation. The ensuing pages weave together narratives told mostly in isolation from one another. The South's political and economic history are customarily told with little reference to environmental history or politics, while environmental histories of the South usually sideline issues of political economy. This book aims to show just how deeply interconnected the political, economic, and environmental strands of the South's twentieth-century history were, even to the point that we cannot fully understand one without the others. I do so through three environmental emphases, each of them pointing to other underappreciated facets of this region's past-century transformation, cultural and social as well as political.

First, whether grasped in a mountain or as metaphor, nature furnished the raw material for Atlantans of many stripes to express their most fundamental hopes and dreams, whether secular or religious, whether past- or future-oriented. Second, much of what was systemic about the racism and classism so pivotal to this history stemmed from how they came to be concretely translated into buildings and plantings, into infrastructure as well as underlying land, and into the city's connective tissues of water and air. In ways that ran deeper than either skin color or paychecks, changes in Atlanta's urban environments solidified advantages and disadvantages, enfolding and shielding some communities while imposing vulnerabilities on others in ways materially sustained from one generation to the next. Third, among the most critical facets of the South's transformation was a new "environmental" vein of politics, which many of today's urban as well as political historians still struggle to address or appreciate. Atlanta's increasingly organized and overwhelmingly white environmental movement of the 1960s and 1970s joined with Atlanta's Black leaders to successfully push for Georgia's democratization. Later on, as an environmental justice movement engaged more Black environmentalists, a neoconservatism gained traction among whites by reframing environmentalism as governmental overreach, even as the environmental consumption of its adherents proceeded apace.

Overall, I mean to show how an environmental history of metropolitan inequality can provide a kind of analytic missing link, better illuminating how economic trends connect to important political transformations. Through historical narrative I argue that the ties between decades-long redistributions of wealth and political change can be direct but also more indirect, as skewing or converging trends in the apportionment of a city's riches were translated into not just paychecks or pocketbooks but urban environmental change. Material consequences ensued for where so many Atlantans lived, worked, and played and also in the extra-economic meanings they themselves attached to these places. Here as well lie many underappreciated dynamics of Atlanta's politics of democratization by the 1960s and 1970s and its replacement by the political divisions and new conservatism of the 1980s and 1990s. By pivoting Atlanta's economic and political history around this environmental fulcrum, this book tells the story of the South's lurching passage from Jim Crow to today, when an inclusive, all-too-amnesic new is beset by an often resentful recharging of the old.

This book couples its environmental emphases with a narrative about Atlanta's democratization over the mid-twentieth century and partial de-democratization by the early twenty-first. After the violence-ridden demise of its Reconstruction-era democracy, the city and its state came under the sway of what political scientist V. O. Key Jr. in 1949 gingerly termed "rustic rule," redubbed more forthrightly by his recent colleagues as "subnational" or "racial authoritarianism."[3] Then, from the 1930s and 1940s onward, governments exclusively dominated by a white elite opened doors to African American power and influence, and not just Blacks but all Atlantans gained a greater say in government, reversing a lopsided favoring of rural voters. In the process new attitudes came to predominate not just about whom government served but about what and how much it should do, a shift pushed, I argue, not just by Black civil rights activists and their white allies but by Georgia's nascent environmental movement. The door opened for expanding public services—education, welfare, and the parks and public health measures then being newly cast as "environmental" causes—which, at least in theory, benefited Blacks as well as whites, the poor as well as the middle class. But democratization here as elsewhere was grounded in contingencies that themselves turned out to be quite vulnerable. By the early decades of the twenty-first century, it was undergoing a partial reversal. Voting and electoral representation faced growing challenges, as government itself was becoming less robustly participatory and less capable, with diminishing boons for a broader public as well as lower costs and loosening strictures for economic elites.[4]

To explain why Atlanta's democratization happened but then turned out to be so assailable, I take as my starting point some basic connections between politics and economy. Most simply, the concentration of wealth nourishes the concentration of political power, whereas a widening or flattening distribution of wealth encourages democratization. As this history seeks to show, this inverse relationship between wealth concentration and democracy is not just some glib truism. Taking it seriously, I frame waning versus waxing redistribution of riches as defining features of the different kinds of capitalism that prevailed in Atlanta during different eras. Under a "cleavage capitalism," distribution of the city's riches relentlessly skewed toward the top. Under a more "compressive capitalism," wealth came to be redistributed toward the middle and lower reaches of the city's economic ladder. Whether the capitalism of a given period inclined toward cleavage or compression profoundly impacted this city's and region's twentieth-century political twists and turns. Over the past decade historians have forged a new history of capitalism that situates the U.S. South more front and center, through a renewed appreciation of slavery's importance to the nineteenth-century global economy.[5] Unpacking how shifts in the twentieth-century South's systems for distributing wealth connected to waxing as well as waning democratization extends this southern focus in the history of capitalism much closer to the present day.

The conflicting visions of the southern past found on Stone Mountain in the early twenty-first century reflect these two broadly contrasting orientations of Atlanta's version of capitalism over the century's course. During the Jim Crow regime, which provides the starting point of this history, what C. Vann Woodward described as Atlanta's and the rest of the region's "long and quite un-American experience with poverty" unfolded in the context of a cleavage capitalism that is equally vital to understanding their undemocratic politics.[6] Compared to northern cities, more of Atlanta's riches lay in the hands of a privileged few, and over the early twentieth century, their share was growing. Not just Blacks were affected; Atlanta acquired a smaller and less prosperous white middle class than cities in other U.S. regions. From the 1930s, however, a new equalizing turn began channeling a growing portion of this city's riches into the pocketbooks and property holding of middle ranks of earners. Atlanta thereby underwent its own version of what economists have recognized as a "Great Compression."[7] While many features of this city's new compressive capitalism were shared across much of the Western industrial world, in the United States those laws and policies that became known as the New Deal spurred and sustained these trends. This widening distribution of wealth and ownership across Atlanta over the midcentury did not just coincide with the fall of Jim Crow authoritarianism, I argue, but helped catalyze it. It did so, in important part, through urban environmental transformations. Then, from the 1970s onward, as cleavage capitalism once more overtook this metropolis, environmental as well as political seeds were successfully sown for curbing or stymying many democratizing achievements.

This book affirms the growing commonalities between the South and West after World War II established by recent scholars: industrialization with its attendant labor struggles; suburbanization with its racial conflicts and anti-tax conservatism; and globalization with its newly arriving trade and immigrants.[8] Through the prism of Atlanta, I seek to square these trends with the persistence of less-than-democratic political institutions across this region, from the "southern cage" imposed on 1930s legislation by southern Democrats to a subnational authoritarianism that endured through much of the South into the 1960s.[9] Atlanta's history also demands a different perspective on the New Deal and its aftermath than can be found in the U.S. North and Midwest, whose urban experiences have bolstered historical explanations of its state building as impelled by "economic" or "consumer citizenship."[10] In this southern city unions were less peopled and less powerful, and pervasive poverty limited the scope of consumer advocacy. As my environmental analysis shows, Atlanta's periphery had a very different look from that of counterparts in richer U.S. regions, from a greater reliance on rentals and Black renters to a harsher and more rural style of poverty than in its downtown. Far from making Atlanta "exceptional," however, I argue that these features made it like more like other metropolises in the Global South, what has long been known as the "developing world."[11] Were I somehow to have ascended Stone Mountain around 1960 with my adult brain and a telescope, along the city's edges I would have seen a mixture of shantytowns as well as treed suburbs, more like Monterrey or Manila than Boston or Minneapolis, where middle-class suburbs dominated. Only afterward did this city jump historical tracks, to become a thriving exemplar of the United States' Sunbelt.[12]

The civil rights movement provided the earliest and in many ways most formidable post–World War II challenge to political control by a white business elite, especially as the Black share of the city's population grew.[13] The class divisions and dynamics underlying this movement and its allies have received much attention from historians, as have the racial inequities, segregation, tensions, and conflicts to which this movement responded, belying the boosterish depiction of this city as "too busy to hate."[14] By framing this post–World War II transition as one from cleavage to compression capitalism and by turning environmental as well as racial and economic lenses on this city's contrasting and clashing corners, I track the roots and rise of this and other parallel political forces. Black as well as white, together they challenged and successfully overturned racial authoritarianism. With workplace organizing stymied through right-to-work laws as well as a racially divided workforce, the consciousness and collective action that drove democratizing arose out of the neighborhoods where Atlantans lived, along with other spaces of civil society—the churches, parks, and meeting halls where they congregated.[15]

In the city's push toward greater democracy, two alternative political projects then proved especially influential: not just its well-studied civil rights movement but an environmental movement whose Georgia variants remain little known.[16] Building on work especially in urban environmental history, this book seeks a more thorough integration of histories of one city's civil rights and environmental mobilizations.[17] Of these two, that for civil rights has received vastly more attention, and justifiably so.[18] By lumping rather than splitting the different strands of civil rights citizenship, from the Atlanta Urban League (AUL) to the Southern Christian Leadership Conference (SCLC) to the Student Nonviolent Coordinating Committee (SNCC), I seek to clarify just how deeply it contrasted with that propounded by Atlanta's environmentalists.[19] At the same time, Atlanta's celebrated civil rights movement had environmental facets and even a nature mindedness that have gone largely unexplored. The harsh ecology of urban slums as well as the massive environmental devastation of "urban renewal" helped propel civil rights activism. Aspirations stirred by a middle-class greenery of parks, homes, and campuses as well as the nature-invoking rhetoric of Black preachers also pulled it along. Additionally, I follow the birth and development of Atlanta's environmental movement, from the Georgia Conservancy and Friends of the River to the Sierra Club, through the later emergence of a movement for environmental justice. Placing the histories of all these post–World War II movements side by side nevertheless demonstrates how, despite abundant contrasts, both shared roots in the new compression capitalism, and both promoted more democratic visions of government than did Jim Crow's rulers.

Few who have followed more recent democratizing transitions around the world will be surprised that an environmental movement was critical to the fall of racial authoritarianism in the U.S. South. From the civic mobilizations that helped catalyze the fall of the Soviet Union, to the new "ecology" groups that have helped spur democratizing in places as diverse as Taiwan and Mexico, to today's China, environmental mobilizations have often provided authoritarian and less democratic regimes with some of their toughest challenges.[20] So it was, as well, in postwar Atlanta. Drawing on different frameworks than its civil rights counterparts, Atlanta's environmental movement was, not surprisingly, much whiter, and those "environments" it found worth promoting and defending were precisely those favored or even already inhabited by a white, suburban middle class. The combined effect of this region's environmental as well as civil rights movements was greater than what either could have achieved alone: reviving democracy in a region long unused to it, thus erasing one other critical difference persisting into the 1960s between Atlanta and other southern cities and their northern and western U.S. counterparts. By the same token, when not-so-democratic political forces began to consolidate around Atlanta from the 1970s and 1980s, not just the aspirations of civil rights leaders but environmental causes, laws, and agencies emerged as prime political targets.

While this history is fundamentally about Atlanta, starting and ending with the city itself, my exploration of its environmental politics also extends into the many relevant levels of government, what political scientists term a "multilevel" approach.[21] The city's new environmental regime had not just a city-level but a regional- and state-level genesis, as Georgia's gubernatorial modernizers from Carl Sanders to Jimmy Carter sought support from a newly empowered urban electorate and went on to thoroughly reorganize Georgia's environmental oversight. Then elected president, Carter also led a final cementing of a new federal environmental regime with far-reaching impacts on Atlanta itself. To compare governmental workings across this period, also to ease my navigation between the many layers of the state involved, I've concentrated especially on those realms that by the 1970s were reframed as "environmental": sanitation, pollution, and park making. By following policy making in these areas before as well as during and after the invention of what I've elsewhere described as the "environmental umbrella," I situate this city's evolving version of environmentalism within the more over-arching rubric of "environmental politics." By that I mean political battles fought over physical threats to places and lives that can be retrospectively identified as "environmental," using today's meaning of that term (broadened as it has become through movements for environmental justice, to "where we live, work, and play").[22] I thereby aim for my history to encompass many, including civil rights activists who never saw themselves as environmentalists, also those who came to oppose the environmentalists' causes, that multiheaded and mutating hydra that Samuel Hays styled the "environmental opposition."[23] After all, as Hays was well aware, the frustrations faced by those favoring environmental causes can be understood only through the study of those mobilizations and politics that arose to systematically oppose environmentalism itself.

The first two-thirds of this book follow the arc of Atlanta's democratization as its brand of capitalism turned increasingly compressive. An initial chapter on Atlanta's early twentieth-century cleavage capitalism looks at the "countrified" environments and "rustic" authoritarian rule associated with it, then follows how a more compressive capitalism began to take shape. Chapters 2 through 4 then look at the expansion of Atlanta's middle classes from the 1940s into the 1960s, Black as well as white; the new politics they spawned; and the democratization that followed. Even as compression capitalism fueled a highly racialized and localized defensiveness among many white property owners, it also fostered new opportunities for ownership and education and, with these, alternative senses of citizenship that were broadly collective and public minded and not so reducible to economic terms.

Chapter 2 looks at how environmental changes across Atlanta's Black communities, poor as well as middle class, fostered its movement for civil rights. From the postwar campaign of the AUL for Black housing to the "slum" destruction of urban renewal to the turn to "direct action" by the SCLC and SNCC, environmental backdrops provoked and nourished a civil rights citizenship increasingly at odds with the racial authoritarianism of Jim Crow. Chapter 3, on water pollution, explores the inequalities of a waterborne waste-disposal system increasingly overburdened by the city's postwar growth. Georgia's racial authoritarians responded, but with a conciliatory approach that left pollution control largely in private and municipal hands. Only as the state democratized did a more evenhanded and forceful oversight of the city's waters arise, though it worked more effectively for Atlanta's middle-class whites than for many of the city's Blacks. Chapter 4 then follows the emergence of Atlanta's environmental movement and its historical contributions to the city's democratization, from groups like the Georgia Conservancy and Sierra Club to the swelling mobilizations against freeway building and for "saving the river" (i.e., the Chattahoochee). Those who pioneered an environmental citizenship for Atlanta lived almost exclusively in the white and more affluent sides of town. Rooted as they and Atlanta's civil rights activists were in middle-class places and circumstances at least until the mid-1960s, both challenged minimalist and marginally democratic governments on behalf of more broadly public interests: asserting all Blacks' rights to spaces reserved for a white public such as restaurants and parks, for instance, or insisting that fewer pollutants be discharged into the city's rivers, air, and dumps. Predictably, the environments and dilemmas of Atlanta's poor and working classes went mostly unseen by the middle-class activists impelling much of Georgia's democratizing. Then, as also explored in chapter 4, civil rights activists from SCLC and SNCC did seek to fold these groups in, initially augmenting their movement's successes. But Atlanta's environmentalists pointedly did not.

By the early 1970s, when I first looked down on Atlanta from Stone Mountain, it was already in many respects joining a national mainstream, with political consequences that are the subject of chapter 5. Georgia's "rustic," democratically challenged rule seemed vanquished, and this city's racial divides were becoming more like those in the rest of the nation, based largely in residential real estate rather than in Jim Crow laws. Atlanta's metropolitan growth no longer moved along the same historical trajectory as cities in Mexico or Central America but instead more closely mirrored the affluent sprawl of cities in the U.S. North and West.[24] If both white environmental activists and Black civil rights leaders still rarely saw much overlap between their causes, enterprising politicians harnessed the electoral power of both. Their alliance at the ballot box helps explains the successes of Jimmy Carter, both as governor and as president, as well as the rise of Black political leadership, from Maynard Jackson's election as mayor to Andrew Young's attainment of a congressional seat. A powerful grassroots tide pushing the democratization of city and state governments crested during the mid-1970s, depriving the city's white business elite of its customary grip on decision making at city hall and instituting, among other changes, a new participatory version of city planning.[25] Such ventures, in conjunction with new state and federal environmental laws, placed a newfound faith in citizens' own choices and judgments, incorporating these into governmental decision making to make it more responsive to those whom it served. At least that was the hope.

As chapter 6 then explores, as Atlanta's growth accelerated over the late twentieth century, cleavage capitalism underwent a revival. Had I returned to look down from the mountain's peak by the 1990s, I would have seen its most visible consequences: glittering "edge cities," whose profusion of subdivisions, malls, and office and industrial parks outshone not just other southern cities but much of the rest of the nation.[26] Over this same while, the capitalism that drove this sprawl was shifting its favor from a middle class toward the upper echelons of earners and owners. For all the accomplishments of the movement for civil rights, the return of cleavage capitalism to Atlanta weighed most heavily on those whose skin was Black, from fewer unions to a lesser dependence on manufacturing to impeded homeownership. With these newer dynamics magnifying older legacies, by 2000 social scientists were characterizing a modern "Atlanta paradox": this seemingly affluent city was afflicted with an inequality that was two pronged.[27] One of these prongs was economic, and more recent studies confirm that Atlanta nears or tops the nation's highest ranks for its income gap between the wealthiest and the rest and also for stymied socioeconomic mobility.[28] The other prong, "of substantial racial segregation in a community with a reputation for good race relations," owed much to what had happened to its downtown. As Black leaders sought ways of bridging between urban-core and suburban Blacks, they waded deeper into environmental issues, becoming among the city's most empowered purveyors of environmental advocacy. These initiatives, in parallel with many others by white environmentalists, made the 1980s into a heyday for Georgia's environmentalism. In the process the base and preferred place of much of Atlanta's environmental movement was shifting cityward, as rising concerns about fossil fuels cast further aspersions on car use and as a "New Urbanism," by selling denser housing and mixed-use neighborhoods with pitches of carless "walkability," helped hitch this era's cleavage capitalism to environmental ideals.

Chapter 7 follows how, with a federal environmental regime in place and with those who could afford suburban homeownership increasingly confined to an upper middle class or else pushed farther out, newer suburbs and exurbs served as launching pads for the third political mobilization featured in this book. Stripping away the connective and communal in property owning, a renewed or neoconservatism favored only private environmental consumption, at the growing expense especially of environmental citizenship. Around Atlanta, as elsewhere in the South, churches undergoing a fundamentalist resurgence provided an important civil-society anchor for this movement, as did a coalescent political project taking aim at the new federal oversight of the environment and workplaces as impediments to market freedom. Over these decades neoconservative politicians in the Atlanta area cobbled together coalitions out of these stirrings that translated into electoral clout, eventually converging on the Republican Party as their primary vessel. Uniting white rural with white suburban voters, enterprising conservative politicians consolidated a white electoral alliance between business owners, propertied professionals, and a working class increasing unsettled by its slipping footholds in the metropolis. Newt Gingrich's political career, launched from the 1970s in the outer suburban reaches of the Atlanta metropolis, exemplifies the centrality of environmental politics to their strategies. Starting off by touting his involvement with the Georgia Conservancy, he then owed much of his political success to his abandonment of environmental issues and advocacy, increasingly associated with downtown and its Black leadership.[29]

Overall, though the Stone Mountain I returned to in 2013 still looked more democratic, metro Atlanta had, over the preceding decades, become a significantly less democratic place. The 1970s dreams of more participatory planning and of a more regional governance had faded, as had the clout and civic vitality of so many of the city's neighborhoods. In agency hearings, the courts, and the media, wealthy families and business interests could marshal far greater sums to make their case than could environmental, civil rights, or other public-interest groups. Congressional and other elections had turned far more professionalized and media dependent, making them much more expensive and dependent on wealthy donors. Politicians now found success by campaigning against the very idea of government and boasted of making the state both less capacious and less oriented to broader public needs. Across electoral playing fields opened decades before by Atlanta's democratizing, as wealth had been concentrating, new imbalances of political power had also consolidated. From a longer point of view, however, running back to the early twentieth century, this twin pooling of wealth and power, attended by swells of racial vituperation, marked something of a restoration.

In revolving the arc of this book around the rise and partial fall of a more democratic Atlanta, I've written a history that draws on political science and economics nearly as much as it does on environmental and urban history. Environmental history was born in the 1970s and 1980s through the carving out of important historical terrain neglected by existing modes of political and economic history, from which the field's pioneers took great care to distinguish it. But that happened in a time when—the first Reagan administration aside—both political parties largely accepted the precepts of environmental citizenship. Our present moment, when a major party long in charge of Georgia's as well as our nation's government has largely turned on those tenets, cries out for more environmental historians to ponder our political economy. That means building bridges to fields that have continued to study it and crafting new methodological hybrids such as this one. Urban historians, long more preoccupied by racial and class inequities and their politics, have also not yet seen a single-city study like this one, integrating these factors with environmental counterparts as well as long-term national and global trends in wealth distribution and urban form.

Situating Atlanta's twentieth century within these larger trajectories helps explain much about not just today's Atlanta and today's South but today's America. Before as well as after the South veered from "colonial" periphery to economic dynamo, Atlanta's historical experience illuminates the vital, if changing, role this region has played in the twentieth-century United States. This city's past also speaks to core dilemmas our whole country faces as we move deeper into the current century. Divagating between reducing and exacerbating inequality, between nourishing and undermining democracy, and between strengthening and softening environmental protections, the unsteadiness of this city's twentieth-century arc lays bare those crossroads at which our nation now stands, on whose navigation all Americans' futures will hinge.

CHAPTER I

Countrified City

As Atlanta struggled through the depths of the Great Depression, two of its most prominent churches, one Black and the other white, brought in new leaders. After losing longtime pastor Adam D. Williams to illness in 1931, Ebenezer Baptist tapped Martin L. King Sr. to take over the pulpit. This son of a sharecropper, now married to Williams's daughter, stepped in to guide what was already a prominent congregation in Atlanta's Black community, lying near the heart of its Black business district, along Auburn Avenue.[1] Three years later Atlanta's First Methodist Church, on the white side of a deeply segregated downtown, brought in Edward G. Mackay, "among the South's leading Methodist ministers," to lead its flock. Born in Ireland and having arrived in the United States nearly thirty years earlier to attend Emory University, just outside Atlanta's eastern city limits, Mackay had served a succession of churches in Alabama and north Georgia alongside brief stints teaching college.[2] Mackay's posting at First Methodist brought his family back to Druid Hills, a subdivision near Emory designed by the nationally renowned landscape architect Frederick Law Olmsted, exclusively for well-off whites (see map 1.1).

King's and Mackay's appointments culminated the social ascent of each into some of the city's most privileged circles, one Black and the other white. Like most other Atlantans of this time, both had been born in a countryside. King had grown up in Henry County, Georgia, and Mackay in rural South Ulster, later part of northern Ireland. Now preaching at such prominent Atlanta pulpits, they and their families would weather the Depression and New Deal ensconced within more affluent houses and neighborhoods on opposite sides of the city's starkly drawn color line. Out of both households would come offspring who helped lead post–World War II movements to overturn the deeply undemocratic governments that ruled their city and state. Martin Luther King Jr.'s part in Atlanta's and the nation's civil rights movement needs no introduction, but Mackay's son James Edward Mackay also had a steady and significant hand in Georgia's anti-authoritarian politics, first as a lawyer-activist, then as state legislator and congressperson, and finally as environmen-

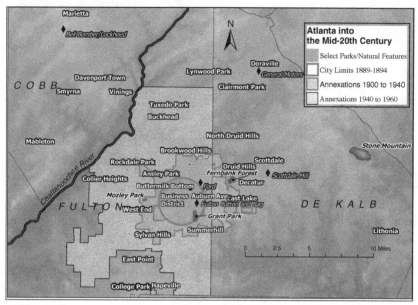

MAP 1.1. Atlanta's places and growth of city limits, 1889–1960. Map by author. *Sources*: "Annexations," Atlanta Regional Commission, accessed November 2, 2022, https://opendata.atlanta regional.com/datasets/coaplangis::annexations-3/explore?location=33.767168%2C-84.436020 %2C12.45; Jonathan Musser, "USGS Digital Elevation Model 1:250,000," U.S. Geological Survey, accessed November 4, 2022, https://apps.nationalmap.gov/downloader/; "Atlanta, Georgia," Google Maps, accessed September 2016, https://www.google.com/maps/place/Atlanta,+GA/@33.7673 806,-84.7076902,11z/data=!3m1!4b1!4m5!3m4!1s0x88f5045d6993098d:0x66fede2f990b630b!8m2! 3d33.7489954!4d-84.3879824.

tal leader. Both sons followed examples set by their pastor fathers. The elder King and Mackay had stepped out from their pulpits to publicly confront a racial authoritarianism that, in the Atlanta and Georgia of the 1930s and 1940s, held the upper hand.

The same 1932 election that propelled Franklin Roosevelt to the White House also inaugurated a Talmadgism that would dominate Georgia for the next three decades, by elevating Eugene Talmadge to the Georgia governor's mansion. Over the ensuing years, the political consequences of Talmadge's ascent would range across all levels of government that held sway over Atlantans and other Georgians. Talmadgists as well as their occasionally victorious opponents belonged to what would remain for many years the region's single viable political party, the Democrats. The party's ruling faction would defend how they were elected to run city and state or to represent both in Washington by an extremely narrow slice of the citizenry, the better-off whites. Beyond the ballot box Talmadge and his allies sought a government of minimal cost and scope, geared mainly to serve white economic elites. They dominated city and state thanks not only to mass disenfranchisement and racial segregation, upheld by laws and social customs, but also to white supremacist and steeply hierarchical notions of civic belonging, a Jim Crow citizenship.

Undergirding these distinctly undemocratic notions and practices was how Atlanta, despite its much-touted reputation as the seat of a "New South," remained smaller, poorer, and less well provisioned than comparable metropolises in richer U.S. regions. The stinginess of its state and local governments was only partly responsible, one facet of more fundamental dynamics. The poverty that plagued the South over the nineteenth into the early twentieth century reflected a "colonial" bind shared with the rest of the developing world as land grabs by Western powers accelerated.[3] Moreover, as the urban hub for such a poor region, Atlanta remained shackled to what historians David Carlton and Peter Coclanis dubbed "the dead weight of [its] impoverished and backward countryside."[4]

Recent literature on the stark and growing concentration of wealth through much of the early twentieth-century world offers an additional context within which to understand this city's and region's "colonial economy." Accompanying Atlanta's relatively slow growth and persistent poverty was a growing unevenness in the distribution of its riches. This gap, characteristic also of many other parts of the world, made for a global trend toward cleavage capitalism. Seen from this angle, Atlanta's early twentieth-century economy was anything but "backward"; rather, it was an American face of unsettling global tides. The growing economic unevenness helped nourish and sustain the racial authoritarianism that both generations of Kings and Mackays confronted, through its effects on Atlantans' sources of livelihood as well as on the environments in which they lived.

In contrast to late nineteenth- and early twentieth-century cities elsewhere in the United States, Jim Crow Atlanta joined other southern cities in having a more "rural environment." The reasons why began not just with the rural backgrounds of so many Atlantans but with their more limited means.[5] And, as a growing share of the city's wealth was channeled to a white elite at the expense of any middle class and as state and local governments operated on shoestrings and ignored Black interests and needs, what was "rural" about different corners of Atlanta varied ever more sharply by race and class. For a few richer whites, it meant mansions or planned, planted, spacious, and racially exclusive suburbs. For most others, it meant living with only a partial share of urban comforts and services that city dwellers in other corners of the nation increasingly took for granted. For poor Blacks as well as the poorest whites, it meant living on the city's periphery, in bare and unprovisioned countryside, akin to urban edges in the developing world. Stark contrasts between the city's living environments furnished visible rationales for those racial and class-based hierarchies of citizenry evoked by racial authoritarians. From their own privileged perches, those like the elder King and Mackay did speak out against the resultant politics. But only as more of these privileges came to be extended to more Atlantans, as those just scraping by then turned more hopeful, would racial authoritarianism finally meet its match.

"New South" City, Deadweight Countryside

Sandwiched between oceans to the south and east and mountains to the north, the Piedmont plateau, where Atlanta arose, had ascended in tandem with the Appalachian Mountains over five hundred million years before, buckling upward from the force of colliding continental plates. A further tectonic convulsion riled vast plumes of magma up from the earth's mantle, congealing huge nodes of granite, or "plutons," and eventually yielding isolated rock faces, or "monadnacks," as the sedimentary layers overlying them wore away. The largest of these in the region became known as Stone Mountain. Two natural break points converged near the place where Atlanta would arise, one between watersheds drained by the Chattahoochee and Flint Rivers, running into the Gulf of Mexico, and another by the Ocmulgee and Oconee Rivers, which wound up in the Atlantic. Toward the north grew a dense hardwood forest dominated by oak, hickory, beech, and elm. Toward the south the sandier soil grew pine trees, chiefly the Southeast's loblolly variety, or mixed pine and hardwood. Land remained in the hands of the Creek tribes into the 1820s, as cotton plantations and slavery were spreading through south Georgia. The first farms penetrating north Georgia's piedmont were smaller, with fewer or no slaves and less wealthy whites, but large-scale cotton agriculture crept north. When in the 1830s railroads began to offer an inland alternative to ships for conveying cotton northward, the convergence point of three railroad routes attracted the establishment of a new town. Christened Marthasville in 1841, some two years later it received a new name that stuck: Atlanta. As a railroad hub, it also served as a social hub for the "moonlight and magnolias" elite of the plantation South, whose concentrations of wealth and power exceeded those of any region in the antebellum United States.

When the Civil War began, Atlanta was only a small town of ten thousand. After the war's end it shook off William Sherman's devastation to grow faster than most southern cities—but at a pace that paled in comparison with cities in other U.S. regions.[6] Though serving as the launching pad for Henry Grady's vision of a "New South," Atlanta by 1930 was still only the fourth-largest city in the Southeast and twenty-eighth biggest in the nation, overtaken by many faster-growing metropolises of the West and Midwest.[7] Just as the explosive urban growth of a nineteenth-century Chicago or a twentieth-century Phoenix owed much to intensifying exploitation of natural resources across the U.S. West, so Atlanta's more sluggish expansion through the early twentieth century stemmed from a less prosperous hinterland, in which the "colonial" character of the South's economy remained rooted.[8]

Inescapably bound to the nation's most rural and agriculturally dependent as well as poorest region, the Atlanta of this era fostered its growing integration into the national economy mainly through commerce in cotton or timber or foodstuffs drawn almost exclusively from the Southland. Like other southern cities, it still leaned on the U.S. North and, increasingly, the West for highly skilled labor, for finished products from more capital-intensive industries, and for capital itself. In the United States' "Global South within its own territory," as Sven Beckert has put it, investors funded textile and other processing factories in Atlanta and other southern cities around the same time as they were pouring funds into similar enterprises in India, Egypt, Mexico, and Brazil.[9] As in these other parts of the Global South, production lines remained labor-intensive and less well-paying than those in more industrialized regions, failing to spark the full-blown industrialization that boosters from Henry Grady to the Forward Atlanta promotion of the 1920s kept envisioning. By 1930 Atlanta still had fewer textile workers than smaller cities like Augusta, and the proportion of Atlantans working in any kind of manufacturing had only just outpaced those employed in trade. Despite the insistent ballyhoo about Atlanta's "New South"–leading factories, its own manufacturing sector was overshadowed not just by cities in the North but by several southern rivals.[10]

The post–Civil War South's low wages and other economic travails owed much to the geographic isolation as well as segregation of its labor markets, especially impactful in the countryside but extending to cities like Atlanta.[11] Persistently dominating the workforce of Atlanta and other southern cities were "personal service" jobs, from barbers and hairdressers to launderers and cooks to servers and housekeepers and "servants"—closely akin to what house slaves had done. By 1919 this category of jobs, at 21.7 percent of Atlanta's workforce, remained bigger than not just manufacturing but all other segments, with twice the share found in similar metropolises in other U.S. regions.[12] Atlanta's jobs also drew hardly any of those immigrants from abroad who peopled the burgeoning cities of Ohio or the Northeast. Mackay's immigration from white, English-speaking Ireland was exceptional; instead, the vast majority of Atlanta's newer residents hailed from the southern countryside.[13] Outside a rare and privileged few, most arrived with few familial assets and little schooling, both scarce in rural Georgia, especially for Blacks.[14] Upon permanently relocating to Atlanta from Stockbridge, Georgia, in 1918, a nineteen-year-old Martin Luther King Sr. realized that "my reading level was barely beyond a rank beginners'" and he "could hardly write." So he enrolled in school starting at the elementary level, while supporting himself through jobs available to someone of his skin color and skills in the Atlanta of this era—working in a tire shop, bailing cotton, and driving a truck.[15]

On the wage front Atlanta's workers fared only somewhat better than those in smaller towns or the countryside but worse than those even in most southern cities. Even in manufacturing, where most all workers in this period were white, the hourly pay hung lower than in nearly every other comparably sized city.[16] That wages across Atlanta stayed so low stemmed from racial discrimination against the 40 percent of the workforce that was Black but also from the weakness of the city's labor unions, Black as well as white. Despite documented episodes of labor mobilizing in late nineteenth- and early twentieth-century Atlanta, by the late 1920s what one labor scholar described as an "intense hostility . . . to unionism" prevailed in textiles, keeping unions out.[17] Some African American workers formed their own unions, but white labor leaders remained either unwilling or unable to reach out across racial lines. Employers deliberately fanned the flames of racial animosity, then took advantage to squelch worker demands and organizing.[18] Union membership in Atlanta did briefly spike to over 7 percent of the city's workers in the late 1920s, a good deal more than in the rest of Georgia, but business leaders and labor scholars alike still pegged the city as predominantly "open-shop."[19]

By the mid-1930s that middle class that the elder King and Mackay had both joined remained smaller than in other U.S. cities and regions and much harder for Blacks to enter than for whites. King worked through a succession of menial jobs, catching up on his education, then earned a bachelor's degree from Morehouse College, to become the city's "best paid Black pastor." But Edward Mackay could count on his degree from private all-white Emory to quickly open doors to pastorates as well as a professorial appointment at Birmingham-Southern that paved the way to his 1934 ascension to Atlanta's First Methodist pulpit. Not just racial discrimination was responsible for the smaller size of the middle class in Atlanta and other southern cities than in other comparably sized American ones.[20] In 1919 Atlanta's white managers and other corporate officials in manufacturing, just 6 percent of that sector's workforce, took home 3.8 times more pay than did the wage workers they employed. That rate surpassed counterparts in northern and western cities and was bested only by less industrial southern rivals such as in Charleston and Nashville. Atlanta also joined other southern cities in having fewer college- or higher-educated professionals, whether doctors, nurses, lawyers, teachers, architects, or college-trained preachers. Not surprisingly, only 3 percent of the city's Black workforce belonged to these professions, and in that capacity or as businesspeople they earned less than white counterparts.[21]

Atlanta's generally lower incomes and diminutive middle class comprised two faces of cleavage capitalism under Jim Crow; the third, most empowered face belonged to its overwhelmingly white elite, the biggest beneficiaries of the city's modest growth. Salaries taken in by its factories' officers, superintendents, and managers approached levels found in the cities of the nation's

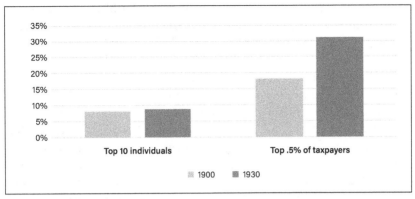

FIGURE 1.1. Increasing wealth concentration in early twentieth-century Fulton County. While the gains of the top ten individual taxpayers were less dramatic, the top half percent of those assessed for taxable assets nearly doubled their share of holdings over the first three decades of the century. "Fulton County Tax Registers for 1900 and 1930," County Property Tax Digests, 1789–2001, RG 34-6-1, Georgia Archives, Morrow.

richest regions.[22] Finance, which would fuel the late twentieth-century resurgence of wealth and income gaps, found special favor in early twentieth-century Atlanta.[23] The sector's preexisting strength drew the southeastern regional branch of the Federal Reserve to the city in 1914, which made it all the more attractive for private banks and insurance firms.[24] Trends in taxable wealth reflected how the cleavage capitalism of the Jim Crow era was channeling the city's expanding riches into a shrinking share of pocketbooks (see figure 1.1). From 1900 to 1930 the share of assessed wealth held by the top half percent of taxpayers in Fulton County, where most of the city and many suburbs lay, rose from just over 18 percent to nearly 31 percent—in all likelihood a considerable underestimate of existing fortunes.[25] Inheritance increasingly vied with business activity to pool Atlanta's wealth at the top, with three families, the Candlers, Inmans, and Grants, together laying claim to 4.4 percent of the county's registered riches. By contrast, the city's Blacks, only two or three generations out from slavery and facing so many other obstacles, stood almost no chance of breaking into the ranks of the city's wealthiest. Among the top three hundred with holdings above $100,000 by 1930, only two were Black.

Among the most telling indicators of how skewed the distribution of the city's riches was becoming was just who owned its most tangible assets, the land and buildings where Atlantans lived, worked, and played. Whites owned 96 percent of the privately held landed property in Fulton County by 1930; only 4 percent belonged to Black owners. Overall, only 30 percent of Atlantans owned their own homes, that asset whose widening availability after World War II would, as Thomas Piketty noted, turn the United States' and other nations' middle classes "patrimonial."[26] Atlanta's white homeownership rate, just over 39 percent, was more than twice that for Blacks. In the throes of a capitalism whose cleavages were exacerbated by Jim Crow, with so many of Atlanta's rural migrants arriving with so little to their name, 70 percent of Fulton County households rented living spaces owned by others.[27] Even white Atlanta remained overwhelmingly a city of renters, while Black Atlantans stood little chance of owning much of anything.

Atlanta and other southern cities were not just poorer than many comparably sized cities in other more industrialized and urbanized U.S. regions, but their geography of ownership also differed, in ways that by the 1920s and 1930s were becoming easy to see as "backward." Atlanta's socioeconomic arrangement, or "ecology," as the contemporary Chicago School of Sociology put it, offered a study in contrast to how they thought modern cities were supposed to grow and be structured, based on other U.S. cities in the North and West. They envisioned an onion-skinned layering of this social ecology that closely corresponded to a city's socioeconomic scale (map 1.2). Toward the inner-most core (with the noted exception of business districts) lay the poorest zones, harboring the city's recently arrived immigrants or Blacks, almost all of whom rented. Rates of homeownership and whiteness then rose with each step outward, peaking at the outer edge with "single family dwellings" and a suburban "commuter zone." By 1940 Atlanta's spatial distribution of ownership clashed with this Chicago School's model, following a regionally distinctive pattern shared with other southern cities far more so than counterparts in the U.S. North and West (map set 1.3).[28] Joining cities like Birmingham or Charleston,

MAP 1.2. City structure according to the Chicago School of Sociology. Downtown, the "slum," and a "zone in transition" lay just outside the business district. "Workingmen's homes" and immigrant settlements came in the next zone, followed by many "double flats" in the next and then a rim of apartment houses. Blacks lived in a thin "belt" running from the slum into this rental rim. Only in the very outer layer were areas dominated by non-"workingmen" homeowners, simply presumed to be all white, living in single-family homes, "restricted residential district," and commuter zones. Ernest W. Burgess, "The Growth of the City," in *The City*, ed. Robert E. Park, Ernest W. Burgess, and Roderick D. McKenzie (1925; repr. Chicago: University of Chicago Press, 1967), 55.

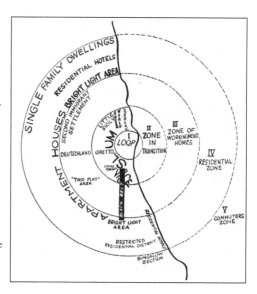

| Atlanta | Charleston | New Orleans | Detroit |
| Cleveland | Pittsburgh | Minneapolis | Seattle |

Homeownership in 1940 Census Tracts
Percentage of Total Housing Units

- 0% - 25%
- 25.01% - 50%
- 50.01% - 70%
- 70.01% - 85%
- 85.01% - 100%

0   5   10   20 Miles

MAP SET 1.3. The dearth of homeowners in southern versus other U.S. cities by 1940. Atlanta and other southeastern cities had markedly fewer home-owning suburbs compared to comparably sized cities in other U.S. regions. Atlanta at this point had a single such tract with more than 70 or 85 percent homeownership, lying as close to downtown as to the city's edge, sandwiched between older picturesque and planned suburbs of Ansley Park and Druid Hills. Charleston and New Orleans had none. Detroit, as well as Cleveland, Minneapolis, and Seattle had many, all along or near their edges. The home-owning middle classes in southern cities remained comparatively smaller and less concentrated, though Pittsburgh, with only seven tracts having homeownership rates of 70 percent or more, lay somewhat closer to the southeastern pattern. Maps by author. *Source:* Steven Manson, Jonathan Schroeder, David Van Riper, Tracy Kugler, and Steven Ruggles, *IPUMS National Historical Geographic Information System: Version 17.0* (Minneapolis: IPUMS, 2022), http://doi.org/10.18128/D050.V17.0.

Atlanta helped define the opposite pole of what was actually more of a continuum, with far fewer predominantly home-owning tracts and with at least half of their outlying suburban tracts having more renters than owners.[29]

An environmental fleshing out of these spatial bones reveals what this distribution of ownership across this more countrified city actually meant for Atlantans living in its contrasting corners. Extending from indoors out to the surrounding lot and neighborhood, those living environments being "consumed" through private housing and rental markets differed deeply by class and race. For a privileged few, whites who could afford their own mansions or full-scale suburban subdivisions, the rusticity of their living environments was first carefully and expensively constructed by developers, with the latest urban amenities installed beneath the greenery. Much more often, however, in this city with such a comparatively small middle class, what was rural about the environments where Atlantans came to live was determined more by developer or landlord stinginess and the meagerness of purchasers' pocketbooks. Theirs were forms of environmental consumption born more of want than of plenty, very close to what many had known in the countryside from which they had come. The rustic character of many such places also stemmed from the inactivity of government: a dearth of public provision, oversight, and planning. In this city, just as in the Georgia countryside, much hardship stemmed from how little public or formal control the government exerted on behalf of any larger citizenry, as opposed to the interests of a well-off and well-connected few.

Decades into the twentieth century, many of those provisions later known as "environmental" were far from universal, from clean drinking water and streams to sanitary protections against infectious disease to public parks. Government officials largely restrained their oversight not just of Atlantans' housing and workplaces but of their shared surroundings of land, water, woods, air, and other natural resources known in the environmental literature as "the commons." Under city leaders' minimalist approach to government, this urban commons resembled rural ones, like the shared pastures of eighteenth-century English towns—the original exemplar of the "commons" term. Without any government stepping in, decisions about usage remained exclusively in the hands of private owners, whether for grazing animals or waterside docks or factories or housing, changing land on which these creatures or structures came to be situated. Less well-off Atlantans, if they could buy their own small lot or use someone else's, could alleviate economic burdens through decidedly rural uses of local land—building their own house, growing their own food. Yet, in a city riven by such deep inequalities, such opportunities remained scarce on the lower-economic rungs, especially for nonwhites. Reinforced by the era's cleavage capitalism and coupled to undemocratic, rustic rule, the dead weight of the southern countryside reached deep into Atlanta's homes and neighborhoods.

The biggest exceptions lay in places like Druid Hills, where the Mackay family moved in 1934. There or in Ansley or Inman Park, within that narrow northerly slice of the city's suburban arc occupied by the city's wealthiest whites, residents lived amid a "country" or "rural attractiveness" that had been carefully and expensively constructed. The work done extended not just to individual homes and lots but to development-wide features, from curvilinear streets lined with lush plantings to neighborhood parks. These newer planned subdivisions, emulating upper-end suburbs in richer parts of the country, also came complete with water and sewer lines and with a racial exclusivity written into their restrictive covenants.[30] Outside these subdivisions Atlanta's "high society" could also choose to surround themselves with the treed and semirural large lots and columned porticos of Peachtree Street or Buckhead. All these upper-end neighborhoods drew first dibs on city services, and in a city more "backward in park development" than any of comparable size in the nation, city leaders poured taxpayer funds into the upkeep of these places' parks, old as well as new. When Asa Candler donated fifty acres right next to Druid Hills in the early 1920s, city leaders promptly moved to convert it into Candler Park, complete with wooded glens, tennis courts, and a golf course.[31]

Where Martin Luther King Sr. took up residence in the 1920s and 1930s next to Auburn Avenue was one of only two neighborhoods on the Black sides of town that offered anything comparable: detached single-family homes with small lawns and, in the case of its West Side counterpart, the nearby greenery of Atlanta University, established for the city's Blacks by northern philanthropists. Even there by the early 1930s, over half the dwellings were rentals, the landscaping was less lavishly rustic or planned, and the city remained much stingier in its public provisions. Indeed, the only public park in which any Blacks were allowed by the end of the 1920s was West Side's Washington Park. And it remained, as a Black newspaper editor put it, a "disgrace," with "no seats in the place, no streets, no sidewalks, simply a mud hole between two hills."[32]

Beyond these middle- or upper-class exceptions, three-quarters of Atlanta's suburban arc, to the west, south, and east, mostly harbored the city's working classes, white as well as Black. Railroads, stockyards, and fertilizer or textile factories, first sited outside the city to avoid taxes and oversight and then annexed, drew workers who often preferred to live nearer to where they worked, since they were unable to afford cars. Whites in Pittsburgh or Scottdale or Reynoldstown might even have a lot and house of their own, with an in-house water connection if they were lucky, a sewer tie-in if doubly so.[33] Black working families, on the other hand, lived in smaller two-to-three-room houses that often looked "like they were built on . . . waste land." Most had to go outside both for water and "sanitary conveniences"—privies shared with their neighbors.[34] More likely tenants than homeowners, both white and Black working classes remained dependent on what was provided by penny-pinching land-lords, who, as long as they could fill rooms and exact rents, had few incentives to pressure city hall for more services. While the wealthier white neighbor-hoods enjoyed a full range of urban public services by the 1920s, those for At-lanta's white working classes remained uneven, even as Black sides of town re-mained the most neglected.

Atlanta's industrial workplaces themselves also suffered from the minimal-ist approach to government in this time and place. Unlike more urban and industrialized regions of the United States, neither the city nor the state of Georgia had factory-inspection laws. The harshness of its textiles mills is best documented: for instance, recounted one spinner, "it was hard to stand on your feet all day. . . . There was no air and you would almost smother." Of-ten stricken with debilitating pulmonary diseases stoked by the pervasive dust, from tuberculosis to the brown lung later documented among them, textile workers also "complained of aching shoulders and arms, sore fingers, catarrh, headaches, and stomach ailments," as historian Cliff Kuhn summarized, "all ostensibly the result of adverse working conditions."[35] While racial barriers kept Blacks out of most textile millwork, those factories that did welcome their labor had conditions widely considered to be still worse. Guano factories, arising around this and other Georgia cities to furnish fertilizer made from bird feces for Georgia cotton farms, featured a labor force of "with the ex-ception of the supervisor and a few professional men, almost entirely . . . un-skilled coloured men."[36] A miserable stench pervaded not just these factories but the neighborhoods around them, to such an extent that guano plants were the only kind of factory banned from the city of Atlanta by its 1910 charter.

In a city deeply riven by racial segregation, those who were both Black and poor faced the fewest choices of living quarters. From Vine City to Butter-milk Bottom, most of those districts available to them had begun as semiru-ral settlements along the city's outskirts just after the Civil War. Buttermilk Bottom arose as an initial settlement of freed slaves known as Shermantown and extended northeastward out Butler Street, taking its own name from a low creek-side location that whites had shunned. As with other southern cities, many towns in Atlanta's urban fringe remained predominantly Black into the early 1900s, a legacy of their forebears' cityward flight from Georgia's plan-tations after the Civil War.[37] Persisting even within wealthy white Buckhead itself by the 1930s was Bagley Park, evolved since the early 1920s into a subdi-vision of small homes, whose residents by 1938 were largely "laborers and do-mestics" working for local households of wealthy whites and living in "poor to dilapidated" rentals.[38] Newer Black suburban enclaves had emerged as well, such as in Scottdale, originally a white mill town that by the 1930s had turned 40 percent Black.[39] Thereby, Atlanta's rural fringes still grew through newer versions of a settlement type that, as Lisa Goff has shown, inhabited the edges of so many U.S. cities in the nineteenth century—shantytowns, built by the working poor.[40]

Among these rural practices were the informal methods of home building that took off in those parts of Atlanta reserved for its poorer and working-class residents, especially if Black. Small houses cobbled together by Black families or aspiring landlords proliferated in backyards and along alleys, "thread[ing]" "the badly drained and dark hollows of the city."[41] Thanks to utter neglect by city hall, not only did such places lack basic urban services such as piped-in water, but the city's lax oversight enabled landlords to make them denser and denser. Atlanta did acquire zoning and building codes over the 1910s and 1920s, yet the city wielded these mainly to protect neighborhoods of well-off whites.[42] Housing inspections remained rare, and inspectors had limited jurisdiction over the alleyways where so much housing for Atlanta's Blacks lay.[43] Citifying improvements in Black housing came almost entirely from Black entrepreneurship and capital. Into the 1920s Vine City, begun as part of a western-edge Black settlement downslope from Atlanta University, remained a place "where [in the words of W. E. B. Dubois's student] slums, dumps, hovels, crime, and want prevailed." When Herman Perry, a Black insurance company owner, then built some homes offering indoor plumbing and electricity, its mix of Black residents shifted from exclusively poor to more working class.[44]

New arrivals to Atlanta from the Georgia countryside also brought agriculture with them: the skill and inclination to grow their own food. Buying even a small plot of land could enable rural styles of self-provisioning, such as the keeping of chickens, cows, and extensive gardens. Even rentals came with stretches of unbuilt land in "homestead" dimensions: narrow street fronts coupled with one or even two hundred feet of depth in back, allowing plenty of room for gardens, chicken coops, and even stables and barns.[45] City ordinances authorized nearly a full range of domesticated animals: into the 1920s the only cows not allowed by the city charter were those "running at large."[46] While farm animals posed fewer intrusions in a sparsely settled and also well-fenced countryside, in densely settled urban neighborhoods even penned animals could bother the neighbors. One A. E. Hogan of Peoplestown complained to the paper in 1925 about the flies drawn by a neighbor's cow "creating filth" as well as his "pigpen in the back yard." "Cows and pigs are not permitted within the corporate limits of any city or village, except in some southern states," the writer bemoaned. "Have we a city council and a board of health interested in health?" In this era of minimalist government, the answer was essentially "it depends on whose health."[47] Neither felt compelled to act, especially for those not among the city's elite, whatever commitments they claimed.

Another rural feature persisting decades into the twentieth century inside Atlanta, adopted out of necessity given the indifference of landlords and city officials, was the privy or outhouse. Whether open-air or enclosed by roof and walls, privies had long been how more rural parts of the world kept human wastes out of their homes, by depositing it into the local ground.[48] While similar practices had prevailed in many cities across the industrialized West up to the mid-nineteenth century, from then into the early twentieth most had moved to interior bathrooms with flush toilets. That shift came much slower in Atlanta and other southern cities than in northern and western U.S. counterparts. Even by the late 1930s, 26 percent of Atlanta homes still had no indoor toilet, and one-third had no interior bathroom, forcing a continued dependence on privies.[49] Part of the reason was that construction of Atlanta's sewers and sewage treatment plants lagged far behind its growing numbers of homes and residents. In the absence of more sewers to channel its wastes out from the city itself, overflow from Atlanta's privies, cesspools, and septic tanks washed into the city's most prominent waterways, stirring episodic jeremiads from health officers that "practically every running stream in the county [is] . . . polluted, and the creeks . . . but running sewers." Not surprisingly, Atlanta had the highest mortality rate among seventy U.S. cities in 1923, and in 1926, along with three other southern cities, led the nation in death rates from typhoid, a disease spread by water or food contaminated by human wastes.[50]

In these and other ways, rural conditions inside Atlanta as well as out along its edges matched up with what Harlan Douglass, author of the first book on the United States' *Suburban Trend* (1925), found more intermittently outside the cities in other, wealthier regions: industrial and Negro suburbs, rural suburbs, also a "veritable suburban hegira of the very poor."[51] These more burdensomely rural edges of Atlanta and other southeastern cities, shared by many western cities in the nineteenth century, over the twentieth century would become associated mainly with cities in the developing world.[52] As a 2003 report from the United Nations would later note, most cities in the Global South had not followed "the classic Chicago School model," expanding "by rings of garden suburbs" and leaving behind a "decaying core." They had grown, instead, through "large tracts of poor-quality low-income housing . . . in squatter zones on the fringe or on . . . fragile land."[53] Far into the twentieth century, Atlanta grew similarly, even while increasingly forced to reckon with its own "decaying core." The resulting "slums" visually confirmed the racial stereotypes of the most ardent segregationists. "Breeding place[s] of crime, childhood delinquency, and epidemics," they threatened the city's "true" citizenry in a host of ways. Even outspoken antisegregationists such as *Atlanta Constitution* editor Ralph McGill thought they needed to be plowed under, for "who can expect" their residents "to have a great and enduring respect for the guarantees of democracy?"[54]

The dead weight of Georgia's countryside heavily encumbered not just Atlanta's slums but people all over the city readily identifiable as country-born. King vividly recalled being "so rural" upon first arriving in the city that "I couldn't say anything . . . without someone laughing or correcting my speech." Not just his "rough country way of speaking" but his "uncreased dusty clothes [and] whole uneducated green farmboy personality" seemed to set off alarm bells among those he tried to impress, from employers and teachers to the minister's daughter he sought to woo, spurring his own pathway to self-improvement. Black Methodist ministers, "formally trained, for the most part" and "college educated," made King with his backwoods Baptist preaching style feel "as though I were nothing to them, almost like I'd been nothing to the white men back in the country." "To be 'country,'" he summarized, "was to be backward, unsophisticated, and hopeless ignorant," and all the more so if the bearer was Black.[55] Mackay left no autobiographic testimony like King's but seems to have escaped much rural stigma through his Irish brogue and his identifying with the city of Belfast (where he attended high school) and entering a Methodist ministry. For whites as well as Blacks in the South of this era, markers of "country"-ness could lock their bearers into the lower rungs of that social hierarchy that structured Jim Crow citizenship. At the same time, urban prejudices against countryness stoked resentment among the city's white working class that fueled its alliance with those rural elites who maintained a choke-hold on Atlanta's as well as Georgia's democracy.

Rustic Rule and the Problem of Citizenship

The senior King's and Mackay's forays into the political arena brought them face to face with what V. O. Key, in his classic 1949 work on southern politics, termed a "rule of the rustics." While Georgia provided the titular example, Key found similar patterns across the midcentury deep South.[56] Though possessing one of the South's largest cities, this state's political leadership came predominantly from its rural counties. Cannily mindful of the state's "rural-urban cleavage," they wielded ideologies and governing practices that back home had subordinated a Black majority to a minority rule by whites. What political scientists today call its "subnational authoritarianism" contrasted to the more democratic regimes in nonsouthern states and the United States as a whole. Like most of today's authoritarian governments, early to midcentury Georgia did have elections, but by political scientist Robert Mickey's criteria for democracy, these were neither "free" or "fair." Even after the all-white primary was abolished in 1943 and the poll tax in 1945, Atlanta-area turnout in 1948 hung down at 20 percent or less, half that of Cleveland, though it then slowly rose. Nor did post–World War II Georgia meet another of Mickey's criteria, a "state apparatus" sufficiently and meaningfully "responsive to election winners."[57] A county unit system, similar to an electoral college, limited urban counties to no more than three times the electoral clout of any rural one. By 1950 a single unit vote from Echols, the smallest county, would represent 1,247 people, while one county unit vote from Fulton County represented 78,292 people, giving each Echols voter *sixty-three times* the electoral clout of each Atlanta voter.[58] And with one party, the Democrats, dominating all the elections, opposing voices and agendas and especially challenges to ruling social and economic elites had few opportunities for gaining electoral traction.

What made post–World War II Georgia, along with many other southern states, "authoritarian enclaves," in sum, was that its "rustic" rule so constricted opportunities for what the sociologist T. H. Marshall termed the "political element" of citizenship. In his classic definition, composed in mid-twentieth-century Britain but also applicable to the contemporary United States, it was one of three "elements" of citizenship that aggrieved and organized residents of Western nations had generally sought. Political citizenship meant, first and foremost, being able to vote, a right considerably more restricted in the South than in the rest of the United States. The severest exclusions were born by Georgia's Blacks, all the more so if poor. But both the poorer and better-off of Atlanta's whites, even the city's elite, also shouldered electoral interdictions. Rustic rule became the political face of a steeply hierarchical gradation of citizenship, from first down to second and lower classes of citizenry—one final way that, even up to 1960, both city and state remained regionally distinctive, not yet a part of any Sunbelt. The electoral dimensions of Jim Crow citizenship were undergirded by equally harsh discrepancies in Marshall's "civil element" of citizenship, those "rights necessary for individual freedom," as well as his "social" element, enabling that modicum of security and aspiration required for "the life of a civilized being according to the standards prevailing in the society."[59] Many Black Atlantans were denied freedoms of speech and movement as well as fair trials. In the social realm they were barred by segregation from the better schools, jobs, housing, and other like opportunities.

While Blacks faced the harshest consequences of Jim Crow's social hierarchies, the protracted pecking order among whites yielded other frictions that for rustic rulers proved politically useful. Disparagement of an all-too rustic white working class by Atlanta's white elite stirred resentments for which Jim Crow citizenship provided expressive channels, diverting frustrations away from the white class divide toward a shared if chimerical white nationhood rooted in the South's own unique history. While often vowing a patriotic allegiance to the United States, Georgia's rustic rulers also periodically pledged a wistful loyalty to the Confederacy, a short-lived nation that had ceased to exist nearly a century before.

Georgia's racial authoritarianism had built off the successful effort to quash Reconstruction's great experiment with biracial democracy. Black voters' share of the city electorate had peaked at 39 percent in 1885, but white political leaders in the city and countryside had then set about curbing their and poorer whites' shares of the Georgia electorate, imposing a poll tax and liter-

acy and property-ownership requirements, and making Democratic primaries all white, among other steps. By 1900 only nine hundred Black Atlantans
cast ballots; the poor or working-class white vote had also shrunk, despite the
"grandfathering" of Confederate veterans. In 1908 this shrunken electorate
then ratified an amendment to the state constitution further legalizing disenfranchisement. Through the ensuing half century, turnout rates for elections
in the city of Atlanta would rarely exceed a fifth of those eligible (or at least
who would be eligible under less restrictive requirements).[60] With countryside-
based politicians like Tom Watson stoking fears about what might happen if
Georgia's cities grew, of "the evil of a pure democracy" in which "the minority
have no protection from the majority," a 1917 Neill Primary Act then codified
an electoral college–type means for ensuring rural political dominance: the
county unit system.[61]

Rooted in practices predating the direct-vote primary, when county representatives themselves chose the party's candidates at a nominating convention, the county unit system locked in a carefully calibrated political parity
between Georgia's many counties that favored rural over urban voters, while
still enabling a popular primary vote. More populous counties received more
units than did the least populated, but at best only three times more. A county
like Atlanta's Fulton wielded six units in statewide primary races, the smallest counties two, and those of intermediate population size four. Raw vote totals in each county determined which candidate received that county's units,
with the victory going to the recipient of a plurality not of the popular vote
but of county unit votes. As these same proportions also determined seats in
the legislature, the least populous counties retained considerable legislative as
well as electoral clout no matter how many people they lost and how many Atlanta, the state's largest city, gained. In synergy with the many ballot box restrictions, the county unit system set the stage for rural control of Georgia for
decades to come.[62]

No one figure personified Georgia's ensuing version of rustic rule better
than Eugene Talmadge, the "wild man from Sugar Creek." Elected governor four times between 1932 and his death in 1946, he famously subscribed
to "four principles" of governing—"white supremacy, states rights, Jefferso-
nian democracy, and old-time religion," the cultural fabric out of which his
party's ascendance had been woven. Though the scion of a well-to-do family, Talmadge strove to personify a hardscrabble rusticity, wearing red sus-
penders ("galluses") fastened to his pants by "ten penny nails" and warning
that Blacks, not "real laborers" (i.e., white workers), would most benefit from
minimum-wage laws.[63] To suppress integration advocacy and combat challenges from political rivals, Talmadge exerted such an iron hand that his opponents dubbed him an "imitation Hitler." It was a comparison he welcomed,
at one point bragging he had read the German dictator's *Mein Kampf* seven

times. Implacably harsh against labor unions, during one strike he declared martial law and "placed textile workers behind barbed-wire 'concentration camps.'"[64] He purged prointegration faculty at the University of Georgia and, when the legislature balked at lowering the fees collected by state commissions, expelled their appointees by calling out the National Guard.[65]

At the same time, for most other public purposes, Talmadge kept state government dialed back. "The way to keep a government good, and keep its citizens prosperous," he declared, "is to have a poor government." He steadfastly opposed the New Deal, railing against its Keynesian spending to "prime" the nation's economic "pump."[66] He and his successors, the Democrats' ruling Talmadge faction, funded what little state government they provided through sales taxes—disproportionately affecting those with lower incomes—rather than income or property taxes.[67] They wielded public resources preferentially, with road and highway building often the highest priority. That choice mainly benefited those who could afford cars and had crops to transport; Talmadge-affiliated leaders thereby rewarded courthouse elites, especially in rural counties that most supported him.[68] Government services that might prove more evenhanded in their distribution, especially those from which the poor or a Black minority could most benefit, received far less. At the dawn of the New Deal, the state's health director complained how "the state is spending $6 per capita for roads, from $1 to $2 per capita for education and only about three cents for public health."[69]

Rustic rule's influence also carried through to the federal level, not only because the state government set election rules for Georgia's senators and congresspeople but because the single party with any chance in statewide elections, the Democrats, often fell under the thumb of Talmadge allies. Through the 1930s, until Democratic landslides diminished the degree to which Roosevelt had to rely on them, the South's single-party legislators constituted the greatest regional bulwark of Democratic support, limiting the aspirations of nonsouthern New Dealers.[70] Georgia's senators Richard Russell and Walter George joined the ranks of "southern cage" builders. They promoted federal laws and expenditures that would bring dollars and uplift to their region yet drew a sharp line against federal initiatives that they feared would undermine their own white supremacist power structures. Southern Democrats filibustered an antilynching law, for instance, and successfully limited the union-bolstering Wagner Act from covering those agricultural and domestic workers who made up so much of the South's Black workforce.[71]

Talmadge himself was even more actively anti–New Deal, vocally resenting the federal administration of funds to Georgians and braking state legislation that would have enabled his state's fuller participation in the New Deal.[72] Only with the anti-Talmadge governorships of Eurith Rivers and then Ellis Arnall, interspersed between Eugene Talmadge's terms, would the state of Georgia reap benefits from many New Deal programs and policies.[73] Even with this burst of federal largesse, by 1942 Georgia's per capita state and local spending lagged far behind national norms, with more robust spending on roads (63 percent of the U.S. average) than on realms such as health (53 percent) or sanitation (55 percent) or recreation and "natural resources" (53 percent).[74] The Talmadge faction of Georgia's Democratic Party retained its hold on political power in important part by cozying up to corporate leaders and minimizing their taxes as well as through its resolute opposition to labor laws and unions. Upon Eugene Talmadge's death in 1946 just after being reelected, his son and related acolytes consolidated their hold on the party apparatus in part by pushing a right-to-work law through the state legislature. More stringent than the federal Taft-Hartley Act still wending its way through Congress, it cut the legal legs off a Georgia labor movement energized by a post–World War II campaign to organize textile workers, which careful observers thought to be "growing."[75] Mostly dominating Georgia's state government into the 1960s, the Talmadge faction would do less for ordinary people, and especially for those in a city such as Atlanta, than counterparts in nearly every other U.S. state or region.[76]

By far the biggest city in Georgia, Atlanta served as the center of the state's anti-Talmadge faction, not least through the activism of those such as pastors King and Mackay. In the mid-1930s King helped lead an Atlanta Civic and Political League and the local branch of the National Association for the Advancement of Colored People (NAACP). He kicked off a Black voter-registration drive by organizing a mass rally at Ebenezer Baptist and a subsequent march to city hall and lobbied for Black teachers to be paid more like their white colleagues. His activism, while stirring disgruntlement not just from whites but from the city's Black leadership, helped initiate what proved an expanding effort to restore Black Atlantans' Reconstruction-era political clout.[77]

Mackay's most prominent political foray came in 1941, when he spoke out against the Ku Klux Klan, the hood-wearing, violence-prone organization of avowed racists that sustained a symbiotic relationship with racial authoritarians like Talmadge. A quarter century after Atlanta's Stone Mountain had provided the cradle for its twentieth-century rebirth, the Klan was still alive and well, especially in white working-class corners of the city. After a "wrecking crew" of the East Point Klan was convicted for a series of brutal floggings targeting Blacks, union organizers, and other Klan enemies, Mackay spoke at a special hearing before Governor Talmadge, arguing against the floggers' appeals for clemency. His stern words about the KKK as "comparable only to the despicable Nazi Gestapo" garnered headlines. Testimony at the hearing cast light, as well, on the Klan as a hidden prop of Jim Crow governance: East Point's sheriff had headed the klavern, and one of his deputies was among the six convicted. While ultimately denying their request for clemency, the governor himself publicly expressed "sympathy" for the Klansmen, admitting that when younger, he had "got mixed up in a thing like that myself."[78]

Despite its many Atlanta supporters, the Democrats' anti-Talmadge faction remained more diverse and loosely organized than its political foe and included many leaders who themselves distrusted democracy. After 1945, with the abolition of the white primary and of Georgia's poll tax, voter registration campaigns among Atlanta's Blacks did begin to make a difference in the city's politics. Mayor William Hartsfield and other white leaders, who'd already begun turning more reform-minded, started taking some concerns of their Black citizenry more seriously, and the city's spending for more broadly public purposes such as education and sanitation also rose.[79] Yet Floyd Hunter's study of who controlled Atlanta over the late 1940s and early 1950s found a government stuck utterly dominated by a white business elite. Interviews showed that many anti-Talmadge faction leaders preferred one-party rule and Jim Crow. Many Atlanta bankers and corporate executives quietly supported the Talmadge faction as "safe."[80]

Revealing how much the pro- and anti-Talmadge factions of Georgia's Democratic Party nevertheless shared, each and every one of the city's state senators joined the Talmadgists in supporting the 1947 right-to-work law. With the express purpose of impeding the unionization of Georgia's workplaces, the unanimous support for this legislation among state senators, if not state house representatives, was loudly acclaimed as "the expressed will of a great majority of people." What actually enabled it, however, was that unique brand of subnational authoritarianism that Atlanta's own rulers shared with their "rustic" counterparts who controlled the state government.[81] Legislators voting for this act had been elected by only a tiny, overwhelmingly white fraction of voting-age Georgians. The legislature that voted was itself heavily stacked to favor rural voices over urban ones. Nevertheless, as we will see, this one law would cast a long and troubling shadow over Georgia's subsequent history. Without as large, assertive, or unifying a labor movement as in other parts of the nation and world, Atlantans would have fewer institutional wellsprings on which they could draw for calling out corporate malfeasance and generally resisting business interests. Instead, more of this resistance would come from other movements, for civil rights and the environment.

While the "courthouse elites" in Georgia's southernly counties served as the prime constituencies for Talmadgism, county leaders in the Atlanta area also cultivated close ties to the state's rustic rulers, even as Atlanta's spreading suburbs brought rising expectations of urban services and protections their way. As rural stretches beyond the city limits got more crowded and as residents clamored for more roads, water and sewer lines, and protection from neighbors and developers, questions arose about whether county governments could step up to handle the demands. Responding to this dilemma, and to the

uptick of Black voters in Atlanta, residents of elite Buckhead as well as suburbs across the metro area's southwest voted to be annexed into the city in
1952, bringing it a hundred thousand new, mostly white residents into Atlanta's polity.[82] In a move that in Georgia had also required authorization from
the Talmadge-controlled legislature, Fulton County also consolidated its public health and other services with the those of the city government. In this and
other ways, including countywide land-use planning and zoning, Fulton became the first metro-area county to undertake a more urban style of governance over what had been lightly governed rural "commons." DeKalb and
Cobb Counties moved in similar directions as they drew more and more of
the metro area's homeowners. Yet with further annexations foreclosed by a
state supreme court decision, these counties also hung onto structures and
styles of governing shared by the rural counties where Talmadgism was based.

Into the post–World War II period, leaders of these two counties had stuck
to a more bare-bones and thinly codified approach to county government.
Singular well-connected leaders wielded personal relationships and connections to accomplish their modernizing, with little resort to expertise, explicit
rules, or spelled-out and publicized plans.[83] In DeKalb the "person of most
influence" was Scott Candler, from the family of the Coca-Cola magnate.[84]
As the county's "Commissioner of Roads and Revenues" over the 1940s and
1950s, like his Cobb counterpart, he undertook initiatives not contemplated
by leaders of more rural counties such as, most notably, extending water and
sewer systems deep into unincorporated territory. But he did so without any
zoning or planning commission or study of land use. Instead, he simply hud-
dled with two main associates to determine where the roads, schools, water
lines, and sewers were to be built; which land uses were to be regulated; and
what industries were to be invited in. Candler was also the Talmadges' man
in DeKalb, exerting a powerful hold on the local Democratic Party to keep
DeKalb's county unit votes in their column.[85]

Rustic rule did posit its own terms for citizenship, racially charged and
starkly unequal as these were. Especially for its leaders and supporters, the belonging felt to a vanquished and vanished nation, the Confederacy, could rival
their allegiance to the United States itself. For working- or middle-class whites
in Atlanta, it could mean not just voting for segregationists but mobilizing to
protect against Black "invasions" of white neighborhoods. It could mean joining the Klan or the Columbians, or voting with their own feet to keep segregation alive through "white flight" to outlying areas.[86] For a wealthy developer like Cobb County's Bill Ward, who joked about being born with a "gold
spoon" in his mouth, it could mean calling up Governor Talmadge to schedule a cozy meet that arranged the state-sponsored conversion of an "unpaved
pig trail" into a four-lane road to Ward's newest subdivision.[87] Over these
years, as most of Atlanta's leaders and white upper-to-middle classes made

their peace with homegrown authoritarianism, the bases grew for constituencies that would prove more restive.

Toward a Compressive Capitalism

If the stock market crash and Depression left even Atlanta's richest denizens with far less wealth than before, at least as transformative of its political economy was that new set of national laws and policies we know as the New Deal. Kick-starting a national shift toward a more compressive capitalism shared across the developed world, this political project overtaking Washington, D.C., in the 1930s would add heft and propulsion to Atlanta's turnaround. Profoundly challenging the minimalist state envisioned by rustic rule, the New Deal sailed through Congress only by making significant concessions to the South's political leaders and generally doing more favors for Atlanta's whites than its Blacks. Those very gaps helped ensure that Atlanta's countryside would impose a continuing drag on its postwar growth. Through the 1940s and 1950s, Atlanta and its region remained in what economic historian Gavin Wright identified as a "distinct transitional phase." It drew fewer high-tech and higher-wage industries that propelled the growth of cities in the Sunbelt West, and even while growing more of a middle class, it failed to shed many rural features and hinterland shackles, economic as well as political, that had long rendered it regionally distinctive from richer parts of the United States.[88] But fewer of the fruits of prosperity went to business and other elites, and more flowed toward a swelling middle class, especially if white. The beachheads were broadening for a more effective opposition to rustic rule.

Not just the dire economic plight of the South but the clout of its leaders in the New Deal coalition had drawn more federal assistance to this region than to any other, making it, as one *New York Times* reporter declared in 1935, the "main laboratory of the New Deal."[89] On the heels of all the new laws and government building in Washington, federal agencies and officials veritably flooded into Atlanta, bearing funds that pooled within the city as well as being channeled into the hard-hit countryside. From public housing and urban renewal to the build out of Atlanta's sewer system, what they funded figures importantly in succeeding chapters of this book. Additionally, a new social security system provided support for elderly retirees, new federal insurance programs backed bank deposits and home mortgages, and new federal rules forbade child labor, limited work hours, and established a national minimum wage. This last measure proved especially influential, imposing new floors on Atlanta's (as other of the nation's) labor markets that benefited many less well-off Atlantans, Black as well as white.[90] Racially speaking, however, many other New Deal interventions were not so evenhanded, helping to freeze long-standing local barriers to Black wealth and attendant amenities into the fixity of federal policy.[91]

Among the most impactful and currently well known of these were far-reaching federal programs to reignite the housing industry. The maps of reputed risks for mortgage loans by the Home Owners' Loan Corporation (HOLC), key tools for redlining, built on those distinctly southern class and racial contours that had arisen in this and other southern cities over the previous half century.[92] Seven of Atlanta's nine A-rated places—deemed the most promising for mortgage lending—included Mackay's Druid Hills but clustered around Buckhead, in a narrow northerly slice of Atlanta's suburban arc. There "private park" subdivisions, not just "well-planned" but "nicely landscaped" and "well-wooded," seemed assured of all-white futures by racially restrictive covenants written into their housing contracts. HOLC thereby lent federal heft to what David Freund has styled as "an alternative theory about the threat [of] black occupancy . . . focused on economics" and property values, which ensured the continued channeling of wealth into northerly upper-end white suburbs.[93] Along the rest of the city's fringes to the west, south, and east, so pervasive were lower-end and less promising mortgage prospects that ratings of D and C prevailed. Alongside built features like industry and "heavy traffic," those features that invited the lowest ratings were excessively rural: unpaved streets, a nearby dairy, oversight by county rather than city police, and a lack of zoning, as well as the sheer presence of Blacks.[94] As for Black sides of town, even the "best Negro district," inhabited by Black "professionals and businessmen" around Atlanta University on the West Side received the lowest rating, a D—as did King's Auburn Avenue neighborhood.[95] While poorer Black quarters closer to downtown, like Buttermilk Bottom and Vine City, also received Ds, the very lowest of D ratings were reserved for predominantly Black outlying districts, industrial sites such as Rockdale Park, and former market towns like College Park and East Point.[96] Directing capital for home building and buying away from all Black neighborhoods as well as the poorer and less-provisioned three-quarters of the city's urban fringe, HOLC helped ensure that those deep contrasts in living environments that Jim Crow and cleavage capitalism had inscribed on the metropolitan landscape would carry over into the post–World War II decades.

Into the 1940s and 1950s, while New Deal laws, agencies, and policies continued to funnel an inordinate share of the federal budget southward, Atlanta grew at a pace that was more modest than breakneck, unlike many cities in the Sunbelt West. Still tethered to a poor and racially troubled Southeast, its steady expansion did raise its U.S. population rank from thirty-third in 1940 to twenty-fourth over the next two decades, but mainly through a mammoth 1952 annexation that tripled its land area. While the populations of cities such as Houston, Miami, Phoenix, and especially Los Angeles grew explosively by drawing in many from outside their own regions, Atlanta's new arrivals still came mostly from its own, unsettled countryside. Its drawing power helped induce a 14 percent population decline in rural Georgia over these same two decades. Yet only in 1960 did urban Georgians finally outnumber the state's rural residents, a demographic watershed that the entire United States had passed some forty years earlier.[97]

Atlanta's wartime and post–World War II gains in manufacturing remained much more modest than many Sunbelt rivals. Factory jobs in the city held steady at 18 percent, just keeping pace with population growth.[98] Many federal investments in large-scale capital- and technology-intensive plants during World War II, like a federally run Bell Bomber factory in Cobb County's Marietta, were shuttered at the war's end. This plant sat empty for seven years, until restarted on a smaller scale by the Los Angeles–based Lockheed.[99] Nor did its restart trigger any takeoff of capital- and technology-intensive production. After high-tech producers kept bypassing Georgia for aerospace hubs in California and New York, and even in other southeastern states, a 1961 study by Georgia Tech scholars bemoaned the dearth of other high-technology plants in the region except for "one lone electronics plant."[100] Far more common in the Atlanta-area were assembly plants like General Motors' or also one set up by Ford, fitting together parts made elsewhere to sell to a southeastern consumer market.[101]

With the South's labor markets shedding their isolation only slowly, most of Atlanta's post–World War II gains in manufacturing still came in low-wage, labor-intensive production, hefting, hewing, and packaging the produce of southern lands.[102] In 1958, as twenty years earlier, Atlanta's biggest factory-based industry remained textiles, based on a mature, established technology and requiring less money for new equipment or operations than did aerospace, electronics, or petrochemicals. Joining its expanding textile plants, by 1963 over 20 percent of the factory workforce in Fulton County handled wood or other forest products, mostly from southeastern trees.[103] And where the Atlanta area actually led the nation was in the factory-style production of chicken flesh, as the nation's biggest source of "broilers"—a new, more consumer-friendly way of packaging chicken.[104] Thereby, its industrial base had less kinship with those of the United States' largest coastal cities and more with industrializing metropolises like Mexico City or Rio de Janeiro in the developing world.[105]

Unlike cities inside developing-world countries, however, post–World War II Georgia's workers also had the advantage of being nestled within a larger and richer developed nation. Being a part of the United States eased the South's economic integration with more prosperous U.S. regions. Despite the exemptions wrested by regional political leaders, New Deal programs emanating out of Washington gradually undermined the tenant and plantation dependence of cotton farming, hastening mechanization and propelling out-migration from the Georgia countryside. Eventually, they led as well to what Wright summarized as "an effective abolition of the low-wage market for in-dustrial labor." Most influential here was the Fair Labor Standards Act of 1938, which had set a nationwide minimum wage, a legal floor on take-home pay that would edge the incomes of the poorest southerners upward toward those in other regions.[106] Rustic rulers could do little to counter the consequences of minimum-wage laws on the low-wage labor on which they and their allies depended, yet by the early 1960s low-wage industries remained an "essential part" of a state economy that needed a "better proportion of high-wage, high skill jobs."[107] Part of the reason for the persistently low wages in many Geor-gia industries was its right-to-work law. Carving out a statewide exception to the New Deal's Wagner Act and quickly backed up with a national Taft-Harley Act, it ensured that by the early 1960s only 13 percent of Georgia work-ers had unionized, compared to the national average of 30 percent and the southern average of 20 percent.[108]

By this time the national shift toward a more compressive style of capital-ism had enhanced the earnings of many Atlantans.[109] The metro area's $7,550 per capita income in 1960 (that is, the average across all jobs) now lay very near the middle of the pack among U.S. cities. Still a full $2,000 away from catapulting this city into the ranks of the nation's richest twenty-five, this av-erage said little about how skewed the incomes were.[110] But census figures suggest a significant convergence between upper and middle levels of income among Atlanta residents over the 1940s and 1950s. As Atlanta's better-off sub-urbs spread, the average incomes of entire counties caught up with some of the richest northern counterparts. By 1960 DeKalb, the metro area's most sub-urban and richest county, had as great a share of residents earning $10,000 or more as New York's suburban Nassau and Suffolk. More broadly, capi-talism's compressive turn had brought the share of Atlantans earning mid-level incomes—$3,000 to $8,000 a year—up to 33.5 percent, comparable to some of richest cities in other regions (vs. 34.7 percent for Minneapolis and 33.9 percent for Seattle).[111] Yet Atlanta's factory workers still earned less than northern counterparts, while nearly a quarter of Atlanta metro-area incomes (23.6 percent) fell below the poverty line.[112] Jim Crow's racial barriers were a powerful reason why. Even as white wages rose, many Blacks had stayed stuck at the bottom of the pay scale, excluded not just from factory jobs but from "firefighting, truck-driving, clerking and auto repair."[113] For poorer white Atlantans as well as Blacks, a dearth of formal schooling—adults with five or fewer years in the classroom were nearly three times as common as in Minneapolis—also delimited opportunities for better-paying jobs.[114]

With this rapid expansion especially of the middle reaches of Atlanta's wealth ladder came a sea change in the contractual ties of so many to where they lived, pivotal to understanding how compressive capitalism came to impact Atlanta's politics and governments. Long a city of renters, by 1960 Atlanta stood at the threshold of becoming a city of homeowners. While its home-owning rates of 45.6 percent in the city and 48.6 percent in Fulton County still lagged behind the national average of 61.9 percent, homeownership among white households came close. Making this surge of home owning possible were not just rising wages and salaries but New Deal housing policies. Government-backed mortgages spread repayment out over thirty years—much longer than private loan markets had allowed—while guaranteeing low interest rates for borrowers. While HOLC maps and most financiers and builders favored white neighborhoods, Atlanta's Black middle class also enlarged and turned propertied. Despite Jim Crow, rising Black incomes joined with a postwar mobilization of housing advocacy to more than double Black homeownership in the two decades to 1960, up to nearly 30 percent of Black households (figure 1.2). In just two decades, nearly twice as many of this city's whites as well as Blacks came to own the property on which they lived. Home owning came to mark membership less in an upper or upper-middle class than in a *middle* one, as postwar Atlanta acquired its own patrimonial (that is, propertied) middle class, undergoing its own version of what Piketty terms "the principle structural transformation of the distribution of wealth in the developed countries in the twentieth century."[115]

If this trajectory paralleled those in other, richer parts of the United States and the world, the post–World War II home-building industry in Atlanta as

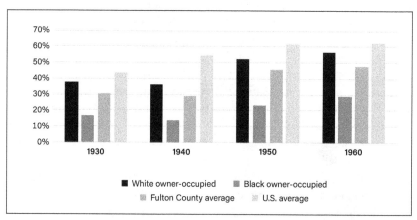

FIGURE 1.2. Black versus white homeownership rates in Fulton County versus the United States, 1930–1960. After a Depression-era lull, white homeownership in Atlanta's main county began catching up with the U.S. average. Even as both Black and white homeownership came close to doubling after 1940, however, the Black rate remained about half of the white one. Manson et al., *IPUMS National Historical Geographic Information System.*

well as in other southern cities still differed in modest but telling ways from that in most other U.S. regions. As late as 1950, Atlanta's professional builders still built more duplexes than single-family detached homes, and 40 percent of new housing consisted of rentals, with more that was self-owned put up by "owner builders," erecting or subcontracting construction of their own homes. By mid-decade more commercial home building of single-family homes had gotten underway, adopting an "operative" or "speculative" guise nearly as often as around New York and Los Angeles, but on a much less massive scale.[116] The closest that the Atlanta area came to seventeen-thousand home Leviathans like Greater New York's Levittown or Los Angeles' Lakewood was the four hundred homes of Belmont Hills in Cobb County's Smyrna, for workers at the recently opened Lockheed plant. Many of these homes wound up rented rather than sold.[117] By 1960 over half of the capital financing Atlantans' homes relied directly on federal backing from the Federal Housing or Veterans Administrations (FHA or VA), yet another way the postwar prosperity of this region leaned more on New Deal programs than did that of the U.S. North or West.[118]

Atlanta's edges absorbed most of its new upper-to-middle class homes, through manicured and well-provisioned suburbs that residents felt befit their class status and which struck many as more like the city than the country. Homebuyers in these reaches of Atlanta's housing market, especially if white, now took for granted much that came with such homes: a water supply, a sewer line for waste disposal, electricity, and streetlights, not to mention all the latest appliances. William Schockley and his wife, Agnes, buying into a new subdivision in North Druid Hills in 1952, were drawn by the "country" features of their lot: how it was "farther out" as well as "new," near a "dairy area" and still with "pure woods" and "a creek in the back." Though he kept a vegetable garden and his wife joined the local garden club, however, they drew a line between these activities and more genuinely rural ones, better exemplified by the neighborhood's "one real vegetable gardener" "from south Georgia" and a chicken yard that was "on the way out."[119] Well-off Blacks, while facing many more barriers to home buying than whites, were similarly disinclined to see the suburban neighborhoods into which they moved as countryside.[120] As some of the first residents to buy into the subdivision known as Collier Heights, developed largely by and for Blacks near the Chattahoochee in the early 1950s, Miriam and William Shropshire, two Black doctors, sought "enough room to move around, to breathe around into," "the openness," and "privacy," as well as "ample space for [their] children to move around." They hired others to handle the landscaping and planted an extensive vegetable garden, yet, like the Schockleys, did not see their home as "rural." That word conjured "outhouses . . . coal lamps and all that type of things, cattle and all that stuff," all of which Collier Heights definitely did not have.[121]

For Atlanta's lower-middle and working classes over the 1940s and 1950s, living environments along the city's edges remained more unmistakably and burdensomely rural, even while offering country-like opportunities. For their largely working-class white clientele, new low-end subdivisions like Belmont Hills did provide rentals with piped-in water, indoor baths, and "improved" roads. Yet compared to the Schockleys' or Shropshires' new abodes, the "suburban countryside" promised in Belmont Hills ads also meant smaller houses and lots and sparser landscaping. In nearby Smyrna, nurse Dorothy Bacon and her husband, Arthur, just starting a dry-cleaning business, bought a lot just blocks off the tiny downtown and "self-built" a duplex there, hiring five or six tradespeople to handle the skilled work. Though in walking distance of the main street, their road remained unpaved and without a sewer line for years. So they put in a septic tank, while renting out the top half of the duplex for extra income.

Less affluent Black migrants to Atlanta's edges had a still harder time. When Gussie Brown and her husband married in the late 1940s, they bought a lot in Scottdale's "colored" subdivision in DeKalb County. The lot had "no paved roads, no lights, no water, no sewer," nor any electricity. A relative who was a brick mason helped them build a two- room house "piece by piece" out of wood and concrete blocks, as they could afford it. For years they fetched water from a neighbor's well, until sometime over the 1950s they got running water from a private supplier. Not just sewer connections but septic tanks and cesspools were slower in coming; in 1960 most Black Scottdalers still relied on outhouses and latrines.[122] Yet for Blacks like the Browns as well as whites like the Bacons, living in such a place meant they could have their own land and grow their own food. As historian Andrew Wiese has noted, ownership of cheaper urban-edge land enabled "self-provisioning"; Gussie's family grew crops and kept chickens, turkeys, and geese, and the Bacons kept chickens, rabbits, bees, and even their own horse.[123]

Nevertheless, the lack of urban amenities in Black Scottdale epitomized those burdensomely rural environments that persisted along Atlanta's edges into the postwar decades, perpetuating the city's bond to the deadweight of its countryside. Far from vanishing over the 1940s and 1950s, this urban-edge shantytown became the fastest-growing African American settlement in DeKalb County.[124] Even as compressive capitalism swelled Atlanta's middle classes, Black as well as white, the continued growth of poorer Black urban-edge enclaves like Scottdale also sustained long-standing differences between southern cities like Atlanta and their comparably sized cousins in the U.S. North and West. Around Atlanta, Scottdale had lots of company, Black enclaves that durably dotted Atlanta's suburban landscape eastward from downtown Decatur to Lithonia, to the north in Lynwood Park, to the south in College Park and Hapeville, and to the west in Louisville and Davenport Town,

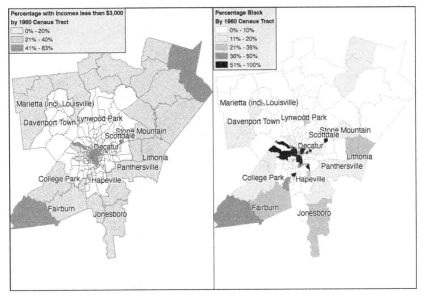

MAP SET 1.4. Concentrations of low-income and Black residence across the Atlanta metropolitan statistical area in 1960. Low income in this case means a family income of less than $3,000 per year, as compared to the median family income of $5,600 for the entire United States in 1959. Both Black and low-income families concentrated together in this era's downtown but also in suburban areas that had long been Black enclaves. Out from downtown white low-income residences now lay beyond richer suburbs largely to the north, Black ones toward the south. Maps by author. *Sources*: U.S. Bureau of the Census, *Per Capita and Median Family Income in 1959, for States, Standard Metropolitan Areas, and Counties* (Washington, D.C.: Government Printing Office, 1965), table 1; Manson et al., *IPUMS National Historical Geographic Information System*; "Atlanta, Georgia," Google Maps, accessed September 2017.

near Smyrna (map set 1.4). Whereas a few of these Black neighborhoods included business districts and better-off households, many, like Scottdale, did not. In them the Atlanta metro area continued to harbor its own versions of the *colonias* springing up outside of Mexico City and the *favelas* outside Rio de Janeiro.[125] Judging by the late twentieth-century definition of slumhood composed by the United Nations, Scottdalers were worse off than residents of Atlanta's downtown "slums." Compared to those living in the notorious Buttermilk Bottom, Black Scottdalers had lower incomes and fewer urban amenities, from indoor bathrooms to piped-in drinking water.[126]

A decade and a half into the nation's post–World War II boom, a compressive capitalism catalyzed by the New Deal had nourished an expansion of middle- and upper-middle-class residents and neighborhoods around Atlanta. Even as the reign of King Cotton appeared to be waning and even as Atlanta's Black as well as white middle classes were waxing, the weight of Georgia's beleaguered countryside continued to be felt, especially along the lower echelons of Jim Crow's racial and class hierarchies, and applied brakes to this city's growth. Not yet having joined the Sunbelt, Atlanta remained tethered to a struggling hinterland not just economically but politically. Even after Eugene Talmadge's death in 1946, his son Herman and his allies had effectively sustained rural control over the political system overseeing Georgia's capital. But the ways they did so, especially in what became known as the Three Governors Controversy, sparked a new generation of Atlanta-based political activists, who began to call for searching and sustained public attention to how undemocratic rustic rule had become.

Already struggling with the cirrhosis and internal hemorrhaging that would fell him, Eugene Talmadge had won the 1946 Democratic primary for governor with only a plurality of county units, while losing the popular vote. Anticipating his father's death, Herman entered the general election for governor and came in second; he then got the state legislature to back his claim to the governorship. But that move violated a newly passed constitution, which had decreed that if a governor died in office, the lieutenant governor was the legal successor. When the departing governor, the anti-Talmadgist Ellis Arnall, insisted that the state's constitution be followed, the junior Talmadge intervened in a move resembling a military coup, sending state troopers to forcibly remove Arnall from office. For two months both Talmadge and the duly elected attorney general ran competing administrations until the court ruled on the attorney general's behalf. The tables then took a final turn, as Talmadge won a special election called to settle the issue and strode triumphantly into the governor's mansion.[127] As historian Dan Carter would later put it, "the war seemed over without a battle," with the more liberal and city-minded candidate summarily cast aside, despite receiving the most actual votes.[128]

Many Atlantans were appalled by this episode, but among those drawn anew into political activism was James Mackay, son of the First Methodist pastor. He had just returned to Atlanta after serving in the war and then earning a law degree at Duke University. The younger Mackay promptly joined an "Atlanta nucleus of a new class of southern rebels," united . . . by frustration . . . [and] hostility to the flourishing injustices of the status quo," who set out to investigate where Georgia politics had gone wrong. A Southern Regional Council led by George Mitchell initiated the effort, a study of *Who Runs Georgia?* As advisers, the investigation drew on board the leaders of groups already mobilizing against rustic rule's notions of citizenship: Black leaders of the Atlanta Urban League (Grace Hamilton) and the Georgia Association of Democratic Clubs (A. T. Walden), leaders from labor (Frank MacAllister of the Georgia Workers Education Service), and the Anti-Defamation League.[129] Joining Mackay as one of the study's two investigators was Calvin Kytle, a journalist teaching at Emory University.

Interviewing key and peripheral players in rustic rule, Mackay and Kytle compiled a richly empirical portrait of just how "essentially undemocratic" the politics of Georgia had become. The power bases of its ruling faction lay mainly in small rural counties whose courthouses could easily be dominated by a tiny group of elites—"a few executives in a few corporations, together with a few skilled politicians." By exploiting the county unit system, often through electoral manipulation and fraud, they maintained their own as well as the Talmadges' grip on power. In addition to the white supremacist and county unit underpinnings of rustic rule, Calvin Kytle and James Mackay's muckraking study found "corporate wealth" and interests dominating the legislature under Talmadgism. Leading legislators "make their living out of corporations," working shoulder to shoulder with corporate lobbyists who flocked through the capital's corridors to ply their influence. The two investigators did not stop there; they also fingered the "ignorance" of Georgians themselves as causative, a "root evil." The "chief reason we are ruled by a coalition of political hacks and corporate wealth is that the people don't know enough to care." The core remedy they envisioned was mass education, to "awaken Georgians to what good government can be." That, however, seemed a tall order, as they found a "really healthy political environment only in those counties where, under the combined stimulus of the Negro vote and an awakened white middle class, active citizens' groups have been organized."[130]

They clearly meant counties mainly around metropolitan Atlanta. Calvin Kytle and James Mackay saw their own county of DeKalb as a wellspring of that enlightened and activated white citizenry for which they hoped. Remarkably, this study itself had special ties to a single one of DeKalb's and Atlanta's best-off white suburbs, Druid Hills.[131] Both Mackay and Kytle lived there, along with Mitchell and another member of the oversight panel, Alexander Miller.[132] Such places were wealthier, better educated, and better connected than most, even within their own counties but especially compared to Georgia as a whole. Significantly, into the post–World War II years, these neighborhoods remained more racially secure than lower-income white counterparts, with less to lose from Blacks' growing economic and political clout. Enjoying higher rates of homeownership and harboring well-established homeowners' associations, abundant churches, clubs, and other groups, they provided training grounds for broader-minded civic leadership especially among women, still largely excluded from Atlanta's ruling elites.[133]

Among the many explanations since proposed for rustic rule's subsequent downfall, political scientists Earl and Merle Black echo Kytle and Mackay in pointing to the advent of a "new middle class" centered in southern cities like Atlanta.[134] But expansion of a middle class itself through the new compressive capitalism was only a first step. For its members to have democratizing impacts, new political projects had to also be forged, to channel middle-class concerns and interests into the public realm. One of these, a new environmental citizenship, would take shape among the more affluent neighborhoods of Atlanta's white middle class, Druid Hills among them. The other, preceding and preparing the way for its environmental compatriot, was an insurgent citizenship of civil rights, arising especially among the city's more aggrieved yet newly hopeful Black middle class.

CHAPTER 2

Civil Rights Citizenship and Its Environments

After several years at a pastorate in Montgomery, Alabama, helping lead a bus boycott and organize the Southern Christian Leadership Conference, Martin Luther King Jr. returned to Atlanta in 1960 to share the pulpit at Ebenezer Baptist Church with his father. Inside that church the podium from which father and son held forth had a cross on the front but, behind, a different kind of iconography: a landscape painting. Installed a few years earlier, shadowed on either side by curtains, the painting showed a river meandering toward the viewer through verdant meadows and trees. No building or cotton field or other sign of human hand intruded on the soothing scene, officially dubbed *The River Jordan*. In the back a mountain poked up against the sky, likely the artist's rendition of Mount Nebo, where an aged Moses caught his only glimpse of the wandering Israelites' Promised Land. As many a brilliant sermon tumbled forth from this pulpit, listeners' eyes might well have strayed up past the preacher and choir to rest on this partly veiled natural scene intimating divine handiwork. That this dreamlike arcadia could occupy such a prominent place in a chamber where so much inspiration for civil rights activism was stirred suggests that there was a good deal more to the *nature* of this Atlanta-based movement than has yet met its historians' eyes.

What might it have meant to hang such a painting in such a place in 1956, at the altar of this core institution of so many Black Atlantans' spiritual and communal life? It suggests, for one thing, that during segregation's apogee nature wasn't exactly missing from Black Atlantans' imaginations or worlds. Nor had such visibly natural places become so entirely or uniformly coded as white. On the contrary, even though Blacks were excluded from "private park" suburbs and kept out of the greenest parks and had many good reasons for fearing what might lie in store for them in Georgia's woods and countryside, they continued to hold onto, even cherish, certain visions and experiences of the natural world. Their aspirations echoed those "landscapes of hope" Black migrants found among the more natural and open spaces around Chicago, as shown by Brian McCammack and Colin Fisher, even as Blacks in this southern city confronted a more severe segregationism and disenfran-

PHOTO 2.1. *The River Jordan* mural in Ebenezer Baptist Church, downtown Atlanta. The mural was completed in 1956 as part of a reconstruction of the baptismal pool; it was restored in the early 2000s. Photos by Christopher Sellers.

chisement.[1] By 1956, as compression capitalism grated against racial barriers by expanding the city's Black middle class, a small but growing portion were finding their way toward suburban homes and surroundings that echoed this painting's pastoral idyll. The then-prosperous businesses and bustle up and down from the church along Auburn Avenue—according to a 1956 report in *Fortune* magazine, "the richest Negro street in the world"—helped to enable such opportunities.[2] Why such imagery found its way into this church sanctuary at this moment hinged not just on its resonance with a growing Black middle class but on the otherworldly respite it conjured for most other of the city's Blacks. They still lived in homes and neighborhoods whose reminders of the countryside were often less idyllic or welcome. Less than half a mile to the north, Buttermilk Bottom epitomized the semirural poverty of this southern city's slums. "Left to flounder in [its] own squalor while the city marched off in shining glory toward the suburbs," it remained shot through with "miserable hovels," "shacks on stilts," and "dismal streets." Since an "essentially white community" next door seemed in "relatively good condition," white architectural students from Georgia Tech visiting the Bottom in the late 1940s decided the main reason why it seemed so miserable was the race of its residents, leading them to dub it Atlanta's "Black heart."[3]

Drive through this area today and search as you may, almost all signs of these slums have been scrubbed away. These same streets are now dominated by a civic center; neat, regimented rows of new apartment and condominium complexes; public housing (Cosby Speers, Bedford Pine) of similarly clean design; and public lands from the wooded pocket park named Renaissance to the seventeen-acre Central Park just west of Bedford Pine, where Buttermilk Bottom used to lie. Now this land is covered with sports fields and grassy hills rimmed with shade trees. Auburn Avenue outside the King Historic District, while seeing some revival through gentrifying, still bears many scars from its preceding half century of decline, chief among them that blocks-wide ribbon of raised earth, concrete, and asphalt that bisected it in the late fifties to finish off the city's first freeway.[4] The transformations have made it all the more difficult to visualize just what these parts of town looked like in the days when "Daddy King" was Ebenezer Baptist's sole preacher. Around when *The River Jordan* first peeked out from behind his pulpit, a veritable juggernaut of environmental destruction had been unleashed that would clear the way for what this part of town now looks like. And there was no better demonstration of just how undemocratic the city's governance remained into the 1950s than the ways choices were made about what was to blame: the land-gobbling projects of urban renewal as well as freeway building. These razed not just neighborhoods but entire swathes of downtown, inhabited mostly by Blacks whose permission was never asked.

Urbanizing as these infrastructual projects were, the closed and elitist decision making about them bore the imprint of rustic rule and its racial authoritarianism, which still prevailed in city as well as state government. Especially within the city of Atlanta itself, however, by 1956 the earliest and most pathbreaking challenge to a white supremacist state was already well underway, a movement for civil rights. Aided by court decisions, this movement first gathered steam as a democratizing force operating largely within confines imposed by a white supremacist state, seeking to circumvent and undermine its bars rather than confront them outright. In its early postwar phases, leaders envisioned a civil rights citizenship that remained deeply and almost exclusively rooted in Atlanta's small but increasingly robust Black middle class. If urban greenery quietly grounded their visions, principles of inclusion and fairness furnished their main moral leverage. Both leading groups, an Atlanta chapter of the NAACP and the Atlanta Urban League, united to get out the Black vote, and, as the NAACP concentrated on the courtroom, the AUL sought to bolster Black opportunities especially in urban and suburban markets for homes. Plying levers of local government as well as businesses, the AUL actively cultivated the building of "modern" surburban housing that more affluent Black families *could* buy, while nourishing civic organizing among the often poorly provisioned existing Black communities nearby.

As Atlanta Urban League's postwar agenda shows, Black Atlantans did mobilize to secure parks as well as more natural-looking home environments for themselves. Yet Urban Leaguers made no mention of protecting "nature" or a larger "environment"; they subsumed these efforts within what they saw as a larger and more compelling project of civil rights citizenship, to secure for Black Atlantans those many rights denied them by a white supremacist regime. Similarly, as the cause of nature preservation began to stir among a white suburban middle class, associated post–World War II political leaders highlighted another goal they deemed more pressing and urgent: challenging those political inequities that rustic rule had foisted on all Atlantans. Though not just Black leaders but a significant share of their white Atlanta counterparts sought democratization, spatial segregation allied with differences in how each conceived their respective political projects to limit their dialogue and collaboration with each other. The divisions between them would prove far more enduring than Jim Crow authoritarianism itself, not just because Atlanta's whites and Blacks still circulated in such separate communities but because these two political projects of civil rights and environmentalism remained so deeply at odds, starting with the "what" to which each aspired to belong.

The Atlanta Urban League's Homescapes of Hope

The 1946 gubernatorial contest, erupting as Martin Luther King Jr. was still attending undergraduate classes at Morehouse, had gained such urgency for Georgia's rustic rulers because of how racial barriers to voting booths seemed to be falling, unleashing a resurgent Black vote especially in Atlanta. In 1944 the U.S. Supreme Court struck down the white primary, that most explicitly racial means by which the dominant Democratic Party had shut out Black voters. That next year the anti-Talmadgist governor Ellis Arnall and the Georgia legislature had repealed the poll tax, largely to enable lower-income white voters but also opening voting booths to more Blacks. Early in 1946 a voter-registration drive by Atlanta's Black leadership and civic groups had successfully swayed a special congressional election, sending Helen Douglas Mankin to finish out the term of Robert Ramspeck for Georgia's Fifth District. For this election Atlanta's most prosperous Black precinct, the home-owning district around Atlanta Univerity, actually had a 50 percent turnout, higher than any white precinct. Among the architects of this and subsequent voter-registration drives was the new leader of the Atlanta Urban League, Grace Towns Hamilton, who also lived there. Tripling the Black electorate in Fulton County, their efforts helped new Black voters across Atlanta to secure Talmadge's defeat in the popular vote for the 1946 gubernatorial race—though the county unit system ensured his victory. City leaders were also put on notice that, for the first time since the end of Reconstruction, the Black vote was gaining real clout.[5]

Voter-registration drives ranked high among the early means by which Atlanta's Black civic leaders forged new avenues of citizenly action to confront the city's racial authoriarianism. Here, as in other nascent citizenship projects, an imaginative effort was necessary at the outset: to step outside the cruel customs and everyday disempowerment of Jim Crow and envision how both the state and an overarching society could be altered for the better, starting with some plausible strategy of advocacy. Getting Blacks to the ballot box entailed contemporary sociologist T. H. Marshall's "political element" of citizenship. In northern U.S. cities, however, much civil rights advocacy had aspired to Marshall's other two "elements," the "civil" and the "social," which were traditionally divvied up between the NAACP and the Urban League. The NAACP had concentrated more on protests and court actions that defended the "civil element," those "rights necessary for individual freedom," including justice itself. The Urban League, on the other hand, pursued citizenship's "social" elements such as decent incomes, housing, and public services. They sought that modicum of security and aspiration for the city's Blacks that would enable them, as Marshall put it, "to live the life of a civilized being according to the standards prevailing in the society."[6]

Within a post–World War II Atlanta regime that imposed second- or third-class citizenship on its Black residents, the Atlanta Urban League and NAACP chapter joined forces to assert Blacks' civil rights to more equitable public provisions—a civil rights citizenship that, for the AUL throughout the 1950s, largely conceded to the supremacist fiction of separate but equal. Seeking out ways of broadening the social citizenship available to Atlanta's Blacks, the AUL settled on an advocacy of Black suburban homeownership that, as Liz Cohen has put it, framed the "purchaser as citizen."[7] If natural spaces and greenery akin to those depicted in *The River Jordan* had a place in the Atlanta Urban League's postwar agenda, these remained subordinated to another overarching goal. The AUL sought to ensure more stable, secure, and "modern" homescapes for Black Atlantans, to foster an environmental consumption that could replace or otherwise ameliorate the all-too-rural environments in which so many of them dwelled.

The Atlanta Urban League had been around more than two decades by 1943, when Grace Towns Hamilton stepped into its directorship. Initially, it had been among the first southern branches of a National Urban League founded in 1910 to undertake the study and betterment "of social and economic conditions among Negroes in cities," along with "the training of Negro social workers." A response to the Great Migration of Blacks from the rural South to the urban North, the league aspired to aid their adjustments to city living. The often decrepit downtown slums to which Blacks were usually confined in the urban North became a major priority of northern chapters. Advocating for new housing as well as proper upkeep and maintenance by landlords, league staff also sought to cultivate moral integrity and respectable behavior among Black newcomers to the city, through education and other more "wholesome" influences including recreational alternatives. Northern chapters prioritized getting Blacks good jobs, providing training and other support to enhance the appeal and "efficiency" of a Black workforce, and reaching out to employers to urge the hiring of skilled Blacks. National Urban League staff, mostly hailing from a small Black middle class, mixed their good intentions with more ambivalent "concerns and apprehensions about migrants and poor African-Americans in general."[8] More than twenty-eight chapters had crystallized in northern cities such as New York and Chicago by 1919, when a new southern regional office in Atlanta gained the league's "first paid staff in the Deep South," which a year later affiliated as an official league chapter.[9]

Up until the 1940s the sponsors and staff of the Atlanta Urban League largely hewed to the mold set by the national office and northern chapters. On the surface the circumstances they faced seemed similar, with Atlanta drawing its own share of Blacks from the southern countryside and with the Atlanta Urban League and its supporters worriedly committed to new arrivals' uplift. At first, shortages of funding in this poorer city hampered the chapter's ability to hire and keep staff, and, after it established a steadier funding stream from Atlanta's white-run Community Chest, league staff had to tread carefully to remain in this funder's good graces. While the chapter periodically collected and conveyed complaints about housing to the authorities, unlike northern counterparts, it concentrated less on influencing government than on reaching and influencing Atlanta's Black communities themselves: informing them about health and hygiene, organizing boys and girls clubs, instructing about canning and setting up community gardens, and sponsoring a Neighborhood Union. Where it hewed most closely to northern models was in seeking to enhance the job prospects for Atlanta's Blacks. Working with willing employers to facilitate the hiring of skilled Blacks, it developed a local "employment bureau" and many training and education programs to better equip Atlanta's Black workforce. In the 1930s it even lent a hand to labor organizing among Black workers.[10] Once Grace Hamilton took up the AUL's reins, however, its job programs would largely evaporate, supplanted by a new priority: providing more decent housing for the city's Blacks.

Growing up among Atlanta's Black elite, Hamilton had just returned to her native city when A. T. Walden, who'd known her from earlier and who headed the city's chapter of the NAACP as well as the AUL's board, promoted her candidacy to become the league's new director.[11] In 1946 she recruited as her chief lieutenant Robert Thompson, a native of Lynchburg, Virginia, with a master's in social work from Atlanta University, who had returned to the city after serving in the war. While the national league office had long seen Black job promotion as part of a "balanced" chapter program, Hamilton and Thompson, after being rebuffed in their early outreach to local GM and Ford plants, then abandoned any such effort.[12] Instead of pounding against these closed doors to what Jefferson Cowie termed "economic citizenship," they sought to expand Blacks' tiny share of the city's economic wealth by building out the home and neighorhood bases of Atlanta's Black communities—as the mantra of the later minority-led movement for environmental justice would have it, "where we live."[13] Lending their own visible and active hand to a capitalism being steered in compressive directions by New Deal ground rules, the league found its greatest post–World War II influence along the city's edges. There it spurred new home building and better public provisions for Atlanta's Blacks, a collective homescape of hope.

Hamilton's Atlanta Urban League confronted a city government under William Hartsfield that since the late 1930s had finally been moving in the "modernizing" and "progressive" directions since accomplished in many U.S. cities outside the South. Most of these reforms served mainly to shore up Atlanta's own Jim Crow regime. Switching to citywide votes for the city council and school board, for instance, or annexing white neighborhoods like Buckhead into the city only fortified the electoral clout of a white majority. Within resolutely white supremacist rule, tightening civil service rules could well further exclude Blacks, reinforcing their status as second- or third-class citizens.[14] Though Hartsfield was initially endorsed by Talmadge, over the mid-1940s, as Black voter registration picked up, he began showing more attentiveness to Atlanta's Blacks than his predecessors.[15] Even though federal funds from the New Deal had begun facilitating public projects on an unprecedented new scale, however, Atlanta's government stayed in the hands of remarkably few. In a 1953 book by the political scientist Floyd Hunter, its city government exemplified the top-heavy urban "power structure" of his title, a less-than-democratic configuration relatively independent of who did or didn't vote. Based on his experience in Atlanta's social welfare bureaucracy and extensive interviewing, Hunter concluded that a tiny cadre of long-standing business leaders and politicians, all of them white, held the true reins of power in Atlanta. The Black "sub-community," as he put it, remained much further down his scale of power and influence. Even among Atlanta's Black civic groups, he ranked the Walden-led NAACP first and the Urban League down at fifth, behind a newly formed Negro Voters League and the Black YMCA.[16]

The AUL's clout remained so limited not just because of the race of its leaders but because of its small size, which forced Hamilton and her chief lieutenant Thompson to carefully pick their battles. Hamilton led a mere handful of paid staff, with a $7,000 budget consisting mostly of salaries. The vulnerability of these purse strings also imposed constraints on how hard the AUL could push against the city's "separate but equal" ways. Unlike league chapters elsewhere, the vast majority of the Atlanta Urban League chapter's funding came out of the city's community chest, which kept a careful eye on how prointegrationist its activities were and moved to clip the league's wings if it strayed too far.[17] Financially and politically precarious as their operations remained, Hamilton and Thompson's decision to concentrate on housing also accommodated the constraints exerted by a white city leadership that remained resolutely segregationist, despite growing lip service to Blacks' concerns. Promoting private-housing developments just for Blacks avoided white officials' determination to maintain a color line and quietly favored that segment of Black Atlanta considered the safest—those already better-off. Rather than pushing for Black jobs that might lift more out of poverty, they plied their advocacy on behalf of Blacks who already had decent-paying work.

Under Hamilton and Thompson's leadership, the league's promotion of new housing for Blacks also addressed a major catalyst for the white resentment and racism that drove the politics of white supremacy in city and state and repeatedly erupted into violence. As Black homeownership in Fulton County nearly doubled over the 1940s, to reach 23 percent of households, Atlanta's West Side became a locus for racial conflict as aspiring middle-class Blacks were able to buy and move into white middle- to lower-income neighborhoods there. White groups from the neo-Nazi Columbians to the Westside Community Development Corporation turned areas transitioning to Black homeownership into focal points for white vigilantism. The Columbians' violence, in the mold of the KKK, was relatively straightforward: bombings and terror-inducing leaflets that tried to scare Black home buyers away. Westside's strategy seemed on the surface of it more civil and reasonable: they sought to raise a pool of money to buy houses from whites who felt compelled to sell, to keep property exchange out of the hands of Blacks.[18] Yet they too wielded violence. One day in 1949, a spokesperson warned a Black woman buying a house on Ashby Street (now Joseph W. Lowery Boulevard, near Clark Atlanta University) that "it wasn't advisable . . . to do so because they were going to bomb it" and that she risked her "own funeral." True to their word, that night an explosion shook the house.[19] While much other violence in mixed areas came from "self-appointed trouble-makers" and not any named group, post–World War II instability in the boundaries between Black and white neighborhoods opened a controversial new front in white supremacist citizenship: scaring off would-be Black home buyers.[20] Stirring an Atlanta base of support for the race-baiting of Talmadgism, such conflicts became an embarrassment for a Hartsfield administration intent on preserving Atlanta's trademark "racial harmony" while also ingratiating itself with a budding Black electorate.

Aggravating the conflicts, Atlanta's white leadership had few legal means to enforce explicitly racial boundaries in private-housing markets, even as it retained the power to racially segregate parks, schools, and other public spaces. Racially defined boundaries had been disallowed in zoning codes since the 1920s, and, after a 1948 U.S. Supreme Court decision, could no longer be legally anchored in the covenants of private-housing contracts. Housing segregation in Atlanta had thus already come to rest, instead, on practices similar to those in other U.S. regions. As scholars of the Sunbelt synthesis such as Matthew Lassiter have noted, calling these *de facto* was a misnomer, since legal and other governmental decisions set the parameters, among other ways, through zoning codes with restrictions on lot or home size that could serve as racial proxies.[21] While housing segregation remained a fact of life in postwar Atlanta, and opportunities for owning or renting stayed much more circumscribed for Blacks than for whites, in reality border zones remained unavoidable. At the same time, private decisions and actions by buyers, sellers, and other agents determined whether a racial boundary would hold, and the willingness of any one white family to sell their home to a Black buyer could breach it. So these borders were inherently unstable—and all the more so as a newly compressive capitalism added to the incomes of Atlanta Blacks, providing them with the means to pay higher rents or become homeowners. Even city hall largely foisted the job of maintaining residential segregation over to private actors: home builders, lenders, realtors, home sellers and buyers, and the less formal or government-sanctioned agreements at which they could arrive. The biracial West Side Mutual Development Committee (WSMDC), set up by Hartsfield in 1952 to foster an "orderly and harmonious" racial transition in that corner of the city, sought mediating agreements that had no force of law behind them. Thereby, it pledged allegiance to *"the primary role of the private real estate market in meeting"* Atlantans' housing needs.[22]

Where the government of this southern city remained regionally distinctive, however, was that, unlike cities of the urban North, it still exercised racially explicit controls over publicly owned buildings and spaces, among these, parks. For many decades its parks committee enjoyed the legally enforceable authority to designate the most lavishly furnished of these green spaces for whites and a much tinier and more neglected share for Blacks. Racial apportioning of the city's titular "public" resources to so blatantly favor whites endured into the 1950s, however loudly solicitous Mayor Hartsfield became of Black voters. The single most notable exception was Mozley Park, thirty-two acres of former estate lands with a clubhouse, swimming pool, and tennis courts. The largest city park on Atlanta's West Side, it remained off-limits for Blacks even as they came to far outnumber white homeowners in the vicinity of the park. Bowing to the burgeoning Black homeownership in this area in 1953, however, with the city's growing Black electorate no doubt in the back of his mind, Hartsfield announced that Mozley Park "would soon be dedicated for Negro use." Appearing alongside his park commissioner, the mayor sought to ingratiate himself with his audience by promising a "Negro golf course" as well as a "full-blast . . . effort" "to meet the Negro citizen's recreational and park needs."[23]

Hartsfield's promise came at a meeting of the local NAACP chapter devoted explicitly to "park and recreation issues," held at an Ebenezer Baptist Church ministered by Martin Luther King Sr. Two years before *The River Jordan* was placed behind its pulpit, Black leaders eagerly welcomed the racial conversion of Mozley in language that could echo that mural's promised-land theme. The *Atlanta Daily World*'s editors' enthusiasm was religiously tinged: "No person can move in the atmosphere of these environments of tranquil beauty and flowing glory without feeling the enchantment common to hallowed ground."[24] For Black Atlantans who had grown up in the rural South, the pastoral setting of the park offered more than just intimations of the sacred. Area churches held picnics on its grounds, and early on a newly Black homeowners' association sponsored religious-themed events there like a film about the Holy Land. More mundanely, the park embodied a smaller-scale and less threatening version of the rural than the Georgia countryside many had left behind. Among the many community groups taking advantage, Campfire Girls and YWCA summer camps met on its visibly natural and tranquil grounds, the latter featuring "cook out lunches, Bible stories, swimming and outdoor recreation."[25]

What made parks like Mozley such beacons of hope, however, was not their freely accessible landscapes and greenery alone, but those built and inhabited spaces that their Black advocates, users, and celebrants so often associated with them. In "hailing" the racial conversion of Mozley, *Atlanta Daily World* noted how a school "on a hill overlooking the park" "is already being occupied by colored children," and a Baptist church nearby added to "the nucleus of what promises to be one of the finest sections in America." Driving all these hopeful changes was how newly arriving Black homeowners had transformed the surrounding neighborhood. "Homes in this vicinity have taken on new life; modern buildings with well-kept grounds and wide streets with their accompanying shade trees and wildflowers." The racial transition of Mozley Park only "cap[ped] the climax" of those larger achievements "credit[ed] to the fine people whose fortune it is to live" there, an expanding Black middle class. Among the virtues being cultivated, enthused *Daily World* editors, were "lessening crime," "health," and even "citizenship" itself. Around Mozley Park, West Atlanta was becoming a homescape of hope.[26]

From the mid-1940s making more such homescapes possible became the Atlanta Urban League's chief goal. Setting aside the elevated and often religiously accented rhetoric of preachers and newspaper editors, however, league leaders sought influence with white city officials through another mode of speech, the language of facts.[27] Following an approach pioneered by W. E. B. Dubois—who by this time had returned to Atlanta and whose classes Hamilton herself had briefly attended—Hamilton and Thompson sought to sway white officialdom principally through the gathering of social and economic data, that lingua franca of the twentieth-century Western state. This resort to social science was not for a white audience alone; it also enabled Urban Leaguers to step out from their own personal and relatively privileged circumstances, to gain a more overarching understanding of the city and local society whose inequities they sought to engage. Concretizing just how unequal Black and white Atlanta were, their social science served to guide both their own and (they hoped) others' decisions about where best to intervene. Culling hard knowledge about the plight of so many Blacks, they judged, also made Black needs and interests more undeniably visible and, the hope was, harder to overlook or neglect. Though Hamilton, at least, was a stalwart churchgoer, she and Thompson systematically avoided biblical language as activists and public figures, taking a resolutely dispassionate and secular approach. Counting up and summarizing the needs of Black Atlanta that could so easily be reduced to invisibility or irrelevance, they pressed Atlanta's white elite to allow for Black homescapes of comparable abundance and provision to those being contemplated for Atlanta's white middle class.

One of the first successes of the Urban League came through its lobbying of a new Metropolitan Planning Commission (MPC) set up in 1947 as the Atlanta area's first stab at regional planning, and, like so many public bodies of this period, it was exclusively white. Aiming at a blueprint for metropolitan development across Greater Atlanta, not just within the city limits but across Fulton and DeKalb Counties, the MPC seemed headed at first toward a conclusion that there was very little room for new Black housing, even out from the city. The AUL was able to counter this conclusion by convening its own shadow planning body, a Housing Council pointedly composed of prominent whites as well as Blacks. It documented the need for new housing for Blacks—existing homes were in "deplorable" condition, with 71.6 percent of them "substandard"—and pinpointed six places out from the city—"presently undeveloped areas" where new and better housing for Blacks could go.[28] The council's fact-based exhortations worked surprisingly well, given the city's long history of simply neglecting Black needs and requests. Planning and city officials reserved the six areas, recognizing them in the MPC's *Up Ahead* planning document of 1952 as "areas of Negro expansion." They also allowed the league to proceed with facilitating new Black housing developments there. Official recognition of these "expansion areas" constituted the single biggest concession the AUL was able to wrench from a white officialdom otherwise fixated on its own white-dominated vision of metropolitan growth.[29] Urban League leaders' willingness to work within Jim Crow's confines won them steady access to city decision makers. They became the only Black group "constantly consulted" by the MPC in formulating plans—a role that the MPC chair then threw back at other Blacks who accused him of an "undemocratic" planning process. The AUL did rebuke the MPC's segregationist assumptions, but only privately and in markedly mild terms. Other Black leaders who had been sidelined then railed against separate-but-equal assumptions in urban planning that the AUL had accepted as "encourag[ing] Jim Crowism."[30]

The AUL's mixture of accommodation with quiet pressure may have won MPC concessions on housing sites but, with the exception of Mozley Park, failed on the parks front. To enhance both the amenities and racial isolation of prospective Black housing areas, the AUL urged these to be "bordered by 'greenbelt' park strips."[31] The "park strips" for these areas never made it into MPC plans. The systematic omission forced the AUL into a characteristically measured retort by private correspondence: "Proper planning must set aside suitable areas" noted "for . . . parks playground and recreational facilities . . . regardless of racial composition."[32] Even while opening more doors to Black housing, the city's white elite seemed to take the long-standing dearth of Black parks as evidence Black Atlantans could still do without them or, at least, that there was little urgency to rectifying such inequities, so long as politicians like Hartsfield could get away with a mere mouthing of promises.

Into the 1950s recreational inequities showed up in nearly all of the league's surveys of outlying Black neighborhoods and of those within the city itself. Not long after Hartsfield pledged his "full-blast" effort, a city-park plan slighting Black needs prompted the Urban League's first report on the issue, in early 1954. It briefly bemoaned Atlanta's overall scarcity of parks—the city's one acre of parkland per two hundred residents was half the minimum recommended by the National Recreation Association. The report then concentrated a barrage of data on how little this park system offered to Atlanta's Blacks. Black Atlanta's parkland amounted to one acre per 1,020 citizens, ten times worse than the minimum standard, compared to one acre for every 155 whites.[33] Even with the addition of Mozley, just four of Atlanta's park areas were reserved for them. As the city dragged its heels even in spending what little it had allotted for Black parks, the league urged a Black appointment to the Parks Department's advisory board, then still all white.[34] Below the level of AUL leadership, league workers themselves were more split over whether "there should be integration" of white parks, or whether, with the looming threat of white violence, more parks should be reserved exclusively for Blacks.[35]

The league's most successful postwar activity was its promotion not of public parks but of new private home building for Blacks. From 1948 it proceeded not just to encourage but to help sponsor the construction of new, more typically suburban "modern homes" in designated "Negro expansion" zones, to remedy how many "fewer houses had been built for our minority group than were needed." Approaching white and Black realtors and builders as well as groups of Black buyers, the league catalyzed the purchase of lands and home construction itself, with the Shropshires' Collier Heights among the most lavish.[36] By 1956 league negotiations had jump-started some eight or nine other subdivisions for Blacks, in addition to Collier Heights. All consisted of single-family homes owned by their occupants, with prices ranging from as low as $6,710 (Fairhaven) to as high as $35,000 (Crestwood Forest, also in the Collier Heights area).[37] The Urban League had also facilitated the building of rentals, starting with Highpoint Apartments, where the Shropshires had first stayed upon moving to the city. By 1956 the league claimed a hand in nearly half of the new private housing units constructed for Blacks in and around the city over the previous fifteen years.[38] Just over half of these 10,550 dwelling units were rentals—Black Atlanta remained a city of renters. But of the new homes owned by Blacks, only a third conformed to the highly publicized pattern of Blacks buying out white homeowners and neighborhoods, featured in narratives of "white flight." Instead, the vast majority of newly owning Black households followed pathways blazed by the Urban League, becoming the first residents to dawn the doorsteps of their new homes.[39] Come 1959, when the national Commission on Civil Rights paid a visit, it praised the city's "beautiful Negro suburbs." They had made Atlanta one of "only a few cities" where "Negroes have access to outlying or suburban areas," while "add[ing] to the city's beauty and greatly impress[ing] the whites."[40]

For the Urban League, and many others Black leaders as well, more was at stake than just bettering Black environmental consumption and growing a Black patrimonial middle class. Their quest for "modern" housing and "decent neighborhoods" also cultivated more "responsible citizenship."[41] Hard to miss here was a denigration of slum dwellers that seemed to echo white critiques, equating personal moral dereliction with the physical conditions that supposedly bred it. But the links drawn by AUL leaders between "modern housing" and "responsible" political engagement articulated the more subversive anti-supremacist thrust of their project. The rustic and ill-provisioned housing of most of Atlanta's Blacks and their miniscule share of the city's wealth under Jim Crow had bolstered white supremacist contentions that they deserved a lower class of citizenship. "Beautiful Negro suburbs," on the other hand, undermined these "proofs" that Blacks remained unworthy of full political or civil rights. Certainly, moving into a "modern" rental or home and yard to which one held the title fulfilled long-standing and historical hopes of many Blacks. But as Marshall's "social citizenship" had also emphasized, for Blacks themselves the stability and confidence of achieving comparable living standards to whites could also raise hopes still further.[42] A newfound optimism that betterment *was* possible could incubate greater citizenly assertiveness in the civil and political realms as well.

Consistent with these broader goals, the Atlanta Urban League also reached out to many of the poorest Black enclaves along the city's edges, to try and catalyze local efforts to alleviate their rural deprivation. Among the most distinctively southern features of Atlanta's edges, impoverished communities of Blacks rimmed all six outlying areas suggested by the AUL and its allies for "Negro expansion," quietly providing the MPC with another powerful reason for approving these areas for new Black housing. AUL surveys in 1952 confirmed how "woefully neglected" these neighborhoods remained "in terms of [as Hamilton put it] the kind of community facilities which one would expect in modern living."[43] Hardly any of these "little isolated groups" had paved roads or sewage connections. Some, like Scottdale, had no piped-in water, and many were without their own Black elementary school. They had little access to stores, doctors, or clinics for health care. Surveyors found public parks and recreation facilities to be especially lacking.[44]

The surveyors also assessed the enclaves for what we might term their citizenship capacity: how ready they were for any collective action that might bring more amenities and services their way. Whereas white homeowners, especially in affluent areas such as Druid Hills, already had strong homeowners' associations, and under white supremacy even many less affluent white neighborhoods could count on some receptiveness from local officials, poor Black communities faced the greatest obstacles both to local self-organizing and to being heard. AUL surveyors found that while most of these edge enclaves had churches, extremely few had many registered voters, and only some had "organized community groups" on which further mobilizing might build.[45] Many were afflicted with a "local inertia or apathy," pessimism born of long-term official neglect and white oppression. The league then sent in organizers to "serve as a catalyst" "to bring together different groups and interests." By "securing a cross section of community participation" and "resolv[ing] obstructive differences and dissention," they aimed "to build up in the communities a new attitude toward its problems and faith in its own potentialities to help itself."[46]

By the mid-1950s, however, with the success of league interventions in individual communities still so "few," the league launched another level of organization, a "Neighborhood Council." This strategy, echoing that of a Neighborhood Union formed decades earlier but which had fallen apart during the Depression, created a Black counterpart to those alliances of white homeowners seeking to stymy the sales and blockbusting turning many of the city's neighborhoods from white to Black.[47] Starting with representatives of seven Black neighborhoods, the council met and began setting up committees to address "concrete problems, namely, securing street lights, better transportation, police patrolwoman [*sic*] safety signs, and recreation facilities."[48] By 1958 some twenty-one civic groups participated, most of them hailing from beyond downtown. The council ran its own newsletter and sponsored other collective events such as cleanup drives. It claimed an array of successes for its member groups at securing "courteous and efficient services" from "the Atlanta Police Department, Water Department, Construction Department, Traffic Department, Atlanta Transit Company and others."[49] Over the 1950s, the league's community-organizing efforts culminating in this Neighborhood Council anticipated later waves of neighborhood organizing that are better known: the foray of youthful activists into Atlanta's slums during the 1960s and a broadening neighborhood movement that by the 1970s would briefly seize the reins of city government.

Even as the league's neighborhood organizing program gained traction over the later 1950s, the challenges grew to its suburban housing initiatives. Despite Atlanta's having three sizeable financial institutions run by Blacks, "the Negro," as Thompson sadly noted, remained "rarely, if ever in the class of favored borrowers."[50] As Atlanta's Blacks remained far less well housed than their white counterparts, with just under half the rate of ownership, governmental programs, like those for returning veterans, and financial conditions, like low interest rates, that had favored home building and homeownership in the early postwar years took turns for the worse.[51] As the AUL's program of cultivating new homescapes of hope appeared in danger of sputtering out, the larger goal these places were supposed to serve, of full and equal citizenship for Atlanta's Blacks, still seemed a distant one.

Back in 1953, standing in front of the altar at Ebenezer Baptist and before a Black audience, Mayor Hartsfield did mouth the appropriate words: "I like to think of Negro citizens as citizens . . . period."[52] But Hartsfield's ingratiating rhetoric and pledges aside, African Americans remained shut out from city efforts that wrought the biggest changes in its physical environment over this period, steered less directly by elections or elected officials and more by their administrative appointees, an increasingly professionalized civil service still operating in white supremacist mode. Public housing offers a case in point. After World War II the Atlanta Housing Authority tapped federal funds to swell its public housing stock, and by 1959 Blacks occupied nearly five thousand of these units, or 66.12 percent of the total. With such a predominantly Black clientele, the Housing Authority at least made a show of seeking Black advice, through a mayor-appointed advisory committee and more informal consultations that included Hamilton and Thompson. Despite a Black majority clientele, however, the Atlanta Housing Authority clung to an internal structure that made no pretense to racial democracy. As late as 1959, its governing board included no Black members, unlike counterparts in sixteen other southern cities.[53] In pushing forward what became Atlanta's most aggressive and disruptive downtown interventions of the postwar era, urban renewal and highway building, the city's white elite sidelined Black voices and interests even more thoroughly, while piling up their most devastating consequences on the Black side of the color line.

The Onslaught against Atlanta's Slums

If the heyday of Atlanta slum eradication had come just twenty years later, we would already know it as the massive *environmental* intervention it actually was. Begun in the 1930s with forerunning projects in the nation's federally funded housing program, it picked up with the national Housing Acts of 1949 and 1954. Federal urban-renewal programs supported by southern lawmakers had furnished the financial means and full legal authority for cities such as Atlanta to raze, then reconstruct, a substantial share of their downtowns. By the late 1950s a full-scale assault was underway on those parts of its core now deemed "slums." Downtown's white business elite, in the guise of a group known as Central Atlanta Progress, was "the prime mover," according to what remains the best account, by the political scientist Clarence Stone.[54] This group worked with Hartsfield and other well-to-do white political leaders to build a coalition from the top down, retaining a tight grip on the decision making that drove and steered the resultant, destructive tide. Federal generosity magnified the impacts: the $39 million price tag for "renewal" of the Bedford Pine portion of Buttermilk Bottom along with two other areas, two-thirds of it covered by federal funds, equaled all the city's annual direct expenditures in 1957.[55] What remained a white supremacist regime set about razing homes inhabited by those it relegated to its lowest class of citizen, poor Blacks utterly deprived of any say. No studies were contemplated of the broader environmental or social impacts, few public hearings were held, and only after key decisions were made was citizenly advice solicited from any Black leaders. Downtown redevelopment gathered steam as a veritable political juggernaut, the most muscular, large-scale, and brutal reconstruction of its built environment this city had seen since Sherman's Civil War torching. The Urban League actually lent their support to the effort early on, seeking to speed Black transfers to more hopeful homescapes. But, as their advice and warnings about those displaced went unheeded and as more homes, businesses, and livelihoods fell to the blades of the federal bulldozer, even Urban Leaguers turned much more critical.[56]

Atlanta's first renewal project, begun in the depths of the Depression, was also the United States' first. Overseeing it was an official with deep qualms about the democratic process, Charles Palmer. This Atlanta real-estate developer was an admirer of the Italian fascist Benito Mussolini; like some other businessmen of the period, he had been inspired on a trip to Italy by the massive building projects of that nation's corporatist dictatorship.[57] All-white Techwood, started in 1935, became the first such public housing project in the nation. As two more all-white projects and three for Blacks got underway, a new Atlanta Housing Authority continued Palmer's work under an executive director, then under an all-white "citizen board" of mayoral appointments.[58] Also gaining charge of the city's urban-renewal program, the AHA then moved quickly to "tear down the slum areas," with housing of the displaced a decidedly secondary priority. Already by 1946 AHA's director estimated they "had eliminated some 15% of slum areas" and were looking to "gradually eliminate" the rest.[59] That same year, planning also got underway for freeway building that would draw the Talmadgist State Highway Department into the redevelopment fray, starting with a north-south route to slash through Auburn Avenue, the Black business district. Soon thereafter, the state constitution was amended to expand powers of eminent domain for such projects, and the U.S. Congress stepped up funding for downtown freeways and expanded the potential scale of urban-renewal projects.[60] With so many checks to their ambitions falling away, Atlanta's slum clearance advocates dreamed bigger and accelerated their timetables.

Their resolve was fortified by how, from the late forties into the fifties, advocates of renewal turned Atlanta's semirural downtown slums into a lurid and increasingly well-known spectacle, at once fascinating and appalling to its visitors. Setting the tone was a two-hour excursion arranged in the fall of 1947 by the Home Builders Association and a Citizens Better Housing Forum. "Representatives of 42 Atlanta clubs and civic organizations" mounted a "suburban coach equipped with a loud speaker" for a whirlwind tour of "at least 20,000 of the 35,000 substandard dwellings in Atlanta." To cap it off, they then all converged on a downtown restaurant for dinner, to share the awfulness of what they'd seen.[61] The Georgia Tech 1949 survey of the city's "worst" slum areas added to the chorus of concern. Dominated by census tracts between 83 percent and 99.5 percent Black, they were, the students found, "encumbered" with "low, ramshackle dwellings . . . chicken coops, pig pens, and other parasitical structures"—all-too-country–like reminders of the city's impoverished and backward "Black heart." Like so many reporters of the time, these architectural students stigmatized these homes apparently without speaking with anyone who lived there, rendering residents invisible except as a "population" defined by impersonal and ominous statistics. Among the worst, they found a "density of 32,600 people per square mile," "more new cases of tuberculosis than any other tract," and "more criminal offenses, juvenile delinquency, and decay of all types than anywhere in Atlanta." "Parks, green areas, and other outdoor recreational areas," which the students believed would promote "crime and disease prevention," were also "practically non-existent." In a foreboding honest expression of the thinking that would drive urban renewal, they confessed to take inspiration from the plans drawn up for London in the wake of the Nazis' bombing campaign. "How wonderful it would be if the 'Black heart' of Atlanta slums were to be leveled by bombs tomorrow. . . . Bloody as it might be, [it] would in the end save more lives lost from crime and tuberculosis than it would destroy."[62]

If soberer euphemisms like "substandard housing" prevailed in official documents and discussions, the press and many civic groups kept up the drumbeat of rawer language and portraiture. "At Least Our Slums Are Well-Publicized," noted an *Atlanta Constitution* editorial in 1955. The accompanying photo essay divulged, once more, how "Blighted Areas Like These Stab at Atlanta's Heart." Half of it featured a section "to the east of Atlanta's downtown 'Golden Heart,'" "variously known as Black Bottom, Blackberry Bottom or Buttermilk Bottom." Photo frames tightened around the fronts of two-story houses, rimmed with rickety porches and stoops right up to the street, or one-story "shacks" "on stilts" or "patched up" with "tar paper and tin." This and other "off the beaten track" "long-neglected areas" belied their town's "New South" self-image of "progress, prosperity, and . . . loveliness." Why—aside from its lurid entertainment value—would media such as the *Atlanta Constitution* trouble their white and well-to-do readers with such unseemly imagery of so ugly, overbuilt, unmodern, chaotic, and disease-inducing an environment? As a public service, averred the editors: these were "potentially highly valuable, strategic areas with unlimited possibilities for redevelopment," after all, especially now that "federal state and urban renewal laws" provided Atlanta's leaders with the instruments for overhaul.[63] More quietly, within a regime that remained white supremacist, stigmatization of the city's slums supported the low rank of their residents in the prevailing political hierarchy: their sorry living conditions graphically demonstrated how just unprepared were Atlanta's Black poor for governing themselves.

The strong implication in slum depictions of the early postwar era was that renters were somehow responsible. Reinforcing this more or less tacit message was the prevailing disregard for those politicoeconomic as well as ecological dynamics at work in Atlanta's "Black heart." Absentee landlords owned the overwhelming majority of slum housing, and a toxic combination of city policies actually incentivized landlord malfeasance. Similar to the slumlords recently studied by historians Nathan Connolly in post–World War II Miami and Beryl Satter in Chicago, the owners of Atlanta's slum housing skimped on maintenance and let their buildings "run down" to reduce city assessments, keeping their taxes low.[64] Because the city's housing code was so porous and so poorly enforced, it actually paid to do so, especially for rentals to those at the bottom of the prevailing hierarchy of citizens, the poorest Blacks. Moreover, racial segregation of rentals combined with lagging capital for Black apartment building to ensure that the demand for slum rentals to Blacks outstripped the supply, "bring[ing] the best return a landlord can get," according to the head of the Fulton County Welfare Department in 1963. Even the most negligent of slumlords could still do steady business while "demand[ing] high rent."[65] With many of the homes in these parts of town self-built or of older construction, and with poor renters having little economic or legal wherewithal to counter landlords' neglectful maintenance, wear and tear steadily accumulated. Natural processes of rot, decay, and erosion stymied through regular upkeep and repairs in other, richer parts of the city went visibly unabated in Atlanta's slums. The wood from which so many were built rotted or drew termites. With many slums having started on low-lying lands or along gullies, rains not only wore down roofs but washed away yards and dirt roads. As landlords failed to fix holes or hire exterminators and as garbage was never picked up by the city's trucks, rats and other pests converged on trash piles, then trouped indoors. The rats got so bad, as one "young Negro mother" put it when a reporter did design to interview her, that "we can't sleep at night."[66]

In what was now an established tradition in Atlanta, depictions of these places came couched in an emotional language of aggression—they were "choking" or "stabbing" the city—or revulsion. The "hovels" were "miserable," the streets "dismal," and visiting council members, at this point exclusively white and male, declared themselves "deeply ashamed" of what they saw, avoiding even lip service to the plight of these places' residents.[67] On occasion the racial cast of such portraits could turn explicit. During an outbreak of rabies in 1959, a headline blared about how a "Safari of Four Guns" was "Down[ing] Dogs in Darkest Atlanta." Supremacist fantasies of an Atlanta Africa aside, it told about how white college students hired by the county pound had carried tranquilizer guns into Buttermilk Bottom to shoot and vaccinate dogs.[68] Such coverage built on old racial tropes that were prov-

PHOTO 2.2. Walker Evans's *Negro Houses: Atlanta, Georgia*, photograph, 1936. Evan's photo of houses in a poor Black neighborhood of Atlanta during the Depression captured the dense construction and dearth of provisions such as paved roads that burnished such places' reputation as "slums." LC-USF342-008033-A [P&P] LOT 1538, FSA/OWI Collection, Prints and Photographs Division, Library of Congress, https://www.loc.gov/item/2017762217/.

ing immensely durable: Black people or "the Negro" seen as less than civilized, closer to nature, and therefore as neither capable nor worthy of citizenship. Fixations on the jungle-like and pathological character of Atlanta's slums nourished assumptions that these environments in and of themselves bred a host of human ills—"poverty, ignorance, disease, crime, mental disturbance, broken homes, high rates of moving and no organized religion." And these assumptions in turn grounded a modernist environmental determinism that in retrospect seems well-nigh magical: that Atlanta's Black poor themselves might somehow be vanquished by bulldozers.[69]

By the end of the 1950s, as criticism of the city's urban renewal program commenced, reporters finally got curious enough to start talking more with these places' residents. What they reported of their conversations still largely matched earlier story lines: of rats that kept residents up at night and of children who became "victims of slums." But another, newer story line also took shape in Atlanta's media, about the greed of the landlord. Starting in 1958, following a full-scale revision of the city's housing code required for federal renewal funds, as the city undertook to register the owners of its residential rentals, the slumlord suddenly began acquiring more visibility and notoriety in local media. A new housing inspectorate then kicking into gear helped to shine a brighter light on these landlords who were actually letting their own properties lapse into slumhood.[70] Many prominent Atlantans had availed themselves of this tremendous investment opportunity, it turned out: "names which appear on fashionable address mailboxes and spot the registers of some of the city's best clubs and civic organizations." "Probably" the largest, according to one report, was Aycock Realty, among the city's oldest realty firms, run by northside resident Carswell Aycock. He and other Aycock family members together owned some one hundred dwellings. The long-standing Atlanta alderman Wayne "Chick" Blanchard also held title to "several pieces" of slum property but had refused to register his property with the city and urged several fellow slumlords also "not [to] bother." Outed by the *Atlanta Journal* in 1959, he tried to save political face by loudly advocating for stricter enforcement of the city's housing code but was soon turned out of office by a political newcomer.[71]

Only much later did local papers begin digging up stories about former residents' lives there—decades after Buttermilk Bottom and other slums had been razed or otherwise transformed by redevelopment. Through the 1950s, though, the boundaries segregating this neighborhood off from others were just "in the atmosphere" and residents "just knew . . . where the line was drawn." But former denizens reminisced about the "sense of community" they had felt within. Like the small rural towns where many of them had grown up, Buttermilk Bottom had had its own movie theater on Forrest Avenue and, nearby, a poolroom and grocery store, undertakers' and doctors' offices, shoe stores and restaurants. There were local juke joints and eating places, an elementary school for the children, C. W. Hill, and local churches where people went to worship. Life in the Bottom was "rough and tough," but in their memories defined not so much by the buildings or physical environment as by "the people living there, interacting." Among other ways, "people went to church there," participating in that most pervasive and enduring of Black institutions.[72]

Ebenezer Baptist lay in walking distance of Buttermilk Bottom. By 1960 the greatest bulk of its members trekked from neighborhoods to the northeast of the church, including the Bottom itself.[73] By then its renovated sanctuary featured that central painting of a swelling river winding from a lumbering peak, an idealized version of the rural background shared by many congregants, including the longtime senior minister. As poorer neighbors filed into its pews, rubbing elbows with better-off congregants, this soothing scenery conjured up rural refuges they remembered and perhaps still visited and also still greater promises. It stirred hopes, amplified by many a scripture reading, that they too might find their way to a Promised Land, whether a "beautiful Negro suburb" or some other place more infused with divine blessings than they now knew.

Though Buttermilk Bottom residents might find balm in this and other downtown churches, the relentless stigmatization of their homescapes justified a racial authoritarianism in the city's urban-renewal and highway programs that sidelined most all of Atlanta's Blacks, not just those who were poor. The laws' requirements for receiving federal funds forced many innovations, among them, an insistence on "citizen participation" in renewal planning. Used to calling the shots, the city's white leaders worked out a self-serving, minimalist method of "participation" that ensured the main decisions lay with their own handpicked planning experts. The recognized "citizens" invited by the AHA were all carefully selected leaders of a Black middle class—"ministers and Negro businessmen." Standing in for all the mostly poor Black residents whose homes and neighborhoods were on the chopping block, these representatives were asked to only "s[i]t in on the initial planning of all the areas, especially where [AHA's own white planners deemed] their interests were paramount."[74] That was it; "experts in city government" then determined the final boundaries of just which areas would be "renewed." By the time the recommended renewal zones were approved by an all-white board of aldermen, no formal citizen's advisory committee had even been appointed, much less met or provided input.[75]

If "citizen participation" in Atlanta's urban renewal meant a short window of consultation and involved only a few carefully selected community leaders, expressway planners and builders made still fewer pretenses to democracy. The original pattern for four-lane limited-access roads in and around the city had been laid out just after the war, with the first leg—quite naturally, given what we've seen of the city's postwar power structure—connecting downtown with Buckhead, that most prominent seat of Atlanta's white wealth. Over the later 1940s into the 1950s, more fine-grained, block-level decisions about routing came mostly through closed-door negotiations between city planners, a State Highway Department under the thumb of Talmadgism, and federal officials who approved their share of the funds. Hardly any other consultation was involved. Even Urban League leaders—arguably the best connected of Black civic groups to planning by Atlanta's white elite at this time—had no say over the north-south expressway's subsequent extension across Auburn Avenue.

When, in the middle of the decade, Atlanta's highway and urban-renewal planners began to converge and collaborate, their decision making remained impervious to input from outside the city's white elite, even as the scale and ambitions of their planning grew. City leaders working with the State Highway Department and those in DeKalb began laying plans to tap an impending 1956 Federal Aid Highway Act to push forward on an east-west expressway route also envisioned in the original plan, around the same time that a 1954 Housing Act spurred a new round of urban-renewal proposals.[76] An eager collaboration ensued between highway and renewal planners: all three zones for urban renewal announced in 1956 designated acreage for freeway routes and interchanges.[77] In two, "clearance" was the priority: the Butler Street area, in the first assault on Buttermilk Bottom; and McDaniel Street, with a Black enclave called Pittsburgh. Only the third around University Avenue, long home to much of Atlanta's small Black middle-class, including league leader Grace Hamilton, allowed for a "combination of clearance and rehabilitation."[78] At least one historian sees this decision as a concession to the Urban League, rewarding their early and steady backing of the urban-renewal campaign.[79]

The AUL's initial support of urban renewal points to the hopes held by a significant share of the city's Black leadership into the early 1950s. Consistent with its own version of civil rights citizenship, which largely conceded the white supremacists' insistence on segregation, the AUL advocated for distributing a more equal share of public goods and spaces and for widening private opportunities for "modern" and improved housing among the city's Blacks. Yet their primary commitment to building a Black middle class, along with their own middle-class backgrounds and concerns with "respectability," inclined them, too, to join the stigmatizing chorus about Atlanta's inner-city slums and their residents. Destruction of these ill-kept and ill-provisioned homescapes of despair in downtown Atlanta even looked like a natural, critical flank for the AUL postwar program. Thereby bolstering its reputation among the city's white elite as a "reasonable" and reputable mouthpiece for Atlanta's Black community, the AUL also edged close to conceding another plank of white supremacist citizenship: treating those who were both Black *and* poor as the lowest and least deserving class of citizen.

By the late 1950s the reservations of Thompson and other AUL leaders about the city's renewal program mounted, especially as they watched just how little priority was being accorded to rehousing those whose homes were being destroyed. Thompson himself had been made aware how indifferent city officials could be to displaced Blacks, as when in the late 1940s a Black community of some three hundred families in Buckhead's Bagley Park had been evicted by Fulton County to make a white park, without so much as a nod to where evictees might go.[80] Though section 221 of the 1954 federal act provided funds and procedures to build homes for the uprooted, the Atlanta Housing Authority dragged its heels on new construction, even as Thompson began to realize the sheer scale of home building that was becoming needed.[81] Already by 1958, some 3,931 families had been forced to move. Nearly twelve thousand households were projected to be made homeless from newly announced plans. Downtown decimation seemed destined to rocket the deficit in Black housing to more than twice what the AUL had faced in the decade after the world war. That then threatened to drive up costs of renting that had already gotten higher than many Black families could afford.[82]

Moreover, what section 221 housing was built often disappointed the AUL as well as its residents. A Santa Barbara subdivision opening in the northwestern suburbs near Collier Drive, among the first for newly displaced residents, enabled first-time homeownership for many residents, but in a physical environment plagued by problems much like those of the downtown slum. Homeowners had to put in their own lawns, since the builder had not bothered. Even as many did so, erosion helped make the new development's "landscaping" "the major problem" for residents, as an *open drainage ditch* and *steep embankment* together [took] up the backyard areas for about 50% of the houses." There was also no public recreational space of any kind. Now, with the housing code revised to secure renewal funds, that was a violation of the city ordinance for new developments. But the City of Atlanta had simply let it happen and showed little interest in addressing it.[83]

Into the late 1950s urban renewal stoked the seeds of a more oppositional civil rights citizenship, as its technocratic top-down control combined with sweepingly destructive environmental impacts to stir up new pressures for a more participatory and democratic vision of urban planning. Black civic leaders began to unite around criticism of Atlanta's urban-renewal program in late 1957, when the biggest renewal project thus far was proposed for the area around Atlanta University. Part of the homescape of the city's most prosperous Black neighborhood, the grassy open spaces of its campus had long added to its hopeful allure as an educational icon of the city's Black community. Only the poorer sections of this part of town would be targeted for demolition, but the renewal juggernaut had now set its sights on the very doorstep of many of the city's Black leaders. In a public hearing at city hall in the course of the Regional Housing Clinic on Urban Renewal, held on the university campus itself, officials defended their top-down decision-making process as built not just on the electoral authority of the mayor but on their own disinterested planning expertise.[84] Others at these gatherings and in a subsequent special issue devoted to the matter in *Phylon Quarterly*, the Atlanta University–based journal, countered that "citizen participation" could surely have been handled better, with a more "democratic process of give and take." "A hand-picked advisory group . . . cannot produce the best results in a community planning project," noted one speaker. "People from all classes should be represented," insisted another, including a "representative group of Negroes." Solicitation of input needed to happen much earlier, "at the initial planning stage of the program"; it was best "not [to] call them in after the decisions had been made."[85] In the wake of these public confrontations, in 1958, a Citizens Advisory Committee on Urban Renewal was finally created, with league board president J. B. Blayton along with Robert Thompson among its eighty-nine appointees.

Meanwhile, as Thompson's concerns about a housing shortfall had mounted, he also gravitated to another realization that altered his priorities: Atlanta's racial geography was coming to look more and more like that of U.S. cities outside the South. Already by the late 1940s, his statistically based generalizations about the living quarters of Atlanta's Blacks had downplayed those edge enclaves that, as we have seen, had historically differentiated this city's racial geography from northern and western counterparts. By the late 1950s he noted how Atlanta and other southern cities were coming to look more and more like Chicago: "increasingly . . . following the established northern pattern of a central concentration of nonwhites, ringed by outlying white areas."[86] White wealth, heretofore essential to the city's tax base, had also been leaving for the suburbs. If the trend "continues or is accelerated, the left behind low income groups and the downtown business district will undoubtedly suffer."[87] In response, Thompson and the Urban League increasingly balanced their quest for "modern" suburban housing of Blacks with an insistence that renovated downtown areas should also quickly restore housing for Blacks. They called for Black public housing to go on inner-city sites, from the recently shuttered Eggleston Hospital to part of Buttermilk Bottom, while also urging follow-through on a "park promised since 1950."[88]

Even after gaining a voice on the Citizens Advisory Committee, the Atlanta Urban League lost these battles, as the white chair urged full-speed-ahead land clearance, asserting that private developers would inevitably provide for the displaced.[89] In the course of these debates, after years of frustration, condescension, and all-too-limited impacts, Thompson's usually cool mode of argument cracked. Beyond facts and social science, he veered into other rhetorical registers. Addressing the chair of Housing Authority's advisory committee, he swerved into echoing the Black national anthem: "Can we afford to fail our less fortunate citizens who live in slum areas? . . . The decision rests with us, so we must be true to our God, our fellowman and ourselves."[90]

By the early 1960s that wish of Georgia Tech architecture students back in 1949 had nearly come true: the Black side of Atlanta's downtown really did look as if targeted by a Nazi bombing campaign. The damage circa 1963 had become so thorough that "within a mile and half radius of the courthouse . . . most of the residential buildings have been razed." Nor were the bulldozers done; they had only just begun to "clear" another major chunk of Buttermilk Bottom to make room for a gleaming new civic center. Surveying this downtown scene, the head of the city Welfare Department noted another consequence that to city leaders convinced they were eradicating poverty must have seemed perverse: "Welfare cases inside [this area] have continued to increase." The reason was a "doubling of habitation of already crowded, substandard buildings." By 1967 mounting complaints and protest forced a more honest and comprehensive survey of what downtown clearance had wrought, with startling results. All told, "government activities" in Atlanta between 1956 and 1966 had displaced some sixty-seven thousand persons, equal to more than half the city's Black population in 1950, "the vast majority of them poor and disadvantaged." More of the displacements came from expressway building than from urban renewal per se. So little public housing had been built that only 11 percent of those who had qualified for it had received it. Yet far from adjusting, the "rents and costs" for other government-supported as well as private housing ran "too high" for "the large number of low income families displaced." A chastened City Planning Department estimated that the city now had a shortfall of inexpensive housing (rents under fifty-five dollars a month) of more than eight thousand units. Black families made up nearly three-quarters of those in need.[91]

While vigilante as well as police violence continued to be visited on the city's Blacks, the ongoing rumble of environmental destruction underway downtown, in a well-nigh Orwellian pursuit of *freeways* and *renewal*, introduced a whole new type of racial repression into the city's disciplinary repertoire. For the first time since Gen. William Sherman's rampage, huge swathes of Atlanta's urban environment were intentionally annihilated. Renewal projects tore their way into Black homes and neighborhoods not just across the city's core but in outlying towns; from Decatur to Marietta, peripheral Black enclaves were also flattened. The greatest victims were thousands of poor Blacks whose very homes were plowed under. But neighboring merchant districts like Auburn Avenue also shriveled and were on their way to shuttering, extinguished by vanishing customers more so than the bulldozer's blade. Across square miles of Atlanta land, decades-long accumulations of Black habitation, investments, and commerce had been swept away. And, as if on a fresh slate, monumental roadways and a coliseum arose, in a mammoth act of creative destruction that everyone in Black Atlanta came to know, whether upper or middle or lower class.

Just over a decade after the 1957 forums where Black leaders lodged protests, highway builders would run up against formidable new walls of resistance, a full-fledged environmental movement around Atlanta that eventually defeated their plans. Why was there such a delayed response? One reason was the continued sway of white supremacy in the city's government over the early post–World War II period. It helped confine the civil rights citizenship sought by groups like the AUL to seeking a separate-but-equal middle class, while enabling freeway building and renewal to proceed full-speed ahead. Another was that the main neighborhoods targeted for razing in 1950s remained poor and Black. From the early 1960s, however, freeway builders began setting sites on neighborhoods with better-recognized and better-defended citizenship rights, not just white but affluent. Still another reason, more subtle, was hugely influential: in 1950s Atlanta no political project of environmental citizenship existed that was comparable to that forged on behalf of civil rights. As a parallel push against rustic rule arose in some of Atlanta's better-off white suburbs, however, the precursors for just such a movement had begun to stir.

White Opposition and the Dawn of Environmental Citizenship

Joining Black groups like the AUL and the NAACP on at least some fronts of the campaign against racial authoritarianism through the 1950s were some powerful and connected white Atlantans. Atlanta's own white "power structure" had benefited nearly as much as rustic rulers from the post-Reconstruction shrinkage of Georgia's electorate. But the city's sharply curbed electoral as well as legislative clout under the county unit system made its overthrow a shared goal of many among the city's white elite and middle classes. These opponents of Talmadgism, however, already enjoyed many of those civil, social, and voting rights for which civil rights advocates were fighting. Focusing their efforts far more against the county unit system itself, they waged this campaign from some of Atlanta's most privileged and powerful niches. Druid Hills resident and lawyer James Mackay, for instance, coauthor of *Who Runs Georgia?*, went on to represent DeKalb in the state legislature, introducing unsuccessful bills to institute direct statewide elections. Mayor Hartsfield was outspoken in his opposition to the county unit system and testified at the lawsuit that finally ended it, brought by James O'Hear Sanders, a white textile-factory manager and "good government" advocate living in a wealthy North Atlanta suburb. Atlanta's better-off suburban whites also reacted with alarm as Talmadgist governors and legislators sought to privatize school systems to prevent their integration, collectively speaking out to preserve public schools as a social right, as Matthew Lassiter has shown.[92] In the process some of these same white politicians and constituencies quietly laid groundwork for what, over the next decade and a half, would emerge as a new political project in and around Atlanta on behalf of environmental citizenship.

This project, while it could conceivably be wedged among Marshall's social elements of citizenship, entertained principles and priorities that went uncontemplated in the larger intellectual traditions to which Marshall's writings on citizenship belonged.[93] Consider, for instance, the single-most favored issue among the new self-identified "environmental" groups in Atlanta by the late 1960s: those "natural areas" they sought to preserve as parks. While Marshallian citizenship imagined a national society and polity to which citizens aspired to belong, valuing land as "natural" meant looking past the social and recognizing and embracing a "nature" there that was distinct and apart from human society itself. To enable that appreciation early advocates of environmental citizenship drew on cultural traditions that were also quite distinct from those in which Marshall wrote: of wilderness celebration, nature writing, and ecological and other natural sciences. Already enjoying much of what civil rights advocates strove to make more available to Black Atlantans, a few white Atlantans began to set their sights on more natural-looking and wilder places, to moralize and politicize their defense. In contrast to the AUL's social science of city- and society-wide racial inequalities, Atlanta's early advocates of environmental citizenship avoided race and social science altogether, slipping into a color-blind rhetoric that contrasted sharply with the explicit race talk of both white supremacists and civil rights advocates. Over against the core ethics of equality and justice that drove civil rights citizenship, an incipient environmental citizenship began to explore an ethic of nature's defense. In so doing, they took up principles that civil rights activists, ever cognizant of the racist trope of Blacks' less-than-civilized closeness to nature, would find difficult to embrace. And the racially tinged environmental determinism wielded against Atlanta's Black slums stoked their suspicions about "environmental" advocacy still further.

Already during the 1950s, as the battles raged over Black housing and public spaces downtown, interest in and support for nature parks simmered across the Atlanta metropolitan region, most visibly in its better-off white suburbs. Only after the grip of rustic rule on the statehouse had been loosened would one of the first political projects to unite Georgia environmentalists become possible: state parks devoted not just to people's recreation but to nature itself, an ecologically defined preservation. Until then penny-pinching Talmadgist leaders had little interest in expanding Georgia's park system and were even willing to sell off the state's public parks to maintain racial segregation. So in and around Atlanta the pursuit of more ecologically authentic parks stayed mostly within private and local civic spheres, and the only sizeable park making undertaken by the state of Georgia bore the imprint not of nature but of white supremacy on its most visible face.

Many roots of the fledgling 1950s support for a more natural style of park ran through those suburban home environments now available for consumption by a white upper-middle class, embodying many of those social rights they already enjoyed. Among the most prominent was DeKalb County's Druid Hills, pivotal not just to the 1947 *Who Runs Georgia?* study but to the Georgia Conservancy's founding twenty years later. For those buying into this subdivision, so carefully planned and planted to look country-like, the environment they thereby consumed, if vaguely pastoral, was not nearly so agrarian as the actual Georgia countryside, plowed, planted, and pastured, that often was to sustain rural residents' livelihoods. Its ornamental picturesqueness stemmed, instead, more from the conspicuous absence of cotton or cornfields, cows or chickens—in distinct contrast to so many of the places rural Georgians, but also many less well-off Atlantans, continued to inhabit.

The least worked, most nonagrarian nature afforded Druid Hills residents was Fernbank Forest, some eighty acres of woods along the edge of Druid Hills' golf course reputedly never cleared either for farming or housing. Up until 1939 this "finest forest and finest forest floor so near a metropolis," in the words of the director of the American Museum of Natural History, had been passed along uncut through the family of a Druid Hills developer. To keep it undeveloped the daughter had then deeded it to a private corporation christened Fernbank, owned and run by "interested citizens in the Druid Hills area," an arrangement out of which the Druid Hills' homeowners' association had also taken a more durable shape. Fernbank's stated purpose was educational, to "provide for the children of the area a place where they could learn about the wonders of nature firsthand." Privately owned and part of Druid Hill residents' homescape, this park mainly served the home-owning families living there, which, from its founding through the active work of its homeowners' association, remained both well-to-do and white.

Through the postwar period Fernbank served many of the same purposes for Atlanta's white northeastern suburbs as Mozley Park did for Black West Atlanta. But not only was Fernbank bigger and more forested; it became a regional center for educating visitors about the natural world, enabling them to see and appreciate its woods and open spaces *as* nature. School classes paid visits, and white Campfire Girls and Boy and Girl Scout troops sponsored day camps there, just as did their Black counterparts at Mozley. But Fernbank also housed a Children's Nature Museum, reputedly the first of its kind in the South, with a live menagerie that included some farm animals but featured small forest creatures. Scouts could visit with caged foxes, squirrels both gray and flying, two skunks, and what most entranced a visiting reporter in 1949: "Raffles, the Fernbank 'Coon." As befit its mostly nonagrarian version of nature, the summer program offered guided tours of its primeval forest, to "get acquainted with the trees, ferns, and wildflowers," and "bird hunting without a gun," so visitors could "learn the names" of "feathered friends in the forest."[94]

Civic contributions to Fernbank's upkeep burnished a private amenity of one of the city's wealthiest neighborhoods but also furnished private dress rehearsals for that later project of citizenship self-identifying as "environmental," as yet without stepping into any political arena. Some garden clubs periodically raised money for its maintenance, but by the early 1950s the museum's disrepair and a trash-strewn forest prompted the homeowners' association to mobilize area residents into more collective action. Druid Hills' "doctors, lawyers, professors, businessmen, high school and college students, boy scouts and girl scouts" then set about "clean[ing] up Fernbank," in a burst of "neighborhood enthusiasm." An Atlanta Bird Club, affiliated with the National Audubon Society by the mid-1950s, then built the forest's first "Nature Trails" and posted "no hunting" signs.[95]

While this bird club joined with Georgia's small Ornithological and Botanical Societies in helping locate and cultivate public spaces for Atlanta's nature lovers and while Atlantans often led a Georgia Appalachian Trail Club and started an Atlanta chapter of the Izaak Walton League in 1953, the most widespread practice of a nature-related civics across the metro region happened in garden clubs.[96] Flourishing during the postwar period especially in white middle- to upper-class suburbs, they rivaled the churches as channels for Atlanta's civil society, at least among white women. While Black counterparts were either less frequent or left fewer traces, the ranks of white garden clubbers swelled. Already by 1940 membership in the state's garden club association had ranked fourth in the nation. A quarter century later the Cobb County town of Smyrna had at least three, and DeKalb County alone had more than the entire state of California.[97] Thereby, the ranks of garden clubbers grew in entangled parallel with the massive expansion of white suburban homeownership under compressive capitalism.

Like agriculture itself, the gardening to which clubs devoted themselves involved hands-on work, a cultivation of the soil. Caring for one's own land and flora in the right way also brought elevation, a confirmation that, socially, a gardener and her family had arrived. The clubs inculcated a middle- or upper-middle-class, leisure-time way of laying hands on one's own surroundings, starting with one's own home lot, precisely to ensure this land was neither *too* farm-like and rustic nor too "raw." But garden clubs also tackled the larger homescapes surrounding their members' own properties, the informal as well more formal commons of publicly owned streets, lots, and town centers that a club's membership shared. We can understand their popularity in and around Atlanta as compensating for rustic rule's minimalist approach to government, which reserved few or no public funds for decorative planting. Whether in North Druid Hills or Smyrna, the clubs also took on collective endeavors, planting in corners of their communities that had been left untended. A coalition of garden clubs even took it on themselves to plant the sides of Atlanta's first freeway, constructed by the State Highway Department, from downtown north to Buckhead in the early 1950s.[98]

For all their swirling activity, Atlanta's garden clubs were no substitute for those groups from Nature Conservancy chapters on the East Coast to those of the Sierra Club out west that had begun to push for preserving "natural areas" or "wilderness" around other U.S. cities.[99] Atlanta's garden clubbers, believing as they did that what the Georgia countryside needed was better cultivation, generally devoted little thought to how or why any corner of it should be left unworked and protected from any kind of human hand.[100] For this reason, as well as their ingrained aversion to politics, Atlanta's garden clubs and other nature-related groups of the 1950s were only proto-environmentalist, not yet conceiving or advocating a full-fledged environmental citizenship. Not surprisingly, politicians sympathetic to their cause, including DeKalb's James Mackay, later a founder of the Georgia Conservancy, concentrated instead on another political project they saw as more urgent: ending rustic rule.

Mackay, one of the authors of the 1947 *Who Runs Georgia?*, had been born in a small town in Alabama and arrived in the Atlanta area in 1934, when his Methodist preacher father accepted a call to ministry and moved into Druid Hills. Attending next-door Emory for college and then serving in the war, he returned to Emory to finish law school, married, and by 1947 had only just begun his law practice, when the Southern Regional Council approached him about undertaking the study that became *Who Runs Georgia?* After completing it, he then pursued a career in electoral politics, mostly as a state legislator representing DeKalb County and living in Druid Hills. Over the postwar decades DeKalb drew an influx of white newcomers, primarily better-off arrivals from the Georgia countryside, to make it the richest and most thoroughly suburban counties in the Atlanta region. It served as a prime example of what Mackay and his coauthor termed a "really healthy political environment," "under the combined stimulus of the Negro vote and an awakened white middle class."[101] Over the 1950s he emerged as one of the Atlanta region's most powerful and influential white voices for democratizing and urbanizing reforms that challenged white supremacist and rustic rule.

Mackay saw his purpose as pushing state and county governments away from white supremacy but not all the way to civil rights citizenship, even though he successfully courted DeKalb's Black vote. As white suburban homeowners, he and much of his electoral base in Atlanta-proximate DeKalb already enjoyed the social as well as civil elements in Marshall's tripartite dissection of citizenship. As Mackay's own election and reelection to the state legislature showed, they also had already obtained a significant measure of political power, however limited by the county unit system and Talmadgism. By steadily seeking ways of abolishing or ameliorating the county unit system, so blatantly weighed against urban counties and voters, Mackay and his allies sought a full measure of political citizenship. At the same time, navigating between the avowedly white state of the Talmadgists and the Black advocacy of civil rights groups, they pursued a vision of governmental color blindness that rarely sought to address accumulated racial inequities or historical injustices.

At the county level Mackay began his political career by taking on Scott Candler, the Talmadge-allied DeKalb County executive who quickly became his political nemesis. Though Candler sought to forestall reform, among other ways, by creating a county Parks Department in 1953 and starting work on three new parks, Mackay and his allies were able to end the single-commissioner government of DeKalb in 1955. They replaced it with what they saw as a more democratic and effective alternative: a five-man commission elected by districts rather than at large.[102] Three years later they pushed "city-type ordinance making authority" for DeKalb through the state legislature, enabling it to carry out policing, zoning, and other enforcement measures. By the decade's end, the *Atlanta Constitution* had declared DeKalb to "no longer [be] a rural county," and a grand jury praised how a successful bond issue was helping develop and expand the county's parks, even though only one of twenty-two had been opened to Blacks.[103]

At the state level the supreme court's 1954 *Brown* decision helped make the fate of Georgia's public schools far more of a defining political issue for legislators like Mackay than were its parks. Instead of privatizing them to keep white schools white, as the Talmadgist legislature voted to do, Mackay and other Atlanta-area politicians pushed for a policy of "local control," an ostensibly color-blind compromise between segregation and integration that left the most critical decisions up to local school boards.[104] Yet the park policies of Talmadgist leaders were especially revealing about what was "rustic" in their approach to government. Already antistatist in inclination, rustic rulers and their constituencies were accustomed to a countryside where woods and fields were never far away, even if privately owned. Often large landowners themselves, they saw little need for public park marking or worried that it might draw out Black city dwellers their way.

In the wake of *Brown*, rustic rulers turned the state park system into a sacrificial pawn to the politics of "massive resistance." In 1956, just as state parkland was growing in other parts of the United States, the Georgia legislature passed a law to enable the privatization of existing state parklands. Terrified by the court-ordered desegregation of schools, Georgia's political leaders worried that state parkland might be next in line for integration. James Mackay slammed the law as allowing officials to "substitute a cornfield for a state park without notice to anyone."[105] That Mackay was one of only two state legislators daring to oppose it testifies to the utter grip that racial anxieties had over the state's white political leadership, urban and suburban as well as rural, and to how politically tenuous any claims to an environmental citizenship were across this region. In the postwar Southeast, most of the forests were second or third growth, federal conservation efforts had long targeted private agriculture (i.e., *soil* conservation), and state and local governments had only recently launched their own conservation programs for forests and game. Public lands devoted entirely to more "passive" recreation such as picnicking, swimming, and hiking remained few and far between. With so few counterparts to the large state-run recreation parks proliferating over previous decades in other U.S. regions, few Georgians had much inkling of what any *more* ecological or natural park might be.[106]

Only in the late 1950s did the State Park Authority finally acquire and develop its first Atlanta-area state park, none other than Stone Mountain. Rising nearly a thousand feet up from the surrounding plain, sixteen miles to the east of Atlanta, the sheer rock face of Stone Mountain qualified it as the largest exposed granite monolith, or monadnock, not just in this region but in the world. It was also home to rare unique ecological communities of plants like the diminutive *Amphianthus*, an aquatic herb that floated and flowered in pools created by spring rains and returned to seed with summer drying. Studies in the early 1960s by Emory biologist Rutherford Platt would help put these communities on the scientific map; later they would become among the first Georgia species protected under the Endangered Species Act.[107] Threatened on Stone Mountain not just by decades of quarrying but tourists' tramples, they would later emerge as some of Georgia's foremost ecological treasures. Within the legislative committee that composed the funding measure for the proposed Stone Mountain Memorial Park, Mackay himself served as the secretary.[108] Their proposal attracted support not only from city leaders like the *Atlanta Constitution* but from DeKalb's own proto-environmental groups—the Druid Hills Civic Association, local garden clubs, and biologists like Platt, some of whom spoke out about preserving the distinctive geology, flora, and fauna.

But more upfront and pivotal in the late 1950s push for the state purchase of Stone Mountain was sponsorship by Gov. Marvin Griffin—Talmadge's successor and also a staunch segregationist. For him this "great scenic wonder" would serve a particular vision not so much of nature as of human history, a state-sanctioned "memorial to the Southern Confederacy."[109] As Griffin and his Talmadgist allies were well aware, this mountain bearing that unfinished monument to Confederate leaders had also given birth to the second Ku Klux Klan, whose followers still sometimes congregated atop. With the sway of Atlanta-area legislators so minimized and with this region being shaken at its

PHOTO 2.3. Gathering of the Ku Klux Klan on Stone Mountain, circa 1950. From the Klan's rebirth in 1915 through the 1950s, this mountain, as well the monument started on its granite flank, occupied a special place in the white supremacist imaginary, culminating in its 1958 acquisition to become a Georgia state park. Courtesy of Marion Johnson Photographs, Kenan Research Center, Atlanta History Center.

political foundations over the late 1950s by the civil rights movement and federal courts, Griffin's outlook on the meanings of the mountain proved more decisive, swaying rural and segregationist legislators.

In 1958 the state legislature finally created a Stone Mountain Memorial Association and gave it $1.5 million with which to work, with Mackay's political foe Scott Candler at its helm. What had made the project politically viable was the message to be delivered by chiseling the faces of Confederate generals into a granite mountainside. Thereby, the only natural land that Georgia's rustic rulers saw fit to acquire and preserve in the Atlanta area prior to 1960 became gouged with a looming, perpetual pledge of allegiance to white supremacist citizenship. That park that rustic rulers finally saw fit to obtain for their state's burgeoning capital city bore a mixture of messages for its residents. On the one hand, a rural-oriented legislature and governor finally began to acknowledge the recreational needs of Atlantans and apportion public funds. On the other, though white civic groups and scientists urged that the park should become a nature preserve, it did not. Instead, the slated completion of its carving would turn the most dominant natural feature on Atlanta's horizon into the region's most towering and visible monument to white supremacy. Soon, however, what had been intended as a bid for timelessness, sculpting the favored heritage of Georgia's racial authoritarians into the face of nature itself, started to look less like an official shrine than an embattled epitaph. Accelerating the fall of Talmadgism was how the civil rights citizenship long sought by Atlanta's Black leaders took a more confrontational turn.

Direct Action as Citizenly Practice

Atlanta stood front and center in a decisive new turn in civil rights activism breaking out across the South circa 1960, as a younger generation, impatient with established civil rights groups like the Urban League and the NAACP, took matters into their own hands.[110] Turning to direct action, a concerted and pointedly civil intrusion into public spaces reserved for whites, they intentionally broke the ground rules of separate but equal, openly defying the white supremacist state. Framing explicitly racial segregation itself not as inescapable but as the biggest barrier to Black equality and discovering ways of challenging a racist power structure that could engage hundreds and even thousands of their fellow Blacks, they transformed the quest for civil rights citizenship. New groups spearheaded this turn. The Southern Christian Leadership Conference (SCLC), founded in 1957, quickly carved out a new and distinctive niche in Atlanta's civil rights movement, especially once Martin Luther King Jr. returned to the city from Montgomery, Alabama, in early 1960. The SCLC soon joined with the Student Nonviolent Coordinating Committee (SNCC), hatched around this same time by local college students. Undergirding the sudden, seemingly spontaneous swell of activism was not just youthful impatience but new hopes, born and nourished under a more compressive capitalism and budding in earlier civil rights groups, that many more Black Atlantans had come to share. As the direct-action campaigns of these groups charged forth, as activism began to spill out across class lines, and as allied courtroom actions also turned more ambitious and bore additional fruit, some of the most egregiously antidemocratic features of city governance gave way.

The new activism had roots among those homescapes of hope now available to many more of Atlanta's Blacks, thanks to a New Deal–steered widening of wealth distribution and years of strenuous effort by the Atlanta Urban League and many others. Nearly 30 percent of Black households now owned their own homes, double the share in 1940, enabling a "generation of young Negroes [to grow] up accustomed to decent housing in good neighborhoods."[111] While Martin Luther King Jr. had grown up along an Auburn Avenue that was now being bisected by a freeway, the treed and lawned living quarters into which he and his family moved upon his return exemplified the plant-festooned living environment to which better-off Blacks could now re-

PHOTO 2.4. The other King house. Martin Luther King Jr. and his family lived in this house on Sunset Drive after returning to Atlanta in 1960. Photo by Christopher Sellers.

alistically aspire. It was located on Sunset Drive near Vine City, closer in than Mozley Park or Collier Heights, but nevertheless a "street of professional people," among them a Black insurance executive and a school principal who, it went without saying, owned their own homes.[112] The Kings' modest, newer ranch house had a more prominent setback and lawn than comparable Atlanta homes from an earlier era, like the one in which the preacher was born, which gave it a distinctly suburban character. Many of SNCC's student leaders as well, from Morehouse College's Julian Bond to Spellman College's Herschelle Sullivan and Roslyn Pope, had been raised—in whole or in part—within Atlanta's expanding neighborhoods of Black homeowners.[113]

The hopes of the new activists also stirred within those other great gardens of African American middle classness: the city's Black colleges and universities. Like students at Atlanta University, those attending Morehouse College, the first to kick off their own sit-in campaign, really did inhabit a kind of garden, a campus carpeted with grass and studded with foliage. That students with less prosperous class backgrounds rubbed shoulders there with scions of Black middle and upper-middle classes points to the partially equalizing alchemy of Black college life in this era. Among the Morehouse leaders of what became SNCC was Lonnie King (no relation), who had grown up on the poorer side of Atlanta, with a former-sharecropper father and a mother who worked as a maid. Just making it into college in a time when only 3.7 percent of Black Atlantans had an undergraduate degree meant entry into a se-

PHOTO 2.5. The Black campus as a haven of greenery, circa 1950. Edward Jones, who taught at Morehouse throughout the post–World War II period, captured its bucolic character during the early 1950s in this and other photos. *Morehouse College*, Edward A. Jones Papers, Archives Research Center, Robert W. Woodruff Library, Atlanta University Center.

lect circle. And the college experience itself could prime a newfound optimism and confidence not just for one's own future but for the possibilities of social change. For students of more modest origins, such as Morris Dillard, the boldness of the ideas encountered in the classroom could inspire leaderly initiative and activism.[114]

Garden-like as these spaces were out of which the direct-action movement arose, they equipped this younger generation of Atlanta's Blacks with a real share of what Marshall called "social citizenship"—that is, they bolstered their denizens' capacity for citizenly practice, nourishing their senses of security, confidence, and possibility. Thereby, such places became springboards for this younger activist generation's head-on breaches of those public and spatial barriers to fuller citizenship still authorized by a white supremacist state. On March 15, 1960, a month and a half after the first Greensboro, North Carolina, lunch-counter sit-ins—a delay largely arising from a concerted effort of Morehouse president Benjamin Mays and NAACP (and sometime Atlanta Urban League) leader A. T. Walden to dissuade them—some 250 Black students fanned out to ten eating places across the Atlanta area. At the train and bus stations, in the capitol building, and at several other locations, they sat down in seats reserved only for whites. Protest leaders would soon christen themselves a Committee on Appeal for Human Rights, and just a few months later welcome to town the headquarters of a newly founded SNCC. Over the coming months these younger activists would find a stalwart ally and spokesperson in the recently arrived minister at Ebenezer Baptist, already hefting a national megaphone as president of the SCLC.

This direct-action campaign parted ways with civil rights elders in the frank dissatisfaction expressed by its leaders "not only with existing conditions, but with the snail-like speed at which they are being ameliorated." Parks offered one of many cases in point. Despite Hartsfield's pledge back in 1953, since Mozley Park's racial conversion not a single new park for Blacks had been built, and there were still just three, despite the forty-two reserved exclusively for whites. Impatience also compelled a new set of tactics, summarized as "direct action."[115] In contrast to the Atlanta Urban League's long-standing inclination to seek safe, separate, and "modern" spaces for Blacks, this generation of civil rights activists stepped out deliberately and collectively into Atlanta's and the South's fraudulently "public" spaces, reserved for whites alone and a constant reminder of Blacks' second-class citizenship. Thereby, they launched Atlanta's civil rights movement into its classic phase. As chief targets, they chose what Winston Grady-Willis terms Jim Crow's "petty Apartheid," the innumerable restaurants, stores, and hospitals as well as parks and other public facilities across which a decades-old color line had been drawn.[116]

While Gandhi and the anticolonial movements in Africa provided new leaders like King with strategies as well as a globalized sense of struggle, a shared Christianity, as a kind of ethical and symbolic garden, provided a most crucial underpinning for their direct action en masse. In southern Black communities, where the church remained such a pillar of collective life, this nonviolent way of protesting looked at once bold and biblical. Its resonance with Jesus's admonitions, for instance, to "turn the other cheek" on those who strike you, inspired the readiness with which ministers, priests, and their religious flocks joined in.[117] Arguably, their behavior also matched up with codes of middle-class respectability, but in this time and place its risks nevertheless remained immense. After all, the point of sit-ins and other "tests" of segregation was to break laws and invite arrest, in a South where lawbreaking by Blacks had long drawn harsh retaliation. Especially for southern Blacks, the dangers were more than just physical. Going to jail left them with a legal record that could dim their future, perhaps barring them from better jobs and generally amplifying effects of racial discrimination that were already formidable.[118] Actively seeking out these risks, while resolving not to strike back in kind, marshaled a moral sway for the activists' cause that is difficult to overestimate. As King noted, "For many white Americans in the North there is little comprehension of the crassness of police behavior and its wide practice. . . . The public only becomes aware of it only during episodes of nonviolent demonstration." That extraordinary restraint with which Black activists met this behavior was easily recognizable to white Christians as well. Highlighting the "barbaric" extremes to which segregationists were willing to go, nonviolent protests by the SCLC and SNCC successfully won over hearts and minds not just in the North but among many southern whites.[119]

Compared to the civil rights citizenship promoted by the Atlanta Urban League, that of this era's SCLC and SNCC leaned more into Marshall's civil than his social elements and also looked less like the citizen-consumer mobilizing emphasized by historian Liz Cohen. While Urban Leaguers *had* quite deliberately sought to open up the market of suburban housing for Black buyers, direct action rested in important part on prior consumption—of housing, of education—that quietly provided underpinnings for its activism.[120] Direct-action protesters did launch their "tests" in the semipublic spaces of private establishments where hamburgers were bought or buses ridden, but they also concentrated on spaces that were publicly owned, parks among these. And they trained their focus less on any particular purchase or public amenity itself than on the southern system of segregation, an untidy patchwork of legal rules and social customs that was as regionally distinctive as the racial authoritarianism that sanctioned it. The main purpose, instead, was to convey protesting bodies en masse into places all too putatively "public," to act out a collective dream that skin color should not serve as a barrier to full rights of entry. The social makeup of their enterprise also entailed a departure from those of the Urban League or the NAACP, deeply reliant on tiny leadership cadres. Instead, while direct action did have its leaders, it worked only *through* broader participation.

Helping to make direct-action protests such a brilliant strategy, at once so threatening and so powerful, was how pervasive and accessible their targets were, opening the door to the support not just from middle class but from working-class or poorer Blacks. As the protests multiplied, King thought he could detect a widening allegiance to the movement across class lines. "Something wonderful is happening in this town," he remarked. "The low-down Negroes are getting tired. . . . White folks never paid them any mind but they're tired. They just aren't going to take it like they always have before," he concluded hopefully.[121] Historian Grady-Willis sees a more working-class orientation emerging in the movement as it began to target cheaper fast-food restaurants like Krystal and as protesters turned more "confrontational . . . [and became] far less concerned with upholding middle-class notions of decorum."[122] Across the Atlanta of early 1960s, as direct action picked up steam and drew in less well-off and more working-class Blacks, its leadership also began moving into workplace issues that Atlanta Urban League had long neglected.[123] As Atlanta's civil rights movement tackled job discrimination and labor conflict, it began to join forces with the city's long-marginalized labor unions in pursuit of that workplace-centered economic citizenship explored by historian Jefferson Cowie.[124]

Thereby, the direct-action campaigns steered Atlanta's civil rights movement even further away from that project of environmental citizenship that would hatch in the Atlanta area over the later 1960s just then still only in the process of being born. If parks and other recreational facilities were among those "tested" in Atlanta, they were among the less prominent of protestors' targets, especially after a new "omnibus" lawsuit sought to stop official segregation in this city, as Tomiko Brown-Nagin has shown.[125] Like many future environmentalists, however, King himself became increasingly critical of the middle-class home-owning affluence that for himself and other leaders had undergirded their new activism.[126] For King as for many advocates of direct action, the sit-ins amounted to a revolt not just against segregation itself but "against those Negroes in the middle class who have indulged themselves in big cars and ranch-style homes rather than in joining a movement for freedom."[127] The "dangerous altruism" of direct action beckoned a redemptive departure both from this complacency and from the safer, nonconfrontative civil rights advocacy it countenanced. Rhetorical dichotomizing aside, King's own circumstances, from his lengthy higher education to his family's modest ranch house on Sunset Drive, suggested a less mutually exclusive choice. Like those middle-class whites who over the next decade began thinking of themselves as environmentalists, middle-class Blacks could and should *choose* to overcome the complacency to which material affluence inclined them, by redirecting their lives toward loftier purposes.

Martin Luther King Jr. also shared one other thing with Atlanta's future environmental leaders: he talked a great deal about the natural world.[128] For King as with other SCLCers, nature-infused rhetoric invoked a vantage point on Jim Crow that was more ethically Archimedean than the social science of Urban Leaguers and that fingered not just inequality but frank injustice. He did so without reference to those legacies usually evoked in histories of environmentalism, in traditions of the "ecological" and other natural sciences, or in nature writing and "wilderness" celebration.[129] Many words and stories on which he drew were thousands of years older, from the Judeo-Christian Bible. Mountains, for instance, abounded in King's sermons and speeches. When he spoke of going to or having been on the mountaintop, he meant something different from what this era's mountain climbers sought.[130] For King the mountaintop was not just awe-inspiring in and of itself, but a place that could bring one closer to God as well as to God's vision for a human world below.[131] He also evoked tempestuous rivers and streams, but, unlike Atlanta's soon-to-be environmentalists, without any thought of rafting or canoeing. Instead, King's water-speak augured an overwhelming and transformative power of divine will, with full capacity to make city and society right. One of his favorite verses, from the Old Testament prophet Amos, called for "justice [to] run down like waters and righteousness like a mighty stream."[132] Biblical verses about rushing torrents helped him evoke the righteous force of the movement he helped lead: justice as a force of nature, sooner or later destined to deluge the human world with its chastening and redemptive waves.

King's biblical talk about tumultuous waters bore little resemblance to the tranquil, meandering River Jordan before which he preached, behind the altar in Ebenezer Baptist's sanctuary. Breaking with this imagery of nature as peaceful refuge, he and the many other pastor-leaders of this phase of the civil rights struggle remixed the secular with the biblical, bringing the flavor of Evangelical revival to Black Atlanta's outcry for civil rights. As they joined with other Black leaders to muster growing political pressure for a fairer share of citizenship, streams and rivers actually running through the city had been made to bear burdens far more noxious.

CHAPTER 3

Water Woes and Democratization

Just over a month after Martin Luther King Jr.'s iconic speech on the steps of the Lincoln Memorial, toward the end of 1963, Georgia state officials finally began to find fault with Atlanta's handling of its sewage. First with a private letter to Mayor Ivan Allen and then publicly at the quarterly meeting of the Georgia Water Quality Council, the head of the State Health Department, James Venable, himself an Atlanta native, warned that his office "cannot condone the action that is now being practiced by the city of Atlanta." Their study of the Chattahoochee River, the region's biggest, showed the city's "water pollution control plants" discharging ton upon steaming ton of "raw and unstabilized sewage" into the river. Fulton County was even allowing wastes from its industries to "bypass . . . [the] existing primary sewage treatment plant" entirely and dump directly into the Chattahoochee. Worsening for years, the problems had overwhelmed even Atlanta's biggest treatment plant. Named for R. M. Clayton, the city's longtime construction chief, it now operated at 57 percent more than its capacity. The result, in the colorless, measured language of the health expert, was "significant damage to the river, resulting in the denial of the use of the river water as a source of drinking water supply to several communities downstream."[1] Reporters swarmed in to elaborate. The *New York Times'* Gladwin Hill found a "nightmarish scene that might have been etched by Gustave Doré" at the Clayton plant's outfall—"skeletal saplings dying in filth-strewn mud, a pervading smell of decay and an endless torrent of sewage gushing into the river."[2]

Tensions between this city and Georgia's government were nothing new, but state officials' sudden move against Atlanta's long-building impacts on the Chattahoochee signaled major changes in who was running Georgia. Not long after the civil rights movement's turn to direct action came the beginning of a cleanup of Georgia's rivers, a little-studied environmental facet of the state's lurch away from the authoritarianism of "rustic rule." Like the urban renewal of the 1940s and 1950s, its thrust was technocratic, empowering expertise.[3] But in contrast to renewal planning that had unfolded within a city still run almost entirely by a white business elite, the 1963 warning to Atlanta came in the midst of a democratizing ferment. It was one of the earliest moves of the first Georgia governor to win election through a majority of the popular vote. With the county unit system rather suddenly overturned and with the votes of Black as well as white Atlantans now counting as much as those of rural Georgians, Carl Sanders had handily defeated the final heir of the Talmadges' "rustic" reign. As the Sanders administration then set about exploring what a more democratic state government could mean for ordinary Georgians, among its first moves was a far-reaching reform of water-pollution control. Countering business interests with the evenhandedness of expertise as well as greater legal authority, its strengthened oversight of Atlanta's and Georgia's waters became more capable of shielding the bodies, environments, and welfare of the less powerful.

The arrival of modern water-pollution control in Georgia reveals a face of democracy beyond the ballot box and beyond the access to public spaces like lunch counters and public goods like schools and parks for which civil rights activists were fighting. The regime change set in motion by the Sanders administration entailed new recognition that Georgians were also *environmental* citizens.[4] Through more robust environmental protections the state of Georgia began to better recognize and defend a hitherto little-recognized subset of citizens' rights, not yet fully acknowledged either by rustic rulers or by a movement for civil rights, to cleaner water and air. As a political project, a self-identified environmental citizenship had not yet coalesced at a grassroots level in 1963, either in Atlanta or other parts of the state. The public outcry against contaminated waters, while significant, had remained scattered and unorganized, in stark contrast to the burgeoning project of civil rights citizenship. The new state laws and programs of the early 1960s emanated largely from the top down, as politicians from Sanders to the legislature strove to curry favor with a newly empowered urban electorate. But, as we will see later, this early environmental state building had an interactive and iterative relationship with grassroots activism. It provided vehicles and visibility and in this case also new incursions of sewer building, all of which spurred a more organized and bottom-up environmental citizenship. By the same token, absent citizenly support and pressure, the evenhandedness of state-based pollution control could falter. Georgia's water-pollution-control effort of the 1960s proved especially ineffective in addressing the many racial and other inequities by then deeply ingrained in the city's aqueous commons, the more or less shared networks of creeks, streams, and rivers through which its waters and wastes coursed. But the power balance did tip against major polluters, as Atlanta along with the rest of Georgia gained growing oversight of the all-too-humanized microbiome and chemistry of rivers and streams running through them.

Strikingly, for all the contemporary emphasis on the deadliness of a contaminated Chattahoochee—its "skeletal saplings" and "smell of decay"—

much of its pollution circa 1963 was actually alive. Take a drop of water from the scene observed by Hill, put it under a microscope, and magnify it five hundred or a thousand times, and you would have espied a bewildering swarm of shapes, circles to rods to rectangles, in a chaotic whir of movement: the bacteria that make up so much of human feces. Innovations in gene-reading technology and big data have now taught us much about that ecosystem out of which such species hailed, what's now called the human microbiome, centered in our own guts. Rivers, too, have microbiomes, often deeply altered as a city grows along their banks.[5] What state health officials and journalists began discovering in the early 1960s was a decades-building transformation of the microbial ecology of Georgia's largest river. From the standpoint of the microscope, as Atlantans had funneled their own waste streams ever more directly into the Chattahoochee over the previous half century, mile after mile of the Chattahoochee had come to look more like their own insides. Combined with what bacterial species had blossomed along sewer lines and in disposal plants, the growing alterations of the river added up to what today's scientists term an "urban stream syndrome." Among its hallmarks was a shrinking diversity not just of microbes but of many other larger species.[6]

The syndrome induced in this and nearby rivers pointed to yet another way that Atlanta and other southern cities remained regionally distinctive, looking less like metropolitan contemporaries in the United States or Europe and more like those found then, as now, in cities of the developing world. As with the Latin American cities with which a U.S.-trained sanitary engineer named Patrick Owens had worked over the late 1950s and early 1960s in Colombia, Atlanta's "problems" were "primarily microbial in nature." Bacterial burdens of the Chattahoochee and other Atlanta-area rivers and streams loomed so large, unlike around Chicago or Boston or Seattle, predominately because so much of Atlanta's housing was only just transitioning to flush toilets and running water. "Septic fringes," like those Owens had come to know around Latin American cities, persisted far into the post–World War II period around cities in the southern states into the 1960s.[7] Contributing as well was the lower profile in and around Atlanta of what Owens termed "microphysicochemical hazards"— "air pollution, microchemical contamination, radiological hazards . . . and the like"—that increasingly afflicted cities in the more developed regions and nations of the West. Not that the Atlanta area was without industrial chemical pollutants, as we will see, but chemical and other heavy manufacturers were fewer and farther between here, and their toxic effluents tended to be overlooked by health as well as political officials or else treated with kid gloves.[8]

Though a movement decrying "environmental injustice" would not arise for another quarter century, government's growing sway over the Chattahoochee's and other Atlanta area stream contamination starting in the 1960s was, in retrospect, a matter of just that, for all its shortcomings in the Black sides of town. By this time, as in many other corners of the planet, the polluting capacity of disposal plants as well as factories had grown enormously, in parallel with accruing economic and political power of those who ran them. In Jim Crow–era Atlanta and Georgia, governmental indifference or leniency toward pollution had eased the ability of big befouling facilities to ride roughshod over the rights of ordinary citizens. Earlier state officials and experts, by refusing to control pollution or just looking the other way, had ensured an environmental face to inequalities that were also economic and racial, between the wealthiest and the rest as well as between whites and Blacks. Over the forties through the fifties, Black Atlantans moving suburb-ward, as well as generally less affluent whites along the western and southerly reaches of the city and beyond, all were *made neighbors* to other more affluent parts of the city, by the streams and rivers that bore the wastes of the better-off their way. Chattahoochee pollution, soon to be fingered as among the country's worst, up until 1963 remained publicly and politically invisible, even if all too odoriferously real for those living or venturing along the river from the Clayton plant southward.

Urbanizing Atlanta's Waterways

Begun along a ridge that happened to be a continental divide, Atlanta as it grew spilled across two watersheds. To the north and west, its lands were drained by Georgia's greatest river, the Chattahoochee, some 430 miles of mobile commons pouring down from the southern Appalachians, famously celebrated in an 1877 poem by the Georgia poet Sidney Lanier. Dashing "All down the hills of Habersham / All through the valleys of Hall" and cutting just seven miles to the northwest of Atlanta's downtown, it drained the westerly side of the city via Peachtree, Proctor, and Utoy Creeks and other tributaries. Ambling southwest through the Georgia Piedmont and skirting the Alabama border, it then joined the Apalachicola to spill into the Gulf of Mexico. Atlanta's other, eastern watershed fed the South River, originating along the southern and eastern slopes of Atlanta itself, carrying only about 6 or 7 percent the volume of water as the Atlanta-area Chattahoochee. From South Fulton and DeKalb, it sluiced a sixty-mile course to feed the Upper Ocmulgee, the Altamaha, and ultimately the Atlantic.[9] From the early 1890s, after decades of reliance on artesian wells and closer-in streams, the city began tapping the Chattahoochee to quench the ever more rapacious thirst; surrounding towns and counties soon followed suit.[10] Over the first half of the twentieth century, while this great watercourse seemed to offer more than enough for thousands of new residents and industries to drink, all the new arrivals created a whole other problem: an ever-mounting burden of wastes.

The growth of Atlanta's human residents alone between 1890 to 1960 hiked up the city's excremental ooze another six times and more, to reach an annual three thousand tons of sheer bacterial biomass. Especially early in this century but also deep into the post–World War II period, an inordinate share of this unseemly yield of the city's human residents went into latrines, cesspools, or septic tanks, what public health experts today refer to as "on-site" disposal systems.[11] Still prevalent in many cities of the developing world and an aspiration of modern closed-loop ecotoilets, these traditional ways of dumping sewage locally spared regional streams and rivers. But they had their own downsides: long-recognized aromatic and other aesthetic disadvantages of on-site disposal gained powerful reinforcement by the early twentieth century with the modern understandings of parasitical as well as infectious disease underscoring public health dangers. Through the first half of the century, Atlanta then went through two major rounds of building what was considered the "modern" solution, sewers that flushed ever more of it into the region's streams and rivers. First, a 1909 bond issue enabled the city to replace a patchwork sewer system with trunk lines along Peachtree (six miles) and two other of the city's largest streams (two and four miles), running into its first three treatment and disposal plants. Then in the 1930s federal capital from the New Deal finally gave this city the wherewithal for a more ambitious sanitary fix: building larger and more modern treatment plants and region-wide trunk lines. Thereby, much more of its sewer-borne wastes could be shunted beyond the city into the region's biggest rivers, especially the Chattahoochee.

Each of these waves of infrastructure building offered only a partial solution to the city's waste problem. For one thing, what treatment was provided by early-to-mid-century disposal plants alleviated only part of the load. By 1960 the city's biggest plant undertook only what was recognized as the first ("primary") of three possible rounds for breaking down wastes. Moreover, the best that sewer building itself could accomplish, however long its trunk lines, was to shunt wastes that had been concentrating in one corner of the city over to another, ideally into a river that would presumably dilute them while also sweeping them farther away. But each build-out of the city's sewer system only transferred Atlantans' inexorable befoulment of waters farther downstream: in 1909 down along intracity streams like Peachtree Creek and in the 1930s out to larger channels along the city's periphery, chief among them the Chattahoochee itself. And if the city's treatment plants during the post–World War II period offered all-too-incomplete cleansing, many sewers running through the city also did not meet the highest contemporary standards of cleanliness. CSOs, or Combined Sewer Overflows (as they are now known), still allowed for episodes of contamination during heavy rains, when an overflowing mixture of raw sewage and runoff would be deliberately diverted right into open streams. Engineered to episodically expose those living along these streams to bouts of putrid smells and pathogens, CSOs saved money but at the expense of noxiousness and ill health. If findings from recent studies of CSOs are any guide, they also led to more local illness and emergency room visits, especially among children living streamside.[12]

That urban stream syndrome Gladwin Hill had witnessed along the Chattahoochee in 1963 had recurred not only around the city's interceptor sewers but in earlier eras in streams threading through the city's heart. Reports in 1908 suggested its appearance along upstream stretches of Peachtree Creek, and in the 1930s farther down that same creek and most others, in each case helping spur new rounds of sanitary reconstruction. While its location changed and its extent grew with each occurrence, the basic biological pattern remained the same. Mixes of bacteria emanated an overpowering odor, just as they do to produce the familiar range of smells given off of human feces.[13] These aqueous stenches came not so much from fecal bacteria themselves as from ecological dynamics set off by their arrival in river water, in the company of organic detritus. In a process lately identified in the rivers around many cities in today's China, among other places, high nutrient levels from untreated waste streams nourished algal blooms that, as they died, drew in oxygen-devouring bacteria to decompose them.[14] The resultant low-oxygen or anaerobic conditions increasingly resembled those found in human intestines. Bacteria from people's own guts then flourished, and the deoxygenated water attracted other microbial anaerobes as well. Stinking vapors emanated from all these oxygen-independent microbes working together, stoking chemical transformations shared with rotting cadavers and eggs and a host of other modes "of decay."[15]

Scientists have found that, where this syndrome occurs, those waters most deeply affected by it choke off the fish and other larger creatures, from frogs to mayflies. Those few sizeable species easily tolerating the plummeting oxygen levels and a surfeit of nutrients, worms and snails, flourish precisely as waters come to be dominated by the algal and bacterial communities most at home with human sewage itself.[16] Many of these come from inside human bodies: *Bacteroides*, for instance, known today as among the most dominant bacteria of the human gut.[17] Anaerobes living and growing exclusively inside mammals, these bacteria can nevertheless survive as long as one or two weeks in sewage-choked streams. Many other enteric bacteria, among them *Escherichia coli* and the *Salmonella* species, have greater staying power outside the gut in fecal-contaminated water. Some varieties of these cause serious diseases in people—diarrheal and intestinal infections in the case of *E. coli* and, with different serotypes of *Salmonella*, either a severe food poisoning or life-threatening typhoid (*typhi*). In the bouts of Atlanta's streams with contamination by human wastes, these tiny migrants from inside Atlantans joined with other microbes multiplying in sewage lines and "primary" treatment plants to overwhelm the many aerobic bacterial species common to the city's less contaminated waters.[18] Among the recurrences of this syndrome as successive versions of Atlanta's sewage system became overwhelmed, the most pertinent to Georgia's democratization was that arising from the New Deal overhaul of the city's sewer system.

Had Atlanta not been a part of a larger, richer nation that, in the early 1930s, suddenly decided to invest heavily in new infrastructure, the bacterial burdens on its streams would have festered for years, if not decades. Of the $10 million expended over the late 1930s to make it happen, only $1.5 million came from city coffers, through a 1935 bond issue. The "lion's share" came from funds dispensed by the Works Progress Administration and other federal agencies.[19] These sums furnished sixty-two miles of new trunk sewers, conveying wastes from thousands more private homes. They then bore their loads (if not overflowing in combination with storm runoff via CSOs) out into larger rivers running beyond the city's boundaries. While the new treatment facilities dumping into the South River lay near the old plant, the biggest change came in the handling of wastes across the city's north and west. Trunk lines built from the Peachtree as well as Proctor disposal plants (set for closure) would begin conveying by far the biggest share of Atlanta's wastes downstream into the Chattahoochee itself. The Clayton treatment and disposal plant constructed there, where Peachtree flowed in, became the largest of the five in Atlanta's new metropolitan sewer system. Opening in 1938, it could handle forty-two million gallons per day of sewage. Effluent was then piped into it from all over the northern side of Atlanta as well as into Fulton County and eastward into northern DeKalb. Wastes underwent a "primary" treatment through four "two-stage digesters." Speeding and spreading the decomposing work of anaerobic bacteria through heating coils and turbine mixers, the technology was considered an advance over the Imhoff tanks used in the city's earliest treatment plants.[20] Not only were Atlanta's wastes to be more thoroughly treated and "stabilized" than before, but the Clayton plant now dumped them directly into the Chattahoochee. Reprieved from serving as receptacle for a disposal plant, Peachtree Creek reportedly ran "clear" by 1939, to the celebration of health officials and their politician backers.[21] Yet the stage had been set for a recurrence of the city's sewage problem both there and on a much larger scale, this time within the state's signature river.[22]

The sanitary triumphalism of this moment did not fully reckon with the city's impending growth, nor with how much of the waste disposal here, as elsewhere in the nation's poorest region, remained dependent on latrines or outhouses, unmistakable markers of Atlanta's and other southern cities' stubborn distinctiveness. Under this region's version of early twentieth-century cleavage capitalism, persisting poverty had sustained a widespread urban and suburban reliance on these low-cost, localized means of waste disposal, whether in the housing of Blacks or for fringe-dwelling poorer whites. Com-

MAP SET 3.1. Southern cities' more septic fringes in 1940. The edges of Atlanta and other southern cities in 1940 had a considerably greater proportion of "septic" housing—without toilets, hence no waterborne flushing of wastes—than cities in other U.S. regions. Thereby, they resembled the cities described by Patrick Owens and others in Latin America and elsewhere in the Global South. In this respect Birmingham, Alabama, actually resembles northern and western counterparts more closely than Atlanta. Maps by author. *Source:* Manson et al., *IPUMS National Historical Geographic Information System.*

pared to cities in richer and more industrialized regions, Atlanta's fringe remained especially, as Owens would later put it in describing some Latin American cities, a "septic one," troubled by infectious risks from latrines or outhouses as well as overflowing sewers or cesspools.[23] A full 35 percent of the households in Atlanta's 1940 census tracts had no indoor toilet. That ranged nearly as high as the 38 percent of housing still reliant on privies in urban Costa Rica in 1963 and considerably more than the 16 percent recorded for Honduran cities in 1961.[24] Just prior to World War II, only Atlanta's best-off tracts had *more* than 40 percent of their housing furnished with the capacity to flush away human wastes. By no means were most offending tracts mainly downtown. Instead, outhouses or privies actually concentrated farther out from the city's core—a persistently *suburban* poverty. Adding further dangers of disease transmission, many of these residents also still got their water from local wells instead of water pipes, hence, from those very water tables into which these wastes might drain. Like most other cities in the U.S Southeast, Atlanta's edges had far fewer sanitary provisions than did cities of comparable size in the Northeast, as well as the West, from Cleveland to Seattle (map set 3.1).

Not surprisingly, given city officialdom's enduring neglect of Black neighborhoods, African Americans predominated in many of these "septic" zones, downtown as well as along the urban fringe. Home environments there continued to sustain their greater susceptibility to many infectious ailments. Partly because of the diarrheal diseases that fecally contaminated water supplies spread among children, Atlanta in 1930 had the third-highest infant mortality rate in the nation. While infant mortality then began improving among whites, by 1947 Black infants born in the city were still twice as likely to die as white babies.[25] Typhoid, that deadly ailment spread via water or food infected by human wastes, continued to provoke special concern.[26] But though a drop in typhoid deaths among whites over the 1930s and 1940s meant that Atlanta no longer led the nation, this disease continued to afflict and kill a disproportionate share of Atlanta's Blacks.[27]

All the new home building and buying wrought by a New Deal–driven compressive capitalism brought indoor plumbing to many more Atlantans, Black as well as white. Once the massive federally funded build-out of the city's sewer system further enabled more and more Atlantans to switch, health and housing officials across metropolitan Atlanta reversed course on privies. Instead of making them more "sanitary," new rules and actions sought to eliminate them altogether. Inside the city as well as outlying towns, the eradication of privies was a major if little publicized goal of "urban renewal," through its bulldozers as well as the stricter housing codes and inspections its federal funding required. More generally, postwar campaigns of Atlanta-area health departments tightened rules for waste disposal in suburban subdivisions, while narrowing loopholes for privies and, in cities and towns, simply outlawing them.[28] Expanding housing opportunities combined with all these governmental pushes by 1960 to shrink the number of metro-area homes without flush toilets by four-fifths in just two decades, from 45 percent to a mere 3.3 percent of households.[29] In the process a growing share of homes adopted other forms of on-site disposal deemed more sanitary, the septic tanks and cesspools whose history has been charted for other parts of the country by Adam Rome.[30] Even as health officials also forged new sanitary rules for these, a growing reliance on sewer lines—their and planners' preferred solution—sluiced a tidal wave of human wastes into metropolitan Atlanta's pipes and treatment plants, then also into the surrounding rivers.

Among the notable consequences of these changes, officials gained growing sanitary rationales for eliminating those fringe settlements of poorer Blacks that had sustained Atlanta's regionally distinctive metropolitan structure. Buckhead's predominantly Black Bagley Park offers a case in point. "Located on the headwaters of a stream that flows southwardly through Fulton County" but "having no sewerage," it was among the earliest targeted for sanitizing demolishment. When white property owners nearby complained about the "health menace," not just "to the entire county" but to white children at the nearby North Fulton Grammar School, Fulton County razed the entire community and replaced it with a white people's park.[31] Other towns around Greater Atlanta brandished the cause of sanitation to eradicate suburban enclaves of poorer Blacks in the name of urban renewal: Decatur cleared out its Beacon Hill, Marietta its Louisville, College Park and East Point completed similar "renewal" projects, and even counties got in on the act.[32] DeKalb arranged a renewal project for 232 acres along the Black edge of Scottdale, to "be redeveloped for public, commercial, industrial and residential uses."[33]

While the biggest new effluent loads on the Chattahoochee as well as South River came from the city of Atlanta, the surrounding counties of Cobb and DeKalb tightened disposal rules as their populations grew, driving additional tides of waste toward the river. An ever more dispersed style of metropolitan growth was no respecter of political boundaries, and political careers were made by ensuring that new housing and industrial development reached this region's outlying counties and municipalities. Reigning political elites saw little reason to address the new, entirely predictable burdens of human as well as industrial wastes until their hands were forced. By the late 1940s in DeKalb, a grand jury and lawsuits targeted the overloaded quarter-century-old disposal plant at Shoal Creek for dumping raw sewage into this tributary of the South River.[34] In Cobb County, Marietta by 1954 was confronting its own disposal dilemma: an aging, overloaded disposal plant that had to be shuttered temporarily for repairs, leading local critics to decry the plant as a "disgrace." As the head of the county medical association put it, "if an epidemic of flyborne diseases like polio or typhoid fever is avoided, it will be 'sheer luck.'"[35] Solutions in both DeKalb and Cobb included federally funded and more sophisticated treatment plants, using a secondary as well as a primary process. Together they got rid of 85 to 90 percent of wastes, far more than what the Clayton plant could manage. By the early 1960s, however, both DeKalb and Cobb still ran other, older plants that offered only primary treatment. Like Clayton, these passed along the vast bulk of incoming wastes through their outfalls, into tributaries like Sweetwater Creek flowing into the Chattahoochee.

Those industries arriving or expanding in the Atlanta area during the post–World War II period added their own growing share to what went into its streams and rivers. Most of Atlanta's postwar industrial growth came either through assembly plants, like General Motors in Doraville, which put together parts made elsewhere, or in textile or food-processing plants. Their detritus consisted mainly of organic materials, not so chemically or physically distinctive from what came out of household toilets or sinks. The discards from broiler production, for instance, consisted mostly of discarded chicken parts. As for textile factories, while they might slough off sulfides, dyes, chromates, and synthetic detergents in river water, Atlanta's health experts, like many of their colleagues not just in Georgia but in other regions, were confident that all these dangers were either minimal or easily correctable through existing procedures, especially "appreciable dilution." While health and environmental scientists elsewhere were already beginning to worry more about these "microphysicochemical hazards," as the sanitary engineer Owens put it, Atlanta-area public health officials of this era believed these substances posed little threat either to human health or to stream life.[36]

In point of fact, these growing industries as well as other arrivals to the Atlanta area during the post–World War II period did offer potential fodder for anxieties about industry-made chemicals. Already these had begun stirring an environmental movement in other regions of the country, from the smog driven by refineries and auto exhaust that swirled through Los Angeles air, to the phenols and cadmium pooled underneath Long Island aircraft plants.[37] While most of Georgia's heavier industries gravitated closer to the coast, the Marietta Lockheed factory opening in 1952 was among the Atlanta-area plants that by mid-decade dumped wastes laden with chemical toxics into local waters, in this case a nearby Nickajack Creek. Four years later neighbors complained about a smell in the creek they thought had come from Smyrna's sewage-disposal plant. But the city engineer and Cobb County Health Department insisted the town's plant was operating "efficiently" and fingered instead "pollution from Cobb County and Lockheed disposals which also dump into the Nickajack."[38] Clearly aware of Lockheed's dumping practices, health officials made no recorded move to address or even monitor them. Only much later would it become known just how much chromium and other toxic chemicals the company had been sluicing into this Chattahoochee tributary for years, with zero treatment.

Throughout the metro region, health officials proved extraordinarily reluctant to monitor or even ask about what was happening to industrial wastes. This disregard was partly due to how much more formidable the problem of human sewage was but also to the ways water pollution was understood and measured at this time. Rather than analyzing streams or rivers for any specifically *industrial* chemicals, health officials assumed both chemical and bacterial impacts could be monitored using a single metric: the biochemical oxygen demand (BOD). This test measured the total oxygen needed by microorganisms to decompose a contaminant in water. The working assumption at the time was that BOD worked equally well whether the danger was infectious or chemically toxic in character. As would later be realized, reliance on BOD measurements failed to account for the chronic harms that heavy metal pollutants like mercury or organic ones like DDT could induce even in tiny amounts. Nor could it track their durability outside the human body; wherever they drifted, their toxicity far outlasted the infectious dangers of most bacteria of concern.[39]

The water woes faced by post–World War II Atlanta were not just a matter of these growing loads; its own sewer system also suffered its share of breakdowns. If even properly functioning CSOs themselves posed episodic threats, by the early 1950s the interceptors began failing, adding to orchestrated storm-fed surfeits. Clogs and insufficient capacity in the main lines led to massive overflows that choked streams like Proctor and Nancy Creeks with raw sewage even during dry weather.[40] As a result, by 1953 the Health Department's chief engineer declared that "most all the major creeks in Fulton County are polluted to some extent."[41] Citizen groups as well voiced their discontent. Representatives of the Grove Park Civic League converged on the city council's sewer committee, for instance, to complain that neighboring Proctor Creek had become polluted by "industrial waste, raw sewage and refuse all the way from a bridge at Francis Street, NW, to the creek's northwest leg," a distance of as many as two miles. Along North Utoy Creek, a homeowner at Cascade Terrace Southwest reported "odors so strong at night we can hardly stand it. . . . [It is] a health hazard . . . because of mosquito breeding and the danger to children in the neighborhood." The Adams Park Civic Club also chimed in, leading city officials to reassure that they were addressing the matter. Yet at least one publicly admitted, "I don't know what could be done about it." Without spending millions more dollars to replace the CSOs, the only solution seemed to be "eliminat[ing] stagnant pools" in the contaminated stream, thereby "insur[ing] a free flow" of sewage-bearing waters.[42]

Aside from those living downstream from CSOs, Atlanta's New Deal–funded solution to its Depression-era pollution problems nevertheless worked well for much of downtown. Before, much of the city's sewage had reached this larger river in a stutter-step manner, via feeder streams, enabling much decomposition to happen prior to its flow into the Chattahoochee itself. But the mammoth Clayton plant, into which all the waste streams from shuttered treatment plants along Peachtree as well as Utoy Creeks had been shunted, dumped all this sewage, once treated, directly into this larger river, out of a single main outfall. In so doing, however, this plant upon opening in 1938 had split the river's environmental history into two. North of the Clayton plant lay a version of the Chattahoochee that after World War II would burnish its gathering reputation as pristine. Many, including some of the city's most priv- ileged whites, would gravitate there. Living and playing along it, they would seek public protections for it as developers drew near, celebrating its value as a visible slice of the natural world. The river south of Clayton, on the other hand, became the dirty Chattahoochee. Abandoned over a growing stretch of miles to the city's excrement, it suffered an elongated version of urban-stream syndrome, of a reach and severity without precedent in the city's or Geor- gia's own history. By the 1960s the volume of Atlanta's waste overwhelmed its largest disposal plant to spill ever more directly and copiously into the state's greatest river. Downstream from this outfall, its bacterial and nutrient loads seethed and festered, wafting up foul odors even as these very banks came to be inhabited increasingly by Atlanta's Blacks.

By the late 1940s into the 1950s, the worsening stink and swirl of dirty wa- ter along this great river as well as within a West Side dotted with many of the city's CSOs adds a further explanation as to why the city's post–World War II white leadership ceded Atlanta's westerly suburbs to the growing ranks of At- lanta's Black homeowners (map set 3.2). White planners as well as Black advo- cates for the city's Black "expansion areas" (see the previous chapter) never ex- plicitly mentioned the interceptors' episodic unleashing of excrement through these neighborhoods, but many white homeowners undoubtedly were aware. As Black homebuyers began to arrive, the noxious backyard smells offered whites an extra incentive to sell.

Silently, but in retrospect unmistakably, an important environmental injus- tice lurked behind one of the proudest post–World War II achievements of the Atlanta Urban League, the westerly wedge of Black "access to suburban and outlying areas" and the "beautiful Negro suburbs" that had arisen there. These as well as the poorer Black housing of its northwest suburbs lay near or beside sluices engineered to carry out, and on occasion to overflow with, the city's ex- crement. The largest public-housing project of the Atlanta Housing Author- ity, the thousand-unit Perry Homes opened in 1955 next to the old Black en- clave of Scotts Crossing, lay alongside Proctor Creek itself.[43] The city's policies of building as well as zoning further amplified how Black Atlantans, new and modern as their housing became, were made to shoulder a disproportionate

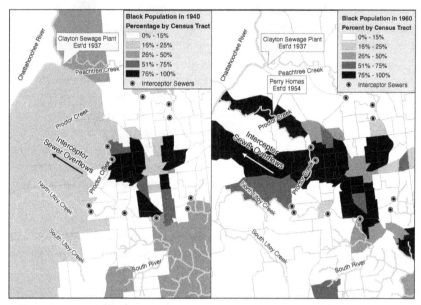

MAP SET 3.2. Black suburbanizing meets interceptor sewer overflow. Racial transitions and Black in-migration to Atlanta's West Side between 1940 and 1960 followed Proctor and North Utoy Creeks, which harbored untreated city sewage after heavy rains. Also depicted here are some of the older Black suburban enclaves such as around Peachtree Creek, which after the war were replaced by white suburban migrants. Maps by author. *Sources*: McGee, "Report on the City"; Manson et al., *IPUMS National Historical Geographic Information System*; "Atlanta, Georgia," Google Maps, accessed August 2018.

share of the city's sanitary noxiousness and threat. During heavy rains, raw sewage streaming in from the whiter parts of the city overflowed into Proctor and North Utoy. And downstream from the outfall of the Clayton plant into the Chattahoochee, bacterial and nutrient loads stewed and putrefied, wafting up foul odors even as these very banks came to be inhabited increasingly by some of Atlanta's most affluent Blacks. Thereby, waterways coursing alongside and among Black homescapes of hope burgeoned with bacteria originating in, among other places, the bowels of white Atlantans.

Empowered Polluters, Constricted State

What enabled this vastly expanded urban imprint on waters running through and alongside Atlanta was not just how much more waste came to dumped into them but, every bit as important, how little government oversight there was either of this pollution or its consequences. In this era prior to the EPA's 1970 creation, when the federal government itself had little enforcement role in water-pollution control, neither local nor regional nor Georgia's state government showed much willingness to take on polluters, even the largest municipal and industrial culprits. The dearth of oversight constituted yet another hierarchy in the citizenship of rustic rule: polluters' rights prevailed, at the expense of anyone else who happened to live, fish, or drink downstream.

Throughout this era the main way metro-area counties and municipalities handled stream pollution was not so much to assess and control it as to seek out water sources that could reliably avoid it. Though within their own boundaries they did try to enforce a growing array of sanitary rules to control household wastes, targeting privies as well as septic tanks and new subdivisions, the scale of pollution accumulating in shared waterways was simply beyond their grasp.[44] Among those tapping the Chattahoochee, the City of Atlanta and Fulton County were the first to site water-pumping stations upstream from the Clayton outfall; DeKalb followed suit in 1939, initiating its county water system running from up-river southward to supply the city of Decatur, its county seat.[45] Cobb County as well, launching its own Cobb County–Marietta Water Authority in 1951, went still farther up the Chattahoochee for its pumping station along with a treatment plant and reservoir.[46] As Cobb and DeKalb joined Atlanta in sluicing their sewerage into this great river, the many municipalities across the city's southern suburbs were forced to adjust, avoiding the resultant, burgeoning streams of waste in their own nearby stretches of the river. In South Fulton the municipalities of East Point and College Park bowed to the Chattahoochee's ineradicable contamination by turning upstream to a smaller tributary, Sweetwater Creek, for their water.[47]

In a region long scarred by poverty, a hands-off approach prevailed to both corporate and municipal facilities, even as factories grew as immense as Lockheed and treatment plants as massive as the R. M. Clayton facility.[48] Starved for industrial development and the wealth it was presumed to bring, bending over backward to woo its corporate agents as well as federally funded sewage works, Georgia and Atlanta officialdom also entertained less-than-democratic notions about the "publics" they served and about just whom their oversight and rules should protect. The reluctance to control or even monitor pollution constituted what would become an increasingly glaring facet of democracy's dearth in post–World War II Georgia. With such constricted electorates, the reins of most governments lay in the hands of small cadres of white officials whose closest ties were often with business and other wealthy elites. They worried far more about offending or embarrassing large-scale polluters, public as well as private, than about protecting communities from the ensuing contamination. A nagging fear reigned that too aggressive action on their part might drive away the factories and other business they and their bosses saw as the region's economic salvation. At the county level prevailing attitudes were captured by a Fulton County health official who decided in 1955 "not to publicize the stream pollution" afflicting so many of the region's streams. His rationale: "it might discourage Industries from coming to Atlanta."[49]

This and other metro counties had nevertheless begun adding more public health and other services as their counties urbanized, parting ways with the bare-bones approach to government dominating rural Georgia, where the classic Talmadge-backed courthouse rings reigned. Personal ties and dealmaking by a commissioner like DeKalb's Scott Candler offered first dibs on water and sewer services to new plants and wealthier white areas, still subscribing to what political scientists term "political clientelism," a governing style leaning on patronage and personalized bargaining to sustain political power.[50] Summarizing both the older and newer literature on this concept, a recent reviewer notes how "clientelism is intimately linked to poverty and inequality, of which it is probably both a cause and a consequence."[51] Clientelism was also a less then democratic citizenship practice, favoring the rights and interests of a select circle of "clients" at the expense of less well-connected, hence, second-class citizens. The authoritarian streak of post–World War II Atlanta's municipal governments acquired an environmental face in how they handled the water pollution of favored clients: sporadically and reactively and only when official hands were forced. While outbreaks of public discontent could lead officials to modernize sewage-treatment plants, and while neighborly spats often drove calls for inspection as well as penalties for improper waste disposal, neither municipal nor county health departments attempted any systematic look at what was getting into Atlanta-area streams and rivers.

What was missing in comparison with later on was a more "programmatic" approach to water-pollution control, one that dispensed governmental services not just to favored "clients" but more evenhandedly. For water-pollution control to work equally well for a fuller range of citizens, professional expertise and testing capacity were necessary conditions, though not sufficient ones. As we saw with urban renewal, whether or not official experts could act more evenhandedly also hinged on larger contexts that were unavoidably political: just how democratic a government was and just whom its political leaders saw themselves as serving. And not only were Atlanta-area municipalities at best only gradually shedding their racial authoritarianism, but they still had little of the necessary equipment or expertise to track water pollution in their midst. Over the entirety of 1957, even the best-endowed county Health Department, for Fulton, ran only ten laboratory tests for stream pollution.[52] By 1964, among the metro area's health departments, only "the city of Atlanta ha[d] the testing laboratories necessary for a careful supervision" of municipal treatment plants, while other health departments "d[id] not."[53]

In the absence of any more genuinely regional governance, the mid-twentieth-century scramble of metro-area cities, towns, and counties after unpolluted drinking water was slow to yield any more overarching framework for decision making. The sluggishness was not surprising, given the siloes within which city and county governments operated and their reluctance even to broach such issues. Atlanta's and Fulton County's Metropolitan Planning Commission (MPC), created in 1947, did begin to address more regional prospects for housing, industry, and road and expressway building but ignored questions of water or sewers. While the 1950 Plan of Improvement suggested another pathway toward a more regional oversight, by consolidating the City of Atlanta's water, sewer, and health department services with Fulton County's, white county leaders elsewhere in the region found consolidation harder to achieve.[54] But even had more consolidations happened or the MPC received more powers, those pollution problems cropping up by the early 1960s would probably not have been forestalled, for Atlanta officials couldn't plan for what they didn't see. The impending burden of waterborne wastes simply failed to register on the radar screen of Atlanta's early regional planners, exclusively worried as they remained about water supply: the volume flowing their way from upstream.[55] Of course, the southern politics of water supply could also turn environmental, as explored by Chris Manganiello.[56] But for the MPC, even after extra counties were added to it in 1960 (Clayton, Cobb, and Gwinnett) and its name changed to the Atlanta Region Metropolitan Planning Commission (ARMPC), some years passed before it took note of the full extent of the region's contaminated waters.[57]

Without any effective regional or municipal oversight, the best prospect for government supervision of the aqueous interconnections wrought by Atlanta's urbanizing lay with Georgia's state government, especially after a 1948 federal water-pollution act set up mechanisms and funding for state-level water-pollution control. But with Talmadgism retaining its grip on political power in Georgia, both greater democracy and more expert-informed policy making seemed distant prospects. As we've seen, Talmadgists, starting with patriarch Eugene, generally frowned on extending governmental services beyond their favored clientele, especially if the benefits were so broad as to reach a Black minority or the poor. Eugene himself also remained highly suspicious of the fundamental science behind water-pollution control, quipping at one point that "country people don't believe in germs."[58] After his death his gubernatorial successors did steer Georgia's ship of state to confront its increasingly fouled waters. But they did so in ways skimpily provisioned with expertise and readily swayed by polluters themselves.[59]

Eugene's son Herman began contending with the issue in 1949, one year after the first federal water-pollution-control act and "after several serious cases of stream pollution were assailed by sportsmen and health officials." At the urging of state legislators, Herman Talmadge then inaugurated the "cooperative" method for addressing pollution episodes that would predominate over the next decade. He appointed a committee to investigate, with representation from all the parties officially deemed "interested." Unlike in states such as New York and Pennsylvania, this board was temporary, and only a single member had any expertise in water pollution: Walter Weir from the State Health Department. A handful of "industry representatives" and legislators garnered most of the slots, along with others from the Game and Fish Commission, a university Agriculture Department, and an association of town officials.[60] Supposedly representative deliberative bodies such as this one, hand-picked to be well stocked with industry spokespeople while marginalizing experts or anyone from affected communities, became the hallmark of the co-operative approach under Talmadgism.[61]

Once this committee dissolved, the State Health Department took over Georgia's efforts under the 1948 act, which consisted almost entirely of approving "water supply, sewage works, industrial waste treatment, and allied activities" for federal funding. Systematically downplaying any hint of enforcement or penalties for the act of polluting, Weir's department confined itself to ushering along these "water and sewage works projects" and providing free training to those in both municipalities and private companies who would run them. Decision making frankly favored "the industrial expansion of Georgia," with those corporations that proposed to establish new plants in the state receiving special solicitude. An "industrial location service" promised to find that one place with "the greatest economic and social advantages with the least damage to natural resources." No matter what the industry, "public health supervision" was to be provided free of charge.[62] State health officials also wielded their clout to tamp down what public opposition arose to companies' plans. In 1951, after the Atlanta Paper Company announced plans to build a new plant on the banks of the Chattahoochee in Cobb County, complaints erupted from local civic groups. But after receiving "more information" on the plant, likely from the company itself, Weir declared it would "have 'no harmful effect on the river' [and] 'not emit objectionable odors.'" His authority, he also tried to clarify, was merely advisory anyway. The company could do what it wanted on its own property, and "the state health department could not raise objections until a nuisance was already created."[63]

Like their Atlanta-area counterparts, state health officials remained far more worried about health dangers from human sewage than from industrial chemicals. They also assumed that municipal plants designed for treating domestic wastes could also handle "most" industrial effluents.[64] Like colleagues in many other parts of the country, they still concentrated primarily on well-known bacteriological problems that their labs were already equipped to handle. In the public health labs of Georgia, still preoccupied with battles against tuberculosis and the lingering malaria that had recently led to the Atlanta establishment of the Centers for Disease Control, that focus seemed to make sense. They had neither means nor know-how even to look for industrial toxins such as pesticides or heavy metals or detergents, only just then starting to be studied in more urban and industrial regions.[65] Through the 1950s they departed only once from prevailing assumptions that industrial wastes could be handled with conventional sewage treatments. That was in 1956, when Lockheed began planning an experimental "atomic plant" in Dawsonville, fifty miles north of Marietta. State officials eagerly issued it a clean sanitary bill of health in advance and, as operations got underway, then "cooperatively" monitored for radioactivity around the plant site and in the streams where waste was dumped. Funding for all these services came not from Lockheed but from Georgia taxpayers.[66]

The reluctance of health officials to scrutinize other industrial pollutants meshed well with postwar variants of Talmadgism, which held fast to white supremacy and the county unit system but eagerly hungered after private capital. With "corporate wealth" and interests dominating the legislature under Talmadgism, its leaders harped on instances of industrial eminence, even though most small counties of the Talmadge political base were dominated by agriculture.[67] Like other southern states, as described by James Cobb, postwar Georgia stepped up governmental support for "industrial progress" on many fronts with little apparent connection to pollution control.[68] Post–World War II Talmadge administrations not only passed right-to-work legislation, suppressing union growth; they created a state Commerce Department, converted Savannah into an official state port, and erased capital-spurning rules and taxes favoring Georgia-based companies over "foreign"—that is, out-of-state—corporations.[69] Herman Talmadge also saw to it that the state's property tax was abolished and replaced by a 3 percent levy on all kinds of consumption. Large landowners, industrialists as well as business-minded farmers, thereby gained tax relief, even as a growing share of state revenues came out of the pockets of less wealthy and unpropertied Georgians.[70]

Talmadgism took its new step toward "cooperative" water-pollution control in the course of an investigation of the state's water resources triggered by the severe drought of 1954. DeKalb's ubiquitous commissioner, the Talmadge ally Scott Candler, headed the commission set up by the legislature to look into water-related issues, of which pollution was just one. Its fifteen members "represented" the relevant state agencies as well as other groups deemed interested, polluting industries prominent among them. Committee members squared off over water pollution early on, with the Health Department representative—Walter Weir again—defending the adequacy of his department's approach against the head of the Georgia's Game and Fish Commission, who "wanted to see more action taken on stream pollution which results in fish kill."[71] To "explain" its own "purposes . . . to Georgia citizens and all parties interested" and possibly to resolve this debate, the committee then took what was still an unusual step for rustic rulers. It opened its proceedings to whoever wished to have a say, by arranging some fourteen public hearings around the state.[72]

Like the Atlanta city officials hosting a public hearing on renewal plans in 1957, state officials hosting these public 1956 gatherings got more than they had bargained for: an upwelling of complaints about how contaminated Georgia's waters had become. From early April through June, the hearings drew out, as "an array of Georgians from private citizens to county officials," including sixty-nine people from in and around the state's biggest city, converged on the Atlanta meeting. Most there "called for a vigorous clampdown on pollution of the state's rivers and streams."[73] Jim Aldredge, head of the Fulton County Commission, joined with the chair of the College Park Lion's Club to ask for investigation of "the condition of the Chattahoochee River below Atlanta." Local sportsmen's groups also attended to express their concern, alongside Fred Sturgess of the Georgia Conservation League, organized just the year before to make this "no longer the only state without a statewide federal federation of fish and game conservation clubs."[74] Sturgess warned that not just sports fishing but the catfish industry, itself a "big business," were both being undone by the pollution threat. Struggling to contain this precipitous outcry, the newspaper coverage as well as the commission's own summaries of the proceedings instead headlined dire warnings from business leaders and others about the many dangers of overly "rigid" antipollution laws. Georgia Chamber of Commerce Walter Cates got top billing in the *Atlanta Constitution* for portraying the choice as between catfish and all the new industry that could "keep our boys and girls from leaving the state." Pointing out it "would be too expensive for industries to have to filter their water," he warned about the threat of pollution control to Georgia's current "good competitive position with other states."[75] The commission's own official account of the testimony, as well, rarely strayed from defenses of industry's right to pollute. "A very strict law," it concluded, "could be very detrimental to the industrial growth of Georgia."[76]

Realizing how mounting anger over water pollution undermined public support for their corporate-friendly autocracy in ways that could not go ignored, Talmadgist officials went through the motions, at least, of taking action. That next year governor and legislature responded by enshrining their cooperative approach to water pollution into law, through the creation of a Georgia Water Quality Council (GWQC). Rebuking Game and Fish's critique of existing efforts as well as its bid for greater say, the council was placed in the state health board. Its composition mirrored the polluter-heavy representation of previous, temporary committees: one from each of the major industries of the state ("Food-Processing," "Textiles," "Pulp and Paper," and "Agriculture") and one each from the various government agencies involved. The biggest addition was a single new member who was now to represent "conservation," channeling the multitudinous concerns brought out at the hearings. While charged with year-round oversight of the state's waters, the council was more like its temporary-committee predecessors than a regulatory agency. Only the Health Department representative claimed any special training in the water-pollution field. Council members all had other full-time jobs, and they met only four times a year. Under the new law the appointment of professional staff remained optional, and none wound up being hired. The council's agenda, rather than being set by steady oversight or any survey of what the state's pollution problems were, remained entirely reactive. Only when some person or group alleged pollution, bringing it to their attention, would they consider it. The council could request an investigation by state health officials, but, no matter how bad the contamination, it administered no rules or laws and had no legal authority to charge anyone with a violation or crime. What power there was actually to penalize still lay in the Board of Health's very hesitant hands; the council could only "make recommendations" to it and "review" its "orders or actions."[77] Another clause written into the 1957 act added to the unlikelihood that the board would fine or prosecute any polluter. To make any penalty stick, the state now had to "prove that a particular discharge is creating a grave and immediate health hazard." With the bar to any punitive enforcement hiked up so high, even when someone could "show that pollution definitely exists," polluters themselves could still rest easy.[78]

Throughout the nearly six years of the Georgia Water Quality Council's existence, it operated largely a kind of political safety valve for swelling complaints about fouled water around the state, publicly acknowledging them only to absorb and allay their sting. Rather than placing additional pressures and demands on polluters, the council, with its limited authority, staff, and expertise, only reinforced the well-established "cooperative" inclinations of Georgia officialdom. The council's sole "conservation" spokesperson, without pollution expertise of his own, was easy to overrule, and the protestations of aggrieved communities easy to absorb through official proceedings. And the solutions offered by the council were almost entirely reliant on the good will of polluters. In 1959, for instance, Col. Charles Russell, the executive director of the Georgia Sportsmen's Federation, then serving as conservation representative, brought up a discharge by "Bona Allen interests" of tannic acid into the Suwannee Creek, another Chattahoochee tributary, which had lately made the newspapers in Atlanta. Weir then took the floor to suggest that Russell needn't have brought it up, since health officials were already "fully aware of the problem" and undertaking studies to assess it.[79] While chicken-processing plants had flourished in north Georgia for decades, the first report of pollution from them came in a July 1959 meeting, when Weir reported on complaints about their wastes coming from city disposal plants in Habersham County's Mud Creek. Russell then prodded the council on what polluting impact chicken processors might be having where they were even more concentrated, around Gainesville. The fix then devised by the council was characteristic:

"invite committee members from chicken and food-processing industries" as well as "other industries concerned with water pollution . . . to sit in on Council meetings for benefit of better understanding of hazards of water pollution that now exist and continue to increase."[80]

The greatest beneficiaries of the council's conciliatory, educational approach were Georgia's biggest polluters. Private industries were implicated in some 58 percent of cases taken up by the council, compared to only 24 percent from municipal sewage plants, yet polluting companies were treated with velvet gloves, as the state's most favored of citizens. The results were all too predictable: an early 1960s federal survey of state pollution-control programs was scathing about Georgia's effort under Talmadgism. As late as 1959 only a single corporate treatment plant around Atlanta actually specialized in industrial wastes, that for Lockheed's small nuclear reactor in Dawsonville. By 1963 only eight factories in the entire state treated what they dumped into rivers or streams in ways federal officials deemed "adequate." The state itself was spending only $126,000 annually on water-pollution control, and its program had no power to set, much less enforce, any water-quality standards. In contrast to the state "control boards" not just in California and New York but in other southern states such as Tennessee, Georgia's had still not brought a single polluter to court.[81]

By the first years of the sixties, however, the growing roster of nonmember attendees at council meetings suggested that, as public worries about river pollution rose, it was turning from absorptive sounding board into a megaphone. The press started showing up, as did more onlookers from implicated corporations and local and state agencies, along with some civic groups and, occasionally, another attendee from the Georgia Sportsmen's Federation or from an affected locale. As with the eruption at the 1956 hearing, this "ad hoc" simmer of discontent, like the 1950s opponents of water pollution that Craig Colten has found in other southern states, hardly added up to an organized or self-identified environmental movement.[82] The most insistent of these groups, the Georgia Sportsmen's Federation, did claim to represent over one hundred local clubs and eight thousand Georgians by 1961. But it had stricken the more politicized project of "conservation" from its name and still got more disturbed about game-law enforcement and corruption in the state's wildlife agency than about water pollution.[83] In these years, nevertheless, a civic club in DeKalb lodged the council's first complaint about the insufficiency of sewage treatment by the City of Atlanta itself, as causing pollution in the South River. The wheels also began to turn that would spotlight what had happened to the Chattahoochee under rustic rule, drawing that river itself into a high-profile role in the state's political history.[84]

By the early 1960s that urban stream syndrome overwhelming the state's largest river, running from Atlanta on down, marked the culmination of decades-long privileging of polluter's rights by all levels of government. It amounted to the most intensive and furthest reaching alteration of riverine ecology that Georgia had ever seen, over three-quarters of it estimated to be from "treated and untreated municipal sewage."[85] Starting at the Clayton plant outfall, a fifty-yard-wide river the color of "coffee-with-cream" turned "much darker in color," carrying "what the engineers euphemistically call 'solids.'" About 80 percent of Atlanta's burden on the Chattahoochee entered here, from a metropolis whose effluent now made up more than half of the bacterial load entering the river along its entire length. Three of the five other city treatment plants (the other two turning to the South River) as well as nine others in the metro area, mostly in Cobb County, also ran their waste into this most massive of Georgia rivers. Most all offered only "primary" winnowing, so the river itself was forced to swallow nearly two-thirds of the actual bacterial mass flowing into treatment plants. And with the Clayton operation running so much above its capacity from the 1950s—by 1964, 157 percent more—and with raw sewage overflowing into Chattahoochee tributaries after rainstorms, even solid chunks that primary systems were supposed to filter out bobbed down the river.

The first systematic testing for fecal coliform species like *E. Coli* along the river, undertaken in the early 1960s, found the Chattahoochee north of the city, around Atlanta's own water intake, to be relatively clean (that is, at 2,000 coliform bacteria per 100 milliliters, usually below the U.S. Public Health Service's criteria for drinking water of 5,000 coliforms). But past the city's main outfalls the readings skyrocketed: coliform counts even nineteen miles downstream registered a whopping thousand times higher than the standard. As so many nutrients as well as bacteria poured into the river in such bulk, the urbanizing dynamic took off. River oxygen levels plummeted, and the diversity of microbial species faltered as aerobic bacteria died off. Anaerobic conditions more like those in human intestines sustained still more enteric species, hobbling the river's capacity to decompose organic wastes. The microbial fruit of metropolitan bowels had made Chattahoochee waters "greatly exceed . . . the bacterial water quality criteria for swimming, skiing, fishing, boating, and general recreational use *along the entire 100 miles reach from Atlanta to upper Lake Harding.*"[86] The city's growth had combined with its fitful sanitizing to spawn a massive urban river syndrome less like those in the contemporary U.S. North or West than in developing nations, then as now: where "urban runoff and sewerage disposal . . . is the major problem of river water quality" (India) and where riverine chemical cascades could catalyze "odorization and Blackening" (China).[87] The dramatic findings prompted health warnings about the potential "disease-producing organisms" and all they could cause: "gastrointestinal diseases, such as typhoid fever, dysentery and diarrhea . . . eye, ear, nose, throat, or skin infections . . . [even] infectious hepatitis."[88]

As with the sewage "solutions" of the New Deal, new federal interventions had begun actively prodding a more aggressive approach to Atlanta's water-borne dilemmas; only this time the state of Georgia itself would also soon step up. Amendments passed by Congress in 1961, to a federal act approved six years before, eased the ability of federal investigators to take enforcement actions against interstate water pollution, flowing from one state into another. The Chattahoochee, which edged into Alabama less than a hundred miles downstream from Atlanta, then became fair game for an intervention by the U.S. Public Health Service, charged with implementing the act. By mid-1962, as USPHS began looking at Georgia rivers, state Game and Fish officials moved to stave off "recourse to P.L. 660 and federal intervention" on the Chatta-hoochee. Gathering with counterparts from Alabama and Florida, they began talks about "devis[ing] a more satisfactory solution to the problem of pollution" in this river.[89] Before either these talks or federal deliberations had gotten very far, however, Georgia's long leadership by the Talmadge faction of the Democratic Party abruptly ended, and new political leadership moved quickly to reconstruct the state's entire approach to water-pollution control.

Toward Science-Based Pollution Fighting

After gathering momentum more slowly over previous decades, the democratization of Georgia's electorate got a sudden boost with a March 1962 decision by the Supreme Court in *Baker v. Carr*, confirming the principle of "one person, one vote" as the law of the land. A lawsuit launched that very day by a white Fulton County voting activist led a federal district court to strike down the county unit system, as shortchanging the state's urban voters. It was, as Jimmy Carter himself reflected three decades later, "one of the most momentous political decisions of the century in Georgia."[90] With both primary and general elections for state offices now to be decided by popular vote, the ballots cast by Atlantans and other city residents suddenly mattered as much as those of rural voters, and turnout in metro-area counties surged. The victor that year, defeating then governor Marvin Griffin in the primary, was Carl Sanders, a moderate Democrat who became the first Georgian from an urban county to ascend to the governor's mansion since the early twentieth century. This watershed election in Georgia's passage from Jim Crow toward greater democracy was fought, in significant part, over the issue of water pollution.

The 1962 gubernatorial campaign unfolded just as an Atlanta-based civil rights movement was gaining considerable traction regionally as well as nationally, keeping segregation as well as explicit race baiting and Atlanta bashing at the forefront of the campaigns. Griffin, true heir to the Talmadge faction, was louder and blunter in his racial stereotyping, accusing Sanders of being backed by a "corrupt Atlanta political machine," "Negro leader Martin Luther King," and a "Negro bloc vote" and of seeking a "Congo on the Chattahoochee," foisting the whole of Atlanta on the Black side of the color line.[91] While Sanders, too, supported segregation and made a point of publicly attacking King and the SCLC's ongoing protest in Albany, Georgia, he was a so-called racial moderate who also pledged to keep public schools open and to "never intentionally foment racial troubles."[92] The new unsettlement produced by abandonment of the county unit system in the governor's race opened the door for Sanders to lay out an alternative strategy of governing, one promising more for those in urban counties and all others ill-served by Talmadgist clientelism, including Blacks. Sanders did take his own turn with racially charged "Africa" talk, yet it was to promise an eradication of cronyism and a more evenhanded dispensation of state powers and resources. Likening Griffin's governorship to "that of an African king holding royal court," Sanders promised a government that would not just dispense favors to supporters buying citizens' "loyalty for one highway" but serve a wider array of citizens, for instance, through a "planned long-range program" for road building. So too with Griffin's meager and conciliatory effort against water polluters: Sanders promised to "see to it that sufficient funds are appropriated to the Georgia Water Quality Council to make it an effective unit to enforce pollution controls."[93]

Going on to boost state authority over water pollution and polluters, Sanders's governorship responded not simply to worsening pollution but to a swelling electorate, whose balance had also suddenly shifted cityward. Thereby, Sanders helped consolidate a new southeastern variant in the U.S. politics and practices of pollution fighting: more programmatic than clientelist, more active than reactive, and, in these important ways, more democratic. Newly empowered and armed with professional full-time staff, it advanced state recognition of the environmental citizenship of ordinary Georgians, by actively monitoring those waterways on which so many of them relied, as well as moving more aggressively against polluters. More science based, it became far more capable and willing to intervene on behalf of ordinary citizens. Ostensibly color blind as it appeared, however, Georgia's new regime of water-pollution control wound up working more effectively for Atlanta's white citizens, especially a home-owning middle class, than it did for many of the city's Blacks.

In the wake of Sanders's electoral victory, state and federal as well as the regional pressures joined with the revealed scale of Georgia's pollution problems to accelerate a rapid transformation in the state's water-pollution control. Even before Sanders's victory, the State Health Department had begun its own survey of pollution along Atlanta's portion of the Chattahoochee, which would culminate in its October 1963 citation of the city. That same fall, on the heels of a U.S. Study Commission's scathing criticism of the existing Water Quality Control Board, a U.S. Public Health Service engineer fingered Georgians' pollution of the Chattahoochee as "endanger[ing] the health and welfare of persons of Alabama."[94] That made the river "subject to abatement under the federal Water Pollution Control Act," triggering a comprehensive six-year study of water pollution in southeastern rivers that would look closely at the Chattahoochee along with the Flint and Apalachicola Rivers that shared its basin.[95] Early that next year Atlanta's regional planners at the ARMPC chimed in, releasing a study that declared the "*regional problem*" of water pollution "one of the more serious problems threatening the Atlanta area." Conditions along the Chattahoochee were worsening, and the South River was now "one grade above being an open sewer."[96] ARMPC planners aligned more with the metro region's developers and a downtown white political leadership by framing new sewer building as a primary solution to the region's pollution problem. But their message of alarm added to the public groundswell.[97]

With all these governmental and quasi-governmental agencies suddenly throwing their spotlights on the region's water-pollution problem, more citizen groups as well as many local officials began making their concerns known. At this moment in Georgia, water pollution remained, in important respects, an issue in search of a more grassroots movement. Nevertheless, attendance at meetings of the Georgia Water Quality Council grew, drawing some members of sportsmen's groups such as the Izaak Walton League as well as women from the League of Women Voters and occasionally from garden clubs. Throughout the early 1960s, however, those representing citizen groups such as these never made up more than 20 percent of the visitors to the council. When overall attendance spiked to sixty or more, they remained always vastly outnumbered by business and governmental officials, paid to be there in pursuit of their company's or agency's interest.[98]

Faced with these and other mounting pressures, the Sanders administration sought not just more money to fight water pollution but a new agency as well as a new law that would have "teeth."[99] The Georgia legislature then took up and passed a bill, going into effect in July 1964, that finally provided full-time staff as well as enforcement powers for a new oversight board. The new law combined investigation and enforcement into the same agency, a new Water Quality *Control* Board (emphasis added) and bolstered its power to do both. Still nominally in the Health Department, it gained authority not just to inspect but to fine or prosecute. And for the first time, the person then appointed to head up Georgia's oversight body for water quality had professional training in the field and a full-time obligation to the work. Sanford chose Ralph "Rock" Howard, a sanitary engineer who had earned degrees from Clemson and the Harvard School of Health, then spent two decades in the Public Works Department of Albany, Georgia, among the state's more rural counties. Starting from scratch, Howard quickly cobbled together an agency laboratory and a staff, starting with just two and burgeoning to ninety-four by the early 1970s. Howard also quickly set out to flex his outfit's newly acquired muscles, melding his own and early colleagues' scientific authority with imperatives enabled by the new law.[100]

Among Rock Howard's first moves as head of the new Georgia Water Quality Control Board was to officially recognize just how far the shadow of the city's urban stream syndrome now stretched. At his first press conference, he announced his agency's conclusion that pollution from Atlanta had made the Chattahoochee River "unfit for use 'for forty miles downstream.'" Then at a meeting of "all city and industrial users" of the river "between Buford Dam and West Point," held in February 1965, he announced that each polluter, the City of Atlanta among them, would be required to come up with "abatement plans," stating exactly how they proposed to reduce what they were dumping into the river.[101] No longer content to await public complaints or polluters' self-reporting, as his predecessors had done, Howard and his scientific staff also began to inventory just who was dumping what into the region's watercourses.

Through field trips and sampling over the next year and more, they wound up inspecting the operations of all the sizeable municipal and industrial polluters along the river near Atlanta, a task that city health officials themselves had never attempted.[102] They studied Peachtree and Nancy as well as Proctor Creeks, across northern Fulton and DeKalb; the South River across these counties' southerly reaches; and Sweetwater, Sope, and Nickajack Creeks, running through Cobb and other westerly corners of the metropolis.[103] "Due to the urgencies" of these problems, the board's technical staff began "cooperating" with the U.S. Public Health Service's survey of the Chattahoochee basin and joined with federal officials at a July 1966 conference to summarize what they had found. Along Georgia portions and feeder streams of the Chattahoochee, around Atlanta and beyond, the Georgia board fingered twenty-two communities and forty-five industries as polluters, far more than the "out-of-date and insufficient" federal study, they proudly noted. And they laid down an ultimatum for the accused. All had to devise viable plans to ameliorate their impacts on Atlanta-area streams and rivers within the year and, by 1971, accomplish what they had planned.[104] That manifold waterborne burden of wastes building across metropolitan Atlanta in the decades after World War II finally began to be reckoned with, not by the city or county or any regional body, nor even by a federal agency, but by the state of Georgia.

What made this new antipollution regime so much more democratic than its Talmadgist predecessor was, first of all, its newfound willingness to make demands on industrial polluters. The greatest benefits here accrued to home-owning neighborhoods that were part of a white middle class swelling under compression capitalism. Especially those living alongside streams that teemed with untreated wastes of corporate polluters, as in Cobb County's Smyrna, had obtained a powerful official ally and thereby a new environmental facet of citizenship. In 1967 a Smyrna resident wrote the governor to get relief from the "alarming" pollution of Nickajack Creek, foisting "smelling, flooding waters" onto every property along his street when it rained. Rock Howard, it turned out, was already on the case. Even as county officials continued to sit on their hands, in 1966 the state's chief pollution fighter cited as the Nickajack's "main sources of pollution" not just the town of Smyrna and Cobb County but Lockheed. He set a 1971 deadline for them to fix the problem. And he personally penned a letter to this aggrieved Smyrnian, averring that though "we all wish the abatement could be affected immediately," at least "relief was in sight."[105]

As complaints kept pouring in from Cobb County residents about the wastes being disposed by Lockheed, Howard and his staff discovered more about what this company along with the Dobbins Air Force were dumping into both the Nickajack and Rottenwood Creeks. The sheer volume was enormous, some 3.6 million gallons *a day*. Still more troubling was that while remaining "'virtually' untreated," the wastes contained highly toxic substances such as "chrome"—presumably chromium. Howard noted some "chrome spills" by the company had been even more concentrated, which "could have been poisonous to people if the water had not been high and the spills small."[106] Despite the now-recognized danger, Lockheed kept dragging its heels on any cleanup plan, insisting on many rounds of study and approval before it could even say when it might have new treatment facilities in place. By late 1969 Howard bemoaned how "we have not obtained meaningful response from Lockheed-Georgia and the U.S. Air Force, and it is our opinion that they . . . will not be able to complete their treatment facilities on time."[107]

In retrospect, wastes and spills such as those Rock Howard and staff documented from Lockheed and Dobbins look a lot more alarming and dire than Howard's contemporary reassurances suggested. He and his colleagues still hewed to an older understanding of industrial dangers, not so in tune with where national and international communities of environmental health scientists were now headed. This very chemical Howard's agency had fingered, chromium, had already been recognized as causing cancer.[108] Over the 1960s into the 1970s, a scientific understanding was consolidating and turning consensual that this and other environmental toxics could, even at miniscule but sustained exposures, induce malignancies as well as a host of other mortal or injurious ailments. Studies of radiation, asbestos, and other substances had already begun establishing these more subtle and pervasive threats in the minds of many health scientists, sowing the seeds for much stricter environmental controls on these more "hazardous" wastes, starting in the 1970s. But in Georgia, where environmental monitoring of industrial chemicals was very new, where inspectors worked off "minimal chemical data," and where corporations had long been coddled by state officials who also faced little countervailing pressure from unions, this new and more alarming understanding of industrial pollutants came more slowly than in other long-industrialized parts of the country.[109] Even the best-trained environmental officials who did start to challenge the state's most powerful companies, such as Howard, took time to grasp its implications for their work.

Howard's reluctance may well have been reinforced by the arrival of a new denizen of the governor's mansion starting in 1966, Lester Maddox. Having skipped college and gone into business as a restauranteur in Atlanta's white working-class northwest, Maddox had made his name politically over the 1950s and 1960s by railing in published newspaper ads against segregation as well as communism, all the while declaiming the virtues of being American, Christian, and white.[110] His gubernatorial victory, uniting working-class whites of Atlanta's city and suburbs with the Talmadges' old rural constituency, showed how an explicitly "white" politics could still draw a plurality in Georgia, even without the county unit system and in the face of a burgeoning Black electorate in and around Atlanta itself. Once in office, like George Wallace and other southern segregationist leaders of the period, Maddox took up the mantle of pollution fighting. The quest to purify Georgia's waters, if properly directed and limited, turned out to harmonize well with his white supremacist notions of progress. At the dedication for a new water-treatment plant in a tiny northwest Georgia town, for instance, he declared how "the Maddox Administration . . . is determined to make water pollution control a top-notch member of Georgia's progressive family." But for Maddox, water-pollution control had little to do with curbing industry; on the contrary, it meant building municipal sewage plants that would "draw . . . new industry to the State." Like the Talmadgist governors before him, he proved far more willing to challenge racial integration than either industrial or municipal polluters. Instead, he sought to revive an approach to polluters in which "cooperation is the key" and for which the overriding goal was not water-pollution control so much as industrial development.[111]

While the new agency, law, and agenda created under Sanders nevertheless endured, Rock Howard faced rising pressures from Washington, D.C., that would carve out some common ground with the state's new chief executive. Foremost among these, he had begun to chafe at the evolving federal effort at pollution control, which seemed to him "to place too much emphasis on enforcement" and to "extend the Federal Administration too much authority to inspect private property."[112] Howard's disgruntlement peaked with a new rule proposed in 1968 by President Lyndon B. Johnson's Water Pollution Control Administration (an Environmental Protection Agency predecessor). It sought a baseline level of pollution for regulators to enforce by forbidding any "significant deterioration" of the nation's waters. The "no significant deterioration" rule was not just unnecessary, Howard felt; it posed a "severe and urgent" threat to a state such as Georgia. The rule could impede his own and other less industrialized and poorer states, where rivers were as yet not so clogged with factory wastes, from catching up economically with the more industrialized parts of the nation. Moreover, "if taken to its fullest extent," he averred, preaching to a gubernatorial choir—it "would place control of the development (especially industrial) of Georgia's interstate waters in the hands of the federal government."[113] Thereby and also through its lagging recognition of the special dangers posed by industrial chemicals, Georgia's oversight agency for water pollution retained a soft spot for private industry over the late 1960s, even as it imposed new environmental obligations on many of the state's corporate citizens.

While the scientific measurements and summaries of its surveys did introduce significant evenhandedness to the work of Howard's agency, it still tended to function better for Atlanta's whites than for the city's Blacks. That was especially true for one of the most recalcitrant of the city's pollution problems, urban runoff. Though it could document the polluted conditions of any streams, at this time the GWCB could move only against the outfalls of factories or sewage-treatment plants, or "point" sources. It was ill-equipped to tackle overflows in Atlanta's combined sewer overflow (CSO) system as well as the "non-point" contributors to stream wastes, such as runoff from streets, yards, houses, factories, service stations, railyards, and other urban or suburban surfaces that fed the urban stream syndrome suffered by smaller streams. Among those watercourses most affected by CSOs and runoff were Peachtree Creek, threading through white neighborhoods across North Atlanta, and streams that ran through the growing Black suburbs of the city's West Side, most notably Proctor Creek. Even as the pollution of Proctor Creek proved the worst, the GWCB showed greater solicitude for the afflictions of Peachtree Creek, running through a white and more affluent part of town.

Along Peachtree and its tributaries, mostly white sections from Gwinnett through DeKalb and Fulton Counties to drain Atlanta's northern flank, the pollution provided shockingly pervasive. Not a single one of thirty-six measuring stations registered as unpolluted or even just lightly polluted. The contaminants ranged from bacterial "organic" loads to industrial effluents, washing in from General Motors and other plants around Doraville or from railside factories and landfills of the city's northwest. One-third of Peachtree basin sites they found "grossly polluted," but even here some were worse than others. Most of these had at least some larger forms of life, those few pollution-tolerant "macroinvertebrates," often air rather than water breathing, that "almost always" thrived in oxygen-starved sewage-choked streams—"pulmonate [air-breathing] snails," for instance, and certain worms. Yet in three sites draining industrial pockets, even these sewage-loving invertebrates were nowhere to be found. Woodhall Creek, running up from industries clustered around the northwest railyards, had a "green-white color" to its water, which carried "floating oil and abundant foam" and gave off "a strong odor of volatile hydrocarbons"—hinting at the "lethal chemicals" biologists "believed responsible," though they still had no tools or directive to assess these. The only living residents of these waters visible were algae, both blue-green and *Sphaerotilus*, wavy spaghetti-like colonies also found in sewage-treatment plants, which grew "abundantly" alongside the burgeoning anaerobic microbes they would have needed microscopes to see. To get the word out about these findings, Howard's Water Quality Control Board published a stand-alone report, complete with a colorful cover, on Peachtree Creek and its tributaries.[114]

Even before investigating and reporting on Peachtree Creek, Howard's agency had completed a much shorter study of Proctor Creek, which coursed through those very slices of west and northwest Atlanta that had opened to Black residents in the post–World War II era.[115] Though Proctor's main channel was actually longer than that of Peachtree Creek (9.0 versus 7.5 miles), fewer monitoring stations were set up, five compared to seven. The study's findings bore out the locals' oft-repeated contentions about the creek.[116] While testing "CLEAN" near its headwaters near Vine City and Atlanta University, three of its four additional stations downstream proved "grossly polluted"—a greater proportion than for any of Peachtree's. Gurgling past the railyards and associated industries in the city's northwest, the stream quickly turned "devoid of macroscopic life" and stayed that way throughout much of its course."[117] At its worst, along Hollywood Road not far from publicly owned Perry Homes, the six-foot-deep flow had turned "an opaque milk white" with "large amounts of garbage and refuse" littering the streambed. The "filthy" water came from the combined-sewer system after heavy rains but also from runoff, worsened by broken utility-hole covers and sewer mains. Among the microscopic, living contaminants might have been *Salmonella typhi*, the tiny progenitor of typhoid, which had not troubled Atlanta's whites since the 1930s. With its sky-high fecal coliform counts, the "gross"-ness of Proctor Creek at Hollywood Road was more than twenty times higher than any found along Peachtree or in the Chattahoochee itself, a stark contrast visible in figure 3.1. No riverine microbiome around Atlanta came closer to that inside the human gut than did this one.

Not just the state agency's findings from Proctor Creek but the way it used them pointed to the lesser measure of environmental citizenship that the new regime of water-pollution control ordained for Atlanta's Blacks. Unlike its Peachtree and Chattahoochee reports, prepared for broad public distribution, Howard's GWQCB handled the Proctor Creek findings privately and "cooperatively," turning a typescript of the report over to city officials as well as an Emory legal-aid clinic. Some of this circumspection may have been due to legal concerns. At least two children from Perry Homes had come down with

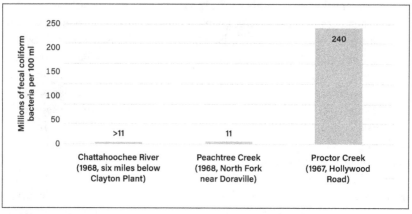

FIGURE 3.1. The all-too-human microbiome of Proctor Creek. Differences in maximum *E. coli* and other fecal coliform levels in Proctor Creek, running through African American suburbs, versus Peachtree Creek and the Chattahoochee were measured by biologists for the Georgia Water Quality Control Board. *Sources*: Georgia Water Quality Control Board, *Water Quality Data, Atlanta Area: Chattahoochee, Flint, and South Rivers, 1968 and 1969 Data* (Atlanta: Georgia Water Quality Control Board, 1970); Georgia Water Quality Control Board, *Peachtree Creek Water Quality Survey* (Atlanta: Georgia Water Quality Control Board, 1969); Edward T. Hall and Max W. Walker, "A Water Quality Study of Proctor Creek," typescript, Georgia Water Quality Control Board, November 10, 1967, http://web.iac.gatech.edu/AHCscans/access/ahc_CAR_015_012_006-access .pdf.

typhoid fever, leading Emory Legal Services Center not only to request the study but to then sue the city for allowing this creek to become the suspected cause.[118] Mayor Allen did respond to the findings by a letter, but with what would become his usual public refrain when accused of heel dragging on environmental cleanup. "Major actions" were now "planned," starting with a "major temporary treatment plant in the vicinity of Hollywood Road" and repair of a broken outfall. But his own water-pollution engineer privately fretted that some of the "problems will be around a long time in the future."[119]

The city engineer was right. Ostensibly color blind, Howard's agency did offer significant boons for Black Atlanta compared to the blatant racism and cronyism of Talmadgism, starting with their demonstration of just how contaminated the Black sides of town had become. But the scientifico-legal arrows in GWCB's quiver could do little against the more diffuse and pervasive pollution of a stream such as Proctor Creek. The environmental vulnerability of those living along its banks had accumulated gradually, as one era of land and infrastructure development after another layered more and more polluting facilities nearby and as zoning and housing construction drew in Black Atlantans often excluded or forced out of other parts of town. Here, as elsewhere inhabited by those with the least economic power—the majority of Atlanta's Blacks—the new state powers against water polluters brought an all-too-marginal corrective to polluted living environments, hence, to *their* residents' rights as environmental citizens. While the city did fix a few of Proctor's travails, more serious repairs would begin only in the 1990s, when protests over these environmental injustices help push a federal EPA to sue the city of Atlanta over its "antiquated" combined sewer system.[120]

Two years later Howard's hand would be strengthened by events in Washington, D.C., most notably the creation of a new federal Environmental Protection Agency. William Ruckelshaus, its first administrator, visited Atlanta for his first address as EPA head, on the eve of the deadline Howard had set for the City of Atlanta to fix that overwhelming riverine burden it imposed on those living downstream. Ruckelshaus singled out Atlanta along with two other cities for the EPA's first official reprimand, as those where "we felt the situation to be most serious." The other two, Detroit and Cleveland, offered classic crystallizations of national worries about industrial contaminants—both lay on the shores of Lake Erie, a body of water that all Americans had come to know as dying, whose tributary Cuyahoga River had famously caught fire. But he fingered Atlanta waters for an older, microbial sort of contaminant, akin to that plaguing rivers of the developing world, then as now. In its extremity but also in its makeup, the Chattahoochee's pollution revealed a long persisting shadow of regional underdevelopment: thirty-two million gallons of untreated sewage from the city steadily pouring in to make the river itself "virtually . . . an open sewer."[121]

Ironically, that same year was when Rock Howard himself first came to recognize how serious toxic pollution—Owens's "microphysicochemical" dangers—had already become in his state. The detection of mercury at alarming levels in the Savannah River and Brunswick estuary seemed to Howard "completely unexpected, and practically unpredictable." It served as a wake-up call: at low levels now shown to be toxic, industrial chemicals such as this one might well be more pervasive than he and other Georgia health officials had long assumed.[122] Howard quickly prepared a proposal to Maddox for "a crash program to determine the exact extent of mercury pollution throughout the more than 4200 miles of Georgia's major river basins" and coastal waters—his agency's first statewide testing for a specifically *industrial* chemical.[123] Maddox, however, seemed to be souring on an agency head who had also taken to publicly tweaking Lockheed—then the state's largest employer—as a "big sacred cow," a quote eagerly seized on by reporters.[124] At first giving Howard what he'd asked for, Maddox then cut the budget of the GWCB by even more, as Howard also had to fight off a legislative initiative to "eviscerate" his agency.[125] Facing headwinds in his work from Georgia's political leadership, that same year Howard overcame his initial suspicions to aid a group of Nader's Raiders traveling in from Washington, D.C., headed by a Harvard undergraduate named James Fallows. Their work, published as *The Water Lords*

(1971), shone a national spotlight on the environmental burdens that industry had foisted on the Savannah River and Georgia coast under Talmadgism, which Howard's agency now struggled to contain.[126]

As for Georgia's own movement on behalf of "the environment," just then coalescing across Atlanta, it harbored a certain ambivalence toward Howard's agency and its work. From the mid-1960s, as this metropolitan region's own environmental citizenship project gained grassroots, it lent some support to pollution fighting. But the new activists also took umbrage at the ecological impacts of a Howard-supported solution: the proliferation of sewer lines along Atlanta's riverbanks. Unlike in many other parts of the county, those involved worried less about pollution itself than about threats to natural landscapes they had come to know.

CHAPTER 4

Making Citizenship
Environmental

One day in March 1970, Roger Buerki parked his car along the highway north-west of Atlanta's downtown and, with his two daughters, slipped down to the banks of a tributary of the Chattahoochee, near where it etches a boundary between Fulton and Cobb Counties. Still new to town, the thirty-year-old Buerki had been working as an engineer at the Lockheed plant in Marietta but had then been let go and so had time on his hands. With his two young daughters, he had set out to explore "for garnets" along sedimentary river-banks near his neighborhood on the edge of town.[1]

On the way they had driven past the latest extensions of the city's tenta-cles into Cobb: a four-lane Interstate 75, now three years old, running out from downtown and meeting up with the perimeter Interstate 285, just opened the previous October. Nearby, the digging had commenced for an apartment complex dubbed Cumberland, soon to be joined by a seventy-two-acre re-gional mall of the same name.[2] Not far away Buerki and his daughters de-scended the treed slopes of Rottenwood Creek "to scramble around on these gorgeous rocks and that little gorge." There he caught a glimpse of a "zon-ing sign" carefully tucked away "back on the dirt road up in the woods," as if hardly "intended to be seen." A rezoning was underway, it announced, so that apartments could be built there. Over the next few weeks, he and a few com-patriots rambled along the northerly Chattahoochee itself, discovering river-side cliffs soon to be dubbed "the Palisades." These were set to be blasted away for a sewer line. Buerki's alarm grew—and with it a sense of mission.[3]

Within the month Buerki had joined a three-year-old Georgia Conservancy and was visiting local campuses and bookstores to promote Atlanta's version of that watershed moment in U.S. environmental history and politics, the first Earth Day. On April 22, 1970, Atlantans, too, celebrated and opined, especially with "teach-ins" on the city's campuses, from Georgia State to Emory to At-lanta University, as well as in an "anti-pollution rally" in Hurt Park. Peachtree Creek, "full of SHIT," according to the city's leading alternative newspaper the *Great Speckled Bird*, emerged as a sudden cause célèbre among Atlanta's fledg-ling white student activists and counterculture, earning a mock "funeral" service.[4] Though the day made front-page headlines in Atlanta's white press, racial and political divides grated against that feel-good sharing of concerns simultaneously unfolding across U.S. cities and suburbs of the North and West. From his governor's mansion Lester Maddox offered among the nation's most hostile responses, affirming his lieutenant governor's insinuation that Earth Day "smacked of a communist plot," since it coincided with Vladimir Lenin's birthday.[5] White media mostly left it to the city's Black newspapers to highlight Proctor Creek's woes, despite how "many Black Atlantans consider[ed]" it "the most important Black pollution issue." With white event organizers and press coverage neglecting the city's Black environments, Atlanta's Black press returned the favor. The *Atlanta Inquirer* devised a different way of portraying "Earth Day": as a "good day to end" a strike by the city's largely African American garbage workers. It mixed in some hostility as well, publishing an op-ed by National Urban League president and former Atlantan Whitney Young that was critical of the protest's neglect of "racism and poverty."[6]

For the many Atlantans who did embrace the first Earth Day, the event nevertheless confirmed the arrival of an *environmental* citizenship that in this metropolis seemed like a new kind of political project. In the U.S. South, as in most other places, disgruntlement about environmental conditions had hardly been absent prior to the mid-1960s, as shown in earlier chapters of this book as well as by most historians who have gone looking.[7] Yet around this city at this historical moment, issues coming to be pegged as "environmental," from water pollution to nature parks, had earlier roused only scattered, episodic, and not-so-effectual public concern. Exemplifying that "weakness of environmental interest" that historian Samuel Hays found across the postwar Southeast, up until 1966 no organized movement existed in or around Atlanta to yoke these issues together as "environmental" or to steadily press their claims on existing governments. The contrast with the gathering social thickness of the push for civil rights could not have been more stark.[8] By the time Buerki turned local activist, however, helping spearhead a long-running, ultimately successful effort to preserve the Chattahoochee north of the Clayton wastewater plant, a much more collective, self-identified, and durable environmental movement had coalesced. In under half a decade, Atlantans had led the formation of lasting environmental groups, from the Georgia Conservancy to a Sierra Club chapter, and had built a growing, increasingly effective opposition to freeway building. Through these three prongs—environmental group formation, freeway fighting, and river "saving"—a modern project of environmental citizenship had rather suddenly erupted around Atlanta. Framing "the environment" as a subject of civic duty, it channeled citizenly engagement into political pressure on behalf of Atlanta's and Georgia's remaining share of the natural world. The arrival of organized environmentalism in and around this city constitutes a vital yet neglected chapter in this state's path away from racial authoritarianism and toward more democratic rule.

This political project played an important role in the next stage of this city's and state's democratizing by stoking and guiding citizenly aspirations within Atlanta's white middle class, now both expanded and (mostly) home owning.[9] Even in this most conservative of regions, post–World War II suburban white activism was not as invariably conservative or antigovernmental as is often retrospectively assumed. In addition to defending public schools from segregationists' efforts to privatize them, Atlanta's white middle-class activists also forged collective action on "the environment's" or "nature's" behalf. Their gathering project of environmental citizenship opened new grounds for civic participation in and around Atlanta and pushed their governments beyond the constricted scope and personalized favoritism of racial authoritarianism. Capitalizing on Georgia's own natural features and building off the preexisting environmental consumption and neighborhood defenses of upper-middle-class suburbs, an Atlanta-centered environmental movement also set about appropriating rhetoric and strategies from well-established groups and movements outside the South. It thereby played an important and as yet underappreciated role in dragging Georgia's political culture closer to the national mainstream. Without the precedent of civil rights activism, whose mass mobilizations and protests successfully drew in round after round of federal interventions, it is difficult to imagine how Atlanta's environmental movement could have been hatched so quickly or to such effect. But while the civil rights movement's importance to this city's and state's democratization is far better known, its environmental movement reinforced these contributions in important ways, by opening new democratizing avenues of its own. As rapidly as it emerged, this more grassroots environmentalism that erupted in and around Atlanta became a second vital pillar for Georgia's ongoing democratization.

If many leaders of Atlanta's early environmental movement also sought to import strategies and agendas from elsewhere, the circumstances they faced in the Atlanta area by around 1970 nevertheless differed from those in the Northeast or urban West in three ways. First, though industrial pollution was elsewhere the single-most important issue around which groups assembled a new "environmental" agenda, in and around Atlanta it remained far less central to mobilizing efforts. A more popular antipollution politics did well up starting in the late sixties, as local Georgia Conservancy chapters began to decry the contamination in some of Atlanta's rivers. Yet the contaminants in question were, as we have seen, mostly considered an older, better-understood pollution, from human wastes whose control seemed on the way, and Atlanta's air pollution at this time was declared relatively mild compared to other more industrialized metropolises. Appreciation and concern lagged around Atlanta for those toxic chemicals, now considered the most troubling pollutants in more industrial parts of the United States. Consistently, opinion polls found the least concern about the chemical industry and pollution broadly writ in the U.S. Southeast.[10] Second, Georgia as yet had little of the conservationist state that governors and legislators in other regions of the country had already built over the middle decades of the century. Outside the creation of a state park at Stone Mountain, so little land had been acquired even for a more recreational style of park that by the midsixties, this metropolitan area's state parks remained a pale shadow of those around Cleveland and Minneapolis, much less those of Long Island or Los Angeles. Third, activists who began to advocate a more ecological style of park around the city were stepping into a civic void. While the Atlanta area had certainly had its hunters, sportsmen, bird-watchers, and especially garden clubs, none had ever sought to assert a steady and systematic influence on political realms. But from the midsixties onward, changes in the composition and character of Georgia's government helped open new opportunities for nature-oriented advocacy. As Georgia's new environmentalism intertwined with a city-centered neighborhood movement to spearhead a next phase of democratizing, however, both remained almost exclusively white.

Half a century later, when asked about the whiteness of Atlanta's early environmental movement, participants recalled the utter separation felt between their cause and those of Atlanta's Blacks and sometimes a lingering puzzlement as to why. Most recall supporting the cause of civil rights, but into the 1970s white environmentalists' recruitment of Blacks remained fitful at best and almost entirely unsuccessful. Whether or not white environmental groups may have been personally unwelcoming to Blacks, the larger foundations for their racial uniformity were structural, often baked into the urban landscape itself layer by layer, from Jim Crow times through the era of more compressive capitalism. If Buerki himself was still a renter, most of those turning activist owned homes in white neighborhoods, had gone to white colleges, and held salaried jobs in white-dominated workplaces. Never having confronted the racial barriers faced by Atlanta's Blacks, many of which were now falling, Buerki's and other early environmentalists' whiteness had quietly secured them ample rights and other benefits that most of Atlanta's Blacks still struggled to obtain. In T. H. Marshall's terms, they were privileged enough to take for granted many "social" and "civil" elements of citizenship. But neither of these elements as described by Marshall in 1950 sounded much like the whole new agendas and distinctive political identities of this early style of environmentalism.[11] Devoted to protecting more visibly natural environments, from northerly stretches of the Chattahoochee to mountains spared from Confederate carvings to suburban parks and neighborhoods near downtown, their desires and actions fleshed out an "environmental" citizenship that Marshall had left uncontemplated.

Like other variants of citizenship, this one involved, as sociologist Bronislaw Szerszynski more recently put it, a "moment of self-absenting," of seeing one's own location "as if from afar or outside."[12] For the new environmental citizens, an aversion of eyes from their city's racial and economic inequalities and their more privileged niches within these helped highlight what their overall society had cast into the shadows, an imperiled natural world. In its genesis around Atlanta, the making of environmental citizenship often leaned on those sciences, sports, and select homescapes that served to single out these perils over most others. Not coincidentally, however, they mainly wound up defending places where more affluent white Atlantans increasingly aspired to play as well as live.

To appreciate just how white this new "environmental" label and political project looked to Black civil rights advocates circa 1970, it helps to consider just where the project of civil rights citizenship was now headed. As we've seen, concerns about where Blacks lived and played had long figured into the civil rights agenda, from housing to parks, yet the impetus of activists, before as well as after the fall of legal segregation, was to enable Black access to spaces and opportunities whites had long enjoyed—inequalities that needed to be addressed on grounds of justice. The project of civil rights citizenship did steer in new directions over the mid-1960s with their own environmental dimensions: seeking to redress the plight and improve the living conditions of Blacks who were working class or poor. Yet legacies of segregationist city building meant that the environments whose improvements they sought harbored little that was visibly or appealingly "natural" about them. Too often these were poorly constructed or maintained and lay along streams and rivers overwhelmed by the city's discards and detritus. As the SCLC and SNCC gravitated toward the problem of poverty, they ventured more deeply into environments that looked ever less like those alluringly natural places this era's environmental movement sought to protect. That trajectory added to their own as well as to the new white environmentalists' sense that the two political projects had little to say to each other, even as by 1970 both propelled the ongoing democratization of city and state.

Civic Ferment and the Birth of the Georgia Conservancy

The first of those groups organized over the mid-1960s to bring a new "environmental" advocacy and politics to Atlanta and Georgia, and for many years the most influential, was the Georgia Conservancy. The earliest moments of its founding dovetailed with the brief congressional career of James Mackay, the DeKalb politician and lawyer who'd long battled against Talmadgism.[13] If Mackay laid networking and institutional groundwork for the conservancy during his turn as a congressperson, many other Atlantans had already become primed to join this group through their own experiences. The pathways toward conservancy involvement of Robert Hanie and Lucy Smethurst, who would join Mackay in the group's leadership, illuminate its roots in the postwar growth of Atlanta's white middle class and the nature-related opportunities afforded its members. Prior to receiving any invitation from Mackay's office, both had forged perspectives and interests that aligned well with the early conservancy's agenda and work.

Mackay's switch from the state to the national legislature came as one-man, one-vote judicial decisions ending the county unit system also compelled a thoroughgoing redistricting of Georgia's congressional districts. Atlanta's single district was split into two, one of which encompassed DeKalb County, which Mackay had been representing in the Georgia House, along with a small portion of Fulton.[14] With "the main points he had worked for . . . fulfilled," in 1964 Mackay drew upon his familiarity to most district voters to enter, then win, the race to represent this new Fourth Congressional District in Washington, D.C.[15] He headed to Congress with the expressed goal of tilting Georgia's delegation "from a point of view oriented to rural and extremely conservative points to the urban and more middle-of-the-road point of view."[16]

In early 1965 Mackay arrived in a Washington, D.C., reconfigured by Lyndon B. Johnson's electoral landslide. Democratic majorities now solidified in both houses of Congress stood ready to make the most of this "liberal hour." A deluge of legislation agenda followed as Johnson sought to make good on his campaign promise of a "Great Society," starting with long-blocked initiatives that, without effective Republican opposition, easily passed. The War on Poverty began, as did federally backed health care through Medicare and Medicaid, and a Civil Rights Act of 1965 secured voting rights. New laws also inaugurated a growing role for the federal government in what was just coming to be understood as "the environment": acts for highway beautification, water and air quality, and solid waste disposal, later strengthened by still more sweeping legislation.[17] Mackay mostly embraced this flood of Democratic initiatives, speaking out for the antipoverty programs and for voting rights and establishing a reputation as a "liberal" and "staunch support of the Great Society." He also carved out a signature government-building issue of his own, traffic safety, by authoring and successfully promoting a law to establish a National Traffic Safety Board. While Mackay himself publicly mused about having "grown" during his stint in Washington, from his first days as a representative he worried about bringing his constituency along with him.[18]

As Mackay had long averred, white and Black Atlantans had adapted to their disenfranchisement under Talmadgism by treating politics as unimportant, as "separate and apart from everything else" in their lives. For Mackay as a congressperson, this encrusted "apathy" was crippling not just to local and regional democracy but to his own political survival. It stood in the way of, among other things, communicating his accomplishments to voters, while easing the distortion of his record by political foes. So from May 1965 he set about creating new doors by which ordinary citizens could learn about and have more input on the direction of his own work as a congressperson. Starting from the top down, he set his office staff to organizing "citizens' panels for progress," through network building that sowed seeds out of which the Georgia Conservancy would soon spring.[19]

Each panel convened together "a group of citizens who are positively interested in a specific area of local and national concern and who want to study, discuss, inform others and act." Echoing the expert task forces set up by President Johnson to design Great Society legislation, Mackay also sought to imbue this effort with a language of "grassroots" implicitly oriented to a college-educated middle or upper-middle class: "well-informed, interested citizens" attending the panels would then "form a closer working partnership with me." He and his staff preselected some twenty-nine "important areas," then assigned chairpeople for each to get the ball rolling.[20] On themes Mackay and his staff knew to be racially divisive, they hewed to a scrupulous color blindness—"Poverty, Welfare, and the Population Explosion" and "Crime Prevention, Youth Programs and Law Enforcement." Bypassing his district's Black civil rights leaders, Mackay installed well-to-do whites at the helm of all these panels, though a third of the panels had female chairs.[21] The initial array of panels was surprising light on what would become known as environmental issues. But, following Johnson administration initiatives, panels started to hold meetings on "air and water pollution" (as the 1965 Water Quality Act was making its way to October passage by Congress) and added "conservation" and "natural beauty" to their names (in the wake of a White House Conference on Natural Beauty in May 1965).[22] A "grassroots Congress" that December brought together 350 people who had worked on the panels, presided over by Mackay himself.

While Mackay had originally envisioned another Grass Roots Congress the next year, by fall of 1966 he faced a surprisingly tough reelection battle, and so he settled on a more limited civic initiative, in "conservation." Mackay himself had long harbored an interest in park making as well as private-land preservation, as we have seen. Panel discussions had also clarified just how underinvested Talmadgism had left his county and state in public land and recreation and how many new federal programs had become available to fund these. Panel participants also brought up successful private preservation models not yet tried in Georgia, most notably the pioneering example of a Western Pennsylvania Conservancy, now decades old. That September Mackay announced his intent to assemble a "private statewide policy group to coordinate all conservation activities in Georgia."[23] His staff then began reaching out to potentially interested civic groups around his district, inviting them to a January 1967 meeting at the Fernbank Science Center in Druid Hills. Some of those invited to the inaugural discussion about this "private statewide policy group" had served on Mackay's Panels for Progress; others were involved in nature-oriented civic groups that Mackay's office invited to attend. But longer personal trajectories of key attendees illuminated those advantages of affluence and education that had already set them apart from most other Atlantans, enabling outside perspectives on Georgia's countryside that had stoked their crystallizing commitments to preserve it.

The young man who had first brought up the model of the Western Pennsylvania Conservancy at a Panel for Progress, Robert Hanie, would become a chief spokesperson for the conservancy in its earliest years. He arrived at the Fernbank meeting on the heels of a personal and religious journey that had steered his interests nature-ward, albeit via avenues someone without his racial and economic privileges could hardly have contemplated. Born in rural Habersham County, Hanie's father was a civil engineer, his mother a teacher. His family's trajectory epitomized the postwar growth of Atlanta's white patrimonial middle class: they moved to DeKalb, and Robert himself grew up in a solidly middle-class home in one of city's most affluent and racially insulated suburbs. His formal education, as well, took advantage of expanding opportunities there: graduating from nearby Emory in 1959, he went on to earn a master's degree in American studies at the University of Richmond. Growing up amid social and economic security, with degrees in hand that assured his own future, he then launched on a years-long hegira to some of the world's remotest corners that would enable him to see his Georgia homeland afresh, as from afar. First traveling up the West Coast to Alaska, he then spent two years teaching for the Peace Corps in Kenya, in East Africa. There he lived in a setting that would "hone his sensibilities to a fine edge": "on the slopes of Mount Kilimanjaro," where "a herd of six thousand zebra had roamed his lawn" alongside other "teeming wildlife," and the flora was "luxuriant . . . jacaranda and flame trees and fields of African violets." The formative influence of these encounters on his later activism points to a vital step toward an environmental conscience as toward other types of social responsibility, seeing his own place from some outside angle. Hanie's written memories of his hegira— which had little to say about this land's human inhabitants, including the Kenyan children with whom he worked—nourished an incipient, sweeping insight that would drive his later environmental activism. "Man needs a dialogue with nature, that in this silent communication man becomes whole."[24]

Returning to Decatur in 1963, while recovering from severe malaria and hepatitis, he found his perspective on his native home had severely darkened, verging on the apocalyptic. It was, he later recalled, "like coming 'straight to hell'": "hideous cities" and "streams . . . burning with pollutants or glutted with human feces or red with the blood of packing houses," "like the bleeding corpus of a sick nation." He took a job teaching history at Druid Hills High School—where the class he taught to Mackay's son would bring his first acquaintance with the congressperson. He also worked as a part-time engineer with the federal water-pollution-control agency, traveling around to assess the contamination in many Georgia streams and coming face-to-face with their current sorry state. "The focal point for his outrage" became Sweetwater Creek, a Chattahoochee tributary flowing through Cobb and Douglas Counties, where he had played as a child. As one reporter later put it after interviewing him, "Sweetwater was to young Hanie what Walden Pond was to Henry David Thoreau—the secret home of his spirit and a microcosm of the world." Formerly trout filled, its waters had run "clear and sweet," surrounded by "moss-furred" "ruins of a mill village" and a "matted forest [that] teemed with deer, squirrel, coons and opossum." He now found it "fetid with pollution," its woods "empty of wildlife," and its ruins "littered with beer cans."[25] "Hideous" as these conditions seemed, as the hopeful scion of an expansively patrimonial middle class, the thirty-one-year-old Hanie was not one to merely throw up his hands. Drawing on his extensive education, worldly knowledge, and a Baptist faith, he believed that not only were this and other environmental desecrations still salvageable but that he himself could and should become a force for the needed change. Jumping at the chance to join Mackay's water-resources Panel for Progress, he then provided a pivotal spark for Mackay's own interest in convening a new "policy group."[26]

Other early stalwarts in the conservancy were newcomers to Atlanta, bringing interests and engagements that were also the fruits, in important part, of familial affluence and privilege. Lucy Cabot Smethurst, for instance, a president of the group by the 1970s, had been born into Boston's foremost Brahmin family, a long line of Harvard graduates renowned for their inherited standing and civic prominence, many of whom were also "avid gardeners." She grew up in a well-to-do Boston suburb, graduated from Wheaton, and for one year attended Harvard Business School but found the entitled New England circles that were her birthright "awfully stuffy." She proceeded to marry a North Carolinian, Wood Smethurst, and moved with him to Atlanta in the early 1960s, "spread[ing] my wings." After time in an apartment, she and her new husband bought a six-acre spread in the northerly, unincorporated part of Fulton County, about a mile beyond the Atlanta city limits. Having been "born loving plants," she "didn't care about the house; I just cared about the potential of the land." What appealed to her was the level lot grown over with pine and a few azaleas, with so much undeveloped land around. Beginning to cultivate her own property as she worked for Rich's, a downtown department store, she also got involved in the local garden club until she found "it had nothing to do with gardening," just with "ladies getting together to coo at each other." She then discovered the Georgia Botanical Society, much more to her liking.

As Mackay was serving his first year in Congress, former Bostonian Smethurst, through the vehicle of the Botanical Society, underwent her own version of seeing Georgia's nature from the outside, even while getting closer to it. Field trips with her fellow Botanical Society members took her "all over Georgia." Falling in love with the state's "rural aspect," its beauty and "diversity of ecology," she felt like she had "really come home." Botanical Society field trips cultivated this love in ways that, despite her deprecatory disavowals as she recalled, meshed well with Smethurst's class background: "snuffing little flowers and throwing out Latin terms." Looking at the Georgia countryside through the lens of science, she gained an additional set of frames for viewing as if from the outside, gleaning a "huge amount" about the native flora of Georgia from "very knowledgeable people." They "didn't care how ignorant you were"—at least if you wanted to learn.[27] But these very ways of traveling and observing magnified differences between how these city-based travelers saw and valued rural Georgia and how the scientifically incurious residents who were its main denizens did. If any kind of citizenship required a sense of allegiance to a vantage point outside one's self, Smethurst's and many others' passage toward environmental citizenship came through an understanding of rural Georgia informed by ecology and other natural sciences. Gathered and honed through national and international communities of natural scientists, scientifically authenticated knowledge about Georgia's ecology, in spreading to Atlantans such as Smethurst, nourished not just new perspectives but more appreciation of its beauty and social value, which rural residents might take for granted or simply not share.

Not coincidentally, governmental projects that had gained little traction under rustic rule were now germinating in Georgia, among them, the idea of "nature preserves." An early 1960s inquiry by the state legislature had called for them, as had the city's metropolitan planning commission.[28] An entire 1964 volume of its regional plan argued the case for them, starting with their definition: "a tract of land (and water) in which a natural plant and animal environment can be sustained, even when regularly visited by large numbers of people." Showing how cities from Chicago to Cleveland to Baltimore were turning to this ecologically authentic style of park, the planners listed Sweetwater Creek among the top prospects for such a site in Greater Atlanta.[29] Unlike other planner suggestions for sewer lines or urban renewal, these fell on deaf ears among the city's and regional power elites. Not until prodded by more citizen-based and collective pressure would they take any action.[30]

By August 1965 Hanie sallied out from Citizens Panel service to make his own foray into political activism on behalf of Sweetwater. He persuaded three of Georgia's congresspeople, Mackay, Charles L. Weltner, and John W. Davis of Summerville, to jointly write the Department of the Interior about acquiring Sweetwater bottom lands as a federal nature preserve.[31] As the months went by without a response, Hanie began looking into another, private vehicle for preservation, the land conservancies. In and around some of the largest cities on the East Coast, where very little land lay in public reserves and local governments were interested only in "recreation" parks, groups had coalesced to raise private funds for buying up and protecting ecologically valued natural lands. The largest of these was the Nature Conservancy, the first of whose chapters had been founded in the Washington suburb of Arlington, Virginia, in 1951. As Hanie began contemplating a similar organization for north Georgia, he concentrated on the independent Western Pennsylvania Conservancy, out from Pittsburgh, as a useful precedent.[32] In May 1966 he wrote a letter to the *Atlanta Constitution* proposing the idea. Though it went unpublished, he continued to shop the letter text around, among other places at the "water resources and conservation" Panel for Progress.[33] Representative Mackay, in attendance and intrigued by Hanie's idea and enthusiasm, then resolved to marshal the many means and connections of an incumbent congressperson's office to make it happen.

At the time Mackay was in the throes of a difficult, ultimately losing campaign for reelection against his Republican opponent, a thirty-eight-year-old lawyer named Ben Blackburn. "A conservative who 'can run a moderate race,'" Blackburn successfully tied Mackay to the national leader of the Democratic Party, President Johnson, and to "boondoggle" poverty programs as well as new federal mandates for civil rights.[34] He harped especially on Johnson's push for the 1965 Voting Rights Act, for which Mackay had voted.[35] Mackay's signature legislative accomplishment, the traffic safety law, left him most vulnerable to Blackburn's second major charge, that the congressperson favored federal action against business interests like the auto industry, which Blackburn also pledged to defend.[36] Effectively capitalizing both on racial anxieties and local business leaders' disgruntlement, Blackburn squeaked out a win, contributing to the Georgia Republican Party's most successful wave election in generations.[37] A recount controversy had just concluded in late January 1967, when some sixty-five people showed up for Mackay's "roundtable of the Present State of Conservation Effort and Activities in Georgia" at Druid Hill's Fernbank. Smethurst, having received an invitation from Lynn Hill, president of the Georgia Botanical Society, accompanied Hill there to see what it was about. Others had gotten invites through their membership in the Georgia Ornithological Society, the Izaak Walton League, bird clubs, and a select few garden clubs.

If the leadership was initially male, the many women also in attendance would soon take up important roles in the group. The place of this first gathering resembled that of many others kicking off like initiatives in other regions of the nation: in Druid Hills, an Atlanta suburb, the purest regional example of what suburbs historian Dolores Hayden termed the "picturesque enclave."[38] Press and the group's own descriptions stressed the "very few big names" among them, how they were "just folks." But characterizations of them such as "a few housewives, a professor or two, some lawyers and businessmen" confirmed how thoroughly white collar they were, and early conservancy mailing address lists showed just how predominantly they hailed from Atlanta's most affluent and whitest suburbs.[39] Here, as in earlier efforts to create private nature preserves, starting with the Nature Conservancy in the early 1950s around Washington, D.C., and New York, the push leaned on the active support, if not always the leadership, of the economically well endowed, the best-off suburbanites.[40]

Mackay and Hanie both addressed the meeting, along with a featured guest, Charles Foster, from the Washington office of the Nature Conservancy. The early rhetoric of Georgia's own version of a conservancy was less secular in tone than that of counterparts in other U.S. regions; it had a distinctly religious ring. Though Georgia scientists like the Emory biologist Robert Platt and the eminent University of Georgia ecologist Eugene Odum were also deeply involved, they let others handle most speeches.[41] Hanie was an active Baptist and sometime preacher himself; in the late 1950s he'd cofounded a Honeydew Baptist Church during a months-long stay in California's "redwood country." For him the conservancy's cause was "not unlike a religious crusade . . . to preserve and restore what the Creator saw fit to put there," for people's "spiritual refreshment."[42] Hanie's harsh forebodings and Evangelical zeal, accented by longish hair and large eyes, burnished his reputation as a "radical" among the mostly staid crowd at this and later conservancy gatherings. Mackay, on the other hand, struck a listener like Lucy Smethurst as more measured and "reasonable." Tone notwithstanding, Mackay was the son of a preacher and an active Methodist, known for sometimes moving speeches in the Georgia House. At this first conservancy gathering, remembered Smethurst, when he "got up and started talking," the "bells began to ring." "Tomorrow is coming," he warned. "If we don't start preparing for it . . . don't start organizing and understanding the kind of resources that we have in Georgia," then "it will start disappearing"; "it'll be gone before we turn around."[43] Mackay's words resonated deeply with Smethurst; she never forgot them. She and her friend "just looked at each other and looked back at Jim as if we had heard the call." The "Come to Jesus meeting," she later called it, with some irony, since she also protested "it wasn't religious in any sense of the word," at least not for her. What she did feel was "the excitement of a group that wanted to do something. It set the tone for my life."[44]

Smethurst was not the only one to feel the flash of inspiration. By the very next meeting a month later, the group had christened itself a "Georgia Conservancy" and started work on bylaws.[45] Mulling over Foster's visit and speech at the January meeting, the conservancy's founders decided not to affiliate with the Nature Conservancy or any other national group. Instead, they would remain "autonomous," "functioning independently" to better address Georgia's own unique needs. Among these, aside from its Appalachian Trail club, the Atlanta area did not yet have any civic organization like the Sierra Club, devoted to hiking or other of what park experts deemed "passive" uses. So conservancy organizers planned each meeting around a nature walk. That choice clearly distinguished the conservancy's budding orientation from that of the garden clubs or of the Georgia Sportsmen's Federation, made up exclusively of "active" hunters and fishermen and the conservancy's main early rival for the mantle of Georgia's "leading conservation group." Early conservancy meetings had their share of policy discussions but also provided ecological as well as experiential training. Participants' eyes, legs, senses, and minds were weaned in less interventionist ways of knowing and appreciating natural settings, without the mediation of trowels, firearms, or fishing rods. "An exciting calendar of field trips" also acquainted members with different faces of that regional "nature" they might seek to preserve. A walk through Fernbank that first January was followed by a February hike in the "beautiful Sweetwater Creek area." In March they traveled to Stone Mountain, where "once again hiking and exploring the park's many interesting natural features were the main activities of the visit."[46] Fourth Saturdays, these blends of meeting and hiking came to be called, for the day held each month.

For Mackay, the new conservancy group embodied much of what he had been trying to achieve with the Citizens Panels: top-down organizing and inculcation that would stir and mobilize interested citizens' own sense of power, energizing political action from the bottom up. "Through our field trips, our exposure to many well-informed individuals, and through new articles and books," he wrote in the group's first newsletter, "we have learned the importance of developing 'ecological' sense." This learning was not confined to ecological or other natural sciences but also civic and political. Whereas that "host of people who share our concern for Conservation" had long been "unorganized and ineffective," "through an organization such as" this one they were learning they could "unite for effective action."[47]

A few years out a sociology dissertator at Emory provided a less rosy depiction. In practice the early conservancy functioned as an oligarchy, with just a handful of people making "virtually all the policy decisions." Starting with Hanie as its first hire (short-lived—he was too "controversial"), it set about building a professional staff. And it brought on a board of trustees envisioned as "establishment-minded," from retired Georgia Power "special assistant" Mamie Taylor to corporate lawyers to a Georgia Power executive. Mackay's

PHOTO 4.1. Georgia Conservancy members atop Panola Mountain, circa 1967. Courtesy of the Georgia Conservancy.

successors as chair-president, including a vice president of development at Emory and a former Georgia Tech football coach and businessperson, helped the board set a course of "responsible action." Restraining militancy and carefully safeguarding its tax-exempt status, conservancy leadership left hard-nosed political lobbying to others. Membership drives met with considerable success: by the early 1970s some four thousand Georgians had signed up. But both members and leaders were "overwhelmingly white, Protestant, well-educated," and high income, so much so as to "suggest real social exclusivity in Conservancy recruitment."[48] From these early days, rural-land preservation emerged as their group's overriding priority, with the Chattahoochee or other pollution and any urban or suburban issues far down the list. While they began pressing for state and federal governments to step up public purchase and protections of land, they also went ahead with their own land conservancy plan.[49] Panola Mountain, in Rockdale County, soon became their first success.

The region's second-biggest monadnock after Stone Mountain, though only a sixth that mountain's size, Panola remained "the only major granite exposure in the southeast that man has spared and left unscarred."[50] Emory biologist and inaugural conservancy member Robert Platt had made a career studying the unique biology of its outcrops. As he explained to reporters, the environment of the outcrop provided "experimental means of gaining fundamental knowledge about evolution," as the gene pools of rare mosses, lichens, and other biota, growing in isolated spots on the rock face, illuminated a "million-year mountain's process of evolution." Upon hearing the property had gone onto the market, Platt hurriedly informed conservancy colleagues. By early August 1967 they had borrowed enough to secure a twelve-month option on the over five hundred acres where this "miniature Stone Mountain" lay.[51] The national Nature Conservancy then covered the loan and more, securing its Georgia cousin more time to raise the $200,000 asked for by the owners.[52] The conservancy then busily set about pursuing similar plans for other natural places they favored, from Sweetwater Creek to Cumberland Island, on the Georgia coast. They also stepped in against destructive state and federal schemes for waterways, from the channelization of the Alcovy River to the damming of the Alapaha.

While a Georgia Natural Areas Council recently created by the legislature became a governmental ally in several of these efforts—and a sometime employer of Hanie—the conservancy often found itself up against the state's elected leader, Governor Maddox, an Atlantan himself. Maddox's bases of support lay among white working-class Atlantans but especially among the actual denizens of the Georgia countryside, nearly absent from the conservancy's ranks. Invoking their interests brought him into repeated clashes with the conservancy, beginning not long after its members ventured their first appearance at a public hearing, in March 1967. There they endorsed the inclusion of the Okefenokee Swamp in the National Wilderness System, to ensure "that the Swamp remain in its present wild, natural condition, unchanged by man."[53] But Maddox threw his political weight against wilderness designation, as "it would not be beneficial from an economic standpoint to the surrounding and adjacent areas of the swamp."[54] Conservancy members nevertheless kept after Maddox, also urging him to stop river-engineering schemes and to commit state funds toward the purchase of Panola, Sweetwater Creek, and other natural treasures.

On this last front they did make some headway with him. In February 1968 Hanie convinced Maddox to come hiking with him along Sweetwater Creek, to show off its charms. Escorting Maddox around, Hanie cannily departed from the conservancy script to emphasize not so much the creek's ecology as its Civil War heritage. Along the creek was a former factory that, prior to its destruction in 1864, had produced yarn and cloth for Confederate uniforms. Walking through the old factory ruins, "enough to the hold the interests of any hiker or governor," Maddox was apparently won over.[55] A month later, with Hanie again at his side, he led another group of hikers to the site— legislators whose support he hoped to win over for state purchase of the property.[56] Yet it was only after Jimmy Carter replaced Maddox in the governor's mansion that Georgia actually bought Sweetwater and also Panola, to convert them into public parks.[57]

Even as conservancy members celebrated and sought to preserve Georgia's natural jewels, they sought protections not just against governmental or developers' designs but against the destructive impacts of these places' human neighbors. After all, ordinary folks living nearby hadn't honed the ecologically informed and aesthetically appreciative perspectives that conservancy members had been teaching one another on their nature hikes. Maddox's own miscalculations for his outings with Hanie suggest other, more subtle ways conservationists distinguished themselves from the uninitiated. There was a dress code: when he showed up in a "blue executive suit, an even bluer tie, white dress shirt, Black shoes, and a diamond-studded fraternal pin," he "didn't look ready for hiking," thought the *Constitution* reporter.[58] But what troubled Hanie more were the kinds of things he found the locals had done at Sweetwater Creek: littering with beer and "pop bottles," hunting and otherwise driving out the birds and other wildlife, and putting up houses that dumped sewage into the creek.[59] So once success arrived—that is, they found funds to purchase and gain control of the place they sought to preserve—their reigning impulse was to cut off most people's access. After they had secured the Nature Conservancy's title on Panola Mountain, they declared it would "not [be] available to the public." It was, instead, to become a site for "research," open only to "sympathetic conservation groups" and, even for them, only "on a tour basis."[60]

Institutionalizing Mackay's earlier vision of effective citizenship, the Georgia Conservancy had become what no short-lived citizen panel ever could be, a durable vehicle for an *environmental* type of citizenship. The right kind of citizens, knowledgeable and admiring of the state's natural treasures, had joined with one another to become a genuine political force for preserving them. The terms it set for environmental citizenship synthesized older strands of obligation into new ways of seeing, focused on the countryside's natural ecology, and new modes of practice, from nature hikes to networking, fundraising, and politicking for the cause of ecological preservation. For Atlantans as other Georgians, it was a newfangled project, and not for everyone. "Significantly excluded" from its ranks, in the Emory sociologist's assessment, were "those earning less than $10,000 a year, those with only a high school education or less, blue collar workers, farmers, and Blacks."[61] Early Georgia Conservancy leaders had little interest in assessing about how socioeconomically and educationally skewed their group was or how this selectivity reflected regional inequities of much longer standing. And the very tools, frameworks, and ethics they'd honed to enable their own activism offered little means for doing

PHOTO 4.2. Georgia Conservancy members on a hike in the late 1960s. White County, in the foothills of the Blue Ridge in the northeast corner of the state, was indeed overwhelming white, like the conservancy itself. Courtesy of the Georgia Conservancy.

so. Some of their number did nevertheless come to recognize how a focus on rural-land preservation could slight those environmental challenges stirring closer in to the city itself.

Of all the absences in their membership, that of African Americans was the one about which they were most aware and at least episodically concerned. "We knew that we were . . . awfully white," recollected Smethurst. "Every now and then we'd go out and find a Black person and drag them to the table."[62] Among these, a Black biologist from Clark, John Withers, briefly served on the conservancy board. While he sought to stir more interest in the air pollution afflicting Atlanta's increasingly Black downtown, his efforts were to little avail. Conservancy leaders already had their agenda, and, as the group's historian put it, their "heart was in the countryside."[63] They strove harder after a membership cut in their own mold. And they wound up with a collective vehicle largely replicating the long-standing exclusivity of the city's power elite, only younger, more female, and more en masse, across a broader swathe of the city's upper middle class but exclusively on the white side of the city's color line.

"The Ghetto Has Come Alive"

While the Georgia Conservancy's whiteness might have stemmed, in part, from some unrecorded cold shoulders to Blacks who sought to join, its roots ran far deeper than any personal dearth of politeness or hospitality. Even after legal segregation had been vanquished, many legacies of this era endured, not just socially but materially, in a racially divided urban landscape whose inequalities persisted or were reinforced through wave after wave of socioeconomic and political change. Despite all that civil rights activists had achieved in the political and civil realms, exemplified by the federal civil rights acts of the mid-1960s, the social and economic obstacles to racial equality remained enormous. Most glaringly, the poorest and least well-endowed corners of the city remained inveterately Black. In response, many of the city's advocates for civil rights citizenship switched their sights from its civil toward its socioeconomic elements. They moved in an opposing direction from those who gathered for the conservancy's monthly meeting and hikes, not just metaphorically but literally. They headed downtown, straight toward those poor, still semirural Black neighborhoods that were among the least likely of places to appeal to a white "nature-lover."

During an historic cold snap in January 1966, a year before the Fernbank gathering that gave rise to the Georgia Conservancy, Martin Luther King Jr. ventured for the first time into the poorer side of Vine City. A Quaker activist handing out blankets there had been arrested for trespassing, at the insistence of a landlord. After his church members convened a meeting in response, King then decided to go see the place himself. Nearly right across the street from his own home, it was in much direr shape, with run-down rentals all-too-penetrable to nature's whims. As captured in a contemporary's notes, "signs of winter poverty" abounded: a "wash basin pipe broken by freezing in pipes . . . boards, lenolium [sic] scraps, rags, tape covering holes in the floor as big as a man's arm . . . paper sacks rolled around legs under stockings to keep warm . . . cracks in doors and windows stuffed with rags . . . honey bucket sitting in [a] 'frozen out' bathroom," and residents who essentially "already [lived] outside."[64] King's horror at what he saw fortified his and the SCLC's budding transition toward poverty and economic injustice that would preoccupy his final years. "This is appalling," he declared. "I had no idea people were living in Atlanta, Georgia, in such conditions." Never had he seen such living conditions, "even in Chicago. . . . I want Mayor Ivan Allen to see this. . . . I don't believe he knows such conditions exist in Atlanta."[65]

SCLC as well as SNCC activists, whose college education and (for many if older) comfortable owner-occupied homes had come courtesy of postwar compression capitalism, had already begun to engage the plight of those living in such places, utterly shut out of Atlanta's postwar spread of wealth and op-

portunities. Compared to a still-coalescent project of environmental citizenship around this city, civil rights citizenship offered more intellectual leverage and ethical resources to bear witness to and advocate for the city's Black poor. Whereas the outside vantage point of this era's environmental citizenship derived from natural sciences, invoking "man" or "society" in whole, that of civil rights citizenship focused on the unequal and unjust divisions within society itself. Even as the direct-action movement had united with Atlanta's least well-off through shared skin color, SCLC and SNCC activists over the mid-1960s found it increasingly hard to ignore how the project of civil rights citizenship had as yet brought little to Black workers and especially the poorest of the city's Black communities. In response, the midsixties shift of both SCLC and SNCC to labor as well as to poverty issues brought their project of civil rights citizenship much closer to Jefferson Cowie's "economic citizenship."[66] As King's own impressions of a place like Vine City show, the ill-maintained and all-too-permeable living quarters of the poor were also at stake, yet neither they nor the new white environmental groups who were their contemporaries identified these concerns as "environmental." Instead, both tended to see the push for improvements in these homescapes as fitting much more comfortably within civil rights citizenship, as an avenue toward full and active belonging for those long at the bottom of racial authoritarianism's citizenly hierarchy.

Nevertheless, poorer neighborhoods like Vine City or Buttermilk Bottom as well as public housing like Perry Homes faced many environmental vulnerabilities, not just from cold snaps or summer heat but from water. As map set 4.1 shows, Atlanta's early slums had lain downhill from the main ridges along which the city had been established, and by 1970 many of the city's poorest areas like Vine City still did. It lay along a gully that during rainstorms served as tributary to Proctor Creek. On Magnolia Street, "the lowest alley" in nearby Lightning, the "floods when it rains" regularly rose up inside people's homes.[67] That was even more true of Perry Homes farther downstream along Proctor Creek. Living alongside what, as we have seen, was just becoming recognized as the most polluted stream in the entire metro area, by the late sixties they "liv[ed] in fear" of its flooding, more so than its contamination. Local parents feared for their children's safety, with one father admitting, "I can't sleep when it rains."[68] Even as families in Perry Homes or Vine City lacked the personally owned yards that came with homeownership, the legacies of Jim Crow had also left them with hardly any public recreation facilities that could stand in. There were none in Vine City and, around Perry Homes, only less developed patches, where roaming children stumbled into additional dangers, like a ten-foot-deep pool in Proctor Creek where a child drowned in July 1966.[69]

Then there were the wildlife favored by such places, most spectacularly (especially for outsiders) the brown rat, or *Rattus norvegicus*. A pest that for centuries had troubled human habitations, gravitating toward settings that combined waste-rich human habitations with nearby waterways and open soil, brown rats found all three in abundance in the craggy, gullied lands around both Vine City and Perry Homes.[70] Their appetite for household wastes was stoked and slaked by the frequent accumulation of garbage, thanks to pickup services that were frustratingly intermittent compared to many white parts of town. A reporter visiting the creek in back of Perry Homes in 1970 found it "strewn with debris of all descriptions—refrigerators, discarded furniture, parts of automobile bodies," and its banks were "honeycombed . . . with holes."[71]

Threatening and troubling as these physical environments were to Atlanta's Black poor, these were only the most visible surfaces of the mammoth challenges they faced. Almost invariably renters, they remained dependent on landlords for addressing these vulnerabilities, and, if they pushed too hard, could be subject to abuse or eviction. Continuing racial discrimination limited their job as well as housing options, further impeding their ability to move. The fruits of a century of public neglect for Black schools meant that in Vine City, half of those older than twenty-five had not attended high school, constraining their job options. With only one-third of Vine City households

MAP SET 4.1. The stubborn geography of Black poverty. By 1970 Vine City and other Black enclaves that in the late nineteenth century had dominated the city's edges had become Atlanta's inner city. All these former suburbs remained poor and, with the notable exception of the old mill village of Cabbagetown, mostly Black. Maps by author. Sources: Manson et al., IPUMS National Historical Geographic Information System; http://doi.org/10.18128/D050.V17.0; John Kellogg, "Negro Urban Clusters in the Postbellum South," Geographical Review 67, no. 3 (1977): 310–21, https://doi.org/10.2307/213725; "Atlanta, Georgia," Google Maps, accessed August 2016.

Late 19th-Century Black Concentrations
Atlanta's Black Population in 1970
Percentage by Census Tract
0% - 5%
6% - 20%
21% - 40%
41% - 75%
76% - 100%

Late 19th-Century Black Concentrations
Poverty and Near-Poverty in 1970
Percentage with Family Income 1.5x Poverty Level or Less
0% - 5%
6% - 10%
11% - 15%
16% - 22%
23% - 40%

having access to a car by 1970, for instance, the vast majority of residents had to take the bus or walk to work. Not only were many men unemployed, but those who did hold down a job worked mostly as laborers or doing nonhousehold "service work"; adult women did either that or domestic work such as serving as maids. In a place like Vine City, severe economic deprivation was shared by over half of the households by 1970, which earned either below or less than one and a half times the poverty level.[72] These neighborhoods also suffered the greatest dearth of those public protections, spaces, and services that racial authoritarianism had long restricted mainly to white Atlantans.

Struggling with so many dilemmas and insecurities not faced by Atlanta's middle classes, Black as well as white, families and individuals in these neighborhoods had less time or stable circumstances and fewer skills to craft collective assertions of political power, even as years or decades of barely getting by had soured hopes. Some took up activism nonetheless, especially encouraged by the direct-action movement. Among them was Dorothy Bolden, who had been born, gone to high school, and raised children in Vine City and who made her living as a maid. Bolden did not start her local civic activism until the midsixties, after she had turned forty. Dr. King provided her "inspiration"; his biblically infused talk about society's inequalities and the imperative for justice was her means for grasping her own dilemmas as from the outside, in a larger motivating context. Still hesitant because of her own financial constraints, her activism began in a distinctly lower working-class key, through a protest of an integration plan that threatened to bus Vine City kids who couldn't afford good clothes to an affluent white high school: "We couldn't integrate the schools out there barefooted." But when Vine City first acquired counterparts to the neighborhood associations of more affluent parts of town, both of them in part through outside aid, Bolden was ready to step in and lend a hand. She became a leader in the Vine City Improvement Association, begun in the wake of a polling effort by a Georgia affiliate of the Southern Regional Council and local college students to inquire about residents' needs.[73] Their first project, after a meeting revealed a widely expressed need for children to have a "place to play," was to construct a playground—though worlds apart from preserving nature, an environmental improvement nonetheless. Bolden then worked on SNCC-leader Julian Bond's campaign for state legislator and, through the Improvement Association, as liaison to SNCC, whose "Black power" turn guided its own entry into Vine City.

SNCC's identification of its evolving strategy as Black power famously began with Stokely Carmichael's coinage of the term in rural Mississippi, though the notion also had longer and broader roots. Vine City served as a first launching pad for SNCC's exploration of what it could mean for urban Blacks. Rather than framing this Black power agenda as a shift of civil rights toward Black "authenticity," as Randolph Hohle has, I concentrate here on the shift it involved in activists' terms of citizenly belonging.[74] In embracing Black power, many whose activism had been hatched within an earlier project of civil rights citizenship, targeting upper levels of government, steered toward a more explicit solidarity with their fellow Blacks that also engaged more local faces of the state. Less constrained by middle-class decorum as well King's religiously inflected notions of an integrated "beloved community," Black power advocates concentrated more on unifying Blacks across class lines, by connecting economic deprivation to racial oppression. In a sense Black power steered civil rights citizenship back toward those economic and social elements of citizenship that had preoccupied the post–World War I Atlanta Urban League, yet without the latter's concessions to separate but equal or its prioritization of Black middle-class housing. SNCC headed, instead, into Atlanta's least economically privileged Black neighborhoods, in pursuit of a revised version of civil rights citizenship that flipped white stigmatization of slums on its head, addressing residents' environmental plights as grounds for mobilizing their political clout.

Already in mid-1963 SNCC had begun lending a hand to Atlanta's poorest communities, starting with a mobilization in Black neighborhoods to the city's south that it dubbed its "Atlanta Project." In alliance with civic groups already stirring there, including an Atlanta Civic Council, SNCC activists helped launched a march of 250 residents to city hall with a list of demands focused on their living environment: "stricter enforcement of the city building code; better parks, recreational facilities and libraries, proper sewage and garbage disposal, and improved street lighting, cross walks, traffic signs."[75] SNCC's reentry into Vine City came in late 1965 or early 1966, when a SNCC team led by Bill Ware and occasionally joined by Stokely Carmichael himself set up a headquarters there, to revivify its Atlanta Project. Responding to the "significant breakthrough in political representation" that had come with the successful election of Bond to the statehouse, they saw a Vine City organizing drive as also offering a demonstration project in how Black power—in important ways more a variation on than a total break with civil rights citizenship—could work in practice. Frustrated over the power dynamics of higher levels of government, they now sought to address "the conduct of local government." That was where they thought poor Blacks stood the best chance of "achiev[ing] a real voice." Especially if this aggrieved community could be brought to understand its grievances through the new lenses on racial oppression being forged by Carmichael and his SNCC colleagues, "we suspect politics can be made most relevant to the ordinary citizen and as a result more susceptible to democratic control."[76]

SNCC quickly joined local allies in taking on the indifference not just of city hall but of those whose pursuit of profits helped keep Vine City residents poor as well as ill-housed: landlords. As historians from Rhonda Williams to

Roberta Feldman and Susan Stall to Roberta Gold have shown, tenant organizing surged around the nation from the mid- through the late 1960s. SNCC helped jump-start its Atlanta version through its Vine City work, directly countering an economic power imbalance at the root of slumhood.[77] They thereby sought to ameliorate, if not reverse, a species of dependency largely alien to neighborhoods of white homeowners or environmentalists in this era but the fount of an overweaning share of Vine City's environmental deprivations, indoors and out.[78]

If labor organizing across this right-to-work city and state had faced substantial obstacles over the postwar period, organized tenant activism around Atlanta had been even quieter and more intermittent. Already by 1965 hopes stirred by civil rights accomplishments had become contagious, and rent strikes began to erupt in places like Mechanicsville, which SNCC's Vine City effort soon joined.[79] Key leadership came from local residents such as Willie Williams, a tenant and a hired carpenter of landlord Joe Shaffer, who left his job to turn activist and neighborhood spokesperson. Days after King's visit, after a SNCC-initiated meeting generated plans for a rent strike, Williams led a delegation to present their grievances to city hall: "because our houses are condemned, because we have no heating system, because our places are unsanitary . . . because many of our windows are broken . . . because the plaster is falling off the walls, because we have holes in our floors"—all flaws in their living environment—and because they had "been overcharged in rent."[80] The rebuffs from the mayor and press were dismissive and sweeping. Allen fulminated that "rent strikes were not in the American way," and landlord Shaffer then promptly evicted those rent strikers who remained his tenants, including Williams. For several subsequent months, into the spring of 1966, as Williams pursued an unsuccessful legal challenge to this law, he wound up living in a tent on vacant Vine City land, next to SNCC activists' own encampment.[81] Undeterred, he and SNCC sketched out groundwork for a bigger housing campaign, one that would unite tenants across all of Atlanta's "Center-City Plantations." "No longer" would they "tolerate the oppression and squalor of the dismal quarters in which they have been entombed." As SNCC staff began contemplating a "tenants' rights handbook," its *Nitty Gritty* newsletter called for a "tenants rights movement" through which "the excessive powers of landlords in Atlanta must be curbed."[82]

By 1968 local activism in this poor corner of the city simmered, so much so that the *Vine City Voice*, a new community newsletter, declared "the ghetto ha[d] come alive." SNCC itself no longer had a hand in the local activism; shunned by a worried group of Vine City residents after being targeted by white alarmism in the wake of looting in Summerhill, it had left town.[83] But the *Voice*'s hopeful summation of where this activity pointed nevertheless echoed SNCC's vision: "There must be local power in the ghetto that the people can share in."[84] At least three prominent groups run by local residents devoted themselves to aiding and improving conditions there: a Vine City Foundation; an army church, "a nonprofit organization composed of residents of Vine City who are interested in the betterment of their community"; and the Royal Knights, begun in 1967 as a recreation club.[85] Much local civic work was devoted to the local living environment: "clean[ing] up Vine City." With college students and even some local financial institutions assisting, for instance, the foundation organized a 1969 effort to "hau[l] away junk cars, stoves, refrigerators, box springs, discarded furniture, and mounts of trash."[86]

Helping spark this hopeful era for Vine City and like neighborhoods inhabited by Atlanta's Black poor were a host of new government initiatives opening more doors to citizenly appeals. In 1967, in direct response to the Summerhill episode and lingering threats of further violence, the city created its Community Relations Commission (CRC). Not even the earlier direct-action movement had spurred a city-hall-turned megaphone like the CRC then became for Atlanta's poor Blacks. Its twenty members, predominantly Black, were charged with actively seeking out and addressing the concerns of those in the city's most aggrieved communities, "the underprivileged of Atlanta"—"to head off additional violence." Its modus operandi was the "town-meeting approach." At its first meeting, held at city hall in February 1967, thirty-five "persons representing areas such as Vine City, Lightning, Blue Heaven, Pittsburgh and Summerhill"—given the small size of the room, an "overflow" crowd—showed up to speak.[87] Later meetings, convened in poor sections of the city themselves, offered the ear of city hall to anyone who wished to attend and bring forth a complaint. "Citizens were told to gripe as much as they wanted, to tell the CRC staff what was wrong with their communities, suggest relief for such wrongs—in fact, tell it like it is." CRC recorded everything, then went to work trying to address what was said, with a first report back in thirty days.[88] The City of Atlanta itself thereby began exploring means for poorer citizens to voice their concerns, without having to create and sustain something like a homeowners' association that could effectively speak for them and their interests.

The largest influx of new opportunities, however, came from the federal government, better enabling the citizenship capacity of Vine City's poor on many levels. A great deal of this support, the local fruit of President Johnson's Great Society, passed through individual families. By one 1969 count, 365 local mothers—some 32 percent of Vine City's adult women—received money from the federal Aid for Families with Dependent Children (AFCD), a program expanded over the 1960s to cover many more Blacks.[89] Much else of what Johnson's Great Society came to mean "on the ground" in this least privileged corner of the city came through Equal Opportunity Atlanta (EOA), what historian Elizabeth Hinton has described as "the most ambitious social welfare program in the history of the U.S."[90] Despite the enabling law's pledge of "maximum feasible participation," its often top-down designs and control continued to stir local criticism, such as that its federal programs "were *designed by people who did not know the poor and their problems*."[91]

Yet from the start EOA built up its Vine City operations with tips of the hat, at least, to local initiatives. A small EOA "satellite center" started there in 1966 had blossomed into a $20,000 recreation center two years later. This center's director acknowledged the role of the Royal Knights in making this expansion possible: "things really began to happen for Vine City recreation" once they had set to work.[92] A Nash Washington Neighborhood Service Center in an adjoining neighborhood to the north channeled in other opportunities: job training, the federally supported preschool education program Head Start, and other welfare and recreation initiatives.[93] Transferring to a brand-new building along with a new middle school in 1970, christened as the John F. Kennedy Center, it had sprouted offices for ten other agencies, becoming a "broker for the poor," or a "castle of hope," as residents and officials variously described it.[94] To break the cycle of poverty, these and other programs aimed "to bring the child out of his cave-like cloister of poverty for 11 hours a day, five days a week, to take him psychologically, if not physically out of his home environment."[95] Additional programs, however, actively sought improvements in the physical environments of Atlanta's poor, edging their homescapes into closer resemblance to those enjoyed by an expanding middle class.

The EOA's rat-control program proved especially effective in addressing an ecological problem of poor neighborhoods, through more of a participatory than a technocratic approach. It got underway slowly at first, starting only with Perry Homes along with Pittsburgh in 1969 and then extending to Vine City and other designated slum areas the following year. But over the next six years, Atlanta's economic-opportunity office wound up administering a $1.2 million effort around Vine City (part of the larger Nash Washington area) and four other poor neighborhoods. Responding to all the community criticism about top-down program design, EOA officials tried to make rat control more responsive to residents' own desires and needs. They emphasized educating and informing, intervening only at residents' invitations. And the entire program wound up being administered largely by residents of the affected communities themselves.[96] Local women selected as "block captains" were instructed how to get rid of rats and then spread the know-how around their neighborhoods. Paid full-time cadres of local youths were hired to clean up "rodent-enticing accumulations" of garbage, construct rat racks "to keep pets from tipping over garbage cans," and bait rat holes with poison.[97] One early result, according to Katie Young, in charge of this EOA program, was that "for the first time in their lives" "many people [in the targeted neighborhoods] are beginning to believe rats are no longer a natural part of their environment." Soon, spurred by this sense of possibility as well as the program's aids, they achieved real ecological results. By 1974 they had brought rat infestations in Vine City and other poor Atlanta neighborhoods down to "acceptable, federally established proportions."[98]

Despite this and other accomplishments, the limitations were nevertheless becoming apparent by the early 1970s in what neighborhood organizing in combination with new federal powers and resources *could* improve in the physical environments of Atlanta's Black poor. Indoor plumbing was a bright spot. Within the decade housing without "all plumbing facilities" plummeted nearly 60 percent in the suburbs and a whopping 83 percent within the central city.[99] Most all of Atlanta's urban as well as suburban poor by 1970 had gained piped water and indoor toilets, from Vine City to Scotts Crossing and Scottdale. Yet among those housing units with full plumbing, the citywide tally of "dilapidated" housing units soared fourfold by 1970, to over ten thousand.[100] While more residents of Vine City and other poor Black neighborhoods gained central heating, most still had only single-room heaters, with less chance of keeping out the cold. Atlanta's poor Blacks also generally enjoyed far less respite from the searing heat of Atlanta's summers, through air-conditioning. And when the CRC held its first meeting in the Kennedy Center in 1971, Vine City residents asked for, among other things, better police protection and more streetlights—concerns that none of the agencies brought into this EOA service center had been able to address.[101]

Compared to what were now identified as "environmental" mobilizations, to protect home-owning neighborhoods, parks, or rivers, poor Black Atlantans also faced much more of an uphill battle to organize themselves and their neighbors and collectively assert themselves against those landlords or even homeowners nearby who wielded power over them. Tenant organizing took off, but mainly across the city's public housing. Residents there pulled together an umbrella group in late 1968, Tenants United for Fairness (TUFF), that would provide a more sustained collective voice for the Atlanta Housing Authority's thousands of tenants.[102] And Vine City resident Dorothy Bolden, by dint of her determination and know-how, carved out a steady activist niche for herself, though not as a neighborhood activist so much as an organizer of her fellow maids. Pulling together in 1968 a group she called the "National Domestic Workers Union," she soon dropped "union" from the name to avoid scaring people with the specter of strikes. For decades her group provided a reference service and advocacy for one of the city's lowest-paid and most vulnerable service workers.[103] On the other hand, as explored by the political scientist Clarence Stone, a group in Bedford Pine that in 1964 had marshaled an unprecedented protest against an urban-renewal plan for that part of town proved incapable of sustaining itself long enough to effectively impact the city's plans. Stone tracks what happened to this neighborhood activist group after a 1968 proposal for a more neighborhood-friendly pathway toward urban renewal. Debates erupted over just who claimed to speak for the neighborhood, punctuated by the occasional militant confrontation with the Atlanta Housing Authority. Ultimately, however, the group failed to hold the city accountable to the promises it had made. "Organizing consumers" always presents "substantial" challenges, he noted, but he concluded that organizing "slum dwellers"— "poor, dependent, and not very educated" as many of them were—constitutes an "especially difficult" and sometimes even "impossible" task.[104]

Facing so many material privations that white middle-class Atlantans did not, both within their homes and around their neighborhoods, over the late 1960s Atlanta's Black poor, joined by segments of its civil rights movement, mobilized more or less explicitly political projects to improve their own living environments. But they as well as this era's environmentalists found it far easier to understand this activism as a species of civil rights citizenship, having little to do with environmentalism. The stubbornly material divide between Atlanta's Black and white homescapes, reinforced by layer on layer of racial barriers over the prior half century, offers one powerful reason. But concepts and values also mattered here. The starkly divergent categories and moralism of civil rights and environmental activists in this time and place cemented their shared sense that their causes had no overlap.

Those Vine City environments that most bothered residents as well as civil rights activists were domestic spaces that they saw as *under*domesticated, from the ill-kempt interiors of rental housing itself to an unruly outdoors nearby, long since visibly shorn of that "ecological" nature that conservancy members now strove to apprehend, appreciate, and save. Moreover, those external vantage points and concepts through which Vine City residents understood and pursued their plight, as reflecting inequality and injustice, came straight out of the toolkit of civil rights citizenship. However environmental we may deem their concerns in retrospect, that environmental citizenship available in this time and place, preoccupied as it was with seeing and forestalling what humans or society as a whole was doing to the natural world, proved utterly incapable of grasping or appreciating the plight of Atlanta's Black poor. Where contemporary environmental citizenship did prove a better fit, extending its reach inside the Atlanta metropolis, was among white neighborhoods long since apportioned with greenery and open space and now confronted with a new threat. Ironically, it came from that same official juggernaut that a decade prior had stoked the ire of civil rights advocates by laying waste to Black neighborhoods: freeway building.

Saving the Neighborhoods

On October 3, 1968, at the DeKalb County Courthouse in Decatur, state highway engineers confronted to their dismay "the roughest opposition to a freeway project in the history of the Atlanta expressway system."[105] Their announced plans to run just over a mile of the I-485 freeway through Druid Hills had rung an alarm bell, drawing five hundred residents to their public hearing, so many that half the crowd had to stand outside. The department's engineers and planners went first, concentrating on how the freeway would solve attendees' and other Atlantans' traffic problems. As soon as the residents' turn came, the verbal onslaught began. Much of it centered on Deepdene Park, twenty acres set aside along Ponce de Leon Avenue, through whose woods the freeway was supposed to run. Twelve local garden clubs, having poured so much "money and time and effort into the beautification of Deepdene Valley," voiced their outrage. The "wooded part" through which the freeway would cut was nothing less than the tiara of the entire neighborhood, the "principal ingredient in perpetuating the desirability of the area for residential use."[106] James Mackay spoke up, along with three other Druid Hills Civic Association presidents, former and current. "Destruction of the natural beauty of Deepdene" was for them "perhaps the most important point," so too the threat to "absolutely unique" Fernbank Forest, that uncut forest patch that was supposed to serve as "the conservation school of this state for generations to come."[107] Fernbank Center's astronomer, the head of the DeKalb School Board, and the leaders of the Georgia Natural Areas Council and the Atlanta office of the federal Bureau of Outdoor Recreation added their voices to the critical throng.[108] The unprecedented outpouring set state highway engineers back on their heels—and the fight against freeways was just getting started.

Highway building stirred some of city's most pointed controversies of the late 1960s and early 1970s, helping rouse many of Atlanta's white communities into a popular mobilizing that drew the sway of environmental citizenship deeper into the metropolis. The synergy between these battles in the city's inner and older suburbs and the conservancy's out in the Georgia countryside ran deep, yet these clashes centered around defense of homescapes, domestic spaces where the mobilized themselves lived. More directly and obviously than Mackay's Panels for Progress or the conservancy, Atlanta's antifreeway mobilization of the late 1960s constituted a bid for greater urban political power by Atlanta's home-owning—patrimonial—upper- to middle-class whites. Unlike other activism of white homeowners portrayed in the literature, from "massive resistance" against school desegregation to later antibusing campaigns, freeway fighters' adoption of environmental citizenship served as grounds for coalition building with the city's rising Black leadership. Many Blacks, after all, had had firsthand experience with the freeway-building juggernaut. As a movement of neighborhoods was born, and with it a larger, less reactive environmental agenda for the city as a whole, white activists joined in provisional alliance with a coalition of Black leaders to wrench the city's power structure toward greater democracy. What Kyle Shelton has termed a project of "infrastructure citizenship" did arise to unite white and Black activists, here as in Shelton's Houston.[109] Yet transportation infrastructure was only one issue among many of those tackled by the two broader citizenship projects explored in this book, and the fault lines between environmental and civil rights movements continued to run deep even during debates over what Atlanta's mass-transit system should look like.

That such a privileged and well-connected neighborhood as Druid Hills should find itself in freeway builders' sights by 1968 proved a wake-up call: despite Georgia's shift toward greater electoral democracy, the city's and state's administrative decision makers continued their autocratic ways. Technocratic planners of freeway megaprojects in particular still retained nearly as tight a control over the routes and siting as they had enjoyed early in the postwar period. Part of the reason was that the Georgia Highway Department remained in charge, one step up the governmental ladder from the city's own leaders and politics. A favorite of the Talmadge faction under rustic rule, its highway builders had nearly as free a hand in and around Atlanta as in the rest of Georgia over the 1950s because of new federal funding as well as the eagerness of city officials for their handiwork. Helping get city and state officials on the same page then, the earliest routes had run largely through poor Black neighborhoods with little citizenship capacity or political clout, especially under Jim Crow. Farther out past many of Atlanta's suburbs, highway builders still faced few obstacles even after rustic rule had ended. They breezed ahead on routes including the sixty-three-mile "beltway" around Atlanta, I-285, completed in 1969. State and city officials had long since envisioned connecting this outer loop with downtown, but the Highway Department put off announcing the exact location of connecting routes until the mid-1960s. Knowing they would have to run these roads through wealthier white areas, they hoped to dampen the anticipated resistance by getting all other routes in place first. Planners hoped that residents would then simply accept the necessity of running mammoth ribbons of concrete right next to their homes, as a bow to the inevitable.

Hints of neighborhood unrest came as early as 1961, when the Highway Department fielded complaints about the vagueness of its proposed route between Atlanta and Decatur. But concerted protest began in earnest after a 1965 announcement of a proposed route for I-485 through the Morningside area, northeast of midtown on the way to Druid Hills (map 4.2).[110] Highway engineers insisted they hadn't yet made up their minds, but the threat led to the formation of a Morningside-Lenox Park Association, which promptly

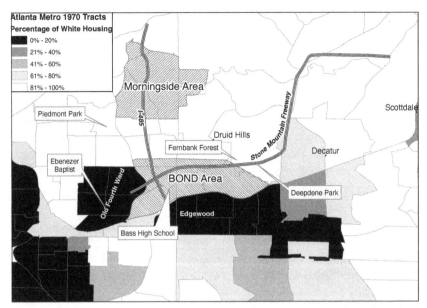

MAP 4.2. Neighborhood origins of Atlanta's freeway revolt by race in 1970. Lined areas show the extent of the Morningside-Lenox Park and BOND associations. Maps by author. *Sources*: Manson et al., *IPUMS National Historical Geographic Information System*; Frank Wells, "Atlanta Toll Roads Move Closer to Reality," *Atlanta Constitution*, August 16, 1968, 7 (map of roads); Greg Gregory, "Draft Report of Recycling an Urban Residential Community: A Framework for Community," June 26, 1972, box 1, Atlanta Coalition on the Transportation Crisis, Virginia Taylor Papers, MSS1222, Special Collections, Emory University (map of BOND); "Atlanta, Georgia," accessed July 2018.

turned out eight hundred worried residents at a meeting on the plan also attended by the district's new congressional representative, James Mackay. Just then fleshing out his plan for citizen panels, he found this the "strongest outpouring of civic expression" he'd ever seen.[111] Over the next year and more, Mackay tried to bring in federal highway officials to mediate. While they supported a reroute, they wound up approving an alternative "route B" that still ran through Morningside. The road plan gained further momentum when the Atlanta Board of Aldermen voted to support the alternative route, in a "wild" meeting that drew some 350 raucous residents. The aldermen's vote in favor of this route, as one reporter saw it, "appeared to be influenced strongly by warnings from the State Highway department that failure . . . to approve Line B would imperil millions of dollars worth of other Atlanta freeway projects."[112] As a last resort, the Morningside-Lenox Association took the Highway Department to court, gaining a temporary injunction that halted the start of construction until the court could deliberate.[113]

What the Morningside residents accused the Highway Department of attempting to do—"bisect[ing] and destroy[ing] a residential community"—

was what it had long taken as its prerogative.[114] That was precisely what it had done during the 1950s to, among other places, Auburn Avenue, then a thriving Black business district. The difference now was that Morningside residents were overwhelmingly white and well-off, denizens of an "attractive and refined neighborhood," where over 70 percent of residents held title to their own homes.[115] Entitled in so many ways, they along with the rest of Atlanta knew all too well the ravages of freeway building, having seen what had transpired over the late 1950s in the city's downtown. They soon lost this lawsuit, but their fight was by no means over. Theirs was only the first sally in a conflict that soon would engulf most neighborhoods in northeast Atlanta, where highway engineers now planned miles of six-to-eight-lane roads slicing through some of the city's whitest and wealthiest neighborhoods lay. Next up among the new neighborhood targets was an even more formidable opponent for the Highway Department: Druid Hills.

In retrospect it hardly seems surprising that the steamroller of post–World War II freeway building first questioned by civil rights activists in the 1950s should finally begin to meet its match in Druid Hills, and that, in so doing, the freeway fight would morph into a matter of environmental citizenship. This Atlanta bastion of white affluence had a civic association decades old, first formed in important part to preserve Fernbank Forest, its own ecologically authentic treasure. When the State Highway Department announced its plans for where exactly its easterly freeway to Stone Mountain would run, Druid Hills was far readier to respond than Buttermilk Bottom or Auburn Avenue or Morningside had been.[116] Testimony from Druid Hills residents in 1968 echoed the defenses of Morningside and of the many other homeowners' associations soon to resound, but Druid Hills was indeed special. With large and richly endowed public parks, it provided freeway opponents with a new kind of moral high ground—defending nature. These advantages had been accumulating for decades, from its Olmstead-crafted design to its strict zoning, to its defenses against block busting, to Fernbank, where Mackay had convened the first meeting of what became the Georgia Conservancy. Now Deepdene Park, to be bisected by the planned route, stood front and center in this neighborhood's nature defense. Authenticated by outside scientists as ecologically valuable, it drew powerful allies into the fray. Not just the county school board now overseeing Fernbank but state and federal agencies now gearing up to preserve the region's "natural areas" all lined up to support the civic association and garden clubs in this struggle. This combined array of support, in addition to the sheer turnout, was what made this protest so unsettling for the highway engineers—and so "effective."[117]

By emphasizing Druid Hills' ecological uniqueness, its defenders dissociated their own battle against the Stone Mountain Freeway, planned to intersect with I-485, from Morningside's struggles as well as efforts of Atlanta's civil rights leaders to steer downtown freeway clearances. Remarkably, however, in an era of rising talk about "the environment" and "ecology" nationally, environmental grounds for defending neighborhoods proved so adaptable and effective that they quickly spread, to freeway fights that soon arose in Atlanta neighborhoods with far fewer of Druid Hills' advantages.

Also targeted by the freeway planners, and most revealing of the frictions that could arise in such neighborhoods between environmental and civil right rights citizenship, was a northeastern district named for the nearby Bass High School, whose white predominance was slipping, even as it remained more working class. Wedged between Druid Hills to the east and Morningside to the north, the Bass neighborhoods area included Inman Park, the city's first upper-end suburban development in the late nineteenth century, as well as Candler Park, Little Five Points, and what's now known as Poncey-Highlands, westward to Lake Claire (map 4.2). Bordered by two predominantly Black districts—the Old Fourth Ward on the downtown side and Edgewood, just across the railroad tracks to the south—by the late 1960s it reverberated with some classic dynamics of racial transition: Bass High School, which also drew students from Edgewood, had by 1970 turned 57 percent African American.[118] Bass area homes, still predominantly occupied by whites of "low to moderate incomes," were older and in need of repair; half of them had registered as substandard in 1960, with some streets verging on slumhood, and, as less well-off older whites moved out, landlords increasingly shouldered in.[119] But from the mid-1960s younger whites also began arriving, drawn by Atlanta's counterculture community around nearby Piedmont Park, along with better-heeled professionals who began buying Inman Park's run-down Victorian homes to fix them up.[120] The Bass area began to undergo what became known as gentrification, a process soon spreading to other inner suburbs and the core of Atlanta.

Not surprisingly, the Highway Department's most ambitiously destructive freeway planning of the late 1960s lanced into these five seemingly fractured and "deteriorating" neighborhoods. As laid out in 1967 plans, I-485 was to slice nearly all the way through them from north to south, and the Stone Mountain Freeway from west to east, with the cloverleaf intersection between them slated for near Little Five Points. As highway officials then confidently set about condemning and clearing some six hundred local homes in the way, residents of these neighborhoods threatened with being "cut to pieces" quickly spawned a citizens' organization.[121] Men's clubs, women's clubs, garden groups, churches, businessmen's associations and civic groups got together and set up the Bass Organization for Neighborhood Development, or BOND, to represent those living in the area around the Bass High School. Initially spurred by the threat of demolition, its early leaders nevertheless insisted it was "not formed to protest" but "based on a positive approach . . . to find out how to make what is going to happen better for the community."[122] Over the next couple of years, however, BOND leaders dug in their heels. By 1971 a Community Congress called by BOND voted two to one against any route for the Stone Mountain Freeway through its neighborhoods, as BOND joined with the Morningside-Lenox Park Association to oppose I-485.[123]

To explain BOND's growing militancy, the *Great Speckled Bird*, a left-leaning underground newspaper begun in 1968 and headquartered nearby, fingered an accelerating transition of the neighborhoods into the hands of better-off whites. Until the late 1960s, the area represented by BOND had remained a "strong working-class neighborhood," which "lack[ed] the power and influence which money brings"; they "felt that about all they could do was push through certain changes in the freeway design." But then those arriving to "restore the few fine old Victorian homes" brought "money, planning expertise and political connections," a citizenship capacity that enabled the newfound resolve.[124] Charles Helms, a sometime president and vice president of BOND who also served as pastor at the Inman Park and then Druid Hills Presbyterian Churches, offered another explanation for why the neighborhood organization turned more resolute. Newcomers had been drawn into the Bass neighborhoods and were more eager to defend them, precisely *because* they had become so diverse, making it "the most interesting" place he had ever lived in. Helms's own neighborhood defense invoked an integrationist variant of civil rights citizenship: its "rich sociological mix" was what deserved protecting, "with . . . middle class whites, blue collar workers, poor whites, an influx of young professional people, Latin Americans . . . academic types . . . a few hip types and young radicals, and a slow trickling in of Blacks, but no panic."[125] Helms was not the only one attracted to this place's diversity, yet the predominantly white parents involved in BOND also feared a "re-segregation" of the now-integrated Bass High School, which in this case meant turning overwhelming Black.[126] And he publicly sparred with reporters from the *Great Speckled Bird* over just how rich and exclusively white an Inman Park restoration group and BOND itself actually were, and whether or not their plans included any place for Blacks, "unless they, too, are affluent and live in beautiful restored mansions."[127]

Bolstering BOND's resolve was how its leaders came to frame their neighborhood defense as a matter of environmental citizenship, thereby aligning their campaign not just with Druid Hills' but with a larger popular groundswell, across the entire nation. Even as BOND was first forming, some of its leaders had drawn on the services of a team of Atlanta architects who had declared a "war on ugliness" in the city. Taking photos and making recommendations for BOND, they helped shape the neighborhood group's initial efforts to remedy "signs of deterioration," starting with a "comprehensive plan" to "overcome our environment" "instead of letting the environment overcome us." The group turned to addressing "problems of health, sanitation, overcrowding of schools, play facilities, traffic, beautification, [and] transportation and social problems." Racial overtones sometimes crept in: for instance, that they were stemming a "tide toward slums."[128] At the same time, a more heroic narrative took hold in the white press, about white "pioneers" moving in to rediscover and restore places such as Inman Park. That meant not just refurbishing old homes but rediscovering a nature close by: "one of the first 'residence' parks in the country . . . [with a] 10-acre park in the center" and the trees along Euclid Avenue "nearly a hundred years old and some of them rare." Over the late 1960s into the 1970s, as the BOND-affiliated neighborhoods became a seat of ecological education and activism, that association cast its opposition to freeways more in the manner of Druid Hills', as protecting not just their own homes and neighborhood but thereby "the environment" largely writ, about which all Atlantans should care.[129]

BOND's increasingly harder line also owed a debt to the evolving mayoralty of Sam Massell, elected in 1968, who opened more doors in Atlanta's city government to the voices of BOND and other freeway fighters. Historians generally see Massell's mayoralty as an interregnum: defeating a candidate of the white business-led elite by drawing widespread Black support, he nevertheless would become the last white Atlanta mayor for another half century. He was able to win by culling support not just from Black voters but from the mostly well-off white neighborhoods fighting freeway building, a stance that placed him at odds with the freeway advocacy of Ivan Allen and the Atlanta Chamber of Commerce. By the end of 1971, Massell successfully prodded the board of aldermen to rescind their 1966 approval of the proposed route for I-485, giving BOND, Morningside-Lenox Park Association, and the other opposition groups much cause for celebration.[130]

Preparing the way for Massell's and the board of aldermen's vote against I-485 was his 1970 appointment of a Citizens Transportation Advisory Committee, which within the year offered a full-throated endorsement of the freeway fighters' arguments. With city appointees "composed largely of Blacks and 'grassrootsy,' non-monied Atlantans," including Vine City's Dorothy Bolden as a voice for low-paid service workers, this committee found that the State Highway Department had settled on this route by omitting "explicit consideration of community goals other than satisfying a demand for vehicular movement." It should, instead, have valued "maintaining and preserving viable neighborhoods." And what that meant, in practice, were a host of considerations hammered home by the neighborhood groups that this official body now styled as "environmental": "The character of the parks and surrounding neighborhoods" and the avoidance of "massive amounts of air pollutants from auto exhaust . . . [and excessive] noise levels." Not only had these impacts been ignored, the committee declared, but state and city officials had confined their deliberations and decision making largely to themselves. "The public, including but not limited to residents of the Morningside community was neither sufficiently nor effectively involved in planning I-485."[131]

Opposition to the freeways came easily for the Citizens Transportation Advisory Committee next to its more formidable political charge: brokering an agreement about a new mass-transit system for Atlanta, envisioned as supplementing and even softening the post–World War II drive for freeways.[132] While the fate of an existing bus system remained central, the main bone of contention was the Metropolitan Atlanta Rapid Transit Authority (MARTA), a proposed new Atlanta subway system soon to become an early fruit of the city's transition to Black political leadership as well as a darling of many environmentalists.

Ironically, Atlanta's push for public mass transit predated any of the state's organized environmental groups. Instead, it hatched out of those very exclusionary power structures that freeway fighters had joined many of the city's Black leaders in challenging. The first full-scale proposals emanated from the five-county Atlanta Region Metropolitan Planning Commission in the early 1960s and were then eagerly endorsed by the business-led Central Atlanta Progress. Mayor Allen quickly jumped on board as well. To this white, business-oriented city leadership, the main attraction of mass transit was its promise for bringing the richest and best consumers—affluent whites—back into downtown stores, after more than a decade of white flight. In a 1964 referendum, however, the proposal stumbled up against suburban racial fears of Blacks riding the metro out from downtown. It won approval in just two of the five metro area counties: DeKalb and Fulton. With the help of Congressperson Mackay, among others, MARTA had nevertheless gained federal funding, leading to a familiar pattern of board appointments: with the white owner of downtown department stores designated as chair, it included only a single Black member. The routes then proposed to voters in 1968 heavily favored the white northside of the city (three routes), with only a single route to the increasingly Black south and west sides. Black and white voters alike thrashed it at the ballot box, just as they were also electing Sam Massell.[133] In the wake of this defeat, the newly elected mayor appointed his own Citizens Transportation Advisory Committee (CTAC) to deliberate over the current plans for freeways as well as MARTA. Among the new committee's charges was to come up a mass-transit proposal actually capable of winning a referendum.

The surging debates within the CTAC laid bare the persisting divide between Atlanta's rising Black leadership, rooted in the tradition of civil rights citizenship, and the largely white freeway opposition, increasingly invested in environmental citizenship. Disagreements also erupted between the committee's blue-collar and "starched" (i.e., white) collar whites, yet its biggest challenge, given the failure of the previous referendum with Black voters, was the racial divide. To make sure their perspective and priorities were taken into account this time, a "Black coalition" of twenty-five political and civic leaders, led by then council member Maynard Jackson, pressed their own list of twenty-six "crucial issues" on the committee, if MARTA was to earn Black voters' support. They insisted that bus as well as subway fare be set at fifteen cents (down from the then-current forty cents for a bus ride), that more lines should run crosstown to Black communities, and that MARTA's workforce should be made 35 percent Black. None of their chief demands made mention of any "environmental" concern; instead, their reason, as then voiced by coalition member Dorothy Bolden (and decades later by Robert Bullard and Glenn Johnson), came straight out of the civil rights repertoire: "about love all around . . . spelling out true human justice."[134] On the other hand, freeway fighters, more concerned about highway planners' obliviousness toward MARTA, hoped not just for its approval but for a "comprehensive transportation plan." They believed that such an plan, "developed for the metropolitan area as a whole," would not only embrace MARTA but reveal the short-sightedness of the Highway Department's freeway fixation and even declare additional downtown freeways obsolete.[135] Through a new Coalition of Civic Organizations that included BOND and other eastern and mostly white neighborhoods threatened by freeway plans, antifreeway activists also increasingly leaned on newer, environmental terms of citizenship, applying talk about "the environment" to the more cityward spaces of those neighborhoods and homes they sought to defend.[136]

The Massell administration's revised proposal for MARTA incorporated many of the committee's proposals, both from the Black coalition—the fifteen-cent fare and additional spurs to the West Side Perry Homes—as well as from the antifreeway neighborhood groups. A political alliance between the city's Black leadership and freeway opponents over MARTA was then consummated in 1971, as pluralities in Fulton and DeKalb approved the new referendum for a $1.4 billion plan to build it, two thirds from the federal government and the rest from a sales tax, with strong support from Blacks as well as antifreeway groups. It was on the heels of that vote that Massell and the board of aldermen also saw fit to rescind approval of I-485.

Even though the mostly white voters in other metro counties—Cobb, Gwinnett, and Clayton—again rejected the referendum, its victory across Atlanta's most urbanized counties brought a new high-water mark for this city's version of Kyle Shelton's "infrastructure citizenship."[137] The debates had nevertheless laid bare a divide between those two underlying political projects whose support had been critical, that of a "Black coalition" rooted in civil rights citizenship and that of a mostly white freeway opposition, increasingly adopting the cause of environmental citizenship. As political machinery for freeway building nevertheless still chugged along, Virginia Harbin, the former Mackay congressional staffer who organized the conservancy's premeeting, helped form and lead an effort to integrate these divergent factions, a Coalition on the Transportation Crisis.[138]

In this coalition's view the city's current transportation plans still leaned on "decisions made as far back as the 1940s and 1950s when there was little knowledge present [of] environmental dangers, complex urban problems, and changing social conditions which characterize Atlanta and all major cities in the 1970s." The coalition called for systematic reconsideration of *both* the city's existing transportation plans to "inundate the central city with automobiles" *and* the unjust and undemocratic processes out of which these had arisen.[139] All freeway building should be banned inside the perimeter, it urged, and a less auto-dependent transportation system envisioned. A better plan should preserve the "unique beauty" of "the remaining sound residential areas" and "maximize the potential of . . . the developing MARTA system" "for citizens of all income levels." "Comprehensive land use planning" should also not be pursued from the top down, as the Highway Department and existing planning groups had done. Instead, it should be "based on citizen generated goals and . . . genuine public participation."[140] Speaking for what was becoming known as Atlanta's neighborhood movement, she soon found herself going toe-to-toe with the Atlanta Chamber of Commerce over the city's freeway preferences and "needs."[141]

Though the conservancy largely kept its official hands off this, as most other cityward environmental campaigns, it provided an early organizational platform for those like Harbin and Roger Buerki to get their feet wet in the new self-identified "environmental politics." As Buerki cycled into and through the conservancy as a temporary hire, he and a growing network of like-minded explorers, canoers, and outdoor enthusiasts began venturing forth along the region's streams and rivers. The natural landscapes and beauty they found there, they quickly realized, were being coveted by developers and sewer-builders, often teetering on the brink of bulldozer blades. Seeking out one another and turning activist, they forged a third leg of Atlanta's early environmentalism: the movement to create a public park along the Chattahoochee.

Saving the River

As with other predominantly white mobilizations that took to sharing the "environmental" or "ecologist" label around Atlanta by the early 1970s, campaigners to "save the Chattahoochee" had trouble recognizing any nature or common cause in downtown places like Vine City. But between the Georgia Conservancy's fixation on more distant countryside and the freeway fighters' focus on their own neighborhoods nearer in, river preservationists forged a middle ground for early environmentalism in Atlanta. Their version of environmental citizenship more closely resembled the effort to preserve Fernbank, another "wilderness that yet remains in our [Atlantans'] backyards."[142] Buerki and his fellow activists, however, faced uphill and political challenges that efforts to preserve this pristine forest in the midst of Druid Hills did not. There was no single owner of these many miles of riverbank. For the most part, the land and waters they sought to preserve lay some distance from their own neighborhoods and homes, so there wasn't any well-established institution like a homeowners' association through which their preservationist advocacy could be channeled. Nor was there (as yet) any regional or single local government to which they might appeal, even as they found themselves pitted against builders and developers, some of the most powerful elements of metro Atlanta's white business elite. Moreover, that northerly part of the river they aimed to save offered fewer grounds than the freeway opposition enjoyed for appealing to Atlanta's Black leaders, whose political power was being augmented by democratization and by an emerging Black electoral majority in the city itself.

Far more evident, even obvious, to Black Atlantans than to so many advocating to "save" this river were the racial bounds to this "wilderness" the river preservationists favored. From the Clayton treatment plant and Peachtree Creek southward, the Chattahoochee in need of saving was the one that bore the bulk of this city's burgeoning sewage and industrial wastes, whose neighborhoods were now increasingly Black. Northward from this same break point, however, a relatively waste-free Chattahoochee didn't smell or seethe with discoloration or algae and was considered safe for boating and swimming. This clean northerly stretch of riverine "wilderness . . . in our backyards" lay much closer to some Atlantans' backyards than to others': residents of those upstream wedges of the city were now almost exclusively white. Not surprisingly, then, so were those who discovered and defended it as a wilderness playground. Among the activists in the Chattahoochee preservation campaign, Claude Terry, an Emory microbiologist who joined forces with Buerki early on, doesn't recall "a single Black member, [of] Friends of the River or any of the groups we worked with."[143] Those two Chattahoochees created through Jim Crow and New Deal city building now seemed naturalized into the river's very fabric, leading liberal activists to conclude that their campaign simply had no connection to Atlanta's heated politics of race.

For many river savers, as for many early joiners of the conservancy as well as the movement for civil rights, personal journeys into Atlanta's middle class, frequently enabled by the growing availability of higher education, laid groundwork for their emergent environmental citizenship. Both Roger Buerki and Claude Terry had risen from more humble working-class and less educated origins. Buerki had grown up in a "far out suburb" of Saint Louis, son of a high school–educated mechanic for McDonnell Aircraft; Terry was born in rural Forsyth County, Georgia, into a household where no one had even attended high school. Higher education—for Buerki an engineering degree from the Missouri School of Mines and for Terry a doctorate in microbiology from the University of Georgia—wound them up in professional jobs that brought them to Atlanta after 1965. Buerki had arrived from the West Coast to work at Cobb County's Lockheed; Terry came for a job teaching microbiology at Emory. After being laid off and taking the part-time conservancy job, Buerki began discovering places like Rottenwood and the northerly Chattahoochee, then emerged as an informal leader of a loosely organized group dubbing themselves the "river rats." Among Atlanta's more staid and established environmental activists, the river rats' aversion to compromise and crowd-drawing tactics garnered a reputation similar to Bob Hanie's, as "radicals." Terry's association with academia and his status as a scientist enabled him to largely escape such a label and gained him a more welcoming ear among some of Atlanta's most elite. At the same time, his own entryway into Chattahoochee appreciation came via another leisure-time way of exploring Atlanta's wilder corners: canoeing. Active in a new Georgia Canoeing Association, Terry's canoeing skills opened additional doors, as a leader of river trips for sympathetic politicians from Mayor Massell to Jimmy Carter.[144]

Like the conservancy itself, the movement to save the Chattahoochee also had strong female leaders, some of them from considerably more privileged backgrounds than Buerki's or Terry's. Both Barbara Davis and Kay McKenzie had been born into privileged circles, Davis as the daughter of a "very prominent lawyer in the state" of Kansas, and McKenzie in Atlanta's own Buckhead, the premier seat of its old-money elite. Her lawyer father had been a president of the Southern Company, the holding company for Georgia Power. Davis had arrived in Atlanta around 1970 from Long Island with a social-work masters in hand; she then began working with her then husband running Lum's, a regional restaurant chain. In Sandy Springs, the couple bought "a big glass house that overlooked the river and the wilderness area. . . . It was just beautiful . . . so peaceful." Barbara Davis Blum's activism began when she discovered that Fulton County was going to run a sewer line along the riverbank of her own property.[145] McKenzie's involvement in the campaign came somewhat later, when first contacted by an old friend from another wealthy Buckhead family who had joined the "river rats," followed by an entreaty from Terry. She used her position on the board of the Atlanta Junior League, a highly selective association of the city's most socially prominent women, to fund and then preside over a new group: Friends of the River.[146]

These four core activists' homes suggest the range of suburbs from which river preservationists hailed (map 4.3). Buerki lived in a white middle- to working-class neighborhood out from the industrial suburb of Marietta; Claude Terry in an ethnically mixed inner suburb within BOND, south of Druid Hills; and McKenzie's Buckhead was in an inner suburban island of

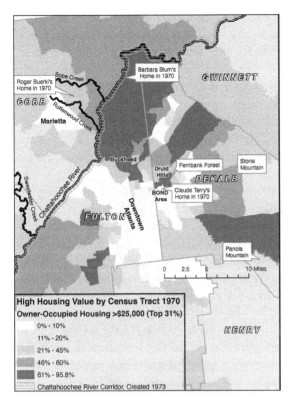

MAP 4.3. Homes of Save the River activists by 1970 housing value. Map by author. *Sources*: Manson et al., *IPUMS National Historical Geographic Information System*; "Georgia: White Pages; Atlanta, Northeast, Nov 70," Library of Congress, accessed November 6, 2022, https://www.loc .gov/item/usteledireco6252/.

wealth. As in other suburbs around U.S. cities over the mid-twentieth century, these property-owning Atlantans enjoying considerable social and economic security and organized mostly to save a nature distinct from their own domesticated "neighborhoods," the wilder stretches of river lying not so far away. Only Blum owned a suburban home along the river itself, by this time a luxury-home segment of Atlanta's growth machine, "Atlanta's answer to the Gold Coast." By 1970 the northerly banks of the Chattahoochee had attracted the greatest share of high-end homes in the metropolis. Developers too were cashing in on the huge premiums the city's most affluent whites were willing to pay for custom-made homes "designed with the view in mind," even with "a view of the river from every room in the house."[147]

What residents already living there or not so far away were up against were impending threats from a multitude of cogs in the city's growth machine, intent as it was on also bringing all other manner of private development to the Chattahoochee's banks. Very near where Buerki and his daughters had gone wandering, near the recently completed interstate beltway, I-285, riverine properties had become among the region's most promising locations for new stores, offices, and, along the riverbanks, apartments with picturesque views. Other allied construction along the Chattahoochee and its tributaries that provoked activists' ire came not from private developers but from a local officialdom newly compelled to lay more sewer lines. Responding to river activists' censure of despoiled or threatened riverbanks, Cobb commissioner Ernest Barrett defended the sewer projects as curbing "pollution," while grumbling, "Now that we're doing something about it, look what thanks we get."[148] Sewer routes castigated by activists had often been authorized by Rock Howard's Georgia Water Quality Control Board and funded by the Federal Water Pollution Control Administration, predecessor to the Environmental Protection Agency (EPA).

A story told by Buerki about an apartment developer who, during the movement's early days, sought his approval captures the clash of mindsets that led activists like Buerki toward other ways of mobilizing support. The developer, whom Buerki met at a conservancy-sponsored dinner, invited the "river rat" out to the site of his riverside apartment complex, hoping to persuade him of his own conservation mindedness. Led by this developer out to the parcel of around fifteen acres, "on top of the hill overlooking the creek," Buerki immediately saw that "it's all bulldozed and there's a tiny little sapling about that diameter [he pointed to a living room lamp stem] in the middle of those only because there was a surveyor's flag on it." Just look around, the developer urged his guest, conjuring up "wood-sided apartments nestled amongst the trees," whose windows would look out on the woods and waterfront. For him rural nature's endurance remained a given; a single development or developer had little chance of threatening it. What Buerki zeroed in on, though, was that "tiny little sapling," a poignant echo of the many trees already lost to the project, of how much riverfront had already been despoiled. For Buerki, in glaring contrast, as for most other "river rats," it had become far more difficult to miss what the hand of developers had wrought.[149]

Unlike this developer and more like those who went on conservancy field trips, Buerki and other proponents of the new environmental citizenship had learned how to see and appreciate this and other less touched nature more from the outside, even when near the places they lived. Compared to the outside lens of ecological science that conservancy brought to bear, Buerki's and other river activists' view came through particular modes of play, another mode of environmental consumption. For him that vehicle was the hiking and other outdoor activities he'd pursued as member of a Sierra Club chapter in the Cascades. Atlanta gained its own chapter of the Sierra Club in 1968, adding to the array of organized hiking or "field trips" available to city residents, those modern and neorustic ways of "getting back to nature."[150] The growth and organization of river-based water sports was also critical to the Chattahoochee preservation movement. For canoers such as Terry, who drove out to north Georgia rivers like the Chattooga when he had time, the clos-

PHOTO 4.4. Palisades of the Chattahoochee, 2013. Cliffs lined the river as it coursed through parts of northern Atlanta, along where activists of the early seventies successfully strove to turn the Chattahoochee into a public park. Photo by Christopher Sellers.

est place to practice lay in Atlanta's shadow—the Chattahoochee (at least up past the Clayton plant).[151] The more explosively popular Chattahoochee sport, however, was rafting. The Great Raft Race, originally sponsored by a fraternity at Georgia Tech, then picked up in 1970 by a popular DJ, began drawing thousands of young people into the Chattahoochee's waves, conveying themselves by "tubes, boats, rafts, and whatever else floats."[152] Preservation activists themselves also began inviting officials and influential figures of all sorts to canoe the river with them—and freely offered training not just in paddling but in *seeing*, presumably also appreciating. One such trip past those "towering tree-lined granite cliffs that overlook the river near 1-285"—the Palisades—drew a floating entourage of fifty, including an impressed reporter for the *Atlanta Constitution*. He recorded a newcomer's surprise at "such an undisturbed corner of the metropolis": "Why, it's just like being in the mountains!"[153]

Activists also forged other ways of spreading word and imagery of just what was at stake. Using his own camera, Buerki produced a slideshow of the banks along the Rottenwood that would be lost and then shopped it around to whomever he could get to watch it. To spark greater appreciation for what might be lost, they coined names for some of the most impressive natural features. Cliffs along one bend of the river, for instance, came to be called "the Palisades." That name reportedly grew out of a conversation Buerki had with Terry, who compared them favorably to cliffs of the same name he had recently visited along the Hudson River, already preserved as parkland. Buerki and others also turned to raft racers as well as weekend tubers to try and build a movement on the river's behalf.[154]

Their frank approval of this demonstrably "mass" enjoyment of the river marked a clear departure from the conservancy's preference for inhibiting public access and for plying influence mainly at top levels, often behind the scenes. It also suggested very different ideas about just what and whom preservation was for: it would not be just for scientists and "conservation" education, nor would entry be strictly controlled, as conservancy spokespeople had envisioned for Panola. Their effort to create a public nature park along the Chattahoochee stood in stark contrast to the more subdued, behind-the-scenes style of conservancy leadership, who gained a reputation among some of them as too corporation-friendly. As a more ecologically authentic preservation took a more broadly participatory turn, river preservationists turned to other newer allies, groups that had also emerged to inspire and channel the new environmental citizenship. Among these were an outfit calling itself SAVE (Save Our Vital Environment), headed by another erstwhile conservancy activist Jane Yarn, and Georgia's Sierra Club chapters.

Securing the time and commitments of like-minded citizen groups was just the beginning to the citizenly work of river activists; a multilayered officialdom also needed to be approached, lobbied, and swayed. Many county, regional, and state officials proved willing to at least be courted, but the most critical ally turned out to be the federal Bureau of Outdoor Recreation (BOR). Its Atlanta office head, Roy Wood, made the activists aware of a new initiative by interior secretary Walter Hickel to nominate lands within metropolitan areas to be made into a new kind of national park, lying within cities rather than far beyond them. In the fall of 1970, Wood's office suggested to federal higher-ups that the Chattahoochee River corridor be nominated to become one of the nation's first urban national parks. Intrigued, their bosses in Washington authorized an in-depth study of how it might happen.[155]

Over the first year of river-saving activism, from the spring of 1970 through 1971, while river savers lost the battle over Rottenwood, they attained some important breakthroughs, aided by how a portion of Atlanta's elite as well as state officials began stepping up.[156] Kay McKenzie secured a grant from the Junior Leaguers to pay for the staff and office of a new group, the Friends of the River, whose first meeting in June 1971 drew some seventy-five people "to begin a major recruiting program."[157] While Cobb and Fulton continued to approve developments along the river's banks, the election of a new governor who was himself a conservancy member, Jimmy Carter, stoked hopes about state-level action.[158] Then, after a year-long extensive study and consultation with its own "citizen's advisory" group, the Bureau of Outdoor Recreation announced its vision for a series of six federally run parks—a "string of pearls" stretching all the way from Peachtree Creek, just above the Clayton plant on the Cobb County side, up through Fulton and DeKalb into Forsyth County, just a few miles shy of Buford Dam. By the federal government's hand, a viable regional blueprint now existed for a public park along the northern Chattahoochee, "a positive, precedent-setting answer to the challenge of Atlanta's urban crisis." "An opportunity exists in the Atlanta metropolitan area," BOR's report declared, "to stem the disregard for the natural and scenic qualities of the environment, to make up in part for yesterday's obscured vision and error."[159]

A park-friendly Carter governorship was meanwhile laying legal groundwork for preserving the river's banks as funds were sought for their public purchase, through an unprecedented (for Atlanta as well as Georgia) empowerment of regional governance. In late 1971 the legislature revamped what had been a strictly part-time and advisory body—the Atlanta Region Metropolitan Planning Commission—into an Atlanta Regional Commission (ARC). It gained actual state financing and, for the first time, some enforceable decision-making power over local governments across the metro region, especially should their planning and zoning efforts clash. The new head of the commission, Dan Sweat, took up the question of Chattahoochee-corridor zoning as his first exercise of the ARC's newfound authority.[160] His hand strengthened considerably in 1973, when the state legislature and governor agreed on an enforceable multicounty plan for land use along the Chattahoochee from Atlanta northward.

For the state of Georgia, it signaled just how far the reigning approach to government had come since Talmadgism. A regional governing body had now received legally actionable oversight over privately owned rural lands.[161] Of course, developmental restrictions alone did not yet fulfill the goals of river defenders; they continued their campaign for public acquisition of many of these lands. But that cause would not find success until Jimmy Carter was elected president. For now the land-use planning bill ensured that enough riverside land would remain suitable for federal park making five years later, when Carter signed the bill finally creating a Chattahoochee National Recreation Area.[162]

Forging new ways for Atlantans not just to save surrounding countryside and wilderness but also many of their own living environments, especially if visibly natural, Atlantans brought a new environmental style of citizenship to their city and state. Like the many new veins of civil rights citizenship, those making up a broadening environmental movement were largely born out of the compression capitalism of the postwar decades, in this case through the expanding ranks, improving education and skills, and higher hopes it brought to white, middle and upper-middle classes. And the several faces of Atlanta's environmental movement quickly joined those of its movement for civil rights to advance the democratization of both city and state. Not just the rapidly rising power and influence of Black politicians in Atlanta but its speedy acquisition of a formidable environmental movement betokened how this southern city was gravitating toward a national mainstream. If Atlanta's Black and environmental leaders began to forge alliances of convenience, however, the perspectives and values of their respective movements, as well as their demographic bases, remained locked in what often seemed separate worlds, even as Black activists actually took up what we can recognize today as environmental concerns.

The arrival of a self-identified environmental movement in Atlanta also helped draw new battle lines in Georgia's enduring contest between city and country. James Dickey's novel *Deliverance* (1970), quickly made into a movie in which Claude Terry and other river rats applied their canoeing skills, captured the internal aspirations as well as new practices sending Atlantans countryward, along with an utter hostility and lack of empathy toward rural whites.[163] Dickey himself, born and bred in the wealthy enclave of Buckhead, portrayed a journey of four white Atlanta men up to a mountain river before it is dammed—a plot based on the damming of the Chattahoochee to create Lake Lanier in the late fifties. Seeking reprieve from humdrum jobs in advertising and too-domesticated suburban home lives through a thrill-seeking trip, they undertake an arduous, unrelenting challenge through which they each hope to reawaken their own more authentic primitive selves. Part and parcel of what brings them this experience, those who survive, is the war into which they fall with hostile mountain folk.

In this corner of the rural South, there are no jungles and no Blacks; it is an all-white wilderness, whose rural denizens have become the unfathomable, and disposable, primitives. The very practices that Dickey's Atlantans come here to pursue augur their sharp differences with the locals: a bow-and-arrow style of hunting rather than mountain dwellers' customary rifles and a plan to canoe the river's rapids that natives find absurd, since "fishing's no good." From the first encounter, old tropes of the "hillbilly" and "white trash" get recycled: "Oree was sleepy and hookwormy and ugly, and most of all inconsequential." Beginning with the conviction that "nobody worth a damn could ever come from such a place," they quickly move from suspecting the natives to assuming the worst and treating them accordingly.[164] Those breaching this code, the two actually reaching out to locals (Bobby with his spurned compliment of a man's hat; Drew who strikes up a guitar/banjo medley with a "demented country kid") are either raped or killed by wandering mountaineers. After the river-riding trip turns into a bloody hunt, in which the canoers must kill or be killed, death of the natives is what elicits the narrator's most stinging disdain. One is "repulsive, useless"; as for the other, "it seemed obvious that he was so nondescript, even for Helms County, that he would probably not be missed by more than a few, and probably not much by them."[165]

As a political allegory, the book and movie echoed the decades-long struggle of Atlantans against the state's rural power and those less-than-democratic governing structures that both Atlanta's environmental and civil rights movements struggled to dismantle and reorder. In stark fashion *Deliverance* channeled its disdain onto a white rural working class that would later emerge as an Achilles heel of the new environmentalism. But over the shorter run of the 1970s, new federal environmental laws wound up tilting Georgia's governments to favor preservation advocates and pollution's victims alike. Ushering in this more environmentally protective state was that same governor who had helped enable Chattahoochee River zoning: conservancy member Jimmy Carter. And in 1976, with Carter's election to the nation's highest office, he advanced to the helm of an executive branch with vastly expanded reach over the many, still swelling set of issues now falling under the "environmental" umbrella. In this most momentous of ways, Atlantans themselves gained impacts on the nation's own environmental politics, even as their city veered into its own democratic heyday.

CHAPTER 5

Jimmy Carter, Black Power, and the New Environmental State

My initiation into the political phenomenon that was Jimmy Carter came in the first months of 1976, when I drove up to Asheville, North Carolina, to attend a first meeting of his primary campaign for president in the western region of my state. That a high school senior should drive for half an hour to walk into a hotel conference room full of people I had never met, for a candidate I knew so little about, bespeaks the promise that a political figure like Carter could hold for southerners such as myself in these years. He seemed far the superior alternative to so many other southern politicians like Lester Maddox or George Wallace, who made national news by standing astride the doorway of regional progress and slinging racial slurs. Carter did win, of course, though with little help from me aside from my vote, bound for a northeastern college as I was. That he won not just the Democratic nomination but the presidency had much to do with what I remember seeing in him: a white southern leader who had somehow stepped out of the Wallace mold.

Prior to his presidential run, that reputation owed mostly to Carter's one-term leadership of his home state. He had ushered Georgia's capital through what became the final leg of the state's midcentury democratic transition, toward a newly inclusive and representative electorate that bolstered the hand of the Democratic Party's civil rights–friendly "moderates." The Carter governorship also consolidated other facets of democratization underway at least since Carl Sanders's term in the governor's mansion, building up state government in more broadly distributive and protective ways. That meant expanding public services to benefit less affluent or privileged swathes of society, Blacks as well as whites; it also meant sweeping new environmental protections. These accomplishments brought Atlanta and Georgia more into the nation's political mainstream, while also staving off the Georgia Republican surge from the mid- to late sixties that had cut short the congressional career of James Mackay. Carter's legacy, the Georgia Democratic Party's own more government-friendly and equitable substitute for rustic rule, would endure there for another two decades and more, until neoconservative Republicans found their way to power.

The springboard for his successful national campaign for president, Carter's gubernatorial record has gone largely unconsidered among historians evaluating his presidency. Most interested in situating Carter against other presidents, they see his administration as pivoting U.S. political history away from a long period of state building: as the "first in a line of post–New Deal/Great Society Democratic Presidents" and as the initiator of the growing, promarket assault on government's size and role now known as neoliberalism.[1] Seen more from the standpoint of the region from which Carter hailed, those antistatist and deregulatory directions he did pursue as president were not that "post" or "neo" at all, but stubborn, nationally projected norms of Georgia's own political economy and culture. In this state, where the business-skeptical orientation of unions had been so effectively marginalized even as per capita income continued to trail those in other U.S. regions, a soft spot for the private corporation prevailed among Georgia politicians, Jimmy Carter among them. But what was customary for Georgia seemed new when emanating from a Carter White House.

Readings of Carter as the first post–New Deal or neoliberal president also have yet to reckon with one area in which his administration did undertake robust state building: the environment. Both as governor and as president, Carter led governments stepping up their restraints on pollution and other harmful interventions in people's surroundings, clarifying and expanding his constituents' rights as *environmental* citizens. Especially from the standpoint of many Atlantans, in no realm were Carter's governorship and presidency more dynamic or influential, often weighing against corporations and other powerful interests on the public's behalf. Through the decade of the seventies, as Georgia implemented new federal environmental rules and added measures of its own, governmental interventions deepened across the Atlanta region into private companies' technologies, routines, and production lines. Some of these, at least, such as the restrictive zoning of the northern Chattahoochee, arose in direct response to Atlantans' own organized expressions of environmental citizenship, especially under a governor who was himself a charter conservancy member. Additionally, from environmental impact statements to tightened rules against air and water pollution, a blizzard of other new tools and programs came more from the top down, as state and federal agencies carried out a slew of new environmental laws.

While many of these new laws were federal, Georgia's late twentieth-century Democratic governors eagerly embraced most of the new environmental state building—with the notable exception of workplace controls—as their own. What Sanders had started, Governor Carter brought to full fruition, ending that freedom to pollute that a white supremacist state had extended to corporations as well as municipalities. The new environmental state also opened up unprecedented avenues of influence for environmentalists and

PHOTO 5.1. Gov. Jimmy Carter paddling along the Chattahoochee River's Palisades, 1972. Carter paddled a canoe on a Friends of the River–sponsored trip to publicize the river's wilder stretches and to back regional restrictions on riverbank development. Courtesy of Steve Jackson/*Atlanta Journal-Constitution* via AP, Atlanta Constitution Photographic Archives, Georgia State University Special Collections.

other civic activists. An entire new architecture coalesced to invite more citizen involvement in environmental policy making and new opportunities for citizenly praxis that took Atlanta and Georgia another step forward in their transition from racial authoritarianism to democracy. When it came to Georgia's workplaces, however, a soft spot for business still reigned, and federal regulators had to repeatedly step in.

Within this reconfigured terrain of environmental politics, a tension also began to stir, with critical implications for the new environmental citizenship. A technocratic ethos began to creep into the environmental regimes coalescing under the Carter governorship and presidency all-too reminiscent of that pervading 1950s planning expertise, whose pursuit of urban renewal and freeway building had invited so little public input. New requirements for public hearings and other participation had been written into the new environmental legislation of the late 1960s and 1970s to keep such inclinations in check. But the evenhandedness of what Adam Rome has dubbed the "environmental management state" leaned not just on its openness to public input but on its resort to science and expertise. Whatever was said at any hearing, measurements or other scientific confirmations of danger or harm were what was supposed to trigger the exercise of all this newfound public power. While expert assessments and metrics provided legally enforceable terms through which an agency could encourage or enforce polluters to comply—driving a corporate environmental citizenship—they posed new hurdles for environmental activism by aggrieved communities. What continuing role could ordinary citizens have in this new environmental oversight? Without specialized scientific and legal knowledge, their concerns might not really be heard by a new environmental officialdom. Though Carter himself recognized the political need for allowing more citizen input, he not infrequently chafed at its messages. He was more inclined toward what political scientists term "managerial liberalism": "undertaken by technocratic, expert-driven bodies and bureaucracies that are at best indirectly accountable to the public."[2] Among the flaws of managerial liberalism, exploited in succeeding decades by a waxing environmental opposition, it took public and political support for its work largely for granted. It did so even while narrowing the input that mattered most in public forums, to what those with deep pockets and their own experts found easiest to provide. Even as its appointed officials proceeded as though detached from political tides, however, the elected leaders on which it depended could not.

In early 1970s Atlanta the separate and sometimes conflicting projects of environmental and civil rights citizenship were both sufficiently organized and influential that politicians seeking to earn support of a majority of Atlantans had to seek out ways of appealing to both. Carter's quest for higher office began by drawing environmental activists to his side; only after becoming governor did he seek more favor from advocates of civil rights. The city's ascendant Black political leadership, on the other hand, from Rep. Andrew Young to Maynard Jackson, started with that civil rights citizenship with which their own careers had begun. They carefully aligned their outreach toward its recent accents on economics and "Black power," albeit a Black power of coat-and-tie wearing and glad-handing rather than raised fists. Both also realized they needed to appeal to white environmental and neighborhood activists. During Jackson's first term his coalition bridging these two political projects effectively overthrew Atlanta's long-standing business-dominated power structure, bringing the city's postwar democratization to its historic peak. Jackson's deeper adherence to the environmental concerns of poorer and Blacker neighborhoods also led his administration's experimentation with a more participatory version of environmental governance, in tension with a predominantly white neighborhood movement and at odds with Carter's more expert-driven mode of governing.

Carter's Ascent and the
New Politics of Inequality

Stepping before his fellow Georgia Conservancy members in November 1969 while prepping a gubernatorial campaign, Jimmy Carter presented himself as the polar opposite of *Deliverance*'s rural stereotypes: a literate and sophisticated country dweller genuinely attuned to the nature around him. Declaiming "man's close and unbreakable tie to nature" with lines from Dylan Thomas, he also flashed through more personal environmental bona fides: a rural childhood "fishing for catfish and eels" and, in the navy, his piloting of an atomic submarine "listening to whales." While praising the conservancy's efforts at "the preservation of remote and relatively exclusive places," he saw these as "skirmishes" anticipating greater struggles to come, as "conservation" strode into the "crowded communities of men." The "multicolored smoke palls" out from Savannah and the South DeKalb streams "covered with foam and thick oily scum" showed that "we have not loved the land." He then suggested a sweeping reparative goal for his own governorship, "a grand design so dynamic and forceful that every decision of government and industry will be guided by its effect on our environment."[3]

Carter probably had little clue at this moment just how far his own political career would carry his state and nation along on this road. For Atlantans and other Georgians, the Carter governorship consolidated a powerful new environmental state, a further step to democratization wrought by the rising influence of a newly affluent and patrimonial middle class. Further wrenching the government of Georgia out of its constricted and decidedly undemocratic mold under Jim Crow, Carter's governing innovations brought it closer to a U.S. mainstream. Yet contrasts persisted with counterparts in north and north-central regions; instead, Georgia joined the Sunbelt, coming to more closely resemble the business-friendly as well as union-hostile Texas and Arizona. Not just Georgia's overall economic growth under compressive capitalism but the continuing unevenness with which its new wealth spread suggest some underlying reasons why.

Only over the 1960s into the 1970s did the average Georgian's economic fortunes finally converge with those enjoyed in other, long wealthier U.S. regions. Georgians' per capita income surged past southeastern rivals such as Alabama, up from three-quarters of the U.S. average in the late 1950s to nearly 86 percent by the early 1970s.[4] By then the 61 percent homeownership among Georgians was also only a couple of percentage points lower than the U.S. average and up nearly nine points from two decades ago.[5] Unions' pushes for higher wages contributed to these rises especially in Atlanta and other union-dense parts of the state, as unionization ticked up by 1970 to 16.1 percent of Georgia's workforce.[6] Historic as that peak was for this state, however, a right-to-work law and the steady stoking of antiunion attitudes helped keep unionization rates half or even lower than those in the western and northern regions of the country.[7] Partly as a consequence, Georgia and other southern states, while on the whole no longer that much poorer than other parts of the United States, remained national bastions of economic inequality. By the standard measure used by social scientists for tallying how skewed incomes are, the Gini index, Georgia's economic inequality ranked the eleventh highest in the United States by 1969, bested by seven southern states and just three outside the South (Oklahoma, South Dakota, and New Mexico).[8] Continuing racial barriers explain much of this persisting inequality in the U.S. Southeast: despite the new civil rights laws, most Blacks still had fewer job, housing, and other economic opportunities than did whites.[9] But the divide between the city and the countryside, dominating Georgia's white politics for so long, also contributed mightily. While Atlanta's own poverty remained obdurate, as we have seen, and concentrated among the city's Blacks, by 1970 Black Atlantans on the whole actually earned a significantly higher median income than did Georgia's rural whites.[10] Even after its economy began to take off after 1960, Georgia's postwar economic gains accrued far less to its rural reaches than to its cities, especially Atlanta, the still-compressive thrust of its capitalism notwithstanding.

Carter exploited this divide especially in his second successful campaign for governor, initially appealing to a disaffected rural vote despite an earlier reputation as a political "moderate." He had first gone into politics after returning from a stint in the navy to his family farm in Plains, Georgia, two-and-a-half hours' drive from Atlanta, which he had famously converted into a peanut agribusiness. Though his father had been a Talmadge man, he entered and won his first race, for the state senate in 1962, by personally taking on the autocratic rule that had long prevailed in rural Georgia.[11] In his first run for Georgia's governorship, in 1966, he had placed a surprising third in the Democratic primary won by Maddox. After a few years shoring up "moderate" credentials especially in an emergent environmental realm—chairing a southwest Georgia planning group, sponsoring the act creating a Natural Areas Council, and joining the Georgia Conservancy itself—he entered the 1970 governor's race. Competing against former governor Carl Sanders, now the odds-on favorite and Atlanta-based, and against the Atlanta lawyer and former SCLC lieutenant Chevenne B. King, who was Black, Carter sought to appeal mainly to white voters in the countryside.

Honing a chameleon-like ability that in this still-transitional period in Georgia's political history would prove eminently useful, the forty-six-year-old Carter played both sides of the state's color line but leaned white, even white supremacist. While he did visit with Atlanta's Black voters, pledging support for their interests, he also conveyed the impression among rural whites that he would defend segregation. He did so not through any policy promises but through "populist symbols" (as his campaign director put it): promising to invite George Wallace to Georgia, declaring Lester Maddox "the essence" of the Georgia Democratic Party, and projecting a rugged, rustic persona through ads that showed him, for instance, harvesting peanuts in family fields. He also effectively tied Sanders to city elites, as "cuff-link Carl." One ad zoomed in on a closed door, identified by voice-over as "to an exclusive country club, where the big-money boys play cards, drink cocktails and raise money for their candidate, Carl Sanders. People like us aren't invited. We're too busy working for a living."[12] Carter's campaign pitch to a white rural working-class leaned on a long and sturdy tradition running back to populist times that had also propped up Talmadgism, pitting ordinary hardworking country folks against the city's moneyed elites.

While Carter also worked hard to draw the votes of the state's newly organized environmentalists, white urban professionals that so many of them were, his campaign was so racially tinged that in his successful runoff with Sanders he drew only 7 percent of the Black vote. In line, also, with Georgia's earlier rustic rulers, Carter's win overcame unanimous opposition from the AFL-CIO and other unions, which endorsed his opponent, Sanders. Playing to the stubborn disdain for unions among so many whites in the Georgia countryside, when a rumor circulated that Sanders had voiced support for a repeal of Georgia's right-to-work law—widely seen as a nonstarter in Georgia politics—he leaped to make that charge stick. Even though Sanders himself denied it, Carter insinuated his opponent had thereby sold out to the "ultraliberal wing" of the Democratic Party.[13] In the runoff Sanders won Atlanta's core and suburban counties of Fulton, DeKalb, and Cobb but wound up with half as many votes as Carter, who swept the rural counties. Then trouncing his Republican opponent in November's general election, Carter cruised into the governor's mansion with few knowing exactly what to expect about his priorities, environmental or otherwise. His political chameleonship was well fitted to winning in a state where established traditions of rule had recently fallen away. But once he was elected, the pressure grew on him to cast his lot, to lean toward one side or another of the state's deep political divides, especially between the white supremacists he had courted and Georgia's strong and outspoken advocates for civil rights. He did that rhetorically from day one, renouncing the race baiting of Maddox and rustic rulers and pledging allegiance to a personalized version of civil rights citizenship.

The "time for racial discrimination is over," he declared in his inaugural address, surprising many who had followed his campaign and disappointing not a few supporters. The *Atlanta Constitution*'s Bill Shipp applauded him: "For a Georgia governor to come out four-square against racial discrimination in his very first speech as governor was, to say the least, precedent-shattering."[14] That pledge constituted the most public break the state had yet seen from the long tradition of overt white supremacist rhetoric Georgians had heard from their governors under rustic rule. Carter's antidiscriminatory talk came to be followed by some walking, symbolic as well as more substantive. He brought a portrait of Martin Luther King Jr. into the governor's mansion and was able to diffuse a racial standoff in Hancock County that threatened to turn violent by sending out three mediators rather than state troopers. He made a concerted effort to appoint more Blacks to state government, starting with important commissions and governing bodies, followed by a mandate for all state agencies to hire more Blacks as well as women. Some of these moves might not have happened without steady outside pressure, as when a Black state representative threatened to request federal scrutiny of the state's discriminatory hiring practices. Carter as governor invested little political capital in policies specifically to serve the cause of civil rights or benefit Georgia's or Atlanta's Blacks. But his distinctly egalitarian notions about just whom government should serve did resonate with principles Atlanta's civil rights activists had urged since the mid-1960s, that "no poor, rural, weak, or Black person should ever have to bear the additional burden of being deprived of the opportunity of an education, a job or simple justice."[15]

Striving after color blindness, the Carter administration sought ways of dispensing public funds that overcame decades of state neglect of Atlanta and other cities as well as Georgia's African Americans, nearly half of whom now lived in urbanized areas and who had long endured the worst of rustic rulers' penury.[16] Carter appointees to state agencies specialized in technocratic fixes, new rules and routines through which they and their staff could redress these long-standing inequities. The Highway Department instituted policies to ensure each part of the state got its fair share of road construction. Educational reforms sought to ensure the same for funding of schools and implemented a statewide public kindergarten program that began with "economically disadvantaged students"—mostly Black.[17] The Carter governorship thereby added a late equalizing boost to Georgia's rising expenditures on public goods and welfare as it democratized. Converging on national norms, state and local per capita spending on education were hiking up from 61 percent of the U.S. average in 1942 to over 80 percent by 1976 and, on health and hospitals, from only 53 percent to a whopping 145 percent—nearly three times as much. In the realm of parks and recreation, the increase was more recent and still lagging, from 47.9 percent in 1957 to 73 percent of the average per capita spending for U.S. states.[18] As to where these funds came from, Carter's tax and other policies abandoned the Talmadgist tradition of asking less of the rich and also sought a scrupulous evenhandedness between what it asked for from the state's urban and rural residents. He kept his pledge not to raise the state sales tax, for instance, a regressive source of income made the state's main revenue source under Talmadgism, and he vetoed an effort to make sales taxes a local option. But the extra taxes earlier imposed on urban Georgia by rustic rulers often led the Carter administration to ask more from rural Georgians, to balance out the burden: increasing fees for hunting and fishing licenses and raising the gasoline tax to pay for more urban road building, while offering tax relief to city homeowners.[19]

In another definitive break with Talmadgism, Carter refused to tout Georgia's lower wages or offer tax breaks and other incentives to bring new industries and jobs to Georgia. In meetings with other southern governors and business leaders, he was outspoken in his criticism of "let[ting] industry take advantage of Southern people" in such ways. Asserting that "wage earners in the Southland should be paid the same wage rates as those in the rest of the nation," he still never went so far as to suggest a repeal of right-to-work law, though by strengthening the state's unions, that could have pushed wages further upward.[20] Instead, his administration concentrated on expanding the industries covered through its unemployment fund, to better provide for laid-off workers who lost their jobs.[21] Moreover, Carter also had an embattled relationship with his own state's Labor Department, run by a separately elected official, Sam Caldwell. This being Georgia, Labor Commissioner Caldwell was no friend of labor unions himself but a Talmadgist protégé, whose pathway into the job had come through the State Highway Department. From within Carter's own executive branch, he and his department became among the governor's most outspoken nemeses, accusing him of neglecting the recruitment of new industries and jobs and seeking to torpedo what Carter came to see as one of his greatest accomplishments: reorganizing the state's bureaucracy.[22]

Carter's first major priority as governor was a reorganization of the state's entire executive branch. He thereby sought to wrest the jerry-built profusion of agencies and offices accumulated under clientelism and rustic rule into a more manageable, effective, and increasingly technocratic shape.[23] On the face of it, reorganization seemed unideological: who could argue against the efficiency and savings that would come from whittling the "muddled maze of nearly 300 separate departments, commissions, bureaus and authorities" down to a few "super-agencies"?[24] Nevertheless, the goal of streamlining also entailed constructing a more hierarchical chain of command, a priority drawing on Carter's engineering and military backgrounds but, perhaps most influentially, on the managerial values and mindset he shared with the business world. Corporate Georgia dominated the group of private citizens helping him craft the restructuring plan. Corporations not being very democratic places, the hierarchical models espoused by their representatives, mostly endorsed by Carter, led to accusations he was an autocrat, that he sought a "power grab" to "concentrate power in the hands of the governor."[25] Taking great pains to stave off these critiques, Carter pitched his reorganization as try-ing to "mak[e] state agencies and government personnel more responsive and effective" to Georgia's elected leadership, hence *more* democratic.[26] Ostensibly to help guide the effort, he also launched an experiment in participatory plan-ning echoing Mackay's citizen panels, christened "Goals for Georgia." Some nineteen daylong meetings were convened across the state to discuss what the reorganization should look like, with "any citizen" welcome to join. Overseen over the spring and summer of 1971 by the Georgia Planning Association as well as regional counterparts, these meetings purportedly gave "thousands of Georgians" the opportunity to provide "hundreds of suggestions about what their government should be doing."[27]

Like the Panels for Progress in the Fifth Congressional District six years earlier, the very format of these meetings favored the college-educated, and here even more constraints were placed on citizens' own input. Attendees' main job at the regional meetings was to provide commentary on eight work-books preassembled by officials and university experts and already winnowed by the state planning board. While discussions could drift away from pre-scribed topics and choices, experts and officials dominated especially the fi-nal roundup conference, held in Atlanta. For the "natural environment," the result was a seventeen-page tally of recommendations based on "goals" of an "average citizen"—neither Black nor white, rich nor poor, city nor country dweller. Whatever ideas and opinions had been voiced were reduced to a few bland generalizations: "He [*sic*] wants a hihg-quality [*sic*] environment to en-joy; where the quality is still high, he wants it protected and preserved; where it is low, he wants it restored, to the full extent that is feasible and economi-cally reasonable; he certainly wants that it not be further degraded." The main obstacles were "fragmentation" or "weakness" in the state bureaucracy; the main fixes were "strong" and "rationally coordinated" agencies, even a "single state authority . . . a single Department of the Environment or Environmen-tal Protection Division."[28] Small wonder reporters found the communication flows in Goals for Georgia gatherings mostly one way, amounting to "public information hearings on the reorganization project."[29]

As the reorganization plan wended its way to passage, it nevertheless gen-erated sparks, becoming "undoubtedly one the of most controversial pieces of legislation in the history of the General Assembly."[30] Bland as changes to a bu-reaucracy might look on paper, Georgia's was riddled with fiefdoms, each with settled outside constituencies who worried about being short-changed or cut off, from teachers to doctors to timber companies, hunters, and fishers. Labor Commissioner Sam Caldwell was among the most outspoken critics, charging that a reorganization scheme to remove the workplace inspectorate from his department originated with a Georgia Power lobbyist.[31] Robert Hanie, still at the Natural Areas Council, as well as Rock Howard of the Water Quality

Control Board both worried a proposed plan to folder their units into a larger agency would reduce their "effectiveness" and "political independence." Hanie went so far as to resign in frustration.[32] Carter nevertheless finally won over first his elected cabinet members, including Caldwell, then the legislature. The workplace inspectors, while they stayed in the Labor Department, were now to be overseen by the Workers Compensation Board rather than the labor commissioner. Howard's and Hanie's environmental agencies were now fused with eighteen separate others into a new, overarching Environmental Protection Division. In the wake of all the requisite approvals, Carter himself publicly expressed his own satisfaction: now, like a president, "I can call a meeting of 21 state department heads who cover the whole gamut of state governmental functions."[33] Legislative approval placed a democratic stamp on Carter's accomplishment: a state government ordered by function, with a clearer—and more hierarchical—chain of command. Drawing still more directly on corporate models, the "zero-base budgeting" also instituted by Carter extended like controls to agency budgets, by requiring every agency to formally justify all of its expenditures each and every year.[34]

Outside of reorganization it was in the realm of "preserving natural resources" that Carter himself remembered having devoted the most time as governor. That is also where some historians find his biggest accomplishments.[35] Julian Zelizer points to an illustrative story that Carter told in his autobiography written for his presidential campaign, about confronting the U.S. Army Corps of Engineers over a dam planned for the Flint River, about fifty miles southeast of Atlanta. The corps had long touted all the recreation, electricity, and even water purification the dam would bring, and former-governor and new-senator Herman Talmadge—as well as Carter himself, initially—supported it. But Carter changed his mind and launched a successful fight against the project, joined by Atlanta's as well as other environmentalists along with state and federal recreation agencies.[36] While affirming Carter's environmentalist bona fides, this one story fails to capture the burgeoning scope of his administration's environmental oversight of private as well as public spaces across metropolitan Atlanta. Nor does it reflect how his technocratic inclinations could not just align but clash with the environmental goals of this city's active and organized citizenry.

The New Environmental Oversight, Phase 1

While Georgia's state government had already been stepping up its oversight of pollution as well its park making, the Carter administration enjoyed two advantages over its predecessors that enabled it to do more. First, its chief executive was already well versed in and committed to many environmental causes. Among Carter's initial moves was to set up a Georgia Heritage Fund to begin public purchase of "special lands," among them, the first acreage for Panola Mountain and Chattahoochee parks.[37] Second, environmentally speaking, Carter faced a different moment in "political time" than any Georgia predecessors, including Sanders.[38] A burst of laws passed in Washington between 1967 and 1972—among the most influential, the National Environmental Policy Act, the Clean Air and Water Acts, and the Occupational Safety and Health Act—that utterly altered the ground rules for environmental conflicts. While the laws themselves and federal agencies implementing them emanated from Washington, the states were supposed to handle most enforcement. In and around Atlanta the Carter administration determined and largely carried out what the new federal laws meant "on the ground." Here Carter and his appointees looked decidedly less probusiness. They took on many corporate water and air polluters, imposing new standards of environmental citizenship for corporate Georgia, and effectively halted some Atlanta-area freeways. But their willingness to take on Georgia businesses also had its limits, especially when it came to downtown highways and workplace dangers, and the rising premium they placed on expertise began to pose new dilemmas for citizens' groups.

Environmental reviews required by the National Environmental Policy Act (NEPA) of 1969 provided Georgia's road fighters, in particular, with new and powerful weaponry.[39] Courts interpreted NEPA as ensuring that federally sponsored or funded projects not deprive anyone of "safe, healthful, productive, and aesthetically and culturally pleasing surroundings." Before a project could be approved, a "detailed statement" came to be required on its projected environmental consequences, what became known as the Environmental Impact Statement (EIS). Before Carter the Georgia State Highway Department had never contemplated any of what NEPA now suddenly required. Another new step under NEPA also delighted highway opponents: before an EIS could be approved, public hearings on it had to be held. There, interested parties could speak directly to administrators under the glare of the media, about additional impacts they foresaw. While the State Highway Department remained in charge of freeway building under Carter, NEPA ensured that a broadening array of environmental consequences would now be considered, whether broached by the state's officials and experts or by an interested public.[40]

For the more rural route of I-75 as well as the Stone Mountain Freeway, hearings and Environmental Impact Statements reinforced one another in the very ways that environmentalists hoped, aided by the new Carter administration's friendliness to their causes. In Carter's first year, the Georgia Conservancy and others expressed opposition to a route across Lake Allatoona. His new head of the Highway Department, Bert Lance, sought to forestall a repeat of earlier freeway fights stirred by his predecessor by initiating just such an impact study. To undertake it he tapped Eugene Odum, the University of Georgia ecologist who'd become involved with the conservancy. Odum's research team, by "put[ting] a value" not just on traffic relief but on "everything" including recreation, came up with what they held to be a less ecologically destructive alternative, and the Highway Department then followed their advice. Downplaying his own values and interests, Odum raved about the Highway Department's responsiveness in a characteristically technocratic manner: "never" had he "seen a more objective and less political decision." An approval by the federal transportation secretary then sealed the decision on the route change.[41] Inside the city's interstate perimeter, those who had battled the Stone Mountain Freeway for several years also marshaled NEPA's requirements effectively. In 1972 a Carter-appointed committee, also including Odum, undertook an EIS of this project, whose hearings drew out hundreds. Following the panel's recommendation that December, Carter killed the project.[42]

For that other inner-perimeter freeway, I-485, around which so much neighborhood activism had surged, Carter's Highway Department took a less accommodating approach. Early on highway officials stonewalled about the need for an environmental impact study of I-485, since the route had been approved prior to NEPA's passage. As Carter highway chief Lance dug in, asserting that that "all future highway development" hinged on its completion, opponents sued the department in 1971 to force an impact study.[43] Losing this case, the Highway Department then hired out an environmental impact study, just as the Morningside-Lenox Park Association as well as a new organized Atlanta Coalition on the Transportation Crisis (ACTC) were declaring their blanket opposition to any freeway at all. The EIS wound up supporting one of the proposed routes, but opponents caught a break when federal transportation officials deemed this EIS insufficient. Mayor Sam Massell and the board of aldermen then voted fifteen to two to reject the project.[44]

In the face of this mounting local opposition, the push for I-485 was kept alive by the stubbornness of Carter himself, belatedly stepping in to see if he could revive its fortunes. Hiring a PR firm, Carter also convened a "Governor's Conference on Transportation," ostensibly just to solicit the diverging opinions on this and other transportation matters. But even more so than in the top-down orchestration of his "Goals for Georgia," Carter's hand on this gathering was unmistakably heavy. He himself spoke at length and with audible irritation especially about I-485, calling the board of aldermen "irresponsible," and accusing them of "yielding to political pressure." Freeway opponents, shut out of conference preparations then strictly limited in the time they could speak, berated it for what it was: "not a seriously planned conference to discuss transportation issues, but rather an exercise in public relations," "to assure the construction of I-485."[45] Over 1974 the political pressure against the project snowballed; without waiting for a revised EIS, the Atlanta Regional Commission and Democratic candidate for governor George Busbee announced their opposition. By September the new mayor Maynard Jackson declared I-485 "dead as a doornail."[46]

The neighborhood movement's decisive victory on I-485 came against not just the Carter administration but a white business elite that had long lobbied for this as for other freeways and in this city was accustomed to having its way. As we will see, with Maynard Jackson's election as the city's first Black mayor, Atlanta's power structure teetered, as democracy in the city lurched toward its historical apogee. Over this same while developments in this and other environmental realms in which Georgia's government was extending its hand would ultimately corrode the capacity and durability of environmental activism by ordinary citizens.

In these early years of environmental mobilizing, a certain looseness prevailed as to who could be called an "ecologist." Early on activists who joined a cause of land or river preservation like Friends of the River could be identified by journalists under the same label they applied to Eugene Odum, as "ecologists."[47] At the same time, while the conservancy had involved academic biologists like Odum and Charles Wharton, more localized and layperson-led groups like Friends of the River soon also discovered needs for technical know-how that went beyond what volunteers such as microbiologist Terry could offer. To marshal the power and resources of government on behalf of their cause, they had to frame their own contentions about environmental damage or threats through vantage points, contexts, and lingo that the new environmental state recognized and considered actionable. They needed to grasp, for instance, the mechanics of the property transfers and easements—demanding, as one journalist put, it "a law degree with special tutoring in legal loopholes." To advocate for "natural areas" that should be spared from developers' schemes, they needed to be able to name and show evidence for the many species of riverine plant communities that needed protecting.[48] In the courts or hearing rooms where they increasingly pursued their cause, having such knowledge on hand or access to a friendly expert who could supply it became increasingly vital, especially if their message was to be heeded.

Even as inexpert activists scrambled after scientific and technical know-how of their own, skirmishes among well-established experts pointed to a growing competition among fields that amplified technical requirements for environmental studies while stirring a growing disdain for the untrained. While sanitary engineer Rock Howard, for instance, argued that "professional biologists, engineers, chemists, geologists, bacteriologists and others" "could very well qualify as professional ecologists," biologist Robert Platt thought that "ecological aspects" were best "added or introduced by ecologists and not by other disciplines." Yet both heartily agreed about those "highly vocal pseudo-ecologists and egocentrics"—without professional scientific qualifications—who "too often" wound up influencing politicians and state officials "on important public environmental issues." In such ways, even while staking out their own, sometimes competing claims, the new environmental experts downplayed or dismissed the value of input from ordinary citizens, even if living in the environment in question.[49]

Howard's own Water Control Board, operating since 1963 on the long-since professionalized turf of water pollution, was arguably the most securely technocratic of all Georgia's existing environmental agencies. Thriving during Carter's governorship, it finally gained the authority to levy fines and by early 1974 a staff of nearly a hundred and a budget reaching $6.9 million. Despite Howard's skepticism about reorganization, once his own unit was absorbed into the new environmental "superagency," Carter promptly put him in charge of all this new outfit's enforcement work. Enabled by new federal laws and programs as well as Carter's support, Howard led a ratcheting up of pressure on both municipal and corporate polluters.[50] Among industrialists seeking to bring new plants to the state, his refusal to compromise environmental standards gained him a reputation for "hardheadedness," along with accusations such as that he had deprived coastal Brunswick of two-thirds of a billion dollars of investments in 1973.[51] Around Atlanta, the still-enormous outpouring of wastes from Atlanta's Clayton plant remained a major headache for Howard. While William Ruckelshaus now praised the city's mayor for "moving more aggressively" to correct the problem, the city's request for a fourth extension to meet a 1971 standard and deadline provoked a far less flattering response from Georgia's lead environmental enforcer. [52] He slapped a new ongoing penalty on the city: until a new treatment plant was finished online, no more sewer taps could be added to the "Clayton Basin"—the pipe networks across North Atlanta feeding into the plant.[53] When that plant was finally completed some three years later, its treatment then failed to meet the somewhat higher standards that had since been set under the 1972 Clean Water Act. So the city had to request another extension for further upgrading.[54]

In implementing this new law, Georgia's water-pollution officials themselves also stepped up their scrutiny of private, industrial polluters around Atlanta. For the first time water-treatment plants like Clayton had to compile a public record of the major private industries pouring effluents their way. Even more sweepingly, under a new National Pollution Discharge Elimination system, every significant Atlanta-area water polluter, actual or potential, had to apply for and receive a permit just to operate legally.[55] State officials also began visiting large industrial polluters regularly, to document just how many toxic substances were being produced and dumped around Atlanta and to begin regulating them.[56] Their records for the big Lockheed plant near Marietta exemplified this intensifying scrutiny and its effects on corporate waste handling. Late in meeting the deadline set by Howard in 1965, Lockheed by 1972 finally operated its new wastewater treatment plant, lessening its toxic toll on the Nickajack and, by extension, the Chattahoochee. The company also stopped using an unsealed "earthen basin," where it had dumped and "treat[ed] concentrated cyanide and metal-plating," allowing leakage into the ground. Instead, Lockheed turned to a more impervious and enclosed aeration basin for treating these wastes, along with a new surface impoundment.[57] From cyanide to cadmium to chromium to lead and mercury, the NPDES system set the first numerical limits for the company's emissions and for the first time required monitoring of eleven toxic chemicals within the thirteen thousand cubic meters of effluent per day that Lockheed's permit now officially authorized it to dump into the Nickajack.[58] The company itself had to do the testing for each of these toxic chemicals, though at best only twice a week. Not all the oily wastes generated by Lockheed's new treatment plant went into the river. Company managers also began shipping some out to other places, including a sanitary landfill closer in to the city of Atlanta, at Westview Cemetery, where it was sprayed on roads to keep down the dust.[59]

Compared to its aggressive oversight of water pollution, the Carter administration took up air pollution more slowly, and only after pushes by federal agencies as well as Atlanta-based civic groups. Though the Georgia Health Department participated in a national air-pollution-monitoring network since 1957, the state legislature and governor began to take up the matter only in the wake of the federal Clean Air Act of 1967, followed by its amendments of 1970. Unlike for water pollution, the State Health Department's capabilities for monitoring air—a necessary condition for it to be able to enforce the new air-pollution laws—remained extremely limited. In the early 1970s it had to borrow tools and experts from a National Air Pollution Control Administration, the EPA's predecessor, to set up the state's first air-pollution-control district, encompassing seven Atlanta area counties.[60] Despite an ill-equipped State Health Department and the dearth of interest among Atlanta's new environmental groups on the issue of air pollution, others across this city evinced greater concern. In the summer of 1970, a conference on Atlanta's new air-pollution standards had drawn what was by some standards the broadest range of participation of any of that era's environmental deliberations. Showing up were "150 selected representatives of more than 30 civic and community organizations, ranging from labor unions to chambers of commerce to women's garden clubs."[61] By the next year the new governor Carter was putting forth his own antipollution package of 1971—including fines for aerial violations—as state officials sought to meet the legal and technical requirements for an EPA-approved air-pollution program.[62]

Under Carter's governorship Rock Howard's consolidated Environmental Protection Division quickly took over air-pollution monitoring and began administering the new federal laws.[63] Like other states without preexisting laws or the capacity to tackle this problem, they ran into early trouble getting their "implementation plan" approved by the federal EPA.[64] For years EPD scrambled to keep its plan in line with evolving federal standards, from a permitting program that could set and enforce rules for "significant" stationary polluters to the kinds and number of staff necessary to carry out the new regulatory work.[65] Its gathering oversight of Georgia Power's Atkinson power plant, across the Chattahoochee River from the Clayton plant in Vinings, illustrates the remarkable new public scrutiny EPD was gaining on the operations of private polluters. State officials making some of their first tests of emissions from Atkinson's smokestacks in March 1971 found its boiler stack number 4 "far in excess of standards set by the state."[66] Georgia Power promised a quick fix, but this coal-burning power plant then faced a tightening noose of nearby monitoring stations looking for exactly the kinds of pollutants it gave off. In addition to officials' episodic smokestack tests at the plant site, their devices at Smyrna, Marietta, and Scott School monitored aerial particulates; at Scott School and the Chattahoochee Water Plant, they scoured the air for both sulfur dioxide and nitrogen dioxide.[67] As with water, Howard and his EPD exercised control over this plant not only through monitoring but with permits, now legally required by every facility with a significant stack or "point source." Each permit set rules not just for aerial emissions but for the operations leading to these releases.[68] Collecting bulk information about what this power plant burned as well as estimating totals for the wastes it pumped into local air, officials also set a 1975 deadline for installing corrective technologies such as precipitators and scrubbers. Though the company insisted it was moving as fast it could, reports made plain just how flagrant its air pollution was. According to one 1973 study, the Atlanta-based company was the second-worst air polluter of all U.S. utilities.[69] So when Georgia Power officials also began to balk at their 1975 deadline, even for such an influential and well-connected firm, Howard pledged to allow no exceptions.[70]

Precisely *as* state officials went after corporate Georgia's polluting ways, civic mobilizing around Atlanta' aerial woes trailed off. With the government now plainly taking action, there was arguably less of an imperative for ordinary citizens themselves to do so. Yet air pollution also never became a front-burner issue for Atlanta's self-identified environmental groups in this period. That was partly because it was not as intensive or as ubiquitous as in northern or western cities, or even in a more industrial southern metropolis like Birmingham. That Atlanta's worst pollution concentrated downtown and in the industrial zone, up the railroad toward the northwest, also contributed to flagging interest in the issue among the city's mostly white environmentalists. Where carbon monoxide was worst was also home to some of Atlanta's poorest and Blackest communities and at some remove from where the city's environmentalists lived or played. Moreover, the back-and-forth between the EPD and the EPA, also scientists, courts, and legislatures made discussions of air pollution increasingly complex and difficult to follow, especially for the untrained but also for those who couldn't afford their own experts. As public hearings shifted from evoking a general need for action to revolving around specialized legal and scientific lingo, companies who could hire their own specialists gained significant advantages over less well-heeled and mostly volunteer citizen groups. By 1973 and 1974 hearings on Georgia's air-pollution standards and policies still drew outside attendees, but the vast majority of them were from state or local agencies or polluting corporations. In one such 1973 gathering, only four of eighty-nine attendees belonged to civic groups, as many as from Georgia Power itself.[71]

Importantly, the new corporate hiring of environmental professionals and accelerating adoption of pollution-curbing technology and practices seemed to augur the possibility, at least, of a new corporate environmental citizenship. The new laws and oversight did require changes in corporate behavior and so *could* also encourage still more internal concerns about environmental impacts, pushing firms beyond the requirements of existing laws and the self-serving blandishments of green advertising. However, within the public forums and court proceedings set up to ensure civic oversight of the new environmental state, corporations like Georgia Power gained a growing ability to dominate sheerly by dint of all the expertise they could afford, making it easier to push back against even the legally enforceable environmental obligations they now faced.

Stirring still less interest in the press and among Georgia's new environmental activists was the indoor pollution that could afflict places of work. In more industrialized states, where unions were generally stronger, a workplace-minded environmentalism largely articulated by labor leaders had led to a new federal law, the Occupational Safety and Health Act of 1970. With centralized oversight in Washington, D.C., in a like manner to new laws for water and air pollution, the Nixon administration created a new Occupational Safety and Health Administration (OSHA) to set and enforce national standards for aerial and other hazards in workplaces.[72] As with NEPA and the Clean Air and Water Acts, while the federal agency set the policies, state agencies, if they met OSHA's requirements, were generally charged with enforcing the rules. While Carter's gubernatorial administration did successfully spearhead Georgia programs for overseeing federal laws for water and air pollution, its effort to do so for workplace environments faltered in the face of personal feuds as well as business-based opposition. Carter's push to meet the new federal requirements in occupational health and safety began belatedly in early 1972, after his reorganization was largely settled. Having lost his battle to take Georgia's existing workplace inspectorate out of Caldwell's Labor Department, Carter then hired Jethro T. Gregory, a fired Caldwell aide, to head a new state office of Occupational Safety and Health within a Labor Department office charged with workers compensation, no longer under Caldwell's direct control. This new unit then became Georgia's liaison to OSHA in the federal Labor Department.[73] Though Carter and Caldwell had mended some fences, in early 1973 impatient federal officials at OSHA declared their own "preeminence" over the new laws, turning out the state of Georgia's inspectors and putting enforcement into their own inspectors' hands.[74]

What this outcome meant for Atlantans was that, unlike for environmental impact statements or water or air pollution, federal agents from OSHA—not Georgia state officials—marched into their factories and other businesses to enforce the rules of the new workplace health and safety law.[75] "Howling" then began about "tough" federal inspectors who could show up unannounced— Caldwell-directed inspectors had never done so. The new federal monitors also refused "courtesy" inspections, and the appeals process turned more formal and arduous.[76] Atlanta building subcontractors and lawyers sued OSHA over the constitutionality of the new law but lost in federal court. Smaller intrastate businesses continued to push for a return to state oversight, but by 1974 larger interstate firms became "pretty pleased with federal enforcement."[77] The "fuss" seemed to have "calm[ed]," even with twelve OSHA inspectors now working Atlanta alone (compared with the twenty-six Caldwell had overseen for the entire state). Despite "more inspections" and "more citations," the "vast majority" of local industry, concluded an *Atlanta Constitution* business reporter, "has been seeking compliance with OSHA rather than defiance" and "recognizing its role in the protection of its workers"—becoming, in this one realm, good environmental citizens.[78]

Yet the biggest challenges posed by the new OSHA law for Atlanta businesses were yet to come, as federal officials began to call into question Georgia's industrialists' prevailing assumptions about what exactly the dangers in their workplaces were. The textile industry, still Georgia's largest employer but now starting to reel from foreign competition, also began to feel pressure on another front that in the early 1970s no longer seemed merely on the horizon—the cotton dust that caused brown lung.[79] Soon federal officials would estimate that as much as a quarter of its workforce suffered from this suffocating pulmonary disease, also known as byssinosis, with the breathing difficulties and fluid-filled lungs that came from long hours and years of working amid the densely clogged air of textile mills. Tightening oversight of cotton dust would come only later in this decade, after amassing science led to new OSHA rules. In an historic twist, this triumph of managerial liberalism, so far-reaching in consequences for Georgia workers as well as industrialists, would come only once a Georgian little known for his worker advocacy ascended to the White House.

Black Ascent, Environmental Alliance, and Peak Democracy

If Carter's governorship wound up ceding oversight of this pivotal plank of Cowie's "economic citizenship" to federal officials, this city's ascendant Black political leadership offered greater affirmation of poor and working-class Atlantans' claims to socioeconomic belonging.[80] Andrew Young, as well as Maynard Jackson, developed and sustained this attentiveness following the evolution of the civil rights movement, despite the relatively elite circles in which they'd been raised. Like many civil rights activists, over the late 1960s their own careers had turned to nourishing and enabling the economic elements of Black citizenship. Before turning to politics, Young had trained as a minister and then served as the executive director of the SCLC, managing its Poor People's March among other events. After law school Jackson had plied his legal expertise toward alleviating the labor and housing struggles of the city's Blacks. Both then entered a political fray transformed by the state's recent democratization and, in Atlanta itself, an expansive Black electorate, just as the city's population turned majority Black. In becoming the bearers of Black political power, both achieved firsts in the political history of Georgia and the entire Deep South: Andrew Young in 1972 became the region's first Black congressional representative since Reconstruction, and Maynard Jackson in 1974 became the first Black mayor of a major Deep South city.[81] As dependent as their political successes were on the votes of both poor and middle-class Blacks, both recognized early on that they also needed white voters. Embracing this city's newly popular and organized environmental movement became part of each's winning formula: mixing pledges of environmental citizenship with others to a civil rights citizenship that had become more economically heedful. Jackson's blended marriage of these two projects, the one still rooted in a white and "ecologist" neighborhood movement and the other among communities of poorer as well as middle-class Blacks, would prove especially consequential. His early mayoralty would pose the deepest political challenge to the city's white business elite since Reconstruction. As a result, democracy in Atlanta, after languishing under Jim Crow for so long, lurched uneasily to its twentieth-century peak.

SCLC leaders, including Young, decided to put one of their own up for election not long after Martin Luther King Jr.'s death. King himself had repeatedly shunned electoral politics, fearing it would taint the SCLC's ability to offer as powerful or objective a critique.[82] But SCLC's new determination to pursue Black political power, following a less separatist strand of a larger Black power movement, came in the face of emerging opportunities in Atlanta itself as well as worries about their own organization's recent "thrust." SCLC staff feared that, compared to their remarkable earlier successes in streets and legislatures, the economic focus of their recent work, from organizing a Poor People's March on Washington to supporting strikes by Black sanitation and hospital workers, had become "too abstract to win new adherents." This concern reflected the persistently middle-class orientation of some staff but also its frustrated search for another immediate and "clear cut victory," like the national legislation of 1964 and 1965 that had followed its direct-action campaigns. By 1970, aside from a favorable settlement of the Charleston hospital workers' strike, the group had few other such accomplishments to which they could easily point. But with the federal government now overseeing the vote, Atlanta had also just turned majority Black, as the 1970 census would soon confirm.[83] So SCLC had the chance to become "the first Black organization" to put one of its own into the U.S. Congress. Such a victory would indeed be "clear cut, "dramatiz[ing] its focus on the power of the electoral process" and "increas[ing] SCLC's stature" even as the successful nominee "increased his own." For their nominee they settled on Andrew Young, a full-time executive for the group since 1964, first under King and then under his successor, Ralph Abernathy. Genial and diplomatic with white allies as well as opponents, Young's candidacy would presumably be "attractive to Black youth, ministers, and white liberal middle-class elements."[84]

Not just the Atlanta-ward migration of Blacks and suburban "flight" of whites but the democratization of the city's electoral system heightened SCLC leaders' hopes. The city had lurched from having a single representative in the state legislature to having twelve; then a takeoff in Black voting had swayed the 1969 mayoral election, the first of the modern era in which the candidate anointed by the city's white business elite had actually lost. Sam Massell's triumph was also Maynard Jackson's, who became the city's first Black deputy mayor. Both victories had hinged so much on the Black vote that the city's Black newspapers celebrated the victors as "our own." But Young's electoral quest beginning that next year faced greater hurdles than had Massell's or Jackson's. The Fifth District, in which he declared his candidacy, was one of the two Atlanta-area congressional districts set up in the wake of one-man, one-vote court decisions (the other, the Fourth District, had been where James Mackay had won in 1964 but then lost) (map set 5.1). Harboring most of the city's Blacks, the district nevertheless had northerly and southerly extensions beyond the city limits that made its electorate 69 percent white.[85]

Knowing just how many white voters he would need to win, Young's first campaign to represent this district took his Black constituency largely for granted and sought to reach out mainly to lower income and more rural whites. Orchestrating appearances with white leaders of the Teamsters, United Auto Workers (UAW), and Alliance for Labor Action, he emphasized his support for "the working man." Attacking his opponent for voting against funding for rat control and hospitals, he voiced a vision for "what I think the 5th

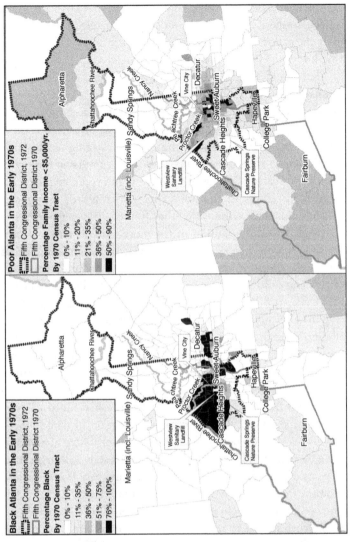

Black Atlanta in the Early 1970s

┋┋ Fifth Congressional District, 1972
☐ Fifth Congressional District 1970

Percentage Black
By 1970 Census Tract

- 0% - 10%
- 11% - 35%
- 36% - 50%
- 51% - 75%
- 76% - 100%

Alpharetta

Chattahoochee River

Nancy Creek

Sandy Springs

Vine City

Decatur

Peachtree Creek

Proctor Creek

Sweet Auburn

Hapeville

Cascade Heights

Marietta (incl. Louisville)

Westview Sanitary Landfill

Cascade Springs Nature Preserve

Chattahoochee River

College Park

Fairburn

Poor Atlanta in the Early 1970s

┋┋ Fifth Congressional District, 1972
☐ Fifth Congressional District 1970

Percentage Family Income < $5,000/yr.
By 1970 Census Tract

- 0% - 10%
- 11% - 20%
- 21% - 35%
- 36% - 50%
- 50% - 90%

Alpharetta

Chattahoochee River

Nancy Creek

Sandy Springs

Vine City

Decatur

Peachtree Creek

Proctor Creek

Sweet Auburn

Hapeville

Cascade Heights

Marietta (incl. Louisville)

Westview Sanitary Landfill

Cascade Springs Nature Preserve

Chattahoochee River

College Park

Fairburn

MAP SET 5.1. Black versus poor Atlanta in the Fifth District, early 1970s. The Fifth Congressional District of Georgia in 1970 (dark, bold line), when Andrew Young first ran and lost, included most of Black Atlanta but was still just 31 percent Black, because of how far it extended to the north as well as the south. In this campaign he railed against Peachtree Creek's and Nancy Creek's pollution in predominantly white North Atlanta, without mentioning Proctor Creek, which was actually worse (see chapter 3) but ran through a Blacker and poorer part of the city. A redrawing of the district by 1972 then excluded Fairburn and other mostly white and rural South Fulton, helping enable Young's victory. Areas excised from the district by 1972, especially those to the south, included many poorer and working-class whites. Maps by author. *Sources:* Manson et al., *IPUMS National Historical Geographic Information System;* Jeffrey B. Lewis, Brandon DeVine, Lincoln Pitcher, and Kenneth C. Martis, "Digital Boundary Definitions of United States Congressional Districts, 1789–2012," UCLA Political Science, accessed May 25, 2021, https://cdmaps.polisci.ucla.edu; "Atlanta, Georgia," Google Maps, accessed September 2017.

District needs," "better schools, housing, and health care"—enhanced public provisions that could especially benefit poorer citizens whatever their race. In a year marked by the nation's first Earth Day, Young also began talking about issues becoming known as "environmental." He pledged support for a "rapid transit system" that would "reduce our need for autos in the city" and especially railed against pollution.[86]

Among a national cohort of young Black politicians now ascending to leadership in cities turning majority Black, Young's espousal of ecospeak came more quickly than many others'.[87] But Young's 1970 messaging on the environment had far less to do with any personal ecological conversion than with pragmatic political outreach; it was an appeal to white voters. Among Atlanta's Black leaders, civic groups, and press, there was still little sign of any self-identified "environmental" citizenship. They framed worries about rats or poor housing as well as water pollution in the more familiar terms of civil rights activism, as reflections of continuing racial discrimination and lagging economic power. Tellingly, even though Proctor Creek's pollution had been fingered by a Black journalist that July, the only streams actually mentioned in Young's campaign literature were the "grossly polluted" Nancy and Peachtree Creeks, running through a North Atlanta that was well-to-do and white. Even as the antipollution rhetoric in Young's 1970 campaign sought to curry favor with white voters, the campaign was slower to recognize how Atlanta's white environmentalists were on the whole more interested in preserving "natural areas" and fighting freeways.[88]

Young lost this, his first race. His campaign strategy had failed to overcome the district's racial divide. He drew only 25 percent of the white vote—not enough, given that only 60 percent of registered Black voters turned out. Though he won a plurality inside the city of Atlanta, he lost by still larger margins in whiter parts of the district lying outside the city, past Hapeville and College Park toward the south, as well as northward into Sandy Springs. Appointed to run the Community Relations Commission (CRC) just weeks after his loss, Young then gained an official platform that he would later credit as one of two key foundations for his victory in the next Fifth District congressional race. Two years later his very public CRC work had burnished his reputation for reaching across racial lines. He also benefited from a redrawing of the Fifth District itself. The new boundaries sloughed off the southern portion of Fulton, chocked with less affluent and more rural white voters, where Young had struggled two years before. Faced with an electorate that was now 38 rather than 31 percent Black, Young's next campaign also turned more proactive toward this core constituency. They registered some twenty thousand Blacks anew and engineered a formidable get-out-the-vote drive on Election Day. He won this time around, in 1972, not just because more Blacks voted but because he had become better at "reach[ing] out to white voters."[89]

He did this, among other ways, by lessening his outreach to white working-class voters as well as absorbing and adopting the environmental priorities of Atlanta's more affluent whites. Toning down his affiliations with unions and talk about pollution, Young aligned his campaign with the main flashpoints for popular environmentalism within Atlanta by the early 1970s. Foregrounding the "transportation crisis" declared by the neighborhoods fighting in-town highways, he also took up the cause of Chattahoochee preservation. He pledged to propose a bill that would turn the Chattahoochee—at least the part north of Atlanta's sewage-treatment plant—into a national park. He would introduce this measure "as my *first* piece of major legislation upon election to Congress, on the *first* day I assume office." While Young pitched a park to be shared by "rich and poor, young and old, Black and white," the proposed preserve as well as the freeway-threatened neighborhoods whose defense he promised lay mostly in the white-dominated and affluent reaches of his district.[90]

Young's 1972 election win inaugurated another longer-term trend for Georgia's environmental politics. A growing friendliness to environmental legislation among Atlanta's representatives in Washington, D.C. dovetailed with the ascension of Black politicians to electoral power within the city itself. Not that Young abandoned his commitment to policies helping the urban poor; he was outspoken in attacking Nixon's efforts to roll back programs like the Neighborhood Job Corps and the Office of Economic Opportunity.[91] But not only did Young keep his promise of a bill proposing a Chattahoochee park as his first legislation; during his first year in Congress, he earned a 100 out of 100 rating by the national League of Conservation Voters, the first perfect score of any Georgia congressperson. Throughout his first term Young's yearly LCV ratings remained at least twice that of the next highest-rate member of Georgia's congressional delegation, until Elliot Levitas, elected in 1974 from Atlanta's other district, nearly equaled him.[92] Young's electoral success in 1972 not only kicked off a slow, gathering greening of Georgia's congressional representatives over the next two decades but also inaugurated a pivotal alliance in Atlanta's environmental politics. From then on issues cast as "environmental" would provide a major avenue by which Atlanta's ascendant Black politicians could reliably curry favor with better-off suburban whites.

Maynard Jackson's victory in the 1973 mayoral race consolidated this pattern. A burgeoning neighborhood movement mostly among whites now largely framing themselves as "environmental" citizens joined with an expanding Black electorate to sweep him into city leadership. Jackson's first victory in the mayoral race would, as political scientist Clarence Stone famously put it, serve as "the linchpin for a new urban regime," by challenging white business leaders' long-standing power and influence in the city's polity.[93] Jackson began his campaign for mayor suggesting he would be more probusiness than his opponent Sam Massell. But, like the SCLC in the late 1960s, Jackson had "cut his teeth as a champion of the poor" and working people. He had done stints as a lawyer for the National Labor Relations Board and for Emory legal services and also helped tally how many were made homeless by postwar urban renewal. As vice mayor, he had also lent prominent support to striking sanitation workers.[94] Jackson's campaign capitalized on this background to appeal to a wide range of Black voters. Even as he pledged to fight crime, he also promised to open doors to grassroots mobilizations and criticized the city's tradition of "slavish, unquestioning adherence to downtown dicta." Approached by three unnamed members of "the so-called downtown power structure" who offered backing in exchange for his support of their candidate opposing SCLC's Hosea Williams for council president, he responded with a pointed "no." Still worse for them, he publicized their backdoor overture and his refusal, turning his willingness to challenge the "power structure" into a campaign talking point.[95]

Taking the cue from Andrew Young's congressional victory, Jackson sought to ingratiate himself with white neighborhoods that had also risen up against "downtown dicta," mostly on the city's north side. He dropped in on small get-togethers with their civic associations.[96] To woo the Coalition on the Transportation Crisis and the Citywide League of Neighborhoods, he released a "comprehensive transportation statement" that said nearly everything these groups wanted to hear.[97] Jackson declared his opposition to I-485, two other pending freeways, and any other expressway "inside of Atlanta": I cannot imagine where another . . . could be built without doing great damage to neighborhoods." Instead, "we should turn to a major expansion of public transportation."[98] The mayoral candidate also brought Kay McKenzie, the founding head of Friends of the River, onto his campaign staff.[99] Allying with Chattahoochee preservationists set him at odds with real-estate developers; siding with the freeway fighters pitted him against the plans of the Chamber of Commerce and Central Atlanta Progress (CAP). Long accustomed to a politics that leaned their way, these civic mouthpieces for downtown businesspeople stuck to their decades-old habit of conflating what was good for their own bottom lines with what was best for Atlanta as a whole. CAP still held on to the hope that the new environmentally minded freeway resistance was merely a passing fad. On the eve of Jackson's victory, one banker anticipated a more "statesmanlike attitude toward these highway opponents" as the new mayor began his term. "I'm for ecology too, but you can't do business on cow pastures you know."[100]

Through his early mayoralty Jackson's stance against Atlanta's white business establishment confronted the difficult politicoeconomic hand he had been dealt. On the one hand, under Jimmy Carter the state legislature had approved a new charter for the city in 1973 that effectively recast the city's governing body, the board of aldermen. No longer would aldermen all be elected at large—the method put in place by mid-twentieth-century reformers as "progressive." Instead, each was to be elected by a single district of the city, a return to a ward-based system long pushed by Black political leaders. That change guaranteed more Black representation on a board long almost exclusively white. Yet the new mayor and his coalition also faced many of the same, long-building challenges as so many other U.S. cities, an "urban crisis." Here, as elsewhere, an expanding white middle class had been conveying its wealth out beyond the city limits, purchasing its patrimony in suburbs. Atlanta over this very period burnished a reputation as a "Black Mecca" in part because its Black middle class had also been growing, but they too had started moving out from the city.[101] These faces of compressive capitalism also meant that the urban core kept losing consumers for its businesses, threatening the city's greatest concentrations of private capital and the tax base out of which city government was funded. The millions of dollars sunk into downtown Atlanta's businesses had led Ivan Allen III, son of the former mayor and himself a business leader, to boast how the city's "business community is committed to the continued strength of the central core, more than . . . any other city in America."[102] Yet white flight as well businesspeople's decisions about where to locate lay largely outside the control of city political leadership, even as that great postwar fount of public resources for cities, the federal government, was dialing down many programs.[103] The Nixon administration shuttered the Office of Economic Opportunity, for instance, and though city funding kept Economic Opportunity Atlanta centers open, its programs became fewer and smaller.[104] Knowing all too well how much Jackson's success hinged on their own, Atlanta's own "racial capitalists," the white leaders of its downtown businesses, repeatedly pitted themselves against any "move toward Black interest" as "undermining economic interest and the city's future."[105]

In his first couple of years, while Jackson tempered his support of city unions, he moved in many other directions little favored by downtown businesspeople yet welcomed by his main constituencies, Black as well as white. He brought many more Blacks into the city's workforce, starting with its police, and sought to address those housing and other neighborhood problems that in this time were less likely to be deemed "environmental," because they involved all-too-unnatural environments of the urban poor.[106] Not long after a rock-throwing episode at a four-year-old public-housing project named Bankhead Courts, Jackson spent a weekend there himself. He found it to resemble a "bombed out World War II building." Rats stalked the courtyard, drainage was poor, dummy heating vents poked out of walls, the grounds had eroded, and vandalism had gone unrepaired. The "intolerable and sickening" conditions prompted the first-year mayor to launch a task force investigating what had gone wrong with public housing in Atlanta over the past twenty years.[107]

Their study recommended "giv[ing] tenants broader control over their housing" in ways that the mayor then promoted: speeding requested maintenance, shifting many residents toward ownership, and removing authority for urban renewal from the Atlanta Housing Authority to city hall.[108] Jackson also lent visible support to nonprofits servicing the poor. He kicked off a community gardening project administered by Economic Opportunity Atlanta across its thirteen service centers, donning "blue overalls and a white workcap" and "dr[iving] a tractor" to break ground for the model garden in Bedford Pine.[109] And when in 1975 the city requested and received $18.7 million in community redevelopment funds from the federal government, the Jackson administration targeted the funds primarily for struggling Black neighborhoods, none of them in the central business district favored by CAP.[110]

The Jackson administration also bolstered the efforts of better-off Blacks to take up the current style of environmental citizenship, centered on more visibly natural (and more ecologically authentic) parks and neighborhoods like Druid Hills. In the early 1970s Jan Meadows, a Los Angeles transplant who had moved with her husband to Cascade Road (next door to SCLC's Joseph Lowery), heard another apartment building was planned nearby, on a steeply sloped, forested patch of land. With the help of a professor at Georgia State and his students, she shepherded research into the site's human as well as its natural history—from its Native American trail to the pastures it provided for Gen. William Sherman's horses to its early twentieth-century "resort area" that drew in many from downtown, then known as Cascade Springs. In 1974 they helped spur a "comprehensive plan" for the entire neighborhood that would turn this unbuilt land, now christened the Cascade Forest, into a city-owned preserve. Demonstrating "that Southwest Atlanta had some history," they also pitched the springs' ecological value, its "rich variety of plant [sic], wildlife, and old trees (100 years)." What became known as the Cascade Forest Neighborhood Association appealed to the Jackson administration, and the city took on the project, buying the first land for the proposed preserve in 1975.[111] Some four years later the city parks commissioner touted the results: "the city's second"—and largest—"wilderness park."[112]

Jackson's mayoralty also brought boons for those white neighborhoods threatened by freeways, beginning early on with his declaration that 1-485 was now "dead as a doornail."[113] As his administration moved ahead with MARTA construction, they also came up with a neighborhood-friendly plan for the land already bought up by the state for this "dead" freeway: a Great Museum Park. Along 2.8 miles of already acquired right of way, they envisioned a "huge . . . complex of museums, lakes, parking decks, shops, housing, an amphitheater and recreational facilities." Upon rollout of the plan, ten neighborhood associations including Morningside-Lenox Park—the first targeted for the 1-485 route—showered the idea with praise.[114] The main opponent here, however, was not CAP but a Georgia Department of Transportation now under the governorship of Jimmy Carter, which promptly proposed another road, a "non-commercial, tree-lined parkway" with "landscaped green belts along medians and roadsides."[115]

Chiefly, however, Jackson's fiercest opposition came from CAP and its downtown allies, heirs of an urban power structure in which white business-people had long called the most important shots. From early in his first term, when the *Atlanta Constitution* declared the city's business leaders "stirred up," they vocally worried that Jackson would "lean to the immediate demands of the little man, rather than the [presumably more long-term] interests of the business community."[116] In September 1974 the CAP head and chair of Rich's board, Harold Brockley, stepped up the pressure, bemoaning "indications of business[es] leaving the city because of a fear of crime, racial problems, doubts about the school system, a poor downtown image, and"—in a few lines that both he and Jackson later downplayed—"the mayor's image as 'anti-white.'"[117] The spat drew national coverage on how businesspeople were being "excluded from city hall" as well larger stories about Atlanta's accelerating "northernization" and a "faltering confidence" at once in the new mayor and the city itself.[118] A significant share of business leaders' frustration rested not with Jackson but with the new city council, whose revised structure, they felt, led members "to show more interest in the people in the neighborhood, who elected them, than in the dollars downtown, which didn't."[119] More democracy, it seemed, was bad for business.

Stepping up the pressure on Jackson, CAP sought his blessing for its own plans for stimulating a private-housing market downtown for the better-off, whose expenditures might help revive central-city commerce. With federal aid for high-density public housing serving low-income tenants diminishing, CAP called on private-sector initiatives to bring in less dense, middle-income dwellings, furthering that "back-to-the-city movement among young people and middle-income families"—overwhelmingly white—who had, ironically, helped mobilize against the freeways.[120] In Bedford Pine, for instance, along the northerly edge of former Buttermilk Bottom, CAP set up a subsidiary named Park Central Communities (PCC), which produced a $250 million plan for a development including "mixed"-income apartments, shopping and recreational facilities. They hoped to site it on land acquired and cleared for urban renewal around the civic center, but a Project Area Committee composed of existing residents remained wary. With the cloud of the Brockley letter hanging over him, Jackson then intervened, sitting down with this committee and PCC representatives in a closed-door "pound cake summit" to iron out differences and seal a deal.[121] Through this and other agreements brokered by Jackson, CAP's plans moved along, introducing a style of development verging on what was later termed "New Urbanism." In subsequent decades such projects would be assailed as first forays of a gentrification that was steadily displacing the city's Black poor from its downtown. But at this time Jackson celebrated his ability to broker this kind of compromise with a testy CAP, as representing a "major follow-through on [his] efforts to strengthen neighborhoods throughout the city," including the poorest among them.[122]

In 1975 the Jackson administration launched its most ambitious democratizing effort yet, a program to spread participatory decision making across the city. The Neighborhood Planning Units stood in a bottom-up counterpoint to the technocratic drift that pervaded so much environmental state building across state and federal governments. The city's new charter had required comprehensive development and zoning plans based on citizen input for the twelve new council districts. A new system of planning units, or NPUs, became the means for doing so.[123] The city's Bureau of Planning divvied up the city into twenty-four units, each of which was to invite residents from its neighborhoods to gather together and come up with their own area development plans. To jump-start the effort and also to navigate difficult questions of zoning and law likely to arise, each unit was also assigned its own professional planner. From their localized scale and accessible meeting places—an available public space within the area—to their openness to any resident, the NPUs offered a more genuinely participatory forum for citizenly involvement than had yet been seen in the city of Atlanta. More localized and neighborhood-level than the CRC, the NPUs enabled a participation that was also far more bottom up than Carter's Goals for Georgia. The NPU's legal sway remained limited: they were only "to advise" their aldermen and other city officials about the preferences and priorities of a given corner of the city. Yet, especially for neighborhoods without their own homeowner or tenant associations, the NPUs opened new opportunities for citizenly practice across the entire city, an officially sanctioned avenue by which residents could speak out and be heard by city hall.[124]

With the advent of the NPUs, Atlanta's democratizing had arrived at what, historically speaking, would prove its high watermark. Forty years prior, the reins of the city had belonged to a very few, its most affluent, themselves elected by an exceedingly narrow portion of its adult populace. The regime had been well-nigh authoritarian, if less so than that of the state government within which it had nested. By the mid-1970s, however, Atlanta's traditional "power structure," run by a few white businesspeople and their politicians, seemed finally to have met its match. With the electorates for both city and state far broader, new forms of governance had also arisen that were more representative, better ensuring that the votes of residents from most corners of the city could influence who served on the council. The NPUs also held out greater hopes for a democracy that was more direct, a forum whereby residents themselves could regularly voice their own visions for their neighborhoods' futures. Adding to the empowering potential of the NPUs was the collabo-

PHOTO 5.2. Mayor Maynard Jackson speaking about the Neighborhood Planning Units. The photo was probably taken at a 1978 conference, where Jackson (*second from right*), whose mayoralty had instituted the participatory planning system, was addressing many NPU members' concerns about how city hall was responding to their work. NPU maps can be seen in background. Courtesy of Maynard Jackson Mayoral Administrative Records, Robert W. Woodruff Library, Atlanta University Center.

rative balance they struck between a neighborhood's often inexpert denizens and planning experts, able to interpret and situate residents' concerns in ways that could be heard and acted on by city officials. Just as many of the region's environmental groups bolstered the passion and commitments of lay residents with the expertise of ecologists or lawyers, the early NPUs built in just such a collaboration on questions of land use, enabling a more informed neighborly citizenship. The NPUs were not at all confined to issues then identified as "environmental"; their ambit remained open to many other concerns of residents across the city's local homescapes. Not so surprisingly, they proved more welcome in those parts of the city where the natural world itself seemed less visible or cultivated, even as the city's organized environmentalism largely ignored their concerns and work.

Indeed, some of the strongest early resistance to the NPUs came from those mostly affluent and white neighborhoods that had led the freeway revolt. They had organized themselves and were already well armed with expertise and connections. As a Morningside lawyer who had been involved in the litigation against I-485 put it, their prevailing attitude toward the NPU system was "don't try to tell us how to organize. We know more about it than you do." NPUs struck them as another layer of bureaucracy to navigate, blocking the ease of access to which they had become accustomed: how "if Virginia High-land want[ed] a play lot," it went straight to the parks director. But as the city's planning director noted, this pre-NPU system had enabled the more organized neighborhoods, often among the city's most advantaged, "to take the available money away from less active areas of the city."[125] Now the NPUs spread some of those citizenly opportunities and capacities already enjoyed by these more organized neighborhoods to other, less privileged corners of the city.

The NPUs also opened the door to new, not-so-advantaged neighborhood leaders, belated beneficiaries of the city's continuing democratization. Among those who emerged in the NPU-I created for Cascade Heights was a Black man named Juner Norris, a worker at the General Motors plant in Doraville, who in the late sixties had bought his family a house in the neighborhood. An autoworker without a college degree, living in a more modest suburban neighborhood that did not yet have as strong an associational voice, Norris attended his first NPU-I meeting sometime in the late 1970s. He then quickly emerged as a respected neighborhood activist, becoming president and holding that position for many years, pushing the rehabilitation of West Atlanta parks and curbing new development projects, from tunnels to condos.[126] While NPUs could hardly overcome all that impeded the citizenly involvement of the city's poor, favoring the voices of businesspeople and homeowners instead, the system did nourish civic activism in some of the poorest corners of the city. For instance, an NPU-M provided a forum through which Bedford-Pine residents disenchanted with a proposed redevelopment project for their neighborhood expressed their opposition. Building on advocacy work already commenced by that project's citizen-led Project Area Committee, it kept up steady pressure to include lower-income housing and shape the shopping center and "central park" for existing residents, while questioning the need for a twenty-four-story office building. When it ran into heavy pushback from CAP, Jackson had to step in to prevent the ouster of this NPU leader, SCLC member Rev. Ted Clark.[127] A 1978 investigation by council members heard some of the highest praise of the NPUs from those living in some of least advantaged parts of the city. One resident of a Black suburb in the city's southeast, Loretta Kimpson, called it "the best thing that has happened to the city of Atlanta . . . the only way that the citizens of Atlanta have a voice in their government."[128]

Maynard Jackson's first term, bringing accomplishments welcomed by civil rights activists or card-carrying environmentalists, and sometimes both, and coinciding with the rollout of a newly protective environmental state, brought democracy in this southern city to a historic high point. Yet the historical conditions enabling this flourishing of democracy proved fleeting. Pressures building on the Jackson administration during his first term came to a head as, in pursuit of a second one, he began mending fences with CAP and Atlanta's business community. Historians Joe McCartin and Maurice Hobson see his 1977 crackdown on a strike of the city's mostly Black sanitation workers as a turning point, with Jackson appeasing a white establishment and Black middle class "instead of championing the people."[129] The same fiscal restraints that justified his strikebreaking also brought a diminution of the NPU system. A first citywide gathering of NPU leaders in 1978 assailed city hall for "not taking NPUs seriously." The second Jackson administration went on to confirm their accusations by reducing NPU planners down from twenty-four to six.[130] Much as the fiscal crisis that befell Atlanta by the late 1970s seemed beyond the control of Atlanta's political as well as business leaders, at this historical moment the continued diminishment of federal funding for cities also played a role. And in that Jackson's fellow Georgian turned president, Jimmy Carter, had an influential hand.

The New Environmental Oversight, Phase 2

Carter's winning presidential campaign of 1976 swept him to the helm of a national government running on a very different political clock than the one he had confronted as Georgia's governor. Most of the United States had not weathered the racial authoritarianism out of which Georgia had recently emerged. Far earlier and more robustly than Georgia, the federal government had acknowledged and supported many economic elements of citizenship, through the New Deal as well as the many new programs of the Great Society. Federal agencies and programs combated urban poverty, funded other metropolitan needs such as mass transit, and protected the rights of unions and the interests of industrial workers. Carter's governorship had brought greater acquaintance with these federal engagements, but his own state building in Georgia had equipped him especially well for the signal environmental accomplishments of his presidency: accelerating the public preservation of natural lands and completing a far-reaching and enduring federalization of environmental regulation in the United States. Still largely overlooked by political historians, this outcome amounted to what the journalist William Greider was suggesting as early as 1979 had become "a more fundamental restructuring of power in America than all of the Great Society programs."[131]

The fiscal crisis that Jackson and other Atlanta leaders confronted in the late 1970s owed in part to the Carter administration's shift away from deficit spending. After first pushing a Keynesian stimulus package to pull the nation out of a mid-decade recession, as the inflation rate continued to rise he and his team switched gears. By mid-1977 they were seeking to curb inflation by cutting federal expenditures, returning to a fiscal restraint long valued in Georgia's political culture.[132] Among the casualties was Carter's quixotic effort to reform the federal approach to cities. Historian Tom Sugrue and many others have characterized Carter's "national urban policy" as prioritizing "small-scale, gradualist,

[and] locally administered" measures, thereby marking a break from the ambitious, centralized managerial liberalism of the New Deal era. In this switch more than just an abandonment of Keynesianism was at work; those same amply funded and centralized federal programs aiding Atlanta's postwar economic growth had roused powerful neighborhood and environmental opposition that Carter knew, in some cases, all too well. But as with these resistance movements, Carter's own urban solutions tacitly favored the moneyed and organized, resting on private-public partnerships and "devolution," brokered by a National Development Bank.[133] According to Sugrue and other critics, larger-scale spending, job creation, and industrial development, if applied with genuine evenhandedness however technocratic, would have stood the best chance of success. Repairing those places from which the private sector had withdrawn, they could have reached into corners of the city too impoverished and politically underorganized to advocate for themselves.[134] As early as 1978, Vernon Jordan, the Black Atlanta-bred lawyer who headed the National Urban League, largely agreed. Despite supporting "many of the things we want," the Carter administration "apparently lacks the will to put its power and prestige on the line for issues vital to minorities and to poor people."[135]

Responding to an "energy crisis" stoked by the world's oil producers, the Carter administration also became the first to articulate a national policy for energy, then shouldering its way into competition with other environmental issues. Declaring a "moral equivalent of war" on the energy front, Carter walked a tightrope between allaying and provoking environmentalists' concerns. His creation of a cabinet-level Department of Energy turned out to be the single largest bureaucratic reorganization of his presidency. Carter and his advisers sought to shift the nation's energy mix away from oil and natural gas toward alternative energy sources like solar and wind, albeit in gradualist and privatizing ways echoing his urban policy, eschewing the ambitious programs for which some environmentalists called.[136] The Carter administration also promoted more use of coal—soon known as the most intensive producer of greenhouse gases. They did seek a greener coal industry, through a stripmining act as well as 1977 Clean Air Act amendments that required scrubbers on new coal-burning plants like those run by Georgia Power. But when oil shortages returned in 1978 and 1979, in the wake of the Iranian Revolution, Carter proposed an Energy Mobilization Board that could explicitly override environmental concerns, which was successfully defeated by environmentalists and their allies.[137] In the face of a spontaneous and grassroots uprising against nuclear power, surging in Atlanta itself over Georgia Power's nuclear plants, Carter continued to push for more nuclear plants. The meltdown at Three Mile Island in 1979 then inspired a protest march of sixty-six thousand through the streets of Washington in the summer of 1980, but Carter stuck to his conviction that closing down the nuclear industry was simply "out of the question."[138] In response, as activists pursued the cause of cleaner energy, they widened the ambit of environmental citizenship in ways that anticipated their response to crises posed by climate change, as yet only dimly adumbrated on theirs as well as the Carter administration's radar screens.

On the most established of environmental fronts, public land acquisition, the Carter presidency ushered in new federal purchases of park lands around Atlanta as in other parts of the United States. Carter's Department of the Interior added much of Alaska into the federal park system, doubling its acreage. In 1978 he signed a National Parks and Recreation Act, hailed by the *New York Times* as "the broadest measure of its kind in history," authorizing expenditure of some $1.2 billion on "more than 100 parks, rivers, and historic sites and trails."[139] That same year the Carter administration also won a long-awaited plum for the Atlanta area: a federal down payment of $72.9 million for a National Recreation Area along the Chattahoochee River, north of the city. While not the national park for which many activists had hoped, its plan hewed to the "string of pearls" strategy laid out by the Bureau of Recreation study some nine years before. Carter proudly signed the measure into law at a White House Rose Garden ceremony in August 1978, with Barbara Blum and many of the river's longtime activists in attendance. The president himself was effusive: "I don't know of any legislation I have signed since I have been in the White House—or will sign—that will give me any more personal pleasure than this." Before the year's end the federal purchases of North Atlanta's riverine lands began, and a new public park was born.[140]

Where Carter and his appointees applied the precepts of managerial liberalism most vigorously was against long-standing environmental prerogatives of private corporations: their freedom to develop, to pollute their own and others' surroundings, and to sicken their own workforces. Most of his leading nominations for the federal environmental agencies hailed from outside the South, exemplifying a new environmental professionalism that had arisen among more city-oriented and union-friendly turfs of environmental citizenship. Northeasterner Doug Costle, a lawyer and former head of Connecticut's environmental agency, was named EPA chief. Eula Bingham, named head of OSHA, was herself an environmental scientist and midwesterner (though born just across the state line from her Cincinnati home, in Kentucky), with a deep familiarity with the rapidly evolving study of environment cancer. The only southerner was someone who had lived in the South for less than a decade: the Atlantan Barbara Blum, the social worker and businesswoman-turned-environmental activist. She sold her home next to the Chattahoochee to go work at the EPA headquarters, as its deputy administrator. Blum's appointment ruffled some feathers precisely because she was an erstwhile activist, not the holder of any qualifying degree. As specialized and variegated as federal environmental officials were becoming, their shared professional ethics and commitments seemed strong. As Blum recalled, "Almost all of them that we worked with were mission-driven and it was—and the morale there and the esprit de corps was incredible. . . . It was just the heyday of the environment. It was full speed ahead."[141] They faced off against what they saw as an old environmentally unenlightened order: private industry, sometimes labor, large rural landholders like farmers and ranchers, and frequently earlier generations of public officials, professionals, and scientists.

Among the most flourishing of the new expert-administered governmental tools honed by the Carter administration was the Environmental Impact Statement (EIS), whose earliest Georgia versions had been crafted by, among others, the conservancy-allied ecologist Eugene Odum. By 1978 some eight thousand Environmental Impact Statements had been issued for federal agencies alone, from the Corps of Engineers to the Nuclear Regulatory Commission. The requirement for an EIS applied not only to what the federal government built but to other projects it funded, which meant environmental assessments for everything from airports to military bases and university libraries. Lawsuits helped stretch many early EISs to thousands of pages. The Carter administration countered by regularizing them further, reigning in their length and requiring some features across the board to stem what had become a tidal tug toward complexity and heterogeneity.[142] During the Carter years the EPA's Atlanta regional office became a national focal point for EIS writing, issuing more than any other EPA region because of the heady pace of government-sponsored or financed construction across the Southeast. Wishing for more thoroughgoing input on the EISs from his own biological specialty, ecology, Eugene Odum expressed his disappointment that they were becoming "almost mass produced" and focused on the "wrong level . . . often, for example, on the species or factor level when the questions and decisions clearly involve the ecosystem level."[143] But around Atlanta, by the late 1970s, the public process of EIS composition also provided many a venue for citizen challenges to powerful actors, from a Coalition on the Transportation Crisis's lawsuit against freeway widenings to the Reverend Ted Clark's attack on CAP's redevelopment plans for Bedford Pine.[144]

The Carter administration also advanced the official assault on water pollution in the Atlanta area, as elsewhere. Since Carter's predecessor, Gerald Ford, had not yet implemented a 1974 Drinking Water Act, that charge fell to Carter's EPA. Under Costle it formulated what became the first legally enforceable "maximum contaminant levels" for toxics in the nation's drinking water, "finally join[ing] the water supply and pollution control fields in a common effort to protect public health." Water officials of the city of Atlanta's drinking water reacted with alarm at the new standards for synthetic organic chemicals in particular, warning these could force "hellish" new expenditures for additional filters.[145] Over this same while the city's waste-treatment plants still struggled to comply with the Clean Water Act in what they released into the Chattahoochee and other area rivers. Under Maynard Jackson the Clayton plant finally opened that secondary treatment plant that environmental regulators had sought ever since Rock Howard's mid-1960s citations of the city. Yet by 1978 that plant had operated another three years without ever bringing its released wastes down to what was permitted, leading Georgia's chief environmental enforcer to declare the Clayton plant the state's "biggest pollution problem." With the support of the Carter EPA, he took the as-yet-unprecedented step of suing the city for its failures of the Clayton plant, not once but twice. Nearby residents meanwhile banded together through their NPU to voice their own protests.[146]

The environmental problem in the Atlanta area drawing the most new governmental interventions during Carter's presidency was air pollution. Concerns about the city's air mounted once a team of federal and state investigators checking for Atlanta's compliance with 1975 standards under the Clean Air Act were surprised to find the city had graduated to a Los Angeles–style of air pollution. By the summer of 1976, agency monitoring revealed levels of ozone and carbon monoxide—both of which came from the burning of hydrocarbons by cars as well as industry—that exceeded state and federal standards. This first, hard evidence of unacceptable pollution from exhaust fumes in the region now fingered the burning of petroleum, rather than coal, as the most concerning source of Atlanta's atmospheric travails. That finding triggered a whole new round of demands and efforts to revise the state's and region's pollution-control programs.[147] After the requisite studies, negotiations, and new legislative pushes got underway in the state capital, new federal legislation then brought a second major shift in the legal landscape of aerial governance.

In mid-1977 Congress passed and Carter signed some far-reaching amendments to the Clean Air Act. Extending deadlines for combating precisely the kind of air-pollution problem that Atlanta had *just* been found to have, they also settled the issue of "prevention of significant deterioration" in places with little or no air pollution, long a bone of contention between the EPA and Georgia's own environmental regulators. The new law's resolution of that issue required much that Georgia's air controllers had not yet undertaken. They had to start monitoring more pollutants, most notably ozone, now shown to be a contaminant of concern around Atlanta, and to undertake detailed inventories of the region's 1,300 stationary emitters of hydrocarbons—precursors to ozone. Especially suspicious of smokestacks, they stepped up aerial oversight of Atlanta-area factories, from Atlantic Steel in northwest Atlanta to Mayo Chemical in Smyrna to Southwire out in Carrollton to Georgia Power's many plants.[148]

To make their job possible, air and other regulators leaned on rapidly evolving science that framed problems of pollution from outside *any* local perspective, through technologies and professional work that no longer required input from communities or citizens whose local environments were at stake. That was especially true with the environmental modeling on which officials came to increasingly rely. For each air-pollution permit they approved for a factory or power plant, they already had to set a maximum level of emissions, calculated to not add unduly to pollutant levels within the metro region. The new rules on "significant deterioration" now required them to project a single facility's impacts across an aerial commons that was more expansive, not just limited to the metropolitan area. Monitors newly set up in state parks, small towns, and agricultural areas provided the "baseline" by which they assessed Atlanta-area pollution impacts, to set the permitted emission level for a single factory.[149] From the air or water that citizens actually experienced, staff singled out, measured, and inscribed within their own schemes those variables that most mattered to pollution control: "sources in the Atlanta area" including automobiles, aircraft, factories, power plants, incinerators, and so on, along with the "meteorological and topographic complexities of the area"—the former of which might include "wind direction, wind speed, atmospheric stability, and [a pollutant's] mixing height."[150]

The great virtue of this technocratic pursuit of pollution control was that, at least in theory, it would not be swayed either by polluters or by those communities and activists who were most organized, who protested most loudly. Environmental policy came to hinge on quantifications calculated without regard to socioeconomics or race or political connections. Rather than requiring or nourishing a more popular and grassroots environmental citizenship, at this point still largely confined to a white middle class, technocratic tools enabled regulators to seek out where pollution itself was often the worst, where the nation's most dangerous pollution problems lay. As Blum herself put it, "the people that live in the urban areas" are "the most impacted." "They breathe the air; they eat the [leaded] paint; they drink the water from the rusty pipes. And yet those are the people who have never had public input into our program."[151] Strictly technical determinations of what pollution would be allowed did tend to leave ordinary citizens on the outside, looking in. Yet with the powerful leverage now available to them, EPA officials *could*, at least under some conditions, persuade the Georgia legislature to take action with minimal support or lobbying from environmental groups. Faced with loss of federal funds for highways and sewers if Atlanta's ozone and carbon monoxide levels did not meet EPA standards, in early 1979 the then governor Busbee "quietly" introduced a bill in the Georgia legislature that set up a mandatory inspection system for cars in the Atlanta area. Forcing drivers to install emission controls at an average cost of $100 each (over $350 in today's dollars), it nevertheless sailed through, passing with little controversy.[152]

The "sharp emphasis on health" at Carter's EPA also aligned it with other environmental agencies, notably OSHA. Most of them were now grappling with the regulatory implications of another growing vein of environmental expertise, on the long-term or "chronic" effects of industrial chemicals. While unsettling health as well as ecological consequences of a "chemical revolution" had long been studied, by the late 1970s scientific studies of chemical after chemical had confirmed just how dire their chronic effects on humans could become. The methodological innovations enabling this knowledge also involved careful constructions that, as with environmental modeling, set scientists' perspectives apart from those of ordinary citizens. Environmental epidemiologists culled medical records and exposure levels from more versus less exposed human populations; environmental toxicologists, of differently exposed laboratory animals standing in for people.[153] Environmental cancer and the scourge of the "carcinogen" absorbed the deliberations of EPA and other policy makers across the Carter administration; it was, after all, still the second-leading killer of Americans and the only major killer whose mortality rate, as of 1980, was still rising. Bolstering the chemical preoccupations of the EPA in particular were two laws passed in 1976, late in the Ford administration: the Resource Conservation and Recovery Act, which drew a distinction between ordinary and more "hazardous" waste disposal, and a Toxic Substances Control Act, which charged the EPA with developing a system for screening the actual or potential toxic effects of chemicals even prior to their being produced or marketed. Not just here but in other regulatory arenas of the federal environmental state—air and water pollution as well as worker and consumer health—the search was on for better ways of singling out the more "hazardous" or "toxic" chemicals from ordinary and presumably safer ones, to find those that might prove to be the next PCBs or asbestos.[154] Through the ministrations of Georgia's own state regulators, this intensifying federal oversight of toxic chemicals reached directly into the Atlanta region's industrial plants.

Their official oversight of toxics at the Lockheed plant in Marietta began in 1976, the same year that Lockheed's industrial waste–treatment plant, completed nearly a decade before under Rock Howard, was named the best in Georgia.[155] Early that year, when a Lockheed official sought state approval of what it had been doing with some of the plant's oily wastes—shipping it to the Westview Sanitary Landfill to tamp down dust—officials found nothing wrong with the practice.[156] But small amounts of chromate, cadmium, and other known toxins then turned up in the analysis of a waste sample, and by midyear, having "stud[ied] the effect of application of this waste to the road at Westview" and "in view of the fact that there are homes in the vicinity," the EPD declared that the "hydrology" was worrisome and rescinded its approval. Now this waste could not just be sprayed about wherever; its disposal required special handling.[157] Three years later, after a complaint that Lockheed had been dumping wastes into a public landfill, an EPD inspector visiting the Lockheed facilities for the first time carefully itemized all the chief waste chemicals that were especially "hazardous." He found seven toxics in the anodizing process, ten in plating, two for painting, and eight for cleaning and stripping, from "dichromate (Cr2O7)" to "residual metals." The inspector then inquired where these wastes were being shipped, at least in large amounts. The "cyanide and cadmium containing wastes" went to Chemical Waste Management in Alabama; empty but unrinsed paint cans were hauled to the Cobb County sanitary landfill; and six thousand gallons a month of waste oil was sold to a buyer firm in Cartersville. Offering several recommendations for making these waste streams less dangerous, she voiced special concerned about the "filter cake" now being poured into a "lagoon on the property." Accumulating via a steady stream of some thirteen thousand gallons a week, this "lagoon" would soon be declared a hazardous waste site. Its composition needed to be analyzed for cyanide, cadmium, chromium, lead, fluoride, "chlorinated hydrocarbons (total)," and other toxics, she urged.[158] Not only had inspectors begun looking much more closely at what was being done inside a plant like Lockheed's; chemically speaking, they were becoming much more inclined to name names.

In addition, by the late 1970s hazardous waste dumps, those repositories of chemicals now generated by the production lines of high-tech companies like Lockheed, were now inspiring an environmental awakening largely independent of any self-identified "environmentalist" group. As substances seeped into backyards and local children sickened, affected, often lower-end neighborhoods organized outcries. The most troublesome for EPA administrators unfolded at Love Canal, New York.[159] Once the federal EPA finally began to intervene there, the person who became the agency's contact with the Love Canal activism was Barbara Blum. Her suburban, homeowner activism in Atlanta had prepared her well for reaching out to the Love Canal Homeowners Association and for chaperoning a federal intervention in this aggrieved New York community. Blum helped lead the EPA's brokering of the final deal that helped the more than seven hundred residents move. The Carter administration then pushed through Congress a federal Superfund program to clean up similar sites around the nation.

Blum's own personal passage illustrates how stepping into this statist vantage point could nourish a critique of self-identified environmentalists and how it could incline officials such as herself toward less visibly natural and often the least healthy environments downtown. She retained much sympathy for environmental groups, finding their stances "either supportive . . . or to the left" of her own and "really good" for countering other political pressures the agency faced. Nevertheless, from the "grander scale" "overview" she had as an EPA administrator, she felt compelled to criticize how "esoteric" and "upper middle class" the self-identified "environmental constituency" remained.[160] Her response was to try and "broaden" the coalitions and issues that counted as "environmental," and she honed in on those places and people neglected by an Atlanta environmental movement she knew so well. She called especially for an emphasis on the "urban environment" and "involvement of minorities," of which there had been "very little." In a speech before the national Sierra Club, Blum made her case: "It's time for all urban residents, inner-city and suburban, to acknowledge that they share a common destiny," "time for the environmental movement to forge a new urban vision and make a sustained commitment to create a healthy urban environment."[161] From the top down Carter officials such as Blum herself sought to broaden the scope of environmental citizenship to include those environments that Black mayors like Maynard Jackson as well civil rights activists now grappled with, not just cityward but factory-ward.

As the Carter administration's EPA imposed these and other new regulatory burdens on industries in and around Atlanta, its OSHA under Eula Bingham meted out the most loudly contested impositions on corporate Atlanta and Georgia. Under Carter and Bingham, the OSHA inspectorate doubled its personnel and consolidated new approaches to occupational ailments that broke definitively with existing industrial-hygiene science and practice, for decades closely allied with the views and needs—and often the funding—of corporate owners and managers.[162] By the time Carter took office, the new laws and agencies elevated the work of scientific and university-based allies already well on their way with innovative investigations in environmental toxicology and epidemiology that compelled tighter standards and stronger sanctions. Though the first rules put out by OSHA in the early 1970s had largely duplicated the so-called Threshold Limit Values established by a corporate-affiliated professional group, the American Conference of Governmental and Industrial Hygienists (ACGIH), the Carter administration began proposing stricter standards, in some cases considerably so. Among the many workplace dangers targeted by Bingham's OSHA, in 1978 alone it issued more demanding rules for lead, benzene, arsenic, acrylonitrile (used in plastics production), DCBH (a pesticide), and cotton dust.

The new rule for cotton dust, clouding the air of textile mills as workers converted plant fibers into fabrics, proposed to effectively overturn a first federal standard, set in 1971, still "not strictly enforced." Whereas this earlier rule had limited the amount of dust to one thousand micrograms per cubic meter in the air breathed by textile workers, the new one under Carter dropped the allowable dust by four-fifths to two hundred, a dramatic tightening. OSHA officials saw this stricter rule as not really a partisan matter, based as it was on reputable scientific studies and begun, as it had been, during the prior Republican administration. But the resistance that greeted the new cotton-dust rule, first flaring inside the administration itself and then extending to an industry largely based in the Southeast, would eventually peg Carter, his appointees, his labor allies, and the Democratic Party broadly writ as the villains.[163] The back-and-forth between his advisers became so intense that by September 1978 Carter was "put[ting] more time on [it] personally" than "any regulation that's been issued within the last 12 months." Carter wound up throwing his weight behind the much-lower standard.[164] Vehemently challenged by the industry, it underwent repeated judicial review but was eventually upheld by the Supreme Court.[165] While formal cost-benefit analyses for environmental rules had commenced under Carter administration, this decision upholding the cotton-dust standard set a far-reaching limit to its usage in all sorts of regulation over the coming decades. Whatever the costs to businesses, the ruling implied, OSHA and other environmental regulators' first obligations were to citizens affected by environmental "externalities" like pollution, whether indoor in workplaces or outdoors. Their protection, the court's decision confirmed, was now enshrined in the nation's environmental laws.

Industrialists running Georgia's textile plants, who for so long had so little to fear from labor unions or state officials, were appalled by federal OSHA's efforts to protect their workforces against brown lung. Having long enjoyed an iron grip over Georgia's labor laws, their political clout had also left the state's workmen's compensation system "in the dark ages as far as occupational diseases are concerned." One-year filing deadlines, for instance, essentially ruled out compensation for most victims of brown lung, since the disease often took more than a year to manifest itself.[166] For many Atlanta-area textile manufacturers, government enforcement of a corporate environmental citizenship toward factory workers went too far and, from what they knew, for no good reason. The vice president of Dundee Mills, in Griffin, questioned the veracity of federal studies, especially their tallies of the disease's victims: "The occurrence of this thing is far less than has been reported."[167] A small manufacturer in Duluth named Lofton Smith refused to let OSHA inspectors in to his ten-person plant, which made machines for cleaning cotton bolls. In 1977 he took the agency to court over its intrusions and won, successfully limiting OSHA inspectors' rights to enter a workplace without suspected hazards.[168] Successfully defending him was a new "public interest" law firm, the Southeastern Legal Foundation (SLF), headquartered in Atlanta and headed by Ben Blackburn, the former Republican Congressperson.[169] In and around Atlanta, businesspeople had begun their own organizing for a political fight, one directed not against workers or unions but against a federal government newly weighing in on workers' behalf.

Carter's energy-related initiatives, the wilderness lands purchased and preserved under his watch, and his shepherding of a massive new Superfund program for toxic wastes have led at least one presidential historian to rank his among the top three "environmental presidencies."[170] But the contribution of the Carter presidency to the new environmental state went considerably beyond its land acquisitions and newest programs. However tame and timid its titularly "urban" policy, its aggressive new oversight of large polluters and dangerous production lines surpassed those of all previous Democratic as well as Republican administrations.[171] Extending governmental recognition and protection of Americans' environmental citizenship, it reached where Atlanta's own organized environmentalism had little interest, into environments that mattered more for Maynard Jackson's nonenvironmentalist constituencies, Black and poor or working class. On these fronts the expanding impacts of federal environmental regulation around this southern city were not nearly as antidemocratic as James Scott and other critics of "seeing like a state" have implied.[172] From the Civil War and the first Reconstruction through the civil rights era, the drama of southern history has often featured the federal government as a democratizing force. So too during the Carter presidency: from initiatives against industrial and other polluters to the protections it imposed on behalf of Georgia's unorganized workers against brown lung, the federal environmental state constrained the locally strong on behalf of the locally weak.

Though "public participation" remained a sine qua non of decision making in all these federal agencies over the late seventies, this triumph of democratizing also brought a countervailing well-nigh tidal countercurrent, a drift toward technocracy. Fresh obstacles were quietly arising to an environmental citizenship of ordinary citizens, as scientific and legal professionalism gained clout and credence. Those with the most means to hire experts, often polluting corporations themselves, gained advantages, as dismissals of "merely" neighborhood-level and local concerns became more frequent. Erstwhile activists like Blum had graduated from seeing like an environmental citizen to seeing "like a state" and now viewed cities from the heights of the new federal environmental regime. Blum gained a perspective on Atlanta's environmental problems that gravitated closer to the project of civil rights citizenship. Technocratic approaches swept past local complexities and interests to illuminate the unevenness and inequity of pollution exposure and other environmental problems. They compelled officials to address concerns that organized environmentalism in Atlanta had not yet recognized, rendering far more visible, for instance, problems of toxics and hazardous waste sites. Soon these issues would catalyze a new movement in Atlanta and elsewhere that was for both the environment *and* civil rights, a movement also by and for Blacks, on behalf of "environmental justice." Carter-era state building made distinct, little-remembered contributions to this movement's birth. It did so even as it also forged new ways of shrugging off or diminishing the voices of communities afflicted by these very problems, impeding their exercise of any distinctive environmental citizenship of their own.

CHAPTER 6

Sprawling, Skewing, and Greening

The late 1980s were a heady time to be an environmentalist in Georgia. The Georgia legislature buzzed with environmental bills and intentions, as the *Atlanta Journal-Constitution* declared "the environment" to have become, "without much fanfare," a "hot topic." During the start of Gov. Joe Harris's second term, bills for groundwater regulation, landfills, and toxics and for surveying and protecting the state's natural heritage passed the legislature. So promising were the political prospects by early 1989 that the Georgia Conservancy, still considered "the state's most visible environmental group," assigned eight people to the capitol building rather than its usual two.[1] Laws "headed for passage in some form" set out to protect mountaintops from overdevelopment, to construct new reservoirs for managing water scarcity, and to restrain soil erosion. Governor Harris, a Democrat then serving his second term, decided to make a statewide land-use planning bill a primary legislative focus of his final year in office, this in a state where less than a third of the hundred or so counties had land-use plans or zoning codes.[2] Its passage would make the state of Georgia something of a bellwether, "one of only about a dozen states in the nation with a strong growth management system."[3]

Rivaling the flurry of new laws in the Carter governorship—as Georgia built up its environmental state—this flood of conservation- and environment-minded legislative successes marked the historical peak of the political project of environmental citizenship in Georgia. Nationally, historians such as Liz Cohen point to the 1970s and 1980s as a time of accelerating an antiregulatory politics that marked the decline of the "purchaser as citizen."[4] The Republican Party certainly sought to revive antistatism here too, as the next chapter shows. But in Georgia up through this decade, more government-friendly Democrats retained the upper hand, in important part through their cordiality to environmental citizenship. Organized environmentalism itself gathered steam and influence in 1980s Georgia through its political channeling of many concerns and anxieties stoked by a new, more sprawling style of metropolitan growth. New York and California cities had spread this way starting in the early postwar decades, but it was only after 1970 that Atlanta's suburban-growth machine kicked into high gear. Drawing in massive influxes of capital and newcomers, it turned this city into a nation-leading exemplar of Sunbelt capitalism.

By the mid-1980s metro Atlanta spanned sixty miles and ten counties, spreading with such rapidity that it seemed to have sprung up all across north Georgia at once. Its heady population growth surpassed that of all southern cities except Houston (by 1990 the country's fourth largest). But what astounded observers even more was how fast and far it spread, gobbling up surrounding countryside. Over this decade into the 1990s, as Greater Atlanta led the nation in starts for single-family homes for five straight years, the hyperboles abounded. This southern city was "sprawling faster than any metro region in history"! It was the nation's "poster child" for sprawl![5] While Georgia's environmentalists quickly adopted sprawl as an environmental issue, their relationship to what it named was more complicated. After World War II that characteristic mix of concerns styled as "environmental" had first congealed into a coherent political project amid the postwar sprawl of cities such as New York and Los Angeles. Especially from 1970 onward, Atlanta came to look much more like these distant landscapes, as its population swelled and so much of its growing riches poured into the development of subdivisions, malls, and office and industrial parks. Residents of this city increasingly confronted a similar array of environmental problems to those encountered amid sprawl elsewhere, though from the 1970s a new environmental regime and its supporters stood at the ready to contend with them. One other important contrast also distinguished Atlanta's later sprawl from these earlier versions: its new riches concentrated toward the top rather than along the middle of the city's wealth ladder.

As this metropolis grew wealthier over the 1970s into the 1990s, even as its sprawl at once enabled and provoked more environmental citizenship, its new wealth increasingly funneled into the hands of a dwindling share of Atlantans. Tides that had been evening out the distribution of income and wealth over the early post–World War II decades began to turn, as the region's capitalism switched gears from compression toward cleavage. Just as compression capitalism had its foundations in the New Deal, so a national retreat from the New Deal as well as the Great Society, beginning in the 1970s but accelerating under the presidency of Ronald Reagan, began widening economic divisions. Under the sway of government-shrinking policies and tax cuts for corporations and the wealthy, the nation veered toward levels of income and wealth inequality last seen in the early twentieth century. But for older, native Atlantans and other Georgians, long accustomed to living among starker divides of wealth and power than in the North or West, the growing skew brought a reversion toward the familiar. As sprawl picked up steam and as poorer as well as middle-class Atlantans began losing ground once more to those at the top, especially if Black, an increasingly fragmented and segmented geography cleaved neighborhoods and residents from one another and from rural places beyond. These trends steered the sway of environmental citizenship, setting new bounds on it even as its aspirants and opportunities grew in realms not just of politics but of private consumption.

As this book has suggested, suburbanization had from its start often involved a kind of environmental consumption, though until the 1960s and 1970s, no one spoke of it as such. Private purchasers had long been drawn to homescapes enveloped by cultivated or wilder greenery, from lawns and trees to parks to countryside nearby. From Druid Hills to BOND and Cascade Heights, from Fernbank to the Chattahoochee's banks, the political project of environmental citizenship had arisen because individual ownership of such places, as private property, had proven insufficiently protective; collective, politically directed action, on the other hand, enabled solutions. From the 1970s onward, with so many government-sanctioned environmental protections now in place and with growing realizations about additional environmental threats, Atlantans explored a host of new ways in which environmental citizenship could inform purchases of food or energy as well as the homes they bought. As environmentalists' politics gained more and more governmental backing, the private opportunities for acting as environmental citizens also proliferated, opening avenues for exercise of those personal ecological virtues that later political theorists from Andrew Dobson to John Barry would unpack.[6] With the return of cleavage capitalism, however, gaps began to yawn between those who could more easily afford to make environmentally virtuous choices and those who could not.

Environmentalism's peaking influence in late 1980s Georgia also stemmed from one other change: a partial rapprochement between environmental and civil rights citizenship. From the early 1970s a new Black leadership had ascended to Atlanta's helm by forging electoral alliances that included white environmentalist as well as civil rights groups, but beyond Election Day activist groups themselves hardly strayed from their separate camps, the one white and the other Black. Compounding their spatial as well as social isolation from each other were the divergent frameworks, values, and priorities of their respective citizenship projects. But some of these dividing lines were now eroding. As a Black middle class grew in scale and security, it gained and also began to advocate for more natural-looking surroundings of its own. As civil rights groups like the SCLC struggled to navigate the growing divides between middle class and poorer Black Atlantans, they also realized that even homeowning Black communities were especially prone to newly recognized environmental problems such as toxics and hazardous wastes. Civil rights activists then started applying their movement's critiques and tactics to those very same problems that white environmentalists had also begun to highlight. As

Atlanta grew explosively through skew and sprawl, its historic role as capital of the nation's civil rights movement also made it a national crucible for a hybrid citizenship project on which white environmental and Black civil rights activists began to collaborate, for "environmental justice."

The Skew and Sprawl of Atlanta's Growth

Greater Atlanta by 1990 spanned 68 miles north to south and was on its way to 128 miles just seven years later. As gargantuan as Los Angeles County in California, it had become the largest "urbanized area" in the Southeast outside of Texas and the twelfth largest in the nation.[7] Atlanta's sprawl, like that of other fast-growing Sunbelt cities from Houston to Phoenix, stemmed from an accelerating metropolitan growth channeled in directions much like those which had earlier transformed New York, Los Angeles, and Chicago. Federal investment provided pivotal underpinnings for this newer sprawl, from the interstate-highway program to an expanded international airport. Between 1958 and 1977 nearly 600 miles of four-lane, limited-access highway rolled across Georgia and into neighboring states, and by the early 2000s the Hartsfield-Jackson Airport would draw more passenger enplanements than any other airport not just in the United States but in the world. Solidifying Atlanta's advantages over southeastern rivals were also federal investments in aerospace and other industries connected to the Cold War. Strategically vital as these public funds were, they likely comprised only a small fraction of the capital flooding into the U.S. South. By the early 1980s surveys such as by the Federal Reserve in Atlanta ranked the region as businesspeople's "no. 1 choice for expansion or relocation."[8] The Atlanta region thereby benefited from not just national but international propellants: newly competitive producers from a recovered Europe and Japan seeking new markets and the continuing transfer of manufacturing from the Northeast and Midwest toward lower-wage regions, Georgia and the rest of the Southeast as well as the developing world. As median household incomes in the U.S. South hiked up from 50 to 90 percent of those in wealthier regions, those of metro Atlantans surged well past the national average.[9]

At least as important to Atlanta's newly consolidated democracy was what average or median figures utterly failed to capture: just how unevenly Atlanta's new wealth, incomes, and opportunities came to be distributed. Off the radar screen of most of environmental citizenship's proponents, yet all too evident to an economically attuned advocacy of civil rights, the "Atlanta paradox" hardened into its modern durability. "Sprawling riches" came to coexist with seemingly ineradicable poverty, much-touted racial harmony with stubborn segregation.[10] Among the federal policies favoring corporations and the wealthy that contributed to this growing "income gap" were deregulatory as well as antilabor measures begun under Carter but taking off under Reagan, along with massive tax cuts for top earners and stockholders.[11] Also contributing to this spreading divergence, according to economists Claudia Goldin and Lawrence Katz, was "skill-biased technological change." The increasingly profitable adoption of new digital and other high-tech tools set new terms for know-how in jobs most in demand, elevating their salaries especially as the education system lagged in spreading those skills to more job seekers.[12] Rising salaries and the rapid growth of computer-related jobs around Atlanta (fourteen times more in 1992 than twenty years earlier) confirm the arrival of the digital revolution there. In the "race between education and technology" characterized by Goldin and Katz, the education of Atlanta's regional workforce may well have been keeping up better than in many other cities. Long a national laggard on education levels, Atlanta's supply of college graduates was also rising quickly, much of it through in-migration of the already educated from the North and West. Across the metro area as a whole, the proportion of adults with a bachelor's degree or more doubled over the two decades to 1990, surpassing 30 percent. But college education had come more easily for white men (42.9 percent) and white women (34.8 percent) than for Black men (20.3 percent) or Black women (24.4 percent).[13] Blacks, especially men, had begun far behind white counterparts, leaving 1980s and 1990s Atlanta with a disproportionately large share of adults who had not finished high school, even as its share of college graduates ranked relatively high.[14]

Whether newly arriving or native to Georgia, those benefiting the most from these changes were Atlanta's most affluent, the executives, administrators, or managers in private corporations and other highly trained professionals: engineers, doctors, and lawyers. Aided by billions of dollars of public investments in its capacities for car, air, and rail travel, along with other infrastructure, by 1988 the city ranked fifth in the number of its headquarters for Fortune 500 companies, tying three other U.S. cities though still behind Houston and Dallas, and had also attracted offices of hundreds of foreign, mostly European companies.[15] Setting up shop in the proliferating office and industrial parks out along its interstates, they drew commutes from high-end employees to their glass-and-steel edifices clustering in "edge cities."[16] Like their fellow highest earners in westerly Sunbelt icons, Atlanta's gained on their counterparts in New York and Los Angeles, pulling away from those across this city's middle echelons as well as its poor, in a reversal of midcentury trends.[17]

That new wealth bulging the wallets and bank accounts of the most privileged Atlantans came not just from paychecks but from investments, symptomatic of a "financialization" fingered by many scholars as contributing to the growing concentration of late twentieth-century Americans' riches.[18] Long home of the southeastern branch of the Federal Reserve Bank, the city benefited from the 1970s unshackling of banking's financial operations from banks themselves, opening wider markets and opportunities for gain.[19] Atlanta's financial firms then veritably burgeoned: over the twenty years to 1993, its herd of banks leaped tenfold; its firms handling stocks, bonds, and commodities multiplied nearly sixfold.[20] The city's investment class was also well endowed: over 36 percent of the stock portfolios held by Atlantans contained more than $100,000, according to one 1984 survey, nearly twice the study's average of 20 percent.[21]

As the financial sector gobbled a growing share of Atlanta's overall wealth, ongoing globalization also may have contributed to the late-century income gap, as other economists and sociologists argue. This influence worked largely through shifts in the location of manufacturing.[22] Closely tied to the United States' converging incomes and wealth over the midcentury, after 1970 factories lost ground in Atlanta as in other parts of the country, as labor-intensive as well as some higher-tech industries chased cheaper labor and other lower production costs abroad.[23] Over the next two decades, manufacturing workers' share of the metro-area workforce—never as great as in northern cities—fell nearly by half, to only 11.8 percent of Atlantans' jobs. Textile factories, the city's biggest manufacturing industry as late as 1960, shrank down to a workforce just over eight thousand by 1992.[24] In aerospace those working at the Lockheed plant in Marietta plummeted from a late-sixties peak of twenty thousand to fewer than nine thousand workers, as GM's Doraville auto assembly plant halved its workforce.[25]

Threats to globalize production by moving factories elsewhere also strengthened employers' hands in negotiations over wages, another reason incomes stagnated along the middle and lower reaches of the city's wealth ladder. A declining membership in labor unions weakened employees' bargaining power. As much as a third of the nation's growing income inequality over the later twentieth century stemmed from unions' declining numbers and "density" in labor strongholds like Detroit and other northern and midwestern cities.[26] Atlanta's workforce shared in this trend, but from a much lower peak. From aerospace to auto making, as corporations sought to automate shop floors and outsource production lines, they forced repeated concessions from Atlanta-area unions.[27] Ununionized companies from Dundee, the textile manufacturer; to Scientific Atlanta, a high-tech instrument maker; to Southwire, a Georgia-hatched manufacturer of wire and cable effectively squelched organizing drives.[28] From its 1970 high the proportion of private-sector workers in Atlanta's (as well as the rest of Georgia's) labor unions shrunk by half over the next two decades, to 8.1 percent in the Atlanta metro area, closer to the 6.9 percent for the entire state's private workforce.[29] Not surprisingly, the average wages in Atlanta-area manufacturing jobs continued to lag behind industrial powerhouses like Detroit, whose industrial workers still made 40 percent more than Atlanta's in 1991, nearly unchanged from fifteen years earlier.[30]

A countercurrent came through the successful unionization efforts of employees in the public sector, by 1989 harboring more of Atlanta's jobs than manufacturing. Unions for teachers, police, and municipal employees all saw steady growth.[31] Alongside the growing outreach of mostly white unions across racial lines, the labor activism of the SCLC and other civil rights groups and the labor-friendliness of many Black political leaders meant that more and more of these public-sector workers and unions were Black.[32]

While metro Atlanta's share of middle-income earners did gain on many northern and western cities' from 1970, its lower starting point combined with other countervailing currents to prevent its middle class from catching up. The fortunes of some households improved; Blacks as well as whites ascended from the lower into more middling income brackets. But, by the end of the 1980s, it had also become clear that the city's sprawling growth was failing to augment the wealth and prospects of a large share of Atlantans. Along the lower echelons of the metro region's wealth ladder, almost 30 percent of whites and half of Blacks still lived on only 60 percent or less of the metro area's mean income.[33] Those in lower-end service jobs were still paid poorly in comparison with other cities. "Contract cleaning" or janitorial work in Atlanta had lower take-home pay not just than northern, midwestern, and western cities but most other cities in the South (only Baltimore's was lower), with "among the lowest" benefits. Over 80 percent of these cleaning workers were Black.[34] While Atlanta's poverty rate fell slightly over the 1970s and 1980s, those improvements concentrated among whoever could make it out to the suburbs. In the downtown area Black poverty rates went in a starkly different direction, hiking up past 50 percent. This ongoing concentration of poverty among downtown Blacks ensured the city an unusually larger share of poor people: a Brookings study of the 2000 census found Atlanta's poverty rate third highest among twenty-six U.S. metropolises.[35]

A spatial mismatch grew as well, between where the most abundant and lucrative jobs lay and where those who most needed work could afford homes, further limiting the opportunities available to poorer Atlantans. Metro-area jobs flocked in the direction of Atlanta's richest whites, toward the more exclusive and expensive neighborhoods of the northside (map 6.1). The burgeoning suburban office parks and malls along I-75, I-85, and I-285, especially toward the north, provided an abundance of white-collar and retail work seemingly independent of downtown. Only the Hartsfield (later Hartsfield-Jackson) Airport on the southside anchored a comparable hub near Atlanta's expanding Black suburbs, and on a remarkably lesser scale. The better-paying new jobs offered in these hubs often required higher levels of education that limited who could aspire to them. Inside the city as well, noted a 1987 study, "the major employment growth . . . has been in high-skill service and technical jobs that minority and low-income groups frequently lack the skills to fill."[36] Even for fast-food companies, a post-1970 growth industry featuring mostly lower-wage jobs, hourly pay in the suburbs surpassed that in downtown restaurants.[37] As Atlanta sprawled, an unequal geography of job opportunities was solidifying. Most all of these new higher-paying jobs lay distant from the homes of most of Atlanta's poorer or working-class residents and largely inaccessible to public transit like MARTA, thanks to the unwillingness of so many suburban counties to fund it.[38]

Two decades later, after the 1980s generation of metro-area children had come of age, social scientists turned to studying just how upwardly mobile they had become. Not very, it turned out. Those growing up poor in the Atlanta commuting zone had less of a chance of moving up into higher-income brackets than those in just about any other metro area in the nation. Compared with ninety-nine of the nation's other largest cities, the expected mobility for a child raised in a family with an income below the median ranked ninety-sixth, fourth from the bottom. The only metro areas worse than Atlanta in enabling socioeconomic mobility among their lower-income residents were Charlotte and Fayetteville in North Carolina and Memphis, Tennessee—three other southern cities. From the 1980s over half of Georgia's more rural commuting zones had actually provided greater opportunities for their poorer children to move up the economic ladder than had this state's capital city.[39]

Especially relevant to the larger political transformations unfolding across the state, however, was how Atlanta's post-1970 growth altered the distribution of riches between the metro area and rural Georgia's small towns and countryside.[40] Outside the South's "ballyhooed urban growth areas," noted the sociologists William Falk and Thomas Lyson in 1988, states like Georgia remained "checkered with pockets of slow growth, stagnation, and poverty."[41] While smaller cities such as Savannah and Macon did better, rural white and especially Black Belt areas bore the brunt of economic disfavor. Holding down far fewer high-wage financial, professional, or managerial jobs, Georgians outside Atlanta were also much less likely to have college degrees, with only 17.5 percent holding at least a bachelor's. Companies seeking the most educated employees showed little interest in relocating to small towns or rural settings. The rest of Georgia also lost manufacturing jobs at a faster clip than the metro area. The metro area's share of the state's overall income rose, even as more of it went into top earners' pocketbooks. As the proportion of Georgians earning lower incomes rose, the share of those earning middle incomes dropped from just over half to 43 percent. As for Georgia's Gini index, that social scientific index of economic inequality (with 0 as perfect equality of incomes and 1 as the most extreme inequality), it had already begun this period on a par with that of the United States. As figure 6.1 shows, over the next three decades, the rise in Georgians' Gini index paralleled that of the nation as a whole, as the upper 10 percent raked in a growing share of the state's income.

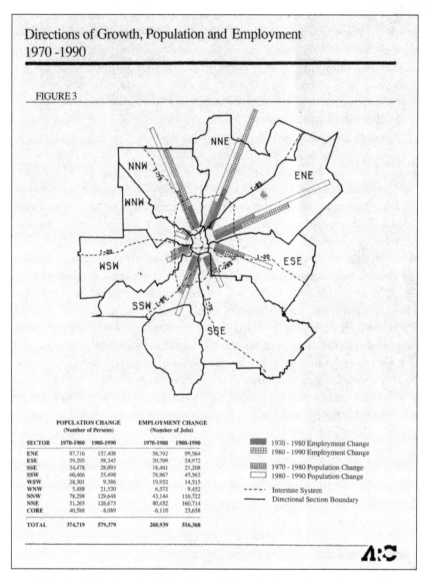

Directions of Growth, Population and Employment
1970 - 1990

FIGURE 3

SECTOR	POPULATION CHANGE (Number of Persons)		EMPLOYMENT CHANGE (Number of Jobs)	
	1970-1980	1980-1990	1970-1980	1980-1990
ENE	87,716	157,408	56,792	99,564
ESE	59,295	58,342	20,709	24,972
SSE	34,478	28,993	18,461	21,208
SSW	60,466	55,498	28,967	45,563
WSW	38,301	9,386	19,952	14,515
WNW	5,488	21,520	6,572	9,452
NNW	78,298	129,648	43,144	116,722
NNE	51,265	126,673	80,452	160,714
CORE	40,588	-8,089	-6,110	23,658
TOTAL	374,719	579,379	268,939	516,368

▓ 1970 - 1980 Employment Change
▦ 1980 - 1990 Employment Change

▦ 1970 - 1980 Population Change
☐ 1980 - 1990 Population Change

- - - - Interstate System
——— Directional Section Boundary

ARC

MAP 6.1. The lopsided trajectories of Atlanta's population and job growth over the 1970s and 1980s. Most of the metro area's new employment as well as new residents headed to the north side, already the wealthiest and whitest segment of the city. Atlanta Regional Commission, *Atlanta Region Outlook* (Atlanta: Atlanta Regional Commission, 1991), Planning Atlanta Planning Publications Collection, Georgia State University Library, 15.

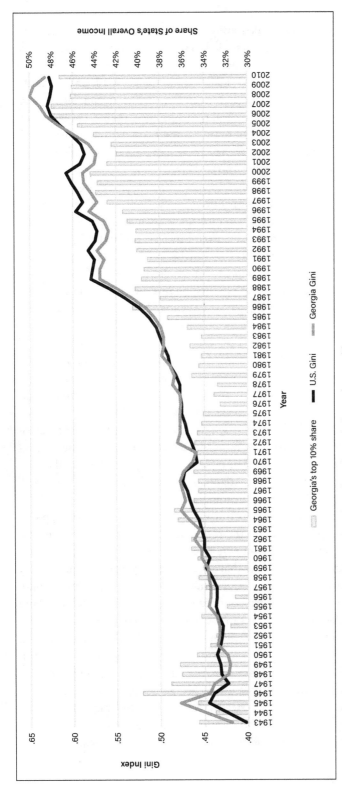

FIGURE 6.1. Redistributing incomes toward the top. The chart shows how Georgia's Gini index, roughly equivalent to that of the United States by 1970, rose in tandem with it into the early 2000s as the share of income taken home by Georgia's top-earning 10 percent grew substantially. Mark W. Frank, "U.S. State-Level Income Inequality Data," Sam Houston State University, 2021, https://www.shsu.edu/~eco_mwf/inequality.html.

As Georgia's wealthiest pulled away from the rest, Atlanta's spread-out growth also had ecological impacts similar to sprawl elsewhere. Far more visible through the lens of environmental than of civil rights citizenship and obscured through the socioeconomic glasses that illuminated its wealth and racial divides, the city's growth wrought a gargantuan destruction of rural lands, flora, and fauna. As new subdivisions, shopping centers, workplaces, and other perquisites of cities like Atlanta shifted outward, their "sprawl" razed mammoth expanses of the informal commons that many had long enjoyed. Fulton and DeKalb County had been nearly two-thirds forested as late as 1967.[42] But by the midseventies, satellite photos showed that across the enlarging metro area, only 50 percent of the land had a heavy tree canopy. Between 1975 and 1985 the metro area lost a further eleven million trees, and by 1996 its denser tree cover had fallen by half, to cover only a quarter of metro-area land.[43] The loss of a living canopy gradually accrued its own further ecological consequences for the Atlanta region: quicker and more voluminous storm runoffs, rising temperatures, and lessening absorption of air pollutants, including diminished sequestration of the carbon driving global warming.[44] Nationally, these consequences nourished a late-century environmental notoriety for metro Atlanta, as epitomizing the ravages of sprawl. They also stirred a strengthening antisprawl movement within the metro area itself.[45] At the same time, and not so paradoxically, more and more Atlantans were themselves moving out from the city, purchasing or visiting places they'd come to associate with "the environment," surrounded by a visible nature of woods, fields, and farms.

The critique of "sprawl" would often draw a sharp line between preexisting forests or meadows that were razed for development and those that remained, enabling a certain ethical and political clarity. Yet the actual consequences of city outgrowth for the Atlanta region's ecology were more mixed, often challenging inclinations to dichotomize. Ecologists themselves had just begun defining the notion of an "urban-rural gradient" that would support a more evenhanded perspective on the resultant ecological patterns along the transect that ran from the downtown across suburbs into the surrounding countryside.[46] Among the changes that ensued as this gradient shifted quickly outward into what had been rural Georgia, agriculture generally lost ground. Land devoted to farms in the ten counties shrank by half between 1969 and 1987. But while the woods on farms in the outer metro counties shrank, farmers let the woods grow back on farmland closer in, in DeKalb and Fulton Counties, anticipating its sale to subdividers. Nor was the fate of farm animals simply one of vanishing. Chickens devoted to egg laying did indeed disappear from most of the metro counties; yet the numbers of those bred to become "broilers" held relatively steady. While cows and calves underwent a more uniform decline across the metro counties, one sector of agriculture flourished anew: the growing of nursery crops. Potting and bedding plants, even sod itself, were the ultimate in intensive agriculture, making far less demands for large acreage and producing goods directly marketable to Atlanta's growing ranks of suburbanites. Nursery crop sales tripled across the region between 1973 and 1987.[47] As so many farmers in the region either left or adjusted to Atlanta's suburbanizing boom, those who refused to sell or change increasingly stood out as strange, even fascinating. One J. C. Hyde, a holdout in East Cobb, captivated local journalists as well as the head of the county's historical preservation commission: "Within a 13-mile radius of Atlanta, where else can you find a man who is farming land that has been farmed continuously for almost 150 years who is still using a mule?"[48]

Among the region's less domesticated fauna, many animals, birds, and other creatures simply lost their habitats, either through outright destruction or fragmentation—when roads and other building projects sliced into what had been continuous stretches of forest or field. Those most vulnerable to the changes were the specialist species, those not inclined to travel very far or most at home in the thick of the forest or in ecotones such as waterways, whose confinement made their denizens still more vulnerable. Of the forty-four animal species now recognized as endangered or rare by Georgia's Department of Natural Resources in the ten metro counties, most were crustaceans, amphibians, or fish.[49] They lived in habitats that were among the most disturbed by urbanizing landscape change: rivers that had been dammed, larger streams long since polluted, and the smaller creeks whose courses clogged with silt and other runoff from building projects.

Exemplary of those most threatened was the Chattahoochee crayfish (*Cambarus howardi*). Among the continent's largest freshwater crustaceans, it is one of some 550 different species worldwide, of which the wet and warm U.S. Southeast harbors the planet's greatest diversity. The bluish-green tint of its carapace, shading into bright yellow-orange rims at the joints, distinguishes it from the duller shades of its more ubiquitous cousins, the common (*Cambarus bartonii bartonii*) and variable (*Cambarus latimanus)* crayfishes. Half the size as well, only an inch and half when full grown, its prospects suffered tremendously from its much more restricted range, especially as it prefers smaller streams and those particular stretches where the water pools or gently runs or "riffles" over sand, cobble, or gravel. Found in only one place in the world beyond the Georgia Piedmont (in Alabama) but not quite as parochial as many other of the twenty species of crayfish declared endangered in Georgia, the Chattahoochee crayfish had the misfortune of establishing its range in that part of Georgia that "essentially straddles the Atlanta metropolitan area." And as this region's streams choked up with pollution or silt, as they were crossed with roads or diverted through culverts, and as developers cleared stream banks of the vegetative detritus on which these crayfish fed, the range of the Chattahoochee crayfish shrank back.[50] Found across most of the metro counties in surveys between 1951 and 1976, by 2006 it had vanished from "historic locations in DeKalb, Fulton, Forsyth, and Lumpkin Counties" and was gone as well from most of its original sites in Cobb. The only place it hung on was one Atlanta's environmentalists had successfully pushed to preserve: "the lower reaches of Sope Creek, in the Chattahoochee River National Recreation Area."[51]

At the same time, Atlanta's sprawl helped other more readily adaptable, "generalist" species to thrive, among them, white-tailed deer. When the state Game and Fish Commission had begun a restocking program just after World War II, these deer, decimated over earlier centuries by hunting, had not been seen in north or central Georgia for many decades. But already by the early 1970s, they numbered around 250,000, and by 1990 over a million, with the greatest concentration across the Georgia Piedmont including where metropolitan Atlanta burgeoned. The forest edges chopped out by sprawl were a big reason why; state game officials noted how "home gardens surrounded by woods are particularly attractive to deer and that they seem to prefer fertilized plants."[52] Other creatures whose needs for food and cover could be served by interspersion of trees and suburbs also prospered: squirrels, chipmunks, raccoons, and opossums. By 1987 the director of the Chattahoochee Nature Center in Roswell was noting how "recent increases in the possum population parallel growth in the suburbs," and a Cobb County animal control official cited a doubling of small wildlife carcasses over the past decade on county roadways.[53]

Bird populations likely underwent a similar transformation. Species diversity tailed off by the time they got downtown, but bird density itself peaked in "moderately disturbed areas," including some parts of the suburbs.[54] Studies done across urban-rural gradients, including one in the Georgia Piedmont itself, suggest why. Most of the region's bird species (66 percent by one study) preferred forested areas for breeding, with only 14 percent selecting urban or suburban nests—including the classic "weedy" bird species such as crows and starlings, but also American robins, northern mockingbirds, and house finches. Some of the forest-breeding birds like the black-and-white warbler did confine their activities to forest canopies, but many also strayed into a wider variety of human-influenced habitat types. Avian counterparts to the squirrels and raccoons, they included not just migrants but many permanent residents: downy woodpeckers, tufted titmice, and, probably the most numerous of all, northern cardinals.[55] When scientists in the early 2000s sought to track exposure to the West Nile virus among bird species along Atlanta's urban-rural gradient, they found cardinals "ubiquitous" throughout. They also discovered a pattern among these cardinals resembling that observed by wildlife officials among opossums: those along the midpoints of the gradient looked the best nourished, "likely" because of the "supplemental food sources (in the form of bird feeders and fruiting vegetation)."[56]

That wildlife did not simply vanish as land suburbanized points to how, for all the paving and house building involved, Atlanta's newer residential landscape actually retained greenery, whether thinner and lower canopies or new plantings.[57] After all, inclinations to seek out urban-edge "nature" drove much of process by which rural land was razed, built on, or otherwise converted, and a significant share of the newfound wealth went not into workplaces or markets nor even into people's houses but into the landscapes that surrounded these. While racially motivated white flight was undoubtedly a powerful force propelling many whites out from downtown, the nature sell, long vital to suburbs' appeal, remained strong among Atlanta's expanding suburban and exurban migrants after 1970.

Homescapes of Environmental Consumption

By this time a sine qua non marker of the middle class in long-richer regions of the United States, the single-family detached home that dominated Atlanta's housing boom reflected the metro area's accumulating wealth. By 1973, 63 percent of Atlanta's new residential construction followed this classically suburban style, finally catching up to where the national average had been in 1965, even as spiking interest rates on home loans pushed that national average itself lower.[58] Over the 1980s Atlanta's housing starts frequently led those of all other U.S. cities, now joining top-ranked counties in Texas and other Sunbelt states and provoking declarations like how "nation's hottest metropolitan counties have a distinctly southern accent."[59] If Atlanta-metro homeownership then reached a historical peak by 1990, its own patrimonial middle class still lagged compared with counterparts elsewhere; the share of Atlanta households holding title to their living quarters still ranked in the bottom third of the hundred biggest cities.[60] The many, often contrasting ways in which nature and "the environment" figured in Atlanta's changing housing markets, as well as the changing floral and cultivational choices Atlantans made about the landed homes they bought, help explain how, in this place and time of growing economic divides, environmental concerns also gained greater prominence.

On the housing front the opportunities for homes enveloped in trees and other greenery did not spill easily across class or racial lines, despite a new civil rights law barring housing discrimination, even as Black suburbs spread out from established beachheads. By the mid-1970s those who were white and poor or working-class (making under $10,000 a year), courtesy of white flight, were still far more likely to live near to a forest patch and in a more suburbward location than Black people. Atlantans with middle incomes were more likely than those who were poorer to live in tracts with some forest, but whites in the middle brackets were more likely to do so than Blacks. A decade and a half later, by 1990, long-standing barriers to Black ownership combined with accelerating white flight and massive home building in the city's outer suburban rings to draw a whopping 84 percent of whites there, up from only half in 1970. Yet by then 45 percent of metro-area Blacks also lived in its outer rings, up from only 14 percent two decades before. Atlanta once more partly defied northern models of a white doughnut with a Black "hole" at the center. Thanks to the suburban migration of its sizeable and growing Black middle class, the doughnut itself had become partly Black.[61]

Those whites with the very highest incomes, the greatest beneficiaries of Atlanta's post-1970 growth, had already begun to dominate tracts with the most tree cover north of downtown, where the clean and preserved portion of the Chattahoochee River also curled. By the mid-1980s national observers of housing markets were declaring the Atlanta metro area "land of the megahouse" and otherwise noting its shift toward "homes with more upscale amenities," with nearby nature among the foremost of amenities buyers sought.[62] Across East Cobb and North Fulton into Gwinnett and southeast DeKalb, luxury home building thrived, complete with perks like complementary tennis courts and golf courses and plenty of open space.[63] Of those houses worth half a million in the metro area in 1990—the top 1 percent for this region—nearly a third lay in just three contiguous northerly census tracts; half if a handful of others nearby were added.[64] Unlike many other U.S. cities, old money still retained its primary stronghold closer to downtown, along West Paces Ferry Road through Buckhead, with mansions like that of Ann Cox Chambers, a newspaper-publishing heir on *Forbes* listings of America's wealthiest. Another listed Atlantan, Ted Turner, the cable magnate who developed CNN into a media empire, had a house in North Atlanta, possibly Alpharetta, by the late 1980s, also home to "perhaps" the region's most pricey subdivision, the "Country Club of the South," occupied by "baby-boomers who struck it rich as entrepreneurs or rose quickly to the top at corporations such as Coca- Cola, Nabisco, Arthur Anderson Co. and IBM." With homes priced between $329,000 and $2 million, it featured a Jack Nicklaus–designed eighteen-hole golf course, where "newly paved streets wind through a forest of towering pines and dogwood blossoms," and a "rolling landscape stretches as far as the eye can see."[65]

Here and elsewhere Atlanta's upper-end homescapes involved what was likely the metro area's most costly as well as lucrative environmental consumption, those expanding consumer markets that comprised much of its "environmental culture." That was what historian Sam Hays named, as he put it, that "set of values that prompt people to emphasize environmental quality."[66] But if residents of the "Country Club of the South" had bought into this development because of its towering pines and rolling landscape, then their purchase may have reflected "environmental values" and "quality" but not necessarily environmental *citizenship*. Treasuring these as emblems of a larger natural world did entail a more outside or overarching perspective on one's own private property, yet the awareness and value purchasers invested in these larger contexts could remain strictly personal and individual. Only when they also bought with more social, collective, or even political ends in mind did their environmental consumption double as an act of environmental citizenship. With the return of cleavage capitalism, high-end aspirations to greater "environmental quality" in housing could entail values that were environmental yet not so citizenly. The quest could devolve into an individualized and competitive pursuit of an "environmental quality" in which a mix of natural surroundings with expensiveness distinguished Atlanta's "high quality" environments from ordinary downtown or suburban living.

As a capital of wealth and income concentration in the South, the Atlanta of the 1970s also gave birth to a print purveyor of these aspirations, *Southern Accents*, "the single consumer magazine of national importance to come out of Atlanta."[67] Pitching horticulture as well as home design for the upper middle class and outright rich, it began in 1975 when the Atlanta-based publisher of the high-end, glossy *Architectural Digest*, Walter Mitchell, fielded a complaint that it never featured homes in the U.S. South. To "fill . . . a gap in the coverage," he launched a new publication for high-end southern readers, covering gardens as well as homes, for "people who can afford fine things, and appreciate them." Its appeal to better-financed as well as more discriminating tastes was also what distinguished it from its main competition, the Birmingham-published *Southern Living*. The new magazine was a smashing success, with a circulation of 205,000 by 1985. According to the publisher, *Southern Accents* readers had an average annual income of $129,000—an especially "affluent lot," given that the U.S. median household income was only around $25,000.[68] Through regular features of "breathtakingly beautiful gardens" and its coffee-table book *Gardens of the South*, *Southern Accents* traded in not just snob appeal but nostalgic impressions of permanence, "the look of being old." And however high-end its featured gardens and homes, the magazine embodied what much other of Atlanta's new environmental culture shared: a pursuit of southernness apparently unshadowed by racial conflict, through choice and cultivation of regional native plants. However white most writers and readers of *Southern Accents* probably were, they favored "typically Southern plant materials"—dogwoods, azaleas, and so on—and explored ways of making "southern gardens . . . distinctive" in look and feel.[69]

Beyond *Southern Accents* the Atlanta-area megaphones prodding this South-minded tailoring of land and plantings included newspaper garden columnists as well as the somewhat less snobbish *Southern Living* itself. Launched in 1966 by the publisher of *Progressive Farmer*, it had been modeled on western regional publications like *Sunset*, with articles covering not just home interiors but the outdoors of a specifically "southern" lifestyle.[70] *Southern Living* also encouraged distinctively southern homescapes among affluent white home-owners. It framed considerations of local soil and climate as well as choices between species of grasses, trees, and shrubs and of right ways to plant as chances "to give a Southern accent to your surroundings."[71] Around Atlan-ta's suburbs even the lawns' nearly identical look to suburban counterparts in the North and elsewhere came through grass species carefully adapted to this region: heat-tolerant Bermuda grasses and, after 1970, new fescue vari-ants, which by the early 1990s composed nearly three quarters of Atlanta-area lawns.[72] While evergreen shrubs became as popular there as in northern sub-urbs, species like yews and blue spruce that prospered to the north did less well in the southern heat. So *Southern Living*'s and other regional horticultur-alists urged the use of nonnatives such as boxwoods but also azaleas, rhodo-dendrons, and mountain laurels and, for trees, magnolias and dogwoods, all of them including natives to the South.[73]

These plantings proliferated not just in the highest-end homescapes but into the middle reaches of the metro-area housing market. With the aver-age Atlanta home price running above $130,000 by 1988, home buyers had many choices down to a modest $75,000, especially if white. Few builders sold houses that were any cheaper. Also discouraging less affluent home buyers, interest rates for mortgage loans had surged to historical highs and hovered above 10 percent into the mid-decade. The city's offerings exemplified what a local reporter also found to be the case nationally, from an Urban Land Insti-tute report: that "housing is becoming less affordable, even widely unafford-able, for middle-class and poor Americans alike."[74] With less affluent white customers also often unwilling to consider cheaper offerings in neighborhoods into which Black families were moving, they did have one other option: living farther out. Hence the attraction of a county like Fayette or Cherokee, here-tofore considered too distant a commute. Over the 1980s these newest exten-sions of the metro area emerged as some of its hottest housing markets, be-cause of their more modestly priced land and houses and still-rural settings as well as their overwhelmingly white racial demographic.[75]

These front edges of metro-area sprawl gained their own distinctive rubric: not "suburbs" but "exurbs." Originating as an ironic caricature of would-be "countrymen" New Yorkers in the early 1950s, by the 1970s "exurb" and "ex-urbia" had gained currency among urban planners and geographers as an ac-tual type of place. The exurb lay out beyond the freeways or beltways, where houses and lots could remain huge or at least sizeable and still encircled by ru-ral land, an informal commons of farms, fields, and woodlots. Even more so than with "suburbia," the outer limits of this "exurbia" remained indistinct. For Atlanta's journalists, just discovering it around this metro area in the late 1980s, it was "land-beyond-the-suburbs-but-just-this-side-of-farm-country."

For Georgia Tech geographers, it named all counties gaining population not more than seventy miles from the state's urban centers.[76] By that definition Georgia's exurbs, led by those around Atlanta, grew faster even than its suburban ones from 1975 to 1985, with counties like Cherokee, Newton, and Forsyth leading the way. The northward migration of Atlanta-area jobs to suburban "edge cities" also eased commutes from farther out, bolstering exurbs' growth. The lower purchase prices in much of exurbia, just being converted from farmland, appealed especially to whites gaining less from the metro area's new wealth, who "do not necessarily have high or middle incomes" but nevertheless "have a strong desire for space and separation." Even if fleeing the prospect of Black neighbors, they were likely also drawn by the "hardwoods," pastures, streams, and lakes ubiquitously mentioned in ads for cheap exurban real estate—and so were "a growing number of middle- to upper-income families." The newcomers joined, as one letter to the editor put it, "us . . . plain country folks who have always, or near 'bout always, lived here," who "became exurbanites only when we got outnumbered by former city dwellers."[77]

From its exurbs and suburbs into its downtown, metro Atlanta's neighborhoods were slowly getting more homogenous not so much racially as economically. On the whole racial segregation waned somewhat from 1970, driven especially by Blacks buying homes in and near mostly white suburbs in Atlanta's outer rings.[78] The forces sustaining racial segregation nevertheless proved remarkably durable within city limits and in inner suburbs like southwest DeKalb turning majority Black.[79] But persisting racial divides coincided with another type of segregation that was on the rise: by income. Atlanta and other southern cities already led the nation on this front by 1970, when 8 percent of its residents lived in the most exclusively affluent tracts and 11 percent in its poorest ones. Three decades later these portions were on their way to doubling: more than a quarter of Atlantans (28.6 percent) lived in neighborhoods either exclusively rich or overwhelmingly poor. Meanwhile, the share of metro Atlantans living in neighborhoods with moderate incomes slipped by 2.3 percent and with high moderate incomes by 9.0 percent. Inside the city limits, middle-income neighborhoods lost even more territory to those dominated by the bottom or top ranks of earners.[80] A mass convergence of the most affluent whites into luxury homes and subdivisions across Atlanta's north drove many of these trends. Another contributor was the opening of more suburban housing to better-off Blacks, who had previously lived in mixed-income neighborhoods alongside poorer Blacks.

Over the 1970s and 1980s, shifts in metro-area income and wealth helped propel more of the city's Blacks into its middle-class suburbs, expanding beachheads of Black homeownership already established along the city's western and southerly edges. As the legal bars to racial discrimination achieved by the civil rights movement helped open new jobs, wealth, and opportunities, including suburban homeownership, the city's Black middle class was discovered in the 1970s by national media and social scientists. This undeclared capital of the civil rights movement now solidified a reputation as a "Black Mecca," despite the growing concentration of poorer Blacks in its downtown.[81] As more and more Blacks moved into neighborhoods with partial tree cover, they too embraced suburban horticulture, a kind of environmental consumption. Yet the ways in which they understood and cultivated their home grounds could resonate less with any recognizably environmental consumption than with modes of belonging to which the project of civil rights citizenship aspired.

Black pathways toward purchase of more typically "suburban" yards and plantings, as exemplified by the experiences of John Evans and James Bussey, embraced their sameness. Unworried about conformity, they read something else in the uniformity of suburban flora: that they as Blacks had joined a lifestyle long considered exclusively white. Evans, by the 1980s a leader of the DeKalb County NAACP, had arrived in Atlanta in 1965 through a job transfer from Chicago, with his new wife. Looking for cheaper options than Cascade Heights, they bought a house in Kirkwood, a sliver of Atlanta city protruding eastward into DeKalb County. Bussey, on the other hand, had himself grown up first in downtown Decatur and in the early 1970s joined other middle-class Blacks moving into DeKalb's unincorporated neighborhoods farther east. Evans found the "modest" trees and landscaping around his home to encapsulate a "community" sense that he valued. Bussey, a professional florist more attentive to plantings, chose his lot in part because of its "very manicured landscaping . . . real cute . . . boxwoods and that kind of thing." For Bussey that "everybody's yard is the same" seemed far more of a virtue than a vice.[82] Neither expressed any desire to seek out native or characteristically southern plantings, nor any eagerness to be surrounded by countryside. In a like vein, garden columns in the *Atlanta Daily World*, the city's most staidly middle class of Black newspapers, instructed readers presumed to be "urban gardeners" in lawn care, mulch, and bug killers.[83]

Those trapped along the lower rungs of the metro area's wealth ladder, especially renters, were largely excluded from any of these opportunities for environmental consumption. Even as overall homeownership rates peaked around 1990, a Black Atlanta still facing racial barriers to mortgages as well as better-paying jobs remained a city of renters, with 54 percent dependent on landlords' control of their living quarters and lots. Black rentals concentrated downtown, while many of the 30 percent of metro area whites who were renters sought living quarters farther out.[84] According to a 1989 report, Atlanta builders' neglect for lower-end markets had given rise to "pervasive and severe" housing deficiencies, from "excessive rent" to "rampant" crowding. Housing prices and rents had grown "much faster than the financial resources of low-income, mostly Black, households," noted a similar investigation, "effectively squeezing them out of the housing market and keeping them trapped in inner-city ghettos." By then, even the editors of the *Atlanta Constitution* bemoaned the scarcity of "cheap housing," as urban planners loudly urged developers in core counties like Fulton to "shift . . . from . . . $100,000-and-up homes to housing affordable to poor and middle-income residents."[85] To close observers the paradoxical character of Atlanta's boom had already become unmistakable: "Growth and its benefits have been unevenly distributed across the metropolitan area and [across] racial and income groups . . . to make the rich richer and the poor at least relatively poorer."[86]

Among the increasingly rich, another vein of environmental consumption echoed the agrarian traditions that still shaped how many thought about the region in which this city lay. Upper-end names and ads frequently invoked the "plantation" ("Lake Charles Plantation") or the "farm" ("Neely Farm") or the "country" ("Country Walk") for landscapes emptied of any actual, productive crops. The Neely Farm development in North Fulton pitched a former estate owner's "fascinat[ion] with agriculture" but then described a subdivision "peacefully stretch[ed] one mile along the Chattahoochee River," with a "private 20 acre riverside park." Cultivation done by the developers was exclusively ornamental, though "landscaping allowances" of as many as several thousand dollars opened the door to new home buyers' choices of plantings.[87] This consumption of formerly or superficially agrarian environments generated little hint of any citizenship, yet a revived interest in the work of agriculture itself could acquire a more citizenly, even critical ring.

Atlanta's foremost spokesperson here was Celestine Sibley, a journalist for the *Atlanta Constitution*, who in the 1960s had decided to move northward to an old cabin in Roswell, some twenty-five miles north of downtown but still in Fulton County. Ensconced in what she christened Sweet Apple, a "funny little log cabin in a still predominantly rural settlement" just a mile from the Atlanta city line, she immersed herself in a "North Georgia" countryside, tending her own garden and orchard, while fondly observing those neighboring "farmers" and "mountaineers" who still hung on. In a North Fulton turning into this city's version of a Gold Coast, Sibley provided ongoing testimonial to a metro-area audience about how the countryside she had sought out was now vanishing around her.[88] By the early 1970s "some 16 or 17 new houses ha[d] been built within a mile or two of us," and a bit farther off "a lovely rolling green pasture and a stand of beautiful woods" became slated for a housing development complete with a lake and golf course. The older houses, dirt roads, barns, mules, milk cows, and "little animal" trails all were on their way out. By 1977 the "pretty, peaceful little white-columned town" of Roswell was "changing, growing, rushing around like a city." A decade later the gig seemed largely up, with "bulldozers growling and whining in what I once regarded as my peaceful woods, putting down curbs and streets and joining power saws and hammers in a harsh chanty."[89] Broadcasting what she saw and felt in newspaper columns over the 1970s and 1980s, Sibley painted her own personal encounters with Atlanta's sprawl seen from the outside, according it a sinister cast that helped to make it a major political issue for Atlanta's environmentalists.

Disturbed as she became over the arrival of "suburbia" in North Fulton, Sibley was far less critical of younger "country-minded" arrivals who themselves sought to take up farming. They were among those many Atlantans seeking "ecology-minded" ways of living that were sustainable over the longer haul—what Daniel Farber has termed "right livelihoods"—who chose to light out from downtown into the countryside.[90] Many of those new periodicals that helped bring back the romanticization of "country living" over this period, such as *Mother Earth News* (by the mid-1970s, out of a small town in North Carolina's Appalachians); *Blair and Ketcham's Country* (out of Vermont); and the *Whole Earth Catalogue*, acquired early audiences in a youthful counterculture, like those clustering near Atlanta's Piedmont Park, but soon gained wider traction. These publications frequently celebrated the superiority of rural living, ecologically as well as ethically, and tried to ameliorate the "lack of expertise" that foiled many of their readers' agrarian inclinations. A significant share of Atlanta's "turned on" youthful generation struck out to suburbs and exurbs around this and other U.S. cities of the 1970s into the 1980s to seek alternative ways of occupying the land centering around food production.[91]

In 1978 "country-eyed cityite" Catherine Harkins put out an invitation in *Mother Earth News* for interested readers in the Atlanta area to join a new back-to-the-land group: Country Bound. Living in DeKalb and working as a human relations consultant, Harkins supplemented her income by growing organic herbs. Two years after Country Bound launched, some two hundred people attended its meetings in DeKalb, and another chapter had begun in Cobb. By that time Harkins herself had pitched in with partners to buy a half-acre lot in southern DeKalb, as well as twenty-two acres in Habersham County, about a hundred miles north of the city.[92] Their efforts paralleled many others on periurban cheap farmland across the southern states (as well as the rural West and New England), as couples, individuals, and larger groups "dropped out" to get "back to the land."[93] From Atlanta's suburbs to its most rural fringes, younger aspirational farmers set out in search of a way of life that shed the compromises and distractions of downtown or suburban living. "Living in the country," as Harkins put it, "means living as a whole person," "in relative simplicity and . . . in touch with cycles and seasons."[94] Seeing city and suburb alike as from the outside, they aspired to live in more palpable connection with the natural world, thereby reclaiming a previously dormant side to their own humanity. In other words, if only for their own small like-minded group of fellow travelers, they sought a radical alternative to reigning modes of environmental consumption, one that would instill a more fully environmental sense of citizenship. Ecologically informed and ambitious as their citizenly vision was, its social and political implications remained more of a question mark. Certainly its basement requirements, the economic means to lease or purchase land, rose as metro-area land became scarcer and more costly.

Countercultural agrarianism constituted only one of the ways that crop growing gained in popularity across the Atlanta-metro area from the 1970s into the 1990s. Home food production joined ornamental horticulture as a new commercial frontier, an eminently marketable strand of a new environmental culture. Attentive to the sales possibilities, local nurseries put out new separate catalogs for vegetable growing and expanded their offerings to "canner cookers" and "pea and bean shellers," whose purchase could help transport customers "back to the good life." By the start of the 1980s, the *Atlanta Daily World* explained how to grow asparagus and make compost from leaves, as *Atlanta Constitution* garden columnist Darryl Riggins declared that "the vegetable garden was finally having its day in the sun."[95] Suburban vegetable gardening fit extraordinarily well with the larger project of *Southern Living* itself, which recruited Celestine Sibley to help it meet the meet the growing demand; she penned the preface to its *Compleat Vegetable Book* (1976). Already by the mid-1970s, critics of the magazine had begun to suggest that *Southern Living* was strategically oblivious not just of the more troubling sides of the South's past but of burning issues in its present, among these: "white flight to the suburbs, low-income housing, and racially integrated neighborhoods." As the magazine's executive editor countered to *Forbes* in 1977—vaguely echoing countercultural lingo—"advocacy journalism isn't our bag." Vegetable growing, on the other hand, fit well into their politically quiescent vision: an environmental awakening through private markets and personal choices of southerners, an environmental consumption informed by only the most noncontroversial veins of environmental citizenship. *Southern Living*, as he succinctly put it, was out to "save the south, but one front yard at a time."[96]

Here, as in many other marketable facets of the new environmental culture, while some consumer offerings actively circumvented environmental citizenship, others as much as demanded it. The choice to garden or farm "organically," for instance, hinged on whether to use pesticides or fertilizers made by big agrochemical companies and routinely promoted and sold in Atlanta's nursery and garden stores. The organic gardener or farmer eschewed these chemicals perhaps for reasons of taste but usually also because of concerns about their deleterious ecological and public health impacts, following historically formative versions of environmental citizenship, such as expressed in Rachel Carson's 1962 *Silent Spring*.[97] Catherine Harkins took these threats very seriously. She described her organic farming efforts as part of her resolve to "learn . . . to live in harmony with the universe, and not exploit . . . it."[98] The most prominent figures in Atlanta's plant trade, on the other hand, from nursery owners like Don Hastings to *Atlanta Constitution* garden columnist Roy Wyatt, scoffed at these worries, insisting that most lawn and garden chemicals, if used correctly, were harmless.[99] The *Atlanta Daily World* offered more ambiguous messages to its predominantly Black readership, suggesting "you might even want to try" organic gardening but later on printing a debunking of organic "myths" by a Fulton County extension agent.[100] Sibley herself embraced organic methods, swearing off "my ninety-eight-cent can of poison spray" and worrying about killing "villains and heroes indiscriminately," from "my invaluable friends, the birds" to "possibly . . . my grandchildren." Yet she remained "almost [but not quite] persuaded by the organic girls and boys" who argued such chemicals "will . . . throw what ecologists call 'the totality of interrelationships' out of kilter."[101] Meanwhile, the ranks of commercial organic producers grew steadily, if not dramatically. A fourth annual meeting of Georgia Organic Growers Association, held in Druid Hills in 1985, drew nearly three hundred attendees.[102] But only wealthier restaurant goers and health-food shoppers in downtown Atlanta bought organic produce, whose high prices and limited availability put them out of reach for most Atlantans, just as with much other environmental consumption establishing market niches under cleavage capitalism.

Farther out from the metro area itself, Atlanta's hinterlands also bore another high-end mode of the city's environmental consumption: the vacation home, immersed within the natural beauty of Georgia's seacoast or northerly mountains. A revived cleavage capitalism shunted a growing share of metro-area wealth into exclusive recreational enclaves and pastimes, ways of enjoying nature available only to the affluent. John Portman, the Atlanta architect who made a fortune through his environmentally inspired developments, built a $6 million vacation "dream home" in the "elite's retreat" of Sea Island, Georgia, their "place of peace, play, and freedom." "Loom[ing] over" a public beach and bordered by planted rows of forty-foot live oaks, it conspicuously interwove seven thousand square feet of living space with "enclosed waterways, . . . reflecting ponds and waterfalls with seven fountains," along with multiple ocean-facing balconies and decks.[103] Ted Turner, the CNN media mogul, by 1986 remembered how his awareness that "the environment was deteriorating" had come "as a sailor" on his yacht. Seeing how "we are polluting the oceans," Turner was reborn as an environmental citizen, turning to environmental philanthropy and restoration, apparently oblivious to the extreme economic privilege reflected in his own conversion story.[104] A step down on the economic ladder, second-home markets for upper-middle-class Atlantans flourished not just along the coasts but in the mountains. "In the last 10 years," noted an Atlanta reporter in 1988, "throughout the knobby ridges and deep valleys of Georgia's high country . . . a cabin directly alongside a babbling brook or a two-story retreat on the steep slopes of a vista-rich mountain are dreams come true for thousands of newcomers."[105] Less lavishly, *Southern Living* pitched abundantly financed trips to the mountains or the beach as part of its aspirational "upscale" lifestyle, with costs of recommended gear or hotels or restaurants, as well as any hint of environmental citizenship, going conspicuously unmentioned.[106]

Environmental Consumption Heads Downtown

While such quests still often propelled Atlantans toward where nature seemed far more visibly *there*, in Georgia's more rural reaches, a newer opposite orientation proved more politically significant: Atlanta's new environmental culture, after first flourishing mainly in its suburbs, gained growing footholds downtown. Amplifying a growing critique of sprawl, environmental concerns about profligate energy usage added impetus to this shift. Over the 1970s and 1980s, ongoing national and international energy crises added new impetus to quests for ecologically minded alternatives to fossil fuels, a newer frontier in the city's environmental culture. As a suburb like Druid Hills turned more "inner" and older, shops and restaurants where organic farmers sold their wares, along with other core elements of the city's environmental culture, took root, especially downtown. That momentum in turn helped bolster private-sector appropriations of many Atlantans' aspirations toward greenness. Among these, in the same time that metro Atlanta's sprawl was stirring national notoriety, a denser style of real-estate development gathered steam inside the city. Anticipating the "New Urbanism" of the 1990s and seeking a mixture of residential and commercial uses, less auto dependence, and more compactness and walkability, it touted a version of environmental consumption that gained investments and municipal backing in certain corners of downtown.[107]

Into the early seventies energy conservation itself had hardly been on the radar screen either of the city's environmental political activists or those more interested in ecologically mindful lifestyles. Debates about transportation, from cars to MARTA to bicycles, had been bedeviled more by the destruction from freeways or the smog from gasoline burning than from energy usage per se. But the nearly unceasing energy crises of this decade amplified what was at stake in fossil fuels themselves, spurring environmentally minded scrutiny of this reliance and other realms of Atlantans' daily lives as consumers. In what Andrew Kirk styled the "pragmatic" wing of the environmental counterculture, new avenues opened for more environmentally informed choices and options for reducing or softening one's ecological impacts as a consumer-citizen. As periodicals like the *Whole Earth Catalogue* and *Mother Earth News* joined with the "small is beautiful" message of E. F. Schumacher, some environmentally minded homeowners took up the cause of small-scale alternative energy production.[108]

Claude and Betty Terry—the microbiologist-activist and his wife—built an additional "sunspace" across the back of their home: a room-long window designed especially to "passively" absorb and store heat from the sun's rays. A Solar Coalition, run by Betty Terry, included their home alongside eight others in a free tour of retrofitted innovations around Druid Hills and elsewhere in town.[109] Not just white but Black homeowners adopted solar methods: Dr. James and Mrs. Rose Palmer installed a heat-catching solar design in a new house into which they moved beside Niskey Lake, in the southwest suburbs beyond Cascade.[110] By the mid-1980s the Solar Coalition estimated there were some 2,500 homes in the metro area with some form of mostly passive solar heating, which the coalition favored over "active" technology such as solar plates or collectors, deemed too expensive and untested. Offices of the Solar Coalition and a Solar Builders' Institute, as well as the Energy Shop, which sold fifteen electric cars in 1981, lay in Little Five Points, one of the BOND neighborhoods, a downtown core for Atlanta's briefly burgeoning solar market.[111]

Though soon stifled by the Reagan administration's shutdown of federal incentives for switching to solar power, Little Five Points' fledgling cluster of alternative-energy enterprises points to how Atlanta's new environmental culture took root in some of those very corners of the city where gentrification had first stirred. Departures of residents, capital, jobs, and wealth, while isolating the poor in the inner city, also lowered property values and rents, drawing in white "homesteaders." In the case of Little Five Points, a 1976 federal $246,000 Urban Area Development Grant also came to the aid of fledgling businesses.[112] Importing the naturalist ideals of an ecology-minded counterculture, newcomers experimented with more environmentally attentive and cooperative uses of land as well as purchases. On nearby public land that had been reserved for the rejected highway project, I-485, but since abandoned, a community organic garden sprouted, run by Susan Chavez and Frank Holtzman, youthful newcomers from California. They had begun it in a neighbor's back yard, then expanded it onto this publicly owned but undeveloped stretch of land, wielding know-how Frank had learned while working on a biodynamic farm near Santa Cruz, California.

Nearby, a small business district formed the early commercial core of Atlanta's new environmental culture, including Sevananda, by late 1970s "perhaps the largest food co-op . . . in the Southeastern United States" and one of the earliest Atlanta food stores where organic produce could be bought.[113] In stark contrast to the corporate and hierarchical structure Atlanta's business elite took largely for granted, Sevananda, a nonprofit cooperative with a membership of some three thousand, was run by worker-members. Half of them were paid; the other half volunteered hours in exchange for lower food prices. A natural foods supply-and-distribution business began in its basement, then joined a bookstore and soy shop in a nearby "new age industrial park." A short walk away alternative-energy offices and businesses plied their trade, and a Radio Free Georgia offered commercial-free broadcasts. A Five Points Pub organized following the 1960s theorist Paul Goodman's notion of *communitas*, as "jointly owned and democratically run." Little Five Points and adjacent neighborhoods like Poncey-Highlands served not just as "Atlanta's funky in-town answer to SoHo" but as experimental loci for less top-down and more shared forms of business enterprise. From the mid to late 1970s, they made up another significant working face of the city's arrival at peak democracy.[114]

By the mid-1980s, however, a transition into a more capital-intensive phase of gentrifying had gotten underway. As one reporter put it, Little Five Points as well as Poncey-Highlands were "suddenly starting to go respectable." Retail shops and popular restaurants were blossoming, and chain supermarkets like Kroger and drug stores like Eckerd had also begun to move in. Mixing restored homes and stores from the mid-1970s, these already eminently walkable areas now attracted larger developments intentionally combining the residential with the commercial, later pitched as a "New Urbanist" innovation. A Ford Factory Square, for instance, going into an old Ford assembly plant on Ponce de Leon, placed stores along its ground floor and some 120 apartments through the upper three. Little Five Points' reputation as "the city's bohemian quarter" was increasingly challenged by the sheer number of its businesses and professional practices. Sevananda was among the sole co-ops to survive, albeit with a declining share of worker-customers and a lessening reliance on Georgia farms.[115] By 1987 reporters marveled at how "a decade of gentrification [in the Highlands] has stimulated a frenzy of commercial growth" by "developers and business-people." Now the prevailing worry of the civic association president, a computer consultant, was not about shabbiness or crime but instead about the influx of big stores, investors, owners, and spenders, which threatened to "spoil the community's village-like atmosphere."[116]

Gentrification moved into other parts of downtown more slowly and selectively, especially in or near urban-renewal zones. By 1981 efforts to renew the Bedford Pine area, along the northerly edge of Buttermilk Bottom, finally bore residential fruit, through groundbreaking on high-rise apartments and condominiums in a development christened Renaissance Park. The style here, as well, presaged a New Urbanism: "relatively spread out," fitting the first 232 two-story units into seventeen acres, and its ads promised "suburban living with urban amenities." Ad testimonials praised not just its proximity to "the High Museum [of Art] and the Civic Center as well many places of work" but its "swimming pool, security adjacent tennis courts, and a beautiful park-like environment in the heart of the city."[117] Despite hopes of a "dawning" of "middle-income ownership," Renaissance Park condos were "by no means cheap," so early buyers were either "people who are retired or are close to it, or . . . young, professional, up-and-coming couples who have no children and who can cover the costs with two substantial paychecks."[118] Early on Renaissance Park faltered, running out of private funds for its second stage of building, only to be saved by Central Atlanta Progress (CAP) and Georgia Power, which stepped in to arrange an unusual six-bank loan of some $2.55 million to complete the project.[119]

As Renaissance Park gained traction in drawing in affluent whites, Blacks still living in homes beyond the easterly edge of Bedford Pine felt misled and pushed aside. "We thought our neighborhood would have some beautification," said one, "but that hasn't materialized," even as offers on their houses multiplied. "Seems like everybody wants us out," one longtime resident opined.[120] Even worse off, however, were those trapped in parts of the city untouched by any such influx of private investment and wealthier whites—places like Vine City. With a conservative Reagan administration quashing any hopes of a revival of federal programs or funds that might compensate for the dearth of private financing, their prospects by 1988 seemed sufficiently dismal that a *Wall Street Journal* reporter found Atlanta to have "all the makings of a big permanent underclass."[121]

For one part of Atlanta's downtown, however, private financiers now showed much more eagerness: its business district. By the early 1980s over twenty new projects were underway there, for hotels and office buildings, entertainment complexes and condominiums in varying combinations. "You can feel the difference now," noted Dan Sweat, the president of Central Atlanta Progress, ever on the lookout for positive news about what was (the reporter covering him noted) "a part of town the *Wall Street Journal* once tagged as a 'war zone.'" Both business and civic leaders agreed about what had enabled all the new private investment, quietly undergirded by massive federal dollars that had been poured into its highways, airport, and MARTA. What they called the "political and economic turbulence of the 1970s" and the historical challenge it had posed to the city's long-standing partnership between public officials and the business elite had "ended at last."[122] Why? The mayor since 1982, Andrew Young, had worked hard to heal the "rift" that had erupted between his predecessor Maynard Jackson and Atlanta's white business community. Young had prioritized redevelopment of downtown, among other ways by beefing up its policing and seconding CAP's vision for a "linear" reconception of just where the renewed investments would run. The downtown of yore, "big" Five Points, made up only the southerly tip of the city's contemplated commercial core. Now it was to extend all the way up Peachtree Street even as far as Buckhead and Lenox Park—historically, the very pathway that residences of Atlanta's white elite had followed out of the city toward its now ever-wealthier northside.[123]

The excitement that CAP leaders expressed about these plans reflected their returning influence on city leaders but also, at least in some small part, how their downtown growth machine had itself set about appropriating Atlanta's new environmental culture. The leading architect behind this downtown renaissance, John Portman, had first won their favor with his design of $200 million Peachtree Center, which sought to bring a semblance in the natural world downtown while creating "a 'walking city' within a city."[124] Portman saw his work addressing how "our cities have run nature out along with the people, no trees, shrubbery, no space." He pitched buildings crafted into architectural instruments of environmental consumption, to serve as "lungs for the city and lungs for the people in an environmental way." The atria running down the center of his designs for the Hyatt-Regency and Peachtree Plaza Hotels brought in sunlight that "allows us to have all kinds of plants and flowers and trees" and, in the case of Peachtree Plaza, also a half-acre lake. He treated his often-lush landscaping plans as a "basic cost of structure" and combined offices, shopping, and entertainment altogether to obviate driving, putting a "full range of man's needs in walking distance."[125] For all his professed idealism about urban nature and walking, however, Portman's designs offered an environmental consumption furnished by corporations for usage by a narrow, moneyed slice of Atlantans, conventioneers, and other visitors. One critic characterized the message of a meander through the Peachtree Plaza this way: "If you have the money and are dressed you may cross the moat and enter the castle."[126] Explicitly favoring a more exclusionary municipal citizenship, Portman griped about Maynard Jackson's allegiances and sought to rid downtown of public housing, replacing it with residences for "middle class" residents.[127] By the mid-1980s architect-developer Portman had turned suburb-ward and was designing and building those office towers and shopping complexes that would compose some of the metro area's most high-end "edge cities."[128]

Only in the 1990s would Atlantans, developers and nondevelopers alike, begin to pick up on Andres Duany's and Elizabeth Plater-Zybeck's now-famous manifestoes for a New Urbanism, as a point-by-point creed of real-estate development.[129] What prepared the way for the buzz about New Urbanism swelling around this city mid-decade, as an alternative to sprawl driven by suburban developers, was precisely how ensconced its operating principles had become within a reviving growth machine in Atlanta's urban core. Aside from the small-town looks and rural or suburban locations of best-known examples (e.g., Seaside, Florida), this purportedly "new" development style largely reaffirmed long-standing goals of a white business elite for this city's downtown. Seen from this angle, the main contributions of New Urbanism's promoters were to make these same principles more portable and sellable, in important part by wrapping them in the mantle of a new environment-minded consumerism. Adding another green wrinkle to the city's cleavage capitalism, multimillion-dollar downtown developers could sell their wares as part of an environmental culture that sought to reduce fossil fuel use in response to climate change and that had growing footholds not just in the suburbs but in a gentrifying downtown. As the more citizenly side to this culture nudged the state's environmental politics in environmentalists' direction over the 1980s, so did the journey of one of the city's foremost civil rights groups toward an environmental citizenship of their own.

The SCLC's Environmental Turn

When SCLC president Joseph Lowery hired the Reverend Albert Love as chief of staff for the storied civil rights group in 1980, members of the organization still saw environmental causes, and environmentalists, as extraneous to their own mission. "White liberals" would ask to visit the first SCLC conventions he organized, to "come and talk about environmental stuff." Among them were young men "with ponytails" and older leaders like Anne Braden, longtime leader of the Louisville-based Southern Organizing Committee. The Reverend Fred Taylor, in charge of the SCLC's Direct Action wing, then encouraged Love to start inviting them, mainly so "there was somebody white" on the program. But "it didn't register that much to the heart and core of SCLC"; "you didn't pay them that much attention." In the nearly decade and a half since its leader Martin Luther King Jr. was assassinated, the SCLC's version of civil rights citizenship had continued its justice-minded mission against Black social and economic inequities. To confront state-sponsored racial oppression and violence, as well—"who was picketing who that caused the police to shoot somebody else"—it still wielded the now-familiar tactics of protest and direct action.[130] But in the last few years, Lowery had also sought to steer the organization in new directions from those of King's immediate successor, the Reverend Ralph Abernathy. This evolution of thought and strategy, which sought to bridge a yawning class divide among Atlanta's and other of the nation's Blacks, would by mid-1982 lead him and other SCLC leaders to embrace a still-emergent environmental issue, the hazardous waste dump, as their own.

After Abernathy took over the reins, from the late 1960s into the early 1970s, the SCLC had continued in the pathway set by King, highlighting poverty, Black labor struggles, and civil rights citizenship with an accent on economic deprivation. But SCLC's own finances increasingly floundered; by 1972 donated funds had dropped to $900,000, down from an annual $2 million in 1968, forcing closure of ongoing endeavors such as the Citizenship Education Project, Operation Breadbasket, and in 1974 its local Atlanta chapter.[131] Aggravating the SCLC's troubles, some disputes and discontent among an opinionated senior staff—King had dubbed them "wild horses"—continued to grow, and departures escalated, some like Andrew Young's more amicable, others less so.[132] In July 1973 Abernathy announced his resignation, pleading some new demands of his West Hunter Baptist pastorate and decrying the SCLC's own shrinking staff, to a point where he felt he could no longer offer a "live and vibrant program." SCLC staff lodged their own complaints as well, about not being heard by Abernathy.[133] The SCLC's board, chaired by Rev. Joseph Lowery, another of Martin Luther King Jr.'s lieutenants, averted Abernathy's departure by adding to his personnel, even as they also tried to reinforce staff opportunities for input and autonomy.[134] But these internal fixes could not address what Abernathy fingered as the biggest problem and his greatest disappointment: "the failure of Black people, who now occupy improved positions because of our struggles, to support SCLC financially."[135] That very Black middle class that had contributed so much to SCLC successes, as it had become more sizable and secure, seemed to be losing its willingness to open its wallet to support SCLC's advocacy for Black workers and the poor. Three years later, faced with continuing financial woes despite a restructured and enhanced staff, Abernathy resigned from SCLC leadership for good.

The SCLC's ongoing challenges over the 1970s had roots in long-standing economic divides among Atlanta's Blacks. As these widened and hardened with the return of cleavage capitalism, they were growing more difficult for a group like SCLC to surmount in its organizing work. Whereas the classic phase of the civil rights movement had spilled across class divisions, uniting Black activists from Atlanta's middle class with poorer Blacks, the growing skew of fortunes between the best and least well-off Blacks raised barriers to further coalition building between them. By 1970 the income gap between top and lower echelon earners in Black Atlanta was 44 percent greater than that among the city's whites. Over the next decade that gap would grow by another third, largely because Atlanta's poor Blacks on the whole remained so much poorer than white counterparts.[136] This widening income gap among the city's Blacks gained geographic reinforcement as a Black middle class increasingly moved out to more suburban and home-owning areas, segregating itself from the poorest Blacks downtown. Exemplifying this contrast, even as the SCLC was taking up the cudgel for Black workers and tenants, Rev. Joseph Lowery—the chair of SCLC's board and since 1968 the pastor at Central United Methodist, between Vine City and Atlanta University—moved with his wife, Evelyn, to a house along Cascade Road. By 1977, with Andrew and Evelyn Young also living nearby and the Abernathys just to the north, this best-off of Black suburbs had drawn much of SCLC's leadership and a "Who's Who of Black Atlanta."[137]

This migration reflected a growing tension between SCLC's poverty and labor emphasis and the personal and familial circumstances not just of its leaders but of a Black middle-class constituency that had long backed its work. Not that better-off Black suburbs were immune from challenges. After its racial transition even the affluent Cascade neighborhood confronted issues its white counterparts did not, from lagging services like trash pickup and street cleaning to frequent rezonings for apartments and other construction plans. Lowery confronted many of these firsthand, as the first Black president of the Cascade Forest Community Association.[138] Yet as these and similar opportunities opened to a growing share of Atlanta's Blacks, citizenly advocacy on their behalf became harder to square with that on behalf of the city's Black poor. Overwhelmingly renters and often educationally deprived, many of them remained trapped in the most run-down corners of downtown. The SCLC's project of civil rights citizenship forged through the 1960s to unite middle-class and poorer Blacks now had to somehow confront this growing class divide between Atlanta's Black communities.

Upon Abernathy's final departure in 1977, longtime chair of SCLC's board Lowery stepped in to serve as the group's president. Lowery was more apt to blame the economy for the group's decline and thought that middle-class Blacks, "hurting too," were not such a lost cause. "The middle-class Black will soon see," he predicted, "that there must be a group to speak his needs."[139] That dilemma went hand in hand with another, of the SCLC's agenda itself. "Our problems are not as sharply defined as they have been. . . . It was easy to see our tasks when dogs and firehoses were in it. . . . But the only thing dogs are used for now is to sniff out dope in bags at airports."[140] Not that they didn't still find plenty of "overt racism": the rural South continued to serve up a steady stream of racially motivated murders and beatings and Klan intimidation. Atlanta itself was hardly immune: a rash of killings lasted from 1979 into the early 1980s in which all the victims were Black children.[141] By that time, too, a pending expiration of the Voting Rights Act enabled the SCLC's return to class-crossing political terrain, which successfully secured this act's renewal. Also riveting the attention and energies of the SCLC leadership was the minimally justified imprisonment of Blacks such as the Wilmington Ten, a North Carolina group led by Ben Chavis who had been thrown into prison for allegedly inciting a riot. Throughout, the SCLC kept up its active support for Black workers and the poor, supporting aggrieved Black employees in Louisiana sugarcane farms and in Mississippi chicken-processing plants and speaking out against the federal government's ongoing retreat from fighting poverty.[142] But Lowery also steered the SCLC into campaigns of clearer relevance to middle-class Blacks that also, not coincidentally, opened more doors to women's leadership.

In 1979 SCLC organized a new women's affiliate, calling itself SCLC/ Women, to be run by Lowery's wife, Evelyn. Sponsoring events on behalf of "Negro child health," SCLC/Women also helped relaunch the group's exercise of a more consumerist style of citizenly power, wielding the economic clout of those with means to buy. Originally, the SCLC's Operation Bread-basket had embarked on like campaigns, mainly to induce businesses to hire Blacks; shut down in 1972, it too was restarted by Joseph Lowery, even as SCLC/Women undertook initiatives of their own. Targeting the hiring practices at Rich's, Evelyn Lowery and her associates also kept a careful eye on the firm's store at Greenbriar Mall, which served the Blackened suburbs of Atlanta's southwest. They "checked merchandise quality, exhibits, [and] organization . . . and even inquired about the extent of the Greenbriar store's lease," with a view to ensuring that "the quality of stores in the Black community has increased substantially."[143] They also explored new ways in which Black suburbanites could wield their buying power on behalf of the less well off. They joined other SCLCers marching in support strikes for better working conditions out in places like Sanderson Farms, a chicken processor in Laurel, Mississippi. They imported the fight to Atlanta's and other suburbs, by calling on affluent Blacks to steer away from the Sanderson brand in their grocery shopping.[144] The group's biggest and most long-running consumer-oriented campaign of this era was led by Joseph Lowery himself. The SCLC led a push to boycott goods and divest from firms that did business in apartheid South Africa—the world's most prominent remaining exemplar of an overtly racist state—among the broadest and most successful of social movements in the 1980s United States.[145]

Also preparing the way for its own embrace of environmental citizenship, the group explored a more citizenly engagement with bodily threats to Black Americans that were less obvious than "dogs and firehoses," those slower modes of violence that, as the Reverend Love put it, required "connect[ing] the dots." SCLC's challenge here was also to show that these dangers were indeed "bona fide civil rights issue[s]" and that they were as relevant to the group's familiar frameworks and critiques "as when they would hit you on the head."[146] Over the late 1970s and early 1980s, the SCLC newsletter began talking more about chronic health threats afflicting African Americans in particular, such as high blood pressure and sickle cell anemia, and advocating for national health insurance.[147] By the mid-1980s Lowery would synthesize these strands into a regular call for a "liberation lifestyle" in the Black community. While "based on a thorough understanding of who we are" that was "spiritual," it also espoused more health-minded choices: "We must not fall victim to . . . our own faults from within," nor should Blacks let themselves be victimized by "assaults from without."[148]

This increasingly programmatic embrace of health sciences by the SCLC offered a new cross-class framing of Blacks' dilemmas, along with an outside vantage point on bodily threats with which the project of environmental citizenship had also engaged. Grounding for the SCLC's crusade against hazardous wastes congealed especially through a growing attentiveness to the dread disease of cancer, by the late 1970s the chief illness of concern for environmental activism and policy. In 1981 "Cancer Facts and Black Americans," by Thomas Calimee Jr., reported how "of every six deaths of Blacks in the U.S., one death is from cancer." While cancer rates over the previous twenty-five years had dropped slightly for whites, for Blacks they had risen. This difference was "certainly not, as some would like to believe, because of inherent biological characteristics." Instead, Calimee reported how cancer researchers "attributed [it] to social and environmental factors"; among them, "because a higher percentage of Blacks than whites are in the lower socioeconomic group, risk of exposure to industrial carcinogens may be increased."[149]

In 1979 a pointed confrontation with the Georgia Conservancy, still the state's best connected and most influential environmental advocate, also raised SCLC leaders' awareness of just how much the ethics and allegiances of civil rights citizenship could clash with those of environmentalists. The seeds of the controversy dated back to World War II, when Harris Neck, a tiny peninsula off the Georgia coast, had been acquired by the military from a group of Black farm families. When in 1979 the government decided to relinquish its control, it devised a deal supported by the conservancy to turn the land into a wildlife refuge. But the original owners and their families begged to differ; their 1940s deal with the military was supposed to be temporary, they insisted, so the land should be given back to them. The SCLC got involved. They did so as part of an ongoing effort to defend rural Blacks who, especially as cleavage capitalism shunted Georgia's wealth toward the city from countryside, were often the first to lose income or farms. An SCLC group traveled down from Atlanta to speak and march on behalf of the farmers' rights to their property claims. Rev. Ted Clark, an SCLC leader who earlier had contested CAP's plans for Bedford Pine, led a direct action in this coastal county, in which he was among four arrested.[150] Defending the property rights of former Black farmers, SCLCers got their first taste of what they would soon see as the socially blinkered citizenship of "mainstream environmentalism," all-too blind to racial inequity and injustice. They squared off against a Georgia Conservancy forthrightly defending the prerogatives of wildlife over those of poor people, in this case, land-deprived Blacks.

That environmental issue that SCLC began to absorb into its vision of civil rights citizenship was the problem of hazardous wastes, first registering in the media and among environmental groups in white communities like Love Canal but then turning up in Black communities in the U.S. South. As Robert Bullard's *Dumping in Dixie* would soon show, despite the environmentally enlightened governments arising in southern states by the 1970s, waste disposal and treatment facilities as well as other polluting industries continued to head southward. They set up shop mostly to be in "poor, working-class and minority communities," taking advantage of their political weakness and economic duress.[151] In 1982 the state of North Carolina hewed to this same pattern by ordering a hazardous waste landfill be built in mostly Black and rural Warren County, to dispose of toxic PCBs illegally dumped along a roadway by the New Jersey hauler. This time, however, Warren County residents were able to put up a fierce resistance, thanks in important part to intervention by the Atlanta-based SCLC.

Widely cited as the original spark of a movement on behalf of "environmental justice" that would spread across the nation and world, the Warren County protests arguably owed their media splash and longer national impact to how Lowery and other SCLC leaders joined in. Their own citizenly arsenal, well honed from two decades and more of civil rights activism, furnished a megaphone for the locals' own protests, without which these might well have had less of an effect.[152] The invitation from the North Carolina SCLC chapter—probably from Rev. Leon White—brought word of the impending September 1982 protest to SCLC's Atlanta headquarters. When the time came, the group sent recruits from other chapters and much of its Atlanta-based leadership, including Joseph and Evelyn Lowery, Albert Love, and Fred Taylor, into the fray. Driving over to the North Carolina Piedmont, they met up with some five hundred others, most of them from the local and surrounding counties, at a local church, where Lowery and others offered inspirational words. They then drove out to the road leading to the landfill and laid down in front of the oncoming dump trucks, refusing police officers' commands to make way. "Like a flashback to the sixties," they were promptly arrested and thrown into jail.[153] Some weeks later they returned to do it all again. On the heels of the Warren County protests came the NAACP's first resolution on the hazardous waste issue (1983) and reports by the Washington, D.C.–based General Accounting Office and by the New York– and United Church of Christ–based Commission on Racial Justice that established just how racially biased the siting of hazardous waste dumps had become.[154] From direct-action tactics to the rhetoric of inequity and injustice, the Atlanta-based SCLC, that iconic flagship of civil rights citizenship, had spawned a version of environmentalism never before seen. Those following its lead soon discovered just how rich the possibilities were for civil rights as well as environmental activists. New terms such as "environmental equity" and "environmental racism" provoked what soon became a flourishing line of analysis and critique, of the differential distribution of environmental dangers and amenities *within* a city or society. This interweaving of principles from civil rights as well as environmental citizenship also gave birth to a powerful new moralism of "environmental justice."

Lowery and his fellow SCLC leaders' motives for appropriating this "environmental" issue as matter of civil rights were not just moral and political but pragmatic. In this first issue on which questions about environmental justice were explicitly honed, hazardous waste dumps, they had found a cause that could unite a Black suburban middle class with rural Black communities such as Warrenton (or Georgia rural locations too). Just as the sociologist Robert Bullard's work on environmental justice had first been sparked by a struggle against just such a dump in a Black home-owning suburb in Houston, Lowery's own Cascade neighborhood in Atlanta also confronted a hazardous waste threat.[155] Since the mid-1970s a Westview landfill had been receiving two thousand gallons of waste oil a month from the Lockheed plant in Marietta.[156] Among those angered by what they learned about the Westview Cemetery landfill and speaking up about it at meetings of NPU-I was Juner Norris. When those in "a neighborhood and a school in that area" "started complaining about sickness," he "drove over to the landfill and just looked and all that dust was going through the neighborhood when the wind changed and to that school."[157] What he had seen led him to raise the issue at a meeting of NPU-I, which over the 1980s would spearhead an effort to have the landfill closed.

Across this southern metropolis Westview Cemetery's landfill turned out to be only the tip of the iceberg. Once investigators went looking for them, some ninety-four hazardous waste disposal sites turned up in the Atlanta area. These lay in zip codes that contained 82.8 percent of the city's Black population, but only 60.2 percent of white Atlantans—a significant racial bias.[158] Whether poor or affluent, rural or suburban, neighborhoods categorized as largely Black had long shared extra vulnerabilities, which we can now recognize as environmental in character, many of which this book has explored. But hazardous waste siting became the first such issue to be widely recognized *at the time* as an "environmental inequity," though initially more by contemporary civil rights than environmental groups. That act of naming was itself new, marking a historical watershed in the relationship between Atlanta's civil rights and environmental movements. Like many affluent and middle-class whites before and since, Black leaders of the SCLC were discovering the political usefulness of environmental language, or ecospeak, even as they went on to twin it with ethical principles long grounding their own movement for equality and justice.

Bridging Environmental and Civil Rights Citizenship

From the 1970s into the 1980s, as the SCLC found its own way toward a kind of environmental citizenship, the expanding concerns and increasingly urban bases of Atlanta's environmental culture pulled environmentalists at least in the direction of civil rights citizenship. Around the city organized environmentalism gained in membership and clout but, despite new coinages like "environmental justice" and "environmental racism," remained almost entirely white. White environmentalists' adoption of civil rights–speak about equity and justice often proved slow and halting at best, yet over the 1980s many began to welcome alliances with groups like SCLC on some identifiably "environmental" issues, bringing a partial rapprochement between environmental and civil rights citizenship. As with the original making of an environmental movement over the 1950s and 1960s in other parts of the country, the successes of Atlanta's environmentalists by the late 1980s reflected the improving match of their agenda to those concerns stirred by their city's sprawling growth. Its consequences spawned environmental worries among many middle-class Blacks as well as whites. At the same time, a resurgent politics of disdain for environmental causes, from the first Reagan administration's assault on environmental agencies to Mayor Andrew Young's reforged alliance with Atlanta's business leadership, helped prod new environmentalist militancy and politicization. These changes helped lead to an upsurge in membership and a thickening alliance with Black political leaders, and environmentalists' influence in the Georgia state capital advanced to a historical high-water mark.

The journey of Atlanta's Sierra Club offers an illuminating window into environmental groups' changing pursuit of activism and politics—the public sides of environmental citizenship—as sprawl took off and they confronted newfound political adversity. From the mid-1970s onward Sierra underwent the biggest transformation of all the metro-area groups. While some soon shriveled (Save Our Vital Environment, Friends of the River), and others rose up anew in the 1980s (the Legal Environmental Assistance Foundation, the Georgia Environmental Project), Sierra along with the Georgia Conservancy provided organizational continuity for what became a broadening swirl of activist networks. The conservancy remained the home of the best connected, highest-status activists. But while key veterans of the Chattahoochee River battles like Claude Terry and Barbara Blum had left the metro area, river rat Roger Buerki, who stayed, found the Sierra Club a congenial fit for continuing his environmental activism. Veritably mushrooming over the next decade and a half, this Sierra chapter came to vie in membership numbers as well as political influence with the Georgia Conservancy, through a less patrician and more confrontational style.

Two important steps taken by Atlanta's Sierrans drew their concerns and strategies closer to those of civil rights advocates from the late 1970s into the 1980s: first, that they stepped decisively beyond the conservancy's focus on natural lands and countryside; and, second, that they stepped up their political engagements. By 1978 their Chattahoochee chapter, which at this point encompassed Alabama as well the whole of Georgia, seemed to have fallen into the doldrums. It included only 2,200 members, mostly living in Atlanta or Birmingham, and most were so minimally engaged that only 90 voted in that year's election for the Executive Committee. A debate then erupted among its leaders about the reasons for member apathy. Some blamed a national office that had strayed from the club's "traditional conservation role." How could they recruit and inspire southern members, one wondered aloud, to a group that endorsed the Equal Rights Amendment and even the "Shell Oil strike" and "sponsor[ed] an Urban Conference instead of a Wilderness Conference?"[159] Not everyone agreed; the environmental merits of working on the Equal Rights Amendment and with labor unions were hotly contested. But support then quickly coalesced within the chapter for the national board's urban emphasis.[160] With so many of Georgia's club members living in metro Atlanta, surely the club had a "place and mandate to work toward a cleaner, more resource-conserving, and more enjoyable urban environment."[161] Polling the membership, the leadership found that, while "wilderness" did rank as their top concern, Chattahoochee Sierrans also prioritized land-use planning, energy, and air and water pollution highly. In addition, 40 percent agreed that "the broad category of urban environment . . . should be a high priority for the club."[162]

A couple of interested Atlanta Sierrans then represented the chapter at a national conference on "City Care," convened in April 1979 in Detroit and jointly organized by the EPA's (former Atlantan) Barbara Blum and other federal officials as well as national offices of Sierra and the Urban League.[163] In the Chattahoochee chapter newsletter, these attendees reported a dialogue they'd had there with representatives of this iconic civil rights group: "We explained our opposition to suburban sprawl which destroys farm and forest resources. The Urban League people explained their opposition to urban disinvestment polices (redlining is one) which suck away a city's vitality, and pushes [*sic*] people to the suburbs." Three years prior to the Warren County protests, one Atlanta Sierran found it "exciting to see the support expressed for what I think of as 'our' programs by urban [read: Black civil rights] groups." In particular, "there was a general consensus among attendees that we would oppose any weakening of pollution control laws."[164]

Significant differences remained, nevertheless, between the ways Atlanta Sierrans and Urban Leaguers spoke about the "urban environment," signaling deeper differences in orientation and priorities. Environmentalists worried about what suburban sprawl did to farms and forests and about the profligate energy use demanded by driving and the ever-more-evident toll on Atlanta's air. While Sierrans did join with Urban Leaguers in criticizing a "white flight" to the suburbs, the urban disinvestment and deteriorating cores emphasized by the Urban League remained far less central to Sierran critiques. Their greatest concerns centered around suburbs' environmental impacts; for them, umbrella language like "the urban environment" could mentally drive past the downtown living quarters of the poor and mainly Black as not really "environmental."[165] But a more urban orientation crept into the Sierra Club's gathering political efforts over the next few years. Individual activists began plugging more cityward issues: staving off a "water doomsday," addressing air pollution, and protecting the Chattahoochee River planning corridor. Also added to this growing list was the promotion of a "new park being purchased by the City of Atlanta, Cascade Park", a project largely hatched by Black residents in racially transitioned suburbs to the city's southwest.[166]

The 1980 elections kicked off another way that the activism of Atlanta's Sierra Club drew closer to that of civil rights activists: through a growing engagement with the political element of citizenship, especially electoral politics. That year the Carter presidency was replaced by a Reagan administration seemingly intent on rolling back the environmental state building of the past decade. Many other "long-time friends of the environment were defeated," in races ranging down to those for Congress and statehouses, in a conservative tide that was also distinctly antienvironmentalist. Atlanta's Sierrans, who had "traditionally considered themselves apolitical" came around to what now seemed "the political reality": some kind of "involvement at election time" was needed.[167] Heretofore, even though "southern legislators have exerted powerful influence on the U.S. Congress . . . the influences on these legislators by the Sierra Club and other environmental groups have been relatively small." That had to change; "letter writing and issue involvement are no longer enough."[168] In 1982 the Georgia chapter made its first endorsements of candidates for the U.S. Congress: Democrats Elliot Levitas for the Fourth District and Wyche Fowler for the Fifth.[169] The very next year the mostly Atlanta-based Georgia Sierrans then split from Alabama Sierrans, turning the Chattahoochee chapter into two state-based ones. For Georgians the main rational was to aid their political work, since they could then concentrate on Georgia's own congressional delegation, legislature, and agencies.[170]

Over this same period Atlanta-area environmentalists also faced new political challenges within the city of Atlanta. Andrew Young, the former SCLC executive and Congress representative, ran for mayor in 1981, pledging his support for the neighborhood movement in his campaign, only to turn his back on neighborhood activists once elected. Instead, by reconsolidating an alliance between city hall and Atlanta's white business elite, Young's mayoralty returned them to their customary position in Atlanta's driver's seat.

This newfound alliance between the city's new Black political leadership and its white business chieftains was forged, in important part, through continued struggle over a long-controversial stretch of city land: that two hundred acres of state-owned and cleared property sitting unused after the plans for I-485 and the Stone Mountain Freeway had been defeated. From the 1970s into the 1980s, the push for a downtown "Great Park" there had been endorsed by Maynard Jackson as well as James Mackay, the former congressperson who came to head the conservancy's urban parks committee, even as the Georgia Department of Transportation stubbornly continued to plan for a "transit facility."[171] Governor Busbee hired architect Portman to put a third compromise design on the table, which favorably impressed Mackay but drew opposition from NPU-M, including Poncey-Highlands and Inman Park. The mounting debate between the Portman plan and another then commissioned by these neighborhoods was cut short when Jimmy Carter, defeated in his 1980 reelection campaign, decided to seek an Atlanta site for his presidential library. Andrew Young, who'd pledged to build no new highways during his successful election campaign to become mayor, then changed his tune, endorsing a four-lane Presidential Parkway on the still-vacant DOT land.

To the dismay of closer-in neighborhoods who had opposed any road larger than two lanes, Young pushed his plan through the city council, starting with a series of town hall meetings as well as intensive lobbying among city council members. Residents of the BOND neighborhoods packed the public meetings, such as the one at the Little Five Points Community Pub, and also marched on City Hall to make their displeasure known. But on the road's behalf, Young successfully marshaled support from the first Black majority city council in Atlanta's history, as well as key civil rights leaders such as Coretta Scott King and SCLC leader Joseph Lowery.[172] Council member John Lewis, a parkway opponent, recalled how "that old bugaboo of racial loyalty was . . . raised," with "a group of Black ministers . . . proclaiming that a vote against" Young's parkway proposal was "a vote against the mayor and against the Black community.'"[173] Jimmy Carter, staying above the fray through most of the debate, intervened at a final, critical moment, and the council in July 1982 voted eleven to eight in favor of his Presidential Parkway.

Here and elsewhere Mayor Young made a point of confronting the city's neighborhood activism head-on and limiting its clout and capacity.[174] He also backed off from a promise to fight a North Atlanta Parkway and that October fired the final six professional planners who'd been working with the twenty-four citizen-run Neighborhood Planning Units. The official rationale was "cost-cutting," but neighborhood activists knew better.[175] As the political scientist Clarence Stone later put it, "Andrew Young's mayoralty quickly demonstrated that the neighborhood movement was outside the governing coalition," now reconsolidated to unite white business leaders with Black politicians such as Young himself.[176] The Atlanta city government's consolidating recalcitrance toward the neighborhood movement offered a paler version of Ronald Reagan's national-level effort to decimate environmental agencies and open up public lands.

In response Parkway opponents introduced a new militancy to the city's environmental politics, drawing directly from the well-honed repertoire of civil rights through lawsuits as well as civil disobedience. A group calling itself CAUTION—Citizens against Unnecessary Thoroughfares in Older

Neighborhoods—coalesced to join those other environment-minded groups and activities stirring in the city's inner, mostly white suburbs. The Atlanta chapter of the Sierra Club lent it a hand, among other ways, with funds to support its lawsuits.[177] When CAUTION and its allies proved unable to halt the start of construction in early 1985, a civil disobedience group, Roadbusters, got underway. Sitting in underneath the cranes and in front of the tractors, they repeatedly got themselves arrested for "criminal trespass." In Shady Side Park, along where the road was to run, they also erected a small "tent city" to hold a twenty-four-hour vigil. For the first time in the history of metro-area environmental politics, Atlanta environmental activists engaged in peaceful lawbreaking to make their opposition known. But in this case that same tactic that had launched the post–World War II struggle for civil rights into its most dynamic and successful phase failed to stop the Presidential Parkway project.[178]

The Sierra Club was able to exploit the resultant sense of besiegement and urgency about environment issues among Atlantans by stepping up recruitment as well as its own political engagements. By 1984 the Atlanta group alone numbered some 2,200, and outside Atlanta the Georgia chapter had inaugurated additional groups in other parts of the state.[179] The Atlanta group's conservation committee was reenergized as well, though still searching for a best operating strategy, from a six-fold agenda tried in 1983 to the one-issue focus in 1984, around acid rain. Falling from clouds acidified by emissions from factories and power plants, it threatened forests and lakes not just in the northeast but elsewhere in Georgia. Under a new conservation chair, Chuck McGrady, an Atlanta lawyer living in the DeKalb suburbs, the club's political priorities were now not so rural at all—"wilderness" lay on the bottom of the list. Instead, they poured their efforts into controlling not just sprawl but the myriad pollution dispensed by private corporations: "Toxics/Hazardous Wastes," "Clean Air Act Reauthorization," "Acid Rain Legislation," "Superfund," "Clean Water Act Reauthorization," and "Nuclear Waste."[180]

Tellingly, this new wave of Atlanta activists, more like those leading the national environmental movement of the 1960s than the Georgians who founded the conservancy, often styled themselves as "environmentalists" rather than "conservationists." Their coalition building was more expansive than any Atlanta-area environmental movement had yet seen, encompassing advocates not just of civil rights but of economic citizenship—Georgia's struggling union movement. A state acid-rain task force, for instance, drew representatives not just from Sierra and the Georgia Conservancy but from the SCLC and the National Urban League, the UAW and the AFL-CIO, and the League of Women Voters.[181] Atlanta-based Sierra by the mid-1980s also undertook a growing amount of politically oriented outreach: putting out their own pamphlets, televising their own public service announcements, and undertaking their own lobbying of political leaders.[182] Since the conservancy had long tracked environmental legislation in the state capital, McGrady and his committee concentrated on Georgia's voices in Washington: its congresspeople. In the space of three months in 1985, a team of three led by McGrady pushed them on the reauthorization of the Clean Water Act; McGrady wrote the entire delegation about acid rain; and at least one other club member worked on each of another seven environmental issues.[183] To make their endorsements less ad hoc, they also set about creating their own standing SCCOPE, or Sierra Club Committee on Political Education, to screen and select candidates while also tapping a fund set up by Sierra's national office for supporting worthy congressional campaigns.[184]

Institutionalizing Georgia Sierra's electoral involvement in these ways, these new politically minded activists created the groundwork for a more sustained electoral alliance between the local Sierra Club and environmentally friendly congressional candidates. Prior to the mid-1980s, environmental appeals in these races had remained ad hoc and candidate driven, like what Andrew Young had pioneered in his successful 1972 congressional run. But now the club acquired the means to make its own evaluation of candidates' records as well as funding mechanisms to back up its endorsements. From this moment onward, less because of the ongoing rapprochement between environmental and civil rights citizenship than because of judicial and other efforts to enable more Black representation in Georgia's congressional districts, most candidates from Atlanta-area districts whom Sierra was willing to endorse were Black. With Atlanta's Black majority now coupled with Black political leadership, Sierra's new political capacities worked largely in support of Black congressional candidates who had established their environmental bona fides, beginning with John Lewis.

By mid-1985 McGrady was reporting to his fellow Sierrans that Lewis, an Atlanta council member, might be running for Congress.[185] During the course of the Presidential Parkway battle, Lewis had been one of three Black council members to vote against Andrew Young's plan, sticking instead to his campaign promise to oppose any parkway. Just elected to the council in 1982, Lewis was a bona fide hero of the civil rights movement, having marched with King, spoken at the 1963 March on Washington, and been beaten on the Edmund Pettus Bridge. A leader in SNCC rather than SCLC, he'd then held several administrative posts: heading up the Voter Education Project, just prior to getting on the council, and serving in the Atlanta office of the National Consumer Cooperative Bank, a federally created institution seeking to support cooperatives as a "means of developing an economic base for rural Black Americans."[186] Though he'd lost a first race for Congress in 1980, after two terms as a council member, he decided to explore another try. McGrady, favorably impressed by Lewis's work on the council, volunteered to help out with a phone survey that would assess the his chances.[187]

Lewis would be running in the Fifth District, whose boundaries as well as racial composition had been substantially altered through court decisions in the early 1980s. Black legal activists had successfully pushed for a redistricting that would make the Fifth District not just majority Black but 65 percent Black. The rationale, agreed to by the courts and the Department of Justice, was that fewer Blacks voted, both because more were younger and because of the long history of discrimination. So an extra majority was necessary for Blacks to compete at the ballot box. "A new group of moderate and conservative Democratic and Republican whites from the suburbs" sided with this redistricting, since putting so many Blacks in the Fifth District would increase the percentage of whites in the Fourth District.[188] With these changes Wyche Fowler, the white congressperson who had represented the Fifth District, stepped down, and it was widely assumed that a Black politician would follow him.

Sierrans' scrutiny of the two main candidates, Julian Bond and Lewis, rivals in the Democratic runoff, illustrated the limited rapprochement achieved between the political projects of civil rights and environmental citizenship by 1986. Bond, the polished, well-connected former Georgia legislator, was the heavy favorite, backed as he was by much of the new Black political establishment. But for Sierrans his deep support among "civil rights leaders and other interests" left "environmentalists less well-positioned to help" his campaign. Moreover, he had "no record" of environmental legislation, and an interview with him showed he "did not know much about environmental issues." Lewis, the son of a sharecropper, was seen as more rough-hewn and working class— the Sierran interviewers found him "not as articulate."[189] But he also hadn't endeared himself nearly as much to the current Black political or civil rights leadership as Bond had and realized he needed every constituency he could get: "blue collar, white collar, gay, Jewish, female, labor, environmentalist—I sought them all," he later recalled. The Sierrans liked that he served on the board of the Legal Environmental Assistance Foundation and during the interview found he "seems to have an intuitive feel for what is right on environmental issues." Lewis himself remembered "protecting the environment" as a main promise of his first winning congressional campaign: "I said it over and over, that people have a right to know what's in the water they drink, the food they eat and the air they breathe."[190]

This version of environmental citizenship, voiced by a civil rights leader turned politician and more centered on toxic pollution than on natural land and resource preservation, matched up well with where Atlanta's Sierra leadership had arrived by the mid-1980s. Georgia Sierra's new SCCOPE committee decided to publicly endorse John Lewis, as well as to send him a $1,000 contribution from Sierra's National SCCOPE fund.[191] After he'd won and gone to Washington, the only Black congressperson from the Deep South, they were not disappointed. Lewis became the staunchest supporter of environ-

PHOTO 6.1. John Lewis with his campaign manager, Judi Gerhardt, during his successful 1986 congressional campaign. Not only was he supported by the Sierra Club, but Gerhardt had previously organized a local version of a Citizens Party, inaugurated by environmentalist Barry Commoner. Courtesy of Kenneth Walker/*Atlanta Journal-Constitution* via AP, Atlanta Constitution Photographic Archives, Georgia State University Special Collections.

mental legislation in the entire Georgia delegation, inaugurating a new tradition. From the end of the 1980s to the time of this writing, the strongest allies that Atlanta environmentalists have had in the Georgia congressional delegation have been Black.

Culminating a decade of coalition building between environmentally interested white and Black activists in Atlanta was a Southern Environmental Assembly convened in 1988, at least partly the brainchild of Sierra's Atlanta-based staff. It was held in late February, nine days before the first "Super Tuesday" presidential primary in many southern states and on the same day as a televised debate between the candidates, to be broadcast from a nearby room in the self-same World Congress Center, the convention center in downtown Atlanta. The assembly featured a panel of Democratic presidential candidates (all the Republican candidates refused repeated invitations) and was cosponsored by the Atlanta-based Southern Christian Leadership Conference as well as over eighty other groups from across the Southeast. Organizer Sam Collier, a white Atlanta lawyer, billed the gathering as a "regional town hall gathering," exemplifying "democracy at its most basic . . . informed and active citizens raising their concerns together and with candidates for the highest office in the land." A thousand people showed up, not just from white, middle-class

{250} CHAPTER SIX

environmental groups but from some labor unions, the SCLC, and "many other Black organizations."[192] "The reason for this is simple," explained Collier in a press release. "In the south, many environmental problems affect blacks directly," among them, Louisiana's cancer alley, "with the highest lung cancer rate in the country for minorities." Here and throughout the assembly, the recent findings of a United Church of Christ study correlating racial and socioeconomic data with hazardous wastes sites reverberated. Doing what the EPA and environmental groups never had, it started with questions about racial equity and drew on social science tools to answer them, conveying an environmental issue into established provinces of civil rights citizenship. The study demonstrated a massive racial skew to the location of hazardous waste dumps: "Three out of every five Black and Hispanic Americans live in communities with uncontrolled toxic waste sites."[193]

Historically remarkable for any environmental gathering to this point was what organizers pitched as distinctly southern about this one: how racially mixed not just its sponsors and attendees but its speakers were. White plenary speakers came from outside the South, whereas most plenary speakers from the South were Black.[194] John Lewis gave the welcoming address. Speaking "as if inspired by our coming together for [a] single purpose," the notes of an assembly organizer on his talk recorded his emphasis on how "we should leave our children and our children's children an environment free from toxic waste and pollution." Twenty-eight years before, to the day, he recalled, he had participated in his first sit-in and arrest for civil rights. Now as then, he suggested, "our purpose is a basic issue, not a Black, or a white, or a rich, or a poor issue, but a human issue."[195] Rev. Ben Chavis, who'd helped organized the protests over a hazardous waste dump in Warren County, North Carolina, spoke to the entire group about leading the United Church of Christ study. Drawing on a regional vision rooted in the SCLC's many civil rights achievements, he insisted that "the struggle for the environment must emerge from the South," which "must rise again," "as it did in the struggle for civil rights." Rev. Joseph Lowery, longtime leader of the SCLC and a Warren County veteran, then delivered the closing address, spinning a version of environmentalism that crossed lines of race and class. Working for a clean environment, he insisted, "went hand-in-hand with struggling to help preserve the rights of blacks, Hispanics and low-income people." Excoriating Republican candidates for snubbing this environmental assembly—as well as an SCLC-sponsored march for the homeless—he invited conferees to join him in a walk "down the hall to see if I can talk to some of those Republicans about why they weren't here." About two hundred attendees then marched over to confront the Republican candidates who had just concluded their debate.[196]

For all the collaborative triumph of this assembly, leading groups were themselves much slower to racially integrate within: Sierra's membership had stayed almost entirely white, and the SCLC's predominantly Black. Yet, by the decade's end, this and other outreach across the color line helped the Atlanta-based Georgia Sierra chapter to become, according to new chair Chuck Mc-Grady, the second-fastest growing of any Sierra chapter in the nation. Mc-Grady attributed its swelling ranks—to six thousand, over half of them Atlantans—to a "movement of the club's agenda" away "from being primar-ily focused on public lands." Reflecting the continuing tensions between civil rights and environmental citizenship, he framed the toxic pollution issues that civil rights leaders now prioritized as just one of a new "wider range of issues" that were "life-threatening": "ozone holes, the greenhouse effect, the medi-cal waste on our coastal shores." Those rights of Black, Brown, and working-class people held up by Lowery in his assembly plenary went unmentioned. Also crediting the "higher visibility" from the chapter's SCCOPE and legisla-tive programs for his chapter's growth, McGrady declared the 1989 session of the Georgia legislature a "success for the Sierra Club" mainly "because of our level of involvement"—by an unprecedented fourteen activists, Roger Buerki among them. Their actual legislative achievements were more mixed: most recommendations of a state Growth Strategies Commission were adopted but in a "weakened" fashion, and a phosphorus ban had been thoroughly de-feated. McGrady insisted that they were on the threshold of achieving much more—"wait until next year!"[197] But many of his hopes would be dashed by a Republican Party in the midst of upsurge, even while turning increasingly hostile to environmental causes. That its national candidates had shunned Si-erra's environmental assembly reflected its ongoing, studied embrace of active opposition to environmental initiatives. Building over previous decades, by the mid-1990s it would furnish the GOP with an important springboard to-ward statewide political dominance.

CHAPTER 7

Conservatism Remade, Environmentalism Eclipsed

Aside from Ronald Reagan, no politician contributed more to the late-century success of Republicans in the Southeast—or their growing aversion to environmental causes—than Newt Gingrich. Born in Pennsylvania but raised in Georgia, he won his first election to Congress in 1978 after two earlier tries, in a district stretching from the suburbs of South Atlanta to the Alabama border. Starting out as a professor of history at Carrollton's West Georgia College (now the University of West Georgia), he had burnished his environmental bona fides by organizing an Environmental Studies Department and becoming active in the Georgia Conservancy. After two campaigns as *the* green candidate, however, his subsequent about-face on the environment was arguably the most dramatic and momentous reversal of his early political career. Abandoning his earlier championing of an environmental state, he abruptly set about castigating and curbing government itself, turning nearly silent about environmental citizenship. The first Republican congressperson from Georgia to achieve durable political success through neoconservative appeals, he won his way to Washington and then into a national Republican leadership. He also helped spur the ascension of the Republican Party in Georgia itself. By 1994 the Gingrich-led Republicans won a majority in the state's delegation for the first time since Reconstruction, initiating a political dominance anchored in Atlanta's white suburbs and exurbs that they would sustain for two decades and more. Not just environmentalists but civil rights advocates and the Georgia Democratic Party were left reeling.

Long in coming, the Republicans' early 1990s success in Georgia arrived through a different route than the oft-cited "Southern Strategy" of Richard Nixon. The Nixon era itself yielded few favors for Georgia's Republicans, bringing major setbacks after some initial successes exploiting Democrats' turnaround on civil rights. As this book has shown, Georgia's transition to electoral democracy culminated over this same period mostly at the hands of a rising, soon victorious faction of the Democratic Party that was more government friendly. Taking on the racial authoritarianism of Talmadgism and shucking off supremacist demagoguery, upstart Democratic politicians like

Jimmy Carter and Andrew Young sustained their party's political fortunes by endorsing many tenets of environmental as well as civil rights citizenship and drawing on them to reshape government. For the next two decades, Georgia Democrats won statewide races by following their example, pursuing greater racial evenhandedness, park making, pollution control, and a generally more positive and expansive view of government as serving a broader public. Yet Georgia's Democratic Party also housed many who continued to favor antistatist and other precepts echoing Talmadgism, not just older—governor-turned-senator Herman Talmadge served until 1981—but younger. Around the same time that Gingrich was gradually learning how a Republican could win an Atlanta-area congressional race, a young Larry McDonald found a way to win as a distinctly hardline conservative on the Democratic ticket, in a congressional district next door. Ultimately, however, the Georgia Republican Party became the main institutional vehicle for a return to power of Talmadge-like approaches to governance. Over the same period, when the SCLC sought out new ways of keeping both poor and middle-class Blacks on board, as Atlanta environmentalists reached out to labor as well as civil rights groups and shifted cityward in their recruitment and orientation, Georgia Republicans wove a cross-class electoral coalition among extra-urban whites that was reminiscent of Talmadgism. But the party itself had begun with a suburban rather than a rural base. With Gingrich in the lead, Republicans jettisoned Georgia conservatism's rustic cast, switching up targets, tactics, and narratives to portray it as new, suburban, and future minded.

The Republicanization of Georgia exemplified what was happening across the entire U.S. South, a shift in partisan control that Earl Black and Merle Black call "the most spectacular example of partisan realignment in modern American history." For them and other political scientists, the GOP's subsequent political dominance has cast the 1970s and 1980s successes of the Georgia Democratic Party in a different light. In retrospect the Democratic Party of this period had become too ideologically diverse for long-term stability.[1] Once the national Democrats' sponsorship of the 1960s Civil Rights Acts had driven many southern whites into independence from any party, they argue, the national GOP's racially coded messaging especially during the 1980s enticed these same voters to take the next step: to identify as Republicans. As we will see, already in 1970s Georgia aspiring conservatives, McDonald as well as Gingrich, had abandoned the explicit racism of the Talmadgists but had set about racially coding the entire, recent generation of state building. With the state Democratic Party increasingly beholden to Black voters, racial coding then became a specialty of Georgia Republicans, with Gingrich leading the way.[2] Adding to the grounds for GOP success with southern whites from the 1970s onward was the party's studied commitment to traditional gender roles, which helped seal a gathering alliance with white Evangelicals.[3] An ascendant

Georgia GOP also tapped into a national conservative movement driven top down by corporate funders and promarket intellectuals and on the ground by conflicts over busing, suburbanization, and white flight.[4] Missing from these many explanations of the rise of the GOP in the South is how it connected to the "environmental reversal" that the national Republican Party underwent over this same period.[5] Gingrich's own evolution offers a local, Georgia-based window into how and why this reversal happened. His state Republican Party won through strategies the national party would quickly make its own: downplaying the urgency of environmental problems, doubting or dismissing environmental science and expertise, and, in an occluded fashion, bemoaning the excesses of environmental laws.

Though many historical forces and developments contributed to the rising power of Republican conservatism in late twentieth-century Atlanta and Georgia, conservatives here as in much of the South enjoyed a distinct advantage: their creeds were far from new. Conservatism had flourished amid the extreme inequalities of the region's early twentieth century, as rustic rulers cozied up to business while flaunting "poor government," white supremacy, and the segregation of Jim Crow. In the post-1970 era, as electoral democracy peaked in this city, it quickly began to be undermined by cleavage capitalism's return. The new economic and racial frictions nourished by it also laid groundwork for a revival of conservatism especially among white Georgians. But for those frictions to be translated into political change, bridges to the region's conservative past had to be built outside the realm of candidates and elections, as well as within. Two new initially separate political projects emerged for doing so. Starting in the religious realm as part of a modern fundamentalist revival, white Evangelical leaders marshaled moral and institutional resources to publicly criticize federal actions on school prayer, abortion, and women's rights. Out of these critiques came a new political project of Evangelical citizenship. As disgruntlement about expanded federal environmental and other powers mounted among businesses and landowners, a new business-first citizenship project also coalesced. In 1970s congressional races, conservative politicians absorbed and spoke to the concerns of both these new conservative political projects, often goading them along. Ironically, both McDonald and Gingrich first wielded these new lines of political attack against Democratic political holdovers from the era of rustic rule. In these and other ways, these two ultimately successful conservatives, one Democratic and the other Republican, led their rivals in conveying Georgia politics into what seemed a more modern era, by marshaling costly new campaign media, a new level of policy fluency, and more effective means of fundraising. They thereby recast conservatism itself as fresh and modern, not just a thing of the past but as means toward what they pitched as a brighter future.

The successes of this new conservative politics also stemmed from how well it dovetailed with Georgia's increasingly skewed growth. Precisely as wealth and income were also concentrating in the state's upper echelons of earners, political campaigning was becoming more financially demanding. As a growing share of new wealth poured into the pockets of the wealthy, they emptied their wallets into politics, shunting ever more cash to candidates they found wealth-friendly. For them that meant tax cuts, smaller and less costly governments, and reduced oversight from an environmental state, positions they saw as entirely compatible with their own eager pursuit of private environmental consumption. In and around Atlanta, where more democratic and environmentally friendly politics was itself of recent vintage, by the mid-1990s conservative Republican leaders were winning electoral majorities from a broader and more urban electorate than rustic rulers had ever known.

A New Evangelical Citizenship in Cobb

Georgia politicians who first seized on "moral" issues like school prayer or abortion in their campaigns were only reading tea leaves. They sought to capitalize on concerns already stirring among local churches and their leaders, in what remained by many measures the nation's most religiously devout region. Responding to a sense of besiegement and cultural crisis, a new generation leading many of Atlanta's Protestant denominations was taking aim at creeping licentiousness, pluralism, and secularism at their doorstep and in the world beyond. Like SCLC's preachers, they drew heavily on the Bible and sought to convey messages not just within their own congregations but to a broader public. Decrying trends whose most visible faces were only tangentially political, at least at first, they laid foundations for a new Evangelical citizenship across Atlanta's white suburbs that most purveyors saw as in stark contrast to the "old-time" fundamentalism of Eugene Talmadge. Their worries centered, instead, on the United States of the sixties and seventies, its culture and media as much as any governmental actions, and many professed a personal antiracism, vocally embracing or tacitly accepting the new civil rights laws. Their core commitment was to revive biblically based values and priorities they saw as threatened. But their common ground of conscience also laid down cultural bases for a new political conservatism. Reaffirming gender hierarchies, it furnished moralistic cover for rank political indifference toward the concentrating riches and curbed social mobility of cleavage capitalism's return, which left many to tread water or sink. Embracing private modes of environmental consumption from hillside homes to hunting, the new Evangelical citizenship also cultivated anew the questioning of scientific expertise, an inclination that could easily spill over into hostility toward the new science-based environmental state. Thereby, its proponents resuscitated key underpinnings of rustic rule.

Cobb County, just northwest of Atlanta's city limits, gave birth to some of the most flourishing and redoubtable bastions of this fundamentalist revival and, a little later, also lay "at the heart of the Republican surge." The large houses and lush lots of East Cobb, some of them perched along the Chattahoochee, and the hillside developments around Kennesaw Mountain drew in many of Atlanta's wealthiest earners, managers, and financial and medical professionals, often newcomers from other parts of the country. By the early 1990s northern journalists found Cobb "the booming suburban South in bold caricature."[6] The Lockheed plant here remained the state's biggest aerospace facility, but its workforce and unions had been shrinking and its wages stagnating. Over the 1970s and into the 1990s, while better-off Blacks buying homes in Cobb's eastern and southern reaches brought some integration to the county, it had continued to draw middle- and some lower-income whites fleeing Atlanta's growing Black suburbs for cheaper subdivisions in West Cobb. Homeowners predominated there, but many houses were "rural" and "deteriorating," and the county also harbored a significant share of mobile homes, those emblematic abodes for "white trash." Their presence would likely have exceeded 10 percent of the housing—as it did in nearly two-thirds of the metropolitan counties—had not Cobb passed restrictive zoning confining them to "parks" of no less than ten acres.[7] Harboring white and some Black affluence, it also was home to a significant share of lower-income whites who over the 1970s and 1980s would face growing economic challenges. Cobb's own changing demographics along with its suburban separateness from downtown made the county into a crucible for the new fundamentalist Evangelism sweeping across Atlanta after 1970 as well as the politics it would help stir.

Exemplifying the mainstream of this religious movement, Marietta's Roswell Street Baptist Church blossomed under the leadership of Rev. Nelson Price. After arriving in Cobb in 1965, he shepherded it through a new chapter in the centuries-old tradition of suburban religious revivalism. Across the metro area Baptist churches harbored far and away the most congregations and congregants of any Christian denomination, and in Cobb itself over three times as many members as the Methodists, the second largest group.[8] Roswell Baptist, a relative newcomer, started in 1943 in an antebellum house and former slave cabins but already had a sizeable congregation of more than a thousand when Price arrived. By the late 1970s, though, it boasted a membership of over six thousand, surpassed in metro Atlanta only by the First Baptist congregation downtown.[9]

Roswell Baptist's main raison d'être, of course, as with other Christian churches that remained the strongest and most pervasive civic institutions across white as well as Black Atlanta, was to put members in touch with millennia-old texts and teachings. Like the leaders of so many other religious groups, the SCLC's preachers not least among them, Price's job was to keep alive and relevant creeds that were genuinely ancient, which he and other believers saw as universal, transcending the human conception of time. What Price and his fellow Evangelicals found in the Judeo-Christian Bible echoed what the new environmental culture found in wild rivers and mountains: an abiding suprahuman reality. Price too was appreciative of the natural world, though in ways less mediated by modern "wilderness" traditions than by Judeo-Christian scriptures, which accentuated the divine handiwork he found there. Over the 1970s he and other Atlantan pastors from among the city's largest Baptist congregations led a resurgent fundamentalism that swept through their own as well as other Christian denominations by decade's end while also foraying into politics.[10] They did so by veering from and sometimes directly attacking many environmentalists' ways of knowing and caring about the natural world.[11] Within suburbs that remained largely segregated by race, halls of worship like Roswell Street Baptist still made Sunday mornings the "most segregated hour in the nation," even as its expanding congregation by the early 1980s led to its being dubbed one of suburban Atlanta's first "mega churches."[12] Beyond his own congregation Price also preached his ostensibly postracist and color-blind righteousness to larger audiences, through revivals that could fill high school football stadiums, televised services reaching some 160,000 Atlantans each week, and a regular column in Cobb County's biggest newspaper.[13]

Driving the growth of Roswell Baptist was not just Cobb County's own rapidly growing population but the evolving thoughts, messages, and entrepreneurship of its leader.[14] Price's ministerial career in Cobb involved his coming to terms with a place that seemed a far cry from that into which he'd been born, the rural and small-town world long dominant across the South. In the "agrarian society" of tiny Osyka, Mississippi, the small Baptist church his family attended served as "the center of community life," unchallenged by any other civic or state institution, especially under the "poor government" principles of Mississippi's own version of rustic rule.[15] The first in his family to attend high school as well as college, his education-enabled mobility reflected the rising opportunities available to white rural Georgians under the compression capitalism of the midcentury. Studying biology and agriculture, initially inspired by a stint of soil "conservation work," to become a county extension agent, after his first year at the university he began to feel called to the ministry. His eventual horticulture degree notwithstanding, he then entered a seminary in New Orleans—his first time living in a city—and spent the first leg of his pastoral career at a rural church on that city's fringe before seeking the position in Marietta.

Prior to his arrival Roswell Street Baptist had a revolving-door pastorate, and upon receiving an invitation to become its minister, Price accepted after some reluctance. A mentor, perhaps thinking he could do better, advised him against taking on this "blue collar congregation," with many lower-paid and less educated whites who worked for the local Lockheed plant. But Cobb's natural scenery tugged at Price: the hilly "topography" and "of course the Chattahoochee, a beautiful stream, and the people." Deciding that God was calling him to this pulpit, he accepted and leaped into the community with both feet. Approaching "every leader in this community," he sought to "get to know" them "on a first name basis and be their friend in the event I ever have to talk to them about an issue." His own understanding of his church's spectacular growth under his leadership was that he successfully recruited the more educated and better-off to a congregation that had been largely working class. His styling of Roswell Street as a "church on the go for God" drew in families of white-collar professionals and businesspeople, many of them new-comers to the area and the chief beneficiaries of the region's gradual tilt toward cleavage capitalism.[16]

Central to that appeal were his conciliatory racial messages, paralleling con-temporary moves by Jimmy Carter as governor. Price helped lead a younger generation of pastors to abandon any defense of segregation and instead to use their pulpits to advocate racial comity and brotherhood. He saw to the for-mal integration of Roswell Street Baptist, even though Black members re-mained few and far between. Having made the acquaintance of Jimmy Car-ter prior to the latter's election as governor, Price's moderate racial views led to his appointment by Carter onto a new Georgia Human Relations Commis-sion. This service work brought him face to face with the flagrant racism that still prevailed (as he saw it) mainly in rural parts of the state.[17] Price personally befriended Carter, also a professed Evangelical, and eventually the Black reli-gious leader Martin Luther King Sr., with whom he occasionally exchanged Sunday pulpits. Over the 1970s, though, as a leader of a growing conservative movement within the Southern Baptist denomination, Price's doctrinal as well as political stances increasingly diverged from those of Carter and many Black southern Baptists. Insisting on the "inerrancy" of the Bible also led Price and other fundamentalists toward ways of seeing and thinking about nature itself that departed significantly from those shared by most environmentalists.[18]

Around the first Earth Day, during the spring of 1970, while images of the earth beamed back from space stirred environmentalists' anxieties about the vulnerability of their planet, Price saw something different: a revelation of God's handiwork. Like so many southerners and others who had grown up or still lived in rural places, he had trouble imagining that human impacts could ever reach a planetary scale.[19] For Price this blue-dot earth dangling amid the blackness of space called to mind another challenge he found more compelling: "show[ing] the people of Marietta and Cobb County that sci-ence and the Bible are compatible." It was a concern with which he had wres-tled ever since his university days, when a faith gleaned from those with little formal education had suddenly collided with views and principles set out in his college textbooks.[20] Price came to accept many, even most scientific accounts of the natural world but felt his faith also compelled textbook-like credence to this foundational Judeo-Christian book. On the lookout for litmus tests where Biblical claims could be weighed against those of establishment science, he settled on a blend of scientific with what we might call *biblical* naturalism. From his columns in early 1970 onward, Price affirmed, praised, and even cited much existing science but drew the line especially at evolution, as "only a hypothesis—no more."[21] As Price saw it, he was neither antiscience nor blindly and strictly traditionalist, for he continued to affirm the values of science and objectivity. But Christians also needed to be ready to challenge the scientific establishment, not just when its assertions clashed with scripture but when they were based on "hypothetical" rather than empirical arguments. His faith, as he saw it, compelled him to test and temper his commitment to science by resort to an ancient, sacred text that he believed told comparable truths about "creation."[22]

Reflecting biblical truths, Price's creationist nature was a divine "gift" eminently deserving both of appreciation and of collective care, unlike in some other fundamentalist variants. An avid Boy Scout in his youth, Price had hiked, camped, hunted, and "enjoy[ed] the beauty of nature and the outdoors and just feeling a sense of free, being free and developing physically."[23] He also ardently admired the national parks and once in Marietta frequented the Okefenokee National Wildlife Refuge. For Price, walking itself brought a "spiritual boost" as well as physical benefits, especially "if one walks amid the beauty of nature . . . where one can get closer to the Lord."[24] His creationist nature proved easily reconcilable with the new environmental consumption gaining traction in so many corners of the Atlanta-metro area and beyond. He too felt the allure of countryside: with friends he bought land farther out, where he raised pumpkins and hunted, culling deer by principles of wildlife management he'd read. When he and his family decided to move out of the church manse in the late 1970s and buy a place of their own, they eagerly turned to some of Cobb's most visibly natural surroundings. They purchased two and a half undeveloped acres on Pine Mountain in West Cobb and built a house there, within a large property owned by a lawyer friend of theirs. What Price especially liked about their new mountainside home was how, with "all sorts of privacy and animals," it "brought me back to nature . . . just the basics." His cherished view—"how, when we'd get up in the morning, with the leaves off the trees this time of year, the sun comes up right between the twin peaks of Kennesaw Mountain"—became so familiar to his congregation at Roswell Street that their parting gift to him upon his retirement was a painting of it.[25]

This private nature that Price so prized in his own backyard was protected in ways that easily went unnoticed by him and his neighbors: by a growing economic segregation of Atlanta's wealthy from other residents, fueled by cleavage capitalism and often bolstered by local land-use policies. Price's house lay in a part of the county still covered into the 1990s with hardwoods and mixed forest and shielded from development by barriers of costliness as well as large-lot zoning. This hilly area attained the county's second-highest housing values—second only to those along the Chattahoochee in East Cobb. Distance also protected it: most of county's main polluters like Lockheed lay on the far side of the county, as did the lower-end suburbs and commercial districts of South Cobb, where cheap land and lax zoning eased invasion by shops and subdivisions. Increasingly isolated from those with middling or smaller incomes, homes, and lots, Price and his neighbors were among Cobb's greatest beneficiaries of privatizing veins of environmental consumption celebrated by *Southern Accents* and *Southern Living*. Having bought their way into their own private yet well-insulated nature preserves, the well-to-do residents of Cobb enjoyed an environmental consumption that brought many comforts and also isolation, which could ripen their willingness to dispense with environmental citizenship. With all these local protections as well as a federal environmental state now quietly working for them, they could afford to spurn new governmental actions, whether against hazardous wastes or for more parkland.

Price never went so far as that, but the few notes of environmental concern he voiced were overwhelmed by what he saw as an ongoing society-wide incursion against Christian values. Associated with cities, including Atlanta, but also with a United States beyond the South, it had ridden into Cobb County homes through television, movies, and other media of modern culture. Thanks to the counterculture, that younger "quality generation" of "vibrant ambitious young Americans" he met through his church work now faced off against a youthful "Beat Generation": "larger in numbers," "deluded," and "defeated," who had "rejected everything."[26] The advent of greater religious diversity had combined with court and other governmental decisions and an excessive faith in scientific authority to propel what he felt was a creeping secularization, exemplified by his own diminishing public and civic access as a church leader.[27] To take rhetorical arms against all these dark forces, Price wielded the timeless naturalism of the Bible, sometimes with and sometimes pointedly against the authority of modern science. While he himself refrained from political organizing or activism, his public stances helped rouse advocacy groups in Cobb and other metro-area counties that, by Reagan's election in 1980, composed a formidable political force.

What most consistently exercised Price throughout the 1970s was how Americans were sliding away from a biblically sanctioned gender traditionalism, how "God created them male and female." Decrying an Equal Rights Amendment (ERA) for women that Congress had passed in 1972 and whose ratification the Georgia legislature then took up, Price declared that already, "America is a matriarchal (feminine) society," since "TV, books and motions pictures" "depict women as smarter than men," and women "own 50% of the money" and "control 87½ % of the buying power." An ERA could only make matters worse for women, he insisted, recounting the dire predictions of Phyllis Schlafly's Stop ERA of forcibly shared restrooms and combat duty. With southerners holding more traditional ideas about gender roles than other parts of the country, many Cobb County readers and congregants already agreed with him.[28]

The Supreme Court's 1973 decision legalizing abortion drew out further vehemence from Price, this time on behalf of the unborn. Not just the Bible but biology itself, the "queen of the sciences," had shown that fetuses were not just "mere globs of jelly" but "babies," a "'he' or 'she'" rather than an "it," "from the moment the ovum is fertilized by the penetration of sperm." Biblical passages anticipated what this science now showed: Jesus, for instance, from the moment of his divine conception was "Jesus Christ, Lord."[29] Price himself was well aware that unwanted pregnancies abounded in predominantly white Cobb, with the third-highest rate among Georgia counties, and his church sponsored a program for mothers to see these to term.[30] His rhetoric, however, grouped abortion with a hellish litany of other ills that, for most of his audience, pointed cityward—"runaway children and runaway spouses, unglued families, divorce, abortion, vandalism, shoplifting, rape, assault, and arson," with "by-products [of] suicide, nervous breakdown, homosexuality, and alcohol and drug problems." Spun with the preacherly purpose of "revitalize[ing] the family," such dystopian visions also confirmed stereotypes about an inner city that, in Atlanta as in cities of other U.S. regions, was mostly both poor and Black.[31] The racial coding here was less direct and likely less intentional than that of conservative politicians railing against crime or welfare, as we will see. Nevertheless, when Evangelical leaders cast abortion as vaguely urban and alien to the suburban Christian family, they and those who followed them helped promote abortion into what was becoming a growing repertoire of racially coded issues on which conservative politicians could draw as more Black than white.

Price's messages helped stir organized opposition in Cobb to both the ERA and abortion. A local Stop ERA chapter coalesced among Cobb County homemakers to help defeat the ERA upon its first vote in the Georgia legislature in 1974 and regained momentum every time the ghost of ERA ratification reared its fearsome head, contributing to its repeated defeat in the Georgia Senate.[32] Of the three hundred Georgia women who converged on the capital in 1977 to make their position known, one-sixth hailed from Cobb.[33] Over the later 1970s antiabortion activism intensified in suburban Atlanta, first in conjunction with anti-ERA groups and then more independently. By 1980 the Atlanta-based Mothers on the March (MOM), formed two years earlier to stave off the institutionalizing of abortion in metro Atlanta, claimed a membership of as many as a thousand, "mostly women and some men," spread across nineteen states and "a cross section of religious denominations."[34] MOM sustained its momentum through events like an "intercession on behalf of the unborn" in 1980 at Atlanta's Omni Coliseum. Protesting the "4,200 babies that die from abortion every day," among the speakers it featured Phyllis Schlafly, this movement's national leader.[35]

For Evangelicals like Price, however, contemporary menaces to the unborn and to womanhood were at least equaled by those to biblically sanctioned masculinity, a worry that spurred his direct criticism of environmentalist concerns. Against the grain of a society he saw as already too "matriarchical," Price strove to affirm the biblical role and values he associated with "fathering." Deeply involved in a local Fellowship for Christian Athletes, he regularly praised "discipline" as well as "compassion" as fatherly virtues, alongside "providing loving consistent authority," showing firmness of resolve, and casting aside the "bad habit" of "worrying."[36] In protesters "unconditionally condemning" the Vietnam War, he brooded about slipping virility.[37] First hoping the energy crisis might compel Americans toward "frugality and restraint," he then worried it was revealing a "shortage of strength in the citizens of our society."[38] As the United States' new environmental state increasingly took on more hazardous and chronic pollutants, Price turned outright dismissive. He shrugged off concerns about nuclear power as overwrought, dispensing pro-nuclear factoids such as that the industry's entire radioactive wastes could "be contained in a single barrel" and that exposures from the Three Mile Island accident were ten times less than what the "average American absorbs" every year from cosmic rays.[39] Price's cultivation of what he saw as right masculinity grounded this as well as another front in his collision with many of Cobb County's environmentally minded: the shooting of animals.

Hunting was a pastime widely shared by men in this time and place, rooted among those like Price who had grown up in the rural South but also drawing in urbanites and regional newcomers. At Roswell Street Baptist, an annual "wild game" dinner, started in 1977, celebrated the manly pursuit of hunting by local "sportsmen and their friends," as they cooked up and served what they had killed and then spun "tall tale[s] about how they came about [that] piece of game." By its third year it drew six hundred participants as well as extensive, jaunty coverage in the *Marietta Daily Journal*, including recipes, such as Price's for wild-game jambalaya.[40] When the event then drew public criticism, Price penned perhaps the most biting satire of a decade of newspaper columns, applying antihunting arguments to the killing of plants. Affirming his "affection" for plants—"they are so live, green and vibrant"—he then noted their sensitivity "to emotion," how "when a plant is cut, there is a vibration produced that is equivalent to a human scream." So vegetarians and lawn mowers were "causing much suffering." Then he made sure his readership did not mistake his mockery of antihunting advocacy by adding that his "conclusions were obviously paradox . . . ridiculous."[41]

As he and his congregants hunted, then feasted together on their prey, a more or less explicitly antienvironmental advocacy of guns was gathering around them. Though hunting itself was strictly limited in Cobb and other metro-area counties, licensed hunters in the state of Georgia had spiked by 1978 to a quarter of a million and by the mid-1980s doubled again, thanks in important part to an ever more robustly conservationist state as well as the federal government and its wildlife management. Not coincidentally, just as Cobb County hunters were grumbling about the "anti-hunting sentiment" among urbanites who "tend to see the pretty side of nature" and miss its "harshness," a push for gun control seemed to be gathering steam in the Georgia state legislature.[42] The main impetus came from Atlanta's representatives as well as city officials like Maynard Jackson—most all of whom were Black—seeking additional legal tools to curb that city's crime. But gun control also emerged as a "hot issue" in mostly white Cobb, albeit with a different thrust. While prospects for legislative action seemed hopeful in 1976, a countermobilization soon shut it down. Pro-gun activism drew together Mariettans Charles Lyles (head of the Georgia Wildlife Federation) and Jesse Benjamin Stoner (a former Klan leader still trying to launch a National States Rights Party), in alliance with the National Rifle Association. The pressure they applied was so effective that three days into the 1978 legislative session, the Georgia House then unanimously declared its "complete support for the NRA position on gun control." Taken aback, Atlanta legislator and leading gun-control advocate David Scott called for investigation of that group's "improper lobbying" and "harassment" of legislators.[43] Yet not only were he and other political advocates for gun control themselves Black, but the crime they hoped to curb was now being pegged as "Atlanta's problem," confined to what was now a majority-Black city. Gun control as well had joined the pantheon of racially coded political causes in Georgia, leaving politicians with white constituents less and less willing to touch it.

Weaving through Evangelical jeremiads like Price's, the conciliatory stances he urged toward established hierarchies furnished quiet underpinnings for a new political conservatism, similarly to how segregationist customs and supremacist attitudes had grounded Jim Crow's citizenly hierarchy. Now, however, gender roles and "the family" were supplanting the racial order as the most explicit targets of righteous fervor, with (implicitly) male dominion over nature through guns as a subtheme. Despite Price's personal antiracist avowals, he and other Evangelicals lent a powerful hand to the racial coding and dissemination of place stereotypes that would be eagerly picked up by conservative politicians: of an (Black) inner city of moral and familial decay versus the righteous (white) suburbs and countryside.

Price's affirmation of existing hierarchies also echoed Jim Crow citizenship in what he had to say about power relations at work. Affirming the "right of the laborer to a square deal" and offering appreciation for masculine virtues among worker-congregants, he had little sympathy for their shop-floor travails.[44] In this era when Lockheed employees faced stagnating wages, shrinking jobs, and retreating unions, his labor-day columns praising "the laborer" paralleled those for mothers on Mother's Day: urging a contentment with one's work life that left little room for personal disgruntlement, much less collective action. "Reflect on your work until you discover reasons for enjoying it," he recommended in his weekly newspaper column. "If you cannot do this, switch jobs."[45] Seemingly unaware of workers' increasingly vulnerable positions within corporate hierarchies and other growing disadvantages faced by those with lower incomes and less education, he urged a "resolute return" "to the old-fashioned American ideal that everyone was responsible for his own welfare."[46] By the late 1970s Price was preaching a meritocratic Gospel frankly congratulatory to those in upper socioeconomic echelons. A chief preoccupation became what scripture taught about fostering personal "productivity." "Anyone who gets things done, an achiever," was "worthy of praise," he declared, anointing Cobb County's upper middle classes with well-nigh biblical blessings. Price's version of the Gospel shored up a receptiveness among his listeners to politicians who harped on the personal flaws and irresponsibility of those on the lower rungs of Atlanta's elongating wealth ladder, as undeserving of government assistance.

The one glaring exception to Price's espousal of the traditionally dominant was science. Dubbing it "the intellectual temple of our times," he acknowledged its contemporary power but chastised what he saw as its usurpation of religious faith. Not infrequently appealing to it himself, Price also saw it as a major engine of U.S. secularization. "Fed through the education system . . . to exclude any mention of God," it had had a "constricting influence on faith."[47] To limit its pernicious influence, by the 1970s Price drew a public line against what he saw as modern science's Achilles' heel: the theory of evolution. Well aware of the rural, antimodern reputation of creationism in the 1920s Scopes "monkey" trial, Price pushed a science-savvy creationism he hoped would bring Cobb County's well-educated managers and professionals on board. Regularly invoking how he "majored in the field" of biology, he wove together select findings and "data" to show how "scientific fact, not faith, is the new instrument in the creationist concept." Claiming to stay abreast of the latest in biology, he highlighted, for instance, the fossil record of an explosion of species in the Cambrian era, for which he thought an evolutionary explanation seemed implausible. Moreover, "no one has found a way to test" evolution's "predictive value." For Price it remained only a "theory" or "hypothesis" rather than "empirical science" and hence had "as much scientific support as" creationism. "Either has to be accepted by faith," he declared, and it actually "takes less faith to believe in creationism."[48]

Just as fellow Evangelical Jimmy Carter was overseeing the maturation of a science-based environmental state in Georgia and the nation, the attacks on evolution by Price and other fundamentalist leaders promoted science questioning to the frontlines of the new Evangelical political project. While our understanding of the modern roots of science denialism usually runs through corporate efforts at product defense, Evangelical activist groups in Georgia had successfully politicized evolution by 1980, with Cobb Countians at the forefront. Under Carter a bill requiring the teaching of creationism alongside evolution had made it through the state senate only to "quietly" die in the house. By 1980 *Atlanta Constitution* reporters ranked a "creation by God" bill second among the legislature's "big issues" and "the most controversial."[49] Helping to drive its rising profile were Mariettans such as Carolyn Sanford, a young homemaker and substitute elementary schoolteacher who belonged to Roswell Street Baptist. She helped found and lead a Citizens for Another Voice in Education (CAVE), a "small but active group." At a meeting "packed" by CAVE members in September 1978, the Cobb County School Board became the first in the state to vote for "equal time" for creationism and evolution in its high school texts; the vote was unanimous.[50] Though Arkansas and Louisiana then quickly moved to approve state-level mandates for "balanced treatment," a hotly contested 1980 initiative at the Georgia capitol faltered.[51] Nevertheless, battles to bring creationism into the public schools had opened a new wedge for widening skepticism among political conservatives about science itself, environmental and otherwise.

While Price and other leaders of the Atlanta area's largest Baptist churches charted a mainstream course for the new Evangelical citizenship, some of their fundamentalist fellow travelers spun a more slashing and sweeping antistatism, surpassing that of Eugene Talmadge himself. By the early 1970s the Armenian American Rousas John Rushdoony, working in an "intellectual Presbyterian tradition" out in California, had fleshed out the tenets of a new frankly authoritarian theology of "Reconstruction" that soon gained an Atlanta-metro following. In Rushdoony's radical vision millennia-old models of law and government in the Bible outlined a "Christian goal for the world [of] the universal development of Biblical theocratic republics . . . under . . . the rule of God's law." Rewriting U.S. history as the civil rights movement waxed, he portrayed the Civil War as a "theological" struggle of a "Christian system" of slavery against atheism and attacked civil rights activism as anti-Christian. For Rushdoony, also influenced by conservative intellectual currents such as Austrian economics, "Christianity is completely and radically anti-democratic." It demanded a "spiritual aristocracy" whose sway could be secured through the razing of most U.S. laws and government built over the past century and more. Schooling, welfare, health, and environmental protections would all be turned over to the church, the patriarchal family, and, as he put it, "capitalization" (wealth accumulation) through markets, so "man" could "subdue the earth and gain wealth as a means of restitution and restoration, as means of establishing God's dominion in every realm."[52]

By 1980 Cobb and other North Atlanta suburbs had become seeding grounds for Reconstruction activism. Most influential within national Reconstructionist circles was American Vision, a small nonprofit set up in Sandy Springs in 1978 by Steve Schiffman, who'd grown up Jewish in Chicago and converted to Christianity upon arriving in Atlanta four years prior. Having earned a college degree in physical education but then fallen into drugs and crime, his conversion turned his life around. Starting with an "Evangelical" ad company, he then launched a platform to popularize the Reconstructionists' far-reaching project. His most productive and energetic recruit for its staff, soon the outfit's leader, was Gary DeMar, a convert from the Catholicism of his Pittsburgh childhood and a recent graduate of a seminary in Jackson, Mississippi.[53] Also converging on the Atlanta area was another like-minded seminary graduate, Joseph Morecraft III, who came from West Virginia by way of a first pastorate in eastern Tennessee. He arrived in the Atlanta suburbs in 1974 to start a new congregation, a Presbyterian church which he dubbed "Chalcedon," after the name of Rushdoony's own California institute.[54] While Morecraft wound up trying his hand at partisan politics, as we'll soon see, Schiffman's and DeMar's American Vision became a fount of literature and media, what religious studies scholar Julia Ingersoll sees as an exemplary "right-wing echo chamber." Their stated intent was to "apply the Bible to all of life," albeit with a special focus on government: the Bible "not just as a spiritual textbook . . . but . . . a political textbook." After eighteen months "supervising research in American history," in 1980 they rolled out a first seminar, drawing nearly 250 mostly laypeople to the Northwest Hilton Inn in Cobb, with "tapes, records, and films" on the way. Authoring a series of "biblical blueprints for government" over the ensuing years, DeMar softened Rushdoony's frank antipathy for democracy without discarding it. Reconstructionists aimed for a "decentralization" of power that, he insisted, was achievable through "democratic process." Once they had won, however, "the best" could justifiably and "vigilantly guard against mob rule."[55]

Already by the start of Ronald Reagan's election to the presidency, even before Jerry Falwell started Georgia's Moral Majority chapter in 1979, a new Evangelical citizenship had gained growing footholds across Atlanta's white suburbs. While polls would find that, nationally, their resurgent fundamentalism had broader appeal in rural areas as well as for blue-collar workers, its successful spread and influence in Cobb and other suburbs pointed to a distinctly metropolitan bent, its engulfment of "conservative areas experiencing rapid modernization."[56] Around southern cities like Atlanta, now fully sharing in the Sunbelt boom, the Evangelical movement made deep inroads into the hearts and minds of affluent whites with white-collar jobs, while also stirring the passions and allegiances of many rural and working-class whites. The personal antiracism of many new Evangelicals did not impede their significant contributions to the racial coding that was becoming a mainstay of the new conservative politics. At the same time, they honed a justifying ethic for the deepening class divides among whites wrought by the return of cleavage capitalism. Affirming and congratulating "the achievers" and disparaging the disgruntled, preachers such as Price often portrayed the lots of the economically or racially deprived as the result of individual moral failings. They channeled their and their listeners' moral outrage toward other alternative targets—against the ERA, abortion, and gun control—and on behalf of the family, faith, gun rights, and a "right to life." Eagerly embracing private environmental consumption, the new Evangelical citizenship generally either downplayed or attacked public environmental concerns and stirred questions about science itself, that mode of truth seeking on which the new environmental state was based. By the late 1970s these many concerns of the new Evangelical citizenship were providing conservative politicians with ample fodder for a white cross-class alliance between suburban and rural voters. Yet a key question remained: Which Georgia political party would become the new Evangelicals' main electoral vessel?

Democratic Conservatism and the Remaking of Business-First Citizenship

From the 1970s into the 1980s, Georgia's Democratic Party vied with Republican rivals to win over not just the metro area's new Evangelical activists but other business-minded upwellings of antistatism among well-to-do whites. With the leader of the national Democratic Party, Jimmy Carter, now also the nation's leading Evangelical politician, and with southern Democrats' long tradition of antistatism far from forgotten, their party provided the earliest vehicle for both new citizenship projects. In congressional races especially in mostly white districts around Atlanta, a newer generation of conservative politicians broke with the government-friendly leadership of Carter Democrats, as well as the Black and urban constituencies who backed them. Larry McDonald's political rise epitomized their recasting of the supremacist conservatism that had prevailed under rustic rule. Supplanting overt racism with racial coding and leading a political charge into electronic media and intensive fundraising, politicians like McDonald made antistatism seem modern and new.

MAP SET 7.1. Suburban to rural congressional districts around metro Atlanta in 1980. These districts, where Larry McDonald (Seventh) and Newt Gingrich (Sixth) forged careers as congresspeople starting in the 1970s, were whiter than the Fifth, but whites there were also deeply and increasingly divided by income. Maps by author. *Sources:* Manson et al., *IPUMS National Historical Geographic Information System;* Jeffrey B. Lewis, Brandon DeVine, Lincoln Pitcher, and Kenneth C. Martis, "Digital Boundary Definitions of United States Congressional Districts, 1789–2012," UCLA Political Science, accessed May 25, 2021, https://cdmaps.polisci.ucla.edu; "Atlanta, Georgia," Google Maps, accessed September 2017.

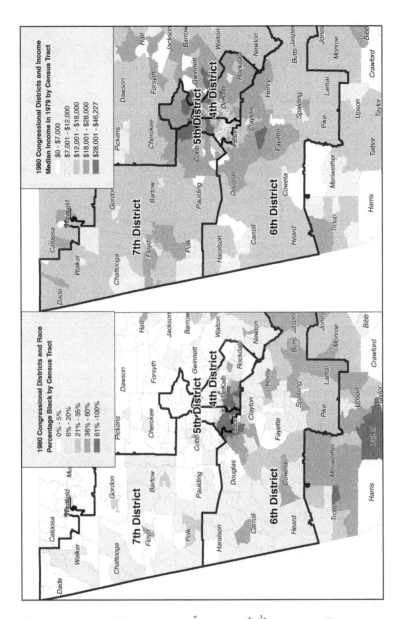

1980 Congressional Districts and Race
Percentage Black by Census Tract
0% - 5%
6% - 20%
21% - 35%
36% - 60%
61% - 100%

1980 Congressional Districts and Income
Median Income in 1979 by Census Tract
$0 - $7,000
$7,001 - $12,000
$12,001 - $18,000
$18,001 - $28,000
$28,001 - $46,227

McDonald won his first victory in 1974, in a Seventh District that embraced Cobb as well as several rural counties to the northwest, and was reelected until 1983, when he lost his life in plane crash. The Seventh District resembled several other Atlanta-area districts that would later become bastions of Georgia Republicanism, including the Sixth District next door, where Republican Newt Gingrich won his first of many congressional races. The most striking trend *within* these predominantly white suburban-to-rural slices of the metro area was that, under an accelerating cleavage capitalism, a white upper-middle class had begun pulling away from more middling and lower-class whites (map set 7.1). To draw funding from the affluent while also garnering votes from less well-off whites, Democrat McDonald set a successful new mold for conservative politics by weaving together the moralistic concerns of the new Evangelical citizenship with the concerns of well-to-do business professionals about governmental intrusion—a business-and-wealth-first citizenship. This last political project gained traction through direct attacks on the newly empowered environmental state, with Larry McDonald leading the way.

Into the 1970s, despite Georgia Democratic leadership's embrace of democratization and more broadly beneficial government, the party's congresspeople representing the Sixth, Seventh, and many other districts were holdovers from the era of rustic rule. McDonald's opponent in 1972 was John Davis, a twelve-year incumbent and self-described "country lawyer" from one of the Seventh District's rural counties, just as Gingrich's opponent in his first two Sixth District races was John Flynt, a former Dixiecrat who had held the seat for three decades. Both had conservative voting records that included systematic opposition to legislation favored by environmental groups: Davis's 1972 rating by the League of Conservation Voters was a mere five out of one hundred, and Flynt's just two.[57] Their antienvironmentalism, however, came couched in the Talmadgist style of politicking that had prevailed in an earlier era of political quiescence. Their allegiance to business interests remained low key and little voiced, largely clientelistic. In public they could remain remarkably silent about policy or "the issues."[58] The political scientist Richard Fenno, observing Flynt's 1972 campaign firsthand, noted how he sat through an entire program about water pollution at a local high school "and said *nothing*."[59] With limited advertising and media outreach, they focused instead on "local-boy, friends-and-neighbors, person-to-person relationships," as Fenno put it. Congressional campaigns in Georgia, as in other southern states, remained mostly "one-man bands," modestly funded by campaign hauls as low as $50,000. While politicians like Carter and Andrew Young countered this muteness with promises of environmental protection, conservatives facing off against this old guard had a different challenge: winning over the wallets of well-to-do whites worried about environmental regulation while turning other less well-off whites against the new environment state.

For McDonald the intellectual alchemy for threading this needle came mainly through the John Birch Society, on whose national council he served. Just as the historian Lisa McGirr found for Orange County in metro-area Los Angeles, Bircher networks and ideology gained an outsized hand around Atlanta, by the early 1980s forging as many as eleven chapters, four of them in Cobb.[60] Here, however, through upper-middle-class businesspeople and professionals turned political activists led by McDonald, the Democratic rather than the Republican Party served as the main vehicle by which they entered politics. Graduating from Davidson College and Emory's medical school, McDonald served as a military flight surgeon then returned to the Atlanta area to practice in his father's urology clinic in the mid-1960s, bringing Birchism with him. Along the way he had befriended Birch Society founder Robert Welch, reportedly also a patient at the McDonald's clinic. Starting a Birch chapter in the city, McDonald became booster and recruiter for that blend of antistatist and conspiratorial thinking with promarket ethos that Birchers had woven.[61]

Like Rushdoony—with whom Welch was also well acquainted—Birchers saw the contemporary United States' reliance on government as deeply at odds with the Founders' vision.[62] Adjusting to a political environment in which the explicit racism of Jim Crow had become stigmatized, Bircher literature harkened back less to the Jim Crow South or the Confederacy than to the U.S. Constitution, espousing what we might call a "constitutional" naturalism. The "collectivism" about which they worried had reared its ugly head not just through Soviet machinations abroad and in the United Nations but through the buildup of a "welfare-socialist system here at home": all the government building over the midcentury that had spread services and protection to so many more Americans. The taxes of fewer and fewer were "pulling the wagon" for the growing numbers relying on government programs, even as more and more state restrictions impeded the "freedom" of the "little guy . . . to rise up." For Birchers nearly as much as for the Christian Reconstructionists, democratization itself, especially in its more recent manifestations, posed a dire threat to U.S. traditions.[63] Birchers' task, then, was to serve as a countervailing force largely by emulating the not-so-democratic strategies and tools by which a victorious cabal of financiers and communists had purportedly connived all the recent state building. Their Bircher-aligned countercabal, in direct opposition to the presumed goals of its communist and socialist foes, sought "less government, more individual responsibility and with God's help a better world."[64]

Bircher recruitment practices illuminate just who was to make up this avowedly oligarchic countervailing force: eager, ideologically inclined advocates of a business-and-wealth-first citizenship. Organizers reached out first and foremost to local businessmen. Cold-calling their way through local business listings (the "yellow pages"), they sought men who were concerned about the government "taking away some of the freedoms of the free enterprise system." High-salary professionals, notably doctors aggrieved over the rise of Medicare and Medicaid, also flocked into chapter ranks.[65] Gathering to discuss prescribed readings and issues and joining their efforts to select political campaigns, Bircher chapters mobilized a political revolt by the biggest beneficiaries of cleavage capitalism's pooling of wealth: an upper-middle-class of white men.

Birchers' constitution fundamentalism—getting back to a much more limited government—harmonized well with their embrace of the new private environmental consumption as well as the conservative religious affiliations to which many were inclined. As Cobb's Bircher organizer and conservative Catholic Allen Rutledge put it, "How can you not love nature? It's provided for us for our wellbeing" by God, "because what is the environment? It's simply a product of creation." In the 1970s both he and Larry McDonald bought homes among the most visibly natural corners of Cobb, McDonald in Chattahoochee Plantation, along the river in East Cobb, and Rutledge, living on a more meager John Birch Society (JBS) coordinator salary, in the less developed western part of the county. Rutledge was an avid fisher and hunter, and McDonald, "according to a published report," kept a "normal sized" gun collection "for hunting and plinking (shooting at tin cans) with my son."[66] But both drew a sharp line between their own private passions for nature and the outdoors and any governmental effort to acquire or protect nature's wonders. That job belonged instead to "the true author of environment . . . God"; market-based allocations of resources and land use were better "reconciled to God" and his law. Here Bircher thinking shaded into the more radical strands of the new Evangelical movement such as Christian Reconstruction. For McDonald himself, that confluence was far from coincidental. Chalcedon Presbyterian Church became his church, and Joseph Morecraft was a "close friend and advisor," who at his funeral eulogized the congressperson's defense of a beleaguered "Christian Republic."[67]

Losing in his first 1972 race against Davis, McDonald beat him two years later by effectively pinning him not just to the ERA and gun control but to the new environmental agencies and laws. In their first face-off, McDonald tried unsuccessfully to position himself as a "middle of the roader," even while insisting Davis was "primarily for big government" and for "our communist enemies." But Davis skewered McDonald for the more outrageous claims of Bircher literature—that Dwight D. Eisenhower was duped by communists, that fighting communism required a "monolithic authoritarian government"—while also dubbing him "the J. B. Stoner of this race," referring to a former Klan leader.[68] McDonald carried suburban Cobb in this first race, but it was not enough to compensate for Davis's big margins in the rural counties.[69] Next time around McDonald hammered harder on new conservative litmus-test issues being pushed among Evangelicals, starting with Davis's vote for the ERA, along with a single vote the incumbent had cast for gun control, which Davis himself now called a "mistake."[70] This time McDonald was more artfully evasive about his stances on broadly beneficial government programs such as social security and minimum wage, while going on the offensive against environmental laws. McDonald set about accusing his opponent of aiding and abetting a "drift down the road to socialism" through "increasing federal controls."[71] Elevating the meddlesome Occupational Safety and Health Administration into a "major campaign issue," he set about pegging Davis as an environmentalist and more.[72] Despite Davis's extremely low rating from the League of Conservation Voters, McDonald ads portrayed "our man in Washington" as someone who "believes you need to be regulated." "His philosophy is that only bigger government can cure the government-caused problem. You get: EPA, OSHA, PSRO, HUD, etc., ad nauseum [sic]. Production is down but the bureaucrats are pleased."[73]

Davis's customarily "quiet, low key" campaign now seemed overmatched by McDonald's media-savvy, expensive, and volunteer-heavy offensive. Offering a mild defense of OSHA, he otherwise neglected McDonald's policy-oriented attacks.[74] But McDonald's railing against "increasing federal controls" on the "little guy," studiously ignoring the realities of corporate power, served his campaign well, as did the media by which he conveyed it. Those many mostly educated and affluent newcomers to the Seventh District were more likely to vote and leaned more on the newfangled medium of television for information about politics and candidates. Television advertising was also considerably more expensive than newspapers or radio, the traditional media of Georgia's congressional races, and in 1974 McDonald's TV-centric ad campaign left the Davis campaign scrambling to catch up. Ads took advantage of McDonald's hulking frame to pitch a rough, tough, and avowedly masculine approach to politics, akin to that which inspired Price's parody of "plant lovers." For instance, one showed McDonald gleefully breaking eggs. By the midpoint of the 1974 primaries, his campaign had spent nearly as much for TV and other media as Davis had spent on the entire race.[75] What enabled McDonald's unprecedented (for Georgia) investments in "media-related" advertising was record-breaking fundraising.[76] Having shocked the Davis campaign by raising five times its war chest in 1972, the McDonald campaign doubled its total in 1974. The bulk of it came from larger (over $100) individual contributions from the district's most affluent citizens—doctors, insurance agents, car dealers, grocery store owners, and other small business owners—making McDonald the best funded of Georgia's congressional candidates.[77]

The McDonald campaign also excelled in inspiring commitments of time and effort from local citizens, drawn largely from the region's burgeoning ranks of Birch recruits. A thousand volunteers knocked on doors on McDonald's behalf during his 1974 campaign, swarming the district's neighborhoods to reach what they supposed to be 90 percent of households. Campaign staff tried to insist to wary journalists that not all were Birchers but still acknowledged a JBS "backbone" to the effort; nearly half of the total canvassers were members.[78] Allied with McDonald's growing financial advantage, this unprecedented canvasing combined with his extensive and effective advertising to, in the judgment of the *Marietta Daily Journal*, "successfully h[a]ng the liberal image around Davis' neck."[79] Besting Davis with 52 percent of the primary vote, he racked up a three-thousand-vote margin in suburban Cobb, still his stronghold. In the final election McDonald then glided to an easy victory over Republican nominee Collins by attacking his conservative credentials.[80] An officer of the John Birch Society then became the first Cobb County resident to represent Georgia's Seventh District in Congress.

Larry McDonald's subsequent congressional career delighted his fellow Birchers as well as a national conservative movement—in 1977 Paul Weyrich's Committee for the Survival of a Free Congress dubbed him the "staunchest conservative" in either the House or the Senate.[81] He began with will-o'-the-wisp resolutions favoring the wealthy—for instance, by totally abolishing the income tax—and protecting rights "to life" (against abortion) and "to work" (against unions), then opened new lines of attack on environmental causes. Up for reelection in 1976, he would offer as sweeping a rejection of environmentalism as any Georgia politician of the period had as yet imagined: it was "part of a drive to cripple industry and take us back to a cave man existence"; moreover, "most environmental bills violated the Constitution's Tenth Amendment," which restricted the federal government to constitutionally defined powers. He rejected not just the EPA itself but over a century of law and jurisprudence authorizing federal interventions into markets through the Constitution's "commerce" clause. He even cosponsored a "Liberty amendment" that would begin turning over the national parks to private ownership.[82] He also became the most outspoken opponent of a bill to turn the northern Chattahoochee into a National Recreation Area, introduced in Congress by Andrew Young and soon brought to fruition under President Jimmy Carter. Adamantly arguing against a public Chattahoochee preserve, he deemed it a "boondoogle" and invoked the "dope addicts, hippies, and criminal elements" that it would draw—specters of an inner city now thoroughly coded as Black. McDonald pioneered a considerably more vocal opposition to federal park making than rustic rulers had dared—and won with it, besting a Republican endorsed by the Georgia League of Conservation Voters LCV. Graphically demonstrating the political viability of attacking environmental citizenship, in 1976 McDonald widened his margins in all his district's more rural counties as well as the more working-class and remote corners of Cobb, while holding onto wealthy suburbs' support.[83] As shown in figure 7.1, McDonald's hardened opposition to most environmental causes favored by

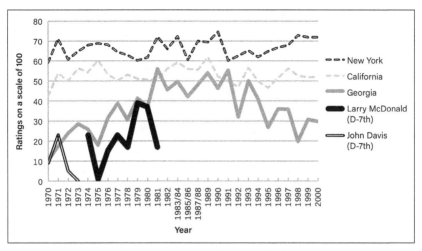

FIGURE 7.1. Larry McDonald bucks the Georgia tide. As rated by the League of Conservation Voters, McDonald's environmental voting countered the trend in Georgia's congressional delegation to favor environmentally friendly bills. Though his antienvironmental voting resembled his predecessor's, John Davis, McDonald turned far more vocal about his environmental opposition. All or mostly Democrats until the early 1990s, the Georgia congressional delegation brought its LCV rating to rival New York's and California's, only to reverse course as more Republicans joined. League of Conservation Voters, "National Environmental Conservation Scorecard Archive," 2022, https://scorecard.lcv.org/scorecard/archive.

the LCV not only anchored his repeated electoral success but stood in growing contrast to the warming embrace of environmentalism by others in the state's Democratic congressional delegation.

Vocally opposed to busing, abortion, gun control, welfare, and unions and skilled at racial coding, McDonald built his political career over the late 1970s into the 1980s by outright attacks on the prize issues of Georgia environmentalism. His pioneering antienvironmental outspokenness solidified his grip on this congressional seat and, with it, a political success for his white coalition of rural voters with upper-middle-class Birchers. So it was that an affluent and highly educated candidate, outspokenly favoring his district's wealthiest echelons and financially backed by them, discovered the political value of an explicit antienvironmentalism.

Beyond his vocal and provocative public stances and voluminous insertions into the *Congressional Record*, McDonald's actual legislative accomplishments remained few. Ideologically at odds with so many in his own party, he eschewed party discipline, alienating national Democratic leaders like Tip O'Neill, against whose campaign for House Speaker he cast the only dissenting vote. He also steadily provoked Democratic Party officials in his own state and county. In 1978 Cobb County's Democrats went so far as to censure him "most of all, for the dishonorable and despicable act of calling himself a Democrat."[84] Even as contemporary political observers attributed the Georgia Democratic Party's continued political dominance over the 1970s to its ideological diversity, McDonald's ongoing clashes with fellow Democrats reflected conservatives' increasingly tenuous foothold within the Democratic Party. And while he himself remained a Democrat up to his 1983 death, his frequent aisle crossing to join Republican-led initiatives anticipated how, in the Atlanta area, the Republican Party would over the next decade firmly supplant its Democratic rival as the primary channel for a conservative political revival.

One quieter way that Georgia's Republicans helped renew a business-first citizenship in this new era of democratic state building was to shepherd along businesspeople's judicial efforts to push back against what they saw as growing government intrusions, environmental and otherwise. As a newly organized Business Roundtable joined with emergent promarket think tanks like the Heritage Foundation to spearhead a national movement of business and free-market advocates, southern businesspeople also joined forces starting in fall of 1975 at the Atlanta headquarters of Western Lumber. Meeting with the president of the National Legal Center for the Public Interest, they determined that the time had come for more active and collective promotion of "policies of government which will permit the strength of a market-oriented economy . . . to reassert itself." They then launched a Southeastern Legal Foundation, two years prior to the start of a Western States Legal Foundation led by James Watt, which helped spur a western "sagebrush rebellion" against environmental laws. The SLF opened a vigorous southern flank in what became a nationwide effort of businesses to use the courts to push back on the United States' expanding regulatory state. It chose Ben Blackburn, the recently beaten Republican congressperson, as its leader. Under Blackburn SLF "had little difficulty raising money" and within two years enjoyed support from over sixty-five of the largest corporations in the South.[85] Front and center in SLF's legal sights were the new environmental laws. Early suits assailed EPA's effort to restrict the use of the carcinogenic pesticide Mirex by Georgia farmers and OSHA's unannounced inspections of Georgia workplaces, along with countering governmental rules for affirmative action and minority hiring. For SLF's first six years, Republican Blackburn steered an Atlanta-based institution dedicated to legal arguments about the burdensomeness and unfairness of the new environmental laws for business, what James Morton Turner and Andrew C. Isenberg term the third plank of the "Republican reversal."[86]

The business-first citizenship of the SLF and allied groups also furnished a second major buttress for a budding conservative skepticism toward science and expertise, soon synergizing with parallel inclinations in the new Evangelical citizenship. Unlike the new fundamentalists, groups like SLF challenged the regulatory science of agencies like the EPA within courtrooms and administrative proceedings. Taking advantage of how these preferred forums of managerial liberalism rarely drew much press or public attention, they advocated rather nakedly on behalf of their clients' economic and legal self-interest. And they concentrated far more on stoking doubt than on shoring up beliefs, with the notable exception of their faith in a free market. Yet similar to those intent on modernizing creationism, SFL's head Blackburn, a lawyer, adduced his own version of modern science to argue against official science-based environmental policies. "No one has proven that Mirex causes cancer," he claimed, since "those tumors in rats disappeared when they stopped feeding them Mirex." As the SFL and other "merchants of doubt" grew in funding and ambition, they would also recruit individual scientists and even scientific institutions to their cause.[87] As with the SFL, contributing efforts in Georgia often had ties to a Republican Party initially based largely in the Atlanta area but finding its way to statewide political power.

From Environmental Citizenship to Consumer Voters

That a four-term Republican congressperson would be available in 1976 to lead the incipient SFL was hardly surprising, given where the Georgia Republican Party stood as Carter ascended to the presidency. Georgia's Republicans appeared to have squandered the headway they had made in the mid-1960s, when their candidates such as Blackburn had successfully vanquished Democrats like congressperson James Mackay by blaming them for the new civil rights laws. By the midseventies, with "the civil rights business . . . all behind us," as one Republican official put it, a gear-shifting Democratic Party had spread its support among Georgia's newly broadened electorate to reap the biggest political benefits of democratization. Watergate added to Democrat-favoring headwinds, contributing to Blackburn's 1974 defeat to a Democrat in the Jimmy Carter and Andrew Young mold, turning the Georgia GOP into "one very sick pachyderm." Republicans held only 24 of 180 representatives in the statehouse and only 4 of 56 state senators—confined to well-off white districts like Paul Coverdell's in North Fulton—and not a single statewide or congressional office.[88] The Republican Party retained only one core advantage: its "top down" appeal among "affluent Southern whites [who] have long voted their economic interests."[89] As Gingrich soon came to realize, the grating of the growing environmental state against the interests of economic elites provided him and his fellow Republicans with new opportunities that built on that advantage. Along with Evangelicals' issues, as McDonald had shown, an antienvironmentalism also beckoned new prospects among rural white voters long won by Georgia Democrats.

Gingrich himself was among the few bright spots for Georgia Republicans in the mid-1970s. This young college professor showed himself to be a "tough campaigner," "scaring 6th District U.S. Rep. Jack Flynt" in 1974 as well as in 1976 by coming within a few thousand votes of beating him.[90] Rare for a Georgia politician up to this point, Gingrich had an itinerant childhood begun in the north; he'd come south only as a high schooler.[91] Moving from Harrisburg to Columbus, Georgia, and studying at Emory, then Tulane, in 1970 he arrived to teach history at West Georgia University in Carrollton, about an hour's drive west of Atlanta's downtown. Already married and with children, he joined the town's First Baptist Church and discovered the Georgia Conservancy. In this time and place, not only were Republicans relatively rare; they were much more inclined to take up environmental causes than they later would become. A Republican president, Richard Nixon, was creating the EPA and OSHA and signing sweeping new environmental laws. Gingrich, with "'moddish' long hair and the tolerant cultural views of a young professor," did more than just join the Georgia Conservancy: he helped bring a local chapter to Carrollton.[92] So enthused did he become about this cause that by 1974 he had left the college's History Department to teach in a new program he had helped create in "environmental studies." During his first two electoral face-offs as well, against a quietly antienvironmentalist Flynt, Gingrich actively strove to become a political voice and vehicle for the new environmental style of citizenship. His own environmental reversal came in three stages: losing as an environmentally friendly Republican; backing away from vocal environmentalism to find electoral success and a growing influence within Congress; and, finally in the 1990s, frontally attacking environment agencies and laws, to help consummate a Great White Shift toward the Republican Party in Georgia and other southern states.

The environmental pitch of Gingrich's first two campaigns fleshed out the "aggressive" and "moderate" sides of his presentation of himself as an "aggressive moderate conservative," an eclectic jumble mirroring the Georgia Democratic Party's now-widened ideological range. Gingrich's espousal of environmental citizenship also demonstrated his "knowledge of Metropolitan problems" in contrast to Flynt's "rural orientation."[93] That pitch increasingly seemed to fit the Sixth District, which, as depicted in map set 7.1, spanned metropolitan tracts—from the Black suburbs of South and West Fulton to the predominantly white suburban and exurban counties of Clayton, Henry, Douglas, Butts, and Fayette—as well as five other counties still classified as predominantly rural. Even its rural counties were turning less agricultural; in Gingrich's home county of Carroll the largest employer was now the wire manufacturer Southwire.[94]

Concentrating his early campaigning in the suburban parts of the district and playing up his involvement "in local environmental affairs," Gingrich went so far as to attack local polluters directly, Southwire among them. Squaring off more generally against "industry," corporations, and the "very rich," he accused his opponent of being "an extremely useful watchdog for big industry" but "not for his constituents." As a political neophyte, Gingrich railed against the federal government as a "horrible creeping bureaucratic mess" but called for a tax reform that would correct how "the very rich pay nothing," even as "federal taxes weigh most heavily on the middle class."[95] His coalition encompassed "groups of people generally not heard from in Georgia Congressional politics—teachers, organized labor, environmentalists," whose organized mouthpieces, including the Georgia League of Conservation Voters, endorsed him. This Gingrich was also unaccommodating to Evangelical or gun lobbyists, refusing to endorse a constitutional amendment outlawing abortion—though he did dutifully play up his Baptist and familial allegiances.[96] His approach won him endorsements from the city's newspapers, Black (*Atlanta Daily World*) and white (the *Journal* and *Constitution*), along with generally glowing coverage of his campaign.

Against an incumbent campaigning in the older style of rustic rulers, low key and personalized, Gingrich in his first two runs marshaled newer electronic media and aggressive fundraising and publicly challenged Flynt's "never analyzed" voting record. Now he also began honing that moralistic critique of a monolithically imagined Democratic establishment that would serve his congressional career so well, less attuned to Carter's and Young's recent revamping of the party than to the Democratic Party under Talmadgism. Flynt was "your classic county unit politician," a "corrupt partisan willing to use his position as House Ethics chairman to protect fellow Democrats." In a time when Atlanta-area Republicans could still embrace environmental citizenship, Gingrich drew in ample funds not just from better-heeled party faithful but from some environmentalists as well. He raised twice as much money as Flynt in 1974, with many more large ($500 or more) contributions, though his spending advantage waned in 1976 as a worried Flynt's fundraising got more vigorous. Political observers found Gingrich's media efforts "slick" and "well-financed," especially the many television ads. But Flynt effectively frustrated Gingrich's eagerness for public confrontation by stonewalling Gingrich's calls for a debate or side-by-side public forum.[97] By election day each time, the challenger repeatedly failed to entice enough white rural voters into abandoning the Democratic standard-bearer and never drew enough suburban Black votes to compensate. Despite Gingrich's *Daily World* endorsement, Georgia Democrats' recent embrace of many tenets of civil rights citizenship now drew Black voters into Flynt's camp. Handing Gingrich two defeats, the district returned to office a Democrat of older vintage who ironically had voted against the 1965 Voting Rights Act.[98]

In 1978, however, after thirty-five years in Congress, Flynt finally retired. No longer pitted against an incumbent, Gingrich finally found a personal pathway to victory and a blueprint for an era of Republican dominance to come. Going into this race, when asked why he didn't abandon the hand-

PHOTO 7.1. Candidate Newt Gingrich reaching out to rural voters. This photo was taken probably during his first successful campaign in 1978, as he began to downplay his environmental allegiances to bolster his appeal to business as well as rural constituencies. Courtesy of *Atlanta Journal-Constitution* via AP, Atlanta Constitution Photographic Archives, Georgia State University Special Collections.

icap of being a Republican by switching parties, Gingrich countered with a long-range vision not just for himself but for Georgia and the nation. He "believe[d] deeply in the need for a conservative majority government." That could come only through the Republican Party, he averred, since nationally the Democrats were "firmly tied to liberal ideology."[99] The first challenge he faced, ironically, was in his own district, where, despite his Republican affiliation, an internal survey by his campaign suggested rural voters viewed him as significantly more "liberal" than Democrat Flynt. While McDonald's campaign against national parks had drawn much rural support, Gingrich chose another more subtle path into environmental opposition, one that he would soon help enshrine as the more characteristically Republican approach. Going near-silent on environmental issues, he set about mending his ties to business leaders he had spent two campaigns attacking. The second stage of his environmental reversal had begun.

Gingrich began his 1978 campaign by promising a small business "bill of rights" and accepting an invitation to visit the Southwire plant. Inaugurating a friendly rapport with Roy Richards, head of this family-owned company and among the *Forbes* 400 richest Americans, he received an earful on Southwire's private efforts to quell pollution and their many squabbles with OSHA and the EPA.[100] Gingrich then jettisoned the strong and vocal environmental advocacy that had helped define his earlier runs. He demoted "environment" far down his list of declared political priorities, to second to last. His campaign literature now hardly mentioned pollution or even corporations at all; a summary of his positions noted only an endorsement by the League of Conservation Voters, vaguely attributed to "his support of various conservation measures" that themselves went unnamed.[101] From here on out his public advocacy of environmental causes turned much quieter and more intermittent. Just as a federal environmental state was maturing under Carter, Gingrich may have sensed that this technocratic and administrative managerialism was burying the political viability of many environmental causes. Proceeding through the second stage of his own "Republican reversal," he largely disappeared the environment from his campaign.

Gingrich was fortunate in the Democrat's choice to replace their incumbent in the Sixth District: Virginia Shapard, then living in the small town of Griffin. She had also been born in the Northeast, negating Gingrich's disadvantage there. As the Georgia senate's only female member, her political career reflected rising opportunities for women in politics but, by the same token, made her a target for the gathering cultural and political concerns of white Evangelicals. Insinuating Shapard would abandon her family if elected, Gingrich presented himself as the advocate of a familial and gender traditionalism, burnishing a hawkish military stance and a perfect rating by gun activists.[102] Fortuitously for Gingrich, Shapard's five years working at a county Welfare Department threw open a door to a Georgia version of Nixon's Southern Strategy: associating her with a vision of government coded Black and thus deeply alienating for many white voters. Ignoring the environmental and other broad benefits of a more democratic and expansive state, he reduced the entire Democratic project of state building to a single program: welfare. Campaign materials fortified the racial coding at work. One notorious Gingrich flyer claimed his "former welfare worker" opponent had "fought to kill" welfare reform while tying her with Julian Bond, Georgia's well-known first Black state senator. "If you love welfare cheaters," it concluded, "you'll love Virginia Shapard." Gingrich spread such messages through a "major effort in the rural counties" among whites whose votes had long gone to Democrats, at this moment starting to find themselves on the losing end of cleavage capitalism.[103]

Ignoring the many additional roles that government had taken on and drawing instead on national conservative currents, the new Gingrich jettisoned any public allegiance to environmentalism or civil rights. Instead, he posited his voters' motivations to be stripped down to a single not-so-citizenly economic core. Voters were consumers, interested mainly in the money government could cost or save them. "The shopping cart" emerged as "the symbol of the Gingrich campaign," "because we represent the people who worry about such things." Doubling down on inflation as the "no. 1 local issue," he now blamed it exclusively on government spending and privately wrote of countering "labor union power by mobilizing the middle class."[104] Images of shopping carts headed the campaign's abundant flyers as well as a run of eighty thousand free "tabloid" newspapers delivered by four hundred campaign volunteers across the district—part of an elaborate Neighbors for Newt outreach resembling what Birchers had done for McDonald.[105] His consumerist reduction of citizenship to voting with one's pocketbook came coupled with an endorsement of the Kemp-Roth bill then on the floor of Congress, seeking a 33 percent cut in income taxes across the board. Tax cuts such as this were becoming Republicans' go-to solution not just for the U.S. economy but for their own political dilemmas. Though it would quietly shower an overwhelming share of sheared tax revenues on the already wealthy, Gingrich pitched Kemp-Roth as "help[ing] all taxpayers," including "low income voters."[106]

In what became Georgia's "most fiercely contested major race" of 1978, Gingrich carried the white suburbs, his established strength in previous races, while gaining on his Democratic opponent especially in the district's rural reaches. Whereas Flynt had racked up four-to-one margins in many of these counties, Gingrich was able to bring down Shapard's rural margins to a mere two to one. Still drawing only 17–22 percent of the votes in his district's Black suburbs, his solid 55–45 percent victory made him the only Republican congressperson from Georgia that year.[107] Gingrich's winning electoral run would nevertheless provide a model for future successful runs by Republicans, not least among them Mack Mattingly's statewide senate race in 1980, which vanquished five-term incumbent Democrat Herman Talmadge.[108]

Favoring the antistatist messaging of Georgia Republicans like Mattingly and Gingrich was a realization previously arrived at by McDonald, that the mounting costs of successful politicking was making it all the more important to ensure backing from the well-heeled, their donations as well as their votes. With the electorate now considerably expanded through democratization as well as demographic change, with television ads now seen as a vital supplement to radio, flyers, and "person-to-person" events, campaigns were becoming much more expensive. Not just despite but partly because of Georgia's democratization, another less democratic line of influence on elections gained in prominence: political candidates required more donations if they were to win. Around this same time, from the mid-1970s Watergate-spawned federal laws and judicial decisions also set tighter and more explicit rules on how money could be channeled into politics. While outlawing unattributed donations and placing caps on individual donations, the reforms featured a new loophole for organizations, the political action committee (PAC). Long adopted by labor unions as well as some companies, by the 1980s PACs had become the most important institutional vehicle for funneling cash into election campaigns.[109] For publicly registered PACs, the sky was the limit on how much they could receive or disburse. In the race that then took off among Georgia's and the rest of the country's organized interests to avail themselves of this new vehicle for tilting electoral outcomes, the wealthiest people and institutions enjoyed a distinct edge, as did those candidates and political parties who promised to put them and their businesses first.

In the Atlanta area these two new and eventually victorious conservatives, McDonald and Gingrich, led the way in circumnavigating these dual challenges. By 1978 McDonald's campaign fundraising continued to outpace those of all other Georgia congressional candidates, with the Gingrich campaign coming in third behind his opponent Shapard, who drew largely on wealth derived from her own family's textile business to finance her campaign. To raise that much Gingrich emulated McDonald's fundraising tactics by setting up a "finance team" tapping wealthier residents in each district county, while taking special care to cultivate political action committees. Their ranks leaped from a mere one hundred in 1972 to four thousand in 1986 and, as early as 1982, channeled some $300 million to candidates nationwide.[110] Some thirty-two individual companies contributed to the Gingrich campaign in 1978; by 1980 that number had soared to over seventy. While many were locally or regionally based—from Southwire to Southern Bell to Piggly Wiggly to the major airlines flying out of the Atlanta airport—many were not, from major oil companies to U.S. Steel and Dow Chemical; most had headquarters not just outside the district but outside Georgia. Alongside these, professional groups from doctors to chiropractors to insurance agents all began to fork over campaign cash. Adding to Gingrich's coffers were a few local labor groups like airline pilots and traffic controllers, employed at his district's Hartsfield Airport, along with PACs organized around conservative causes like the NRA and, by 1980, the American Family Political Action Committee. Whereas McDonald led the quest of Georgia congressional candidates for large individual donations, it was Gingrich who pioneered congressional fundraising in the Brave New World of PACs. From these candidates' as well as their many donors' perspectives, environmental as well as civil rights advocacy groups could hardly compete. By the mid-1980s, when the Georgia Sierra Club began to channel funds from the club's national fund to Atlanta-area candidates, they were arriving late to the political financing party.

As a congressperson into the 1980s, Gingrich also went beyond McDonald in absorbing the moralizing of the Christian Right, wielding rectitude as a cudgel against a Democratic establishment as well as more staid and moderate members of his own national party. Like McDonald, Gingrich rarely spoke publicly about his faith, but "a religio-political current r[an] strong in the congressman's office." His staff became a "magnet for young Christian activists": a first chief of staff kept a Bible nearby, "as a research tool to shape his political positions on issues like welfare and defense." An early press secretary was a former Baptist youth minister.[111] Alongside these quieter roots in the new Evangelical citizenship, there was Gingrich's stark, righteous line drawing, a "defining theme" of his political career from his first campaigns against Flynt throughout his career in Congress.[112] He lobbed corruption charges against House Democrats, from Baltimore congressperson Charles Diggs, who happened to be Black, to House Speaker Jim Wright. Not surprisingly, however, Gingrich turned his righteous indignation mainly on politically advantageous targets. He all but ignored the moral imperatives promoted by either civil rights or environmental advocates, aside from occasional pivots such as to support a national holiday for Martin Luther King Jr. to help deflect their criticism. While bowing to the Sierra Club on some bills such as to combat acid rain, his "pragmatic" environmental allegiances remained far from consistent, readily expendable to the main channels of his rhetorical fire. A "constant thorn in the side" even of his own party leaders, his righteous tone, along with support for issues like prayer in schools, made him a favorite of the Christian Right. "What a great guy," gushed Jerry Falwell in 1986. "He votes his conscience."[113]

As Georgia's only Republican congressperson during much of Ronald Reagan's presidency, Gingrich came to play a supporting but significant role in the national politics that would drive a "Great White Switch" toward the Republican Party across the South. Under Reagan many southern whites who had come to think of themselves as independents rather than Democrats began identifying as Republicans, speeding a Republicanization of the white South that in the 1990s would come to full fruition. The jovial cowboy-hatted former actor presided over an administration that sought much of what Gingrich himself had in his 1978 campaign, and Gingrich was among those in charge of pulling together a "conservative coalition" to provide House backing.[114] Corralling Republicans' votes, he also drew conservative Democrats like Larry McDonald into the fold, for instance, for a 1981 Reagan-proposed tax cut, later hailed as the first victory of a "supply-side revolution." The chief goal was to deliberately bolster the fortunes of the wealthiest Americans, spurring economic growth that would then create jobs and other benefits for the rest of Republicans' consumer voters, "trickling down." Reassuring his fellow Congress representatives about the appeal of lower taxes to voters further down the wealth ladder, the Georgia Republican successfully rallied colleagues around this measure, slicing the rates for top earners from 70 to 50 percent—on its way to 28 percent by the administration's end.[115] Also shepherding along the

Reagan effort to shred the federal safety net for the unemployed and other poor, Gingrich became a significant player in Reagan's successful wielding of federal power to accelerate the tipping of U.S. capitalism toward cleavage.

The Gingrich-aided economic agenda of the Reagan administration amounted to a direct and thoroughgoing rebuke of that economically attuned civil rights citizenship the SCLC had promoted since the late 1960s. SCLC's leader Joseph Lowery realized as much. While a handful of former SCLCers, including Ralph Abernathy, flirted with Reaganism, Lowery's outspoken opposition to Reagan started with the 1980 election campaign, when he worried about the "racist forces" the former California governor was attracting through his "code words." As the new administration's plans to gratify consumer voters took shape, no public figure in Atlanta or Georgia was clearer or harsher than Lowery about their "reverse Robin Hood economics . . . tak[ing] from the poor and giving to the rich." The new conservatism, Lowery admitted, had snuck up on civil rights advocates: "While we were celebrating in 1975 what we did in 1965, they were planning how to take over the country in 1985."[116] Having grown up in a time of rustic rule, older civil rights leaders like Lowery were also acutely aware that what the Reagan administration and supporters were seeking, on so many fronts, was to "turn back the clock" to a less democratic era. To stave off the worst, SCLC focused its early efforts on a renewal of the 1965 Voting Rights Act that was set to expire, without which "our political future is in jeopardy." A sixty-four-day "Pilgrimage" march from Birmingham to Washington, D.C., in 1982 helped win an extension, stymying a congressional effort to weaken this foundational law won by an earlier movement for civil rights. While Lowery and other civil rights leaders kept mobilizing and organizing, however, they were unable to stop how, as an SCLC resolution put it, "the present administration . . . has [worked] to dismantle, subvert, reduce or abolish" that "broad range of social programs" that was a legacy of "half a century." The effect was to make "the rich richer, the poor poorer, the privileged more privileged, the needy needier, the bigoted more bigoted." For SCLCers it amounted to "an assault on the moral fabric, the generous spirit, the creative energies, and the sense of justice amongst the people of this nation."[117]

The SCLC's 1982 turn to protesting toxic waste broadened their political front against Reagan still further, by taking on his administration's assault against environmental citizenship. The early Reagan administration had commenced a sweeping scaleback of federal environmental agencies, while opening federal lands to all manner of private extractive enterprise. The most controversial of his appointees, James Watt at the Department of the Interior and Anne Gorsuch at the EPA, carried to Washington an opposition to environmentalism in the suburban and rural West and for two years sought a systematic rollback of a federal environmental state. By 1983 the near-universal outcry had forced them and many other appointees out, showing Republican conservatives the political dangers of too overt an attack on the new environmental state.[118] Though Reagan himself then appointed more environmentally allied leadership at the EPA and the Department of the Interior, this federal assault sparked an upsurge of environmental organizing and activism around Atlanta and Georgia, as in the rest of the country, that was slow to abate.

Over these years Gingrich, still in the second stage of his environmental reversal and wary of this popular blowback, had to walk a fine line. In early letters to constituents, he still claimed to "think of myself as an environmentalist" but rarely spoke out about any such issue, except when environmental groups began inquiring about his positions.[119] He quietly supported many of Reagan's environmental budget cuts, and, when his colleagues sought to cite Anne Gorsuch for contempt (after she refused to respond to a House committee's subpoena), Gingrich and Larry McDonald became the only two Georgia representatives to vote no. By mid-1983 he called on Reagan to fire James Watt, but only after the secretary's derogatory comments about Blacks, Jews, and women.[120] Never initiating any significant environmental bills, Gingrich preferred to cosponsor those that would not rankle his business base: declaring an "environmental health week" or providing tax breaks for solar energy or pursuit of shale oil.[121] While he did support the regulation of noise around airports and some controls for acid rain, more and more of his time and attention went toward quests for the "relief" of business and other well-heeled constituents from environmental rules.[122] He cosponsored measures to waive OSHA's coverage of "non-hazardous" businesses, to weaken the Clean Air Act, and to delay deadlines and penalties for polluters. Threading together many of his antienvironmental votes was his hesitancy toward what were increasingly framed as matters of "environmental justice": from the Superfund and toxic wastes to communities' environmental right to know.[123] But Gingrich tended his growing flame of environmental opposition so quietly that, as late as 1984, national reporters saw him as "moderate" on environmental issues, especially as compared to his "hard-right conservatism on economic issues, foreign policy and the family."[124]

In 1982, irked by the Reagan administration's acceptance of a tax hike and by electoral defeats that retained a House Democratic majority, Gingrich and some of his like-aged colleagues took it on themselves to come up with a sharper-edged and more attention-grabbing vision for their party. Drawing on conservative intellectual currents while dabbling in the futurism of Alvin Toffler and John Nasibitt, Gingrich and his fellow "young Turks" began touting the virtues of a "Conservative Opportunity Society." Intended as a thoroughgoing alternative to a "liberal welfare state," Gingrich's COS pitch portrayed the past twenty years of democratization as driven "largely by cries to serve the poor and reshape society"—a stunning feat of racial coding that reduced those many forces propelling democratization "largely" to civil rights groups' advocacy for the Black poor.[125] While still in the second stage of his own environmental reversal, Gingrich had set about erasing the environmental movement from his own as well as his fellow conservatives' past and present, laying the groundwork for their later, outright assault on the United States' environmental state. The technocratic, managerial liberalism of the new environmental state may have made this rhetorical vanishing act easier, but it owed much more to a willful authorial sleight of hand. In the "Conservative Opportunity Society" program, environmental citizenship already looked like what it would later prove to be through his voting record and the Contract with America: a necessary casualty of his quest for a conservative majority.

Gingrich's 1984 *Window of Opportunity*, coauthored with the science fiction writer David Drake, elaborated this program. It interwove elements of Evangelical and business-first citizenships with the consumer voter idea to make a narrative of conservative progress. Chastising the "hedonistic society" that the United States had "essentially" become over the past "two generations," the book pointed an accusatory finger at, first of all, the liberal welfare state. With government itself limned as mainly about "welfare"—that most racially coded of all federal programs—other imbalances of power and wealth that democracy-minded state building addressed, environmental and otherwise, could be conveniently ignored. Gingrich could now claim that the modern federal state was hostile to the interests and needs of most Americans, reprising an enmity that linked Talmadgists with Birchers. "Systematically biased against achievement" and fixated on stealing voters' tax dollars and "entangling [them in] government regulations," it had become "a threat to the average person" and the single biggest obstacle to Americans' ability to harness the potential of the digital revolution. Now markets and "decentralized initiative," politically supported by "a new model of citizen as customer-oriented," offered "the best mechanisms for . . . responding to the changes." Regulations, "job-killing anti-capital tax codes," and "welfare and other make-work governmental programs" had to be left "by the wayside." If only the state confined its scope to job retraining and the reward of initiative and individual achievement, our society would rediscover its work ethic, and "morale and elan" would return. "Our children and grandchildren" would then inherit and "live in a positive optimistic America." The Conservative Opportunity Society's proponents actively celebrated the widening gaps and divisions of cleavage capitalism, doing everything in their power to speed these along. To make sure any disgruntlement or other irresponsibility did not get out of hand, a "strong criminal justice system" was necessary, including more prisons to serve as "permanent" "holding tanks for the genuine criminal."[126] For Gingrich mass incarceration looked like a more honest and superior solution to poverty than did welfare, especially if selling the labor of prisoners could finance the prisons that caged them.

By the mid-1980s neither Gingrich's nor Reagan's successes in Washington had won much additional traction for Georgia Republicans in statewide races. Party switchers signaled the Republicans' growing appeal for conservative Democrats, as when Rev. Joseph Morecraft, McDonald's ministerial protégé, decided to run for the deceased congressperson's former seat not as a Democrat but as a Republican. But he lost, as did Mattingly in his run for re-election, both of them bested by moderate Democrats. The only bright spot for the party was Pat Swindall's successive victories in 1984 and 1986 to represent the congressional Fourth District. A thirty-four-year-old lawyer and furniture store owner living in wealthy Dunwoody, his campaigns largely followed the Gingrich model: assailing the "liberalism" of his opponents and "call[ing] for less government involvement and more creative ideas," in his case combining "Reagan-style Republicanism" with a more sleeve-worn Christianity explicitly aligning his campaign with Evangelicals. Thereby, he was able to win over the more rural and lower-income Rockdale, long Democratic, while holding the Republican base across DeKalb's wealthy white suburbs.[127] In Congress Swindall had found newer ways of appealing to both Evangelical and business-first citizenships while keeping up the racial coding—as when he voted against emergency aid for African famine victims "as a matter of principle."[128] On the environment Swindall joined Gingrich in favoring local, defensive strands of environmental citizenship, often led by more affluent white homeowners, even while attacking environmental regulations and other governmental initiatives.[129] Swindall's ratings from the League of Conservation Voters slid slightly lower than Gingrich's during these years, to become the second lowest of the entire Georgia congressional delegation—barely undercut by a conservative Democrat from a south district. But his loss in a 1988 re-election campaign also reflected the political risks of antienvironmentalism. The winner, Democratic Ben Jones, formerly "Cooter" on the TV series *Dukes of Hazzard*, had repeatedly accused Swindall of being "in the pocket of the polluters."[130]

Across Atlanta's predominantly white suburbs and exurbs in these years, however, the Republican Party was nevertheless forging a growing dominance over local government. In 1980 Cobb became the first county in the metro area to elect mostly Republican officials, with the party taking ten of thirteen county-wide elections there, as Mattingly and Reagan also won there by large margins.[131] By 1986, though Mattingly lost statewide, his margins held at 1980 levels across white suburban and exurban counties, as Republicans also racked up sweeping wins for local offices in Atlanta's "doughnut." Across Cobb, Gwinnett, Clayton, and Fayette, the GOP won fourteen of nineteen county-wide races, including all the county commission seats in Gwin-net and Fayette. Reagan's presidency may have opened the door to these successes, but state as well as county Republican officials were also striving to recruit and support more candidates, as a "Republican ideology" for county government also coalesced.[132] It promised more "prudent management practices," largely "learned through their experience in business." Whether that meant a "streamlining" of government (Gwinnett) or more top-level agenda setting, limiting the windows for public input (Cobb), their approach, however fresh and modern they made it seem, echoed rustic rule in its inclinations toward minimalist, business- and development-favoring, and top-down governance.[133]

A closer look at Fayette County in Gingrich's district suggests just how the Republicanization of these parts of the Atlanta metropolis fed off an environmental consumption of the privileged that diminished any locally felt need for environmental citizenship. Fayette, along with Gwinnett, was the fastest growing county in Georgia during the 1980s, doubling its population. Republican leadership preferred to think of the newcomers as coming from other regions, but many, if not most, came from other parts of Georgia and the South, moving "as close to the city as they could stand."[134] An expansive Hartsfield International Airport in next-door Clayton County—close but not too close—contributed mightily to Fayette's growth, reportedly employing 65 percent of its workers. With a workforce that otherwise was mostly composed of "professionals and executives," the county also remained 95 percent white. That skew toward the greatest beneficiaries of Atlanta's cleavage capitalism owed much to how, by the mid-1980s, the unincorporated parts of the county still retained a "rural flavor." County-wide zoning had reserved these areas for a spacious-style residential use, with one-acre minimum lots. Fayette also had a thriving version of the kind of planned, walkable community celebrated by the New Urbanists: privately developed Peachtree City. Started in 1959 but taking off in the 1970s, it blended a variety of homes "buff[ed]" with "open spaces and wooded golf cart paths," along with schools, parks, a village green, shopping districts, and a golf course within walking or biking distance.[135] Fayette residents' environmental amenities seemed as secure and deserved as their incomes—the state's highest household median. Having "achieved by working," as one Republican leader put it, the electorate of this upper-middle-class white county readily bought into Republican antistatism and its commitment to market-mediated, meritocratic rule.[136]

Into the early 1990s Fayette provided a reliable electoral bastion for Gingrich as he lurched into the final stage of his own environmental reversal. From 1989, when Gingrich was named the Republican minority's second-in-command in the House, his legislative votes turned harshly and consistently antienvironmental. As shown in figure 7.2, his League of Conservation Voters rating plummeted to ten, and after a slight rebound, to zero. As he came

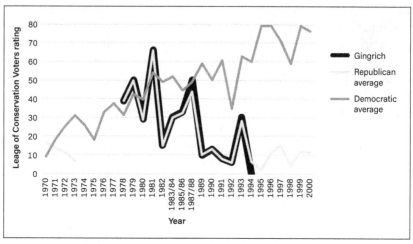

FIGURE 7.2. Gingrich's long environmental reversal. Already during his moderate LCV ratings from the late 1970s into the mid-1980s, he talked relatively little about environmental issues compared to the mid-1970s. From 1989 or so, however, his favorability ratings with environmental groups collapsed and, after a 1993 tick back upward, fell to zero in 1994, the year of the Contract with America. Georgia's suddenly growing ranks of House Republicans followed suit. League of Conservation Voters, "National Environmental Conservation Scorecard Archive."

out against every single recommendation of the national Sierra Club, Georgia Sierrans now excoriated his "abysmal environmental voting record . . . [as] the worst in the Georgia delegation." "It is becoming apparent," they declared hopefully, "that despite G's high visibility and stature, constituents are tired of his antics and rhetoric." In the 1990 race for his congressional seat, they enthusiastically supported his opponent, a young Democratic lawyer named David Worley, who "has taken a pro-environment position on nearly every bill that has come up in Congress."[137] Worley gave Gingrich an election-night scare, but the veteran representative squeaked out another win, then persevered in his antienvironmental turn. Joined by his fellow Republican congresspeople and what soon became a Republican majority in the U.S. House of Representatives, he forged that national "conservative majority" to which he had long aspired, in part by dropping any pretense to environmental citizenship.[138]

Race and the Republicans' Burial of Environmental Citizenship

Sociologists tracking the Republican Party's environmental reversal through polls and congressional voting patterns have singled out the early 1990s as marking a definitive break. Looking at the nation as a whole, they find a considerable drop-off in Republican support of environmental issues from 1991, after two decades of only slightly lagging behind the Democrats. These social scientists finger contemporaneous developments as responsible. With the end of the Cold War, Republican leaders turned to fighting environmentalism rather than communism. Republicans' business allies, especially alarmed by the then emergent issue of climate change, geared up their science doubting and antiregulatory initiatives.[139] Powerful as these national and global influences were, a closer look at the Atlanta metro area's experience suggests other reasons. From this angle climate played a relatively minor role: while Gingrich voted against the few climate bills introduced, Atlanta news coverage of climate change situated the debates in international circles and in Washington, D.C., with little immediate relevance for Georgians. More important to this southern corner of the Sunbelt was a Republican environmental opposition that had quietly gathered steam for over two decades, fed by new political projects of Evangelicals and business interests. Between 1988 and 1994, precisely as Georgia's congressional delegation went from a single Republican member—Gingrich—to a Republican majority, the party's opposition to an environmental state turned more prominent, firm, and sweeping. This political culmination of Georgia's Great White Shift came from the continuing effort of Gingrich and other party leaders to sharpen Republican messaging, from breakthrough fundraising and favorable new media and redistricting, along with new political opportunities on the environmental front. With so many white Republican voters now ensconced among their own private environmental amenities and with a new rapprochement consolidating between environmentalism and civil rights, public environmental causes were becoming a new frontier of racial coding: as more urban than suburban, as more Black than white.

Gingrich himself had an outsized hand in his party's final push for a Great White Shift. His own relentless dichotomizing and political hardball drew media fascination; he also led through organizing, fundraising, and teaching other candidates to emulate his style. His own political action committee, GOPAC, advised and supported Republican candidates nationwide but zeroed in on "congressional districts where Reagan consistently polls at least 55 percent but where few local Republicans have sought office"—a rural and suburban South still ruled by conservative white Democrats. Starting in the late 1980s, Gingrich also helped recruit dozens of Republicans to run for office in his own district and across Georgia.[140] By 1989 Gingrich had won over Georgia emulators like R. T. "Tom" Phillips, a state senator from Gwinnett who characterized himself as "in line with Gingrich," since "I am abrasive." Among the training materials GOPAC distributed by the thousands to candidates were cassettes and videos of Gingrich's speeches and a revealing 1990 memo on how to speak like him. It urged a Manichean and moralizing verbiage on Republican candidates: the "optimistic positive" for articulating your own governing vision and those "contrasting words" to "help define" your Democratic opponent—among these, "red tape," "unionized bureaucracy," "sensational-ists," and "destructive" (twice listed). As environmentalists excoriated his vot-ing record, he spun exemplary new "contrasting words" to return the favor, declaring "thirty-five percent of the environmental movement . . . just stupid" and "their solutions . . . essentially socialism."[141]

As Gingrich sought to spread his slash-and-burn political style among like-minded Republicans in Georgia and elsewhere, over the early 1990s new me-dia allies arose to echo and magnify their attacks. Atlanta was also becoming a mecca for flamboyantly conservative talk-radio hosts, whose barbs reached further into the Talmadge toolbox of explicit racism than Gingrich himself dared. Profiting off a "format . . . geared for 25- to 54-year-old white males," stations began turning over their airwaves to the likes of Neil Boortz, who ar-gued that those on welfare be denied the right to vote, and New York–native Sean Hannity, who arrived at Atlanta's WGST-AM in 1992 at the age of thirty. Working out of a Buckhead studio, he "decr[ied] the [Black] Atlanta City Council's vote to give itself a fat pay hike" and "joke[d] about 'hos.'" As the *Atlanta Journal-Constitution* summarized the new style of radio show, "it's an-tagonistic, it's provocative . . . And, in Atlanta," a city now two-thirds Black, "it's almost all white."[142] Beyond the spheres of Evangelical churches and ac-tivists, a conservative media cocoon was being woven, soon to be joined by Fox News, then later by Breitbart, Facebook, and Twitter.

Over the early 1990s the fundraising of Gingrich and other Georgia Re-publicans also shot past that of their Democratic rivals, more effectively tap-ping corporations and the wealthy to meet the growing expenses of cam-paigns. Media and staff expenses for congressional campaigns had risen to $529,000 for successful ones by 1994, over five times as much as in 1976, even accounting for inflation.[143] And as demands had risen, the legal limits on donations helped make candidates ever more dependent on a broad as well as deep-pocketed donor base, a need well-met as the total number of corpo-rate PACs involved in congressional elections mushroomed. By 1990 it shot past one thousand nationally, with well over $100 million in available funds. With the Realtors Political Action Fund also topping $5 million and the NRA's "Victory Fund" $3 million, the GOP's antistatist agenda literally paid off. By contrast, the financial counterweight of environmental advocates remained all too meager: only the League of Conservation Voters' fund exceeded $1 mil-lion, and the Sierra Club's remained just over half that.[144] As Gingrich and other GOPs discovered, combining promises of tax cuts with a quietly gath-ering opposition to environmental regulation could prove highly lucrative. Gingrich's own congressional campaigns, already the best-funded in Georgia, from 1990 came to rank among the top ten most well-heeled in the nation. Across Atlanta's congressional races Republicans' fundraising from large indi-vidual donors ($500 or more) already surpassed that of the opposing party by

1984. As Gingrich and his Republican colleagues turned more overtly antienvironmental from 1990, they quickly doubled that lead. By the 1994 campaign their overall intake of $5 million surged 30 percent past what Democratic opponents mustered.[145]

As Republicans' increasing opposition to environmental causes nurtured their growing financial advantage, the late 1980s rapprochement between civil rights and environmental advocates opened another front for attacking environmentalism: its proponents were turning partly Black. That environmental citizenship could itself become coded as Black was deeply ironic, given how uniformly white Atlanta's environmental movement had long been and mostly remained and how critical environmental justice advocates were of white "mainstream" environmentalists. Already with their own well-established agendas, activists in both the Sierra Club and the SCLC generally framed environmental justice as a side collaboration, less central to their main political project. But racial coding had little to do with accuracy, and Black-white gatherings like the 1988 Southeastern Environmental Conference provided new fodder for a racial coding to which white Georgians remained keenly attuned. Over the early 1990s Jesse Jackson and Robert Kennedy Jr. both flew in to give well-covered speeches on "environmental racism." *Atlanta Constitution* editors wrote their own editorials decrying it and featured op-eds by pathbreaking voices of the environmental justice movement, from SCLC activist Ben Chavis to Black sociologist Robert Bullard. In 1992 the EPA's Atlanta regional office held "the nation's first government-sponsored conference about whether minorities suffer more than other Americans from toxic waste and pollution." That same year Atlanta congressperson John Lewis introduced the first Environmental Justice Bill in Congress, and a state-level version was proposed by an Atlanta representative. Two years later Clark Atlanta University lured Bullard from California to lead its new center devoted to environmental justice.[146]

No doubt noticing these trends and the political opportunities they provided, Gingrich and his fellow Republicans probably missed another change that came with this newfound attention to what were now recognized and labeled as genuinely *environmental* challenges in Black communities. More quietly, environmental citizenship in Atlanta gained a new bulwark: the Black environmentalist. A Black activism arose that was centrally engaged with environmental issues, more so than SCLC or even NPU leaders, resembling a white environmentalism in the focus and steadfastness of its commitments. But Black environmentalists also brought something new to table: their environmentalism came deeply interwoven with a concern for racial justice. Among the early practitioners of this Black environmentalism on Atlanta's West Side was Richard Bright. A newcomer to the city in the late 1980s, after a childhood in Florida, he worked on pesticide safety for the EPA during his early career in Washington, D.C. Already having earned a pharmacology degree, while at the agency he earned a master's degree in divinity and took on a part-time pastorate—an unusual step for an EPA staff member but a familiar one for civil rights activists. In the mid-1980s he helped persuade the agency to begin "develop[ing] environmental and environmental health programs" for historically Black colleges and universities, and by 1989 he had moved from D.C. to Clark Atlanta University to set up a prototype program. Among his early students and mentees was another newcomer to Atlanta who would lend a hand in Bright's environmental activism and then spearhead her own: Na'taki Osbourn Jelks. She had grown up in Louisiana, in the petrochemical region known as "Cancer Alley," an experience that shaped her direction after she left to study at Spelman in Atlanta. As a college student, she was drawn to the Clark University program, to better understand not just the effects of environments like that but the ways in which they might be changed. Out of her own and other budding environmental activism during the early 1990s, a new Black environmentalist identity was being hatched around Atlanta. One of its early targets was an environmental problem that the Black side of the city had faced for decades: combined sewer overflows (CSOs).[147]

Republicans like Gingrich, whose districts and voter bases ranged from Atlanta's white suburbs out into the country, had little reason to follow the inner-suburban campaign undertaken by Bright and Osbourn. In the now-Black southwest, starting in 1993, they helped to organize a series of neighborhood meetings among those living near Utoy Creek, still regularly polluted by design, when heavy rains caused an overflow of sewage lines into the stream. A city renovation plan currently in motion would fall short of fixing this problem, the activists explained, and a much better solution was available: separating the storm and sewage waste flows. Pressing city officials for a full separation of waste flows, they formed what they dubbed an "Environmental Trust," a "small but well-organized group" that successfully pushed the case for separation. It was both better for the neighborhoods, they argued, and less expensive than planned treatment plants. Three months later they had won, persuading the city council to unanimously override a mayoral veto and call for an end to combined sewers.[148] On the heels of their push, the Environmental Trust was joined by other citizen groups such as Save Atlanta's Fragile Environment and Chattahoochee Riverkeeper in a mobilization over the mid-1990s for an overhaul of the city's "'third world' sewers" that would more effectively clean up the city's worst streams. Among the targets for repair was that waterway that since the first Earth Day in 1970 had emblematized the environmental travails of Black Atlanta: Proctor Creek. Winning a lawsuit and drawing the EPA and Georgia's EPD to their cause, some forty years after the creation of a new environmental state, environmental activists finally got its gears to grind more effectively against the downtown's most glaringly polluted of streams.[149]

If Gingrich and other Republicans were likely less aware of these and other

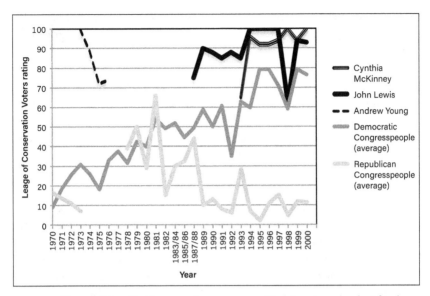

FIGURE 7.3. The racializing of environmental support among Georgia congresspeople. After the departure of Ben Jones, representatives from Atlanta's Black majority districts became the strongest environmental supporters in the Georgia delegation. From 1994 all three remaining Democratic congresspeople were Black. Black representatives from the third Black majority district, in south Georgia, more mixed in their environmental support. League of Conservation Voters, "National Environmental Conservation Scorecard Archive."

environmental efforts simmering within the city of Atlanta itself, they could not miss or mistake the changing complexion of environmental advocacy at the highest levels of government. Among Georgia's congresspeople, Ben Jones turned out to be the last white Democrat elected to the House with a more uniformly proenvironment voting record. Jones lost his seat in 1992, leaving two more "moderate" white Democrats in office until 1994. Throughout what turned out to be a transition period, John Lewis, from the Atlanta-centered Fifth District, emerged as far and away Georgia's most consistent and strongest environmental voice in Congress (see figure 7.3). Coming to Congress as African Americans were becoming more engaged with environmental causes and an environmental justice movement was gaining clout and influence, Lewis, the veteran of the 1960s civil rights movement, now made himself a political figurehead for this new movement, intersecting environmentalism with civil rights. By 1994 he campaigned for reelection alongside another Black candidate for office in the neighboring Eleventh District, Cynthia McKinney, also a vocal proponent of environmental causes. She soon joined Lewis as Georgia's strongest environmental voices in Congress, and her election would further bolster the racial coding of environmental advocacy in Georgia. It came to be reflected by the very faces of those Georgians supporting state-based environmental protections in the U.S. House of Representatives—the very realm Gingrich himself was busily making his own. And Gingrich certainly noticed when, on February 11, 1994, President Bill Clinton signed an executive order conceding environmental justice advocates' point. It required the EPA and other government agencies to begin addressing the disproportionate impact of pollution on minorities and the poor, "to make environmental justice a part of all they do."[150]

The redrawing of congressional district lines, compelled by the 1990 census results and guided by the courts, accelerated the Great White Shift into Republican Party ranks, enabling this party's near sweep of Georgia's congressional seats by mid-decade. With Georgia's first majority-Black congressional district already occupied by its single Black congressperson, Lewis, the state's population gains in the new census earned it an additional eleventh seat in the House of Representatives. Black leaders pushed for two more majority-Black districts so that Georgia's House delegation would better reflection Blacks' 27 percent share of the state's population. A white Democratic leadership long frustrated by Department of Justice rejections of its redistricting plans accepted their demands, and the reshuffling of Black precincts to create minority-majorities in three of the eleven districts went forward, sanctioned by the legislature as well as the federal government and courts.[151] These solutions also required making other districts more overwhelming white; however, as subsequent studies then showed, the Republican-favoring effects in these redrawn districts went far beyond merely substituting white voters for Black ones. The new district lines concentrated split-ticket voters, those now regularly voting for Republican presidents but Democratic legislators, making that discrepancy easier for Republican candidates to exploit. The extent of the redistricting also undercut reigning Democrats' advantages of incumbency, putting them on a par with Republican challengers in needing to win over new voters unfamiliar with their reputation or record. Thereby, redistricting sped along the exodus of white Georgians from the Democratic into the Republican Party that was already well underway.[152]

Around Atlanta, with Ben Jones's Fourth District now harboring somewhat fewer Black voters and more of the privileged northside, wealthy and white, it had become "a tough road to hoe for a Democrat." Switching to the remade Tenth District, also "with lots of Republicans on both ends," he lost in the primary to a Democrat who was then bested by a Republican. Gingrich, too, had to make a switch, but to a Sixth District that still included parts of Cobb, with "all the makings of a Republican stronghold."[153] In addition to Gingrich's victory, Georgia Republicans picked up two other House seats in 1992, as well as "enough state legislative seats to be reckon[ed] a real power for the first time." If those victories made for what one journalist declared "unquestionably the greatest day in [the Georgia Republican Party's] history,"

MAP SET 7.2 Georgia's new congressional color line. The carving out of two more Black-majority congressional districts in Georgia after the 1990 census combined with other changes in the electoral landscape to give rise to a Republican majority in the Georgia congressional delegation by the mid-1990s. Maps by author. *Sources:* E. Scott Alder, "Congressional District Data File, 101st and 104th Congress," University of Colorado, Boulder, accessed November 8, 2022, https://sites.google.com/a /colorado.edu/adler-scott/data /congressional-district-data; Lewis et al., "Digital Boundary Definitions."

they paled next to the party's congressional triumph two years later.[154] They won seven of eleven seats, their first majority on Georgia's congressional delegation since Reconstruction. As shown in map set 7.2, with the defection of Nathan Deal from the Democratic Party that next April, Republicans then claimed all eight of Georgia's congresspeople who were white.[155] Southern Republicans' victories propelled their party to a majority in the House for the first time in forty years, and Gingrich himself into its speakership.

The Contract with America, the Republican platform shared by Gingrich on September 27, 1994, on the steps of the nation's capitol in the midst of that year's campaign, succinctly encapsulated the endgame of the Georgia Republican's long quest to become the political face of cleavage capitalism. Tapping the deepening pockets of the region's wealthiest and synthesizing the platforms of business first and Evangelical citizenship, the contract more and less explicitly attacked a lion's share of the state building that Georgia's democratization had wrought. The most explicit targets were the familiar racialized obsessions of the "Southern Strategy," now neatly wrapped in the "personal responsibility" moralism of the Christian Right: cutting welfare and aid to the poor, building more prisons, and hiring more cops. The Contract with America signaled its own whiteness by countering not just welfare programs but a larger protective scope of government that Joseph Lowery and other civil rights advocates had long advocated on Black communities' behalf. Republican "Contractors" called for the government to be shrunken across the board except for the military, through a balanced budget amendment as well as "family reinforc[ing]" and "middle-class tax relief," as consumer voters reigned. In the wake of the Republicans' victory, Lowery himself, deeply concerned about the changing political landscape, helped convene an "emergency" meeting of Black leaders in Washington to try and persuade new House leadership not to balance the federal budget "on the backs of the poor."[156]

The Contract with America, the third and final stage in Gingrich's environmental reversal, also culminated the Republican Party's environmental about-face. With more Black people joining the environmental movement and its combination of Black and white political spokespeople offering racial cover, Republicans jettisoned any and every environmental pledge as of diminishing interest to their white constituents. That abandonment in turn enabled a more thoroughgoing embrace of businesspeople whose cash increasingly infused their campaigns, through promises of freedom from "absurd regulations and oppressive laws." After the Republicans had won, a worried Sierra Club launched a national petition drive against the "Contract," starting with an Atlanta rally on the banks of the Chattahoochee, just downstream from Gingrich's own Sixth District. By then it was becoming crystal clear to others, as well, that, as an *Atlanta Journal-Constitution* reporter put it, the Contract with America "takes a swipe at the environment at just about every turn."[157]

The House sought to require the federal government to figure in the costs to business of all environmental regulations, to financially compensate those affected, and to slash the enforcement budget of the EPA by a third.[158] A Democratic Senate and president applied the brakes to much of what Gingrich and his House Republicans passed. Yet in the House itself those Georgian congresspeople who voted against these measures were now doubly a minority. Not only were they all Democrats, in a state delegation now overwhelmingly Republican, but all the GOP's congressional victors were also white, and the remaining Democratic representatives, all three of them, were Black. In and around Atlanta the divide between pro- and antienvironmental politics had reconsolidated in such a way that racial coding was no longer necessary, since party lines now hewed to the region's color line.

Back to the Future?

Georgians had not seen anything like it "since the days of Gene Talmadge in the 30s and 40s," commented one longtime political observer. He was talking about Donald Trump's visit to Atlanta in February 2016, fresh off a resounding victory in the South Carolina Republican primary. The front-runner for his party's presidential nomination spoke at the Georgia World Congress, a downtown convention center, on his way to a Super Tuesday win in Georgia and other southern states that locked up his party's nomination. His Talmadge-like "cult of personality" was on full display, all "instinct and passion," "in which facts take a back seat to the affirmation of an audience's greatest fears." As in the time of Talmadgism and massive resistance, "race never seemed to be far from the minds of many in the audience and on the stage." Candidate Trump railed against "illegal immigrants," "treated much better, in some cases, than our vets," and pledged to "build that wall." Two terms of a Black president had deepened his listeners' inclinations to see the very idea of government as conspiratorial: Trump told his audiences they'd been "hoodwinked. Bamboozled. Led astray" by "political hacks." In Trump's "plainspoken 'class solidarity' with the common man," other Atlanta observers also heard echoes of Talmadge's "crude, folksy showmanship." Yet Trump was no suspender-clad "rustic" but a New York City–bred businessperson; as a reality-TV billionaire, his fealty to wealth lay in plainer sight. Foulmouthed and tough talking, he pledged to do in Washington what he insisted was needed: cracking down on immigrants, ISIS, and the Chinese but otherwise shredding and muscling government out of the private sector's way.[1]

For Atlantans and other Georgians, a Republican Party captivated by Trump stood on the verge of taking the entire nation through an odd time warp, to a place eerily reminiscent of Georgia in the 1940s. Promising to "Make America Great Again," the Republican front-runner assured that he would turn around a government that for too long, he insinuated, had coddled and protected the interests of nonwhites. In the name of a more or less explicit white nationalism, he would launch a concerted assault against the government building of the past half century and more, the fruit of Georgia's democratization recorded in the preceding pages. For the Republicans' new standard-bearer, no federal powers needed more reigning in than those protecting Americans' environment. Instead of the quieter sabotage of Gingrich Republicanism, Trump exuded outright scorn: climate change was a Chinese hoax, and the EPA needed breaking up into "little tidbits." Upon his November victory he would indeed try to steer the federal environmental state in the direction Georgia had adopted under Talmadgism: more thinly staffed, less scientifically driven, and more "cooperative" with industries it oversaw.[2]

Just four years later Georgia itself seemed headed through another wrenchingly dissimilar time tunnel. Led by the Atlanta-metro area, the state's electoral votes went to the Democratic candidate for president, Joe Biden, for the first time since Carter's 1976 triumph. Ralph Warnock and David Ossoff also won runoffs for Senate seats, tipping their party to a chamber majority through the first statewide victories for any nonincumbent Democrat since Roy Barnes's 1998 win for governor. Not just the victories but the ways they'd been won recalled the avenues by which mid-twentieth-century Atlantans and other Georgians had toppled Talmadgism and its rustic rule. As in the 1950s and 1960s, long-standing efforts to reach and mobilize a broader electorate were crucial, in this case led by Stacey Abrams's Fair Fight and New Georgia Project and a host of others. That latest heir of civil rights citizenship, a Black Lives Matter movement, drew promises from all the winning Democrats to reform policing and the justice system. Warnock himself, the pastor at Atlanta's Ebenezer Baptist, that churchly cradle of civil rights activism previously led by both Martin Luther Kings, senior and junior, vividly personified this legacy. The winning Democrats also pointedly espoused a grassroots climate movement that had surged after Trump's election, a latter-day face of environmental citizenship that had even wended its way into Warnock's church. They committed to reversing the Republicans' environmental rollbacks and to acting more aggressively to combat climate change, Warnock through policies "placing equity and justice at the center" and Ossoff through a "historic infrastructure plan" to invest in clean and efficient energy.[3] For all the resonances with Georgia's midcentury politics of democratization, however, Democrats' state-level wins in 2020 and 2021 remained far narrower than those of the 1970s and 1980s. While Biden's national margin of victory was more formidable, in all three races Georgians chose Democrats over Republicans by only a few thousand votes, a hair's breadth.

With only one of our two major parties now interested in a more active, equitable, and foresightful government, this state and our nation stand athwart what may prove an enduring crossroads. Each election season, Americans stand on a precipice, facing the prospect of losing our ability to prepare together, to secure a future that would serve more than a fortunate few. The receptiveness of many Atlantans and other Georgians to Trumpian Republicanism suggests that for all their urbanizing and newfound prosperity from the 1940s, for all their democratization over the 1960s and 1970s, in critical ways this city and state have now come full circle. One of this book's chief arguments points to just what that common thread between the Talmadge era and the 2010s and 2020s might be: the return of concentrated wealth. Then, as over the past few decades, the swelling coffers toward the top of the region's wealth ladder have wound up slowly and ineluctably choking the governing vision and practice of Georgia's rulers, elected though they still are. Whereas today it is the Republican Party that seeks to pinch and pare the scope of government, back then it was Talmadge-aligned Democrats whose "poor government" principles and policies deeply favored the wealthiest at the expense of a middle class but especially those who were poor and Black. Two overweening historical differences nevertheless distinguish this latter-day journey past democracy from its predecessor. Rustic rule itself had followed on the heels of a democratization forced on white southerners after their loss in the Civil War and commenced with a radical, violence-strewn shrinkage of the southern electorate. But Republicans' more recent revival of antistatism has triumphed at the ballot box: in Georgia by the 1990s, and by the late 2010s across the nation. As this book has shown for Georgia, it took over governments that over preceding decades had been rendered far more democratic, largely through bottom-up mobilizations by Atlantans and Georgians themselves, Black as well as white.

As this book has explored, democracy did not come easily to a mid-twentieth-century U.S. South bedeviled by gaping inequalities and the grip of racial authoritarians. However high the hopes of small cadres of African American as well as white moderate activists and voters in the 1940s, democratization took much longer and required deeper and more sustained wellsprings. It did not come as Karl Marx or many labor historians might expect, through some uprising of an industrial working class. The main roots of Georgia's democratization lay instead in a metropolitan, expanding, and cross-racial middle class. Slowly building civil rights, neighborhood and environmental activism were favored by an equalizing jet stream blowing through the region's political economy. New Deal policies, driven in important part by other regions' more successful labor movements, combined with the wartime recovery to craft a compression capitalism, one whose newfound riches poured more robustly into ordinary people's pocketbooks, bolstering middle-class wealth.

Despite Georgia's suppression of organized labor and the New Deal's many racial barriers and exclusions, spreading affluence and rising living standards across some Black communities and more white ones heightened hopes for further change. Despite the New Deal's notorious countercurrents from redlining and white flight to freeway building, homeownership mounted among

Blacks and whites alike. Within Atlanta's newly expansive and patrimonial middle class, segregated as it was, new impetuses for democratization arose, claims not just on individual properties but on places that were, or could be, shared—neighborhoods, parks, and other public spaces. Rising hopes helped catalyze political projects that proved transformative: both civil rights and environmental citizenship. These two citizenship projects, nurtured as well as provoked by federal programs, had tidal consequences. This book has charted how, over the 1960s into the 1970s, they effectively toppled Atlanta's and Georgia's democracy-constricting political regimes, both a city government overseen by white business-oriented elites and a state government controlled by rural "courthouse rings."[4]

As a new generation of politicians came to power and set about changing the scope and sway of government, electoral and participatory democratization reached historic peaks in and around Atlanta. Over the course of these struggles, proponents of civil rights and environmental citizenship often wound up on the same political side but rarely saw eye to eye. While environmentalists allied with the city's new Black leaders, starting in the pivotal elections of the early 1970s, their sense of purpose revolved around saving what was recognizably natural or of ecological value. Meshing readily with the priorities of Atlanta's better-off whites, it mirrored or defended private amenities many of them already enjoyed. When civil rights activists sought to better Black living environments, on the other hand, they articulated a different sense of what was at stake. From the 1940s into the 1960s, they sought more equitable and just access to well-provisioned homes, parks, and other public spaces. From the mid-1960s into the 1970s, they also called for improvements in Black working-class and poorer quarters and workplaces, in stark contrast to Atlanta's environmentalists. As Black leaders like Maynard Jackson famously ascended to the city's most powerful political posts, what has gone less remarked on is how many white Atlantans also benefited from the concomitant recasting of city as well as state governments. As civil rights– and government-friendly white Democrats also ascended to Georgia's helm, the remaking of government at multiple levels served and shielded a wider citizenry, white as well as Black, and invited more participation. Compared with Jim Crow counterparts, the new models of government were dramatically more equitable and protective as well as more expansive and more steadily open to the voices of their citizenry.

For all the celebrated achievements of this era's civil rights movement, the resulting transformations in the environmental realm were at least as sweeping. Environmental laws and agencies furnished aggressive new safeguards shielding ordinary citizens against powerful polluters. While the new protections often turned technocratic, embodying a managerial liberalism, they also opened more doors for public input and court challenges, giving many neighborhood or environmental leaders new avenues for asserting their own and the public's interests. If the democratization of city and state was peaking, however, the new state powers and participatory structures also ushered in new vulnerabilities, ways they might be gamed through moneyed or other forms of privilege. Environmentalists, for instance, discovered to their dismay that the increasingly technical requirements for contributing to public hearings and administrative proceedings could work to the advantage of corporate intruders and polluters, whose accumulated wealth bought legal and scientific expertise that could dominate the dialogue. And as activists at the SCLC realized, the new environmental oversight could prove more solicitous of the environmental travails of better-off whites than of Blacks, a realization that then drove the birth of a movement for environmental justice. In addition, the broadened and equalized electoral systems of city and state proved susceptible to a new antiregulatory politics spearheaded by the well-heeled, especially as cleavage capitalism returned to Atlanta and its Georgia hinterlands.

From the 1970s, pressures toward economic and racial cleavage once more picked up across this southern city and region. More newly created wealth began flowing into upper-end pocketbooks, especially those held by white hands. Thereby, the northern reaches of the metropolis as well as whiter counties to the south magnified their advantages over the southern and western sides of town, where so many better-off Blacks moved. Among these, whites moving to the more affluent suburbs and exurbs now enjoyed a host of private environmental amenities, from woodsy lots and neighborhoods to parks and other open spaces. What they already enjoyed through their own consumption could undermine their appreciation of public environmental needs. Moreover, within the city's limits gentrification gathered steam, drawing inmigration and investments from well-off whites. In these parts of the downtown, rising rents began to price out long-standing Black residents, even as the poorest Blacks remained trapped in other parts of the city that wealth continued to shun. The shrinking job, housing, and other opportunities for many downtown combined with the concentration of wealth across the North Side and its edge cities turned Atlanta into an early twenty-first-century icon for inequality. Poorer Blacks and whites alike became ensnared, whether in the more strapped of downtown neighborhoods, in run-down suburbs, or in an increasingly desperate countryside beyond.

Like the compression capitalism that reigned during and after World War II, the cleavage capitalism of the late century owed much to attendant political changes. A new antistatist politics arose recalling that of the Jim Crow era but with its own distinctive emphases, coalitions, and policies. From the 1970s a rekindled Christian fundamentalism, sharpening its critiques of secularism and societal decadence, flourished in Atlanta's white suburbs. Out of it came a new Evangelical citizenship that challenged perceived intrusions of the modern state, defended gender traditionalism and a "right to life," and sought a place for science-skeptical creationism in the public schools. Businesspeople as well, disgruntled with the new environmental and other governmental oversight, dove into new rounds of political organizing, crafting a new business-first citizenship. It assailed new environmental policies through lawsuits, attacks on the science on which these were often based, and growing financial support of politicians who would take up its cause. Absorbing and channeling these political currents, enterprising Republicans such as Newt Gingrich forged a new conservatism that could win at the ballot box, not least through its success at campaign fundraising. Through rhetorical sleights of hand that were also feats of racial coding, they impugned the newly broadened scope of government as mainly serving the poor (and Black) and reconceived voters as consumers, primarily interested in protecting their own pocketbooks from Uncle Sam. Tax cuts became their economic cure-all and "family values" a wellspring for politicized righteousness, as their ambitions for shrinking government escalated.

Even as the popularity of environmental causes in Georgia soared over the 1970s and 1980s in tandem with metropolitan sprawl, stimulating further rounds of environmental state building, Georgia's beleaguered Republicans commenced their own environmental reversal. In some ways the mounting Republican opposition took advantage of environmentalism's successes: the private environmental amenities now proliferating across many of Atlanta's spreading suburbs and exurbs as well as a new environmental state quietly performing its protective job in the unobtrusive manner envisioned by managerial liberalism. An early step in their abandonment of environmental citizenship was to split off that more defensive environmentalism of private homeowners, which they favored, from the environmental oversight and regulation undertaken by government agencies, which they increasingly called into question. Republican antienvironmentalism then turned more sweeping and resolute in the early 1990s as Atlanta-area environmentalism turned less exclusively white, helping Republicans win the contest for campaign funds while drawing more votes from rural and less wealthy whites.

The electoral rewards of Republican antienvironmentalism turned still greater as climate change surged up environmentalists' agenda, with far-reaching implications for businesses that burned fossil fuels. The Southern Company, Georgia Power's parent, had realized the ramifications for its coal-burning operations by the 1980s, when it began funding initiatives to question the underlying science.[5] Since then the Georgia Republican Party's solicitude for business and penchant for politically massaging racial divisions have led it down the pathway of climate denialism. As an increasingly Black and metropolitan Democratic Party has taken climate change seriously, leading Georgia

Republicans have shunned climate policy, while inveigling against even the mildest regulations to tackle it as well as other environmental problems. Georgia Republicans from Sonny Perdue to Brian Kemp, who won Georgia's governorship in 2018, turned mum about climate trends while loudly pledging antiregulatory "chainsaws."[6]

This state's reigning Republicans also tilted the redistributive balance of Georgia's government back toward where it stood under Talmadgism: relieving burdens on the well-to-do while shearing or limiting programs that benefited the less well-off. Their tax cuts started, predictably, with corporate and income taxes. Like the Talmadgists, they treated new taxes as an anathema, but what little new revenue they sought came through sales and other regressive taxes, placing proportionally greater burdens on those with less.[7] Republican legislators were especially resourceful at finding ways of cutting funds for public education, even while funneling public revenue to private charter schools. By 2016 Georgia had once more had slid down into the lower ranks of U.S. states on education spending. Recalling the Talmadge response to New Deal largesse, Republican leadership balked at accepting $40 billion to expand Medicaid under the 2010 Affordable Care Act, complaining that the process of distributing it to millions of needy Georgians would cost too much.[8]

Republican rule in Georgia also sought curbs on the environmental oversight that from the 1970s through the 1990s had become a keystone of government's protective role. The rollbacks began with the Georgia Regional Transportation Agency, a legislated effort at regional governance pushed by Georgia's last Democrat governor, Roy Barnes, in the late 1990s in response to EPA sanctions imposed on the sprawling Atlanta-metro area for its air pollution. Sonny Perdue then defeated and replaced Barnes, becoming the state's first Republican governor since Reconstruction. The agency then quickly lost its way: by 2005 outside observers and even the director himself agreed that it had "largely failed to live up to its promise."[9] The state's Republican leadership also steadfastly refused to fund MARTA or other transit projects. It turned an increasingly cold shoulder to infrastructure projects of any kind and diverted funds designated for landfill and waste site cleanups to nonenvironmental uses.[10] Since then, while Georgia's environmental agencies have not suffered as much as Republican chainsaw-to-regulations rhetoric suggests, the state's Republican leadership has barely lifted a finger to address climate change. Gov. Nathan Deal, through his two terms, could only muster an advisory committee to study how coastal counties should adapt to rising sea levels. Georgia's Republican attorney general meanwhile joined national lawsuits to challenge federal efforts to widen water-pollution controls and curb greenhouse gases. Reluctant to admit that greenhouse gases need regulating, the state's Republican leadership anticipated, then embraced, the outright antienvironmentalism of Trump Republicanism, turning dead set against a vein of citizenship that, four decades earlier, had easily found sympathies among Republican candidates and officeholders.[11]

That climate along with almost all other environmental issues have been so effectively driven from the agenda of Georgia's ruling party is symptomatic of how corrupted by amassed wealth American democracy has already become. Most directly, Republicans' sustained majority of Georgia's congressional delegation by the 1990s came through a swelling river of campaign cash, as congressional campaigns were getting more expensive, and Republicans were quicker off the mark in tapping the region's upper echelons of income. Decades before the Supreme Court's *Citizens United* decision of 2011, the search for bigger donors then created a cycle in which politicians pioneered a host of new policies benefiting the better-off, whose padded bank accounts then furnished them with still more money to donate to their political friends. National networks also played a role: an American Legislative Exchange Council, richly funded by corporate moguls like Charles and David Koch (owners of Georgia-Pacific from 2005), created a further line of influence on bills proposed, then passed, by Georgia's Republican leaders. As wealth concentration has picked up in a state already bearing some of the nation's harshest legacies of racial and economic inequity, those holding the reins of power have effectively channeled white Georgians' fiercest and most righteous ire against government itself. Shearing away the services and protections it provides for a broader public, they have also imposed another less concrete toll. They have impaired our collective ability to imagine and plan *any* shared future for our society, much less one that is more broadly equitable.

As Atlanta has replaced rural Georgia as the redoubtable bastion of the state's Democrats, it too has been profoundly shaped by the reversal of those trends that underwrote its mid-twentieth-century democratizing ferment. Already by the 1980s most of the city's Black political leaders had made their peace with a white business elite, whose backing and clout once more came to be seen as essential to the city's welfare and future. In response to the Great White Shift toward Republicans, Georgia's Democratic Party has become increasingly Atlanta centered and multiracial in its leaders and interests. It retains many commitments made in the 1960s and 1970s to a broader, more evenhanded, and democratic governing vision. Especially within the city limits and closer-in suburban counties of the metro area, Democratic control has perpetuated more active roles for government. Yet, especially after Republicans gained control of the state government, Atlanta mayors Shirley Franklin, Kasim Reed, Keisha Bottoms, and Andre Dickens have hesitated to push against business interests, lest they reaccelerate the long-standing flight of private investment from downtown and alienate the state's promarket and city-wary leadership.

Atlanta's own government could and did undertake ambitious projects in environmental realms. It planned and constructed a Freedom Park in the mid-1990s that resolved the long-running dispute over the land around the Carter Center. It undertook a massive repair and reconstruction of its sewers first sketched in the late 1990s and, under Shirley Franklin, finally began tackling the combined-sewers problem. A 2005 commission launched a "Beltline" project that would bring parks, trails, and transit into the city along many of its old railroad corridors. But with hopes for GRTA largely dashed and with the still largely advisory Atlanta Regional Commission once more in nominal charge of metro-area governance, plans and projects reaching beyond the city itself to outlying suburbs and exurbs turned wispier and less certain. With so much of the metropolis's wealth having fled beyond the city limits, especially northward, the city's modest tax base also left it with limited financing for sizeable projects. In the Democratic downtown, as property or other taxes shouldered more by the wealthy were liable to provoke further business departures, sales taxes seemed the brightest way forward for financing an infrastructure project like MARTA or the sewer overhaul. Pushing back against their regressive reputation, mayor advocates insisted that sales-tax financing would not impose any greater burden on the less-well-off, since "visitors and commuters would help shoulder the costs."[12] The other pathway forward pursued by city officials was "public-private partnerships," which would leave a considerable share of any project, and the city's future, largely in the market's hands.[13]

This leaning on private entrepreneurship as engine and shaper of Atlanta's future has turned out to be extraordinarily compatible with a New Urbanism. The severe collapse of the region's suburban-growth machine in the wake of the 2008 financial crisis hit Black homeowners and suburbs especially hard but also helped speed the channeling of more capital and investment into purportedly unsuburban New Urbanist developments.[14] As economic growth returned to the region after 2010, it became apparent just how much of the construction market had tilted in this direction. "Atlanta, once known as the poster child of sprawl," reported the *Journal-Constitution* in 2014, "has seen an emergence of denser, walkable urban developments since the 1990s," with these New Urbanist designs taking up "more than 50 percent of the market share."[15] One consequence of stymied wage growth was also a rising demand for rentals, and New Urbanist projects, with their bristling apartments and condos, raked in residents and profits from this shift. Their successes led the omnipresent urban planner Christopher Leinberger to change his tune about Atlanta. "The market has spoken," he declared, echoing what suburban developers had long claimed while winning the battle for market share. "Metropolitan Atlanta, 'the poster child of sprawl,'" pronounced Leinberger in typically grand fashion in 2013, "is now experiencing the end of sprawl."[16]

Lost in this eager triumphalism was how many Atlantans still lived in suburban landscapes predating this New Urbanist ascendancy. So dominated by earlier waves of development did the region remain that a 2014 survey still assessed Atlanta's sprawl as the nation's eighth most extreme, lagging behind only a few other smaller southeastern cities.[17] New Urbanist triumphalism also skimmed past just how many certifiably "walkable" developments lay in suburbs rather than downtown, including over half of the forty-six identified by Leinberger himself. Environmentally speaking, for both suburban and downtown "walk-ups," the substitution of walking for car travel was not nearly as complete as New Urbanist rhetoric promised. The walkability they delivered did not extend, for instance, to the jobs of apartment residents, who might still have to commute to workplaces miles away. Arguably the most stunning blind spot of the New Urbanist triumph came in the realm of "social equity"—the racial and socioeconomic distribution of the opportunities these developments offered. As Leinberger's own report somewhat euphemistically noted, "walk-ups" that did best economically were the very ones that had the lowest equity ratings—that is, with the least income and racial diversity. Most lay in the white northside, that most economically and racially "favored" of suburbs. Within the city as well, the skewing effects would soon become unmistakable: "Atlanta's post-recession building boom has been overwhelmingly concentrated in luxury housing—particularly high-end rental."[18]

Still less noted were the larger consequences afoot from a reshuffled distribution of wealth now decades in the making across this metropolis. That patrimonial middle class that had arisen over the mid-twentieth century, whose gathering economic power had prepared the way for a politics of democratization across city and state, was losing traction. As fewer and fewer owned the land on which they lived, Atlanta veered once more toward what it had been in an earlier era of racial authoritarianism: a city of renters rather than of homeowners, especially for Blacks.[19] If more and more of these rentals were high end, that only heightened the contrast identified by studies in both 2014 by Brookings and 2018 by Bloomberg, pegging the city of Atlanta itself—not the larger metro area—as the nation's most unequal.[20] By no coincidence, cleavage capitalism's escalating dynamics have diminished the leverage available to city leaders for confronting these larger metropolitan undertows. Consequently, "the city's African American population," as the environmental justice scholar and former Atlantan Robert Bullard put it in 2010, has been largely "left on the side of the road because of residential segregation, inadequate public transportation, location of major job centers, and persistent inequality."[21] And city officials' efforts to "go green and sustainable," though far more sincere and significant than those of the state's Republican leadership, have struggled to avoid exacerbating the longer-term deepening of disparities that has been underway between rich and poor, white and Black.

The fate of the widely celebrated Beltline illustrates these dilemmas. From its start in 2006, the construction of this twenty-two-mile walking trail around downtown has been dogged by how, at nearly every step, it has tended to reassert rather than reduce Atlanta's enormous underlying inequities. When the first land purchases just happened to take place in the affluent northeast around the Carter Center, the protests of south and west siders led to a systematic effort to concoct an "equitable development" plan for the Beltline's rollout. A 2013 study captured just how far short this plan had fallen, thanks to the severely unequal landscape along which the Beltline project itself had unfolded. Three large project areas—the most expensive of these in the northeast—had gobbled up three-quarters of the $200 million spent so far. No comparable large-scale project had as yet begun in the south or southwest parts of the route: the Blacker suburbs. With half of those living near the line at one income extreme or the other, either poor or affluent, and with northern and eastern neighborhoods considerably whiter and southerly and westerly ones Blacker, study authors concluded that "Atlanta's inequity story is the Beltline's inequity story."[22] And as the forces of gentrification have prevailed through Atlanta's post–Great Recession boom—cheered on by Leinberger's and others' calls to remake the city for a "creative class"—the Beltline as well as a new streetcar line have threatened not just to duplicate existing inequities but to worsen them.[23] Affordable housing promised along the trail has lagged overall, but especially in Atlanta's poorer and Blacker West Side, echoing the dashed promises of post–World War II urban renewal. Meanwhile, the east-side trail, through the city's gentrifying heartland, has drawn "boutiques, restaurants, and craft breweries" into the Old Fourth Ward but little of the promised affordable housing, as longtime Black residents are driven out. In other Black enclaves like Reynoldstown as well, the Beltline's recent arrival continues to "price out" those who can no longer afford the rising rents or property taxes.[24]

In the past few years, city leaders have tried harder to ensure that their environmental initiatives better protect Black and poor residents from new as well as older fallout of real-estate developers' and polluters' "freedom." Long-overdue measures require that at least 15 percent of the units in apartment projects be priced affordably, and prominent mixed-use developments allot twice that; a city "anti-displacement fund" now aids less well-off existing residents to stay put in gentrifying areas.[25] Tightening federal controls on power plants as well as cleaner vehicles have brought down Atlanta's air pollution from its 1990s peaks, though by 2018 it still ranked twenty-third in the nation for ozone and twenty-second for year-round particles.[26] Even Proctor Creek, that aqueous avenue by which the city's worst water pollution had long pooled on the Blacker and poorer sides of town, has seen a remarkable, if still partial, revival. Though as late as 2018, levels of coliform bacteria were still fifty times greater than the EPA standard, that was significantly lower than only five years before. With the help of federal as well as city and private funds, dozens of citizens now help monitor for spikes and pinpoint sources of the creek's pollutants. A new greenway and trail are opening along Proctor Creek's banks, "to provide historically isolated neighborhoods greater access to nearby parks, schools, and restaurants."[27] Especially over the past decade, city officials have also tackled climate change with a growing seriousness and verve that have sharply contrasted with the approach of the state's Republican leaders. Mayors now publicly pledge their allegiance to climatory as well as environmental citizenship, and Atlanta has a response team for climate-related storms, efficiency and energy standards for city-owned buildings and cars, and a commitment to transition to "100% Clean Energy."[28]

Not just on the climate front but with many other issues, Democratic priorities and plans have come to contrast ever more sharply with the antistatist ideology of a Republican Party committed to only the fuzziest and most market-friendly of futures. Based in the downtown and suburbs of Atlanta and other Georgia cities and bringing together Black and white voters on behalf of a more expansive, protective, and projective role for government, by the late 2010s Georgia Democrats finally appeared to be gaining traction statewide, after two decades in the electoral wilderness. Their winning 2020 campaigns turned this state into a much-consulted crystal ball for where Americans' thoroughly fractured political culture may be headed.[29] The stakes are monumental. And this city's and state's long historical voyage toward, then away from, democracy over the past half century also points to a difficult road ahead for democracy's advocates. Beyond the now nearly defunct Voting Rights Act, the main electoral and governmental achievements secured by the South's democratization over the 1960s and 1970s remain in place, at least for now. But this very system has also proven vulnerable to big money and racially coded demagoguery, giving us a Republican Party that is not just Talmadge-like in its conservatism but willing to go further than Talmadge ever did, to reject outright the results of a national election. Their opponents may need a good deal more than successful get-out-the-vote drives to secure our democracy's prospects.

Changing demographics have become the most oft-cited grounds for anticipating a political shift ahead. By 2020 even Cobb County, the last majority white among the city's five core counties, was down to 56 percent white, with 30 percent Black and the rest Latino. Minority gains in this and other suburban counties, successfully targeted by voting drives, translated directly into Republican losses. That year not just Fulton and DeKalb but Cobb, Gwinnett, Rockdale, Clayton, Douglas, and Henry Counties all voted for Democrats, both at the top of the ticket and for county leadership. A similar changeover might be in store for Georgia as a whole if it loses its white majority just after

2030, as some project.[30] But will demographic change come soon enough, or prove politically transformative enough, to scatter those clouds gathering out along this state's horizons, casting ever sharper and darker shadows?

The skewing of wealth and income that has picked up not just across Georgia but the rest of the nation and world over the past few decades shows no signs of slowing. Recent work by economic and labor historians suggests we should expect no less: the compression capitalism of the mid-twentieth-century United States and other nations may well have been the exception and the cleavage capitalism of Jim Crow as well as more recent times the historical rule.[31] Thomas Piketty and other economists predict that income and wealth will continue amassing at the top over the rest of the century, short of some disruptive catastrophe or else unprecedented public interventions worldwide.[32] As the modern Republican Party now forthrightly spearheads and applauds this ongoing redistribution of riches in the United States and seeks to further it, its temporary control of two branches of the federal government between 2016 and 2020 has enabled a more enduring hand on the third: a Supreme Court with a conservative majority. Whether or not the Democrats can also win through the 2020s, the Republican Party shows little sign of fading into irrelevance in Georgia or other less embattled strongholds across the nation. And nationally the structural advantages of today's conservative Republicanism mirror those of Georgia's rustic rulers under the old county-unit system until the 1960s: an Electoral College and Senate that favor rural states and electorates over urban ones, despite the shrinking share of voters living there. With the Republican skepticism of science and expertise having bloomed into full-blown dismissal of any reality principle beyond the claims of an authoritarian leader and with the revealed willingness of many Republicans to seek or support an outright coup to overturn an election, the future of U.S. democracy remains deeply uncertain.

Among all the other shadows lurking along Georgia's horizon but ignored by today's Republicanism, none is more certain than climate change. Despite denials by politicians, corporations, and many citizens, temperatures and extreme weather from global accumulations of greenhouse gases are inexorably, relentlessly on the rise. Atlanta's average temperature rose two degrees over the past twenty-five years, with 2019 the hottest year on record. Temperatures are set to spike another four to nine degrees on average over the next eighty to a hundred years. Days of extremely high (over ninety degrees Fahrenheit) temperatures will no longer be episodic but recur over nearly a quarter of the year, aggravating the effects of air pollutants like ozone and of the city's "heat islands."[33] The region is also likely to witness more "extreme precipitation events"—massive rainfalls like those which made 2018 Atlanta's second-wettest year on record.[34] That same year the October charge of Hurricane Michael through Georgia offered a portent of the destructiveness ahead. Not so paradoxically, another outcome is drought, often bringing with it outbreaks of wildfires. Already droughts in 2007 and again in 2016 served up a foretaste of how pregnable Atlanta has become, as the biggest city in the United States to tap such a moderately sized river system for its water supply.[35]

Just as with the coronavirus pandemic, the hardships of climate-caused disruption will not be shared equally; indeed, as scientists concluded by 2017, "climate change tends to increase preexisting inequality."[36] With Atlanta's average temperatures escalating, the least privileged places and people bear the greatest climatological burdens. By 2014 the contrast between heat-absorbing tree canopies in well-off suburbs and exurbs and the city's treeless downtown, inhabited by many poor Blacks, made their outdoor air two degrees hotter. That gap promises to widen as temperatures rise, with the downtown's poor the least able to afford air-conditioning bringing indoor respite. Pollutants worsened by rising heat, such as ozone, also pool in these parts of town, and studies have already begun to show hot-weather-related spikes in hospital visits for asthma among Black children living there.[37] Worsening downpours and flooding wreak their biggest damage in low-lying parts of the city, where poorer neighborhoods have long clustered. Intensifying storms and droughts are also bad news for farm-dependent rural Georgians, already squeezed under a cleavage capitalism that enriches mostly the metropolis. In 2018 Hurricane Michael wrung over $2.5 billion out of Georgia agriculture, and with seasonal weather ever more erratic, late frosts and high winds have hurt crops.[38] Yet Georgia officials have reacted to climate-related crises only as and after they happen. They have done very little either to prepare or to reduce the emissions that accelerate climate change, essentially trusting to corporate interests still deeply invested in fossil fuels to handle the state's transition toward more renewable energy.

The ongoing dismissal of climate change by Georgia's Republican leadership aside, neither inequitable wealth distribution nor autocracy necessarily stand in the way of national curbs on greenhouse emissions or better anticipation of climate change's devastating impacts. Historical examples abound of authoritarian nations tackling environmental problems, from Nazi Germany's conservation policies to the Soviet Union's forest reserves under Joseph Stalin to China's recent, more robust embrace of climate policy. But, as these examples also demonstrate, authoritarian regimes with environmental projects also visit immensely destructive designs on unfavored people and places, leaving victims, with as Robert Wilson has noted, "fewer avenues for redress or recourse."[39] A conservative regime that simply ignores or dismisses the reality of climate change enables a similarly uneven impact, but at the hands of markets and private capital. While those with means will be able to protect themselves and even profit, those without will bear the brunt of its ravages.

With such storm clouds ahead, we have ample grounds to be fearful for the future of democracy in this and other similar corners of our nation. The hour is late, and recent countercurrents should not obscure how the South and the rest of our nation still stand at or near a tipping point into a still more illiberal and undemocratic era. If the corrosive effect of wealth concentration on democracy we have seen in past times continues into our future, then the prospects will turn even more daunting and dire. This history of Georgia's democratizing offers a historical example of just how such trends may be countered: by the sustained collective action of many ordinary citizens. Here, however, a caveat is necessary: in midcentury Atlanta middle- and lower-class residents enjoyed favorable tailwinds at their backs. A broadening distribution of economic means and clout, if still blocked for many Blacks, nourished the sprouting of civic hopes. Now those tailwinds have become headwinds. How can future movements for democratizing sustain and grow themselves, as a middle class steadily loses out in means and prospects?

This historical study counsels, first of all, the virtues of patience and perseverance. While Democrats may defeat the Republicans in the next statewide election or the next, any more robust and sustainable reversal will likely be much longer in coming. A succession of progressive-minded waves may be necessary, each one building on its predecessor over a matter of decades. The greatest governmental impetus for democratizing change may have to come from Washington, D.C., as it did in this as in so much other of the South's history. Looking closely at the New Deal and other policies that made the compression capitalism of the mid-twentieth century possible, we need to seek viable ways of replicating those today. New wealth or other kinds of taxes might launch a return to a more progressive tax structure. We also need to encourage those democracy-nourishing conditions that compression capitalism created independent of federal or state policies. Might digital connections help replicate those historical experiences of collective economic clout and felt or aspired-to "commons" that, in and around Atlanta, nourished movements for civil rights, neighborhood advocacy, and environmentalism? Given the growing obstacles to homeownership for so many, under what conditions might tenancy provide similar grounds for collective sensibilities and activism, and how may we encourage these? Certainly, the passage of more robust and powerful labor laws could encourage stronger workplace democracy in a right-to-work state like Georgia. It might even reverse a long-standing weakness of labor unions so fundamental to maintaining this state's probusiness political culture.

Unlike the democratizing political ferment over the mid-twentieth century that is followed by this book, those sprouting within today's cleavage capitalism will more likely be driven by shared economic woes and diminishing hopes, more like the working-class immiseration about which Karl Marx and Friedrich Engels wrote. With the return of a more explicit style of racism and white supremacy in recent years, racial animosities have once more served to divert many whites from the economic dilemmas they share with those whose skin is Brown or Black. The insularity of a conservative media sphere has limited the effectiveness of civil rights tactics forged during the 1960s, of peacefully provoking racial violence that is then shamed through national media. Yet phone-filmed videos of police choke holds and shootings have catalyzed a Black Lives Matter movement that has drawn both whites and Blacks into the streets. If this book has stressed the importance of religious values and frameworks to both sides of Georgia's political fences, the elections of Ralph Warnock, a Baptist minister, as well as Joe Biden, a practicing Catholic, show that moral muscles of a Christian Left are far from exhausted. And while the SCLC's earlier campaign against poverty eventually stumbled over the growing divide between middle-class and poorer Blacks, current trends could make for another story. The revival of a national "Poor People's campaign" led by the Reverends William Barber and Liz Theoharis, inspired by the SCLC's initiative of half a century before, and the new "jolt" to labor organizing and activism in the wake of the COVID pandemic offer promising channels for a more collective confrontation with what lies ahead for so many Georgians and other Americans, whatever their skin color. For these and other like-minded groups, the assault on voting rights and election results, picking up steam at the time of this writing, may well provide a unifying thread.[40]

What today's and future mobilizations on behalf of democracy cannot afford, given all that is arrayed against them, is the largely sundered character of Atlanta's democratizing movements of the 1960s and 1970s. Back then those advocating what this book has termed "civil rights citizenship" saw it as distinct and separate from the project of "environmental citizenship" being crafted by environmentalists, and the latter returned the favor. In retrospect, however, not any single one of these movements so much as their *coincidence* and synergy spurred the successful democratization of their city and state. Of the two, only civil rights citizenship's proponents stepped out from their middle-class beachhead to encompass economic versions of citizenship, on behalf of workers and the poor. Only much later, in the wake of an environmental justice movement also initiated largely by civil rights advocates, would these two veins of citizenship come to better acknowledge and work with each other.

A starting point for building a denser and more durable solidarity across these causes is to acknowledge how, ideally, a more democratic political system, a fairer economy, and a healthier environment are not separate projects. For each goal to stand a better chance, especially in a time increasingly hostile to them all, all three must be pursued in tandem, through mobilizations that more forthrightly rely on, coordinate with, and draw from one another. While movements as different as those for civil rights, the environment, and labor have long coursed separately, not infrequently clashing, they've also benefited from one another's efforts and successes. Especially given the continued corrosion of a middle class that helped muster the mobilizations bringing democratization to Atlanta and the rest of the South, the need is now greater than ever for their latter-day counterparts to see eye to eye. My hope is that a book such as this, examining how two such citizenship projects were pursued side by side to historic effect, can lay groundwork for further alliances and collaborations to come.

If Atlantans, Georgians, and Americans as a whole do not become better at mobilizing to protect our democracy, the risk is rising that we will indeed lose it. If concentrated economic power continues to gain sway over our politics and if our electorates are made to shrink further, then our democracy will become even less genuinely representative, with dwindling responsiveness to the bulk of its citizens. As for what comes next, those wealth-favoring political changes we have seen thus far—governments shrunk back and their broadly public services and protections increasingly privatized or stripped away—will likely pale in comparison. As storms and droughts worsen and as the seas rise, governments will not likely vanish, but just how democratic they will be? Will they exist only to enable the rich—or others willing to ride roughshod over election results and laws—to gain or maintain power or simply to save themselves? To forestall such a future, those who care about sustaining democracy can't just assume that upcoming demographic changes will do the job for them. Instead, we all have to get to work.

NOTES

Introduction. The View from Stone Mountain

1. Grace Elizabeth Hale, "Granite Stopped Time: The Stone Mountain Memorial and the Representation of White Southern Identity," *Georgia Historical Quarterly* 82, no. 1 (1998): 22–44; Paul Stephen Hudson and Lora Pond Mirza, *Atlanta's Stone Mountain: A Multicultural History* (Charleston, S.C.: History, 2011); David B. Freeman, *Carved in Stone: The History of Stone Mountain* (Macon, Ga.: Mercer University Press, 1997).

2. William Faulkner, *Requiem for a Nun* (London: Chatto and Windus, 1919), 85.

3. V. O. Key and Alexander Heard, *Southern Politics in State and Nation* (1949; repr. Knoxville: University of Tennessee Press, 1984); Edward L. Gibson, *Boundary Control: Subnational Authoritarianism in Federal Democracies* (Cambridge: Cambridge University Press, 2013), Kindle; Robert Mickey, *Paths Out of Dixie: The Democratization of Authoritarian Enclaves in America's Deep South, 1944–1972* (Princeton, N.J.: Princeton University Press, 2015).

4. In other words, my working definition of democracy here is not just "procedural" but also "substantive" and not just "representative" but also "deliberative." Representatives of the interdisciplinary literature on which this working definition draws include James E. Bell and Lynn A. Staeheli, "Discourses of Diffusion and Democratization," *Political Geography* 20, no. 2 (2001): 175–95; Carole Pateman, "APSA Presidential Address: Participatory Democracy Revisited," *Perspectives on Politics* 10, no. 1 (2012): 7–19; Laurence Piper, "How Participatory Institutions Deepen Democracy through Broadening Representation: The Case of Participatory Budgeting in Porto Alegre, Brazil," *Theoria: A Journal of Social and Political Theory* 61, no. 139 (2014): 50–67; John S. Dryzek, *Democracy in Capitalist Times: Ideals, Limits, and Struggles* (New York: Oxford University Press, 1997); Quan Li and Rafael Reuveny, "Democracy and Environmental Degradation," *International Studies Quarterly* 50, no. 4 (2006): 935–56; and Arthur Lupia and Anne Norton, "Inequality Is Always in the Room: Language and Power in Deliberative Democracy," *Daedalus* 146, no. 3 (2017): 64–76.

5. Sven Beckert and Seth Rockman, eds., *Slavery's Capitalism: A New History of American Economic Development* (Philadelphia: University of Pennsylvania Press, 2016); Alan L. Olmstead and Paul W. Rhode, "Cotton, Slavery, and the New History of Capitalism," *Explorations in Economic History* 67 (January 2018): 1–17, https://doi.org/10.1016/j.eeh.2017.12.002; "Interchange: The History of Capitalism," *Journal of American History* 101, no. 2 (2014): 503–36.

6. C. Vann Woodward, *The Burden of Southern History* (1960; repr. Baton Rouge: Louisiana State University Press, 2008), 17.

7. Paul Krugman, "Wages, Wealth and Politics," *New York Times*, August 18, 2006, sec. Opinion, https://www.nytimes.com/2006/08/18/opinion/18krugman.html; Krugman, *The Conscience of a Liberal* (New York: Norton, 2007); Thomas Piketty and Emmanuel Saez, "Income Inequality in the United States, 1913–1998," *Quarterly Journal of Economics* 118, no. 1–39 (February 2003): 1–39; Claudia Goldin and Robert A. Margo, "The Great Compression: The Wage Structure in the United States at Mid-century," *Quarterly Journal of Economics* 107, no. 1 (1992): 1–34, https://doi.org/10.2307/2118322; Timothy Noah, *The Great Divergence: America's Growing Inequality Crisis and What We Can Do about It* (New York: Bloomsbury, 2012).

8. Jennifer Rittenhouse and Jason Morgan Ward, "From the Great Depression to the 'End of Southern History,'" in *Reinterpreting Southern Histories: Essays in Historiography*, ed. Craig Thompson Friend and Lorri Glover (Baton Rouge: Louisiana State University Press, 2020), 364; Dennis Doyle and Marko Maunula, "The South in Global and Transnational Contexts," in Thompson Friend and Glover, *Reinterpreting Southern Histories*, 385–414. The growing similarities between the U.S. South and West over the late twentieth century have led to arguments that the postwar South's trajectory needs to be understood within a more overarching regional concept, the Sunbelt, as involving this region's "steady integration into the mainstream of American life." Rittenhouse and Ward, "From the Great Depression," 384. See also Michelle Nickerson and Darren Dochuk, eds., *Sunbelt Rising: The Politics of Space, Place, and Region* (Philadelphia: University of Pennsylvania Press, 2011).

9. Ira Katznelson, *Fear Itself: The New Deal and the Origins of Our Time* (New York: Liveright, 2013); Mickey, *Paths Out of Dixie*.

10. Jefferson Cowie, *The Great Exception: The New Deal and the Limits of American Politics* (Princeton, N.J.: Princeton University Press, 2016); Jefferson Cowie and Nick Salvatore, "The Long Exception: Rethinking the Place of the New Deal in American History," *International Labor and Working-Class History*, no. 74 (2008): 3–32; Lizabeth Cohen, *A Consumers' Republic: The Politics of Mass Consumption in Postwar America* (New York: Vintage, 2003).

11. Kevin M. Kruse, *White Flight: Atlanta and the Making of Modern Conservatism* (Princeton, N.J.: Princeton University Press, 2007); Matthew D. Lassiter and Joseph Crespino, eds., *The Myth of Southern Exceptionalism* (New York: Oxford University Press, 2010); Matthew D. Lassiter, *The Silent Majority: Suburban Politics in the Sunbelt South* (Princeton, N.J.: Princeton University Press, 2006).

12. Lassiter and Crespino, *Myth of Southern Exceptionalism*.

13. Clarence N. Stone, *Regime Politics: Governing Atlanta, 1946–1988* (Lawrence: University Press of Kansas, 1989).

14. Ronald H. Bayor, *Race and the Shaping of Twentieth-Century Atlanta*, rev. ed. (Chapel Hill: University of North Carolina Press, 2000); Tomiko Brown-Nagin, *Courage to Dissent: Atlanta and the Long History of the Civil Rights Movement* (New York: Oxford University Press, 2011); Alton Hornsby, *Black Power in Dixie: A Political History of African Americans in Atlanta* (Gainesville: University Press of Florida, 2009); LeeAnn Lands, *The Culture of Property; Race, Class, and Housing Landscapes in Atlanta, 1880–1950* (Athens: University of Georgia Press, 2011); Kruse, *White Flight*; Lassiter, *Silent Majority*; Andrew Wiese, *Places of Their Own: African American Suburbanization in the Twentieth Century* (Chicago: University Of Chicago Press, 2005).

15. Liz Cohen stretches her "citizen consumers" to fit the collective aspirations emerging in such places, especially Blacks pushing for fuller access to markets and other public life.

Yet she portrays the shift from buying to owning, especially of homes, in a more sinister light, as mainly giving rise to homogenous neighborhoods, racial defensiveness, and a narrowed, localistic conception of the "public good." *Consumers' Republic*, 190, 228.

16. To probe just what citizenship projects did impel Atlanta and Georgia toward greater democracy, I've employed the broad economic abstractions of Jefferson Cowie and Liz Cohen as reference points, but in the main adopted that empirical, descriptive approach suggested by John Clarke, Kathleen Coll, and others. This book treats citizenship itself as a terrain of historical contest. More like Kyle Shelton, who coined the notion of "infrastructural citizenship" to capture challenges to postwar transportation planning in Houston, I start by categorizing those "divergent views of citizenship, voiced by differently situated subjects, in [the] particular context" of postwar Atlanta. Cowie, *Great Exception*; Lizabeth Cohen, *A Consumer's Republic: The Politics of Mass Consumption in Postwar America* (New York: Vintage Books, 2003); John Clarke et al., "Recentering Citizenship," in *Disputing Citizenship* (Bristol: Bristol University Press, 2014), 14, https://doi.org/10.2307/j.ctt9qgzqg.5; Kyle Shelton, *Power Moves: Transportation, Politics, and Development in Houston* (Austin: University of Texas Press, 2017), 5 ("infrastructural citizenship").

17. Andrew Hurley, *Environmental Inequalities: Class, Race, and Industrial Pollution in Gary, Indiana, 1945–1980* (Chapel Hill: University of North Carolina Press, 1995); Matthew Klingle, *Emerald City: An Environmental History of Seattle* (New Haven, Conn.: Yale University Press, 2008); Robert Gioielli, *Environmental Activism and the Urban Crisis: Baltimore, St. Louis, Chicago* (Philadelphia: Temple University Press, 2014); Ellen Griffith Spears, *Baptized in PCBs: Race, Pollution, and Justice in an All-American Town* (Chapel Hill: University of North Carolina Press, 2014).

18. Yet beyond the immense scrutiny of voting, this literature offers relatively little explicit analysis of activists' claims about citizenship. A notable exception, by Randolph Hohle, emphasizes mainly the performative contrasts between direct action and Black power activism, more so than any broader inclinations they shared. *Black Citizenship and Authenticity in the Civil Rights Movement* (New York: Routledge, 2013).

19. Tom Bottomore and T. H. Marshall, *Citizenship and Social Class* (London: Pluto, 1987); Michael Lister, "'Marshall-ing' Social and Political Citizenship: Towards a Unified Conception of Citizenship," *Government and Opposition* 40, no. 4 (2005): 471–91.

20. Marjorie Sun, "Environmental Awakening in the Soviet Union," *Science* 241, no. 4869 (1988): 1033–35; Mike Bowker and Antje Grebner, "The Referendum on the Construction of a Nuclear Heating Plant in Voronezh in 1990: An Example of Grassroots Democracy in the Soviet Union," *Slavonic and East European Review* 85, no. 3 (2007): 543–59; Jordi Díez, "The Rise and Fall of Mexico's Green Movement," *Revista Europea de Estudios Latinoamericanos y del Caribe / European Review of Latin American and Caribbean Studies*, no. 85 (2008): 81–99.

21. Jefferey M. Sellers, Anders Lidström, and Yooil Bae, *Multilevel Democracy: How Local Institutions and Civil Society Shape the Modern State* (Cambridge: Cambridge University Press, 2020), https://doi.org/10.1017/9781108672337.

22. I thereby define "environmental politics" with a similar breadth to that looser definition of "environmentalism" employed by many of my colleagues.

23. Samuel P. Hays, *Beauty, Health, and Permanence: Environmental Politics in the United States, 1955–1985* (New York: Cambridge University Press, 1989).

24. Gibson, *Boundary Control*; Mickey, *Paths Out of Dixie*.

25. Stone, *Regime Politics*.

26. Joel Garreau, *Edge City: Life on the New Frontier* (New York: Anchor, 1992); David

Goldberg, "Survey: Metro Area Tops in Urban Sprawl," *Atlanta Journal-Constitution*, September 10, 1998, sec. B; Robert Bullard, Glenn S. Johnson, and Angel O. Torres, eds., *Sprawl City: Race, Politics, and Planning in Atlanta* (Washington, D.C.: Island, 2000); Center on Urban and Metropolitan Policy, *Moving beyond Sprawl: The Challenge for Metropolitan Atlanta* (Washington, D.C.: Brookings Institution, 2000).

27. David L. Sjoquist, ed., *The Atlanta Paradox* (New York: Sage Foundation, 2000), 1 ("Atlanta paradox").

28. Alan Berube, "All Cities Are Not Created Unequal," Brookings Institution, February 2014, http://www.brookings.edu/research/papers/2014/02/cities-unequal-berube; Rebecca Burns, "Atlanta: Highest Rate of Income Inequality in the U.S.," *Atlanta Magazine*, February 21, 2014, http://www.atlantamagazine.com/news-culture-articles/atlanta-highest-rate-of-income-inequality-in-the-us/; Raj Chetty, Nathanial Hendren, Patrick Kline, Emmanuel Saez, and Nicholas Turner, "Is the United States Still a Land of Opportunity? Recent Trends in Intergenerational Mobility," *Opportunity Insights* (blog), January 4, 2014, https://opportunityinsights.org/paper/recentintergenerationalmobility/.

29. Jacob S. Hacker and Paul Pierson, *Winner-Take-All Politics: How Washington Made the Rich Richer—and Turned Its Back on the Middle Class* (New York: Simon and Schuster, 2010).

CHAPTER 1. Countrified City

1. Martin Luther King Sr., *Daddy King: An Autobiography* (Boston: Beacon, 2017); Clayborne Carson and Ralph Luker, eds., introd. to *The Papers of Martin Luther King, Jr.*, vol. 1, *Called to Serve, January 1929–June 1951* (Berkeley: University of California Press; Martin Luther King, Jr., Research and Education Institute, 1992), https://kinginstitute.stanford.edu/sites/mlk/files/publications/vol1intro.pdf#page=10.

2. "Dr. Mackay Transferred," *Birmingham News*, October 22, 1934, 14 ("leading"); "Sketch of Rev. Mackay," *Atlanta Constitution*, December 2, 1934.

3. C. Vann Woodward, *Origins of the New South, 1877–1913*, rev. ed. (Baton Rouge: Louisiana State University Press, 1971); Gavin Wright, *Old South, New South: Revolutions in the Southern Economy since the Civil War* (Baton Rouge: Louisiana State University Press, 1997).

4. David L. Carlton and Peter A. Coclanis, *The South, the Nation, and the World: Perspectives on Southern Economic Development* (Charlottesville: University of Virginia Press, 2003), 100 ("dead weight").

5. David R. Goldfield, *Cotton Fields and Skyscrapers: Southern City and Region* (Baltimore: Johns Hopkins University Press, 1989).

6. Andy Ambrose, "Atlanta," *New Georgia Encyclopedia*, March 15, 2004, http://www.georgiaencyclopedia.org/articles/counties-cities-neighborhoods/atlanta.

7. Barton Shaw, "Henry W. Grady Heralds 'The New South,'" *Atlanta Historical Journal* 30, no. 2 (1986): 55–66. Atlanta was the fourth-largest city after New Orleans, Louisville, and Houston; see U.S. Bureau of the Census, *Fifteenth Census of the United States: Population*, vol. 1, *Number and Distribution of Inhabitants* (Washington, D.C.: Government Printing Office, 1931), 18–19.

8. William Cronon, *Nature's Metropolis: Chicago and the Great West* (New York: Norton, 1992); Andrew Needham, *Power Lines: Phoenix and the Making of the Modern Southwest* (Princeton, N.J.: Princeton University Press, 2014).

9. Sven Beckert, *Empire of Cotton: A Global History* (New York: Knopf, 2014), 393 ("Global South"), 395.

10. In 1930, 2,964 were employed in cotton and knitting mills and "other textile industries" in Atlanta versus 3,424 in Augusta, Georgia. U.S. Bureau of the Census, *Fifteenth Census of the United States: 1930; Population*, vol. 3, pt. 1, *Reports by States: Showing the Composition and Characteristics for Counties, Cities, and Townships; Georgia* (Washington, D.C.: Government Printing Office, 1930), 527. In 1919 Atlanta's percentage (17.4 percent) and number (17,222) of workers in manufacturing were dwarfed by Louisville's (32.1 percent; 36,008), Richmond's (32.2 percent; 25,661), and Birmingham's (25.6 percent; 20,260). U.S. Bureau of the Census, *Fourteenth Census of the United States Taken in the Year 1920*, vol. 3, *Population 1920: Composition and Characteristics of the Population by States; Occupations* (Washington, D.C.: Government Printing Office, 1920), table 19, pp. 132–240.

11. Wright, *Old South, New South*, 177; James C. Cobb, *The Selling of the South: The Southern Crusade for Industrial Development, 1936–1980* (Baton Rouge: Louisiana State University Press, 1982); James C. Cobb, *Industrialization and Southern Society, 1877–1984* (Lexington: University Press of Kentucky, 1984); Joshua L. Rosenbloom, *Looking for Work, Searching for Workers: American Labor Markets during Industrialization* (New York: Cambridge University Press, 2002).

12. By contrast, Toledo's share was 8.5 percent, Syracuse's 9.3 percent, and Minneapolis's was 10.4 percent. Calculated from U.S. Bureau of the Census, *Residential Financing: 1950 Census of Housing*, vol. 4 (Washington, D.C.: Government Printing Office, 1951), table 19, pp. 132–240. Also by 1919 nearly as many Atlantans performed clerical work in offices (14.4 percent) or were involved in trade (16.7 percent) or transportation (10.5 percent) as were employed in manufacturing (17.4 percent).

13. Wright, *Old South, New South*, 177.

14. Illiteracy in the Atlanta workforce was twice as high as in comparable nonsouthern cities, and by 1930 a larger share of Atlanta's school-age children had dropped out of school than in nearly any similarly sized city in the country. U.S. Bureau of the Census, *Fourteenth Census*, vol. 3; U.S. Bureau of the Census, *Twelfth Census of the United States, 1900: Census Reports; Population*, vol. 2, pt. 2 (Washington, D.C.: Government Printing Office, 1900).

15. King, *Daddy King*, 52 ("reading level").

16. At $919.14 per year in 1919, the average manufacturing wage of Atlantans was considerably lower than in Hartford ($1,197.13), Toledo ($1,267.83), Portland ($1,445.50), Birmingham ($1,152.33) and Houston ($1,054.94) and also lower than in Louisville ($966.03) and New Orleans ($923.21); U.S. Bureau of the Census, *Fourteenth Census of the United States Taken in the Year 1920*, vol. 9, *Manufactures, 1919, Reports for States, with Statistics for Principal Cities* (Washington, D.C.: Government Printing Office, 1923); Rosenbloom, *Looking for Work*, 128–30.

17. Tera Hunter, *To 'Joy My Freedom: Southern Black Women's Lives and Labors after the Civil War* (New York: Cambridge University Press, 1997); Clifford M. Kuhn, *Contesting the New South Order: The 1914–1915 Strike at Atlanta's Fulton Mills* (Chapel Hill: University of North Carolina Press, 2001); Mercer Griffin Evans, "The History of the Organized Labor Movement in the State of Georgia" (PhD diss., University of Chicago, 1929), 29, 43, 44 ("intense hostility").

18. "Strike Ended: All at Peace," *Atlanta Constitution*, August 8, 1897; "Brown Answers Labor Leaders," *Atlanta Constitution*, July 26, 1914, sec. B.

19. Ivan Allen Sr. wooed out-of-state investments by praising the "judgment and good sense" of local union leaders in allowing the entire city to become "open-shop," a pattern affirmed by a contemporary study of Georgia's unions that was more labor friendly. Ivan Allen, *Atlanta from the Ashes* (Atlanta: Ruralist, 1928), 81 ("judgment and good sense"); Evans, "History of the Organized Labor Movement," 48 ("open-shop").

20. Historians of the region's middle class, while illuminating its gender, social, and political dynamics, have had less to say about its relative dimensions. Don Doyle, *New Men, New Cities, New South: Atlanta, Nashville, Charleston, Mobile, 1860–1910* (Chapel Hill: University of North Carolina Press, 1990); Jonathan Daniel Wells, "Reconstructing the Southern Middle Class: Professional and Commercial Southerners after the Civil War," in *The Southern Middle Class in the Long Nineteenth Century*, ed. Jonathan Daniel Wells and Jennifer R. Green (Baton Rouge: Louisiana State University Press, 2011), 225–43; Glenda Elizabeth Gilmore, *Gender and Jim Crow: Women and the Politics of White Supremacy in North Carolina, 1896–1920*, 2nd ed. (Chapel Hill: University of North Carolina Press, 2019).

21. U.S. Bureau of the Census, *Fourteenth Census*, vol. 9 (on comparative pay in manufacturing by city), vol. 4 (on professional workforces by city); and for racial breakdowns, U.S. Bureau of the Census, *Fifteenth Census*, vol. 3, pt. 1, p. 527. The equivalently sized cities to which Atlanta was compared were Syracuse and Hartford in the Northeast; Toledo and Minneapolis in the central North; Denver and Portland in the West; and Birmingham, Charleston, Houston, Richmond, Louisville, Nashville, and New Orleans in the South.

22. U.S. Bureau of the Census, *Fourteenth Census*, vol. 9.

23. Joel I. Nelson and Jon Lorence, "Metropolitan Earnings Inequality and Service Sector Employment," *Social Forces* 67, no. 2 (1988): 492–511, https://doi.org/10.2307/2579192; Saskia Sassen, *The Global City: New York, London, Tokyo* 2nd ed. (Princeton, N.J.: Princeton University Press, 2001); Joseph E. Stiglitz, *The Price of Inequality: How Today's Divided Society Endangers Our Future* (New York: Norton, 2012).

24. By the mid-1920s its fire-insurance industry was "fourth place in importance . . . in the United States." "Atlanta Center of Insurance in Southern Region," *Atlanta Constitution*, June 14, 1928, sec. A. See also "A History of the Federal Reserve Bank of Atlanta, 1914–1989," Federal Reserve Bank of Atlanta, 1990, https://www.frbatlanta.org:443/about /publications/atlanta-fed-history/first-75-years/droning-through-the-roaring-twenties; U.S. Federal Reserve Bank Organization Committee, "Exhibits and Letters Submitted at Hearings . . . (Atlanta)," U.S. Federal Reserve Bank Organization Committee, 1914, https:// fraser.stlouisfed.org/files/docs/historical/nara/nara_rg082_e02_b2651_02.pdf; Allen, *Atlanta from the Ashes*, 34; "Atlanta Center of Insurance in Southern Region," *Atlanta Constitution*, June 14, 1928, sec. A.

25. This count itself likely underestimated just how concentrated the city's riches were, starting with the richest of all, Coca-Cola founder and former mayor Asa Candler. His realty business, formed after he had sold his beverage company, enjoyed a county assessment of just over $4 million, less than a fifth of its estimated $25 million value upon his death in 1929. "Asa G. Candler, Millionaire, Philanthropist and Civic Leader, Dies after Long Sickness," *Atlanta Constitution*, March 13, 1929.

26. Thomas Piketty, *Capital in the Twenty-First Century*, trans. Arthur Goldhammer (Cambridge, Mass.: Belknap, 2014), 260–62.

27. Among Blacks the three thousand households and businesses owning any property the county considered worth taxing, as reflected in local tax digests, comprised only a tiny fraction of its twenty-five thousand Black households counted in the 1930 census.

Fulton County, "Tax Digest 1930 for Fulton County," 1930, Tax Digest Collection, Georgia Archives, Morrow; U.S. Bureau of the Census, *Fifteenth Census of the United States, 1930*, vol. 4, *Population: Families; Reports by States, Giving Statistics for Families, Dwellings and Homes, by Counties, for Urban and Rural Areas and for Urban Places of 2,500 or More* (Washington, D.C.: Government Printing Office, 1933).

28. HOLC, "HOLC Residential Security Map of Minneapolis, Minn.," 1938, folder "Minneapolis, Minn.," box 124; HOLC, "HOLC Residential Security Map of Essex County, N.J.," 1938, folder "Essex County, N.J. Master Security Map and Area Descriptions, 2 of 2," box 46; HOLC, "HOLC Residential Security Map of Columbus, Ohio," 1938, folder "Columbus, Ohio Security Map and Area Descriptions #1," box 104, all in RG 195, Records of the Home Owners' Loan Corporation, National Archives, Bethesda, Md.

29. HOLC, "HOLC Residential Security Map of Birmingham, Alabama," 1938, folder "Birmingham, Alabama Security Map and Description," box 156, RG 195, Records of the Home Owners' Loan Corporation, National Archives.

30. Rick Beard, "Hurt's Deserted Village: Atlanta's Inman Park, 1885–1911," in *Olmsted South: Old South Critic/New South Planner*, ed. Dana White and Victor Kramer (Westport, Conn.: Greenwood, 1979), 195–222; Richard Eric Beard, "From Suburb to Defended Neighborhood: Change in Atlanta's Inman Park and Ansley Park, 1890–1980" (PhD diss., Emory University, 1981); Gayle E. Sanders, "Frederick Law Olmsted's Plan for Druid Hills," *Atlanta History: A Journal of Georgia and the South* 31, nos. 1–2 (1987): 39–47; Robert Hartle, *Atlanta's Druid Hills: A Brief History* (Charleston, S.C.: History, 2008); LeeAnn Lands, *The Culture of Property; Race, Class, and Housing Landscapes in Atlanta, 1880–1950* (Athens: University of Georgia Press, 2011), chap. 3, esp. 98.

31. "Mayor and Board Are Harmonized; Druid Hills Gets Water," *Atlanta Constitution*, June 25, 1908 (first dibs on water); "Our Parks!," *Atlanta Constitution*, July 4, 1923; "Ansley Parks Are Accepted," *Atlanta Constitution*, November 8, 1911; "Candler Park to Be Most Beautiful in All America According to Plans of City Engineers," *Atlanta Constitution*, January 7, 1923, sec. C; Clarence Nixon, "Women's Play Today to Open Public Links," *Atlanta Constitution*, April 9, 1926.

32. *The Negro American Family* (Atlanta: Atlanta University Press, 1908), 66; HOLC, "Best Negro Section in Atlanta D17," 1937, folder "Atlanta, Ga.," box 185, RG 195, Records of the Home Owners' Loan Corporation, National Archives; "Inequality among People Is Inhumanity among People," *Atlanta Independent*, January 26, 1928.

33. Beard, "Suburb to Defended Neighborhood"; Lands, *Culture of Property*; "The Park's Cool Spring," *Atlanta Constitution*, March 31, 1896; "The Board of Aldermen," *Atlanta Constitution*, March 21, 1896.

34. Board of Trade of London, *Cost of Living in American Towns* (London: His Majesty's Stationery Office, 1911), http://hdl.handle.net/2027/uc2.ark:/13960/t00z7641v, 57.

35. Kuhn, *Contesting the New South Order*, 72 ("aching shoulders").

36. Board of Trade of London, *Cost of Living*, 53–54 ("coloured men").

37. U.S. Bureau of the Census, "1900 Census Fulton County Enumeration District #39: Edgewood"; U.S. Bureau of the Census, "1900 Census Fulton County Enumeration District #34: Adamsville"; U.S. Bureau of the Census, "1900 Census Fulton County Enumeration District #36: Including East Point, College Park Town, Hapeville Town"; U.S. Bureau of the Census, "1900 Census Fulton County Enumeration District #30: Black Hall Including Oakland City Town"; U.S. Bureau of the Census, "1900 Census DeKalb County Enumeration District #14: Decatur Town," all in United States Federal Census, https://www.ancestry.com.

38. HOLC, "Buckhead Negro Area DI," 1937, folder "Atlanta, Ga.," box 185, RG 195, Records of the Home Owners' Loan Corporation, National Archives; Susan M. Conger, "Historic Bagley Park (Frankie Allen)," Heritage Preservation Program, Georgia State University, December 9, 2008, http://buckheadheritage.com/sites/default/files/Mt.%20 Olive,%20BagleyPark-FrankieAllen-CONGER%20REPORT.pdf.

39. HOLC, "Scottdale Mill Section and Ingleside," 1937, folder "Atlanta, Ga.," box 185, RG 195, Records of the Home Owners' Loan Corporation, National Archives.

40. Lisa Goff, *Shantytown, USA: Forgotten Landscapes of the Working Poor* (Cambridge, Mass.: Harvard University Press, 2016).

41. HOLC, "North Avenue to Edgewood Avenue, between Piedmont Avenue and Southern R. R. Belt Line D20," 1937, folder "Atlanta, Ga.," box 185, RG 195, Records of the Home Owners' Loan Corporation, National Archives.

42. Lands, *Culture of Property.*

43. United States Public Health Service, *Municipal Health Department Practice for the Year 1923: Based upon Surveys of the 100 Largest Cities in the United States,* bulletin (Washington, D.C.: Government Printing Office, 1926), 512.

44. HOLC, "Bellwood to Atlanta University, East of Ashby Street and West of Marietta Street," 1937, folder "Atlanta, Ga.," box 185, RG 195, Records of the Home Owners' Loan Corporation, National Archives; Kevin Moore, John Stuart, and Mabel Wilson, "Incubating Uncertainty: Anticipating Change in Vine City, Atlanta," ACSA, https://www.acsa-arch.org/chapter/incubating-uncertainty-anticipating-change-in-vine-city -atlanta/; Louie Delphia Davis Shivery, "The History of Organized Social Work among Atlanta Negroes, 1890–1935" (master's thesis, Atlanta University, 1936), https://radar.auctr .edu/islandora/object/cau.td%3A1936_shivery_louie_d_d/ , 76 ("slums, dumps, hovels").

45. See "Insurance Maps of Atlanta, Georgia," Digital Library of Georgia, 1899, https://dlg.usg.edu/record/dlg_sanb_atlanta-1899; for an example, see Lands, *Culture of Property,* 28.

46. City of Atlanta, *Charter and Ordinances of City of Atlanta* (Atlanta: City of Atlanta, 1910), 391; Clifford Kuhn, E. Bernard West, and Harlon Joye, *Living Atlanta: An Oral History of the City, 1914–1948* (Athens: University of Georgia Press, 1990), 3.

47. A. E. Hogan, "Says City No Place for Cows or Hogs," letter to the editor, *Atlanta Constitution,* April 28, 1925 ("pigpen").

48. United States Public Health Service, *Municipal Health Department Practice,* 512.

49. Stuart Galishoff, "Germs Know No Color Line: Black Health and Public Policy in Atlanta, 1900–1918," *Journal of the History of Medicine and Allied Sciences* 40, no. 1 (1985): 22–41.

50. W. N. Adkins, "Every Stream in County Polluted and Menace to the Health of Entire Community, Says Health Officer," *Atlanta Constitution,* August 7, 1932, sec. D; Louis Dublin, "Typhoid in the Large Cities of the United States," *American Journal of Public Health* 17, no. 6 (1927): 644; Louis Dublin, "Vital Statistics," *American Journal of Public Health* 14, no. 3 (1923): 263–65.

51. Harlan Paul Douglass, *The Suburban Trend (the Rise of Urban America)* (1925; repr. New York: Arno, 1970).

52. T. Lynn Smith, "Urban Growth and Urban Problems in Latin America," in *Population and Urbanization Problems of Latin America,* ed. Philip B. Taylor and Sam Schulman (Houston: Latin American Studies Committee, Office of International Affairs, University of Houston, 1971), 1–19; Colin Clarke, introd. to *Urban Population Growth and Migration*

in Latin America: Two Case Studies, ed. Bryan Roberts and Stella Lowder (Liverpool, UK: Centre for Latin-American Studies, University of Liverpool, 1970), 1–5; Arturo Calle, "La población de las 'Barriales Marginales,'" in *Problemas de urbanización en América Latina* (Friburgo, Switzerland: Oficina Internacionale de Investigaciones Sociales de FERES, 1963), 221–40.

53. United Nations Human Settlements Programme, *The Challenge of Slums: Global Report on Human Settlements, 2003* (New York: Routledge, 2003), 22.

54. Ralph McGill, "One Word More," *Atlanta Constitution*, October 26, 1939, 8 ("breeding"); McGill, "One Word More," *Atlanta Constitution*, April 23, 1940; "Low-Rent Homes Called Insurance for Democracy," *Atlanta Constitution*, October 19, 1939.

55. King, *Daddy King*, 7 ("say anything"), 48 ("uncreased"), 52 ("college educated"), 8 ("backward").

56. V. O. Key and Alexander Heard, *Southern Politics in State and Nation* (1949; repr. Knoxville: University of Tennessee Press, 1984).

57. Edward L. Gibson, *Boundary Control: Subnational Authoritarianism in Federal Democracies* (Cambridge: Cambridge University Press, 2013), Kindle; Gibson, "Politics of the Periphery: An Introduction to Subnational Authoritarianism and Democratization in Latin America," *Journal of Politics in Latin America* 2, no. 2 (2010): 3–12, https://doi.org /10.1177/1866802X1000200201; Robert Mickey, *Paths Out of Dixie: The Democratization of Authoritarian Enclaves in America's Deep South, 1944–1972* (Princeton, N.J.: Princeton University Press, 2015), 12.

58. William G. Cornelius, "The County Unit System of Georgia: Facts and Prospects," *Western Political Quarterly* 14, no. 4 (1961): 942–60, https://doi.org/10.2307/445093; Albert B. Saye, "Georgia's County Unit System of Election," *Journal of Politics* 12, no. 1 (1950): 93–106, https://doi.org/10.2307/2126089; Herman E. Talmadge, "Georgia's County Unit System, Fountainhead of Democratic Government," *Georgia Review* 5, no. 4 (1951): 411–22.

59. Tom Bottomore and T. H. Marshall, *Citizenship and Social Class* (London: Pluto, 1987), 172–73.

60. Eugene J. Watts, "Black Political Progress in Atlanta: 1868–1895," *Journal of Negro History* 59, no. 3 (1974): 268–86, https://doi.org/10.2307/2716767; Sarah Mercer Judson, "Building the New South City: African-American and White Clubwomen in Atlanta, 1895–1930" (PhD diss., New York University, 1997), 40 (1908 disenfranchisement); Michael Perman, *Struggle for Mastery: Disfranchisement in the South, 1888–1908* (Chapel Hill: University of North Carolina Press, 2003), esp. 293; Ronald H. Bayor, *Race and the Shaping of Twentieth-Century Atlanta*, rev. ed. (Chapel Hill: University of North Carolina Press, 2000).

61. C. Vann Woodward, *Tom Watson: Agrarian Rebel* (New York: Beehive, 1973), 340.

62. Laughlin McDonald, *A Voting Rights Odyssey: Black Enfranchisement in Georgia* (Cambridge: Cambridge University Press, 2003); J. Morgan Kousser, *The Shaping of Southern Politics: Suffrage Restriction and the Establishment of the One-Party South, 1880–1910* (New Haven, Conn.: Yale University Press, 1974); Perman, *Struggle for Mastery*; Cornelius, "County Unit System of Georgia"; Saye, "Georgia's County Unit System."

63. "Talmadge Asks Votes on Record While in Office," *Atlanta Constitution*, August 26, 1934; L. A. Farrell, "Talmadge Scoffs at Foes' Charge He Opposes FDR," *Atlanta Constitution*, August 16, 1934 ("ten penny," "real laborers").

64. William Anderson, *The Wild Man from Sugar Creek: The Political Career of Eugene Talmadge* (Baton Rouge: Louisiana State University Press, 1975); Pippa Holloway, *Other*

Souths: Diversity and Difference in the U.S. South, Reconstruction to Present (Athens: University of Georgia Press, 2008), 272; Joseph Shaplen, "Many Mills Open; 80,000 of Strikers Still Out South," *New York Times*, September 25, 1934.

65. Luke Greene, "Arnall 'Enters' Governor Race; Flays 'Tyrant,'" *Atlanta Constitution*, June 28, 1941; "Daily and Weekly Press of Georgia United in Condemning Dictatorship by Governor Talmadge," *Atlanta Constitution*, March 8, 1936, sec. K.

66. "Paid 23 Million on State Debts, Talmadge Says," *Atlanta Constitution*, August 2, 1942, sec. A; Sarah McCulloh Lemmon, "The Ideology of Eugene Talmadge," *Georgia Historical Quarterly* 38, no. 3 (1954): 226; Numan V. Bartley, *Creation of Modern Georgia* (Athens: University of Georgia Press, 1983), 189–90; Randall L. Patton, "A Southern Liberal and the Politics of Anti-colonialism: The Governorship of Ellis Arnall," *Georgia Historical Quarterly* 74, no. 4 (1990): 599–621.

67. John E. Allen, Gary M. Fink, and Merl E. Reed, "Eugene Talmadge and the Great Textile Strike in Georgia, September 1934," in *Essays in Southern Labor History: Selected Papers, Southern Labor History Conference, 1976* (Westport, Conn.: Greenwood, 1977), 224–43; Robert Preston Brooks, "Economic Progress and Taxes in Georgia," *Georgia Review* 6, no. 4 (1952): 381.

68. "Ku Klux Hosts to Talmadge and Hamilton," *Atlanta Constitution*, December 18, 1943.

69. "Abercrombie Urges More Health Funds," *Atlanta Constitution*, April 24, 1935.

70. Gibson, *Boundary Control*, locs. 1487, 1483, Kindle.

71. Ira Katznelson, *Fear Itself: The New Deal and the Origins of Our Time* (New York: Liveright, 2013).

72. Key and Heard, *Southern Politics*, 116.

73. Lemmon, "Ideology of Eugene Talmadge," 226; Bartley, *Creation of Modern Georgia*, 189–90; Patton, "Southern Liberal."

74. U.S. Bureau of the Census, *Census of Governments: State Finances, 1942*, vol. 1, *Individual State Reports: Georgia* (Washington, D.C.: Government Printing Office, 1943); U.S. Bureau of the Census, *Revised Summary of State Government Finances, 1942–1950* (Washington, D.C.: Government Printing Office, 1953).

75. M. L. St. John, "Harris-Made White Primary Bill Sails through House Committee," *Atlanta Constitution*, January 21, 1947; John Couric, "Georgia's House Must Figure Way to Raise Funds to Meet Expenses," *Atlanta Constitution*, February 23, 1947, sec. A; St. John, "Labor's Intentions and the Rev. Rabun," *Atlanta Constitution*, August 13, 1947 ("growing").

76. Lemmon, "Ideology of Eugene Talmadge," 228n6; Anderson, *Wild Man from Sugar Creek*; Eugene Talmadge, "Text of Talmadge's Speech Flaying Roosevelt, New Deal," *Atlanta Constitution*, December 7, 1935.

77. Carson and Luker, introd. to *Papers of Martin Luther King, Jr.*; King, *Daddy King*, 97.

78. "Sordid Flog Drama Played at Hearing," *Atlanta Constitution*, November 26, 1941 ("despicable," "mixed up"); Luke Greene, "Six Floggers' Clemency Plea Is Declined," *Atlanta Constitution*, December 2, 1941 ("sympathy"); Willard Cope, "Klan Operations Bared; Deputy Is Exalted Cyclops," *Atlanta Constitution*, March 14, 1940; "Three Deputies in Sheriff's Choir Named in Probe," *Atlanta Constitution*, March 14, 1940.

79. Bayor, *Shaping of Twentieth-Century Atlanta*, 20–38.

80. Floyd Hunter, *Community Power Structure: A Study of Decision Makers* (Chapel Hill: University of North Carolina Press, 1953); Harold H. Martin, *William Berry Harts-*

field: Mayor of Atlanta (Athens: University of Georgia Press, 2010); Bayor, *Shaping of Twentieth-Century Atlanta;* Key and Heard, *Southern Politics,* 116 ("safe").

81. Calvin Kytle and James A. Mackay, *Who Runs Georgia?* (1947; repr. Athens: University of Georgia Press, 1998) (on Talmadgist leaders dominating anti-Talmadgist counties like Fulton and DeKalb, see pages 43 and 177); "Mr. Thompson Shows Courage," *Atlanta Constitution,* March 28, 1947 ("expressed will"); M. L. St. John, "Veto Eliminates White Primary Bill; Thompson Pen Outlaws Closed Shop," *Atlanta Constitution,* March 28, 1947; "Our Transportation Tie-Up," *Journal of Labor,* May 6, 1949. Atlanta, still the stronghold of Georgia's labor movement, harbored an estimated fifty thousand union members around this time—about the same as the total votes cast in Fulton County during 1948—but union members probably compose only a small fraction of the 17 percent who actually turned out.

82. Larry Keating, *Atlanta: Race, Class and Urban Expansion* (Philadelphia: Temple University Press, 2001), 71–72; Martin, *William Berry Hartsfield,* 42.

83. Thomas Allen Scott, *Cobb County, Georgia, and the Origins of the Suburban South: A Twentieth-Century History* (Marietta, Ga.: Cobb Landmarks and Historical Society, 2003).

84. Kytle and Mackay, *Who Runs Georgia?,* 16 ("most influence").

85. Julius McCurdy, interview by Clifford Kuhn, November 21, 1988, http://digital collections.library.gsu.edu/cdm/ref/collection/ggdp/id/3515; Morris Shelton, *Mr. DeKalb* (Atlanta: Dickson's, 1971); Griffenhagen and Associates, *Report on the Governments of DeKalb County and the Municipalities Therein* (Decatur: Griffenhagen and Associates, 1954); DeKalb County Local Government Commission, "Final Report of the DeKalb County Local Government Commission," November 30, 1954, Local History Room, Decatur Public Library, Decatur, Ga.

86. Kevin M. Kruse, *White Flight: Atlanta and the Making of Modern Conservatism* (Princeton, N.J.: Princeton University Press, 2007).

87. Bill Kinney, "Rambunctious Bill Ward Helped Cobb and Smyrna Grow Up," *Marietta Daily Journal,* September 10, 1987, sec. A.

88. Wright, *Old South, New South,* 241, 264–65 ("transitional"); C. Vann Woodward, "The Search for Southern Identity," *Virginia Quarterly Review* 34, no. 3 (1958): 321–38. Building on C. Vann Woodward's declaration of a "bulldozer revolution" in the post–World War II South, historians of the Sunbelt synthesis have generally focused on the continuities between southern cities of the 1940s and 1950s and the 1960s and 1970s in ways that skip past its actual slowness in joining the national mainstream.

89. Anne O'Hare McCormick, "The Main Laboratory of the New Deal," *New York Times,* January 6, 1935, sec. SM.

90. Douglas L. Fleming, "The New Deal in Atlanta: A Review of the Major Programs," *Atlanta Historical Journal* 30, no. 1 (1986): 23–45; Frank Ruechel, "New Deal Public Housing, Urban Poverty, and Jim Crow: Techwood and University Homes in Atlanta," *Georgia Historical Quarterly* 81, no. 4 (1997): 915–37; Associated Press, "New Deal Pours $147,000,000 into Georgia in Year," *Atlanta Constitution,* November 24, 1938, sec. C.

91. Fleming, "New Deal in Atlanta"; Ruechel, "New Deal Public Housing"; Associated Press, "New Deal Pours."

92. Thomas W. Hanchett, *Sorting Out the New South City: Race, Class, and Urban Development in Charlotte, 1875–1975* (Chapel Hill: University of North Carolina Press, 2000).

93. David M. P. Freund, *Colored Property: State Policy and White Racial Politics in Suburban America* (Chicago: University of Chicago Press, 2010), Kindle, loc. 274; HOLC, "Explanation: Atlanta, Georgia," 1937, folder "Atlanta, Ga.," box 185, RG 195, Records of the Home Owners' Loan Corporation, National Archives ("well-planned").

94. HOLC, "Grant Park Section," 1937, folder "Atlanta, Ga."; HOLC, "Hancock Subdivision, Atkins Park, Western Edge of Druid Hills, and University Park," 1937, folder "Atlanta, Ga."; HOLC, "Mayfair (Outside City)," 1937, folder "Atlanta, Ga.," all in box 185, RG 195, Records of the Home Owners' Loan Corporation, National Archives.

95. HOLC, "Best Negro Section in Atlanta."

96. HOLC, "Negro Area of East Point," 1937; HOLC, "Two Negro Sections of College Park D31," 1937, both in folder "Atlanta, Ga.," box 185, RG 195, Records of the Home Owners' Loan Corporation, National Archives.

97. U.S. Bureau of the Census, *U.S. Census of Population, 1960: Supplemental Reports; Population of Standard Metropolitan Statistical Areas, 1960 and 1950* (Washington, D.C.: Government Printing Office, 1961), https://www2.census.gov/prod2/decennial/documents/41953654v1ch3.pdf; U.S. Bureau of the Census, *Census of Population, 1960*, vol. 1, Characteristics of the Population: Georgia (Washington, D.C.: Government Printing Office, 1961).

98. U.S. Bureau of the Census, *County and City Data Book, 1962* (Washington, D.C.: U.S. Department of Commerce, 1962).

99. Robert Lewis, "World War II Manufacturing and the Postwar Southern Economy," *Journal of Southern History* 73, no. 4 (2007): 837–66, https://doi.org/10.2307/27649570; Scott, *Origins of the Suburban South.*

100. Kenneth Cameron Wagner and Milton Dale Henson, *Industrial Development in Georgia since 1947: Progress, Problems, and Goals* (Atlanta: Georgia Institute of Technology, 1961), 32 ("electronics plant"); Margaret Pugh O'Mara, *Cities of Knowledge: Cold War Science and the Search for the Next Silicon Valley* (Princeton, N.J.: Princeton University Press, 2004), 208–9.

101. Richard S. Combes, "Aircraft Manufacturing in Georgia: A Case Study of Federal Industrial Investment," in *The Second Wave: Southern Industrialization from the 1940s to the 1970s*, ed. Philip Scranton (Athens: University of Georgia Press, 2001); Scott, *Origins of the Suburban South.*

102. American Federation of Labor, "Subsidizing the Migration of Industry: A Study from Labor's Point of View," 1955, American Federation of Labor Papers, Georgia State University Archives; Cobb, *Selling of the South.*

103. David Scott, interview by Christopher Sellers, Decatur, January 16, 2004; Douglas Flamming, *Creating the Modern South: Millhands and Managers in Dalton, Georgia, 1884–1984*, 2nd ed. (Chapel Hill: University of North Carolina Press, 2000); "Textile Union Demands Immediate Wage Boost for Southern Workers," *Wall Street Journal*, November 29, 1959; "Georgia Forests Now Yield $600 Million Each Year," *DeKalb New Era*, February 12, 1953, sec. A.

104. "Competition among Areas in Supplying Broilers to the New York Market," *Maine Agricultural Experiment Station Bulletin* 582 (1959): 5–6; Arthur Gannon, "The Georgia Broiler Industry," *Georgia Poultry Times*, May 18, 1956; Bernard Tobin and Henry Arthur, *Dynamics of the Broiler Industry* (Cambridge, Mass.: Harvard University Press, 1964); William Boyd, "Making Meat: Science, Technology and American Poultry Production," *Technology and Culture* 42 (2001): 631–64.

105. For varying angles on this pattern in Latin America, see Ruth C. Young, "The

Plantation Economy and Industrial Development in Latin America," *Economic Development and Cultural Change* 18, no. 3 (1970): 342–61; William C. Thiesenhusen, "A Suggested Policy for Industrial Reinvigoration in Latin America," *Journal of Latin American Studies* 4, no. 1 (1972): 85–104; Fernando Cardoso and Enzo Faletto, *Dependency and Development in Latin America*, trans. Mariory Urquidi (Berkeley: University of California Press, 1979).

106. Wright, *Old South, New South*, 238 ("abolition"), esp. 219–25.

107. Amy Collins, *Industrial Development in Georgia, 1958–1965* (Atlanta: Engineering Experiment Station, Georgia Institute of Technology, 1967), iii ("better proportion"); Wagner and Henson, *Industrial Development in Georgia*; Jim Montgomery, "$1.40 Wage Floor Starts Tomorrow," *Atlanta Constitution*, January 31, 1967; Cobb, *Selling of the South*.

108. Jim Montgomery, "Georgia Ranks 8th as Least Unionized," *Atlanta Constitution*, April 27, 1964.

109. Claudia Goldin and Robert A. Margo, "The Great Compression: The Wage Structure in the United States at Mid-century," *Quarterly Journal of Economics* 107, no. 1 (1992): 1–34, https://doi.org/10.2307/2118322; Thomas N. Maloney, "Wage Compression and Wage Inequality between Black and White Males in the United States, 1940–1960," *Journal of Economic History* 54, no. 2 (1994): 358–81; Chinhui Juhn, "Wage Inequality and Demand for Skill: Evidence from Five Decades," *Industrial and Labor Relations Review* 52, no. 3 (1999): 424–43, https://doi.org/10.2307/2525143; Carola Frydman and Raven Molloy, "Pay Cuts for the Boss: Executive Compensation in the 1940s," *Journal of Economic History* 72, no. 1 (2012): 225–51.

110. Data Integration Division, U.S. Bureau of the Census, "Income: Table 3. Per Capita Income by Metropolitan Statistical Areas (MSA): 1959, 1969, 1979, and 1989; U.S Census Bureau," accessed May 31, 2016, https://www.census.gov/hhes/www/income/data/historical/metro/msa3.html.

111. Figures on $10,000 and up were 12.5 percent versus 5.5 and 10 percent; all statistics from U.S. Bureau of the Census, *County and City Data Book, 1962* (Washington, D.C.: Government Printing Office, 1962).

112. Herbert Schaffer, *Factory Workers' Earnings in Selected Manufacturing Industries, June 1959*, Bureau of Labor Statistics, 1960, https://fraser.stlouisfed.org/scribd/?title_id=4551&filepath=/docs/publications/bls/bls_1275_1960.pdf; U.S. Bureau of the Census, "CPH-L-186: Poverty Rates by Metropolitan Statistical Areas (MSA): Selected Years 1959 to 1989," U.S. Bureau of the Census, 1990, https://www2.census.gov/programs-surveys/decennial/tables/cph/cph-l/cph-l-186.pdf.

113. Gavin Wright, *Sharing the Prize: The Economics of the Civil Rights Revolution in the American South* (Cambridge, Mass.: Belknap, 2013), 17; Herbert Hill, "Patterns of Employment Discrimination," *Crisis*, March 1962, 137–47.

114. "City and County Data Books Online," University of Virginia Library, accessed May 31, 2016, http://ccdb.lib.virginia.edu/ccdb/ccdb/index.

115. Piketty, *Capital in the Twenty-First Century*, 260 ("structural transformation").

116. U.S. Department of Labor, *Structure of the Residential Building Industry in 1949* (Washington, D.C.: Government Printing Office, 1949), 32, table 21; George Erwin, "Building Hits New Heights; Georgia Sees $475 Million," *Atlanta Constitution*, January 2, 1956.

117. "Lockheed Heights; Put Yourself in This Picture," ad, *Marietta Daily Journal*, March 19, 1951; "Shopping Center Just a Dream Four Years Ago," *Marietta Daily Journal*, 1955; "Belmont Hills; Before You Buy or Rent Anywhere!," ad, *Marietta Daily Journal*,

February 11, 1953; "Firm Pays $875,000 for 93 Homes," *Marietta Daily Journal*, August 30, 1955.

118. U.S. Bureau of the Census, *Residential Finance: 1960 Census of Housing*, vol. 5 (Washington, D.C.: Government Printing Office, 1961); U.S. Bureau of the Census, *Residential Financing*.

119. "LaVista Acres," ad, *Atlanta Constitution*, May 16, 1956; "Brookwood Subdivision," ad, *Marietta Daily Journal*, August 25, 1957; U.S. Bureau of the Census, *Census of Population 1960: Georgia; General Social and Economic Characteristics* (Washington, D.C.: Government Printing Office, 1963); Charles Schockely, interview by Christopher Sellers, North Druid Hills, Ga., March 23, 2001; Harold McNeel, interview by Christopher Sellers, Smyrna, Ga., February 5, 2013.

120. Kruse, *White Flight*.

121. Alan Patureau, "Collier Heights: Community Pride, Involvement Flourish in Suburb Split by I-10," *Atlanta Journal Constitution*, November 25, 1990, sec. H; Miriam Shropshire and William Shropshire, interview by Christopher Sellers, Atlanta, February 15, 2013.

122. Gussie Brown, interview by Christopher Sellers, Decatur, July 30, 2002; "Report on Scottdale," 1947, folder 2, box 224, Special Collections, Atlanta University Library, Atlanta. Confirming these accounts is a study undertaken by Black high school students out of downtown Atlanta, in 1947, which reported only 10 percent of local Black housing with running water and 35 percent with chickens.

123. Harry Mickelboro, interview by Christopher Sellers, Marietta, Ga., February 13, 2011; Dorothy Bacon, interview by Christopher Sellers, Smyrna, Ga., February 14, 2013; Andrew Wiese, *Places of Their Own: African American Suburbanization in the Twentieth Century* (Chicago: University of Chicago Press, 2005).

124. Goff, *Shantytown, USA*.

125. Clarke, introd. to *Urban Population Growth*; Philip Hauser, *Urbanization in Latin America*, Technology and Society (New York: Columbia University Press/UNESCO, 1961); Andrew Pearse, "Some Characteristics of Urbanization in the City of Rio de Janeiro," ed. Philip Hauser (New York: Columbia University Press/UNESCO, 1961), 191–205; Peter M. Ward, *Colonias and Public Policy in Texas and Mexico: Urbanization by Stealth* (Austin: University of Texas Press, 1999); Angela J. Donelson and Adrian X. Esparza, *The Colonias Reader: Economy, Housing and Public Health in U.S.-Mexico Border Colonias* (Tucson: University of Arizona Press, 2010).

126. Only on the "poor structural quality of housing" and "insecure residential status" did Buttermilk Bottom fare worse, in large part because its housing was older and almost entirely rented. For the three other criteria, Black Scottdale ranked worse. On clean water—UN's number-one criterion—whereas all Buttermilk Bottom residents had access to city water, a few Scottdalers still relied on their own wells and *only 6 percent on a public supply*. As for the second criterion, while no Bottom dwellings still relied on latrines or outhouses, nearly 40 percent of Black Scottdale still did. Based on data gathered from NHGIS: U.S. Bureau of the Census, *U.S. Censuses of Population and Housing, 1960: Final Report* PHS(1)-8; *Census Tracts: Atlanta, Ga. Standard Metropolitan Statistical Area* (Washington, D.C.: Government Printing Office, 1962), https://www2.census.gov/prod2/decennial/documents/41953654v1ch3.pdf; also United Nations Human Settlements Programme, *Challenge of Slums*, 12.

127. Scott E. Buchanan, "Three Governors Controversy," *New Georgia Encyclopedia*, December 11, 2015, http://www.georgiaencyclopedia.org/articles/government-politics/three-governors-controversy; Charles S. Bullock III, Scott E. Buchanan, and Ronald Keith

Gaddie, *The Three Governors Controversy: Skullduggery, Machinations, and the Decline of Georgia's Progressive Politics* (Athens: University of Georgia Press, 2015).

128. Dan Carter, foreword to Kytle and Mackay, *Who Runs Georgia?,*. xv ("battle").

129. Kytle and Mackay, *Who Runs Georgia?*, xix; Bayor, *Shaping of Twentieth-Century Atlanta*; Tomiko Brown-Nagin, *Courage to Dissent: Atlanta and the Long History of the Civil Rights Movement* (New York: Oxford University Press, 2011); Martin, *William Berry Hartsfield*.

130. Kytle and Mackay, *Who Runs Georgia?*, 80 ("essentially undemocratic"), 6 ("few executives"), 34 ("make their living"), 86 ("root evil"), 48 ("really healthy").

131. Kruse, *White Flight*.

132. Associated Press, "Vets Press War on Unit System," *Atlanta Constitution*, August 11, 1946, James Mackay Papers, Special Collections, Emory University, Decatur, Ga.

133. Kytle and Mackay, *Who Runs Georgia?*, 54.

134. Earl Black and Merle Black, *Politics and Society in the South* (Cambridge, Mass.: Harvard University Press, 1989).

CHAPTER 2. Civil Rights Citizenship and Its Environments

1. Brian McCammack, *Landscapes of Hope: Nature and the Great Migration in Chicago* (Cambridge, Mass.: Harvard University Press, 2017); Colin Fisher, *Urban Green: Nature, Recreation, and the Working Class in Industrial Chicago* (Chapel Hill: University of North Carolina Press, 2015).

2. Edward Hatfield, "Auburn Avenue (Sweet Auburn)," *New Georgia Encyclopedia*, June 2, 2006, http://www.georgiaencyclopedia.org/articles/counties-cities-neighborhoods /auburn-avenue-sweet-auburn; Georgina Hickey, "From Auburn Avenue to Buttermilk Bottom: Class and Community Dynamics among Atlanta's Blacks," in *Historical Roots of the Urban Crisis: African Americans in the Industrial City, 1900–1950*, ed. Henry Louis Taylor and Walter Hill (Abingdon: Taylor and Francis, 2000), 109–42; William L. Calloway, *The "Sweet Auburn Avenue" Business History, 1900–1988* ([Atlanta?]: Central Atlanta Progress, 1991); Emmet John Hughes, "The Negro's New Economic Life," *Fortune*, September 1956.

3. Albert Riley, "Blighted Areas Like These Stab at Atlanta's Heart," *Atlanta Constitution*, July 25, 1955 ("miserable hovels"); D. A. Crane, "The Black Heart of Atlanta," reprint from *Georgia Tech Engineer* 10, no. 4 (1949): 1 ("essentially").

4. Emanuella Grinberg, "Martin Luther King Jr.: Life Returns Slowly to Area," CNN, January 17, 2016, http://www.cnn.com/2016/01/16/living/king-historic-district-auburn-avenue-feat/index.html.

5. David Andrew Harmon, *Beneath the Image of the Civil Rights Movement and Race Relations: Atlanta, Georgia, 1946–1981* (Abingdon: Taylor and Francis, 1996), 20–24; Ronald H. Bayor, *Race and the Shaping of Twentieth-Century Atlanta*, rev. ed. (Chapel Hill: University of North Carolina Press, 2000), 20–25.

6. Tom Bottomore and T. H. Marshall, *Citizenship and Social Class* (London: Pluto, 1987), 172–73.

7. Felix L. Armfield, *Eugene Kinckle Jones: The National Urban League and Black Social Work, 1910–1940* (Urbana: University of Illinois Press, 2014); Guichard Parris and Lester Brooks, *Blacks in the City: A History of the National Urban League* (Boston: Little, Brown, 1971); Lorraine Nelson Spritzer and Jean B. Bergmark, *Grace Towns Hamilton and the Politics of Southern Change* (Athens: University of Georgia Press, 2009); Sharon Mitch-

ell Mullis, "The Public Career of Grace Towns Hamilton: A Citizen Too Busy to Hate" (PhD diss., Emory University, 1976); Lizabeth Cohen, *A Consumer's Republic: The Politics of Mass Consumption in Postwar America* (New York: Vintage Books, 2003), 8.

8. "Report 1911–1912," National League of Urban Conditions among Negroes, 1912, https://babel.hathitrust.org/cgi/pt?id=chi.14025482&view=1up&seq=11&skin=2021, 6 ("conditions"); Touré F. Reed, *Not Alms but Opportunity: The Urban League and the Politics of Racial Uplift, 1910–1950* (Chapel Hill: University of North Carolina Press, 2009), 43 ("concerns and apprehensions"); Parris and Brooks, *Blacks in the City*; Nancy J. Weiss, *The National Urban League, 1910–1940* (New York: Oxford University Press, 1974).

9. Jesse O. Thomas, first head of the league's southern field office, quoted in Alton Hornsby Jr. and Alexa Benson Henderson, *The Atlanta Urban League, 1920–2000* (Lewiston, N.Y.: Mellen, 2005), 2.

10. Hornsby and Henderson, *Atlanta Urban League*.

11. Hornsby and Henderson; Tomiko Brown-Nagin, *Courage to Dissent: Atlanta and the Long History of the Civil Rights Movement* (New York: Oxford University Press, 2011).

12. Hornsby and Henderson, *Atlanta Urban League*, 20–27, 38–39, 29; Spritzer and Bergmark, *Grace Towns Hamilton*, 39; Hornsby and Henderson, *Atlanta Urban League*, 45–49.

13. Jefferson Cowie, *The Great Exception: The New Deal and the Limits of American Politics* (Princeton, N.J.: Princeton University Press, 2016). 24; Robert D. Bullard, ed., *Unequal Protection: Environmental Justice and Communities of Color* (San Francisco: Sierra Club Books, 1994).

14. "Many Reforms in Government Urged by Group," *Atlanta Constitution*, December 15, 1940, sec. A; League of Women Voters, "Facts Published by Atlanta League of Women Voters; Mayor and Council," *Atlanta Constitution*, September 2, 1945, sec. B; Harold H. Martin, *William Berry Hartsfield: Mayor of Atlanta* (Athens: University of Georgia Press, 2010); Louis Williams, "William Berry Hartsfield: The Reluctant Accommodationist and the Politics of Race in Atlanta, 1900–1961" (PhD diss., [Emory University?], 1996); Louis Williams, "William Berry Hartsfield and Atlanta Politics: The Formative Years of an Urban Reformer, 1920–1936," *Georgia Historical Quarterly* 84, no. 4 (2000): 651–76.

15. Bayor, *Shaping of Twentieth-Century Atlanta*, 19–25, 24; Lorraine Nelson Spritzer, *The Belle of Ashby Street* (Athens: University of Georgia Press, 1982).

16. Floyd Hunter, *Community Power Structure: A Study of Decision Makers* (Chapel Hill: University of North Carolina Press, 1953), 126.

17. Spritzer and Bergmark, *Grace Towns Hamilton*, 137–38.

18. Kevin M. Kruse, *White Flight: Atlanta and the Making of Modern Conservatism* (Princeton, N.J.: Princeton University Press, 2007).

19. Rose Torrence, "[Typescript on Threat and Bombing of House]," March 8, 1949, folder 37, box 240, Atlanta Urban League Papers, Special Collections, Atlanta University Library, Atlanta.

20. Ortelus Shelman to William Hartsfield, August 29, 1961, folder 24, box 224, Atlanta University Library.

21. Matthew D. Lassiter, "De Jure/De Facto Segregation: The Long Shadow of a National Myth," in Lassiter and Crespino, *Myth of Southern Exceptionalism, 25–47*; Arnold R. Hirsch, *Making the Second Ghetto: Race and Housing in Chicago, 1940–1960* (Chicago: University of Chicago Press, 1998); Thomas J. Sugrue, *The Origins of the Urban Crisis* (Princeton, N.J.: Princeton University Press, 1996); Colin Gordon, *Mapping Decline: St.*

Louis and the Fate of the American City (Philadelphia: University of Pennsylvania Press, 2009); N. D. B. Connolly, *A World More Concrete: Real Estate and the Remaking of Jim Crow South Florida* (Chicago: University of Chicago Press, 2016).

22. West Side Mutual Development Committee, "Policy Proposal of the West Side Mutual Development Committee Regarding the Operation of the Real Estate Market with Respect to Race of Occupancy," August 20, 1958, folder 3, box 27, Atlanta University Library, esp., 3 ("orderly and harmonious," *"private real estate"*; emphasis in original), 1.

23. "NAACP Meet Hears Mayor, Others on Park Problems," *Atlanta Daily World*, Octo-ber 14, 1953.

24. "We Hail Mozley Park," *Atlanta Daily World*, April 10, 1954.

25. "Camp Fire Girls Day Camp Near Mozley Park," *Atlanta Daily World*, May 27, 1954; "Monday Opening Day for YWCA's Summer Program," *Atlanta Daily World*, June 5, 1954; "Stone Mountain," *Atlanta Daily World*, August 22, 1954; "Mozley Park Civic to See Film," *Atlanta Daily World*, October 20, 1955.

26. "We Hail Mozley Park."

27. "Urban League Report," *Atlanta Constitution*, April 7, 1954; Dupont Wright, "Negro Sub-division Proposed," *Atlanta Constitution*, April 12, 1949.

28. Robert Thompson, "Where Are People Going to Live?," May 31, 1949, folder 4, box 246, Atlanta University Library; Robert A. Thompson, Hylan Lewis, and Davis McEn-tire, "Atlanta and Birmingham: A Comparative Study in Negro Housing," in *Studies in Housing and Minority Groups*, ed. Nathan Glazer and Davis McEntire, Special Research Report to the Commission on Race and Housing (Berkeley: University of California Press, 1960), esp. 22–25 (for its housing initiatives); "Plan Defines Six Areas for Negro Housing," *Atlanta Constitution*, November 14, 1947.

29. Atlanta Metropolitan Planning Commission, *Up Ahead: A Regional Land Use Plan for Metropolitan Atlanta* (Atlanta: Atlanta Metropolitan Planning Commission, 1952), 88–90.

30. A. T. Walden, I. H. Burney, Mrs. G. T. Hamilton, R. A. Thompson, "Atlanta Urban League to Metropolitan Planning Commission," June 5, 1952, folder 2, box 32, Atlanta University Library.

31. "Plan Defines Six Areas."

32. Walden et al., "Atlanta Urban League."

33. Atlanta Urban League, "A Report on Parks and Recreational Facilities for Negroes in Atlanta, Georgia," 1954, folder 13, box 252, Atlanta University Center.

34. "Urban Leauge [*sic*] Report," *Atlanta Constitution*, April 7, 1954.

35. "Atlanta Urban League Information Data Sheet: Bush Mountain (Oakland City)," January 24, 1955, folder 5, box 224, Atlanta University Library.

36. Thompson, "Where Are People Going to Live?," 1 ("fewer houses"); R. A. Thomp-son to Housing Incorporated, c/o Morris Abram, January 9, 1950, folder 4, box 246, Atlanta University Library; Hornsby and Henderson, *Atlanta Urban League*, 57–60; Spritzer and Bergmark, *Grace Towns Hamilton*, 93–98; Andrew Wiese, *Places of Their Own: African American Suburbanization in the Twentieth Century* (Chicago: University Of Chicago Press, 2005).

37. Atlanta Urban League, "Outline of Tour: 'From Slums to Decent Neighborhoods and Responsible Citizenship,'" May 5, 1956, folder 57, box 240, Atlanta University Library.

38. Spritzer and Bergmark, *Grace Towns Hamilton*, 98.

39. Thompson, Lewis, and McEntire, "Atlanta and Birmingham," 35–36; *"Testimony*

of *Robert A. Thompson, Housing Secretary, Atlanta Urban League, before the United States Civil Rights Commission: "Housing"* (Atlanta: Government Printing Office, 1959), 523 (for slightly different figures).

40. U.S. Commission on Civil Rights, *Report of the United States Commission on Civil Rights* (Washington, D.C.: Government Printing Office, 1959), 511 ("beautiful"), 367 ("access").

41. Atlanta Urban League, "Outline of Tour."

42. For a recent sociological study of similar questions, see Kim Manturuk, Mark Lindblad, and Roberto G. Quercia, *A Place Called Home: The Social Dimensions of Home-ownership* (New York: Oxford University Press, 2017).

43. "Minutes of Atlanta Urban League Board of Directors," November 18, 1952, folder 5, box 1, Atlanta University Library, 2 ([summarizing a presentation by Hamilton]: "woefully neglected," community facilities").

44. "Atlanta Urban League Information Data Sheet: Avondale-Scottdale," June 20, 1952, folder 2, box 224; "Atlanta Urban League Information Data Sheet: Scott's Crossing," April 28, 1953, folder 11, box 225; Howard Roberts, "Atlanta Urban League Information Data Sheet: Johnstown (Buckhead)," June 20, 1952, folder 21, box 224; Roberts, "Atlanta Urban League Information Data Sheet: College Park," June 20, 1952, folder 9, box 224; "Atlanta Urban League Information Data Sheet: Hunter Hills," June 20, 1952, folder 20, box 224; Roberts, "Atlanta Urban League Information Data Sheet: Lamar Heights," June 20, 1952, folder 23, box 224, all in Atlanta University Library.

45. "Atlanta Urban League: Avondale-Scottdale," 4; "Atlanta Urban League: Scott's Crossing," 4.

46. Zettie Ables Blayton, "Community Organization Processes for Neighborhood Development Emphasizing Coordinating Efforts by the Atlanta Urban League" (master's thesis, Atlanta University, 1956).

47. Blayton; Brittany L. Hancock, "The Neighborhood Union and the Transformation of the West Side of Atlanta" (PhD diss., University of Houston, 2015); Louie Davis Shivery and Hugh H. Smythe, "The Neighborhood Union: A Survey of the Beginnings of Social Welfare Movements among Negroes in Atlanta," *Phylon Quarterly* 3, no. 2 (1942): 149–62, https://doi.org/10.2307/271522.

48. Blayton, "Community Organization Processes."

49. Council of Neighborhood Organizations, "Council Members," *Community Action for a Better Atlanta*, January 1958, folder 5, box 225, Atlanta University Library; Council of Neighborhood Organizations, "City Departments Very Cooperative," *Community Action for a Better Atlanta*, January 1958, folder 5, box 225, Atlanta University Library.

50. Thompson, Lewis, and McEntire, "Atlanta and Birmingham," 44; U.S. Commission on Civil Rights, *Report of the United States*.

51. Robert A. Thompson, "The Effect of Monetary and Fiscal Policy upon the Supply of Housing with Special Reference to Housing for Nonwhites," June 1, 1956, folder 1, box 27, Atlanta University Library.

52. "NAACP Meet Hears Mayor."

53. "Opening Statement of Jesse B. Blayton, Sr.: Civil Rights Commission's Hearing on Housing; Atlanta, Georgia," April 10, 1959, folder 2, box 27, Atlanta University Library, 1 (figures on public housing); "$10 Million Carver Community for Negroes Is Dedicated," *Atlanta Constitution*, April 27, 1953; U.S. Commission on Civil Rights, *Report of the United States*, 427.

54. Clarence N. Stone, *Regime Politics: Governing Atlanta, 1946–1988* (Lawrence: University Press of Kansas, 1989), 16.

55. Herman Hancock, "$135,561,500 20-Year Plan for Slum Clearance Offered," *Atlanta Constitution*, November 3, 1959; U.S. Bureau of the Census, *1957 Census of Governments: Government in Georgia*, vol. 6 (Washington D.C.: Government Printing Office, 1959), 48, table 39 Stone, Regime Politics, 16, 38 ("prime mover").

56. See Clarence N. Stone, *Economic Growth and Neighborhood Discontent: System Bias in the Urban Renewal Program of Atlanta* (Chapel Hill: University of North Carolina Press, 1976).

57. Stephen Wayne Grable, "From Private Realtor to Public Slum Fighter: The Transformation of the Career Identity of Charles F. Palmer" (PhD diss., Emory University, 1983); Frank Ruechel, "New Deal Public Housing, Urban Poverty, and Jim Crow: Techwood and University Homes in Atlanta," *Georgia Historical Quarterly* 81, no. 4 (1997): 915–37; Florence Fleming Corley, "Atlanta's Techwood and University Homes Projects: The Nation's Laboratory for Public Housing," *Atlanta History: A Journal of Georgia and the South* 31, no. 4 (1987): 17–36.

58. Ruechel, "New Deal Public Housing."

59. "City to Build 2,500 Housing Units as Part of Slum Clearance Plan," *Atlanta Constitution*, March 11, 1946 ("tear down," "gradually").

60. Stone, *Regime Politics*, 38–39.

61. "Club, Civic 'Envoys' to Make Slum Tour," *Atlanta Constitution*, August 10, 1947, sec. D; Katherine Barnwell, "Civic Workers Blast Slum Area Tour Sights," *Atlanta Constitution*, August 13, 1947.

62. Crane, "Black Heart of Atlanta," 1.

63. "At Least Our Slums Are Well-Publicized," *Atlanta Constitution*, December 17, 1955; Riley, "Blighted Areas Like These Stab."

64. Connolly, *World More Concrete*; Beryl Satter, *Family Properties: Race, Real Estate, and the Exploitation of Black Urban America* (New York: Metropolitan Books, 2010).

65. Jack Strong, "Dorough Wants to Ease Slum Areas," *Atlanta Constitution*, June 21, 1963.

66. Ed Hughes, "Growing Atlanta Slums Mean a Growing Menace," *Atlanta Constitution*, May 17, 1959, sec. C ("can't sleep").

67. "Slums May 'Choke' City, Douglass Says," *Atlanta Constitution*, August 9, 1956; Riley, "Blighted Areas Like These Stab"; Marion Gaines, "2 Aldermen to Press for Action to Force Clean-Up of Slums," *Atlanta Constitution*, May 29, 1959 ("deeply ashamed").

68. Phil Smith, "Safari of Four Guns Downs Dogs in Darkest Atlanta," *Atlanta Journal*, June 23, 1959.

69. Ed Hughes, "Children of the Slums," *Atlanta Journal*, May 22, 1959.

70. "Value of Housing Code Is in Its Enforcement," *Atlanta Constitution*, October 6, 1959.

71. Hughes, "Growing Atlanta Slums"; Marion Gaines, "Massell Wins over Evans," *Atlanta Constitution*, September 23, 1961; Ed Hughes, "Housing Code Unenforced," *Atlanta Journal*, May 19, 1959.

72. Ra Khabeer, interview, 1994, folder 3, "Entering BMB—Research—Interviews," REPOhistory Papers, Special Collections, Bobst Library, NYU University; Bo Emerson, "Uncovering Buttermilk Bottom," *Atlanta Journal Constitution*, September 14, 1995; John E. Williams, *Race, Place, and Politics: Urban Renewal, Redevelopment, and Stories of the*

Historic Buttermilk Bottom Neighborhood in Atlanta (Atlanta: Georgia State University, 2018).

73. "Table I: Geographic Distribution of Members of Ebenezer Baptist Church and the Nonwhite Population," April 1960, folder 20, box 247, Atlanta University Library.

74. "Citizen Participation," *Phylon Quarterly* 19, no. 1 (1958): 115–17.

75. Though "much discussion and exploration" was reported, questions arose in the minds of some participants about how "public" these conversations had been; that word was only penciled between "much" and "discussion" after the final report had been typed. Citizens Advisory Committee for Urban Renewal, "Fact Sheet for Atlanta's Urban Renewal Program," January 1960, clippings folder "Citizens Advisory Committee for Urban Renewal," Atlanta History Center, Atlanta; Malcolm Jones, "Year-End Review of Urban Renewal," December 31, 1958, folder 1, box 27, Atlanta University Library.

76. Ronald H. Bayor, "Urban Renewal, Public Housing, and the Racial Shaping of Atlanta," *Journal of Policy History* 1, no. 4 (1989): 419–39.

77. "3 Slums to Be Cleared Are Listed, Plans Given," *Atlanta Constitution*, April 27, 1956; Malcolm Jones, "The Workable Program of a Southern Metropolis, Atlanta, Georgia," *Phylon Quarterly* 19, no. 1 (1958): 60–63.

78. "3 Slums to Be Cleared."

79. Irene Valerie Holliman, "From 'Crackertown' to the 'ATL': Race, Urban Renewal, and the Re-making of Downtown Atlanta, 1945–2000" (PhD diss., University of Georgia, 2010).

80. Thompson, "Where Are People Going to Live?"

81. Thompson to Housing Incorporated, Atlanta University Library.

82. Robert Thompson, "Summary Analysis of Deficit in Negro Housing," 1958, folder 1, box 27, Atlanta University Library.

83. Edward Cartert, "Formation of a Community Organization in Santa Barbara Subdivision," August 1959, folder 2, box 27, Atlanta University Library; U.S. Commission on Civil Rights, *Report of the United States*, 487.

84. "Urban Planning," *Phylon Quarterly* 19, no. 1 (1958): 113, https://doi.org/10.2307/273027; Herman Hancock, "Urban Renewal Project Cited at Public Hearing," *Atlanta Constitution*, December 14, 1957.

85. "Citizen Participation," 115 ("democratic process"), 117.

86. "Testimony of Robert A. Thompson"; Robert Thompson, "Social Dynamics in Demographic Trends and the Housing of Minority Groups," *Phylon Quarterly* 19, no. 1 (1958): 31–43.

87. U.S. Commission on Civil Rights, *Report of the United States*; "Testimony of Robert A. Thompson"; "Opening Statement."

88. Robert A. Thompson, "The Construction of Public Housing Units in Census Tract F-18 (Buttermilk Bottom Area) and in Census Tract FC-20 (Thomasville Area)," January 28, 1958, folder 1, box 27, Atlanta University Library.

89. Cecil Alexander, "Letter of Cecil Alexander, Chair of Citizens Advisory Committee for Urban Renewal, to Mr. J. B. Blayton, President, Atlanta Urban League," December 14, 1959, folder 2, box 27, Atlanta University Library.

90. Thompson, "Construction of Public Housing Units."

91. City Planning Department and Housing Resources Committee, "A Review of Atlanta's Housing Program: Its Problems and Prospects" (Atlanta: City of Atlanta, October 1967).

92. "Meet Segregation Crisis with Facts, Mackay Urges," *Atlanta Constitution*, February 12, 1959; Jame Sheppard, "Rural Domination a 'Bitter Fruit' of Unit System," *Atlanta Constitution*, January 31, 1958; "Unit May Be in the Soup—But Judge Is in the Swim," *Atlanta Constitution*, April 28, 1962; Matthew D. Lassiter, *The Silent Majority: Suburban Politics in the Sunbelt South* (Princeton, N.J.: Princeton University Press, 2006).

93. Tom Bottomore and T. H. Marshall, *Citizenship and Social Class* (London: Pluto, 1987); Andrew Dobson, *Citizenship and the Environment* (New York: Oxford University Press, 2004). Marshall also wrote in a different rights tradition than the more recent spate of works on environmental and ecological citizenship: Andrew Dobson and Ángel Valencia Sáiz, *Citizenship, Environment, Economy* (New York: Routledge, 2013); John Barry, "Sustainability, Political Judgement and Citizenship: Connecting Green Politics and Democracy," in *Democracy and Green Political Thought: Sustainability, Rights and Citizenship*, ed. Brian Doherty and Marius de Geus (New York: Routledge, 1996), 115–31; John Barry, "Citizenship and (Un)Sustainability: A Green Republican Perspective," in *The Oxford Handbook of Environmental Ethics*, ed. Stephen Gardiner and Allen Thompson (New York: Oxford University Press, 2016), https://doi.org/10.1093/oxfordhb/9780199941339.001.0001.

94. Paul Jones, "Museum Expansion a Goal: Raffles, the Fernbank 'Coon, Swigs Pop," *Atlanta Constitution*, January 23, 1949; Yolande Gwin, "Fernbank: Nature's Museum," *Atlanta Constitution*, July 10, 1951; Emily Harrison, "South's First Children's Nature Museum Is Established Near Heart of Atlanta," *Atlanta Constitution*, August 24, 1941.

95. "Work Parties State to Put Fernbank in Good Shape," *Atlanta Journal*, May 16, 1953.

96. "Region Reports at Savannah GOS Meeting: Mss. No. 1219," October 9, 1964, Official Correspondence, Georgia Ornithological Society Papers, Special Collections, University of Georgia, Athens; "Affiliate: Atlanta Bird Club," May 26, 1964; Carl Buchheiser, "To Gladys Buckner," September 16, 1954, both in folder "Georgia," box B-246, National Audubon Papers, New York Public Library; Jean Rooney, "Trail Blazing," *Atlanta Constitution*, January 16, 1953; Bill Allen, "Izaak Walton Clubs Are Expected to Expand in Georgia This Year," *Atlanta Constitution*, January 11, 1954.

97. "Annual Meeting of the National Council," *Garden Gateways* 17 (1941): 3; Dorothy Nix, "Where a Flower Grows," *DeKalb New Era*, October 1, 1964.

98. "Expressway Beautification Complete as over 10,000 Trees Area Planted," *Metropolitan Herald*, February 29, 1956.

99. Christopher Sellers, *Crabgrass Crucible: Suburban Nature and the Rise of Environmentalism in Twentieth-Century America* (Chapel Hill: University of North Carolina Press, 2012).

100. While 45 percent of the eighty-eight certified in 1959 listed themselves as "general," some 30 percent mentioned evergreens as a specialty, and 17 percent boxwood; others listed included camellias, *Ilex* (holly), magnolias, and azaleas. Georgia Department of Agriculture, "List of Georgia Certified Nurseries, 1959–60."

101. Kytle and Mackay, *Who Runs Georgia?*, 86, 87, 48 ("really healthy").

102. "Neighbor DeKalb Is Looking Ahead," *Atlanta Constitution*, May 21, 1956; "Fleming Named to Direct DeKalb Parks Planning," *Atlanta Constitution*, November 11, 1953; "Development Plans Laid for Two DeKalb Parks," *Atlanta Constitution*, December 16, 1953.

103. "Neighbor DeKalb Is Looking Ahead"; DeKalb County Grand Jury, "Parks: DeKalb County Grand Jury Presentments," *Atlanta Constitution*, September 4, 1959;

Charles Turner, "He Calls for Parks for DeKalb Negroes," letter to the editor, *Atlanta Constitution*, September 27, 1960. The one "Negro park" was Tobie Grant on the edge of Scottdale, donated to the city by Grant herself, an African American woman who became relatively wealthy as a fortune teller.

104. Lassiter, *Silent Majority*.

105. Celestine Sibley, "Parks Swap Bill Voted as No-Mix Aid," *Atlanta Constitution*, February 15, 1956, 1, 9.

106. Frank Veale, "Georgia Parks: A Disgrace," *Atlanta Journal*, February 2, 1963, sec. D, 6.

107. Madeline P. Burbanck and Robert B. Platt, "Granite Outcrop Communities of Piedmont Plateau in Georgia," *Ecology* 45 (1964): 292–306; Jerry L. McCollum and David R. Ettman, Georgia's Protected Plants (Atlanta: Georgia Department of Natural Resources, 1977).

108. "State Purchase of Stone Mountain Still 'a Feat,'" *Atlanta Journal*, March 4, 1958.

109. "Griffin Hails Legislature, Lists Gains," *Atlanta Constitution*, February 21, 1958, 32; Scott E. Buchanan, *Some of the People Who Ate My Barbecue Didn't Vote for Me: The Life of Georgia Governor Marvin Griffin* (Nashville: Vanderbilt University Press, 2011).

110. Brown-Nagin, *Courage to Dissent*; Winston A. Grady-Willis, *Challenging U.S. Apartheid: Atlanta and Black Struggles for Human Rights, 1960–1977* (Durham, N.C.: Duke University Press, 2006).

111. U.S. Commission on Civil Rights, *Report of the United States*, 28 ("generation of young").

112. Rose Palmer, interview by Christopher Sellers, Niskey Lake, Ga., May 25, 2012.

113. Brown-Nagin, *Courage to Dissent*, 145–49; "Herschelle Sullivan Challenor, C'60, Played a Significant Role in the Atlanta Student Movement," *Our Stories*, Spelman College, March 2016, http://www.spelman.edu/about-us/news-and-events/our-stories/stories/2016/03/29/herschelle-sulivan-chanellor; "Celebrating Roslyn Pope, Ph.D., C'60, and the Alumnae of the Atlanta Student Movement," *Our Stories*, Spelman College, March 2016, http://www.spelman.edu/about-us/news-and-events/our-stories/stories/2016/03/29/roslyn-pope.

114. Brown-Nagin, *Courage to Dissent*, 146–47; Morris Dillard, interview by Carole Merritt, October 11, 2005, Voices across the Color Line, Atlanta History Center, http://album.atlantahistorycenter.com/cdm/ref/collection/VACL/id/41; U.S. Bureau of the Census, "Social and Economic Data for Persons in SMSAs," in *Standard Metropolitan Statistical Areas: 1960 Census of Population* (Washington, D.C.: Government Printing Office, 1960), esp. 600–601.

115. Willie Mays et al., "An Appeal for Human Rights," *Atlanta Constitution*, March 9, 1960; Jack L. Walker, "Protest and Negotiation: A Case Study of Negro Leadership in Atlanta, Georgia," *Midwest Journal of Political Science* 7, no. 2 (1963): 99–124, https://doi.org/10.2307/2108669.

116. Grady-Willis, *Challenging U.S. Apartheid*.

117. Among the expositions of these religious roots are Dennis C. Dickerson, "African American Religious Intellectuals and the Theological Foundations of the Civil Rights Movement, 1930–55," *Church History* 74, no. 2 (2005): 217–35; David L Chappell, *A Stone of Hope: Prophetic Religion and the Death of Jim Crow* (Chapel Hill: University of North Carolina Press, 2004).

118. Richard Ashworth, "17 Negro Students in Sitdown Bound over to Criminal Court," *Atlanta Constitution*, March 17, 1960.

119. Martin Luther King Jr., "Pilgrimage to Nonviolence," in *A Testament of Hope: The Essential Writings and Speeches of Martin Luther King Jr.*, ed. James M. Washington (New York: HarperCollins, 1986), 40. By 1964, however, King concluded a bit too summarily that "Negroes have found nonviolent direct action to be a miraculous method of curbing force"; soon it would famously rejected by SNCC leader Stokely Carmichael as inconsistent with true "Black power." King, *Testament of Hope*, 172 ("white Americans"), 173 ("miraculous method").

120. Lizabeth Cohen, *A Consumers' Republic: The Politics of Mass Consumption in Postwar America* (New York: Vintage, 2003).

121. Grady-Willis, *Challenging U.S. Apartheid*, 31 (King, quoted in Jack L. Walker, *Sit-Ins in Atlanta: A Study in the Negro Revolt* (New York: McGraw Hill, 1964), 91–92.

122. Grady-Willis, 46 ("far less concerned").

123. By 1962, two years after Grace Hamilton had resigned from its leadership, the AUL was "concentrating . . . on job development and employment." Bruce Galphin, "Quiet Progress Aim of Urban League," *Atlanta Constitution*, June 25, 1962; Hartwell Hooper and Susan Hooper, "The Scripto Strike: Martin Luther King's 'Valley of Problems': Atlanta, 1964–1965," *Atlanta History: A Journal of Georgia and the South* 43, no. 3 (1999): 5–34; G. S. Carlson, "Must Fight for Better Jobs, King Tells 250 Scripto Strikers," *Atlanta Constitution*, December 21, 1964.

124. Cowie, *Great Exception*.

125. Brown-Nagin, *Courage to Dissent*, 195–98.

126. Daniel Horowitz, *Betty Friedan and the Making of "The Feminine Mystique": The American Left, the Cold War, and Modern Feminism* (Amherst: University of Massachusetts Press, 2000); Sellers, *Crabgrass Crucible*.

127. Brown-Nagin, *Courage to Dissent*, 153.

128. On the SCLC's turn to natural settings for many deliberations, see Andrew Young, *An Easy Burden: The Civil Rights Movement and the Transformation of America* (Waco, Tex.: Baylor University Press, 2008), 145, 149, 189; Tomiko Brown-Nagin, "The Transformation of a Social Movement into Law? The SCLC and NAACP's Campaigns for Civil Rights Reconsidered in Light of the Educational Activism of Septima Clark," *Women's History Review* 8, no. 1 (1999): 81–137.

129. For recent examples of the latter see Thomas R. Dunlap and William Cronon, *Faith in Nature: Environmentalism as Religious Quest* (Seattle: University of Washington Press, 2005); John Gatta, *Making Nature Sacred: Literature, Religion, and Environment in America from the Puritans to the Present* (New York: Oxford University Press, 2004); Mark Fiege, *The Republic of Nature* (Seattle: University of Washington Press, 2012).

130. The best-known example is Martin Luther King, "American Rhetoric: Martin Luther King, Jr.—I've Been to the Mountaintop," *American Rhetoric*, April 3, 1968, http://www.americanrhetoric.com/speeches/mlkivebeentothemountaintop.htm; on mountain climbers, see Joseph E. Taylor, *Pilgrims of the Vertical: Yosemite Rock Climbers and Nature at Risk* (Cambridge, Mass.: Harvard University Press, 2010); for religious appropriation of mountains, see especially Jared Farmer, *On Zion's Mount: Mormons, Indians, and the American Landscape* (Cambridge, Mass.: Harvard University Press, 2010).

131. Martin Luther King Jr., "Our God Is Marching On," and King, "The Time for Freedom Has Come," both in King, *Testament of Hope*, 230, 164.

132. Martin Luther King Jr., "I Have a Dream," and Martin Luther King Jr., "The American Dream," both in *Negro History Bulletin* 31, no. 5 (1968): 16–17, 10–15.

CHAPTER 3. Water Woes and Democratization

1. Georgia Water Quality Council, "Minutes of the Regular Quarterly Meeting," October 3, 1963, folder 10/3/63, box 1, subgroup 7, series 8, DCO-2645, RG 26, Department of Public Health Archives, Georgia Archives, Morrow, 3 ("resulting in"); Majory Rutherford, "Atlanta, Fulton Warned on Pollution," *Atlanta Constitution*, October 4, 1963; Rutherford, "An 'Able Man, Big Job' Still True for Venable," *Atlanta Constitution*, September 30, 1963.

2. Gladwin Hill, "Atlanta Loses Ground in Fight on Pollution: Debris Overwhelms Attempts to Purify Drinking Supply $30 Million Project to Ease Problem Is Under Way," *New York Times*, March 2, 1965 ("gushing").

3. Marjorie Sun, "Environmental Awakening in the Soviet Union," *Science* 241, no. 4869 (1988): 1033–35; Mike Bowker and Antje Grebner, "The Referendum on the Construction of a Nuclear Heating Plant in Voronezh in 1990: An Example of Grassroots Democracy in the Soviet Union," *Slavonic and East European Review* 85, no. 3 (2007): 543–59; Jordi Díez, "The Rise and Fall of Mexico's Green Movement," *Revista Europea de Estudios Latinoamericanos y del Caribe / European Review of Latin American and Caribbean Studies*, no. 85 (2008): 81–99.

4. James F. Cook, *Carl Sanders: Spokesman of the New South* (Macon, Ga.: Mercer University Press, 1993); Carl Edward Sanders, oral history interview by Randy Sanders, March 28, 1989, Georgia Government Documentation Project Oral Histories, Special Collections, Georgia State University, Atlanta; V. O. Key and Alexander Heard, *Southern Politics in State and Nation* (1949; repr. Knoxville: University of Tennessee Press, 1984).

5. Julliane Dutra Medeiros et al., "Comparative Metagenome of a Stream Impacted by the Urbanization Phenomenon," *Brazilian Journal of Microbiology* 47, no. 4 (2016): 835–45, https://doi.org/10.1016/j.bjm.2016.06.011; Judy L. Meyer, Michael J. Paul, and W. Keith Taulbee, "Stream Ecosystem Function in Urbanizing Landscapes," *Journal of the North American Benthological Society* 24, no. 3 (2005): 602–12, https://doi.org/10.1899/04-021.1.

6. Derek B. Booth et al., "Global Perspectives on the Urban Stream Syndrome," *Freshwater Science* 35, no. 1 (2016): 412–20, https://doi.org/10.1086/684940; Christopher J. Walsh et al., "The Urban Stream Syndrome: Current Knowledge and the Search for a Cure," *Journal of the North American Benthological Society* 24, no. 3 (2005): 706–23, https://doi .org/10.1899/04-028.1.

7. Patrick N. Owens, "The Training of Sanitary Engineers and Other Environmental Health Specialists in Latin America," *American Journal of Public Health and the Nation's Health* 56, no. 11 (1966): 1948–53; N. R. E. Fendall, "Public Health and Urbanization in Africa," *Public Health Reports* 78, no. 7 (1963): 569–84.

8. Owens, "Training of Sanitary Engineers"; Fendall, "Public Health"

9. Annually, the volume for the city's streams averaged 1,632 seconds-feet, a unit capturing the directed speed of water flow (dividing distance traveled in feet by the number of seconds taken to travel them, based on the USGS 1951 estimate of 1.36 seconds-feet per square mile); whereas that for the Chattahoochee in the Atlanta area was between 1,408 and 4,780 seconds-feet averaged annually; figures and final calculation (based on an estimate of 1,200 square mile drainage area derived from the map in the appendix) are from R. W. Carter and S. M. Herrick, "Water Resources of the Atlanta Metropolitan Area," United States Geological Survey, November 1951, http://pubs.usgs.gov/circ/1951/0148 /report.pdf.

10. "The Water Question Settled," *Atlanta Constitution*, May 14, 1891.

11. "Feeling the Pulse, Scanning the Tongue of, and Probing Hygienic Conditions in

Atlanta," *Atlanta Constitution*, August 2, 1908; Booth et al., "Global Perspectives"; Günter Langergraber and Elke Muellegger, "Ecological Sanitation: A Way to Solve Global Sanitation Problems?," *Environment International* 31, no. 3 (2005): 433–44, https://doi.org/10.1016/j.envint.2004.08.006.

12. EPA, *Report to Congress: Impacts and Control of CSOs and SSOs* (Washington, D.C.: Government Printing Office, 2004); Cole Brokamp et al., "Combined Sewer Overflow Events and Childhood Emergency Department Visits: A Case-Crossover Study," *Science of The Total Environment* 607–608 (2017): 1180–87, https://doi.org/10.1016/j.scitotenv.2017.07.104.

13. On the bacterial composition of human feces, see David Christian Rose et al., "The Characterization of Feces and Urine: A Review of the Literature to Inform Advanced Treatment Technology," *Critical Reviews in Environmental Science and Technology* 45, no. 17 (2015): 1827–79, https://doi.org/10.1080/10643389.2014.1000761; Alison M. Stephen and John H. Cummings, "The Microbial Contribution to Human Faecal Mass," *Journal of Medical Microbiology* 13, no. 1 (1980): 45–56, https://doi.org/10.1099/00222615-13-1-45.

14. Zhiwei Liang et al., "Blackening and Odorization of Urban Rivers: A Biogeochemical Process," *FEMS Microbiology Ecology*, accessed February 12, 2018, https://doi.org/10.1093/femsec/fix180; Chen Song et al., "Key Blackening and Stinking Pollutants in Dongsha River of Beijing: Spatial Distribution and Source Identification," *Journal of Environmental Management* 200 (2017): 335–46, https://doi.org/10.1016/j.jenvman.2017.05.088.

15. Jechan Lee et al., "The Role of Algae and Cyanobacteria in the Production and Release of Odorants in Water," *Environmental Pollution* 227 (2017): 252–62, https://doi.org/10.1016/j.envpol.2017.04.058; Liang et al., "Blackening and Odorization."

16. Georgia Water Quality Control Board, *Peachtree Creek Water Quality Survey* (Atlanta: Georgia Water Quality Control Board, 1969), 24–29; Walsh et al., "Urban Stream Syndrome"; Booth et al., "Global Perspectives"; Larry R. Brown et al., "Urban Streams across the USA: Lessons Learned from Studies in 9 Metropolitan Areas," *Journal of the North American Benthological Society* 28, no. 4 (2009): 1051–69, https://doi.org/10.1899/08-153.1.

17. Alyssa Bell et al., "Factors Influencing the Persistence of Fecal Bacteroides in Stream Water," *Journal of Environmental Quality* 38, no. 3 (2009): 1224–32, https://doi.org/10.2134/jeq2008.0258; Aaron G. Wexler and Andrew L. Goodman, "An Insider's Perspective: Bacteroides as a Window into the Microbiome," *Nature Microbiology* 2 (2017): 17026, https://doi.org/10.1038/nmicrobiol.2017.26.

18. W. N. Adkins, "Every Stream in County Polluted and Menace to the Health of Entire Community, Says Health Officer," *Atlanta Constitution*, August 7, 1932, sec. D.

19. Herman Hancock, "Maze of Sewers Is Nearing Finish," *Atlanta Constitution*, December 11, 1939.

20. Van P. Enloe, "Mechanical Mixing of Digesting Sludge at Atlanta, Georgia," *Sewage and Industrial Wastes* 31, no. 6 (1959): 732–33; Gordon E. Mau, "Applying Recent Research to Design of Separate Sludge Digesters," *Sewage and Industrial Wastes* 28, no. 10 (1956): 1199–1210; Walter A. Sperry and Williard P. Pfeiffer, "Can Digester Recirculation Be Overdone?," *Sewage and Industrial Wastes* 25, no. 6 (1953): 741–44.

21. "Clayton Sewage Approved," *Atlanta Constitution*, January 26, 1938; Hancock, "Maze of Sewers."

22. "Clayton Sewage Approved"; Hancock, "Maze of Sewers."

23. Owens, "Training of Sanitary Engineers."

24. Department of Engineering and Environmental Sciences, *Community Water Supply and Sewage Disposal Programs in Latin America and Caribbean Countries*, Technical Series 5 (Washington, D.C.: Pan American Health Organization, 1969), 42, 51.

25. City of Atlanta Health Department, *Annual Report, 1947* (Atlanta: City of Atlanta Health Department, 1947), Fulton County Board of Health Archives, Director's Office, Fulton County Health Department, Atlanta, 16; "Infant Mortality Rate Here Third Highest in Nation," *Atlanta Constitution*, July 1, 1930.

26. "Typhoid Figures Indicate Georgia Leads All States," *Atlanta Constitution*, May 20, 1923.

27. City of Atlanta Health Department, *Annual Report, 1947*, 26.

28. "Minutes of Fulton County Board of Health," January 26, 1946; May 5, 1948, Minute Book 1940 to 1949, Fulton County Board of Health Archives.

29. U.S. Bureau of the Census, *Data for Small Areas: Housing; Sixteenth Census of the United States: 1940* (Washington, D.C.: Government Printing Office, 1943); U.S. Bureau of the Census, *Atlanta, Ga. Standard Metropolitan Statistical Area: U.S. Censuses of Population and Housing* (Washington, D.C.: Government Printing Office, 1962).

30. Adam Rome, *The Bulldozer in the Countryside: Suburban Sprawl and the Rise of American Environmentalism* (Cambridge: Cambridge University Press, 2001).

31. Susan M. Conger, "Historic Bagley Park (Frankie Allen)," Heritage Preservation Program, Georgia State University, December 9, 2008, http://buckheadheritage.com/sites /default/files/Mt.%20Olive,%20BagleyPark-FrankieAllen-CONGER%20REPORT.pdf.

32. Larry Irby, "Negro Houses Still Scarce in Marietta," *Marietta Daily Journal*, October 7, 1962, sec. B; "College Park Gets $2 Million for Its First Renewal Project," *Atlanta Constitution*, March 12, 1963; "U.S. Sets Aside $4.7 Million for East Point Slum Project," *Atlanta Constitution*, June 7, 1961.

33. "DeKalb Gets $1,707,000 for Renewal," *Atlanta Constitution*, November 24, 1965, sec. 10.

34. "$20,000 Sought in Sewerage Suits," *Atlanta Constitution*, August 18, 1949; Gordon Sawyer, "Decatur Sewerage Vote Is Seen after Petition," *Atlanta Constitution*, August 16, 1949.

35. "Marietta Disposal Plant Is Called Peril to Health," *Atlanta Constitution*, July 23, 1954.

36. Robert S. Ingols, "Textile Waste Problems," *Sewage and Industrial Wastes* 30, no. 10 (1958): 1273–77.

37. Christopher Sellers, *Crabgrass Crucible: Suburban Nature and the Rise of Environmentalism in Twentieth-Century America* (Chapel Hill: University of North Carolina Press, 2012).

38. "Injunction Threat Facing Smyrna over Plant Odors," *Marietta Daily Journal*, August 12, 1956.

39. M. Starr Nichols, "Uses and Abuses of Biochemical Oxygen Deman," *American Journal of Public Health* 29 (August 1939): 91–97; F. Wellington Gilcreas, "Standard Methods: Past, Present, Future," *American Journal of Public Health* 46 (June 1956): 754–62.

40. Roy W. McGee, "Report on the City of Atlanta Sanitary Sewage Interceptors," August 6, 1951; "Minutes of Fulton County Board of Health," July 31, 1952; May 28, 1953, all in Minute Book, 1950 to 1953, Fulton County Board of Health Archives.

41. "Minutes of Fulton County Board of Health," December 17, 1953, Minute Book, 1950 to 1953, Fulton County Board of Health Archives.

42. Herman Hancock, "Pollution of Creek Reported," *Atlanta Constitution*, October

28, 1953; "West Enders and City to Talk 'Odor Plaint': Adams Park Rally Will Air Report of Sewer Hazards," *Atlanta Constitution*, September 16, 1953, sec. D.

43. Albert Riley, "No New Housing Plans to Follow Harris Project," *Atlanta Constitution*, December 27, 1955.

44. Rome, *Bulldozer in the Countryside*.

45. Morris Shelton, *Mr. DeKalb* (Atlanta: Dickson's, 1971).

46. Thomas Allen Scott, *Cobb County, Georgia, and the Origins of the Suburban South: A Twentieth-Century History* (Marietta, Ga.: Cobb Landmarks and Historical Society, 2003), 241–44.

47. Frank Wells, "No Dearth of Water Seen Here," *Atlanta Constitution*, April 18, 1960.

48. On the symbiosis between Talmadgist and corporate leaders, see Calvin Kytle and James A. Mackay, *Who Runs Georgia?* (1947; repr. Athens: University of Georgia Press, 1998), especially 20–24; see also James C. Cobb, *The Selling of the South: The Southern Crusade for Industrial Development, 1936–1980* (Baton Rouge: Louisiana State University Press, 1982).

49. "Minutes of Fulton County Board of Health," December 17, 1953, Fulton County Board of Health Archives, 12 ("discourage").

50. Griffenhagen and Associates, *Report on the Governments of DeKalb County and the Municipalities Therein* (Decatur: Griffenhagen and Associates, 1954); DeKalb County Local Government Commission, "Final Report of the DeKalb County Local Government Commission," November 30, 1954, Local History Room, Decatur Public Library, Decatur, Ga.

51. Susan C. Stokes, "Political Clientelism," in *Oxford Handbook of Political Science*, July 7, 2011, https://doi.org/10.1093/oxfordhb/9780199604456.013.0031; Allen Hicken, "Clientelism," *Annual Review of Political Science* 14, no. 1 (2011): 289–310, https://doi.org/10.1146/annurev.polisci.031908.220508; Raju Parakkal, "Developing Countries, Political Clientelism, and Weymouth's 'Tug of War' Model of Antitrust Reform," *Antitrust Bulletin* 61, no. 2 (2016): 317–19, https://doi.org/10.1177/0003603X16644123.

52. Fulton County Health Department, *Annual Report of Fulton County Health Department, 1957* (Atlanta: Fulton County Health Department, 1958), 12.

53. Atlanta Region Metropolitan Planning Commission, *Water and Sewer Problems in Metropolitan Atlanta* (Atlanta: Atlanta Region Metropolitan Planning Commission, 1964), https://digitalcollections.library.gsu.edu/digital/collection/PlanATL/id/38167/, 36 ("careful supervision").

54. "County Assailed as 'Backing Down' on Sewer Bargain," *Atlanta Constitution*, September 26, 1937, sec. A; "Fulton Withdraws Support of Sewers," *Atlanta Constitution*, July 7, 1939; "$12,669,00 City Budget Okayed; Ends Fulton War," *Atlanta Constitution*, June 18, 1944; "Merging of Governments in DeKalb Asked by Jury," *Atlanta Constitution*, May 27, 1954; Burt Spender, "DeKalb Mayors Assail Jury's Merger Proposal," *Atlanta Constitution*, May 28, 1954.

55. Atlanta Metropolitan Planning Commission, *Up Ahead: A Regional Land Use Plan for Metropolitan Atlanta* (Atlanta: Atlanta Metropolitan Planning Commission, 1952), 85.

56. Christopher J. Manganiello, *Southern Water, Southern Power: How the Politics of Cheap Energy and Water Scarcity Shaped a Region* (Chapel Hill: University of North Carolina Press, 2015).

57. "Metropolitan Board Set Up to Guide 5-County Planning," *Atlanta Constitution*, July 6, 1960.

58. William Anderson, *The Wild Man from Sugar Creek: The Political Career of Eugene Talmadge* (Baton Rouge: Louisiana State University Press, 1975), 86 ("germs"). As early as

1941, however, the governor had at least come to believe in water pollution's deadly effects on fish. Apprised of a fish kill in the Chattahoochee just south of Atlanta, reported by two citizens of South Fulton's Fairburn, Talmadge ordered his commissioner of natural resources to "stop the pollution of Georgia streams which is killing fish in many sections." The commissioner then pleaded with the governor that there was "no special law covering the pollution of streams." Talmadge shot back that he simply should find one, since "we might as well abolish the fish and game department if we can't do anything about this." "Cravey Given Orders to Halt River Pollution," *Atlanta Constitution*, June 5, 1941. Nothing appears to have come of either idea, however. Water pollution remained a problem that meagerly funded state agencies for fish and game or health—not to mention the National Guard—were ill-equipped to solve.

59. Where Georgia's dealings with water pollution began but also ended by the time Ernest Vandiver, last leader of the Talmadge faction, left office, suggests that the recent characterizations of this and other pre-1965 regimes in the U.S. South as subnational authoritarianism need some qualifying. While fitting the undemocratic character especially of Georgia's electoral system, it does not very well accord with the postwar state government's oversight of rivers and streams. Edward L. Gibson, *Boundary Control: Subnational Authoritarianism in Federal Democracies* (Cambridge: Cambridge University Press, 2013), Kindle; Robert Mickey, *Paths Out of Dixie: The Democratization of Authoritarian Enclaves in America's Deep South, 1944–1972* (Princeton, N.J.: Princeton University Press, 2015).

60. "Herman Talmadge Signs Re-registration Bill," *Thomasville Times-Enterprise*, February 15, 1949; "Talmadge Orders Employees to Ink Anti-Red Oaths," *Thomasville Times-Enterprise*, March 4, 1949.

61. "Talmadge to Air 'Package' Tax Bill," *Atlanta Constitution*, October 3, 1950; Georgia Department of Public Health, *Georgia Water Pollution Control Comprehensive Report* (Atlanta: Georgia Department of Public Health, 1950); Division of Water Pollution Control, *Twenty-Five Years of Stream Pollution Control Progress in Georgia: A Review of Sewage Treatment Planning and Plant Construction; 1930–1955* (Atlanta: Georgia Department of Public Health, 1955).

62. Georgia Department of Public Health, *Annual Report, 1955* (Atlanta: Georgia Department of Public Health, 1955), 19, 20 ("location service").

63. "Paper Plant on Chattahoochee Appears Doomed," *Marietta Daily Journal*, July 1, 1951; Ben Miles, "Guarantees New Paper Mill to Emit No Offensive Odor," *Marietta Daily Journal*, July 8, 1951 ("more information," "until a nuisance").

64. Georgia Department of Health, *Clean Streams in Georgia* (Atlanta: Georgia Department of Public Health, 1952), 8.

65. Elizabeth W. Etheridge, *Sentinel for Health: A History of the Centers for Disease Control* (Berkeley: University of California Press, 1992).

66. Bill Kinney, "A-Plant to Add Further Permanency at Marietta," *Marietta Daily Journal*, April 10, 1956; B. F. Berens, "Lockheed Aircraft Corporation: Georgia Division; Minutes of Meeting Held with Dr. A. E. Gorman of the A.E.C. Reactor Development Division," April 9, 1956, folder "1956 Water Pollution Control," box RCB-27623 #70, Public Health—Directors Office—Directors Subject files, Georgia Archives, Morrow; Georgia Department of Public Health, *Annual Report, 1957* (Atlanta: Georgia Department of Public Health, 1957), 20.

67. Kytle and Mackay, *Who Runs Georgia?*, 34 ("make their living").

68. Herman Talmadge, "Former Gov. Talmadge Looks Back with Pride," *Atlanta Constitution*, January 12, 1955; Cobb, *Selling of the South*.

69. Herman Talmadge, "Text of Gov. Talmadge's Address at Opening of General Assembly," *Atlanta Constitution*, January 15, 1952; Herman Talmadge, "Here's Text Talmadge Talk before Joint Session," *Atlanta Constitution*, January 14, 1953; "Talmadge Seeks Tax Plan for 'Foreign' Corporations," *Atlanta Constitution*, December 14, 1949; "Nuisance Taxes Out on July 1," *Atlanta Constitution*, February 20, 1951.

70. "Gov. Talmadge Looks to Future," *Atlanta Constitution*, January 14, 1953.

71. "Minutes: Organization Meeting of the Georgia Water Law Revision Commission," April 20, 1955, folder "Georgia Water Law Revision Commission Minutes," box RCB-53449 #18B, 026-02-003, Public Health—Directors Office—Directors Subject files, Georgia Archives; "Water Revision Unit Studies 5 Laws," *Atlanta Constitution*, August 29, 1956 ("more action").

72. "Minutes: Georgia Water Law Revision Commission," September 30, 1955, folder "Georgia Water Law Revision Commission Minutes," box RCB-53449 #18B, 026-02-003, Public Health—Directors Office—Directors Subject files, Georgia Archives, 2.

73. Georgia Water Law Revision Commission, "Summary of Results of the Commission's Public Hearings Held in Georgia, April 4–June 25, 1956," August 24, 1956, folder "Georgia Water Law Revision Commission Minutes," box RCB-53449 #18B, 026-02-003, Public Health—Directors Office—Directors Subject files, Georgia Archives, 3 (list of hearings and numbers of participants).

74. "Georgia Conservationists Unite, Elect Fred Sturges President," *Atlanta Constitution*, October 22, 1955.

75. Dorothy Kremin, "State Facing Choice on Fish or Industry, Water Unit Told," *Atlanta Journal*, April 4, 1956, "array"; "Industry, Fish Interests Argue Pollution at Inquiry," *Atlanta Constitution*, April 5, 1956, "no rigid laws."

76. Georgia Water Law Revision Commission, "Summary of Results," 21–22.

77. "Minutes of Meeting of Georgia Water Quality Council," October 3, 1957, folder "1957 Minutes," box 1, subgroup 7, series 8, RG 26, Department of Public Health Archives, Georgia Archives, 5, 4 ("make recommendations").

78. Georgia Department of Public Health, "Water Quality Council Hears Comments on Water Law Inadequacies," press release, Water Quality Control Board minutes, January 9, 1964, folder "January 8, 1964," box 2, subgroup 7, series 8, RG 26, Department of Public Health Archives, Georgia Archives ("definitely exists").

79. "Minutes of Meeting of Georgia Water Quality Council," July 2, 1959, folder "July 2, 1959," subgroup 7, series 8, RG 26, Department of Public Health Archives, Georgia Archives, 3; Harry Gage, "Fishing and Boating Big Biz—And How!," *Atlanta Constitution*, May 28, 1959 (on Russell being executive director).

80. "Minutes of Meeting," October 1, 1959, Georgia Archives, 3, 5 ("sit in on").

81. Ronald Harvey Tebeest, "Water Pollution Control in Georgia as a Governmental Concern" (master's thesis, Emory University, 1965), 30–32; U.S. Study Commission, Southeast River Basins, *Plan for the Development of the Land and Water Resources of the Southeast River Basins* (Washington, D.C.: Government Printing Office, 1963).

82. Craig E. Colten, *Southern Waters: The Limits to Abundance* (Baton Rouge: Louisiana State University Press, 2014), esp. 182–84, 182 ("ad hoc").

83. "'Sportsmen' Censure of Lovell Tabled as Convention Ends," *Atlanta Constitution*, October 16, 1961; "Sportsmen Ask Specialist for Wildlife Helm," *Atlanta Constitution*, Sep-

tember 30, 1963; "Freeman to Head Sportsmen's League," *Atlanta Constitution*, October 22, 1957.

84. "Minutes of Meeting of Georgia Water Quality Council," October 5, 1961, folder "October 5, 1961," subgroup 7, series 8, RG 26, Department of Public Health Archives, Georgia Archives.

85. Federal Water Pollution Control Administration, *Proceedings: Conference in the Matter of Pollution of the Interstate Waters of the Chattahoochee River and Its Tributaries, from Atlanta, Georgia, to Fort Gaines, Georgia*, vol. 1, *Atlanta: July 14–15, 1966* (Washington, D.C.: Government Printing Office, 1966), 32.

86. Federal Water Pollution Control Administration, 32, 47 ("bacterial water quality"; emphasis added).

87. Surindra Suthar et al., "Water Quality Assessment of River Hindon at Ghaziabad, India: Impact of Industrial and Urban Wastewater," *Environmental Monitoring and Assessment* 165, nos. 1–4 (2010): 103–12, https://doi.org/10.1007/s10661-009-0930-9; Liang et al., "Blackening and Odorization."

88. Federal Water Pollution Control Administration, *Proceedings*, 1–45, 37 ("gastrointestinal").

89. Murray Stein, "Legislation on Water Pollution Control," *Public Health Reports* 79, no. 8 (1964): 699–706; "Minutes of Meeting of Georgia Water Quality Council," July 12, 1962, folder "July 12, 1962," subgroup 7, series 8, RG 26, Department of Public Health Archives, Georgia Archives, 15.

90. Jimmy Carter, *Turning Point* (New York: Crown, 1992).

91. "No Congo in Georgia—Griffin," *Augusta Chronicle Herald*, August 5, 1962, sec. A; "Griffin, Sanders Press Duel," *Augusta Chronicle*, May 22, 1962; "Griffin Says Bloc May Decide Race," *Augusta Chronicle*, August 26, 1962.

92. "A Dangerous Gamble," *Augusta Chronicle*, July 31, 1962; "Sanders Says King for Marvin," *Marietta Daily Journal*, August 5, 1962.

93. "'African King' Says Sanders of Griffin," *Augusta Chronicle Herald*, August 12, 1962, sec. A ("African," "loyalty")."

94. U.S. Study Commission, *Plan for the Development*; Tebeest, "Water Pollution Control."

95. "U.S. Sets Up River Pollution Survey," *Atlanta Constitution*, October 31, 1963.

96. Atlanta Region Metropolitan Planning Commission, "Water and Sewer Problems," 5 ("more serious"), 12 ("open sewer").

97. For instance, see earlier reports of MPC and media coverage such as Albert Riley, "'Crazy-Quilt' Duplication of Services Result of Atlanta, Fulton Expansion," *Atlanta Constitution*, November 27, 1949, sec. A; and Atlanta Region Metropolitan Planning Commission, "Water and Sewer Problems." The ARMPC's criticism of a "water-sewer lag" centered on the extra expenses and troubles entailed by putting in sewers later and said very little about the cesspool risks and pollution emphasized for other nonsouthern metro areas by Rome, *Bulldozer in the Countryside*.

98. Sellers, *Crabgrass Crucible*, on antipollution movements elsewhere; "Minutes of Meeting of Georgia Water Quality Council," April 5, 1962, folder "April 5, 1962," subgroup 7, series 8, RG 26, Department of Public Health Archives, Georgia Archives, 21; "[List of Attendees at GWQCB with Addresses and Affiliations]," 1965, folder "Minutes: GWQCB, 1965," box 5, RG 26, subgroup 7, series 62, Archives of Georgia State Department of Health, Secretary's Subject Files, 1966–1975, Environmental Protection Division Archives, Georgia Archives.

99. "Water Laws Weak, State Told," *Atlanta Constitution*, October 29, 1963; "Governor Backs Stiff Water Law; Hints Own Plan to Fight Pollution," *Atlanta Constitution*, November 3, 1963; "Pollution Control Is Need, Not Boards," *Atlanta Constitution*, November 5, 1963; "Increased Funds, Staff Urged for Pollution," *Atlanta Constitution*, December 4, 1963; William O. Smith, "Unit Sought to Cut Pollution of Water," *Atlanta Journal*, January 1, 1964; "Our Pollution Problems Will Get Worse Unless Positive Steps Are Taken Now," *Atlanta Constitution*, January 6, 1964.

100. [Rock Howard?], "Water Pollution Control Program in Georgia]," 1974, folder "1972 Environmental Protection Division," box 1, RCB 2144, Water Quality Control Board, Executive Secretary's Subject Files, 1966–75, Georgia Archives.

101. Bill Shipp, "State Calls Urgent Talks to Stem Chattahoochee Pollution," *Atlanta Constitution*, January 8, 1965; "Minutes of Meeting of Georgia Water Quality Control Board," April 1, 1965, folder "Minutes, April 1, 1965," subgroup 7, series 62, RG 26, Department of Public Health Archives, Georgia Archives, 3 ("abatement plans").

102. [Howard?], "Water Pollution Control Program."

103. "Minutes of Meeting of Georgia Water Quality Control Board," July 1, 1965, folder "Minutes, July 1, 1965," subgroup 7, series 62, RG 26, Department of Public Health Archives, Georgia Archives, 3 ("urgencies").

104. Achsah Nesmith, "Cleanup Date Set for Chattahoochee; Polluting Cities, Industries Get a Year to Submit Plans," *Atlanta Constitution*, July 16, 1966 ("out-of-date").

105. R. S. Howard, Executive Secretary of GWQCB, to W. C. Rowland, Smyrna, Georgia, September 14, 1967, folder "Governor's Office 1967," box 2, RG 26, subgroup 7, series 62, Archives of Georgia State Department of Health, Secretary's Subject Files, 1966–75, Georgia Archives.

106. "Lockheed Vows New Steps to Clean Up Industry Waste," *Atlanta Constitution*, November 7, 1969, sec. A ("chrome spill"); "Polluters Pressed on River Cleanup," *Atlanta Constitution*, October 16, 1969, sec. A.

107. R. S. Howard, Executive Secretary of GWQCB, to Harry R. Jones, December 10, 1969, folder "Governor's Office, 1967," box 2, RG 26, subgroup 7, series 62, Georgia Archives ("not obtained meaningful").

108. Wilhelm C. Hueper and William W. Payne, "Experimental Cancers in Rats Produced by Chromium Compounds and Their Significance to Industry and Public Health," *American Industrial Hygiene Association Journal* 20, no. 4 (1959): 274–80, https://doi.org/10.1080/00028895909343716; Thomas F. Mancuso and Wilhelm C. Hueper, "Occupational Cancer and Other Health Hazards in a Chromate Plant: A Medical Appraisal. I. Lung Cancers in Chromate Workers," *Industrial Medicine and Surgery* 20, no. 8 (1951): 358–63.

109. Edward T. Hall and Max W. Walker, "A Water Quality Study of Proctor Creek," typescript. Georgia Water Quality Control Board, November 10, 1967, http://web.iac.gatech.edu/AHCscans/access/ahc_CAR_015_012_006-access.pdf, 1 ("minimal").

110. Justin Nystrom, "Segregation's Last Stand: Lester Maddox and the Transformation of Atlanta," *Atlanta History: A Journal of Georgia and the South* 45, no. 2 (2001): 34–51; Bob Short, *Everything Is Pickrick* (Macon, Ga.: Mercer University Press, 1999); Lester Maddox, *Speaking Out: The Autobiography of Lester Garfield Maddox* (Garden City, N.Y.: Doubleday, 1975).

111. Lester Maddox, "For Immediate Release (Text of Remarks Prepared for Delivery by Governor Maddox for the Dedication of Joint Water Pollution Control System for the City of Cove Spring and the Georgia School of the Deaf)," April 19, 1968, folder "Gov-

ernor's Office 1968–69," box 2, RG 26, subgroup 7, series 62, Archives of Georgia State Department of Health, Secretary's Subject Files, 1966–75, Georgia Archives ("new industry, "cooperation is the key").

112. R. S. Howard, Executive Secretary of GWQCB, to Governor Carl Sanders, October 5, 1966, folder "Governor's Office, 1966," box 2, RG 26, subgroup 7, series 62, Georgia Archives.

113. R. S. Howard to Governor Maddox, June 4, 1968; R. S. Howard to John Love, Governor of Colorado, 1968, both in folder "Governor's Office, 1968–9," box 2, RG 26, subgroup 7, series 62, Georgia Archives.

114. Georgia Water Quality Control Board, *Peachtree Creek Water Quality Survey* (Atlanta: Georgia Water Quality Control Board, 1969) 28 ("grossly polluted," "almost always"), 48 ("green-white").

115. Hall and Walker, "Water Quality Study," 1.

116. For instance, see Tom Sherwood, "Williams Assails Half-Day Classes," *Atlanta Constitution*, May 5, 1967; and Hall and Walker, "Water Quality Study" ("We have received a number of complaints in this office pertaining to pollution in Proctor Creek," Rock Howard to Honorable Ivan Allen, November 17, 1967, included as frontispiece).

117. Hugh Nations and Leonard Ray Teel, "State's Pollution Problem Real but Solvable," *Atlanta Constitution*, May 3, 1970, sec. C; Hall and Walker, "Water Quality Study," 5 ("CLEAN"), 4 ("devoid").

118. Nations and Teel, "State's Pollution Problem."

119. Ivan Allen to R. S. Howard, December 19, 1967 ("major actions," "major temporary"); Robert Morris to Ivan Allen, November 22, 1967 ("long time"), both in Georgia Water Quality Control Board, http://web.iac.gatech.edu/AHCscans/access/ahc_CAR _015_012_006-access.pdf.

120. Joseph R. McConnell, *Impact of Urban Storm Runoff on Stream Quality Near Atlanta* (Cincinnati: U.S. Environmental Protection Agency, 1980), 36, table 4 (lead, arsenic, and chromium readings); Charles Seabrook, "Atlanta Sewer Deal: Antiquated System, and Efforts to Fix It, Were Found Wanting," *Atlanta Journal-Constitution*, April 14, 1998, sec. A; Kenneth Rollins, "A Special Life of Service," *Atlanta Constitution*, June 23, 1997; Charles Seabrook, "$2.5 Million Effort Making Proctor Creek Clean Again; Project in South Atlanta Will Take Year to Complete," *Atlanta Journal Constitution*, October 24, 1998, sec. D; U.S. Environmental Protection Agency, *Atlanta's Proctor Creek: Making a Visible Difference* (Atlanta: Environmental Protection Agency, Region 4, 2015).

121. "U.S. Warns 3 Cities to Halt Pollution," *New York Times*, December 11, 1970; "Chattahoochee Cleanup Ordered," *Marietta Daily Journal*, December 10, 1970, sec. A ("open sewer"); "Environment Administrator Hits 3 Cities," *Augusta Chronicle*, December 11, 1970, sec. D ("most serious").

122. R. S. Howard, Executive Secretary of GWQCB, to Governor Lester Maddox, September 2, 1970, folder "Governor's Office, 1970," box 2, RG 26, subgroup 7, series 62, Archives of Georgia State Department of Health Secretary's Subject Files, 1966–1975, Environmental Protection Division Archives, Georgia Archives ("unpredictable"); Michael Egan, "Communicating Knowledge: The Swedish Mercury Group and Vernacular Science, 1965–1972," in *New Natures: Joining Environmental History with Science and Technology Studies*, ed. Dolly Jørgensen, Finn Arne Jørgensen, and Sara B. Pritchard, 103–17 (Pittsburgh: University of Pittsburgh Press, 2013); Simone M. Müller, "Corporate Behaviour and Ecological Disaster: Dow Chemical and the Great Lakes Mercury Crisis, 1970–1972," *Business History* 60, no. 3 (2018): 399–422, https://doi.org/10.1080/00076791.2

017.1346611; Slaffan Skerfving, "Methylmercury in Fish: An Important Health Problem," trans. from Swedish, *Läkartidningen* 67, no. 45 (1970): 5235–43; Philip H. Abelson, "Methyl Mercury," *Science* 169, no. 3942 (1970): 237–37, https://doi.org/10.1126/science.169.3942.237.

123. "Minutes of Meeting of Georgia Water Quality Control Board," October 1, 1970, folder "Minutes, October 1, 1970," subgroup 7, series 62, RG 26, Department of Public Health Archives, Georgia Archives.

124. "Lockheed Vows New Steps" ("big sacred cow").

125. Hugh Nations, "State's Pollution Problem No. 5," *Atlanta Journal*, May 7, 1970, sec. A.

126. James M. Fallows, *The Water Lords: Ralph Nader's Study Group Report on Industry and Environmental Crisis in Savannah, Georgia* (New York: Grossman, 1971), xxi; James Fallows to R. S. Howard, Executive Secretary, Georgia Water Quality Control Board, June 17, 1970, folder "Nader," box 2, Water Quality Control Board, Executive Secretary's Subject Files, 1966–75, Georgia Archives.

CHAPTER 4. Making Citizenship Environmental

1. Roger Buerki, interview by Christopher Sellers, Marietta, Ga., February 12, 2013.

2. "5-Mile Link Opens I-75 into Marietta," *Atlanta Constitution*, January 27, 1967, 75; Sallye Salter, "Community Complex Planned in Cobb," *Atlanta Constitution*, July 12, 1969; Harry Murphy, "Perimeter Effect? Tieup Not Worse," *Atlanta Constitution*, April 12, 1970, sec. A; "Covers 72 Acres," *Atlanta Constitution*, August 16, 1973, sec. S.

3. Roger Buerki, interview; Keith Coulbourn, "The Chattahoochee Has Friends," *Atlanta Constitution Magazine*, October 16, 1976.

4. Sam Hopkins and Terry Adamson, "Earth Day Marks Assault on Pollution," *Atlanta Constitution*, April 23, 1970; "Antipollution: It's Earth Day—Georgia Style," *Atlanta Journal*, April 22, 1970, sec. A; Jeff Nesmith, "Georgia Students to Join in Earth Day," *Atlanta Constitution*, April 17, 1970; Maxine Rock, "Emory Conservation Group Seeks Clean Environment," *Atlanta Journal*, April 22, 1970, sec. B; Stephanie Coffin and Perry Treadwell, "Peachtree Creek Is Full of SHIT!," *Great Speckled Bird*, February 23, 1970.

5. Bill Shipp, "Earth Day on Lenin's Day; Bentley Fears a Red Plot," *Atlanta Constitution*, April 10, 1970, sec. A.

6. Ernest Pharr, "Our Polluted Environment—Part Two; 'Proctor Creek Will Rise Again,'" *Atlanta Inquirer*, July 11, 1970 ("most important"); Boyd Lewis, "Garbage Strike Over: But Wage Hike Slighted; April 22, 'Earth Day,' Good Day to End Strike," *Atlanta Inquirer*, April 26, 1970; Whitney Young, "Slum and Pollution," *Atlanta Inquirer*, April 26, 1970. Proctor Creek sometimes received attention when reporters looked at multiple examples of pollution; see Hugh Nations and Leonard Ray Teel, "State's Pollution Problem Real but Solvable," *Atlanta Constitution*, May 3, 1970, sec. C.

7. Robert Gottlieb, *Forcing the Spring: The Transformation of the American Environmental Movement* (Washington: Island, 1993); Robert Gioielli, *Environmental Activism and the Urban Crisis: Baltimore, St. Louis, Chicago* (Philadelphia: Temple University Press, 2014); Chad Montrie, *The Myth of Silent Spring: Rethinking the Origins of American Environmentalism* (Oakland: University of California Press, 2018); Ellen Spears, *Rethinking the American Environmental Movement Post-1945* (New York: Routledge, 2019).

8. Samuel P. Hays, *Beauty, Health, and Permanence: Environmental Politics in the United States, 1955–1985* (New York: Cambridge University Press, 1989), chapter 4, p. 53 ("weakness"); Otis L. Graham Jr., "Again the Backward Region? Environmental His-

tory in and of the American South," *Southern Cultures* 6, no. 2 (2000): 66, https://doi.org/10.1353/scu.2000.0000; Albert E. Cowdrey, *This Land, This South: An Environmental History*, rev. ed. (Lexington: University Press of Kentucky, 1995).

9. Kevin M. Kruse, *White Flight: Atlanta and the Making of Modern Conservatism* (Princeton, N.J.: Princeton University Press, 2007); Matthew D. Lassiter, *The Silent Majority: Suburban Politics in the Sunbelt South* (Princeton, N.J.: Princeton University Press, 2006).

10. Frank Wells, "Enforcement of Rules, Not Slogans, Called Water Key," *Atlanta Constitution*, April 24, 1970; Robert Claxton, *The History of the Georgia Conservancy, 1967–1981* (Atlanta: Georgia Conservancy, 1985); Louis Harris and Associates, *The Harris Survey Yearbook of Public Opinion, 1970* (New York: Louis Harris and Associates, 1970); Hazel Erskine, "The Polls: Pollution and Industry," *Public Opinion Quarterly* 36, no. 2 (1972): 263–80; Erskine, "The Polls: Pollution and Its Costs," *Public Opinion Quarterly* 36, no. 1 (1972): 120–35; Arvin W. Murch, "Public Concern for Environmental Pollution," *Public Opinion Quarterly* 35, no. 1 (1971): 100–106.

11. Tom Bottomore and T. H. Marshall, *Citizenship and Social Class* (London: Pluto, 1987), 172–73.

12. Bronislaw Szerszynski, "Local Landscapes and Global Belonging," in *Environmental Citizenship*, ed. Andrew Dobson and Derek Bell (MIT Press, 2005), 91 ("as if from afar"). This point of departure for the new environmental citizenship had a curious kinship with the "veil of ignorance" over one's own origins and position in society being proposed at the time by political philosopher John Rawls, in *A Theory of Justice* (Cambridge, Mass.: Belknap, 1971).

13. "Failure to Reapportion State Senate Shortchanges Majority of Georgians," *Atlanta Constitution*, February 16, 1962.

14. Toombs v. Fortson, 205 F. Supp. 248 (Dist. Court 1962); Peyton McCrary and Steven F. Lawson, "Race and Reapportionment, 1962: The Case of Georgia Senate Redistricting," *Journal of Policy History* 12, no. 3 (2000): 293–320; Wesberry v. Sanders, 376 U.S. 1 (1964); Gray v. Sanders, 372 U.S. 368 (1963), Justia Law, accessed April 23, 2018, https://supreme.justia.com/cases/federal/us/372/368/case.html.

15. Eugene Patterson, "Mackay: A Man Who Fought," *Atlanta Constitution*, August 18, 1964; "Mackay Is Expected to Run for Congress," *Atlanta Constitution*, February 15, 1964 ("main points").

16. "Negativism Dead, Says Mackay," *Atlanta Constitution*, February 18, 1964.

17. Robert Weisbrot and G. Calvin Mackenzie, *The Liberal Hour: Washington and the Politics of Change in the 1960s* (New York: Penguin Books, 2008); Randall B. Woods, *Prisoners of Hope: Lyndon B. Johnson, the Great Society, and the Limits of Liberalism* (New York: Basic Books, 2016); Joshua Zeitz, *Building the Great Society: Inside Lyndon Johnson's White House* (New York: Penguin Books, 2018); Julian E. Zelizer, *The Fierce Urgency of Now: Lyndon Johnson, Congress, and the Battle for the Great Society* (New York: Penguin Books, 2015).

18. Art Pine, "Can Mackay Be Beaten? Question Gets Down to Earth," *Atlanta Constitution*, June 2, 1966 ("liberal"); Remer Tyson, "You Grow Up in Congress, Face Issues, Mackay Says," *Atlanta Constitution*, September 25, 1965 ("staunch support"); "Mackay Fights for Safety Law," *Atlanta Constitution*, March 16, 1966; "Mackay's Victory Is Public's Too," *Atlanta Constitution*, August 27, 1966.

19. Betty Carrollton, "Solon Calls for Anti-apathy Drive," *Atlanta Constitution*, March 1, 1961 ("apathy").

20. James A. Mackay, "A Report to the New 4th District from Your Congressman James A. Mackay," newsletter, April 1965, item 19, box 7, collection 456, James Mackay Papers, Special Collections, Emory University, Decatur, Ga.

21. James Mackay, "Citizens Panels for Progress for the 89th Congress: Fourth Congressional District," December 1965, box 16, item 34, Mackay Papers, Emory University.

22. Mackay, "Report to the New 4th District," Emory University; James Mackay, "What Can a Strong Citizens Panel for Progress Do? We Found Out Last Week When Caraker Paschal and His Panel on Water Resources Held a Seminar on 'Air, Water and Our Health' . . . ," *Looking at Washington*, November 1, 1965, item no. 23, box 7, collection 456, Mackay Papers, Emory University; Diane Thomas, "River Basin Management Plan Is Urged to Control Pollution," *Atlanta Constitution*, October 30, 1965.

23. "Mackay Asks Conservation Policy Panel," *Atlanta Constitution*, September 28, 1966.

24. Betsy Fancher, "Profile of Bob Hanie," 1970, box 14, shelf 30-8-43, Georgia Natural Areas Council Collection, Georgia Archives, Morrow.

25. Fancher; Robert Hanie, "Curriculum Vitae: Robert E. Hanie," 1972, folder "Ossabow 1972," box 6, shelf 30–8–43, Georgia Natural Areas Council Collection, Georgia Archives.

26. "Mackay Asks Conservation Policy Panel"("policy group").

27. Lucy Smethurst, interview by Christopher Sellers, Atlanta, January 20, 2004.

28. "Committee Report on Natural Areas," 1967, folder "Natural Areas Council: Minutes, 1966–67," box RCB-36646, Game and Fish Commissioner's Office, Commissioner's Subject Files, 1957, Department of Agriculture Papers, Georgia Archives.

29. Atlanta Region Metropolitan Planning Commission, *Atlanta Metropolitan Region Comprehensive Plan/Nature Preserves* (Atlanta, 1964), 15 ("plant and animal environment").

30. Jeff Nesmith, "They Had a Park Plan—But That's All," *Atlanta Constitution*, September 26, 1966.

31. "3 Georgia Solons Support Sweetwater Wildlife Area," *Atlanta Journal*, August 5, 1965.

32. Bill Birchard, *Nature's Keepers: The Remarkable Story of How the Nature Conservancy Became the Largest Environmental Group in the World* (Hoboken, N.J.: Jossey-Bass, 2005); Christopher Sellers, *Crabgrass Crucible: Suburban Nature and the Rise of Environmentalism in Twentieth-Century America* (Chapel Hill: University of North Carolina Press, 2012).

33. Legislative Committee on Natural Areas, "Committee Report on Natural Areas (BR 161)," n.d., folder "Natural Areas Council: Minutes, 1966–67," box RCB-36646, Department of Game and Fish Archives, Commissioners Office, Georgia Archives.

34. Pine, "Can Mackay Be Beaten?"; Art Pine, "Blackburn Called a Sure Mackay Foe," *Atlanta Constitution*, May 28, 1966.

35. Duane Riner, "Mackay, Blackburn Clash at Forum," *Atlanta Constitution*, October 7, 1966.

36. Jeff Nesmith, "Mackay, Blackburn Toe-to-Toe," *Atlanta Constitution*, October 21, 1966; "Blackburn Hits Laws on Powers," *Atlanta Constitution*, October 29, 1966.

37. Pine, "Can Mackay Be Beaten?"

38. Robert Hartle, *Atlanta's Druid Hills: A Brief History* (Charleston, S.C.: History, 2008); Dolores Hayden, *Building Suburbia: Green Fields and Urban Growth, 1820–2000* (New York: Vintage, 2004), 45–70 ("picturesque enclave").

39. Jeff Nesmith, "Little Group Has Big Ideas," *Atlanta Constitution*, June 11, 1967, sec. B; "Georgia Conservancy Receives Charter: Officers, Committees Named," *Geor-*

gia Conservancy Quarterly 1, no. 1 (1968): 3; "Membership List," July 1967, folder "Conservancy: General," box 7, shelf 30–8–43, Georgia Natural Areas Council Collection, Georgia Archives.

40. Sellers, *Crabgrass Crucible*.

41. Mark Finlay, "The Counterculture Meets Georgia Politics: Ecology, Human Ecology, Christianity, and the Battles to Save the Georgia Barrier Islands," 2013, in possession of the author.

42. Bob Harrell, "Wilderness Hike Near Atlanta," *Atlanta Journal and Constitution*, September 15, 1968.

43. Lucy Smethurst, "Founders Look Back and Think Ahead," *Georgia Conservancy Panorama* 30 (June 2000): 6; Smethurst, interview.

44. Smethurst, "Founders Look Back and Think Ahead"; Smethurst, interview.

45. Claxton, *History of the Georgia Conservancy*, 7; Smethurst, interview.

46. "Field Trips—Rare Good Fun," *Georgia Conservancy Quarterly* 1, no. 1 (1968): 2.

47. James A. Mackay, "Letter from Chairman Mackay," *Georgia Conservancy Quarterly* 1, no. 1 (1968): 1.

48. Merle Schlesinger Lekoff, "The Voluntary Citizen's Group as a Public Policy Alternative to the Political Party: A Case Study of the Georgia Conservancy" (PhD diss., Emory University, 1975) ("virtually all"), 46 ("overwhelmingly"), 47 ("exclusivity").

49. Claxton, *History of the Georgia Conservancy*.

50. Nesmith, "Little Group Has Big Ideas"; Georgia Department of Natural Resources, "Panola Mountain State Conservation Park: Brief Historical Background," n.d., Georgia Department of Natural Resources, folder "Panola Mountain State Conservation Park," DeKalb County Historical Society, Decatur, Ga.

51. Duane Riner, "$200,000 Gets Them a Mountain for Science," *Atlanta Constitution*, August 2, 1967.

52. Charlotte Hale Smith, "Life on a Spectacular Rock," *Atlanta Constitution*, September 8, 1968; John Pennington, "Georgia's First Wilderness Park," *Atlanta Constitution*, June 20, 1971.

53. James A. Mackay, "Statement of the Georgia Conservancy at the Public Hearing under the Wilderness Act: Friday April 21, 1967, Waycross, Ga.," *Georgia Conservancy Quarterly* 1, no. 1 (1968): 2.

54. Wayne Kelley, "Maddox: Leave Okefenokee Out of Wilderness System," *Atlanta Constitution*, September 21, 1967, sec. A.

55. Harrell, "Wilderness Hike Near Atlanta."

56. Bob Harrell, "A Walk into History to an Old Mill," *Atlanta Constitution*, October 24, 1968.

57. Smith, "Life on a Spectacular Rock"; Pennington, "Georgia's First Wilderness Park"; "In Douglas: State Buys 867 Acres for Park," *Atlanta Constitution*, May 12, 1972.

58. Harrell, "Wilderness Hike Near Atlanta."

59. Fancher, "Profile of Bob Hanie."

60. Riner, "$200,000 Gets Them a Mountain"; "Panola Mountain Purchase First Important Project," *Georgia Conservancy Quarterly* 1, no. 1 (1968): 1.

61. Lekoff, "Voluntary Citizen's Group," 146 ("excluded").

62. Lekoff, 46 ("Black person"); Smethurst, interview.

63. Tom Henderson, "Peril Cited in Atlanta Pollution," *Atlanta Constitution*, June 18, 1970.

64. "Vine City," 1966, folder 24, "Vine City, Georgia Slum Project, 1966," box 9, SCLC Papers, Special Collections, Emory University.

65. Junius Griffin, "News: Press Release of Southern Christian Leadership Conference," Southern Christian Leadership Conference, Atlanta, February 1, 1966.

66. Jefferson Cowie, *The Great Exception: The New Deal and the Limits of American Politics* (Princeton, N.J.: Princeton University Press, 2016), 24.

67. "Hector Black: White Power in Black Atlanta," *Look*, December 13, 1966, 137; Bartow Elmore, "Hydrology and Residential Segregation in the Postwar South: An Environmental History of Atlanta, 1865–1895," *Georgia Historical Quarterly* 94, no. 1 (2010): 30–61.

68. Philip Gailey, "Proctor Creek Residents Protest Flood Problems," *Atlanta Constitution*, May 31, 1968 ("in fear").

69. Kathryn L. Nasstrom, "'This Joint Effort': Women and Community Organizing in Vine City in the 1960s," *Atlanta History: A Journal of Georgia and the South* 48, no. 1 (2006): 28–44; "Creek Here Yields Body of Boy, 12," *Atlanta Constitution*, June 9, 1966.

70. Doris Traweger and Leopold Slotta-Bachmayr, "Introducing GIS-Modelling into the Management of a Brown Rat (*Rattus Norvegicus* Berk.) (Mamm. Rodentia Muridae) Population in an Urban Habitat," *Journal of Pest Science* 78, no. 1 (2005): 17–24, https://doi.org/10.1007/s10340-004-0062-5; Thomas Madsen and Richard Shine, "Rainfall and Rats: Climatically-Driven Dynamics of a Tropical Rodent Population," *Australian Journal of Ecology* 24, no. 1 (2009): 80–89, https://doi.org/10.1046/j.1442-9993.1999.00948.x; Alice Feng and Chelsea Himsworth, "The Secret Life of the City Rat: A Review of the Ecology of Urban Norway and Black Rats (Rattus Norvegicus and Rattus Rattus)," *Urban Ecosystems* 17, no. 1 (2014): 201, https://doi.org/10.1007/s11252-013-0305-4.

71. Nations and Teel, "State's Pollution Problem" ("honeycombed").

72. U.S. Bureau of the Census, *1970 Census of Population and Housing: Census Tracts; Atlanta, Georgia* (Washington, D.C.: Government Printing Office, 1972), P-30–37, P-72–79, https://www2.census.gov/library/publications/decennial/1970/phc-1/39204513p2ch02.pdf.

73. Marcia Halvorsen, "An Analysis and Interpretation of Data on the Social Characteristics of Residents of 'Vine City': A Negro Slum Ghetto within the City of Atlanta, Georgia," Spellman College, June 15, 1967, https://files.eric.ed.gov/fulltext/ED015225.pdf.

74. Randolph Hohle, *Black Citizenship and Authenticity in the Civil Rights Movement* (New York: Routledge, 2013); Rhonda Y. Williams, *Concrete Demands: The Search for Black Power in the 20th Century* (New York: Routledge, 2014); Peniel E. Joseph, *Stokely: A Life* (New York: Civitas Books, 2016); Clayborne Carson, *In Struggle: SNCC and the Black Awakening of the 1960s* (Cambridge, Mass.: Harvard University Press, 1995).

75. Ronald H. Bayor, "The Civil Rights Movement as Urban Reform: Atlanta's Black Neighborhoods and a New 'Progressivism,'" *Georgia Historical Quarterly* 77, no. 2 (1993): 286–309; "Negroes Protest Facilities," *Atlanta Constitution*, August 6, 1963.

76. SNCC, "Prospectus for Atlanta Project," 1966, Archives Main Stacks, SC3093, WIHVS260-A, Mendy Samstein Papers, 1963–66, Freedom Summer Online Collection, Wisconsin Historical Society, https://content.wisconsinhistory.org/digital/collection/p15932coll2/id/17696, 1 ("significant breakthrough"), 2 ("democratic control").

77. Rhonda Y. Williams, *The Politics of Public Housing: Black Women's Struggles against Urban Inequality* (New York: Oxford University Press, 2005); Roberta M. Feldman and Susan Stall, *The Dignity of Resistance: Women Residents' Activism in Chicago Public Housing* (Cambridge: Cambridge University Press, 2004); Roberta Gold, *When Tenants Claimed*

the City: The Struggle for Citizenship in New York City Housing (Champagne-Urbana: University of Illinois Press, 2014).

78. SNCC Vine City Project, "Prospectus for an Atlanta Project, " Freedom Summer Digital Collection, Wisconsin Historical Society, 1966, http://content.wisconsinhistory.org/cdm/ref/collection/p15932coll2/id/17747.

79. Ted Simmons, "Rent Strike Brews in South Atlanta," *Atlanta Constitution*, September 25, 1965; Bill Westbrook, "Slum Fighter Okay City Hall 'Tent-In,'" *Atlanta Constitution*, October 1, 1965.

80. Bill Shipp, "Tenants Open Rent Strike in War on Markham Slums," *Atlanta Constitution*, February 5, 1966; Shipp, "King Says Slum Here Is the Worst He's Ever Seen," *Atlanta Constitution*, February 1, 1966.

81. Shipp, "Tenants Open Rent Strike"; SNCC Vine City Project, "These Affidavits Come from People Living in a Roughly Five Square Block Area," Freedom Summer Digital Collection, Wisconsin Historical Society, 1966, http://content.wisconsinhistory.org/cdm/ref/collection/p15932coll2/id/17747, 2 ("American way"); Bill Shipp, "Spy Cut Tent, Wanted Him, Rent Strike Leaders Says," *Atlanta Constitution*, March 24, 1966.

82. SNCC Vine City Project, "We of the Atlanta Project of SNCC Can Not Overlook the Suffering and Exploitation," Freedom Summer Digital Collection, Wisconsin Historical Society, 1966, http://content.wisconsinhistory.org/cdm/ref/collection/p15932coll2/id/17747; SNCC Vine City Project, "Nitty Gritty Urges Launching of Tenants Rights Movement," Freedom Summer Digital Collection, Wisconsin Historical Society, 1966, http://content.wisconsinhistory.org/cdm/ref/collection/p15932coll2/id/17747; SNCC Vine City Project, "Rough Design for a Tenant's Rights Handbook," Freedom Summer Digital Collection, Wisconsin Historical Society, 1966, http://content.wisconsinhistory.org/cdm/ref/collection/p15932coll2/id/17747.

83. Wayne Kelley, "Factions Feud in Vine City as Poverty Crushes People," *Atlanta Journal*, July 18, 1966; Don McKee, "U.S. Probes Snick's Finances," *Atlanta Constitution*, December 8, 1967.

84. Helen Howard, "The Ghetto Comes Alive," *Vine City Voice*, December 1968, folder "Vine City," Clippings Collection, Atlanta History Center, Atlanta; David Nordan, "'Nickel, Prayer' Started Clinic," *Atlanta Journal*, October 23, 1967; B. J. Phillips, "The Poor Must Work Together," *Atlanta Constitution*, June 25, 1968.

85. David Alexander Russell, "Cosmopolitan A.M.E. Church and the Problem of the Vine City Community of Atlanta, Georgia" (master's thesis, Interdenominational Theological Center, 1969).

86. Bill Collins, "12,000 Pitch in to Clean Up Vine City Section," *Atlanta Journal and Constitution*, May 18, 1969, sec. A ("box springs").

87. Frank Wells, "Underdogs Have Defenders at City Hall," *Atlanta Constitution*, October 4, 1970, sec. A ("underprivileged"); Phil Garner, "Angry Groups Bring Dramatic Changes," *Atlanta Constitution*, January 18, 1970 ("additional violence"); Margaret Hurst, "Atlantans in Slums Explain Problems," *Atlanta Constitution*, February 17, 1967 ("persons representing").

88. Frank Wells, "Underdogs Have Defenders at City Hall" ("gripe as much"); Community Relations Commission [Atlanta], "A Report to the People," 1968, Planning Atlanta Digital Collection, Georgia State University Archives, https://digitalcollections.library.gsu.edu/digital/api/collection/PlanATL/id/36322/download.

89. Russell, "Cosmopolitan A.M.E. Church," 2 (figures on AFCD mothers, apparently given in 1969 interview).

90. Elizabeth Hinton, *From the War on Poverty to the War on Crime: The Making of Mass Incarceration in America* (Cambridge, Mass.: Harvard University Press, 2016), 49 ("most ambitious").

91. Howard, "Ghetto Comes Alive," 3 ("*designed*"; emphasis in the original).

92. Harmon Perry, "Recreation Model Built in Vine City," *Atlanta Constitution*, July 21, 1968, sec. A ("things really").

93. "No Job for Linda? ACEP Held Answer," *Atlanta Constitution*, January 11, 1969, sec. L; Russell, "Cosmopolitan A.M.E. Church."

94. Junie Brown, "A New Kind of School," *Atlanta Constitution*, March 28, 1971, sec. SM; Alex Coffin, "Poverty Chief Predicts New Sense of Mission," *Atlanta Constitution*, March 7, 1971, sec. A ("broker," "castle").

95. "Experimental Program Designed to Break the 'Cycle of Poverty,'" *Atlanta Constitution*, December 1, 1969, sec. A.

96. Nancy Long, "Women Turn Out to Help EOA," *Atlanta Constitution*, January 17, 1969; "Zap-A-Rat Drive Begins Here Today," *Atlanta Constitution*, May 18, 1971, sec. A.

97. Jim Montgomery, "Funds Off 83 Pct. but Rat Pack's Busy," *Atlanta Constitution*, September 14, 1969, sec. C ("rodent-enticing"); Jean Tyson, "Women Continue Rodent Fight," *Atlanta Constitution*, March 22, 1970, sec. G.

98. Montgomery, "Funds Off 83 Pct." ("natural part"); Faye S. Joyce, "Metro Atlanta Rages Rat War," *Atlanta Constitution*, May 23, 1975, sec. B ("federally").

99. U.S. Bureau of the Census, *General Population Characteristics: Georgia, 1970* (Washington, D.C.: Government Printing Office, 1971), 12–31, table 5.

100. U.S. Bureau of the Census, *Plumbing Facilities and Estimates of Dilapidated Housing* (Washington, D.C.: Government Printing Office, 1973), table 2.

101. "Law Enforcement Top Complaint of CRC Summer Town Hall Meetings," *Atlanta Inquirer*, September 19, 1970; Frank Wells, "Town Hall Meeting Airs Old Grips in New Setting," *Atlanta Constitution*, May 14, 1971, sec. A.

102. Phil Garner, "Shall the Tenant Voice Be Heard?," *Atlanta Constitution*, December 1, 1968, sec. C, pp. 4, 6.

103. Jean Tyson, "Dorothy Bolden Speaks for Herself, Others," *Atlanta Constitution*, November 21, 1976; Elizabeth Beck, "The National Domestic Workers Union and the War on Poverty," *Journal of Sociology and Social Welfare* 28, no. 4 (2001): 195–211; Premilla Nadasen, "Power, Intimacy, and Contestation: Dorothy Bolden and Domestic Worker Organizing in Atlanta in the 1960s," in *Intimate Labors: Cultures, Technologies, and the Politics of Care*, ed. Rhacel Salazar Parreñas and Eileen Boris (Stanford, Calif: Stanford University Press, 2010), 204–16.

104. Clarence N. Stone, "Atlanta's Neighborhood Renewal and Rehabilitation," in *Neighborhoods in Urban America*, ed. Ronald H. Bayor (Port Washington, N.Y.: Kennikat, 1982), 236–37 ("dependent").

105. Bob Hurt, "Opposition Voiced to New Freeway," *Atlanta Constitution*, October 4, 1968 ("history").

106. State Highway Department of Georgia, "Transcript of Proceedings in Public Hearing Held by State Highway Department of Georgia at DeKalb County Court House: Decatur, Georgia, October 3, 1969; Section of Stone Mountain Freeway U-061-1(2) DeKalb County: Terrace Avenue to Scott Boulevard," October 3, 1968, folder 1, Stone Mountain Freeway: Public Hearing, October 1968, box 11, Druid Hills Civic Association Records, Special Collections, Emory University, 34 ("beautification"), 29 ("principal ingredient").

107. P. M. Prescott, "Statement of P. M. Prescott, President, Druid Hills Civic Association, in Protest of the Extension of the Stone Mountain Expressway through Druid Hills," in State Highway Department of Georgia, "Transcript of Proceedings," 21 ("most important point").

108. State Highway Department of Georgia, "Transcript of Proceedings."

109. Kyle Shelton, *Power Moves: Transportation, Politics, and Development in Houston* (Austin: University of Texas Press, 2017).

110. Dick Hebert and Frank Wells, "All 3 Routes for I-485 Are Opposed," *Atlanta Constitution*, April 30, 1965, 25; Sam Hopkins, "Morningside Routes Cheaper, State Says," *Atlanta Constitution*, June 3, 1965.

111. Hebert and Wells, "All 3 Routes for I-485" ("outpouring").

112. Marion Gaines, "Aldermen Back Morningside B in Wild Session," *Atlanta Constitution*, June 17, 1966.

113. Newell Edenfield, "Morningside Sues to Block 'Line B,'" *Atlanta Constitution*, October 25, 1966; Reuben Smith, "Morningside Writ Reviewed by Court," *Atlanta Constitution*, May 11, 1967.

114. Edenfield, "Morningside Sues," ("residential community").

115. Gaines, "Aldermen Back Morningside B" ("refined").

116. Hurt, "Opposition Voiced to New Freeway."

117. State Highway Department of Georgia, "Transcript of Proceedings," 27.

118. Bill Seedon, "Bass School Fears Aired," *Atlanta Constitution*, May 5, 1970; U.S. Bureau of the Census, *1970 Census of Population*, P-9–16.

119. Alex Coffin, "Can Avoid Being Displaced Mayor Assures Bass Residents," *Atlanta Constitution*, October 29, 1968; U.S. Bureau of the Census, *U.S. Censuses of Population and Housing, 1960: Final Report* PHS(1)-8; *Census Tracts: Atlanta, Ga. Standard Metropolitan Statistical Area* (Washington, D.C.: Government Printing Office, 1962), https://www2 .census.gov/prod2/decennial/documents/41953654v1ch3.pdf.

120. Andrew Sparks, "Turmoil among the Turrets," *Atlanta Constitution*, March 7, 1971, sec. SM.

121. "krista," "I-485: Highway to Nowhere?," *Great Speckled Bird*, January 7, 1974.

122. Diane Stepp, "Once Wealthy Area Unites to Retain a Community," *Atlanta Constitution*, October 16, 1967.

123. D. Railleur, "BOND Fights Hiway [*sic*]," *Great Speckled Bird*, July 5, 1971.

124. "krista," "I-485," 10 ("working-class," "all they could do").

125. Charles G. Helms, "Groovy People," letter to the editor, *Atlanta Constitution*, August 20, 1970 ("rich sociological"); Sparks, "Turmoil among the Turrets," 34 ("no panic").

126. Seedon, "Bass School Fears Aired."

127. Railleur, "BOND Fights Hiway" ("affluent"); D. Railleur, "BOND Raps Steadfast Railleur," *Great Speckled Bird*, July 12, 1971.

128. Stepp, "Once Wealthy Area Unites" ("environment," "beautification"); Sallye Salter, "3 Atlanta Architects Fighting War on Community Ugliness," *Atlanta Constitution*, November 23, 1968 ("toward slums"); Bob Rohrer, "Voter Drive Turned Down," *Atlanta Constitution*, August 28, 1969."

129. Sparks, "Turmoil among the Turrets" ("pioneers"); Richard Miles, "Couple Pushing Cleanup of 5 Neighborhoods," *Atlanta Constitution*, October 23, 1970, sec. B.

130. Railleur, "BOND Fights Hiway"; Railleur, "BOND Raps Steadfast Railleur"; Jean

Tyson, "I-485 Stops; Citizens Plan Next Move," *Atlanta Constitution*, November 21, 1971, sec. G.

131. Hugh Nations, "Feud Hindering Transit Group?," Atlanta Constitution, May 2, 1971, "grassrootsy"; Citizens Transportation Advisory Committee of the Atlanta Area Transportation Study, "Summary and Recommendations," November 22, 1971, 2 ("vehicular movement"); Citizens Transportation Advisory Committee, "Review of Findings," November 22, 1971, both in folder "City of Atlanta," box 1, Atlanta Coalition on the Transportation Crisis/Virginia Taylor Papers MSS1222, Special Collections, Emory University, Decatur, Ga., 1 ("viable"), 2 ("parks," "noise").

132. Citizens Transportation Advisory Committee, "Review of Findings," Citizens Transportation Advisory Committee, "Summary and Recommendations."

133. Jacob Anbinder, "The South Shall Ride Again: The Origins of MARTA and the Making of the Urban South," *Yale Historical Review*, Spring 2013, 37–57; Ronald H. Bayor, *Race and the Shaping of Twentieth-Century Atlanta*, rev. ed. (Chapel Hill: University of North Carolina Press, 2000), 190–93; Ivan Allen, *Mayor: Notes on the Sixties* (New York: Simon and Schuster, 1971), 32–36; Atlanta Region Metropolitan Planning Commission, *Implementing Rapid Transit for the Atlanta Metropolitan Region* (Atlanta: ARMPC, 1962).

134. Alex Coffin, "Blacks Ask 10-Year 15-Cent MARTA Fare," *Atlanta Constitution*, July 3, 1971; Robert D. Bullard and Glenn Johnson, eds., *Just Transportation: Dismantling Race and Class Barriers to Mobility* (Stony Creek, Conn.: New Society, 1997).

135. Prescott, "Statement of P. M. Prescott," 20 ("comprehensive"); for more detail on the case being made prior to the 1971 MARTA vote, see "The Case for Rapid Transit," *Facts Published by League of Women Voters of Atlanta-Fulton County* 44, no. 4 (1971).

136. Bill Seldon, "Rapid Transit Hearings Open to Public Beginning July 22," *Atlanta Constitution*, July 16, 1971. For an emphasis on the problems with BOND's physical environment, including housing deterioration and vacancies as well as trash, litter, and vacant lands, see Greg Gregory, "Draft Report of Recycling an Urban Residential Community: A Framework for Community," June 26, 1972, box 1, Atlanta Coalition on the Transportation Crisis, Virginia Taylor Papers, MSS1222, Special Collections, Emory University.

137. Doug Monroe, "Where It All Went Wrong," *Atlanta Magazine*, August 2012, https://www.atlantamagazine.com/great-reads/marta-tsplost-transportation/; Lester Neidell, "Analysis and Demand Implications of the Rapid Transit Vote in Atlanta," *Transportation Journal* 13, no. 4 (1974): 14–18; Shelton, *Power Moves*, 5 ("infrastructure citizenship").

138. Maxine Rock, "Diary of a Toll Road Fighter," *Atlanta Journal and Constitution Magazine*, April 30, 1972.

139. Bayor, *Shaping of Twentieth-Century Atlanta*, 190–95; Clarence N. Stone, *Regime Politics: Governing Atlanta, 1946–1988* (Lawrence: University Press of Kansas, 1989), 78–85.

140. Atlanta Coalition on the Transportation Crisis, "Statement of Goals and Purposes," 1972, box 1, Atlanta Coalition on the Transportation Crisis, Virginia Taylor Papers, MSS1222, Special Collections, Emory University.

141. Chuck Bell, "Foes Attack: C of C Poll Shows Toll Road Support," *Atlanta Constitution*, August 17, 1972; Rock, "Toll Road Fighter."

142. Pritt J. Vesilind, "A Matter of Imagination: Chattahoochee—Frontier or Intruder," *Atlanta Constitution*, June 22, 1969.

143. Claude Terry, interview by Christopher Sellers, Atlanta, November 14, 2012.

144. Terry, interview, May 21, 2012; November 14, 2012.

145. Barbara Davis Blum, interview by Christopher Sellers, Washington, D.C., March 17, 2015; Gregory Jaynes, "Sewer Line Causes Concern," *Atlanta Constitution*, June 18, 1971.

146. Kay McKenzie, phone interview by Christopher Sellers, March 29, 2013; April 2, 2013.

147. "The Rush Goes On at Chattahoochee," *Atlanta Constitution*, September 7, 1968.

148. Maurice Fliess, "Beauty and the Bulldozer Quarrel in Cobb," *Atlanta Constitution*, August 23, 1970, sec. A (quotes from Barrett).

149. Buerki, interview.

150. Bob Harrell, "Camp Sites 'Grow' Small," *Atlanta Constitution*, May 12, 1968, sec. F; "Atlanta Bird Lovers Join Audubon Society," *Atlanta Constitution*, October 10, 1968; Bob Harrell, "Cold of Winter Can't Stop the Sierra Schedule," *Atlanta Constitution*, June 24, 1971, sec. F; Bob Harrell, "Recommended for Hikers—The Appalachian Trail," *Atlanta Constitution*, April 18, 1971, sec. F; Barbara Casson, "Back to Nature: How to Get There," *Atlanta Constitution*, August 27, 1972, sec. A.

151. Terry, interview, November 14, 2012.

152. Jack Spalding, "The Great River Raft Race Grows in Appeal," *Atlanta Constitution*, May 31, 1970, sec. A; Buerki, interview; Charles Bethea, "Woodstock on the Water: An Oral History of the Ramblin' Raft Race," *Atlanta Magazine* (blog), June 15, 2015, http:// www.atlantamagazine.com/great-reads/woodstock-on-the-water-an-oral-history-of-the -ramblin-raft-race/.

153. Buerki, interview; "They Row to Keep River Unspoiled," *Atlanta Constitution*, August 2, 1970, sec. B ("granite cliffs," "mountains").

154. Claude Terry, "Palisades Naming," email correspondence with the author, April 30, 2013; Buerki, interview; Terry, interview, May 21, 2012.

155. "They Row to Keep River"; Buerki, interview; John Pennington, "Friends and Enemies of the River," *Atlanta Constitution Magazine*, June 4, 1972.

156. Jaynes, "Sewer Line Causes Concern"; Gregory Jaynes, "Cobb Sewer Tunnel Low Bid Is $997,360," *Atlanta Constitution*, May 26, 1971, sec. A; "Conservationists Win Two," *Atlanta Constitution*, July 4, 1971, sec. A.

157. Mike Corbin, "'Friends of River' Organize Here," *Atlanta Constitution*, June 6, 1971; Pennington, "Friends and Enemies."

158. Margaret Hurst, "Rezonings on Chattahoochee Approved," *Atlanta Constitution*, July 17, 1971.

159. Maurice Fliess, "New Song for Chattahoochee," *Atlanta Journal and Constitution*, August 29, 1971.

160. Pennington, "Friends and Enemies."

161. Barbara Casson, "Time's Critical for River Friends," *Atlanta Journal and Constitution*, January 20, 1974.

162. Claudia Townsend, "McDonald Blocks Chattahoochee Bill," *Atlanta Constitution*, September 23, 1976; Craig Hume, "Park Bill Signed by President," *Atlanta Constitution*, August 16, 1978.

163. James Dickey, *Deliverance* (New York: Delta, 2008).

164. Dickey, 64 ("fishing"), 55 ("hookwormy," "worth a damn"); Nancy Isenberg, *White Trash: The 400-Year Untold History of Class in America* (New York: Viking, 2016).

165. Dickey, *Deliverance*, 60 ("country kid"), 124 ("repulsive"); 204 ("nondescript").

CHAPTER 5. Jimmy Carter, Black Power,
and the New Environmental State

1. William Leuchtenberg, "Jimmy Carter and the Post-New Deal Presidency," in *The Carter Presidency: Policy Choices in the Post-New Deal Era*, ed. Gary M. Fink and Hugh Davis Graham (Lawrence: University Press of Kansas, 2001), "Great Society"; Jefferson R. Cowie, *Stayin' Alive: The 1970s and the Last Days of the Working Class* (New York: New Press, 2010); Julian E. Zelizer, *Jimmy Carter*, American Presidents Series (New York: Times Books, 2010); Iwan Morgan, "Jimmy Carter, Bill Clinton, and the New Democratic Economics," *Historical Journal* 47, no. 4 (2004): 1015–39, https://doi.org/10.1017/S0018246X0400408X; Paul Sabin, "'Everything Has a Price': Jimmy Carter and the Struggle for Balance in Federal Regulatory Policy," *Journal of Policy History* 28, no. 1 (2016): 1–47, https://doi.org/10.1017/S0898030615000366; W. Carl Biven, *Jimmy Carter's Economy: Policy in an Age of Limits* (Chapel Hill: University of North Carolina Press, 2003); Phillip J. Cooper, *The War against Regulation: From Jimmy Carter to George W. Bush* (Lawrence: University Press of Kansas, 2009).

2. K. Sabeel Rahman, "Conceptualizing the Economic Role of the State: Laissez-Faire, Technocracy, and the Democratic Alternative," *Polity* 43, no. 2 (2011): 269 ("technocratic"); Adam Rome, "What Really Matters in History: Environmental Perspectives on Modern America," *Environmental History* 7 (April 2002): 303–18; Paul S. Sutter, "The World with Us: The State of American Environmental History," *Journal of American History* 100, no. 1 (2013): 94–119, https://doi.org/10.1093/jahist/jat095; Richard N. L. Andrews, *Managing the Environment, Managing Ourselves: A History of American Environmental Policy*, 2nd ed. (New Haven, Conn.: Yale University Press, 2006).

3. Jimmy Carter, "Goergia [*sic*] Conservancy: Columbus," November 6, 1969, ARC identifier 894701, Carter Family Papers, ca. 1940–76, Collection JC Family, Jimmy Carter Presidential Library, Atlanta, Georgia; Kenneth E. Morris, *Jimmy Carter, American Moralist* (Athens: University of Georgia Press, 1996), 82–83 (on ambiguities of his claiming to be "from Plains").

4. "Georgia vs. Southeast: Comparative Trends Analysis; Per Capita Personal Income Trends over 1958–2015," United States Regional Economic Analysis Project, 2016, https://united-states.reaproject.org/analysis/comparative-trends-analysis/per_capita_personal_income/tools/130000/950000.

5. U.S. Bureau of the Census, "Historical Census of Housing Tables: Homeownership," Census of Housing, October 31, 2011, https://www.census.gov/hhes/www/housing/census/historic/owner.html.

6. U.S. Department of Labor, *Directory of National Unions and Employee Associations, 1973* (Washington, D.C.: Bureau of Labor Statistics, 1973), 84; U.S. Department of Labor, *Directory of National Unions and Employee Associations, 1979* (Washington, D.C.: Bureau of Labor Statistics, 1980), 71.

7. U.S. Department of Labor, *Directory of National Unions* (1973), 81.

8. Thomas R. Dye, "Income Inequality and American State Politics," *American Political Science Review* 63, no. 1 (1969): 157–62, https://doi.org/10.2307/1954291; David Ruthenberg and Miro Stano, "The Determinants of Interstate Variations in Income Distribution," *Review of Social Economy* 35, no. 1 (1977): 55–66.

9. Mark W. Frank, "A New State-Level Panel of Annual Inequality Measures over the Period 1916–2005," SHSU Economics and International Business Working Paper (Hunts-

ville, Tex.: Department of Economics and International Business; Sam Houston State University, 2008) (based on database made available by this author).

10. U.S. Bureau of the Census, *1970 Census of Population*, vol. 1, *Characteristics of the Population*, pt. 12, *Georgia* (Washington, D.C.: Bureau of the Census, 1973), table 194.

11. Robert C. McMath Jr., "Old South, New Politics: Jimmy Carter's First Campaign," *Georgia Historical Quarterly* 77, no. 3 (1993): 547–59; Jimmy Carter, *Turning Point* (New York: Crown, 1992).

12. Randy Sanders, "'The Sad Duty of Politics': Jimmy Carter and the Issue of Race in His 1970 Gubernatorial Campaign," *Georgia Historical Quarterly* 76, no. 3 (1992): 612–38.

13. Bill Shipp, "A Zany Year for Georgia?," *Atlanta Constitution*, April 22, 1970, sec. A; Duane Riner, "Negro Vote to Split Evenly, Suit Predicts," *Atlanta Constitution*, October 17, 1970 (7 percent); "Sanders Meets with Labor Leaders," *Journal of Labor*, February 27, 1970; Bill Shipp, "Union for Sanders; Hargrett Hits Carter," *Atlanta Constitution*, August 11, 1970, sec. A; "Carter Charges Sanders Sold Out to Ultra-Liberals," *Atlanta Constitution*, August 23, 1970, sec. A.

14. Bill Shipp, "Carter's Pledge to End Bias Shows Times Have Changed," *Atlanta Constitution*, January 13, 1971, sec. A.

15. Jimmy Carter, "Inaugural Address: January 12, 1971," in *Addresses of Jimmy Carter (James Earl Carter): Governor of Georgia, 1971–1975*, ed. Frank Daniels (Atlanta: Fortson, 1975), 80 ("no poor"); "Sen. Johnson Praises Carter," *Atlanta Constitution*, March 4, 1971; Milo Dakin, "Hike Minority Hiring, State Officials Are Told," *Atlanta Constitution*, December 4, 1973; Peter G. Bourne, *Jimmy Carter: A Comprehensive Biography from Plains to Post-presidency* (New York: Scribner, 1997), 211–12 (Hancock County episode); Zelizer, *Jimmy Carter*, locs. 511, 531 (King portrait), Kindle.

16. U.S. Bureau of the Census, *General Population Characteristics: Georgia, 1970* (Washington, D.C.: Government Printing Office, 1971), 55, table 18.

17. Dick Pettys, "Road Chief Bert Lance Building Solid Power Base," *Atlanta Constitution*, May 7, 1972; Deanna Michael, "Educational Reformers or Keepers of the Status Quo: Governors Reubin Askew and Jimmy Carter," *Paedagogica Historica* 42, nos. 1–2 (2006): 220, https://doi.org/10.1080/00309230600552146.

18. Figures compiled from U.S. Census of Governments for the stated years. U.S. Bureau of the Census, *Census of Governments: State Finances, 1942*, vol. 1, *Individual State Reports: Georgia* (Washington, D.C.: Government Printing Office, 1943), 5; U.S. Bureau of the Census, *1977 Census of Governments: Historical Statistics on Governmental Finances and Employment* (Washington, D.C.: Government Printing Office, 1979), https://www2.census.gov/programs-surveys/state/tables/1977/volume-6/1977-vol6-no4-hist-stats-on-gov-fin-and-emp.pdf, 83.

19. Prentice Palmer, "An Up and Down Year for State Taxes," *Atlanta Constitution*, March 14, 1971, sec. A; Milo Dakin, "Cities Get Break on Tax Relief," *Atlanta Constitution*, April 18, 1973, sec. C; Rex Granum, "Option Tax Bills Made It," *Atlanta Constitution*, March 27, 1975, sec. A; David S. Jones and Maureen M. McIntosh, "Revenue Options for Georgia Localities," *Georgia Government Review* 6, no. 2 (1974): 6–8; Pettys, "Road Chief Bert Lance."

20. Howell Raines, "Carter Urges Wage Equality," *Atlanta Constitution*, August 19, 1974; David Morrison, "It Doesn't Take Much to Scare Off New Industry," *Atlanta Constitution*, April 8, 1974.

21. Neil Swan, "Unemployment Trust Fund Healthy, Growing," *Atlanta Constitution*, December 8, 1974.

22. Phil West, "Non-farm Jobs Drop in Georgia," *Atlanta Constitution*, November 21, 1974.

23. Carter, "Inaugural Address," 79, 80; Gary M. Fink, *Prelude to the Presidency: The Political Character and Legislative Leadership Style of Governor Jimmy Carter* (Westport, Conn: Praeger, 1980); Morris, *Jimmy Carter*, 195–96.

24. Jimmy Carter, "State of the State Address: January 14, 1971," in Daniels, *Addresses of Jimmy Carter*; "Gov. Carter Will Sign Revamp Bill Thursday," *Marietta Daily Journal*, April 2, 1972 ("maze").

25. A "blue ribbon" committee in charge included the president of the Georgia Business and Industry Association and some sixty businesspeople, who joined a slightly greater number of state officials and a few token union spokespeople in the subcommittees hashing out the reorganization plan. "Carter to Form Unit to Aid in Revamping," *Augusta Chronicle*, March 2, 1971, sec. A; "Lobbyist Is on Carter's Committee," *Augusta Chronicle*, June 3, 1971; "Caldwell Calls Plan a 'Power Grab,'" *Augusta Chronicle*, November 20, 1971; "Burson, Forester Denounce Carter Reorganization Plan," *Augusta Chronicle*, December 17, 1971.

26. "Chronicle Tops GPA in Local Sports, Editorials," *Augusta Chronicle*, June 19, 1971.

27. "A Blueprint for Action: Goals for Georgia in the Seventies," 1972, folder "Goals for Georgia, General, 1971," box 9, RCB-36656, Department of Game and Fish, Commissioner's Office, Assistant Director's Subject Files, 1998–49A, Georgia Archives, Morrow.

28. "Governor's Citizens Council on Environmental Protection," September 1, 1971, folder "Environmental Quality Governor's Council on 1971," box 8, RCB-36649; "Outline; Goals for Georgia; The Natural Environment," 1971, folder "Goals for Georgia, General, 1971," box 9, RCB-36656, both in Department of Game and Fish, Commissioner's Office, Assistant Director's Subject Files, 1998–49A, Georgia Archives.

29. "Carter Plan Expected," *Marietta Daily Journal*, November 29, 1971, sec. A.

30. "Gov. Carter Will Sign."

31. "Caldwell Calls Plan"; Bill Shipp, "Carter Sends Reform Proposal Out Today," *Atlanta Constitution*, December 10, 1971, sec. A; Tom Linthicum and Bill Jordan, "Ga. Safety, Health Unit Gains Panel Approval," *Atlanta Constitution*, February 17, 1972.

32. Raleigh Bryans, "State Water Quality Board Joins Howard in Battling Carter," *Atlanta Journal*, January 6, 1972, sec. B; Robert Hanie, "Telegram to Donald Scott," October 14, 1971, folder "Natural Areas Council: Corr 1968–69," box RCB-36646, Department of Game and Fish, Commissioners Office, Assistant Director's Subject Files, Georgia Archives; "Conservation Head Resigns in Opposition to Carter," *Atlanta Constitution*, October 15, 1971.

33. "Gov. Carter Will Sign."

34. "Just Who Began 'Zero Budgeting'?," *Atlanta Constitution*, September 5, 1976, sec. B; Thomas Lauth, "Zero-Base Budgeting in Georgia State Government: Myth and Reality," *Public Administration Review* 38, no. 5 (1978): 420–30.

35. Bourne, *Jimmy Carter*, 250; Zelizer, *Jimmy Carter*, loc. 547.

36. Jimmy Carter, *Why Not the Best: The First Fifty Years* (Fayetteville: University of Arkansas Press, 1996), 118–20; Zelizer, *Jimmy Carter*.

37. John Pennington, "A Plan to Save Special Places," *Atlanta Constitution*, October 8, 1972; John Pennington, "Georgia's First Wilderness Park," *Atlanta Constitution*, June 20, 1971.

38. Stephen Skowronek, *Presidential Leadership in Political Time: Reprise and Reappraisal* (Lawrence: University Press of Kansas, 2020).

39. Maxine Rock, "Diary of a Toll Road Fighter," *Atlanta Journal and Constitution Magazine*, April 30, 1972; Marilyn Grist, "Neighborhood Interest Groups and Public Policy" (master's thesis, Georgia State University, 1984).

40. Stephen Hildebrand and Johnnie B. Cannon, eds., *Environmental Analysis: The NEPA Experience* (Boca Raton, Fla.: Lewis, 1993); Roy Clark, "NEPA: The Rational Approach to Change," in *National Environmental Policy: Past, Present and Future*, ed. Roy Clark and Larry Canter (Boca Raton, Fla.: St. Lucie, 1997), 17–21; Robert Lazear, *The National Environmental Policy Act and Its Implementation: A Selected, Annotated Bibliography* (Madison: Wisconsin Seminars on Resource and Environmental Systems, Institute for Environmental Studies, University of Wisconsin, 1978); Lynton K. Caldwell, *Science and the National Environmental Policy Act: Redirecting Policy through Procedural Reform* (Birmingham: University of Alabama Press, 1982); Wendy Read Wertz, *Lynton Keith Caldwell: An Environmental Visionary and the National Environmental Policy Act* (Bloomington: Indiana University Press, 2014).

41. "Ecologists Try to Sink Lake Road," *Atlanta Journal and Constitution*, January 10, 1971; Bill Jordan, "Athens Ecology Leader Hails New Route of I-75," *Atlanta Journal Constitution*, July 14, 1971 ("values," "objective"); "New I-75 Route," *Atlanta Constitution*, March 22, 1972, sec. A; Robert Claxton, *The History of the Georgia Conservancy, 1967–1981* (Atlanta: Georgia Conservancy, 1985), 43, 53 (on "persuasive politics" enabled by Carter's election), 55–56.

42. Bob Fort, "Carter to Name Study Panel on Stone Mountain Freeway," *Atlanta Journal and Constitution*, October 12, 1971; Gregory Jaynes, "Stop Mountain Tollway, Panel Told at Decatur," *Atlanta Constitution*, December 7, 1972, sec. A; Bill MacNabb, "No Tollway; What Now?," *Atlanta Constitution*, January 21, 1973, sec. A.

43. Barbara Casson, "I-485 Study Draws Mixed Reactions," *Atlanta Constitution*, July 30, 1972, sec. A ("development").

44. Howell Raines, "Carter Backs I-485 Amid Wide Criticism," *Atlanta Constitution*, August 8, 1973, sec. A; Raines, "Carter Denies I-485 Stand Bias," *Atlanta Journal and Constitution*, July 25, 1973; Claudia Townsend, "I-485 Critics Say Carter Limited Their Input," *Atlanta Constitution*, August 7, 1973, sec. A.

45. Raines, "Carter Backs I-485"; Howell Raines, "Carter Defends Hiring of PR Firm for Tollways," *Atlanta Constitution*, August 10, 1973, sec. A.

46. Bill King, "Jackson Declares I-485 Issue Dead," *Atlanta Constitution*, September 26, 1974, sec. A.

47. "Ecologists Try to Sink"; Margaret Hurst, "River Ecologists Chose Council," *Atlanta Constitution*, September 21, 1971; Duane Riner, "Ecologists Chide Industry," *Atlanta Constitution*, December 1, 1971, sec. A.

48. Keith Coulbourn, "The Chattahoochee Has Friends," *Atlanta Constitution Magazine*, October 16, 1976, 18 ("legal loopholes").

49. Rock Howard, "Letter to Dr. Robert Platt," June 7, 1973; Robert Platt, "Letter to Mr. R. S. Howard," July 2, 1973, both in folder "Misc. Letters for RSH," box 1, RCB 2144, Water Quality Control Board, Executive Secretary's Subject Files, 1966–75, EPD Papers, Georgia Archives.

50. [Rock Howard?], "Water Pollution Control Program in Georgia]," 1974, folder "1972 Environmental Protection Division," box 1, RCB 2144, Water Quality Control Board, Executive Secretary's Subject Files, 1966–75, Environmental Protection Division Archives, Georgia Archives; Rex Granum, "Howard Will Retire as Chief of EPD," *Atlanta Constitution*, December 31, 1974, sec. A; "Ravan Officially Named Southeast Ecology

Chief," *Atlanta Constitution*, September 2, 1971, sec. A; "Howard Praised by Top Official," *Atlanta Journal*, July 26, 1977, sec. C.

51. Morrison, "It Doesn't Take Much."

52. Alex Coffin, "City Receives $3.9 Million to Clean Rivers," *Atlanta Constitution*, October 12, 1972, sec. A.

53. Tom Linthicum, "Sewer Ties Banned in Basin," *Atlanta Constitution*, November 9, 1973, sec. A.

54. Bill Shipp, "A River Still in Need of Friends," *Atlanta Constitution*, January 5, 1976, sec. A; Ken Willis, "Chattahoochee Cleanup Is Promised," *Atlanta Constitution*, January 22, 1976, sec. A.

55. City of Atlanta, "Fact Sheet: Application for National Pollutant Discharge Elimination System; Permit to Discharge Treated Wastewater to Waters of the State of Georgia: Application No. GA0021482," August 30, 1974, folder "Atlanta Ga (NPDES) GA0021482," box 4, RG 26, subgroup 7, series 62, Georgia Health Department Archives, Georgia Archives.

56. James A. Evans, "Federal Water Pollution Control Act Discharge Permit System: An Industrial Viewpoint," *Natural Resources Lawyer* 10, no. 4 (1978): 761–67.

57. CH2M Hill, "For Air Force Plant 6, Georgia," March 1984, folder "Lockheed–Ga. Company, Marietta: Cobb County," box 28, RG 88, subgroup 7, series 29, EPD Hazardous Waste Program Archives, Georgia Archives, VI-10 ("concentrated").

58. "Authorization to Discharge under the National Pollutant Discharge Elimination System: Permit No. GA001198; United States Air Force: Air Force Plant #6," June 25, 1974, folder "Lockheed–Ga. Company, Marietta: Cobb County," box 28, RG 88, subgroup 7, series 29, EPD Hazardous Waste Program Archives, Georgia Archives.

59. Clyde F. Fehn, "Memo: Waste Oil Generated at Industrial Waste Water Treatment Plant at Lockheed Aircraft Co.—Cobb County," March 31, 1976, folder "Lockheed–Ga. Company, Marietta: Cobb County," box 28, RG 88, subgroup 7, series 29, EPD Hazardous Waste Program Archives, Georgia Archives.

60. NAPCA, Region IV Office, "Meeting to Gather Data for Atlanta AQCR Status Report," March 4, 1970; G. T. Helms, "Memo: Location of Air Sampling Trailer in Atlanta AQCD," August 19, 1970; Office of Public Information; HEW News, Region IV Office, "Press Release: Proposed Boundaries for an Intrastate Air Quality Control Region in the Metropolitan Atlanta, Area," February 2, 1970; Department of Health, Education and Welfare, "Transcript of Proceedings: Air Quality Control Region; Atlanta, Georgia: 13 February, 1970," ACE Federal Reports, all in folder "Atlanta AQCR," box 5, Access 79A0045, State Implementation Plan Files, EPA Archives, National Archives, Southeast Region, Atlanta.

61. Jim Morrison, "Air Quality in the Atlanta Region: A Workshop for Citizens," *Newsletter of the Georgia Conservancy*, June 26, 1970.

62. "A Summary of the Governor's Pollution Package as Enacted by the 1971 Georgia General Assembly," 1972, folder 2, "Environmental Quality Governor's Council on 1971," box 8, RCB-36649, Department of Game and Fish, Commissioner's Office, Assistant Director's Subject Files, 1998–49A, Georgia Archives; Bill Shipp, "Carter to Offer Tough Ecology Package," *Atlanta Constitution*, December 2, 1971, sec. B.

63. "Minutes of Ad Hoc Advisory Committee on Ambient Air Standards," September 18, 1970, folder "Atlanta AQCR," box 5, Access 79A0045, National Archives.

64. Bob Hurt, "Two of Ga.'s Air Pollution Rules Vetoed," *Atlanta Constitution*, June 1, 1972, sec. A; Lawrence Carter, "Implementation Plan Evaluation: Report for the State of

Georgia," July 25, 1972, folder 8.2.3.11 "Control Strategies," box 5, Access 79A0045, State Implementation Plan Files, National Archives.

65. "EPA Hits State Plan on Waste," *Atlanta Constitution*, May 10, 1973, sec. A; Chuck Bell, "New Pollution Proposal Hit," *Atlanta Constitution*, July 27, 1973, sec. A; Ken Willis, "State Air Quality Experts Supports Stricter Controls," *Atlanta Constitution*, September 5, 1973, sec. C; Ken Willis, "Should Relax Controls, Says EPA Official Here," *Atlanta Constitution*, September 6, 1973, sec. A; Air Program Branch, "Argument of NRDC vs. EPA: Air Program Branch's Comments," December 6, 1972, folder 8.2.3.11 "Control Strategies," box 5, Access 79A0045, State Implementation Plan Files, National Archives; James I. Hamby, "The Clean Air Act and Significant Deterioration of Air Quality: The Continuing Controversy," *Boston College Environmental Affairs Law Review* 5, no. 1 (1976): 145–74; Barbara Casson, "How Dirty Is Georgia's Air?," *Atlanta Constitution*, November 25, 1973, sec. C.

66. "Georgia Power Plans for Pollution Abatement," *Atlanta Constitution*, March 11, 1971, sec. A.

67. "Georgia Air Sampling Network," May 5, 1976, box 1, Environmental Protection Division, Air Quality Control Administrative Files, 1971–78, Georgia Archives.

68. Chuck Bell, "Pollution Controls Tightened," *Atlanta Constitution*, March 29, 1972, sec. A.

69. Bill Collins, "Report Labels Southern Co. One of the Worst Polluters," *Atlanta Constitution*, July 2, 1972, sec. E; Casson, "How Dirty Is Georgia's Air?"

70. Ken Willis, "Some Industries Balk at Clean Air Deadlines," *Atlanta Constitution*, October 17, 1974, sec. C.

71. "Public Hearing: 'Proposed Rules on Prevention of Significant Air Quality Deterioration'; Held in Atlanta, Georgia, September 4–5, 1973," September 4, 1973, folder "Significant Deterioration—Misc," box 6, Access 79A0045, State Implementation Plan Files, National Archives.

72. Nicholas A. Ashford, *Crisis in the Workplace: Occupational Disease and Injury* (Cambridge, Mass: MIT Press, 1976); Daniel M. Berman, *Death on the Job* (New York: Monthly Review, 1979.

73. Milo Dakin and Jim Stewart, "U.S. Report Due on Ga. Labor Probe," *Atlanta Constitution*, September 20, 1972.

74. Jim Stewart, "U.S. Preempts State's Labor Safety Laws," *Atlanta Constitution*, January 3, 1973, sec. A.

75. Linthicum and Jordan, "Ga. Safety, Health Unit."

76. Milo Dakin, "Carter Abandons Job Safety Plan," *Atlanta Constitution*, May 9, 1973, sec. A ("tough"); James Hightower, "Compliance, Not Defiance; Safety Act Fuss Calms," *Atlanta Constitution*, April 14, 1974.

77. Nick Taylor, "Work Safety Rules Upheld," *Atlanta Constitution*, May 25, 1972; Billie Brown, "Just Who Will Enforce Industrial Safety Law?," *Atlanta Constitution*, October 24, 1973.

78. Hightower, "Compliance, Not Defiance," ("calm[ed]," "compliance").

79. Joe Brown, "Crisis in Textiles," *Atlanta Constitution*, January 12, 1971; "U.S. Textile Industry Entering Critical Period," *Atlanta Constitution*, May 15, 1977.

80. Jefferson Cowie, *The Great Exception: The New Deal and the Limits of American Politics* (Princeton, N.J.: Princeton University Press, 2016), 24.

81. Alton Hornsby, *Black Power in Dixie: A Political History of African Americans in Atlanta* (Gainesville: University Press of Florida, 2009); Maurice J. Hobson, *The Legend of the Black Mecca: Politics and Class in the Making of Modern Atlanta* (Chapel Hill: Uni-

versity of North Carolina Press, 2017); Mack H. Jones, "Black Political Empowerment in Atlanta: Myth and Reality," *Annals of the American Academy of Political and Social Science* 439 (September 1978): 90–117; Andrew Young, *An Easy Burden: The Civil Rights Movement and the Transformation of America* (Waco, Tex.: Baylor University Press, 2008); David Andrew Harmon, *Beneath the Image of the Civil Rights Movement and Race Relations: Atlanta, Georgia, 1946–1981* (Abingdon: Taylor and Francis, 1996); Robert A. Holmes, *Maynard Jackson: A Biography*, 2nd ed. (Miami: Barnhardt and Ashe, 2011).

82. Jones, "Black Political Empowerment"; Clarence N. Stone, "Atlanta: Protest and Elections Are Not Enough," PS 19, no. 3 (1986): 618–25, https://doi.org/10.2307/419184.

83. "Blacks Now a Majority in Atlanta," *Atlanta Constitution*, February 11, 1971.

84. "Memo: The Candidacy of Andrew Young for Congressman; 5th District of Georgia," 1970, folder 1 "Strategy," box 52, Andrew Young Papers, Auburn Avenue Library, Atlanta; Young, *Easy Burden*, 504–8.

85. Andrew Young for Congress Support Committee, "The Candidacy of Andrew Young for Congressman: 5th District of Georgia," memo, May 1970, folder 1 "Strategy," box 52, Young Papers, Auburn Avenue Library.

86. Bill Shipp, "Young Seeks Thompson's House Post," *Atlanta Constitution*, March 5, 1970, sec. A; Jones, "Black Political Empowerment," esp. 103; Hornsby, *Black Power in Dixie*, 132–33; Young Campaign, "Face the 70's: The Platform of Andrew Young; Democrat: Fifth Congressional District," October 19, 1970, folder 8, "Position Statements and Research," box 66, Young Papers, Auburn Avenue Library.

87. Andrew Hurley, "Challenging Corporate Polluters: Race, Class, and Environmental Politics in Gary, Indiana, since 1945," *Indiana Magazine of History* 88, no. 4 (1992): 273–302; Andrew Barnes, "3 Candidates Back D.C. Cleanup," *Washington Post*, February 28, 1971, sec. D; David Stradling and Richard Stradling, *Where the River Burned: Carl Stokes and the Struggle to Save Cleveland* (Ithaca: Cornell University Press, 2015); Robert Gioielli, *Environmental Activism and the Urban Crisis: Baltimore, St. Louis, Chicago* (Philadelphia: Temple University Press, 2014).

88. Young Campaign, "Face the 70's"; Ernest Pharr, "Our Polluted Environment—Part Two; 'Proctor Creek Will Rise Again,'" *Atlanta Inquirer*, July 11, 1970.

89. Boyd Lewis, "Historic Victory Escapes Andy Young in Campaign," *Atlanta Voice*, November 1, 1970; Young, *Easy Burden*, 510–18, 516.

90. Andrew Young, "Environment (Chattahoochee) Talking Points," 1972, folder "Position Papers and Research: Environment," box 67, Young Papers, Auburn Avenue Library, 9 (emphasis in the original); Young, *Easy Burden*, 518 ("rich and poor").

91. Bob Fort, "Nixon Cuts Will Hit State Hard," *Atlanta Constitution*, January 30, 1973, 14; Bob Allison, "Nation in Serious Trouble, Young Warns on Fund Cuts," *Atlanta Constitution*, March 12, 1973.

92. "National Environmental Scorecard," League of Conservation Voters, 2012, https://scorecard.lcv.org/scorecard/archive.

93. Clarence N. Stone, *Regime Politics: Governing Atlanta, 1946–1988* (Lawrence: University Press of Kansas, 1989), 85 ("linchpin").

94. Hobson, *Legend of the Black Mecca*, esp. 52 ("champion"), 59; Holmes, *Maynard Jackson*.

95. Stone, *Regime Politics*, 87 ("dicta"); Tom Linthicum, "City's Mayoral Candidates Carve Out Their Positions," *Atlanta Constitution*, September 30, 1973, sec. A; Tom Linthicum, "Jackson Claims He Refused Support of 'Power Structure,'" *Atlanta Constitution*, June 30, 1973, sec. A ("so-called").

96. Hank Ezell, "Maynard Aims to Woo White Northsiders," *Atlanta Constitution*, April 15, 1973, sec. A.

97. Tom Linthicum, "Residential Group Eyes Candidates," *Atlanta Constitution*, March 28, 1973, sec. A.

98. Tom Linthicum, "Must Seek Alternatives to Highways—Jackson," *Atlanta Constitution*, August 10, 1973, sec. A ("damage," "expansion").

99. Kay McKenzie, phone interview by Christopher Sellers, March 29, 2013.

100. Ernest Holsendolph, "Atlanta's Black Mayor and Its Business Image: Can He Please the Poor and Big Business, Too? Atlanta's Black Mayor," *New York Times*, November 4, 1973, sec. BF ("cow pastures").

101. Phyl Garland, "Atlanta: Black Mecca of the South," *Ebony* 26, no. 10 (1971): 152; Hobson, *Legend of the Black Mecca*.

102. B. Drummond Ayres Jr., "Amid Signs of Racial Division, Atlanta's Black Mayor Begins Second Year under Fire," *New York Times*, February 26, 1975.

103. Hobson, *Legend of the Black Mecca*; "Atlanta: New Mecca for Young Blacks," *Ebony* 28, no. 11 (1973): 62.

104. Keith Coulbourn, "Tightening the Lines at EOA," *Atlanta Constitution*, October 12, 1975; Colleen Teasley, "City Funding to Keep EOA in Operation," *Atlanta Constitution*, March 21, 1973; Chuck Bell, "EOA's Achievements Here May Insure Its Survival," *Atlanta Constitution*, September 24, 1973, sec. A.

105. Roger M. Williams, "America's Black Mayors: Are They Saving the Cities?," *Saturday Review World*, May 4, 1974; on racial capitalism as a framework of analysis, see Cedric J. Robinson, *Black Marxism: The Making of the Black Radical Tradition*, 3rd ed. (1983; repr. Chapel Hill: University of North Carolina Press, 2020); and Robinson, *On Racial Capitalism, Black Internationalism, and Cultures of Resistance*, ed. H.L.T. Quan (London: Pluto, 2019); Gargi Bhattacharyya, *Rethinking Racial Capitalism* (Lanham: Rowman and Littlefield International, 2018); Justin Leroy and Destin Jenkins, eds., Histories of Racial Capitalism (New York: Columbia University Press, 2021).

106. Ken Willis, "Atlanta Police Force Changing Color Fast," *Atlanta Constitution*, June 16, 1976; Carol Askinaze, "Mayor Promises Women a Better Deal on Municipal Jobs," *Atlanta Constitution*, June 20, 1978.

107. Jim Stewart et al., "One Weekend . . . Mayor Jackson Finds Apartments Unlivable," *Atlanta Constitution*, October 21, 1974; John Head and Chet Fuller, "Public Housing; It Will Take Much, Much More Than Money, Bricks or Mortar to Solve the Ugly Dilemma of the People Who Must Live Here," *Atlanta Constitution*, November 10, 1974, sec. B; "The Welfare Mess; Assistance More than Money . . . It's Housing, Help for Mobless," *Atlanta Constitution*, May 23, 1975, secs. 1, 6 ("intolerable"); "Conditions in Project Shock Atlanta Mayor," *New York Times*, October 21, 1974.

108. Jim Merriner, "Jackson Signs Bill on Housing Powers," *Atlanta Constitution*, May 22, 1975, sec. A; Jim Merriner, "Mayor's Task Force Plan; AHA May Lose Managing Role," *Atlanta Constitution*, May 31, 1975, "tenants broader control."

109. Valerie Price, "Mayor Plows Bedford-Pine Area Garden," *Atlanta Constitution*, March 15, 1975.

110. Harmon, *Beneath the Image*, 285–86; Hobson, *Legend of the Black Mecca*.

111. Jan Meadows, interview by Christopher Sellers, Atlanta, February 7, 2013. Cascade Forest Planning Committee, *Cascade Forest Neighborhood Comprehensive Plan: One-Five-Fifteen Year* (Atlanta: Cascade Forest Neighborhood Association, 1975), 26,

29; Meadows, interview; Cascade Forest Planning Committee, *Cascade Forest Neighborhood*, 36 ("wildlife").

112. Henry Eason, "Feds Ante Up $440,000 for Cascade Park," *Atlanta Constitution*, January 9, 1979, sec. C ("wilderness park"); Bob Harrell, "Nature Preserve Slated for Southside at Cascade Spring," *Atlanta Constitution*, March 23, 1987, sec. D.

113. King, "Jackson Declares I-485 Issue Dead."

114. Jim Merriner, "Jackson Sees No Problems Blocking I-485 Corridor Park," *Atlanta Constitution*, October 2, 1974.

115. Frederick Allen and Rex Granum, "DOT Plans Parkway for I-485 Corridor," *Atlanta Constitution*, October 9, 1974.

116. Hank Ezell, "Jackson Has the Business Community Buzzing," *Atlanta Constitution*, April 7, 1974, sec. A ("stirred up").

117. Colleen Teasley, "Racism Killing City, Ivan Allen Tells Forum," *Atlanta Constitution*, September 26, 1974; John Huey, "Jackson, Brockey Sending Corrections," *Atlanta Constitution*, November 15, 1974, sec. A.

118. Wayne King, "Atlanta's Confident Hope Is Faltering," *New York Times*, October 7, 1974.

119. Ezell, "Business Community Buzzing" ("more interest").

120. Jim Gray, "Housing Revival Report Studied," *Atlanta Constitution*, June 29, 1974, sec. B.

121. Alexis Scott Reeves, "Area Panel Again Hits Plan for Bedford-Pine," *Atlanta Constitution*, September 10, 1974, sec. A; Jim Merriner, "'Pound Cake Summit' Partially Breaks Bedford-Pine Deadlock," *Atlanta Constitution*, November 23, 1974, sec. A.

122. Ernest Pharr, "Thousands of Atlantans to Affirm the City's Spirit," *Atlanta Inquirer*, October 5, 1974.

123. Maxine Rock, "Democracy Comes to City Planning," *Atlanta Constitution*, December 8, 1974, sec. SM.

124. Clarence N. Stone, "Preemptive Power: Floyd Hunter's 'Community Power Structure' Reconsidered," *American Journal of Political Science* 32, no. 1 (1988): 82–104; Grist, "Neighborhood Interest Groups"; Ann Woolner, "New Legal Clout: Neighborhoods Talk and City Listens," *Atlanta Journal*, September 27, 1976, sec. A.

125. Ann Woolner, "Neighborhood Planning Units Accorded Mixed Reviews," *Atlanta Journal*, September 21, 1978, sec. C.

126. Meadows, interview; Juner Norris, interview by Christopher Sellers, Atlanta, February 5, 2013.

127. Dale Russakoff, "City, Residents Face Off on Poor Process of NPUs," *Atlanta Constitution*, June 11, 1978; Lyn Martin, "CAP Asks Mayor to Declare Clark Election Invalid," *Atlanta Constitution*, June 6, 1978; Martin, "Jackson Says Clark Will Keep NPU Chairmanship," *Atlanta Constitution*, June 7, 1978.

128. Woolner, "Neighborhood Planning Units."

129. Joseph A. McCartin, "'Fire the Hell Out of Them': Sanitation Workers' Struggles and the Normalization of the Striker Replacement Strategy in the 1970s," *Labor: Studies in Working Class History of the Americas* 2, no. 3 (2005): 67–92, https://doi.org/10.1215/15476715-2-3-67; Hobson, *Legend of the Black Mecca*, 85–89, 86 ("championing").

130. Steven Holmes and Lyn Martin, "NPU Members Tell City Hall: 'You Can't Ignore Us,'" *Atlanta Constitution*, June 13, 1978, sec. C ("not taking"); John Carter, "Ailing NPUs Face Critical Malady," *Atlanta Constitution*, February 14, 1980.

131. William Greider, "Facing Up to the New Economic Order: The New Economic Order," *Washington Post*, April 22, 1979, sec. Outlook Columnists Editorials.

132. Morgan, "Jimmy Carter," 1020; Skowronek, *Presidential Leadership*; Fink and Graham, *Carter Presidency*.

133. Stuart Meck and Rebecca Retzlaff, "President Jimmy Carter's Urban Policy: A Reconstruction and an Appraisal," *Journal of Planning History* 11, no. 3 (2012): 243, 242–80, https://doi.org/10.1177/1538513212444565; Thomas J. Sugrue, "Carter's Urban Policy Crisis," in Fink and Graham, *Carter Presidency*, 138–49; Tracy Neumann, "Privatization, Devolution, and Jimmy Carter's National Urban Policy," *Journal of Urban History* 40, no. 2 (2014): 283–300, https://doi.org/10.1177/0096144213508623.

134. Sugrue, "Carter's Urban Policy Crisis," 149; Neumann, "Privatization."

135. Meck and Retzlaff, "President Jimmy Carter's Urban Policy," 257 ("apparently lacks").

136. Barry Commoner, "Discussant: Barry Commoner," in *The Presidency and Domestic Policies of Jimmy Carter*, ed. Herbert D. Rosenbaum and Alexej Ugrinsky (Westport, Conn.: Praeger, 1993), 600–602.

137. J. William Holland, "The Great Gamble: Jimmy Carter and the 1979 Energy Crisis," *Prologue* 22, no. 1 (1990): 63–79; John C. Barrow, "An Age of Limits: Jimmy Carter and the Quest for a National Energy Policy," in Fink and Graham, *Carter Presidency*, 158–78; Sidney Plotkin, "Corporate Power and Political Resistance: The Case of the Energy Mobilization Board," *Polity* 18, no. 1 (1985): 115–37, https://doi.org/10.2307/3234735; Philip Shabecoff, "Environmentalists Fear a Retrenching by Carter: Official Reassurances Energy Department Reports Concern on Mobilization Board," *New York Times*, July 17, 1979, sec. Business and Finance; Meg Jacobs, *Panic at the Pump: The Energy Crisis and the Transformation of American Politics in the 1970s* (New York: Hill and Wang, 2016), 161–95.

138. Margaret Shannon, "New Energy Boosts the Fight against Nuclear Power in the South," *Atlanta Constitution*, February 25, 1979; Bourne, *Jimmy Carter*, 440 ("out of the question").

139. Seth S. King, "Carter Signs a Bill to Protect 104 Million Acres in Alaska: Warning about Pollution; A Balance Is Sought Allowing Oil Exploration; Stevens Pledges Further Action," *New York Times*, December 3, 1980; S. King, "President Signs a Bill for Record Spending of $1.2 Billion on 100 Parks, Rivers, Historic Sites and Trails," *New York Times*, November 12, 1978.

140. Craig Hume, "Park Bill Signed by President," *Atlanta Constitution*, August 16, 1978; Jerry Schwartz, "Park Service to Buy 2 Chattahoochee Parcels," *Atlanta Constitution*, December 27, 1978.

141. Barbara Davis Blum, interview by Christopher Sellers, Washington, D.C., March 17, 2015.

142. Philip Shabecoff, "Environment Policy of U.S. Faces Change: 'Impact Statements' on Federal Projects to Be Simplified under New Regulations," *New York Times*, December 18, 1977; "Implementation of the Environmental Impact Statement," *Yale Law Journal* 88, no. 3 (1979): 596–611, https://doi.org/10.2307/795664; Richard A. Carpenter, "Ecology in Court, and Other Disappointments of Environmental Science and Environmental Law," *Natural Resources Lawyer* 15, no. 3 (1983): 573–95.

143. Leonard Ray Teel, "Get Rich? EPA's Impact Statements Bulky but Very Profitable," *Atlanta Constitution*, January 8, 1978; Eugene P. Odum, "The Emergence of Ecology as a New Integrative Discipline," *Science* 195, no. 4284 (1977): 1291 ("mass produced").

144. Barbara Moran, "Highway Widening Challenged in Court," *Atlanta Constitution*, July 5, 1979; Stephen Holmes, "Clark Threatens a Court Fight over Bedford Plans," *Atlanta Constitution*, April 15, 1978.

145. Richard P. McHugh, "The Impact of the Safe Drinking Water Act," *Journal American Water Works Association* 70, no. 12 (1978): 666–69 ("pollution control"); Frederick Allen, "EPA's Water Rules Could Prove Costly," *Atlanta Constitution*, January 27, 1978 ("hellish").

146. Lyn Martin, "City's Treatment Plant Is Biggest Polluter," *Atlanta Constitution*, April 13, 1978; John Carter, "Plant Draws State Order," *Atlanta Constitution*, August 21, 1980; David Secrest, "Zoning and Pollution Cause NPU Rift," *Atlanta Constitution*, December 11, 1980.

147. Leonard Ray Teel, "Georgia Told: Clean Up Air," *Atlanta Journal*, July 2, 1976, sec. A; Chuck Bell, "Ozone Problem Here," *Atlanta Journal Constitution*, November 29, 1976, sec. A; "Air in 11 Metro Counties Won't Pass EPA Smog Test," *Atlanta Journal*, February 24, 1978, sec. A.

148. Environmental Protection Division, "Monthly Report," March 1978; Environmental Protection Division, "Monthly Report," October 1978; Environmental Protection Division, "Monthly Report," November 1978, all in folder "Monthly Report Air Branch, 1978," box 4, RG 88, subgroup 4, series 16, Air Quality Division, Environmental Protection Department Archives, Georgia Archives, Morrow.

149. Environmental Protection Division, "Monthly Report," May 1978, folder "Monthly Report Air Branch 1978," box 4, RG 88, subgroup 4, series 16, Air Quality Division ("baseline").

150. Office of Air Quality Planning and Standards, *Guideline on Air Quality Models*, OAQPS Guideline Series (Washington, D.C.: U.S. EPA, 1978), 14 ("meteorological and topographic"); Office of Air Quality, *Air Quality Modeling: What It Is and How It Is Used* (Research Triangle Park, N.C.: U.S. EPA, 1980) 9 ("wind direction"); see also Catherine G. Miller, *Case Studies in the Application of Air Quality Modeling in Environmental Decision Making: Summary and Recommendations* (Research Triangle Park, N.C.: Environmental Sciences Research Laboratory, 1981).

151. Barbara Blum, "Interview: EPA Deputy Administrator Barbara Blum," *Journal Water Pollution Control Federation* 50, no. 5 (1978): 817 ("most impacted").

152. Environmental Protection Division, "Monthly Report," March 1978, Georgia Archives; Fran Hesser, "Car Emission Checks Approved," *Atlanta Constitution*, October 2, 1980, sec. C; Beau Cutts, "Legislature Votes 81 Auto Exhaust Tests," *Atlanta Constitution*, March 22, 1979; Beau Cutts, "Metro Motorists to Face Air Pollution Inspections," *Atlanta Constitution*, January 26, 1979 ("quietly").

153. Douglas Costle, "Dealing with the Chemical Revolution," *EPA Journal* 4, no. 8 (1978): 2–3; Rachel Carson, *Silent Spring* (Boston: Houghton, 1962); Christopher C. Sellers, *Hazards of the Job: From Industrial Disease to Environmental Health Science* (Chapel Hill: University of North Carolina Press, 1997); Robert N. Proctor, *Cancer Wars: How Politics Shapes What We Know and Don't Know about Cancer* (New York: Basic Books, 1996); Soraya Boudia and Nathalie Jas, eds., *Toxicants, Health and Regulation since 1945* (London: Pickering and Chatto, 2013).

154. Eileen McGurty, *Transforming Environmentalism: Warren County, PCBs, and the Origins of Environmental Justice* (New Brunswick, N.J.: Rutgers University Press, 2009); Emily Brownell, "Negotiating the New Economic Order of Waste," *Environmental His-*

tory 16, no. 2 (2011): 262–89, https://doi.org/10.1093/envhis/emr030; Charles Davis, "Implementing the Resource Conservation and Recovery Act of 1976: Problems and Prospects," *Public Administration Quarterly* 9, no. 2 (1985): 218–36.

155. Office of Planning and Evaluation, Environmental Protection Agency, *National Accomplishments in Pollution Control, 1970–1980: Some Case Histories* (Washington, D.C.: Environmental Protection Agency, 1980), 25.

156. Fehn, "Memo."

157. Clyde F. Fehn, "Letter to Mr. Cliff Griffin, Lockheed-Georgia Company," April 12, 1976; Shirley Maxwell, "Letter to Mr. Cliff Griffin, Lockheed-Georgia Company," July 30, 1976, both in folder "Lockheed –Ga. Company, Marietta: Cobb County," box 28, RG 88, subgroup 7, series 29, EPD Hazardous Waste Program Archives, Georgia Archives.

158. Sid Akers to John D. Taylor, "Lockheed Disposing of Wastes at Cobb County Landfill Located on Olie Creek," August 22, 1979; Shirley Maxwell to John D. Taylor, "Memo: Inspection of Lockheed Georgia on August 22, 1979," December 14, 1979, both in folder "Lockheed –Ga. Company, Marietta: Cobb County," box 28, RG 88, subgroup 7, series 29, EPD Hazardous Waste Program Archives, Georgia Archives.

159. Elizabeth D. Blum, *Love Canal Revisited: Race, Class, and Gender in Environmental Activism* (Lawrence: University Press of Kansas, 2008); Thomas H. Fletcher, *From Love Canal to Environmental Justice: The Politics of Hazardous Waste on the Canada-U.S. Border* (Peterborough, Ont.: University of Toronto Press, 2003); Amy M. Hay, "Recipe for Disaster: Motherhood and Citizenship at Love Canal," *Journal of Women's History* 21, no. 1 (2009): 111–34.

160. Blum, "Interview," 881 ("esoteric").

161. "Major Urban Conference," *EPA Journal* 4, no. 8 (1978): 32–33.

162. Frank Goldsmith and Lorin E. Kerr, "Worker Participation in Job Safety and Health," *Journal of Public Health Policy* 4, no. 4 (1983): 447, https://doi.org/10.2307/3342222.

163. "Eula Bingham Administration, 1977–1981: Of Minnows, Whales and 'Common Sense,'" U.S. Department of Labor, accessed August 16, 2019, https://www.dol.gov/general/aboutdol/history/osha13bingham.

164. "Jimmy Carter: Interview with the President: Remarks and a Question-and-Answer Session with Members of the National Association of Farm Broadcasting," American Presidency Project, September 29, 1978, http://www.presidency.ucsb.edu/ws/?pid=29892 ("personally"); David Burnham, "Carter Gets Warning on Cotton Dust: Marshall Chides Economic Aides; Reason Given for Delay Cited Carter: Warned on Cotton Dust Ruling," *New York Times*, June 1, 1978, sec. Business and Finance.

165. "2 U.S. Judges Block Enforcement of OSHA Cotton Dust Standard," *Atlanta Constitution*, October 5, 1978, sec. D; American Textile Manufacturers Institute, Inc., et al. v. Donovan, Secretary of Labor, et al., 452 U.S. 490 (1981); Linda Greenhouse, "Justices Decide U.S. Must Protect Workers' Safety Despite High Cost," *New York Times*, June 18, 1981, sec. A; W. Kip Viscusi, "Regulating the Regulators," *University of Chicago Law Review* 63, no. 4 (1996): 1423–61, https://doi.org/10.2307/1600278.

166. Roger Witherspoon, "Quirks in Georgia's Law Block Worker Compensation," *Atlanta Constitution*, February 19, 1981, sec. B.

167. Robin Schatz, "Brown Lung: The Dust Hasn't Settled," *Atlanta Constitution*, February 19, 1981, sec. B ("this thing").

168. Hal Gulliver, "The Right Not to Be Fooled With," *Atlanta Constitution*, January 19, 1977, sec. A.

169. Sallye Salter, "Businessmen Hail Curbing of OSHA Inspection Powers," *Atlanta Constitution*, May 24, 1978, sec. A; Michael Schwartz, "Law Firm Fights Government Control," *Atlanta Constitution*, December 16, 1979, sec. J.

170. Emma Bryce, "America's Greenest Presidents," *New York Times*, September 20, 2012; David Roberts, "The Greenest Presidents," *Corporate Knights: The Magazine for Clean Capitalism* 1, no. 4 (2012), https://www.corporateknights.com/leadership/greenest -president-u-s-history/; "America's Greenest Presidents," *Green Blog*, accessed July 5, 2014, http://green.blogs.nytimes.com/2012/09/20/americas-greenest-presidents/.

171. Blum and other EPA officials also made significant, accepted contributions to Car- ter's urban policy itself; see Blum, "Interview," 815–18.

172. James C. Scott, *Seeing Like a State: How Certain Schemes to Improve the Human Condition Have Failed* (New Haven, Conn.: Yale University Press, 1998).

CHAPTER 6. Sprawling, Skewing, and Greening

1. David Beasley, "Key Bills' Success Is Encouraging to Environmentalists; Growth, Water Supply Are Hot Issues," *Atlanta Journal and Constitution*, February 18, 1989, sec. C ("hot topic," "most visible").

2. David Beasley, "On Eve of Statewide Planning Law, Its Clout Still Unclear," *Atlanta Journal and Constitution*, March 13, 1989, sec. D.

3. David Beasly, "State Land-Use Plan: 'Hardest Part Is Yet to Come'; Ga. Localities Likely to Fight Growth Rules," *Atlanta Journal and Constitution*, April 17, 1989, sec. E ("strong").

4. Lizabeth Cohen, *A Consumer's Republic: The Politics of Mass Consumption in Postwar America* (New York: Vintage Books, 2003), esp. 8–9.

5. "Atlanta Leads Way," *Boston Globe*, March 25, 1988, 3rd ed., sec. Real Estate; Jay Bookman, "Growing a New Atlanta," *Atlanta Journal Constitution*, June 15, 1997, sec. F ("faster"); David Goldberg, "Survey: Metro Area Tops in Urban Sprawl," *Atlanta Journal-Constitution*, September 10, 1998, sec. B ("poster child").

6. Andrew Dobson, *Citizenship and the Environment* (New York: Oxford University Press, 2004), 103; John Barry, "Citizenship and (Un)Sustainability: A Green Republican Perspective," in *The Oxford Handbook of Environmental Ethics*, ed. Stephen Gardiner and Allen Thompson (New York: Oxford University Press, 2016), https://doi.org/10.1093/oxfor dhb/9780199941339.001.0001.

7. "1990's: Metropolitan Area Tables," Data Integration Division, U.S. Bureau of the Census, accessed June 18, 2014, http://www.census.gov/popest/data/historical/1990s/metro .html; Campbell Gibson, "Population of the 100 Largest Cities and Other Urban Places in the United States: 1790 to 1990," U.S. Bureau of the Census, June 1998, http://www.census .gov/population/www/documentation/twps0027/twps0027.html; Tony Giarruso, "Com- bating Urban Sprawl in Georgia," *ArcUser Online* (blog), December 2003, https://www .esri.com/news/arcuser/1003/sprawl1of2.html.

8. Reginald Stuart, "Post-boom Difficulties Seize Industrial Center of Sun Belt: The Sun Belt Today Growth Pains Amid Prosperity," *New York Times*, July 6, 1982, sec. A ("no. 1 choice"); James S. Fisher and Dean M. Hanink, "Business Climate: Behind the Geographic Shift of American Manufacturing," *Economic Review* 67, no. 6 (1982): 20–30; Roger W. Schmenner, *Making Business Location Decisions* (Englewood Cliffs, N.J.: Prentice-Hall, 1982), http://archive.org/details/makingbusinesslooooschm, 42, 159; for other factors in the region's growth, see Tony H. Grubesic, Timothy C. Matisziw, and

Matthew A. Zook, "Global Airline Networks and Nodal Regions," *GeoJournal* 71, no. 1 (2008): 53–66, http://www.jstor.org/stable/41148238; Truman Asa Hartshorn, *Metropolis in Georgia: Atlanta's Rise as a Major Transaction Center* (Cambridge, Mass.: Ballinger, 1976), 3–5; William Toal, "The South's Share of the Federal Pie," *Monthly Review of the Federal Reserve Bank of Atlanta*, April 1977, 47–53; Toal, "Southeastern Industrial Investment," *Monthly Review of the Federal Reserve Bank of Atlanta*, June 1977, 63–68; Bruce J. Schulman, *From Cotton Belt to Sunbelt: Federal Policy, Economic Development, and the Transformation of the South, 1938–1980* (New York: Oxford University Press, 1991); and David Carlton, "The American South the U.S. Defense Economy: A Historical View," in *The South, the Nation, and the World: Perspectives on Southern Economic Development*, ed. David L. Carlton and Peter A. Coclanis (Charlottesville: University of Virginia Press, 2003), 160–62.

9. By 1989 Metro Atlanta's median household income was $36,051 versus $30,056 for the United States. "IPUMS USA: 1990 Census Papers," 1990, Bureau of the Census, https://usa .ipums.org/usa/voliii/pubdocs/1990/cphls/cphl122.shtml.

10. David L. Sjoquist, ed., *The Atlanta Paradox* (New York: Sage Foundation, 2000).

11. David Jacobs and Jonathan C. Dirlam, "Politics and Economic Stratification: Power Resources and Income Inequality in the United States," *American Journal of Sociology* 122, no. 2 (2016): 469–500, https://doi.org/10.1086/687744. Taxes on capital gains—from financial investments such as stocks and bonds—fell in half, and the top income tax rate, which had averaged over 80 percent during the previous half century, plummeted to 28 percent. Jacob S. Hacker and Paul Pierson, *Winner-Take-All Politics: How Washington Made the Rich Richer—and Turned Its Back on the Middle Class* (New York: Simon and Schuster, 2010), 133–34; Ronald P. Formisano, *Plutocracy in America: How Increasing Inequality Destroys the Middle Class and Exploits the Poor* (Baltimore: Johns Hopkins University Press, 2015), 78.

12. Claudia Goldin and Lawrence F. Katz, *The Race between Education and Technology* (Cambridge, Mass.: Belknap, 2010), 292 ("skill-biased").

13. "1990's"; Sjoquist, *Atlanta Paradox*, 150, table 7.17.

14. Brookings Institution Center on Urban and Metropolitan Policy, *Atlanta in Focus: A Profile from Census 2000* (Washington, D.C.: Brookings Institution, 2003), 42. pt. 2.

15. Grubesic, Matisziw, and Zook, "Global Airline Networks."

16. Charles Rutheiser, *Imagineering Atlanta: The Politics of Place in the City of Dreams* (London: Verso, 1996), 181; Tom Walker, "RJR Nabisco Tops Atlanta-Based Firms on 1988 Fortune 500 List," *Atlanta Constitution*, April 7, 1988; Joel Garreau, *Edge City: Life on the New Frontier* (New York: Anchor, 1992); Norman Peagam, "Why the Foreigners Flock In," *Euromoney*, December 1984.

17. Truman Asa Hartshorn, *The Dynamics of Change: An Analysis of Growth in Metropolitan Atlanta over the Past Two Decades* (Atlanta: Policy Research Center, Georgia State University, 1993).

18. Ken-Hou Lin and Donald Tomaskovic-Devey, "Financialization and U.S. Income Inequality, 1970–2008," *American Journal of Sociology* 118, no. 5 (2013): 1284–1329, https:// doi.org/10.1086/669499; David A. Zalewski and Charles J. Whalen, "Financialization and Income Inequality: A Post Keynesian Institutionalist Analysis," *Journal of Economic Issues* 44, no. 3 (2010): 757–77, http://www.jstor.org/stable/20778712; Till van Treeck, "The Political Economy Debate on 'Financialization': A Macroeconomic Perspective," *Review of International Political Economy* 16, no. 5 (2009): 907–44, http://www.jstor.org/stable /27756199.

19. Mike Billips, "Since '78, Atlanta Lost Banks, but Not Economic Power," *Atlanta Business Chronicle*, June 15, 1998, https://www.bizjournals.com/atlanta/stories/1998/06/15 /focus8.html; Thomas D. Hills, "The Rise of Southern Banking and the Disparities among the States Following the Southeastern Regional Banking Compact," *North Carolina Banking Institute* 11 (February): 48.

20. U.S. Bureau of the Census, *Population and Housing Unit Counts: Georgia* (Washington, D.C.: Government Printing Office, 1992); U.S. Bureau of the Census, *1970 Census of Population: General Population Characteristics; Georgia, General Population Characteristics* (Washington, D.C.: Government Printing Office, 1971), http://www2.census.gov /library/publications/decennial/1970/pc-v2/15872858v2ch2.pdf; U.S. Bureau of the Census, *1992 Census of Financial, Insurance, and Real Estate Industries* (Washington, D.C.: Government Printing Office, 1995), https://www.census.gov/library/publications/1995/econ/fc92 -n-1.html, 366; Bureau of Labor Statistics, *Industry Wage Survey: Banking, 1985* (Washington, D.C.: Government Printing Office, 1986).

21. This average was based on survey data from six other U.S. cities besides Atlanta: New York, Houston, Los Angeles, Minneapolis, Chicago, and Tampa. Tom Walker, "Poll Discovers Investors Don't Put a Lot of Stock in Advice," *Atlanta Constitution*, October 29, 1984.

22. Bennett Harrison and Barry Bluestone, *The Great U-Turn* (New York: Basic Books, 1988); Robert B. Reich, *The Work of Nations: Preparing Ourselves for 21st Century Capitalism* (New York: Vintage, 2010); Christopher Kollmeyer, "Globalization and Income Inequality: How Public Sector Spending Moderates This Relationship in Affluent Countries," *International Journal of Comparative Sociology* 56, no. 1 (2015): 3–28, https://doi.org /10.1177/0020715215577869.

23. William S. Moore, "Income Inequality and Industrial Composition," *Public Administration Quarterly* 33, no. 4 (2009): 552–81, http://www.jstor.org/stable/41219998; Albert Chevan and Randall Stokes, "Growth in Family Income Inequality, 1970–1990: Industrial Restructuring and Demographic Change," *Demography* 37, no. 3 (2000): 365–80, https://doi.org/10.2307/2648048.

24. U.S. Bureau of the Census, *Population and Housing Unit Counts*"; U.S. Bureau of the Census, *General Population Characteristics*.

25. Marilyn Geewax, "Lockheed Move Happy News for Atlanta Area," *Atlanta Constitution*, May 11, 1990, sec. A; "GM Pact Gains in Vote," *Atlanta Constitution*, October 10, 1984; Matt Kempner, "UAW's Choice of Ford a Bad Sign for GM Talks," *Atlanta Constitution*, September 5, 1996, sec. E.

26. David Bradley et al., "Distribution and Redistribution in Postindustrial Democracies," *World Politics* 55, no. 2 (2003): 193–228, https://doi.org/10.1353/wp.2003.0009; David Jacobs and Lindsey Myers, "Union Strength, Neoliberalism, and Inequality: Contingent Political Analyses of U.S. Income Differences since 1950," *American Sociological Review* 79, no. 4 (2014): 752–74, https://doi.org/10.2307/43187562; Bruce Western and Jake Rosenfeld, "Unions, Norms, and the Rise in U.S. Wage Inequality," *American Sociological Review* 76, no. 4 (2011): 513–37, http://www.asanet.org/sites/default/files/savvy/images/journals/docs /pdf/asr/WesternandRosenfeld.pdf.

27. Mike Christensen, "Lockheed, Government Haggling over C-5 Costs Again," *Atlanta Constitution*, September 30, 1986, sec. D; Chris Burritt, "Issue of Job Security Looms over Carmakers-UAW Talks," *Atlanta Constitution*, July 19, 1987, sec. E.

28. Victor Gary Devinatz, "'To Find Answers to the Urgent Problems of Our Society': The Alliance for Labor Action's Atlanta Union Organizing Offensive, 1969–1971," *Labor*

Studies Journal, no. 2 (2006): 69; "Unions Target Atlanta," *Atlanta Constitution*, January 28, 1982; Gayle White, "Fear Keeps Unions from Enfolding Textile Work Force," *Atlanta Constitution*, February 4, 1981; Ann Wood Kimbrough, "Southwire Will Appeal Ruling That It Broke Law in Fighting Union," *Atlanta Constitution*, May 2, 1985; Ann Wood Kimbrough, "Scientific-Atlanta Employees Defeat Campaign by Union," *Atlanta Constitution*, July 3, 1984.

29. Barry Hirsch and David McPherson, "Union Membership and Coverage Database," Unionstats, 2019, http://unionstats.gsu.edu/.

30. Bureau of Labor Statistics, *Employment, Hours, and Earnings, States and Areas, 1939–82*, vol. 1, *Alabama-Nevada* (Washington, D.C.: Government Printing Office, 1984); Bureau of Labor Statistics, *Employment, Hours, and Earnings, States and Areas, Data for 1987–92* (Washington, D.C.: Government Printing Office, August 1992).

31. Reagan Walker, "State Teachers Drop to 40th on Salary List," *Atlanta Constitution*, October 5, 1994; Richard Greer, "Police Unions on the Rise," *Atlanta Constitution*, February 9, 1992, sec. E; Ann Wood Kimbrough, "Union Warns Government against 'Contracting Out,'" *Atlanta Constitution*, December 12, 1983.

32. Bureau of the Census, *1990 Census of Population: Social and Economic Characteristics, Georgia* (Washington, D.C.: Government Printing Office, 1993).

33. Hartshorn, *Dynamics of Change*; Keith Ihlandfelt and David L. Sjoquist, "Earnings Inequality," in *The Atlanta Paradox*, ed. David L. Sjoquist (New York: Sage Foundation, 2000), 128–57.

34. Bureau of Labor Statistics, *Industry Wage Survey: Contract Cleaning Services, August 1986* (Washington, D.C.: Government Printing Office, 1988), 2 ("among the lowest"); Bureau of the Census, *1990 Census of Population*.

35. Brookings Institution Center, *Atlanta in Focus*. Over these two decades poverty did resist the rise seen in most other U.S. metropolises, even falling by 1989 not just among metro-area whites (from 6.9 to 5.1 percent) but among Blacks (28.6 to 20.6 percent), but that was compared to a halving over the 1960s from 19.0 to 9.1 percent. Sugie Lee, "Metropolitan Growth Patterns' Impact on Intra-regional Spatial Differentiation and Inner-Ring Suburban Decline: Insights for Smart Growth" (PhD diss., Georgia Institute of Technology, 2005); William H. Frey and Elaine L. Fielding, "Changing Urban Populations: Regional Restructuring, Racial Polarization, and Poverty Concentration," *Cityscape: A Journal of Policy Development and Research* 1, no. 2 (1995): 66.

36. Susan Wells, "Poor Paying More for Less Adequate Housing," *Atlanta Constitution*, October 16, 1987 ("lack the skills").

37. Keith R. Ihlanfeldt and Madelyn V. Young, "Intrametropolitan Variation in Wage Rates: The Case of Atlanta Fast-Food Restaurant Workers," *Review of Economics and Statistics* 76, no. 3 (1994): 425–33, https://doi.org/10.2307/2109968.

38. Robert Bullard, Glenn S. Johnson, and Angel O. Torres, eds., *Sprawl City: Race, Politics, and Planning in Atlanta* (Washington, D.C.: Island, 2000).

39. Raj Chetty et al., "Where Is the Land of Opportunity? The Geography of Intergenerational Mobility in the United States," *Quarterly Journal of Economics* 129, no. 4 (2014): 1553–623, http://www.equality-of-opportunity.org/images/mobility_geo.pdf; Raj Chetty, Nathanial Hendren, Patrick Kline, Emmanuel Saez, and Nicholas Turner, "Is the United States Still a Land of Opportunity? Recent Trends in Intergenerational Mobility," *Opportunity Insights* (blog), January 4, 2014, https://opportunityinsights.org/paper/recent intergenerationalmobility/.

40. One measure of the metro area's economic inequality stayed relatively stable: its

Gini index (a social scientific index of the evenness with which income is distributed). Plateauing, the Atlanta metro area's Gini index continued to rank among the more unequal of U.S. metropolises, even as the Gini index for the city of Atlanta, not including most suburbs, edged upward. For the city, see Christina Stacy, Brady Meixell, and Tanaya Srini, "Inequality versus Inclusion in US Cities," *Social Indicators Research* 145, no. 1 (2019): 117–56, https://doi.org/10.1007/s11205-019-02090-3.

41. William W. Falk and Thomas Lyson, *High Tech, Low Tech, No Tech: Recent Industrial and Occupational Change in the South* (Albany: State University of New York Press, 1988), 11 ("checkered").

42. Ray Shirley, "Report of Activities for Atlanta Area since July 1964," 1967, folder "Forestry Assistance in Metropolitan Areas," box 4, RG64-1-12, Director's Office Subject Files, Georgia Archives.

43. "Urban Ecosystem Analysis: Atlanta Metro Area; Calculating the Value of Nature," American Forests, August 2001, http://arboretum.agnesscott.edu/tree-walk/learn-more /american-forests-urban-ecosystem-analysis-atlanta/; Margaret Usdansky, "Tree Protection Is Taking Root in Metro Laws," *Atlanta Journal-Constitution*, September 12, 1988, sec. A.

44. American Forests, "Urban Ecosystem Analysis."

45. Atlanta was number one in the country in sprawl, according to the Sierra Club, and, though only number four in a 2004 Smart Growth Study, by 2014 it had achieved number one in that ranking as well. "Sprawl: The Dark Side of the American Dream," Sierra Club, 1998, http://vault.sierraclub.org/sprawl/report98/report.asp; "Measuring Sprawl and Its Impact," Smart Growth America, 2004, http://www.smartgrowthamerica.org/research /measuring-sprawl-and-its-impact/; Rebecca Burns, "Atlanta: Highest Rate of Income Inequality in the U.S.," *Atlanta Magazine*, February 21, 2014, www.atlantamagazine.com /news-culture-articles/atlanta-highest-rate-of-income-inequality-in-the-us/.

46. Mark J. McDonnell and Steward T. A. Pickett, "Ecosystem Structure and Function along Urban-Rural Gradients: An Unexploited Opportunity For . . . ," *Ecology* 71, no. 4 (1990): 1232; Elizabeth A. Johnson and Michael W. Klemens, *Nature in Fragments: The Legacy of Sprawl* (New York: Columbia University Press, 2005).

47. U.S. Bureau of the Census, *1969 Agricultural Census*, vol. 1, *Area Reports*, pt. 28, *Georgia* (Washington, D.C.: Government Printing Office, 1972), https://agcensus.library. cornell.edu/wp-content/uploads/1969-Georgia-1969-01-full.pdf; U.S. Bureau of the Census, *1974 Census of Agriculture*, vol. 1, *State and County Data*, pt. 10, *Georgia* (Washington, D.C.: Government Printing Office, 1977), https://agcensus.library.cornell.edu/wp -content/uploads/1974-Georgia-1974-01-intro.pdf; U.S. Bureau of the Census, *1987 Census of Agriculture*, vol. 1, *Geographic Area Series*, pt. 10, *Georgia: State and County* (Washington, D.C.: Government Printing Office, 1989), https://agcensus.library.cornell.edu/wp -content/uploads/1987-Georgia-1987-01-full.pdf.

48. Sam Heys, "East Cobb's Last Holdout Land on River Worth Millions, but J. C. Hyde, 76, Not about to Sell Beloved One-Mule Farm," *Atlanta Journal and Constitution*, July 13, 1986, sec. Dixie Living, http://global.factiva.com/redir/default.aspx?P=sa&an =atjc00002001119di7doouyt&cat=a&ep=ASE.

49. "Georgia Rare Species and Natural Community Data: Georgia DNR; Wildlife Resources Division," Georgia Department of Natural Resources, accessed June 28, 2014, http://www.georgiawildlife.com/node/1370.

50. "*Cambarus Howardi*: Crayfishes of Georgia," Georgia College, accessed June 28, 2014, http://www.gcsu.edu/crayfishes/chattahooch_crayfish.htm; Christopher Taylor et

al., "A Reassessment of the Conservation Status of Crayfishes of the United States and Canada after 10+ Years of Increased Awareness," *Fisheries* 32 (2007): 372–89, https://doi .org/10.1577/1548-8446(2007)32[372:AROTCS]2.0.CO;2, 3; Radu C. Guiaşu, "Conservation, Status, and Diversity of the Crayfishes of the Genus *Cambarus Erichson, 1846* (Decapoda, Cambaridae)," *Crustaceana* 82, no. 6 (2009): 721–42, http://www.jstor.org /stable/27743327; Christopher E. Skelton, "History, Status, and Conservation of Georgia Crayfishes," *Southeastern Naturalist* 9, no. 3 (2010): 127–38.

51. "Georgia Rare Species"; George Stanton, "Evaluation of Conservation Status of Six West Georgia, Chattahoochee-Flint River Crayfish Species" (unpublished report, Georgia Department of Natural Resources, Georgia Natural Heritage Program, 2006), 8 (in possession of the author); Stanton, "Crayfish in Greater Atlanta Area," email correspondence with the author, June 30, 2014.

52. Leon Kirkland, "Ga. Deer Herds on the Increase," *Farmers and Consumers Bulletin* 74, no. 43 (1987): 1, 16; Gib Johnson, "Managing Georgia's Deer Herd," *DNR Outdoor Report* 3, no. 3 (1988): 2–5; Kent Mitchell, "This Week's List Outdoors," *Atlanta Journal-Constitution*, October 22, 2000, sec. Sports.

53. Cynthia Durcanin, "Possums Are Dying Flat but Happy, on Streets of Suburbia," *Atlanta Journal*, October 26, 1987, sec. E.

54. Jameson F. Chace and John J. Walsh, "Urban Effects on Native Avifauna: A Review," *Landscape and Urban Planning* 74, no. 1 (2006): 46–69, https://doi.org/10.1016/j .landurbplan.2004.08.007.

55. Michael Parrish and Jeffrey Hepinstall-Cymerman, "Associations between Multiscale Landscape Characteristics and Breeding Bird Abundance and Diversity across Urban-Rural Gradients in Northeastern Georgia, USA," *Urban Ecosystems* 15, no. 3 (2012): 559–80.

56. Catherine A. Bradley, Samantha E. J. Gibbs, and Sonia Altizer, "Urban Land Use Predicts West Nile Virus Exposure in Songbirds," *Ecological Applications* 18, no. 5 (2008): 1090 ("bird feeders").

57. American Forests, "Urban Ecosystem Analysis."

58. Tom Walker, "Study: Cities to Have More Vital Role in South's Economy," *Atlanta Journal and Constitution*, February 4, 1985, sec. C, http://www.ajc.com/s/vendor/news bank/; Falk and Lyson, *High Tech, Low Tech*; U.S. Bureau of the Census, *1982 County and State Data Book* (Washington, D.C.: Government Printing Office, 1982); Hartshorn, *Metropolis in Georgia*, 37–39.

59. G. Scott Thomas, "America's Hottest Counties," *American Demographics*, September 1, 1991, http://global.factiva.com/redir/default.aspx?P=sa&an=ad0000002001108dn 910005b&cat=a&ep=ASE; "Atlanta Leads Way." In the previous decade Atlanta's housing starts had ranked third or fourth in the nation during the early 1980s and spiked to second in 1985. "New Housing Starts to Remain Stable in 1986," *Chicago Tribune*, November 23, 1985, sec. N.

60. Brookings Institution Center, *Atlanta in Focus*, 64, pt. 2.

61. Christopher Sellers, "Tree Cover versus Demographics in a Changing Atlanta, 1970s to 1990," *Suburban Nature* (forthcoming), https://sites.google.com/a/stonybrook .edu/suburban-nature2/trends; Lee, "Metropolitan Growth Patterns' Impact."

62. John Helyar, "The Big Hustle—Atlanta's Two Worlds: Wealth and Poverty, Magnet and Mirage; The Metropolitan Area Grows as the Core City Shrinks: Will a Shooting Star Fall? New Waves at the Bus Station," *Wall Street Journal*, February 29, 1988, http:// global.factiva.com/redir/default.aspx?P=sa&an=j000000020011117dk2t005ea&cat

=a&ep=ASE. As economist Tara Watson explains, "a housing market in a booming metropolitan area is very responsive": "if inequality is rising," it concentrates on meeting "the increased demand for high-amenity houses in the good neighborhood." "Metropolitan Growth, Inequality, and Neighborhood Segregation by Income," *Brookings-Wharton Papers on Urban Affairs* 2006, no. 1 (2006): 1–52, https://doi.org/10.1353/urb.2006.0029.

63. Alfred King, "New Housing Is an Upscale Venture," *Atlanta Constitution*, April 11, 1987; Connie Green, "Luxury Finds a Home in Southeast DeKalb," *Atlanta Constitution*, August 18, 1987; Alfred King, "Experts Optimistic on '88 Housing Market," *Atlanta Journal Constitution*, May 14, 1988.

64. U.S. Bureau of the Census, *1990 Census of Housing: Detailed Housing Characteristics, Georgia* (Washington, D.C.: Government Printing Office, 1993).

65. Susan Laccetti, "When Home Must Be a Castle: Atlanta's Young Rich Find Suburbs Ready to Please," *Atlanta Journal-Constitution*, October 25, 1988, sec. Local News ("baby-boomers"); "The Roads Are In," advertisement, *Atlanta Constitution*, April 6, 1986; "There Will Never Be a Better Time to Purchase a Homesite at the Country Club of the South," advertisement, *Atlanta Constitution*, March 4, 1990.

66. Samuel P. Hays, "Environmental Political Culture and Environmental Political Development: An Analysis of Legislative Voting, 1971–1989," *Environmental History Review* 16, no. 2 (1992): 13, https://doi.org/10.2307/3984926; Hays, *A History of Environmental Politics since 1945* (Pittsburgh: University of Pittsburgh Press, 2000); Hays, *Explorations in Environmental History* (Pittsburgh: University of Pittsburgh Press, 1998), esp. 86–89. Hays was echoing terminology used by national intellectual and political leaders of the 1960s described by Adam Rome, scions of a new liberalism devoted to better "quality of life." "'Give Earth a Chance': The Environmental Movement and the Sixties," *Journal of American History* 90, no. 2 (2003): 525–54, https://doi.org/10.2307/3659443.

67. Richard Morgan, "New Magazine Will Accent Atlanta," *Atlanta Constitution*, October 15, 1980, sec. A.

68. Kathy Trocheck, "Beauty and Tenacity of Region Reflected in Southern Gardens," *Atlanta Journal Constitution*, October 27, 1985, sec. L ("affluent lot"); Tom Walker, "Monday Profile: Accenting Life in the South Was a Winner," *Atlanta Journal-Constitution*, January 21, 1985, sec. C, 27 ("fine"); Bureau of the Census, *Money Income of Households, Families, and Persons in the United States: 1985*, Current Population Reports: Consumer Income, P-60, no. 156 (Washington, D.C.: Government Printing Office, 1987).

69. Trocheck, "Beauty and Tenacity of Region" ("breathtakingly," "old," "distinctive").

70. Andrew C. Baker, *Bulldozer Revolutions: A Rural History of the Metropolitan South* (Athens: University of Georgia Press, 2018); Christopher Sellers, *Crabgrass Crucible: Suburban Nature and the Rise of Environmentalism in Twentieth-Century America* (Chapel Hill: University of North Carolina Press, 2012).

71. Sam G. Riley and George Frangoulis, "Southern Living," in *Regional Interest Magazines of the United States*, ed. Sam G. Riley and Gary W. Selnow (Westport, Conn.: Greenwood, 1991), 289–94; Sam G. Riley, "The New Money and the New Magazines," *Journal of Regional Cultures*, Fall–Winter (1982): 107–15; John Logue and Gary McCalla, *Life at Southern Living: A Sort of Memoir* (Baton Rouge: Louisiana State University Press, 2000); "Let's Go to the Southern Living Show," *Southern Living*, May 1969 ("accent"); "The Most Profitable Magazine in the U.S.," *Forbes*, June 15, 1977.

72. Joe Earle, "Made in the Shade: Fescue Grows Big Sales for Private Georgia Firm; Pennington's Grass Spreads across U.S.," *Atlanta Journal and Constitution*, September 4, 1992, sec. F.

73. Tom Hallman, "A Plant Industry Has Sprouted," *Atlanta Journal-Constitution*, May 13, 1985, sec. C; Roy Wyatt, "Q&A/Garden Clinic: Don't Expect Blue Spruce, Balsam to Survive Here," *Atlanta Journal-Constitution*, February 2, 1986, sec. L; Roy Wyatt, "Atlanta a Stronghold for Fast-Growing Lawn Services," *Atlanta Journal-Constitution*, October 5, 1986, sec. L.

74. Alfred King, "Beyond Suburbia: Urban Villages Invade Recently Rural Areas," *Atlanta Journal Constitution*, April 9, 1989, sec. P; McKay Jenkins and Cynthia Durcanin, "Suburbs Lack Affordable Housing for Growing Ranks of Working Poor," *Atlanta Constitution*, September 10, 1989; King, "Experts Optimistic" ("widely unaffordable"); John Cunniff, "Is a Home Really Affordable Now?," *Atlanta Constitution*, March 7, 1986.

75. Alfred King, "Market Expected to Remain Strong," *Atlanta Constitution*, April 26, 1987; Betsy White, "'87 Looks Promising in DeKalb," *Atlanta Constitution*, March 26, 1987; Jeanie Franco Hallem, "Housing Market Down, but Stable," *Business Atlanta*, August 1, 1988, http://global.factiva.com/redir/default.aspx?P=sa&an =bal0000020011117dk81000b&cat=a&ep=ASE; Susan Wells, "Peachtree City's Best-Laid Plans Prove Boon for Fayette," *Atlanta Constitution*, December 31, 1987.

76. Tom Walker, "The New 'Burbs: Families, Businesses Find a New Vitality on the Urban Fringe," *Atlanta Journal-Constitution*, October 29, 1989, sec. A; Robert Reinhold, "Suburbs Face More of Ills Already Troubling Cities," *New York Times*, November 18, 1978, sec. B; William Schmidt, "Once-Rural Georgia County Now Has Fastest Growth in U.S.," *New York Times*, June 2, 1985; Arthur C. Nelson, William Drummond, and David Sawicki, *Exurban Industrialization* (Atlanta: School of Architecture, Georgia Institute of Technology, 1990).

77. Walker, "New 'Burbs," 21 ("space and separation"); King, "Beyond Suburbia," 1; Jim Minter, "Southside: Life in Exurbs Can Be Blissful—or a Picnic Shared with Fire Ants," *Atlanta Journal-Constitution*, October 6, 1994, sec. K ("outnumbered").

78. Douglas S. Massey, "Residential Segregation and Neighborhood Conditions in U.S. Metropolitan Areas," in *America Becoming: Racial Trends and Their Consequences*, ed. National Research Council (Washington, D.C.: National Academies Press, 2001), 1:391–444, https://doi.org/10.17226/9599; Daniel H. Weinberg and Erika Steinmetz, *Racial and Ethnic Residential Segregation in the United States: 1980–2000*, Census 2000 Special Reports (Washington, D.C.: U.S. Bureau of the Census, 2002); Melissa Mae Hayes, "The Building Blocks of Atlanta: Racial Residential Segregation and Neighborhood Inequity" (PhD diss., Georgia State University, 2006).

79. Karen Pooley, "Segregation's New Geography: The Atlanta Metro Region, Race, and the Declining Prospects for Upward Mobility," *Southern Spaces*, 2015, http://southern spaces.org/2015/segregations-new-geography-atlanta-metro-region-race-and-declining -prospects-upward-mobility.

80. George Galster, Jackie Cutsinger, and Jason C. Booza, *Where Did They Go? The Decline of Middle-Income Neighborhoods in Metropolitan America* (Washington, D.C.: Brookings Institution, 2006), 8, 10, tables 5 and 6.

81. Phyl Garland, "Atlanta: Black Mecca of the South," *Ebony* 26, no. 10 (1971): 152; "Atlanta: New Mecca for Young Blacks," *Ebony* 28, no. 11 (1973): 62; Maurice J. Hobson, *The Legend of the Black Mecca: Politics and Class in the Making of Modern Atlanta* (Chapel Hill: University of North Carolina Press, 2017).

82. John Evans, interview by Christopher Sellers, Decatur, Georgia, July 21, 2002; James Bussey, interview by Christopher Sellers, Decatur, Georgia, January 18, 2004.

83. Herb Lester, "How Long to Water Your Lawn," *Atlanta Constitution*, August 16, 1979; Lester, "Mulches Serve Many Purposes," *Atlanta Daily World*, April 24, 1980; Lester, "Bug Killers," *Atlanta Daily World*, October 9, 1980.

84. Bill Dedman Staff Writer, "The Color of Money, Part 1: Atlanta Blacks Losing in Home Loans Scramble," *Atlanta Journal*, May 1, 1988, sec. Local News, http://global .factiva.com/redir/default.aspx?P=sa&an=atjc000002001117dk5300jmz&cat=a&ep=ASE; Lee, "Metropolitan Growth Patterns' Impact"; Brookings Institution Center, *Atlanta in Focus*.

85. Jenkins and Durcanin, "Suburbs Lack Affordable Housing" ("excessive rent"); Wells, "Poor Paying More for Less" ("financial resources"); "Public Housing Out in the Cold," *Atlanta Constitution*, March 25, 1985; Gary Abramson, "Fulton Could Price Moderate Housing Out of County," *Atlanta Constitution*, December 12, 1989 ("affordable to poor").

86. Wells, "Poor Paying More for Less" ("unevenly distributed").

87. "Neely Farm Reflects Past Traditions," *Atlanta Constitution*, November 15, 1987, Business ed., 545; Buckhead Brokers, Realtors, "Imagine a Home on the River," advertisement, *Atlanta Constitution*, September 18, 1988 ("peacefully").

88. Celestine Sibley, *The Sweet Apple Gardening Book.* (Garden City, N.Y.: Doubleday, 1972), 26 ("funny"); Margaret T. McGehee, "A Plague of Bulldozers: Celestine Sibley and Suburban Sprawl," *Southern Spaces*, March 9, 2009, http://southernspaces.org/2009 /plague-bulldozers-celestine-sibley-and-suburban-sprawl; Lucy Smethurst, interview by Christopher Sellers, January 20, 2004; Hartshorn, *Dynamics of Change*, 44.

89. Celestine Sibley, "Favorites Vanish before My Eyes," *Atlanta Constitution*, March 4, 1973 ("rolling green," "little animal"); Sibley, "Nothing Like Change of Pace," *Atlanta Constitution*, March 28, 1977 ("changing"); Sibley, "Trauma of Change Rooted in the Past," *Atlanta Constitution*, September 7, 1987 ("bulldozers growling").

90. David Farber, "Building the Counterculture, Creating Right Livelihoods: The Counterculture at Work," Sixties: A Journal of History, Politics and Culture 6, no. 1 (2013): 1–24, https://doi.org/10.1080/17541328.2013.778706.

91. John Moretta, "Down on 'The Technicolor Farm' of Summertown, Tennessee: The Hippie Era's Most Eclectic and Visionary Commune," *Tennessee Historical Quarterly* 75, no. 4 (2016): 276–321; Neal Rassman, "Second of a Series: The Communal Landscape," *Landscape Architecture* 68, no. 1 (1978): 65–69, http://www.jstor.org/stable/44664441.

92. Sara Cash, "Love of Herbs Sprouts into Blooming Business," *Atlanta Constitution*, June 10, 1973, sec. G; "City Dwellers Pool Resources, Help Others Find the Country," *Atlanta Constitution*, February 4, 1979; Charles Taylor, "City Folks Can Return to the Land but First They Gotta Gain Savvy," *Atlanta Constitution*, April 22, 1979; Ellie Sussman, "Country Bound Develops Self-Sufficiency," *Atlanta Constitution*, September 4, 1980.

93. Gardens for All, *The Impact of Home and Community Food Gardening on America* (Burlington, Vt.: Gardens for All, 1981), quoted in William Fischel, "The Urbanization of Agricultural Land: A Review of the National Agricultural Lands Study," *Land Economics* 58 (1982): 249; "Country Bound," *Mother Earth News* 64 (July–August, 1980).

94. Harkins, quoted in Taylor, "City Folks Can Return" ("whole person").

95. Hastings Company, "1978 Growing and Preserving for the South," 1978, folder 2, box 20, Hastings Nursery Collection, Atlanta History Center, Atlanta; "Asparagus Provide Years of Harvest," *Atlanta Daily World*, March 10, 1983; "Spring, Good Times for

Planting Grapes," *Atlanta Daily World*, April 2, 1981; "Home Gardner [sic] Says Compost Those Leaves," *Atlanta Daily World*, November 6, 1980; Darryl Riggins, "Vegetable Garden Finally Having Its Day in the Sun," *Atlanta Constitution*, March 23, 1980, sec. H.

96. Celestine Sibley, introd. to *The Compleat Vegetable Book* (Birmingham, Ala.: Book Division of the Progressive Farmer, 1976), vii–x; Riley, "New Money"; John White, "Safe to Have on Your Coffee Table: 'Southern Living' Reconsidered," *Alabama Review* 47, no. 3 (1994): 185–209; Tracy Lauder, "The Southern Living Solution: How the Progressive Farmer Launched a Magazine and a Legacy," *Alabama Review* 60, no. 3 (2007): 186–221, 209 ("isn't our bag," "one front yard").

97. Rachel Carson, *Silent Spring* (Boston: Houghton, 1962).

98. Harkins, quoted in Sussman, "Country Bound Develops Self-Sufficiency" ("with the universe").

99. Don Hastings, *Rich Harvest: A Life in the Garden* (Atlanta: Longstreet, 1998); Roy Wyatt, "Organic Gardening a Matter of Choice," *Atlanta Journal and Constitution*, May 26, 1985, sec. K.

100. Portia Scott Brookins, "High School Beat," *Atlanta Daily World*, April 1, 1976 ("want to try"); Herb Lester, "Urban Gardener," *Atlanta Daily World*, May 29, 1980 ("myths").

101. Sibley, *Sweet Apple Gardening Book*, 101 ("ecologists").

102. USDA Study Team on Organic Farming, *Report and Recommendations on Organic Farming* (Washington, D.C.: United States Department of Agriculture, 1980); Virgil Adams, "Organic Gardeners Dispel Myths," *Atlanta Journal-Constitution*, November 3, 1985, sec. L.

103. Margaret Knox, "Georgia's Xanadu," *Atlanta Constitution*, May 20, 1984, sec. G; Jingle Davis, "Portman Paradise," *Atlanta Constitution*, October 1, 1984, 17 ("waterways"); Scott Thurston, "Like Something Out of Star Trek," *Atlanta Constitution*, October 25, 1986, 14 ("enclosed waterways").

104. Raad Cawthorn, "Ted Turner's High-Flying Mind," *Atlanta Journal Constitution*, June 29, 1986 ("sailor," "oceans").

105. John Harmon, "Floods, Slides Will Return to Mountains," *Atlanta Constitution*, July 24, 1988, 66 ("knobby ridges").

106. For instance, see Tom Adkinson, "Racing the Rapids of the Chattooga," *Southern Living*, September 1973; Phillip A. Morris, "The Southern Seacoast—Keeping Its Balance," *Southern Living*, March 1973.

107. Peter Katz, *The New Urbanism: Toward an Architecture of Community* (New York: McGraw-Hill Education, 1993); Andres Duany, Elizabeth Plater-Zyberk, and Jeff Speck, *Suburban Nation: The Rise of Sprawl and the Decline of the American Dream* (New York: North Point, 2001).

108. Andrew G. Kirk, *Counterculture Green: The Whole Earth Catalog and American Environmentalism* (Lawrence: University Press of Kansas, 2007); E. F. Schumacher, *Small Is Beautiful: Economics as If People Mattered* (New York: Perennial Library /Harper and Row, 1975).

109. "Home Tour Showcases Efficient Solar Design," *Atlanta Journal and Constitution*, November 10, 1985, sec. L; Claude Terry, interview by Christopher Sellers, Atlanta, November 14, 2012.

110. Rose Palmer, interview by Christopher Sellers, Niskey Lake, Ga., May 25, 2012.

111. Midge Yearley, "Solar Group Sheds Light on Energy," *Atlanta Constitution*, June 12, 1983, sec. J.

112. David Johnston, "Revival a Step Ahead in Little Five Points," *Atlanta Constitution*, February 17, 1981, sec. C; Christopher Hammett, "The Blind Men and the Elephant: The Explanation of Gentrification," *Transactions of the Institute of British Geographers* 16 (1991): 173–89.

113. Rutheiser, *Imagineering Atlanta*, 59–60, 194, 205; more generally on the mix of countercultural and environmental concerns sprouting in U.S. downtowns in this time, often connected to early gentrification, see, Sharon Zukin, *Loft Living: Culture and Capital in Urban Change* (Baltimore: Johns Hopkins University Press, 1982); Neil Smith, "New City, New Frontier: The Lower East Side as Wild Wild West," in *Variations on a Theme Park*, ed. Michael Sorkin (New York: Hill and Wang, 1992), 61–93; Interview with Susan Chavez, interview by Christopher Sellers, August 26, 2004, Atlanta; "Food Co-ops: Good Food and Good Prices," *Mother Earth News* 59 (September–October, 1979).

114. Mark Bruce Kelmacher, "Where Magic Works and Dreams Come True," *Atlanta Constitution*, September 9, 1979, sec. SM ("jointly owned"); John Carter, "The 'New Age Industrial Park,'" *Atlanta Constitution*, November 8, 1979, sec. D; Kathy Trocheck, "Poncey-Highlands Area Regaining Respectability," *Atlanta Journal Constitution*, December 8, 1985 ("SoHo").

115. Beverley Hall, "From Old Shabby to New Chic: Business District at Little Five Points Has Come a Long Way," *Atlanta Journal Constitution*, April 18, 1985, sec. C; Diane Loupe, "Little Five Points Big on Growth," *Atlanta Journal Constitution*, January 3, 1993, sec. R ("bohemian"); Trocheck, "Poncey-Highlands Area"; Cynthia Jubera and Anne Byrne, "The Organic Alternative," *Atlanta Journal Constitution*, March 29, 1989, sec. W.

116. Tom Walker, "Growth Reaches Crossroads: Virginia Highlands Faces Pressure from Developers and the Community," *Atlanta Journal Constitution*, October 19, 1987, sec. E ("frenzy," "village-like").

117. Hank Ezell, "Renaissance Park: Urban Living Is Born in a Suburban Style," *Atlanta Constitution*, September 13, 1981 ("suburban"); "Why Did Atlanta Ballet's General Manager Buy His Home at Renaissance Park?," advertisement, *Atlanta Constitution*, November 3, 1984 ("park-like").

118. Ezell, "Renaissance Park."

119. Maria Saporta, "Arranging Renaissance Park's Financing a Complicated Task," *Atlanta Constitution*, December 18, 1983, sec. E.

120. Thonia Lee, "Bedford Pine's Progress Worries Longtime Residents," *Atlanta Constitution*, April 25, 1991, sec. E.

121. Helyar, "Big Hustle."

122. Tom Walker, "Downtown Sits on Threshold of Dramatic Growth," *Atlanta Constitution*, December 18, 1983, sec. E ("tagged," "turbulence"); Tom Walker, "City's Skill in Getting Funds Called a Boost to Downtown," *Atlanta Constitution*, August 10, 1983, sec. D.

123. Tom Walker, "A New Downtown Atlanta Concept: Growth Master Plan May Embrace Entire Peachtree Corridor," *Atlanta Journal Constitution*, February 13, 1985, sec. B.

124. Ken Willis, "John Portman Still Dreaming of a 'Walking City,'" *Atlanta Constitution*, February 15, 1981, sec. E ("walking").

125. Marian Smith, "John Portman Is an Architect Determined to Dress Up the City," *Atlanta Constitution*, November 4, 1979, sec. F ("nature," "lungs," "man's needs").

126. Willis, "John Portman Still Dreaming" ("castle").

127. Tom Walker, "Portman Proposes Futuristic Complex," *Atlanta Constitution*, June 14, 1983, sec. D; Willis, "John Portman Still Dreaming."

128. John Finotti, "Portman in the Suburbs: The $1.2 Billion Northpark," *New York Times*, May 15, 1988.

129. Duany, Plater-Zyberk, and Speck, *Suburban Nation*; Katz, *New Urbanism*; S. A. Reid, "City Faces: In Praise of New Urbanism Activist Preaches That Neighborhoods Should Be Walkable," *Atlanta Journal and Constitution*, April 10, 1997, sec. D.

130. Rev. Albert Love, interview by Christopher Sellers, Atlanta, May 29, 2013; "Rev. Albert E. Love Joins SCLC Staff," *Southern Christian Leadership Conference National Magazine*, July–August 1980.

131. Peter Range, "S.C.L.C.: What's Happened to the Dream," *Atlanta Magazine*, April 1, 1972, http://www.atlantamagazine.com/civilrights/sclc-whats-happened-to-the-dream/; Chauncey Eskridge, Executive Director, SCLC, to Roger Wilkins, Ford Foundation, December 22, 1969; Chauncey Eskridge, "Proposal for Grant to the Southern Christian Leadership Conference," December 22, 1969, both in folder "Correspondence 1970" and "Correspondence 1969," box 466, series 1, Board of Directors Records, 1958–2004, Southern Christian Leadership Conference Papers, Manuscript Collection 1083, Special Collections, Emory University, Decatur, Ga.; John Huey, "Atlanta Chapter of SCLC Closes," *Atlanta Constitution*, October 15, 1974.

132. Andrew Young, *An Easy Burden: The Civil Rights Movement and the Transformation of America* (Waco, Tex.: Baylor University Press, 2008), 490; Bernard Scott Lee et al. to SCLC Board Member, 1973, folder "Memoranda, Internal, 1971–2000," box 6, series 1, Board of Directors Records, 1958–2004, Southern Christian Leadership Conference Papers, Emory University.

133. Ralph Abernathy to Joseph Lowery, July 5, 1973, folder "Correspondence, 1972–85," box 466, series 1, Board of Directors Records, 1958–2004, Southern Christian Leadership Conference Papers, Emory University; Austin Scott, "Funds Are Dwindling as SCLC Seeks Future in New Directions: SCLC, with Dwindling Funds, Takes Subtle New Directions," *Washington Post*, April 1, 1973; Bernard Scott Lee et al. to Ralph Abernathy and Joseph Lowery, 1973, folder "Memoranda, Internal, 1971–2000," box 6, series 1, Board of Directors Records, 1958–2004, Southern Christian Leadership Conference Papers, Emory University.

134. Bernard Scott Lee to Executive Committee of the Board, September 18, 1973, folder "Correspondence 1970" and "Correspondence"1969," box 466, series 1, Board of Directors Records, 1958–2004, Southern Christian Leadership Conference Papers, Emory University; Joel Dreyfuss, "Dissent-Torn SCLC to Try to Regroup behind Abernathy," *Washington Post*, August 16, 1973.

135. Abernathy to Lowery, July 5, 1973, Emory University; Scott, "Funds Are Dwindling."

136. Tara Watson, "Inequality and the Measurement of Residential Segregation by Income in American Neighborhoods," working paper (Cambridge: National Bureau of Economic Research, 2009).

137. Tina McElroy, "Cascade Road Neighborhood: Who's Who of Black Atlanta," *Atlanta Constitution*, December 10, 1977.

138. "Another Crisis in S.W. Atlanta," *Atlanta Voice*, February 1, 1970; Ernest Pharr, "Protest May Mushroom to All Affected Areas; Black Coalition May Form on Apartments; Cascade Homeowners Bitter over Rezoning," *Atlanta Inquirer*, February 7, 1970, sec. A.

139. "20th Anniversary Finds SCLC Facing Change," *SCLC Magazine and Newsletter*, September 1977, 14, 15.

140. Joseph E. Lowery, "National SCLC Retreat," *SCLC Magazine and Newsletter*, February 1978.

141. Dennis McCluster, "Rash of Child Killings in Atlanta," *SCLC Magazine and Newsletter*, December 1980; Joseph E. Lowery, "Children Will Not Have Died in Vain," *SCLC Magazine and Newsletter*, April 1981.

142. "Focus On: The Economic Front," *SCLC Magazine and Newsletter*, April 1979; "SCLC Denounces Impending Democrat Betrayal of the Poor," *SCLC Magazine and Newsletter*, February 1979; "SCLC Pledges Solidarity to Sugar Cane Workers Head," *SCLC Magazine and Newsletter*, February 1979; "Laurel, Mississippi, Marks the Unification of Labor, Civil Rights, Women's and Church Coalitions," *SCLC Magazine and Newsletter*, August 1980.

143. "SCLC/Women Urges Rich's to Employ Black Managers," *SCLC Magazine and Newsletter*, December 1980.

144. "SCLC Tradition: A Review of the Past 23 Years," *SCLC Magazine and Newsletter*, August 1980; "Laurel, Mississippi, Marks."

145. Jessica O'Connor, "'Racism Anywhere Threatens Freedom Everywhere': The Legacy of Martin Luther King, Jr. in Black America's Anti-apartheid Activism," *Australasian Journal of American Studies* 34, no. 2 (2015): 44–58, http://www.jstor.org/stable/44779733; Frederic I. Solop, "Public Protest and Public Policy: The Anti-apartheid Movement and Political Innovation," *Policy Studies Review* 9, no. 2 (1989): 307–26, https://doi.org/10.1111/j.1541-1338.1989.tb01127.x.

146. Love, interview; Rob Nixon, *Slow Violence and the Environmentalism of the Poor* (Cambridge, Mass.: Harvard University Press, 2013).

147. Ronald Danzig, "Living with Your Heart," *SCLC Magazine and Newsletter*, November 1977; Marion Wells, "Healths A-Poppin," *SCLC Magazine and Newsletter*, November 1977; Bernard Bridges, "National Health Insurance Policy," *SCLC Magazine and Newsletter*, February 1978.

148. Lois Benjamin, *The Black Elite: Still Facing the Color Line in the Twenty-First Century* (Lanham, Md.: Rowman and Littlefield, 2005), 209.

149. Thomas Calimee Jr., "Cancer Facts and Black Americans," *SCLC Magazine and Newsletter*, April 1981.

150. Cynthia Tucker, "Clark Takes Rights Battle to Strike Front," *Atlanta Constitution*, May 6, 1979; Rick Dunn, "Black Community Fights U.S. Government for Ancestral Land," *SCLC Magazine and Newsletter*, February 1979; Kathy Trocheck, "Black-Owned Land Going at Fast Clip," *Atlanta Constitution*, August 2, 1981.

151. Robert D. Bullard, *Dumping in Dixie: Race, Class, and Environmental Quality*, 3rd ed. (Boulder, Colo.: Westview, 2000), 27–29.

152. Even before the news of the Warren County landfill's opening wound up on his doorstep, Lowery himself had appeared at "environmental" events like the 1980 Atlanta roundtable "Environmental Ethics: The Theological Perspective." "Atlanta Environmental Symposium III: 'The Ethics of Scarcity,'" *SCLC Magazine and Newsletter*, December 1980; "Leukemia Victim Challenges NRC in Court," *SCLC Magazine and Newsletter*, May 1982.

153. "100 Held in Protest of PCB's Dumping," *Atlanta Constitution*, September 16, 1982; "Lowery Jailed in N.C. Protest," *Atlanta Journal*, September 21, 1982; Eileen McGurty, *Transforming Environmentalism: Warren County, PCBs, and the Origins of Environmental Justice* (New Brunswick, N.J.: Rutgers University Press, 2009); "PCB Rights Meets Environmentalists," *SCLC Magazine and Newsletter*, February 1983, 7 ("flashback").

154. General Accounting Office, *Siting of Hazardous Waste Landfills and Their Cor-*

relation with Racial and Economic Status of Surrounding Communities: Report (Washington, D.C.: General Accounting Office, 1983); Robert D. Bullard, "Solid Waste Sites and the Black Houston Community," *Sociological Inquiry* 53, nos. 2–3 (1983): 274–88; Benjamin Chavis and Charles Lee, *Toxic Wastes and Race in the United States: A National Report on the Racial and Socio-Economic Characteristics of Communities with Hazardous Waste Sites* (New York: Commission on Racial Justice/United Church of Christ, 1987).

155. Robert D. Bullard, "The Mountains of Houston," *Cite* (blog), 2014, https://offcite .rice.edu/2014/02/Cite_93_Mountains_of_Houston_Bullard.pdf; Bullard, "Environmental Racism and 'Invisible' Communities," *West Virginia Law Review* 96 (1994): 1037–50.

156. Clyde F. Fehn, "Memo: Waste Oil Generated at Industrial Waste Water Treatment Plant at Lockheed Aircraft Co.—Cobb County," March 31, 1976, folder "Lockheed –Ga. Company, Marietta: Cobb County," box 28, RG 88, subgroup 7, series 29, EPD Hazardous Waste Program Archives, Georgia Archives; C. K. Griffin, "Memo: 'Waste Oil Analysis from B-10 Industrial Waste Plant,'" April 27, 1976, folder "Lockheed Hazardous Wastes"; "Site No. 538, Westview Landfill, Inc.," February 10, 1980, folder "Westview Cemetery Landfill," all in Correspondence Files, Environmental Protection Division, Georgia Archives; Randy Jay, "Southwest Group Renews Fight against Westview Landfill," *Atlanta Constitution*, June 25, 1987, sec. E.

157. Juner Norris, interview by Christopher Sellers, Atlanta, February 5, 2013.

158. Bullard, *Dumping in Dixie*, 42.

159. Ironically, they sounded notes very much like those of California's chapters back in the 1950s, before an embrace of health-threatening issues like smog, as well as sprawl-threatened places like urban parks, had catapulted Sierra from a small West Coast group into nationwide membership and prominence. "Ugh!," *Chattahoochee Sierran* 4, no. 3 (1978): 4; Ron Mayhew, "Chairman's Corner," *Chattahoochee Sierran* 8, no. 2 (1983): 4; Mary Jane Brock, "Chapter Excom Raps National Board Policies," *Chattahoochee Sierran* 4, no. 3 (1978): 4; J. Walden Retan, "Cahaban Exchanges Policy Views with Club's National President," *Chattahoochee Sierran* 4, no. 4 (1979): 5; Victor Cohen, "Sierran Resigns Membership in Protest of Board Policies," *Chattahoochee Sierran* 4, no. 5 (1979): 2; Sellers, *Crabgrass Crucible*.

160. Denny Shaffer, "'Mayhew Mayhem' Is Destructive, National Treasurer Tells Excom," *Chattahoochee Sierran* 4, no. 9 (1979): 5; Ted Snyder, "Here Is the Text of National President Ted Snyder's Letter to Wally Retan," *Chattahoochee Sierran* 4, no. 4 (1979): 5; Theodore Snyder, "President Responds to Member's Resignation," *Chattahoochee Sierran* 4, no. 8 (1979): 5.

161. Saly Sierer, "Urban Environment Important, New Excom Member Asserts," *Chattahoochee Sierran* 4, no. 4 (1979): 5.

162. Sally Sierer, "Urban Issues Need Support," *Chattahoochee Sierran* 4, no. 8 (1979): ("broad category").

163. "Major Urban Conference," *EPA Journal* 4, no. 8 (1978): 32–33.; Barbara Blum, "Helping Cities," *EPA Journal* 5, no. 5 (1978): 16–17; Bill Futrell, "Urban Issues Need Support," *Chattahoochee Sierran* 4, no. 7 (1979): 2.

164. Sven Lovegren, "Atlanta Conservation Committe [*sic*] Funds Issues 'Too Numerous,'" *Chattahoochee Sierran* 4, no. 5 (1979): 2.

165. Lovegren, 2.

166. Sally Sierer, "Is a Water Doomsday in Atlanta's Future?," *Chattahoochee Sierran* 4, no. 7 (1979): 1, 4; Donna Mull, "Clean Air 'Principles' in Actuality a Rip-Off!," *Chattahoochee Sierran* 7, no. 4 (1981): 1; Mull, "Ozone Pushes Pollution to Unhealthy Levels,"

Chattahoochee Sierran 9, no. 1 (1983): 5; Roger Buerki, "MRPA, MRPA, Will She Wake If We Burp Her?," *Chattahoochee Sierran* 7, no. 11 (1982): 4; Lovegren, "Atlanta Conservation Committe."

167. Rachel Frantz-Rottschafer, "Club 'SCCOPING' Out More Political Involvement," *Chattahoochee Sierran* 7, no. 10 (1982): ("long-time friends," "involvement").

168. Ron Mayhew to the Core Group, "Grassroots Training 1983," February 12, 1983, folder 1, "Atlanta Group Executive Committee, 1983," box 2, Georgia Sierra Club Records, UA97-072, Hargrett Rare Book and Manuscript Library, University of Georgia, Athens.

169. Pat Dunbar, "Chapter Backs Levitas, Fowler for Congress," *Chattahoochee Sierran* 7, no. 17 (1982): 1.

170. "Georgia Prepares for Chapter Split," *Chattahoochee Sierran* 7, no. 4 (1981): 4; "Split Georgia and Alabama?," *Chattahoochee Sierran* 4, no. 5 (1979): 4.

171. "A Great Park," *Atlanta Constitution*, July 13, 1977, sec. A; Keith Graham and John Carter, "Atlanta Looks for a Way to Park," *Atlanta Constitution*, December 6, 1979, sec. E ("transit facility"); Catherine M. Howett, "Atlanta's 'Great Park' Controversy: A Crisis in Urban Landscape Values," *Environmental Review* 10, no. 1 (1986): 17; Suzanne M. Hall, "Progress or Preservation: The Presidential Parkway Controversy, 1946–1986," *Atlanta History: A Journal of Georgia and the South* 31, nos. 1–2 (1987): 22–38.

172. Mark Platte, "Mayor's Plan Is Assailed," *Atlanta Constitution*, June 25, 1982, sec. A; Gail Epstein, "Parkway Opponents Jam Public Hearing," *Atlanta Constitution*, June 30, 1982, sec. A.

173. Michael D'Orso and John Lewis, *Walking with the Wind: A Memoir of the Movement* (New York: Simon and Schuster, 2015), 458–59.

174. Gail Epstein, "Carter Lobbying for Young's Park Plan," *Atlanta Constitution*, July 10, 1982, sec. B; Anne Cowles, "City Council OKs Great Park Plan; Battle Not Over," *Atlanta Constitution*, July 11, 1982, sec. D.

175. Maria Saporta, "Neighborhood Planners Will Be Cut to Save Funds," *Atlanta Journal-Constitution*, October 25, 1982, sec. A; Robert Anderson, "Many Leaders in NPU See Decline in Effectiveness of the System," *Atlanta Journal and Constitution*, June 20, 1985, sec. E.

176. Clarence N. Stone, *Regime Politics: Governing Atlanta, 1946–1988* (Lawrence: University Press of Kansas, 1989), 135 ("outside the governing").

177. Maria Saporta, "Neighborhood Groups Unite to Fight Park Road," *Atlanta Constitution*, September 7, 1982, sec. A; Ron Mayhew, "Chapter Excom Ratifies Diversity of Actions," *Chattahoochee Sierran* 7, no. 15 (1982): 4; Howett, "Atlanta's 'Great Park' Controversy"; Hall, "Progress or Preservation."

178. Nancy White, "Trying to Beat Parkway Path: 'Roadbusters' a Mixed Bag of Protesters," *Atlanta Journal Constitution*, February 27, 1985, sec. B; Debbie Newby, "2 Parkway Protesters Arrested," *Atlanta Journal*, July 2, 1985, sec. D.

179. Robin Raquet, "Sierra Club Atlanta Group Fact Sheet," 1984, folder 2, "Atlanta Group Executive Committee, 1984," box 2, Georgia Sierra Club Records, UA97-072, Hargrett Rare Book and Manuscript Library, University of Georgia, Athens.

180. [Chuck McGrady?], "1985–86 Conservation Priorities," 1985, folder 1, "Conservation Committee, 1984–1985," box 3, Georgia Sierra Club Records, UA97-072, Hargrett Rare Book and Manuscript Library, University of Georgia.

181. Bob Dart and David Secrest, "Environmentalists Call for Action to Stem Acid Rain Threat in South," *Atlanta Constitution*, June 8, 1984, sec. A.

182. Stewart Stokes, "Minutes: Atlanta Group Executive Committee," April 26,

1984, folder 2, "Atlanta Group Executive Committee, 1984," box 2, Georgia Sierra Club Records, UA97-072, Hargrett Rare Book and Manuscript Library, University of Georgia.

183. Chuck McGrady to Judy, Arte, Bill, and Jean, July 31, 1985, folder 1, "Conservation Committee, 1984–1985," box 3, Georgia Sierra Club Records, UA97-072, Hargrett Rare Book and Manuscript Library, University of Georgia.

184. Stewart Stokes, "Atlanta Group ExCom Minutes," October 25, 1984, folder 2, "Atlanta Group Executive Committee, 1984"; Chuck McGrady, "SCCOPE Committee [Report]," 1986, folder 15, "Atlanta Group Executive Committee, 1986," both in box 2, Georgia Sierra Club Records, UA97-072, Hargrett Rare Book and Manuscript Library, University of Georgia.

185. Jean Sokol, "Minutes: Atlanta Group Executive Committee, Georgia Sierra Club," May 23, 1985, folder 9, "Atlanta Group Executive Committee, 1985," box 2, Georgia Sierra Club Records, UA97-072, Hargrett Rare Book and Manuscript Library, University of Georgia.

186. "National Task Force Established by Conference," *Atlanta Voice*, April 12, 1980, 5 ("rural Black Americans").

187. Stokes, "Atlanta Group ExCom Minutes"; Jean Sokol, "Minutes: Atlanta Group Executive Committee, Georgia Sierra Club," June 27, 1985, folder 9, "Atlanta Group Executive Committee, 1985," box 2, Georgia Sierra Club Records, UA97-072, Hargrett Rare Book and Manuscript Library, University of Georgia.

188. Reginald Stuart, "Plan for 65% Black District in Georgia Is Approved," *New York Times*, August 14, 1982.

189. Chuck McGrady and Georgia Chapter SCCOPE, "Request for Approval of Activities for Federal Candidates, Sierra Club; John Lewis," May 11, 1986, folder 15, "Atlanta Group Executive Committee, 1986," box 2, Georgia Sierra Club Records, UA97-072, Hargrett Rare Book and Manuscript Library, University of Georgia.

190. D'Orso and Lewis, *Walking with the Wind*, 467 ("environmentalist"), 468 ("air they breathe").

191. McGrady, "SCCOPE Committee [Report]"; McGrady and Georgia Chapter SCCOPE, "Request for Approval of Activities."

192. Sam Collier, "Saving the Southern Environment: We Need a Regional Strategy," 1988, folder 45, "Southern Environmental Assembly," Sam Collier Papers, 1985–2008 Y009, Georgia State University Archives ("democracy," "Black"); Charles Seabrook, "The Presidential Campaign: Environment Issues Get Mostly Yawns, Token Talk from Presidential Hopefuls," *Atlanta Journal and Constitution*, December 6, 1987, sec. A.

193. Benjamin Chavis and Charles Lee, *Toxic Wastes and Race in the United States* (New York: Commission on Racial Justice, United Church of Christ, 1987); Sam Collier, "'Regional Town Meeting' to Look at South's Environmental Issues," 1988, folder 45, "Southern Environmental Assembly," Collier Papers, Georgia State University Archives.

194. "Southern Environmental Assembly '88: Agenda," 1988, folder 45, "Southern Environmental Assembly," Collier Papers, Georgia State University Archives.

195. Patricia Giblin, "Summary of Conference," 1988, folder 45, "Southern Environmental Assembly," Collier Papers, Georgia State University Archives, 1 ("human issue").

196. Scott Bronstein, "Environmentalists Protest at GOP Debate," *Atlanta Constitution*, February 29, 1988, sec. E ("rise again," "hand-in-hand"); "Southern Environmental Assembly '88."

197. Chuck McGrady, "Chairman's Corner," *Georgia Sierran*, April 1989.

CHAPTER 7. Conservatism Remade, Environmentalism Eclipsed

1. Earl Black and Merle Black, *Divided America: The Ferocious Power Struggle in American Politics* (New York: Simon and Schuster, 2007), 52 ("most spectacular"); see also Earl Black and Merle Black, *The Rise of Southern Republicans* (Cambridge, Mass.: Belknap, 2003); David Lublin, *The Republican South: Democratization and Partisan Change* (Princeton, N.J.: Princeton University Press, 2004); Seth C. McKee, *Republican Ascendancy in Southern U.S. House Elections* (Boulder, Colo.: Westview, 2009); and Frances Fitzgerald, *The Evangelicals: The Struggle to Shape America* (New York: Simon and Schuster, 2017).

2. For samples of the literature on the politics of racial coding, see Martin Gilens, "'Race Coding' and White Opposition to Welfare," *American Political Science Review* 90, no. 3 (1996): 593–605; Fred Slocum, "White Racial Attitudes and Implicit Racial Appeals: An Experimental Study of 'Race Coding' in Political Discourse," *Politics and Policy* 29, no. 4 (2001): 650–69, https://doi.org/10.1111/j.1747-1346.2001.tb00609.x; Rachel Wetts and Robb Willer, "Privilege on the Precipice: Perceived Racial Status Threats Lead White Americans to Oppose Welfare Programs," *Social Forces* 97, no. 2 (2018): 793–822.

3. Fitzgerald, *Evangelicals*; Angie Maxwell and Todd Shields, *The Long Southern Strategy: How Chasing White Voters in the South Changed American Politics* (New York: Oxford University Press, 2019); Darren Dochuk, *From Bible Belt to Sunbelt: Plain-Folk Religion, Grassroots Politics, and the Rise of Evangelical Conservatism* (New York: Norton, 2012); Seth Dowland, *Family Values and the Rise of the Christian Right* (Philadelphia: University of Pennsylvania Press, 2015); Glenn Feldman, ed., *Painting Dixie Red: When, Where, Why, and How the South Became Republican* (Gainesville: University Press of Florida, 2014).

4. Nancy MacLean, *Democracy in Chains: The Deep History of the Radical Right's Stealth Plan for America* (New York: Viking, 2017); Jane Mayer, *Dark Money: The Hidden History of the Billionaires behind the Rise of the Radical Right* (New York: Doubleday, 2016); Jason Stahl, *Right Moves: The Conservative Think Tank in American Political Culture since 1945* (Chapel Hill: University of North Carolina Press, 2016); Jonathan Schoenwald, *A Time for Choosing: The Rise of Modern American Conservatism* (New York: Oxford University Press, 2002); Christopher Leonard, *Kochland: The Secret History of Koch Industries and Corporate Power in America* (New York: Simon and Schuster, 2019); Matthew D. Lassiter, *The Silent Majority: Suburban Politics in the Sunbelt South* (Princeton, N.J.: Princeton University Press, 2006); Elizabeth Tandy Shermer, *Sunbelt Capitalism: Phoenix and the Transformation of American Politics* (Philadelphia: University of Pennsylvania Press, 2015); Lisa McGirr, *Suburban Warriors: The Origins of the New American Right* (Princeton, N.J.: Princeton University Press, 2002).

5. James Morton Turner and Andrew C. Isenberg, *The Republican Reversal: Conservatives and the Environment from Nixon to Trump* (Cambridge, Mass.: Harvard University Press, 2018); Judith A. Layzer, *Open for Business: Conservatives' Opposition to Environmental Regulation* (Cambridge, Mass.: MIT Press, 2012).

6. Peter Applebome, "A Suburban Eden Where the Right Rules," *New York Times*, August 1, 1994 ("the heart"; "booming"); Tad Friend, "Does America Hate New York . . . or Has It Just Stopped Caring," *New York Magazine*, January 23, 1995.

7. Denise Thomas, "Mobile Home Industry Unhappy with Zoning Laws," *Marietta Daily Journal*, April 18, 1982, sec. A. Mobile homes made up about 3 percent of Cobb's housing units in 1990 (or 4,888 units), compared to around 4 percent (or 2,502) in 1970; by 1990 eleven of eighteen metro-area counties had more than 10 percent of their housing in

mobile homes, compared to just three of this same eighteen in 1970. Steven Manson, Jonathan Schroeder, David Van Riper, Tracy Kugler, and Steven Ruggles, *IPUMS National Historical Geographic Information System: Version 17.0* (Minneapolis: IPUMS, 2022), http://doi.org/10.18128/D050.V17.0.

8. Billie Cheney Speed, "Baptist Country: Top Protestant Group Has Stronghold in State," *Atlanta Journal-Constitution*, October 9, 1982.

9. Susan Miles, "Dedication of New Sanctuary Caps Decade of Growth," *Marietta Daily Journal*, May 25, 1979, sec. A; "Antebellum Plantation Was Church's First Home," *Marietta Daily Journal*, May 27, 1979; Tucker McQueen, "Pastor of Roswell Street Baptist: Price Believes Bigger Is Better," *Marietta Daily Journal*, August 22, 1980, sec. B; David Secrest, "Nelson Price Tends Cobb's Largest Flock," *Atlanta Constitution*, November 1, 1979.

10. Fitzgerald, *Evangelicals*, 240; Ken Willis, "Clergy Forum Stirs Faith with Politics in Quiet Campaign," *Atlanta Constitution*, July 10, 1980.

11. James W. Watkins, "Fundamentalist, Militant Southern Baptist Group Foments Tension, Turmoil," *Atlanta Constitution*, May 25, 1986.

12. C. Kirk Hadaway, David G. Hackett, and James Fogle Miller, "The Most Segregated Institution: Correlates of Interracial Church Participation," *Review of Religious Research* 25, no. 3 (1984): 204–19, https://doi.org/10.2307/3511119; Diana L. Hayes, "Korie L. Edwards, the Elusive Dream: The Power of Race in Interracial Churches," *Journal of Religion* 90, no. 3 (2010): 447–49, https://doi.org/10.1086/651998; Kathleen Garces-Foley, "New Opportunities and New Values: The Emergence of the Multicultural Church," *Annals of the American Academy of Political and Social Science* 612 (July 2007): 209–24.

13. Secrest, "Nelson Price Tends."

14. McQueen, "Pastor of Roswell Street Baptist," "mega-church."

15. Rev. Nelson Price, interview by Christopher Sellers, Marietta, Ga., February 13, 2013; V. O. Key and Alexander Heard, *Southern Politics in State and Nation* (1949; repr. Knoxville: University of Tennessee Press, 1984), 229–53.

16. Price, interview.

17. "Price Included on Racial Panel," *Marietta Daily Journal*, October 17, 1971, sec. A.

18. While Price and Carter had struck up a friendship in the early seventies, and in the latter's early presidency were "prayer partners," by time Carter was running for reelection they had a falling out.

19. Nelson Price, "God Is Only Source Sufficient to Creation," *Marietta Daily Journal*, March 15, 1970, sec. A.

20. Price, interview.

21. Nelson Price, "Evolution Is Only Hypothesis—No More," *Marietta Daily Journal*, March 22, 1970, sec. A; Nelson Price, "Fossil Data Weakens Theory of Evolution," *Marietta Daily Journal*, April 15, 1970, sec. A.

22. Nelson Price, "Evolution Is Only Hypothesis"; Nelson Price, "Creationist Theory Gains New Credence," *Marietta Journal*, February 20, 1972.

23. Price, interview.

24. Nelson Price, "Walking Does Give One Spiritual Boost," *Marietta Daily Journal*, August 19, 1973, sec. A.

25. Susan Miles, "After 23 Years, Prices Move to Dream Home," *Marietta Daily Journal*, January 12, 1979, sec. A; Susan Miles, "Price Can Take Look at History from Home on Pine Mountain," *Marietta Daily Journal*, January 12, 1979, sec. A; Cathy Cleland-Pero,

"Artist Profiles Mountain from Many Angles," *Atlanta Journal-Constitution*, September 8, 1994, sec. G.

26. Nelson Price, "Cross-Country Tour Finds Youth Polarized," *Marietta Daily Journal*, June 14, 1970, sec. A.

27. Price, interview.

28. Nelson Price, "ERA Sounds Good, But What Does It Do?," *Marietta Daily Journal*, January 20, 1974, sec. A ("matriarchal," "50% of the money"); Tom W. Rice and Diane L. Coates, "Gender Role Attitudes in the Southern United States," *Gender and Society* 9, no. 6 (1995): 744–56; Laura M. Moore and Reeve Vanneman, "Context Matters: Effects of the Proportion of Fundamentalists on Gender Attitudes," *Social Forces* 82, no. 1 (2003): 115–39.

29. Nelson Price, "Abortion Is a Complex Issue," *Marietta Daily Journal*, September 28, 1980.

30. Pat Kinney, "Teen Pregnancy: Problem in Cobb," *Marietta Daily Journal*, June 19, 1980, sec. B; Donna Espy, "'Love Life' Seeks to Offer an Alternative to Abortion," *Marietta Daily Journal*, May 18, 1985, sec. A.

31. Nelson Price, "Taking a Look at Our Do-Your-Own-Thing Society," *Marietta Daily Journal*, December 2, 1979, sec. A.

32. "Dr. McDonald Recognizes Three Smyrna Members," *Marietta Daily Journal*, April 13, 1973, sec. A.

33. Kristina Marie Graves, "Stop Taking Our Privileges! The Anti-ERA Movement in Georgia, 1978–1982" (master's thesis, Georgia State University, 2006); Rick Beene, "Cobb Women Joining in Capitol 'Stop ERA' Bid," *Marietta Daily Journal*, January 1, 1977, sec. A.

34. Mary Duckworth, "Mothers on the March Strive to Preserve Unity of the Family," *Augusta Chronicle*, August 23, 1979, sec. A.

35. Mothers on the March, "Day of Intercession for the Unborn," advertisement, *Marietta Daily Journal*, October 5, 1980, sec. A ("4,200 babies").

36. Nelson Price, "A Father's Responsibility," *Marietta Daily Journal*, June 26, 1977, sec. A.

37. Price, "Taking a Look"; Nelson Price, "Don't Let America's Dream Die," *Marietta Daily Journal*, March 16, 1980, sec. A.

38. Nelson Price, "Don't Weaken under Spectrum of Scarcity," *Marietta Daily Journal*, December 9, 1973, sec. A; Nelson Price, "It's No Longer Business as Usual," *Marietta Daily Journal*, July 22, 1979, sec. A.

39. Nelson Price, "Hoping That the Future Is Good to Human Beings," *Marietta Daily Journal*, November 9, 1980, sec. A.

40. Rie L. Carnes, "Banquet Cook Starts Preparation in Advance," *Marietta Daily Journal*, February 6, 1980, sec. C ("sportsmen," "piece of game"); Carnes, "For Hunters Feed: Chef Roasts Ram, Boar," *Marietta Daily Journal*, February 6, 1980, sec. C.

41. Steve Cook, "Killing Animals Is Appalling," letter to the editor, *Marietta Daily Journal*, February 12, 1980, sec. A; Price, "Abortion Is a Complex Issue"; Nelson Price, "Our Influence for Good Can Change the World," *Marietta Journal*, April 5, 1981.

42. Leon Kirkland, "Game and Fish," *Outdoors in Georgia* 9 (June 1979): 11–13.

43. Rebecca Reetz, "Gun Control Issue Is Hot One in Cobb," *Marietta Daily Journal*, January 13, 1976 ("hot issue"); "Crime Tagged as Atlanta's Problem," *Marietta Daily Journal*, February 5, 1975; J. B. Stoner, "Stoner Warns against Gun Control Bills," *Marietta Journal*, March 1, 1976; Barry King, "Legislator Demands Probe of National Rifle Association," *Atlanta Constitution*, January 12, 1978.

44. Nelson Price, "A Break in the Labor Action," *Marietta Daily Journal*, September 2,

1979, sec. A; Price, "Spelling Was Bad but He Got Results," *Marietta Daily Journal*, April 8, 1974, sec. A.

45. Nelson Price, "Give Labor Day Thanks for Labor," *Marietta Daily Journal*, September 1, 1974, sec. A; Price, "Inventory Your Work Attitude," *Marietta Daily Journal*, August 31, 1980, sec. A.

46. Nelson Price, "Some Thoughts on Worry," *Marietta Daily Journal*, March 9, 1979, sec. A; Price, "Don't Let America's Dream Die" ("resolute"); Price, "Now Is the Time to Jog America's Short Memories," *Marietta Daily Journal*, November 11, 1979, sec. A.

47. Nelson Price, "A Principle of Science," *Marietta Daily Journal*, July 16, 1978 ("temple"); Price, "Gallup Pollsters Take Up an Important Question," *Marietta Journal*, January 27, 1980.

48. Nelson Price, "Queen of the Sciences," *Marietta Daily Journal*, November 12, 1978 ("majored"); Price, "Creationist Theory Gains New Credence," *Marietta Journal*, February 20, 1972 ("scientific fact"); Price, "Principle of Science."

49. Prentice Palmer, "Solons Key on Purse," *Atlanta Constitution*, March 17, 1973, sec. A ("quietly"); "The Big Issues," *Atlanta Constitution*, March 9, 1980; Frank Heflin, "General Assembly Was Correct in Keeping Out of Creation," *Atlanta Constitution*, March 13, 1980 ("most controversial").

50. Susan Miles, "Creation Plus Evolution: Group Calls for 'Equal Time,'" *Marietta Daily Journal*, September 20, 1978, sec. D; Rebecca Reetz, "Creation, Evolution 'Equal Time' Urged," *Marietta Daily Journal*, September 29, 1978, sec. A; Edward J. Larson, *Trial and Error: The American Controversy over Creation and Evolution*, 3rd ed. (New York: Oxford University Press, 2003); Ronald M. Numbers, *The Creationists* (New York: Knopf, 1992).

51. After a reconciled version was passed by the Senate but stood four votes short in the House, amid "air . . . thick with charges of atheism," the House's Democratic leader used a parliamentary maneuver to kill it. "Legislature," *Atlanta Constitution*, March 10, 1980; "Ten Best, Ten Worst Legislators," *Atlanta Constitution*, March 23, 1980.

52. Frederick Clarkson, "Christian Reconstructionism: Theocratic Dominionism Gains Influence," Political Research Associates, March 1, 1994, http://www.politicalresearch.org /1994/03/01/christian-reconstructionismtheocratic-dominionism-gains-influence ("theocratic republics"); Fitzgerald, *Evangelicals*, 339–41 ("theological," "radically anti-democratic"); Rousas J. Rushdoony, *The Institutes of Biblical Law*, vol. 1 (Vallecito, Calif.: Ross House Books, 1973), 524 ("subdue the earth"); Fitzgerald, *Evangelicals*; Julie J. Ingersoll, *Building God's Kingdom: Inside the World of Christian Reconstruction* (New York: Oxford University Press, 2015); Molly Worthen, "The Chalcedon Problem: Rousas John Rushdoony and the Origins of Christian Reconstructionism," *Church History* 77, no. 2 (2008): 399–437.

53. Ingersoll, *Building God's Kingdom*, 167–68; John Hightower, "Atlanta Organization Helps in Promoting Year of the Bible," *Atlanta Constitution*, December 23, 1983; Billie Cheney Speed, "American Vision Says Aim Is to Apply Bible to All of Life," *Atlanta Constitution*, February 5, 1983; Gayle White, "A 'World View' Based on the Bible," *Atlanta Journal-Constitution*, September 26, 1992, sec. E.

54. Herb Schild, "Minister to Run for Congress," *Atlanta Constitution*, August 1, 1985; Rev. Joseph Morecraft III, interview by Christopher Sellers, Cumming, Ga., May 23, 2012.

55. Ingersoll, *Building God's Kingdom*, 184 ("echo chamber"); Speed, "American Vision"; Jim Walls, "Christian Group Plans Nationwide Campaign," *Atlanta Constitution*, October 23, 1980 ("political textbook," "research in American history"); Kathey Alexander,

"Focus On: American Vision," *Atlanta Constitution*, July 5, 1994; Gary DeMar, *Ruler of the Nations: Biblical Blueprints for Government* (Forth Worth, Tex.: Dominion, 1987), 30 ("decentralization"); White, "World View" ("democratic process," "mob rule").

56. Nancy Ammerman, *Baptist Battles: Social Change and Religious Conflict in the Southern Baptist Convention* (New Brunswick, N.J.: Rutgers University Press, 1990), 128–42, 146–49; Fitzgerald, *Evangelicals*, 366 ("rapid modernization").

57. "National Environmental Scorecard Archive," League of Conservative Voters, 2012, https://scorecard.lcv.org/scorecard/archive.

58. Richard F. Fenno, *Congress at the Grassroots: Representational Change in the South, 1970–1998* (Chapel Hill: University of North Carolina Press, 2000) (emphasis in original); Earl Black and Merle Black, *Politics and Society in the South* (Cambridge, Mass.: Harvard University Press, 1989), 23–43.

59. Fenno, *Congress at the Grassroots*; Black and Black, *Politics and Society*, 23–43.

60. McGirr, *Suburban Warriors*; Lisa McGirr, "A History of the Conservative Movement from the Bottom Up," *Journal of Policy History* 14, no. 3 (2002): 331–39; Barbara S. Stone, "The John Birch Society: A Profile," *Journal of Politics* 36, no. 1 (1974): 184–97, https://doi.org/10.2307/2129115.

61. Joseph Nocera, "Larry McDonald for the Right, the Far, Far Right," pt. 1, *Atlanta Constitution*, April 20, 1980; Nocera, "Larry McDonald for the Right, the Far, Far Right," pt. 2, *Atlanta Constitution*, April 27, 1980.

62. G. Edward Griffin, Edward, *The Fearful Master: A Second Look at the United Nations* (Boston: Western Islands, 1964), http://archive.org/details/TheFearfulMaster.

63. Darren J. Mulloy, *The World of the John Birch Society: Conspiracy, Conservatism, and the Cold War* (Nashville: Vanderbilt University Press, 2014); Randle Joseph Hart, "The Truth in Time: Robert Welch, the John Birch Society and the American Conservative Movement, 1900–1972" (PhD diss., University of Toronto, 2007), https://tspace.library .utoronto.ca/handle/1807/120481; Schoenwald, *Time for Choosing*; McGirr, *Suburban Warriors*; Stone, "John Birch Society"; Alan F. Westin, "The John Birch Society: Fundamentalism on the Right," *Commentary* 32, no. 2 (1961): 93–104.

64. "Core Principles," John Birch Society, accessed January 21, 2019, https://www.jbs .org/about-jbs/core-principles.

65. Allen Rutledge, interview by Christopher Sellers, Powder Springs, Ga., February 11, 2013.

66. Rutledge, interview; Jim Stewart and Paul Lieberman, "McDonald's Records Subpoenaed," *Atlanta Constitution*, April 1, 1977, 13 ("hunting").

67. Rutledge, interview ("true author"); David Secrest, "Morecraft Challenges Darden to a Series of Weekday Debates," *Atlanta Constitution*, October 16, 1986 ("close friend"); Ann Woolner, "McDonald Mourners Warn U.S.," *Atlanta Constitution*, September 16, 1983 ("Christian Republic").

68. Bill Carbine, "Davis vs. McDonald: Incumbent Attacks Birchers; Challenger Sees 'Sickness,'" *Marietta Daily Journal*, July 24, 1972, sec. A; Carrol Dadisman, "Congress Foes Unleash Attacks," *Marietta Daily Journal*, July 30, 1972.

69. Bill Carbine, "McDonald Confident as Race Hits Stretch," *Marietta Daily Journal*, August 2, 1972, sec. A.

70. "Dr. McDonald Recognizes"; Dee Bryant, " ERA Deprives Women—McDonald," *Marietta Daily Journal*, August 28, 1973, sec. A.

71. Frederick Burger, "McDonald Hits Davis' Record," *Marietta Daily Journal*, July 25, 1974, sec. A.

72. "OSHA: An Unwieldly Bureaucratic Agency," *Marietta Daily Journal*, August 25, 1974, sec. A.

73. Larry McDonald, "Where I Stand," advertisement, *Marietta Daily Journal*, June 23, 1974, sec. A; Ruth Schuster, "Davis Running a Quiet Low-Key Campaign," *Marietta Daily Journal*, August 11, 1974, sec. A.

74. McDonald, "Where I Stand"; Schuster, "Davis Running."

75. Frederick Burger, "Demos Outspend Republicans," *Marietta Daily Journal*, August 5, 1974, sec. A.

76. "7th District: Cobb, Conservatives in Saddle," *Marietta Daily Journal*, August 14, 1974, sec. A; Frederick Burger, "McDonalds Campaign Draws Devoted Helpers," *Marietta Daily Journal*, October 20, 1974, sec. A.

77. Burger, "Demos Outspend Republicans."

78. Burger, "McDonalds Campaign Draws"; Nocera, "Larry McDonald for the Right," pt. 2, p. 203 (figure of 90 percent of households).

79. "7th District."

80. Frederick Burger, "Seventh District Foes Heading to Wire," *Marietta Daily Journal*, November 1, 1974, sec. A.

81. "McDonald Gets Group's 'Yea,'" *Atlanta Constitution*, October 31, 1977.

82. Pat Cariseo, "'Dirty Dozen' Tag Expected," *Marietta Daily Journal*, March 15, 1976, sec. A; Rick Beene, "On Parks: Collins Raps at McDonald," *Marietta Daily Journal*, August 19, 1976, sec. A; "McDonald Sponsors EPA Bill," *Marietta Daily Journal*, February 5, 1975, sec. C.

83. Buzz Weiss, "McDonald Warns: Dope Addicts to Ruin Park," *Marietta Daily Journal*, October 5, 1976, sec. A ("criminal elements"); Henry Eason, "McDonald Reelected; Newt Gingrich Fails to Unseat Rep. Flynt," *Atlanta Constitution*, November 4, 1976; Buzz Weiss, "Collins Gets Backing of Conservation Voters," *Atlanta Constitution*, n.d.

84. Bob Dart, "Straightforward Larry McDonald Keeps Conservative Faith," *Atlanta Constitution*, February 23, 1983; "Rep. McDonald Labels Party Censure 'Illegal,'" *Atlanta Constitution*, February 9, 1978.

85. Oliver A. Houck, "With Charity for All," *Yale Law Journal* 93, no. 8 (1984): 1498–500, 1498 ("to reassert"), 1499 ("little difficulty"), https://doi.org/10.2307/796163. On the sagebrush rebellion, see Turner and Isenberg, *Republican Reversal*; R. McGreggor Cawley, *Federal Land, Western Anger: The Sagebrush Rebellion and Environmental Politics* (Lawrence: University Press of Kansas, 1993); Jacqueline Vaughn Switzer, *Green Backlash: The History and Politics of Environmental Opposition in the U.S.* (Boulder, Colo.: Rienner, 1997); and Jonathan Lash, David Sheridan, and Katherine Gillman, *A Season of Spoils: The Reagan Administration's Attack on the Environment* (New York: Pantheon Books, 1984).

86. "Georgia May Fight Plan to Ban Mirex," *Atlanta Constitution*, December 9, 1976; Craig Hume, "No Warrant, No Look In," *Atlanta Constitution*, August 4, 1977; Turner and Isenberg, *Republican Reversal*.

87. "Georgia May Fight Plan" ("no one has proven"); Naomi Oreskes and Erik M. Conway, *Merchants of Doubt: How a Handful of Scientists Obscured the Truth on Issues from Tobacco Smoke to Global Warming* (New York: Bloomsbury, 2010); David Michaels, *Doubt Is Their Product: How Industry's Assault on Science Threatens Your Health* (New York: Oxford University Press, 2008); David Michaels, *The Triumph of Doubt: Dark Money and the Science of Deception* (New York: Oxford University Press, 2020).

88. Frederick Allen, "Georgia's GOP: Can It Make a Comeback?," *Atlanta Constitution*, November 14, 1977 ("civil rights business," "pachyderm").

89. Black and Black, *Rise of Southern Republicans*.

90. Allen, "Georgia's GOP."

91. "Flynt Fights Off Gingrich Bid," *Marietta Daily Journal*, November 3, 1976.

92. David Osborne, "The Swinging Days of Newt Gingrich," *Mother Jones*, 1984 ("moddish"); Craig Shirley, *Citizen Newt: The Making of a Reagan Conservative* (Nashville: Nelson, 2017); Robert Claxton, *The History of the Georgia Conservancy, 1967–1981* (Atlanta: Georgia Conservancy, 1985).

93. "We Support Gingrich Too," *Atlanta Daily World*, November 5, 1974; John Crown, "Newt Gingrich in the 6th," *Atlanta Journal*, [1974?], box 3, "Precongressional Materials," Newt Gingrich Papers, West Georgia University, Carrollton, Ga. ("conservative"); Kay Brown, "Upsets Possible for Two Incumbents," *Marietta Daily Journal*, October 23, 1974, sec. D.

94. Charles Price, "Contest in Sixth, Unfair?," *Atlanta Daily World*, November 5, 1978.

95. "The Politicians Had Their Chance. Now You Can Have Yours," flyer, 1976; "Newt Gingrich for Congress," flyer, 1976; "Tax Reform Is Possible," flyer, 1976, all in box 3, "Precongressional Materials," Gingrich Papers, West Georgia University ("mess").

96. Robert Claxton to Mark Hatfield, October 29, 1975, box 5, Gingrich Papers, West Georgia University ("groups of people"); Osborne, "Swinging Days of Newt Gingrich"; "Building Newt Inc.: Money and Politics; The Change a 'Flip-Flop' on Business," *New York Times*, February 12, 1995; Crown, "Newt Gingrich in the 6th"; West Georgia Right to Life Chapter, "Pro-life Questionnaire," 1976, folder "W," box 17, Gingrich Papers, West Georgia University.

97. Price, "Contest in Sixth, Unfair?" ("never analyzed"); "The Sixth District," *Atlanta Constitution*, October 29, 1976 ("classic county unit"); Henry Eason, "Flynt Leads Sixth; McDonald Beats Collins in Seventh District," *Atlanta Constitution*, November 3, 1976, 1, 12 ("slick"); Reg Murphy, "Jack Flynt May Be Losing His Race," *Atlanta Constitution*, October 30, 1974); Bead Cutts, "Candidates' Aid Sources Varied," *Atlanta Constitution*, November 5, 1974; Eason, "Flynt Leads Sixth," 12.

98. "Negro Vote Gave Flynt Victory," *Atlanta Daily World*, November 15, 1976.

99. Newt Gingrich, "Newt Gingrich Fund-Raising Dinner," October 29, 1977, box 3, "Precongressional Materials," Gingrich Papers, West Georgia University.

100. Newt Gingrich to Ruby and Charles Hooper, October 27, 1976, folder "Right to Work," box 17, Gingrich Papers, West Georgia University; Jeff Gerth and Stephen Labaton, "The Local Forces That Helped Shape Gingrich as a Foe of Regulation," *New York Times*, February 12, 1995, sec. National Report; "Building Newt Inc."; Gail Sheehy, "The Inner Quest of Newt Gingrich," *Vanity Fair*, September 1995, https://archive.vanityfair.com/article/1995/9/the-inner-quest-of-newt-gingrich.

101. Newt Gingrich for Congress, "Newt Gingrich [versus] Virginia Shephard," 1978, folder "Flyer Issues Comparison," box 23, Gingrich Papers, West Georgia University.

102. Jim Morrison, form letter to sportsmen, August 5, 1978, box 20, Gingrich Papers, West Georgia University.

103. Beau Cutts, "Shapard Calls Flier 'Racist,'" *Atlanta Constitution*, October 31, 1978 ("love welfare"); Newt Gingrich to William Brock, January 24, 1977, box 14; Newt Gingrich to Mister Carlyle, May 18, 1978, box 20, both in Gingrich Papers, West Georgia University ("major effort").

104. Friends of Newt Gingrich, "If You're Worried about Rising Prices, You Need Newt Gingrich," *New Georgia Leader*, June 1978 ("shopping cart"); Friends of Newt Gingrich, "Gingrich Poll: Inflation Number One Concern," August 22, 1978, box 25, Ging-

rich Papers, West Georgia University; Gingrich to Brock, January 24, 1977 ("labor union power").

105. Gingrich to Carlyle, May 18, 1978, West Georgia University.

106. Newt Gingrich to Friend and Supporter, July 6, 1978, box 20, Gingrich Papers, West Georgia University; Gingrich to Carlyle, May 18, 1978, West Georgia University; "Cut Taxes One-Third Says Newt Gingrich: 'Good for You and Good for America,'" *New Georgia Leader*, April 1978; Friends of Newt Gingrich, "We Need a Real Tax Cut," *New Georgia Leader*, Gingrich campaign flyer, April 1978 ("taxpayers," "low income").

107. "Gingrich: Sacrifice Required for 2-Party," *Atlanta Journal and Constitution*, November 19, 1978, sec. B; Newt Gingrich for Congress, "Newt Gingrich [versus] Virginia Shephard."

108. Fingering the "real problem" as "inflation" and "cutting taxes" as the solution, Mattingly also called for "government withdrawal from many areas of our economy." Like Gingrich, Mattingly also ran a more expensive and television-centric campaign than his sixty-seven-year-old opponent. Up against an icon of rustic rule, Mattingly gained an endorsement from the Georgia League of Conservation Voters, and his espousal of tax incentives for inner-city enterprises led the *Atlanta Constitution* to speculate that "his program should appeal to every Black voter." The race was close nevertheless, with Mattingly eking out a victory through his large margins in Georgia's urban and suburban counties. John Crown, "Mattingly: The Problem Isn't Herman," *Atlanta Constitution*, March 29, 1980 ("real problem"); "Mack Mattingly," *Atlanta Constitution*, October 27, 1980 ("government withdrawal," "Black voter"); Carole Ashkinaze, "Mattingly Outruns Talmadge by 22, 008," *Atlanta Constitution*, November 6, 1980.

109. J. David Gopoian, Hobart Smith, and William Smith, "What Makes PACs Tick? An Analysis of the Allocation Patterns of Economic Interest Groups," *American Journal of Political Science* 28, no. 2 (1984): 259–81, https://doi.org/10.2307/2110873; Michael Unseem, "Business and Politics in the United States and the United Kingdom: The Origins of Heightened Political Activity of Large Corporations during the 1970's and Early 80's," *Theory and Society* 12, no. 3 (1983): 281–308; Emily J. Charnock, *The Rise of Political Action Committees: Interest Group Electioneering and the Transformation of American Politics* (New York: Oxford University Press, 2020).

110. Jacob S. Hacker and Paul Pierson, *Winner-Take-All Politics: How Washington Made the Rich Richer—and Turned Its Back on the Middle Class* (New York: Simon and Schuster, 2010); Theodore J. Eismeier and Philip H. Pollock III, "An Organizational Analysis of Political Action Committees," *Political Behavior* 7, no. 2 (1985): 192–216.

111. Tracy Thompson, "'Sanctified': The Staffers Who Influence Rep. Gingrich's Ideas," *Atlanta Constitution*, October 5, 1981.

112. Julian E. Zelizer, *Burning Down the House: Newt Gingrich, the Fall of a Speaker, and the Rise of the New Republican Party* (New York: Penguin, 2020), 35 ("defining theme").

113. Diane Granat, "Perspective: Junior House Republicans Seeking 'Zzazip,'" *CQ Weekly*, November 5, 1983 ("thorn"); Merrill Foote, "Falwell Praises Gingrich, Condemns Abortion at Church Service in Fayette," *Atlanta Constitution*, April 28, 1986 ("great guy").

114. Andrew L. Johns, ed., *A Companion to Ronald Reagan* (Malden, Mass.: Chichester, UK: Wiley-Blackwell, 2015); Doug Rossinow, *The Reagan Era: A History of the 1980s* (New York: Columbia University Press, 2015); Daniel S. Lucks, *Reconsidering Reagan: Racism, Republicans, and the Road to Trump* (Boston: Beacon, 2020); Hacker and Pierson, *Winner-Take-All Politics*; Ronald P. Formisano, *Plutocracy in America: How Increasing Inequal-*

ity Destroys the Middle Class and Exploits the Poor (Baltimore: Johns Hopkins University Press, 2015).

115. Brian Domitrovic, "Gingrich's Connection to the Supply-Side Revolution Confirmed," *Forbes*, January 30, 2012, https://www.forbes.com/sites/briandomitrovic /2012/01/30/gingrichs-connection-to-the-supply-side-revolution-confirmed/; Monica Prasad, "The Popular Origins of Neoliberalism in the Reagan Tax Cut of 1981," *Journal of Policy History* 24, no. 3 (2012): 351–83, https://doi.org/10.1017/S0898030612000103.

116. Clem Richardson, "SCLC Leader Calls for an End to Complacency," *Atlanta Constitution*, November 22, 1981.

117. Henry Eason, "Lowery Endorses Carter, Claims Reagan Drawing Racist Support," *Atlanta Constitution*, October 24, 1980 ("turn back the clock"); Joseph E. Lowery to Friend of Justice, "Voting Rights! Jobs! Peace! Fight Back!," April 21, 1982, box 96, Joseph Lowery Correspondence, series 2, Office of the President Records, Manuscript Collection 1083, SCLC Archives, Emory Manuscripts and Archives, Decatur, Ga.; Edward D. Sargent, "Protest: Demonstrations Staged for Rights, Housing Rights Activists March to Capitol; Housing Protesters Set Up Tent City," *Washington Post*, June 24, 1982, sec. Metro Federal Diary Classified Comics; SCLC, "Resolution on the 'Budget,'" 1984, box 1, series 1, "Board of Directors Records, 1958–2004," Manuscript Collection 1083; SCLC Archives, Emory Manuscripts and Archives ("reduce or abolish," "assault").

118. Lash, Sheridan, and Gillman, *Season of Spoils*; Turner and Isenberg, *Republican Reversal*; Richard N. L. Andrews, *Managing the Environment, Managing Ourselves: A History of American Environmental Policy*, 3rd ed. (New Haven, Conn.: Yale University Press, 2020); Jacob Hamblin, "Ronald Reagan's Environmental Legacy," in Johns, *Companion to Ronald Reagan*, 257–74; Leif Fredrickson et al., "History of U.S. Presidential Assaults on Modern Environmental Health Protection," *American Journal of Public Health* 108, no. S2 (2018): S95–103, https://doi.org/10.2105/AJPH.2018.304396.

119. Newt Gingrich to R. E. Ridley, April 23, 1979, folder "Legis/Environment/General," box 80, Gingrich Papers, West Georgia University.

120. "How Georgia's Delegation Voted," *Atlanta Journal-Constitution*, December 26, 1982; Associated Press, "House Votes to Return EPA to Budget at Pre-Reagan Level," *Atlanta Constitution*, June 3, 1983; Bob Dart, "Gingrich Tells Reagan to Get Rid of Watt for GOP's Sake," *Atlanta Constitution*, September 30, 1983.

121. Jack Brinkley and Newt Gingrich, «A Joint Resolution Designating the Week Beginning July 20, 1980, as 'National Environmental Health Week,'» H.J. Res. 508, 96th Cong. (1980), March 11, 1980, https://www.congress.gov/bill/96th-congress/house-joint-resolution/508?q=%7B%22search%22%3A%5B%22gingrich%22%5D%7D; Ken Kramer and Newt Gingrich, «Energy Production Incentive Act of 1979,» H.R. 5090, 96th Cong. (1979), August 2, 1979, https://www.congress.gov/bill/96th-congress/house-bill/5090?q =%7B%22search%22%3A%5B%22gingrich%22%5D%7D; Edgar Jenkins and Newt Gingrich, "Shale Oil Production Tax Incentive Act of 1979," H.R. 4565, 96th Cong. (1979), June 21, 1979, https://www.congress.gov/bill/96th-congress/house-bill/4565?q=%7B%22search %22%3A%5B%22gingrich%22%5D%7D.

122. Newt Gingrich to Jesse Freeman, June 3, 1979, folder "Legis/Environment/General," box 80, Gingrich Papers, West Georgia University; Gerry E. Sikorski, "Acid Deposition Control Act of 1986," H.R. 4567, 99th Cong. (1986), June 20, 1986, https://www .congress.gov/bill/99th-congress/house-bill/4567. When farmers and other property owners complained about not being able to use certain pesticides, Gingrich commiserated with them and spoke of contemplating "some method, such as the congressional veto

idea . . . to bring all regulatory agencies into a more responsive condition." Newt Gingrich to Ray Newbold, April 11, 1979, folder "Legis/Environment/General," box 80, Gingrich Papers, West Georgia University.

123. David Stockman and Newt Gingrich, "Motor Vehicle Regulatory Improvement Act of 1979," H.R. 5413, 96th Cong. (1979), September 26, 1979, https://www.congress .gov/bill/96th-congress/house-bill/5413?q=%7B%22search%22%3A%5B%22gingrich%22 %5D%7D; League of Conservation Voters, "Representative Newton Gingrich's Environmental Voting Record," *League of Conservation Voters Scorecard* (blog), February 10, 2014, https://scorecard.lcv.org/moc/newton-leroy-gingrich; Wes Watkins and Newt Gingrich, "A Bill to Amend the Clean Air Act to Postpone for One Year the Application of Certain Restrictions to Areas Which Have Failed to Attain National Ambient Air Quality Standards and to Delay for One Year the Date Required for Adoption and Submission of State Implementation Plans Applicable to These Areas, and for Other Purposes," H.R. 1150, 96th Cong. (1979), January 18, 1979, https://www.congress.gov/bill/96th-congress/house -bill/1150?q=%7B%22search%22%3A%5B%22gingrich%22%5D%7D; Bob Traxler, "Mobile Source Clean Air Act Amendments of 1981," H.R. 4400, 97th Cong. (1981), September 23, 1981, https://www.congress.gov/bill/97th-congress/house-bill/4400; James T. Broyhill, "A Bill to Modify the Deadlines Applicable to Hazardous Waste Disposal Facilities Required to Certify Compliance with Certain Financial Responsibility Requirements under the Solid Waste Disposal Act," H.R. 3692, 99th Cong. (1985), November 13, 1985, https://www .congress.gov/bill/99th-congress/house-bill/3692.

124. Osborne, "Swinging Days of Newt Gingrich" ("hard-right").

125. UPI, "'Boring' GOP Image Subject of Meeting," *Atlanta Constitution*, October 30, 1983; Newt Gingrich, *Window of Opportunity: A Blueprint for the Future* (New York: Tor Books, 1984), 99 ("cries to serve the poor").

126. Gingrich, *Window of Opportunity*, 97 ("average person"), 140 ("decentralized"), 111 ("customer-oriented"), 140 ("best mechanisms"), 86, 39 ("elan," "positive"), 34 ("holding tanks").

127. Wendy Parker, "Swindall Contends Heritage Is Being Attacked by Levitas," *Marietta Daily Journal*, November 1, 1984, sec. A; John Buchanan, "Political Issues Should Not Be Tests of Religious Faith," *Atlanta Journal-Constitution*, March 9, 1985, sec. A; Parker, "Swindall Contends Heritage."

128. Swindall courted Christian fundamentalists in his support for a "pro-life" constitutional amendment. He also applied his legislative hand to rolling back the "welfare state" and taxes on the United States' wealthy by pushing a bill to replace the current progressive income tax, in which those with higher incomes paid the greatest share, with a "flat" tax and proposed a sweeping voucher system for public funding of schools including private ones. Frederick Allen, "Unorthodox Pat Swindall," *Atlanta Journal-Constitution*, March 28, 1985, sec. C; Chuck Bell, "Swindall, Maloof Square Off in Unexpected Public Debate," *Atlanta Journal Constitution*, September 5, 1985, sec. A; Frederick Allen, "Cooter's Race in the 4th Will Be Hazardous Duty," *Atlanta Journal-Constitution*, May 18, 1986; Gayle White, "Jones Skips Primary Foes, Attacks Swindall," *Atlanta Journal-Constitution*, July 15, 1986, sec. D; Ben Jones, *Redneck Boy in the Promised Land: The Confessions of "Crazy Cooter"* (New York: Crown, 2008), 190.

129. Swindall was a foe of the Carter Presidential Parkway, which had stirred such controversy in the western part of his district in these years, just as Gingrich publicly advocated on behalf of neighborhoods around Hartsfield International Airport that complained of excessive noise. John Vardeman, "Dole Says Parkway Local Issue, Won't

Withdraw Federal Funding," *Atlanta Journal-Constitution*, April 9, 1985, sec. C; Julie K. Miller, "Residents Say Airport Noise 'Unbearable,'" *Atlanta Constitution*, January 23, 1986; Mike Christensen, "Gingrich, Worley Clash over Social Security in Televised Debate," *Atlanta Constitution*, October 24, 1988.

130. David Pendered, "Swindall Is New 4th District Rep after Upsetting Levitas Last Fall," *Atlanta Journal-Constitution*, May 16, 1985, sec. A; Billy Mallard, "Sierra Club Gives Fowler Good Marks but Finds Fault with Barnard, Gingrich," *Atlanta Journal-Constitution*, March 18, 1986, sec. C; Amy Wallace, "Jones Says Swindall 'Weak' on Environment: Asserts Incumbent's Record Has Endangered Ga. Resources," *Atlanta Journal-Constitution*, September 15, 1988, sec. B ("pocket").

131. David Secrest, "Do Republicans Own Cobb Politically? After Last Week, Looks Like They Might," *Atlanta Constitution*, November 13, 1980.

132. Bert Roughton, "Republican Victories in 'Doughnut' Leave Democrats in the Hole," *Atlanta Constitution*, November 6, 1986 ("doughnut"); Bert Roughton and David Secrest, "GOP Launches Offensive to Gain Ground in Suburbs," *Atlanta Journal-Constitution*, October 12, 1986, sec. D ("ideology").

133. Gail Epstein and Ellie Novek, "Republicans Making Changes in Cobb, Fayette, Gwinnett," *Atlanta Constitution*, March 10, 1985.

134. Roughton and Secrest, "GOP Launches Offensive"; Priscilla Painton and Bert Roughton, "Southside Counties Gung-Ho for Growth," *Atlanta Constitution*, August 19, 1985 ("as close").

135. Alan Gordon, "Both Clayton, Fayette Bustling with Growth," *Atlanta Constitution*, June 1, 1986 ("professionals," "rural flavor," "open spaces"); see also Painton and Roughton, "Southside Counties Gung-Ho"; Keith Graham, "Residents Cherish Their Privacy as Well as Quiet Life; It's Close to Jobs but Still Country, the Citizens Say," *Atlanta Constitution*, June 1, 1986; and Maria Saporta, "Peachtree, Shenandoah: A New Tale of Two Cities," *Atlanta Journal Constitution*, September 21, 1986, sec. M.

136. Painton and Roughton, "Southside Counties Gung-Ho"; Bert Roughton, "Democrat Faces Stiff Challenge," *Atlanta Constitution*, October 12, 1986 ("achieved by working").

137. "David Worley Receives Sierra Club Endorsement in Sixth District U.S. House Race," *Georgia Sierran*, October 1990 ("abysmal," "antics").

138. Gingrich, "Newt Gingrich Fund-Raising Dinner," 3 ("conservative majority").

139. Aaron M. McCright, Chenyang Xiao, and Riley E. Dunlap, "Political Polarization on Support for Government Spending on Environmental Protection in the USA, 1974–2012," *Social Science Research* 48 (November 2014): 251–60, https://doi.org/10.1016/j.ssresearch.2014.06.008; Aaron M. McCright and Riley E. Dunlap, "The Politicization of Climate Change and Polarization in the American Public's Views of Global Warming, 2001–2010," *Sociological Quarterly* 52, no. 2 (2011): 155–94, https://doi.org/10.1111/j.1533-8525.2011.01198.x.

140. Greg McDonald, "Gingrich, Bo Callaway Plan to Head GOP Fund," *Atlanta Constitution*, June 5, 1986 ("few local"); Rhodes Cook, "CQ Roundtable: Can Gingrich Nurture a Georgia Legacy?," *Congressional Quarterly Weekly*, July 1, 1989.

141. Al L. May, "Conservative Likely to Become Senate GOP Leader," *Atlanta Constitution*, April 28, 1989 ("abrasive"); Mike Christensen, "Gingrich's PAC Enlarges His Realm," *Atlanta Constitution*, June 11, 1992; Newt Gingrich, "Language: A Key Mechanism of Control," GOPAC, 1990, https://www.transcend.org/tms/wp-content/uploads/2019/11/Newt-Gingrich-Language-A-Key-Mechanism-of-Control-1990.pdf; Nicole Asmus-

sen Mathew and Mathew Kunz, "Recruiting, Grooming, and Reaping the Rewards: The Case of GOPAC in the 1992 Congressional Elections," *Congress and the Presidency* 44, no. 1 (2017): 77–101, https://doi.org/10.1080/07343469.2016.1263249; Tom Baxter, "What's a Candidate to Talk About? Economy," *Atlanta Constitution*, June 4, 1990 ("socialism").

142. Gerry Yandel, "Talk Radio Realigns Its Forces for Next Battle," *Atlanta Journal-Constitution*, October 14, 1992, sec. B; Jim Auchmutey, "Ragin' Radio: Talk Hosts Are Angry, Callers Are Fired Up and Ratings Are Hot," *Atlanta Journal-Constitution*, February 3, 1993, sec. B; Bo Emerson, "A Voice Not Heard," *Atlanta Journal-Constitution*, November 10, 1994 ("format," "hos," "provocative").

143. Joseph E. Cantor, "Congressional Campaign Spending: 1976–1996," Congressional Research Service, August 19, 1997, https://www.everycrsreport.com/reports/97-793.html, 4.

144. "1989–1990 Election Cycle Data Summaries through 12/31/90," Federal Election Commission, 2019, https://www.fec.gov/resources/campaign-finance-statistics/archive/1991/19910315_Party-24M.pdf.

145. Christensen, "Gingrich's PAC Enlarges His Realm"; "Campaign Finance Data," Federal Election Commission, last accessed September 20, 2022, https://www.fec.gov/data/browse-data/.

146. Scott Bronstein, "Atlantans Hear Jesse Jackson's New Cry for Justice: 'Clean the Air, Clean the Water,'" *Atlanta Constitution*, March 31, 1990; Scott Bronstein, "Robert F. Kennedy Jr. Issues Call for 'Environmental Justice' for All," *Atlanta Constitution*, May 2, 1992; "What Is 'Environmental Racism'?," *Atlanta Constitution*, December 29, 1993; "Who Gets Dumped On?," *Atlanta Constitution*, February 25, 1993; Tony Anaya and Benjamin Chavis, "Race and the Environment: Protecting the Have-Nots," *Atlanta Constitution*, October 27, 1991; Robert D. Bullard, "Victims of Their Environment," *Atlanta Constitution*, January 19, 1995; Scott Bronstein, "'This Is an Issue of Life and Death': EPA Gets an Earful on Alleged Racism in Pollution Policy," *Atlanta Constitution*, September 15, 1992; "Coming Up," *Atlanta Constitution*, June 3, 1992; "Bill before Legislature," *Atlanta Constitution*, February 22, 1993.

147. Rev. Richard Bright, interview by Christopher Sellers, Atlanta, February 6, 2013.

148. Scott Bronstein, "Sewer Plan Critics to Be Heard Today by Council Panel," *Atlanta Constitution*, May 10, 1993; Scott Bronstein, "City Panel Recommends Halting Proposed Combined Sewer Overflow Plant," *Atlanta Constitution*, May 11, 1993 ("small but well-organized"); Mary Louise Kelly, "'Sewer-Separation' Plan Ok'd over Mayor's Veto," *Atlanta Constitution*, July 7, 1993.

149. Julie Hairston, "'Third-World Sewers'; Upscale Buckhead Tires of Manhole Geysers Spewing Sewage," *Atlanta Constitution*, February 1, 1999, sec. F.

150. Associated Press, "Clinton Seeks 'Environmental Justice,'" *Washington Post*, February 12, 1994.

151. Laughlin McDonald, *A Voting Rights Odyssey: Black Enfranchisement in Georgia* (Cambridge: Cambridge University Press, 2003), esp. 211–13.

152. Seth McKee, "Review Essay: The Impact of Congressional Redistricting in the 1990s on Minority Representation, Party Competition, and Legislative Responsiveness," *Journal of Political Science* 32, no. 1 (2004): 1–46; Black and Black, *Rise of Southern Republicans*; John R. Petrocik and Scott Desposato, "The Partisan Consequences of Majority-Minority Redistricting in the South, 1992 and 1994," *Journal of Politics* 60, no. 3 (1998): 613–33; David Lublin and D. Stephen Voss, "Racial Redistricting and Realignment in Southern State Legislatures," *American Journal of Political Science* 44, no. 4 (2000): 792–810, https://doi.org/10.2307/2669282.

153. Charles Walston, "Remap OK Opens Door for Congressional Campaigning," *Atlanta Constitution*, April 4, 1992 ("road to hoe"); "New Congressional Districts and Their Candidates," *Atlanta Constitution*, April 4, 1992 ("both ends"); Rhonda Cook, "Feds' Redistricting OK Sets Up Primaries; Tussles Leave Legislators with Fences to Mend," *Atlanta Journal-Constitution*, April 3, 1992, sec. A; Walston, "Remap OK" ("stronghold").

154. Tom Baxter, "Election Was Mixed Bag for Both Georgia Parties," *Atlanta Constitution*, November 5, 1992 ("real power," "unquestionably").

155. Dick Williams, "Delegation Now Has One White Democrat; Deal's Switch Completes a Chapter of History," *Atlanta Journal*, April 11, 1995, sec. A.

156. "Contract with America," Republican Members of the House of Representatives, 1994, http://www.gvpt.umd.edu/jgloekler/documents/contract.pdf; Dan Freedman, "Blacks to GOP: Don't Abandon Poor," *Atlanta Constitution*, December 29, 1994 ("emergency," "backs of the poor").

157. "Environmentalists Rally," *Atlanta Constitution*, March 22, 1995; Tom Teepen, "A Damaging Environment," *Atlanta Journal-Constitution*, February 21, 1995, sec. A ("swipe").

158. Jay Bookman, "Vicious Assault on EPA," *Atlanta Journal-Constitution*, August 6, 1995, sec. B; Mike Christensen, "Clinton, Senate Stand in Way of Restrictions on EPA," *Atlanta Journal-Constitution*, August 2, 1995, sec. A.

CONCLUSION. Back to the Future?

1. Jim Galloway, "Trump's Id and Kasich's Super-Ego," *Atlanta Journal-Constitution*, February 25, 2016, sec. B ("cult"); "Trump," *Atlanta Journal-Constitution*, June 16, 2016, sec. A, p. 6 ("race never seemed"); Galloway, "Trump's Id" ("political hacks").

2. Lindsey Dillon et al., "The Environmental Protection Agency in the Early Trump Administration: Prelude to Regulatory Capture," *American Journal of Public Health* 108, no. S2 (2018): s89–94, https://doi.org/10.2105/AJPH.2018.304360 ("tidbits"); U.S. Environmental Protection Agency, "EPA Releases Administrator Pruitt's Year One Accomplishments Report," press release, Speeches, Testimony, and Transcripts, U.S. EPA, March 5, 2018, https://www.epa.gov/newsreleases/epa-releases-administrator-pruitts-year-one -accomplishments-report ("cooperative"); Leif Fredrickson et al., "History of US Presidential Assaults on Modern Environmental Health Protection," *American Journal of Public Health* 108, no. S2 (2018): s95–103, https://doi.org/10.2105/AJPH.2018.304396.

3. Zoya Teirstein, "What the Georgia Senate Candidates Think about Climate Change," *Grist* (blog), January 5, 2021, https://grist.org/politics/what-the-georgia-senate -candidates-think-about-climate-change/; James Bruggers, "In Georgia Senate Race, Warnock Brings a History of Black Faith Leaders' Environmental Activism," *Inside Climate News* (blog), December 31, 2020, https://insideclimatenews.org/news/31122020/warnock -Black-church-environmental-justice/.

4. Calvin Kytle and James A. Mackay, *Who Runs Georgia?* (1947; repr. Athens: University of Georgia Press, 1998), 99 ("courthouse rings"); Charles S. Bullock III, Scott E. Buchanan, and Ronald Keith Gaddie, *The Three Governors Controversy: Skullduggery, Machinations, and the Decline of Georgia's Progressive Politics* (Athens: University of Georgia Press, 2015), 29; Dewey W. Grantham, *The Life and Death of the Solid South: A Political History* (Lexington: University Press of Kentucky, 1992).

5. David Anderson, Matt Kasper, and David Pomerantz, *Utilities Knew: Documenting*

Electric Utilities' Early Knowledge and Deception on Climate Change from 1968–2017 (San Francisco: Energy and Policy Institute, July 2017); Greg McDonald, "'Citizens Group' Lobbying against Acid Rain Legislation Really Run by Utilities," *Atlanta Constitution*, September 26, 1986.

6. Ryan Bort, "These Georgia Republican Campaign Ads Are Somehow Not Fake," *Rolling Stone* (blog), July 20, 2018, https://www.rollingstone.com/politics/politics-news /brian-kemp-ads-701456/.

7. James Salzer, "GOP Gains Ground on Core Issues," *Atlanta Constitution*, April 3, 2005, sec. E; Salzer, "Spurning Delta, State Passes Tax Cut," *Atlanta Constitution*, March 2, 2018, sec. A; Jim Galloway, "Tea Party Victory in Fight over Roads, Rail," *Atlanta Constitution*, January 17, 2010, sec. B.

8. Ty Tagami, "Georgia Ranks Near Bottom on School Funding," *Atlanta Constitution*, June 16, 2016, sec. B; Misty Williams, "Federal Money May Entice States to Expand Medicaid," *Atlanta Constitution*, October 25, 2014, sec. A.

9. Paul Donsky, "Transit Agencies May Join Forces; Vote Today Could Lead to Metro Plan," *Atlanta Journal-Constitution*, December 15, 2005, sec. E.

10. James Salzer, "Also at the Capital: Amendment Aims to Keep Fees from Being Diverted," *Atlanta Constitution*, February 23, 2016, sec. A.

11. Samuel Olens, "Olens Urges EPA to Delay Implementation of WOTUS Rule," Office of Attorney General of Georgia, July 29, 2015, https://law.georgia.gov/press -releases/2015-07-29/olens-urges-epa-delay-implementation-wotus-rule; Ariel Hart, "Some Leaders Cool to Global Warming," *Atlanta Constitution*, January 2, 2015, sec. A; Dan Chapman, "Power Plant Ruling Hailed; Ga. Officials Say Carbon Reductions Would Hurt Businesses, Ratepayers," *Atlanta Constitution*, February 11, 2016, sec. A; Adam Liptak, "Chief Justice Won't Block Mercury Limits," *Atlanta Constitution*, March 4, 2016, sec. A; Greg Bluestein, "Climate Change Barges into Governor Race," *Atlanta Constitution*, October 21, 2018.

12. "The AJC Atlanta Project," pt. 3, "Sewers: Mayoral Candidate Views; Kasim Reed," *Atlanta Constitution*, October 3, 2009, sec. A ("shoulder").

13. Dan Chapman, "Partnerships Help Parks Cut Costs, Raise Revenue," *Atlanta Journal-Constitution*, December 28, 2011, sec. B; Joseph G. Martin Jr., "Public-Private Partnerships: Atlanta Style," in *Planning Atlanta*, ed. Harley Etienne and Barbera Faga (Chicago: American Planning Association, 2014), 69–77.

14. Norma Stanley, "National Urban League Addresses the Economy of Black America," *Atlanta Constitution*, January 2, 2009; Christopher Leinberger, *The WalkUP Wake-Up Call: Atlanta*, white paper (Washington, D.C.: George Washington University School of Business, 2013), https://smartgrowthamerica.org/resources/the-walkup-wake-up-call-atlanta/; Federal Reserve Bank of St. Louis et al., "The Homeownership Experience of Minorities during the Great Recession," *Review* 99, no. 1 (2017): 139–67, https://doi.org /10.20955/r.2017.139-67.

15. Andria Simmons, "MARTA's Plans Include Walker-Friendly Villages; Apartments, Shops Could Transform Transit Areas, Boost Ridership," *Atlanta Journal-Constitution*, February 7, 2014, sec. A.

16. Leinberger, *Walk-Up Wake Up Call*.

17. Deborah Dietsch, "Report: Atlanta, Nashville Areas Rated among Worst for Sprawl," *Urban Land Magazine*, April 2, 2014, http://urbanland.uli.org/infrastructure -transit/atlanta-nashville-rated-among-worst-cities-sprawl/; Rebecca Burns, "Atlanta: Highest Rate of Income Inequality in the U.S.," *Atlanta Magazine*, February 21, 2014,

www.atlantamagazine.com/news-culture-articles/atlanta-highest-rate-of-income
-inequality-in-the-us/.

18. Scott Trubey, "Civic Center Sale Sets Stage for Development," *Atlanta Constitution*,
November 22, 2017, sec. A, 10 ("building boom").

19. Tommy Andres, "Divided Decade: How the Financial Crisis Changed Housing,"
Marketplace (blog), December 17, 2018, https://www.marketplace.org/2018/12/17/what-we
-learned-housing/.

20. Alan Berube, "All Cities Are Not Created Unequal," Brookings Institution, February 2014, www.brookings.edu/research/papers/2014/02/cities-unequal-berube; Sarah
Foster and Wei Lu, "Atlanta Takes Top Income Inequality Spot among U.S. Cities,"
Bloomberg, October 10, 2018, https://www.bloomberg.com/news/articles/2018-10-10
/atlanta-takes-top-income-inequality-spot-among-american-cities.

21. Odette Yousef, "State of Black Atlanta Summit Paints Bleak Picture," WABE, 2010,
http://wabe.org/post/state-Black-atlanta-summit-paints-bleak-picture; Robert Bullard,
"Black Atlantans Stranded by Legacy of Inequality," pt. 2, *OpEdNews*, March 27, 2010,
http://www.opednews.com/articles/Black-Atlantans-Stranded-b-by-Robert-Bullard
-100324-319.html.

22. Atlanta Beltline Partnership and Davidson Consulting, *An Atlanta Beltline for All:
Equitable Development Assessment* (Atlanta: Atlanta Beltline Partnership, 2014), https://
saportakinsta.s3.amazonaws.com/wp-content/uploads/2014/09/Equitable-Development-
Assessment_FINAL-VERSION.pdf ("Beltline's inequity story"); Alexander Garvin,
"Atlanta's Beltline: The Emerald Necklace Shaping the City's Future," in Etienne and
Faga, *Planning Atlanta*, 204–16; David Pendered, "BeltLine: Construction Returns as
Advisory Group Ponders Equity Issues," *SaportaReport* (blog), February 25, 2013, http://
saportareport.com/beltline-construction-returns-as-advisory-group-ponders-equity-issues/.

23. Christopher Leinberger, "'Hotlanta' Isn't What It Once Was," *Atlanta Journal-
Constitution*, January 26, 2012, sec. A.

24. Leon Stafford, "Housing Concerns Grow along Beltline," *Atlanta Constitution*,
May 22, 2017, sec. A; Ernie Suggs, "Gentrification Wave Hits Historic Atlanta," *Atlanta
Constitution*, May 12, 2019, sec. A ("boutiques"); Bill Torpy, "What Reynoldstown's 50-50
Split Says about Idea of 'One Atlanta,'" *Atlanta Constitution*, January 11, 2018, sec. B.

25. Stafford, "Housing Concerns Grow along Beltline"; Trubey, "Civic Center Sale Sets
Stage."

26. "Atlanta Air Quality Worsened, Finds 2018 'State of the Air' Report," *Gwinnett Citizen Newspaper*, April 21, 2018, https://gwinnettcitizen.com/local-news/4008-atlanta-air-
quality-worsened-finds-2018-state-of-the-air-report; Aaron Gould Sheinin, "Region Meetings EPA Standard for Air Quality," *Atlanta Constitution*, June 3, 2017, sec. A; "New Air
Quality Report Finds Georgia's Short-Term, Ozone Pollution Worsened, Year-Round Pollution Improved," American Lung Association, April 18, 2018, https://www.lung.org/local
-content/_content-items/about-us/media/press-releases/state-of-the-air-2018-ga.html;
Nedra Rhone, "Deeper Findings: Five Metro Atlanta Counties Earn a Failing Grade for
Air Quality," *Atlanta Journal Constitution*, April 24, 2019, https://www.ajc.com/news/five
-metro-atlanta-counties-earn-failing-grade-for-air-qualityC6Csmoq45khlpJMACqocKM/.

27. U.S. Environmental Protection Agency, *Atlanta's Proctor Creek: Making a Visible
Difference* (Atlanta: Environmental Protection Agency, Region 4, 2015); Marshall Lati-
more, "Proctor Creek Greenway: Mayor Opens First Phase of Greenway," *Atlanta Voice*,
May 18, 2018; Nedra Rhone, "Citizens Help Fill Gaps in Water Quality Monitoring,"
Atlanta Constitution, November 4, 2018, sec. B; Na'Taki Osborne Jelks, "Combined Envi-

ronmental and Social Stressors in Northwest Atlanta's Proctor Creek Watershed: An Exploration of Expert Data and Community Knowledge" (PhD diss., Georgia State University, 2016); Katie Leslie, "Millions in Fixes Fail to End Sewer Woes," *Atlanta Journal Constitution*, January 23, 2014, sec. A.

28. Katie Leslie, "Reed Makes His Case in Paris," *Atlanta Constitution*, December 5, 2015, sec. A; Stephanie Stuckey, "Sustainability Work Helping Put Atlanta at Forefront in U.S.," *Atlanta Constitution*, April 23, 2016, sec. A; Keisha Lance Bottoms, "Why Cities Must Lead the Way to Cleaner Air," *HuffPost*, January 25, 2018, https://www.huffpost .com/entry/why-cities-must-lead-the-way-to-cleaner-air_n_5a677295e4b0e56300742179.

29. "The Partisan Divide on Political Values Grows Even Wider," *Pew Research Center for the People and the Press* (blog), October 5, 2017, https://www.people-press.org/2017 /10/05/the-partisan-divide-on-political-values-grows-even-wider/; "Climate Change, Russia Are Partisan Flashpoints in U.S. Views of Global Threats," *Pew Research Center for the People and the Press* (blog), July 30, 2019, https://www.people-press.org/2019/07/30/climate-change-and-russia-are-partisan-flashpoints-in-publics-views-of-global-threats/; Daniel T. Rodgers, *Age of Fracture* (Cambridge, Mass.: Belknap, 2012); Yuval Levin, *The Fractured Republic: Renewing America's Social Contract in the Age of Individualism* (New York: Basic Books, 2016); Kevin M. Kruse and Julian E. Zelizer, *Fault Lines: A History of the United States since 1974* (New York: Norton, 2019).

30. Saurabh Datar, "Map: Watch as Georgia's Racial and Ethnic Changes Unfold," AJC, 2017, https://www.ajc.com/news/state—regional/map-watch-georgia-racial-and -ethnic-changes-unfold/UWVTVqmkLK9wU9DC6jv6KL/; Jim Galloway, "Power Changed Hands in Cobb and Gwinnett, Too," *Atlanta Constitution*, November 15, 2020, sec. B.

31. Steve Fraser, *The Age of Acquiescence: The Life and Death of American Resistance to Organized Wealth and Power* (New York: Little, Brown, 2015); Jefferson Cowie, *The Great Exception: The New Deal and the Limits of American Politics* (Princeton, N.J.: Princeton University Press, 2016); Robert J. Gordon, *The Rise and Fall of American Growth: The U.S. Standard of Living since the Civil War* (Princeton, N.J.: Princeton University Press, 2016).

32. Thomas Piketty, *Capital in the Twenty-First Century*, trans. Arthur Goldhammer (Cambridge, Mass.: Belknap, 2014).

33. "How Does Climate Change Affect Georgia?," *Climate Reality* (blog), September 28, 2018, https://www.climaterealityproject.org/blog/how-does-climate-change-affect -georgia; "Georgia's Climate Threats," States at Risk, accessed June 26, 2019, http://states atrisk.org/georgia.

34. Rene Duff, "Dozens of Cities in Eastern, Southern U.S. Set New Rainfall Records in 2018," AccuWeather, January 2, 2019, https://www.accuweather.com/en/weather-news /2018-leaves-its-mark-in-the-rainfall-record-books-across-eastern-southern-us/70007024.

35. Jeff Masters, "Top U.S. Weather Story of 2007: The Southeast U.S. Drought," Weather Underground, January 1, 2008, https://www.wunderground.com/blog/Jeff Masters/top-us-weather-story-of-2007-the-southeast-us-drought.html; "The Southeast U.S. Drought of 2016: Evolution, Climate Perspectives, and Impacts," Southeaster Regional Climate Center, October 2016, https://sercc.com/SERCC_drought_report _Oct_2016.pdf; Dan Chapman, "This Georgia Drought Bears the Mark of Fire," *Atlanta Journal Constitution*, November 19, 2016, https://www.ajc.com/news/state—regional -govt—politics/this-georgia-drought-bears-the-mark-fire/eoHCaitIKTpBjQCkJ1S0NL/.

36. Solomon Hsiang et al., "Estimating Economic Damage from Climate Change in the United States," *Science* 356, no. 6345 (2017): 1362–69, https://doi.org/10.1126/science. aal4369 ("preexisting inequality").

37. Judith Curry, "Local Warming: Consequences of Climate Change for Atlanta," white paper (Atlanta: Georgia Institute of Technology, 2008), https://curry.eas.gatech.edu /climate/policy.htm; Keith T. Ingram et al., *Climate of the Southeast United States: Variability, Change, Impacts, and Vulnerability* (Washington, D.C.: Island, 2013); Cassandra R. O'Lenick et al., "Evaluation of Individual and Area-Level Factors as Modifiers of the Association between Warm-Season Temperature and Pediatric Asthma Morbidity in Atlanta, Ga.," *Environmental Research* 156 (July 2017): 132–44, https://doi.org/10.1016/j. envres.2017.03.021; "Georgia's Climate Threats"; Rebecca Philipsborn et al., "Health," Georgia Climate Information Portal, October 27, 2020, https://www.georgiaclimate project.org/portal/health/; "How Does Climate Change?"

38. Nedra Rhone, "Weather Disasters in U.S. Cost $45B in 2019," *Atlanta Constitution*, January 11, 2020; Pam Knox, "Georgia Climate Project: What Are the Costs and Benefits of Climate Change to Agriculture?," *Climate and Agriculture in the Southeast* (blog), June 3, 2018, https://site.extension.uga.edu/climate/2018/06/georgia-climate-project-what-are -the-costs-and-benefits-of-climate-change-to-agriculture/.

39. Robert Wilson, "Authoritarian Environmental Governance: Insights from the Past Century," *Annals of the American Association of Geographers* 109, no. 2 (2019): 314–23, https://doi.org/10.1080/24694452.2018.1538767 ("fewer avenues"); James McCarthy, "Authoritarianism, Populism, and the Environment: Comparative Experiences, Insights, and Perspectives," *Annals of the American Association of Geographers* 109, no. 2 (2019): 301–13, https://doi.org/10.1080/24694452.2018.1554393; Stephen Brain, *Song of the Forest: Russian Forestry and Stalinist Environmentalism, 1905–1953* (Pittsburgh: University of Pittsburgh Press, 2011); Yuan Xu, *Environmental Policy and Air Pollution in China: Governance and Strategy* (New York: Routledge, 2020); Barbara Finamore, *Will China Save the Planet?* (Cambridge, UK: Polity, 2018).

40. Jelani Cobb, "William Barber Takes on Poverty and Race in the Age of Trump," *New Yorker*, May 7, 2018, https://www.newyorker.com/magazine/2018/05/14/william -barber-takes-on-poverty-and-race-in-the-age-of-trump; Christian Knox, "Pandemic Sparks Unionization Jolt across Georgia," *Atlanta Civic Circle* (blog), July 21, 2022, http:// atlantaciviccircle.org/2022/07/21/pandemic-sparks-unionization-jolt-across-georgia/; Kendall Glynn, "Labor, Voting Rights Groups Aim to Seize the Moment," *Atlanta Civic Circle* (blog), March 24, 2022, http://atlantaciviccircle.org/2022/03/24/labor-voting-rights -groups-aim-to-seize-the-moment/ ("jolt").

INDEX

Commission on Racial Justice (United Church of Christ), 241

Commissioner of Roads and Revenues (DeKalb County), 33

Committee for the Survival of a Free Congress (conservative group), 274

Committee on Appeal for Human Rights (civil rights group), 80

Commoner, Barry, 250

commons, 22, 315; aerial, 202; aqueous, 86, 88; informal, 218, 224

communism, 131, 272, 291

Community Chest, Atlanta, 50, 52

Community Congress, 152

Community Relations Commission (CRC), Atlanta, 143, 145, 188

compressive capitalism, 5, 78, 209; 1930s–50s, 4–8, 36–40, 93, 163, 258, 303, 305, 313–15; 1960s–70s, 91, 170–71; Black communities and, 8, 46, 51–52, 78, 93, 136, 191; racial boundaries and, 52, 53; white communities and, 8, 73, 93, 111, 191. *See also* capitalism; income and wealth distribution

Confederacy, 1–3, 28, 33, 122, 133

Congress, U.S., 31, 61, 124, 186, 204

congressional districts: Eleventh, 295; Fifth, 48, 175, 186, 245, 249, 295; Fourth, 123, 186, 245, 249, 288, 296; Seventh, 270, 272, 274; Tenth, 296

Connolly, Nathan, 62

conservation and preservation: in 1960s, 125, 129–35, 156–58, 160–63; 1970s onward, 165–66, 170, 176–79, 188, 208, 219, 240. *See also* environmental citizenship; environmental movement; parks

conservatism and antistatism, 121, 268; as intellectual movement, 254–55, 266; new fundamentalism and, 259; science and, 266, 276. *See also* business-first citizenship; Evangelical citizenship; Jim Crow citizenship; racial coding

—Democratic: 1900s–1930s, 11, 14, 22, 24, 27–34; 1940s–60s, 9, 30, 33, 73, 98–106, 113; 1970s onward, 249, 254, 266–75

—Republican: 1960s–70s, 11, 129, 276–83; 1980s–90s, 208–9, 234, 245, 249, 253–56, 278–93, 295–99, 303

Conservative Opportunity Society, 286–87

Construction Department, Atlanta, 59

consumer citizenship, 6, 49, 146, 231, 282. *See also* citizenship

consumer voters, 285, 287. *See also* Gingrich, Newt

Contract with America, 287, 298

Corps of Engineers, U.S. Army, 176

Cosby Speers (public housing), 47

Costle, Doug, 199–200

cotton, 41; antebellum, 16; fertilizer for, 24; after World War II, 17

cotton dust, 24, 184, 205–6

Country Bound, 228

Country Club of the South (subdivision), 222

county governments. *See specific counties*

County Parks Department, DeKalb, 75

county unit system, 27–29, 33, 43, 49, 103; undermining of, 70, 108. *See also* rustic rule; voters and voting

courthouse elites. *See* rustic rule; Talmadgism

Coverdell, Paul, 277

Cowie, Jefferson, 51, 82, 136, 321n16

cows, 25, 72, 218

Creek tribes, 16

Crestwood Forest (subdivision), 57

crops, 30, 40, 227, 229–30, 314; nursery, 218–19; sod, 219; sugarcane, 238. *See also* agriculture and agrarianism; cotton

Cumberland Island, 119, 133

Cuyahoga River, 117

Davenport Town, 40

Davidson College (N.C.), 271

Davis, Barbara, 158

Davis, Jefferson, 1

Davis, John W., 129, 270, 272

Dawsonville, Ga., 103, 106

Deal, Nathan, 298, 307

Decatur, Ga., 40, 69, 94, 99, 126, 147–48, 226

Deepdene Park, 147, 150

DeKalb County, 33, 37, 55, 72–75 passim, 94, 145, 222; environmental concerns, 94–95, 99–100, 114, 163, 220; environmentalism in, 73, 76, 228; natural features of, 88, 113, 218; politics of, 74–76, 288, 312; racial composition, 40, 43, 225. *See also* Druid Hills; Mackay, James Edward; Scottdale

Deliverance (film), 164–65, 170

DeMar, Gary, 267

democracy and democratization, 4–5, 91, 108, 303–4, 316; civil rights and, 3, 6–7, 48, 78, 163, 303–4; county unit system and, 70, 108, 123; economic power and, 4–5, 282–83, 298, 310, 317; environmentalism and, 3, 7–8, 86, 108, 120–21, 148, 163, 168, 303–5; Jim Crow and, 27–34, 51, 60, 68–70, 98–106; neoconservative business interests and, 206, 255, 276–77; neoconservative politicians and, 11, 268–76, 282–83, 286–87, 298, 301–3, 312; participatory efforts, 125, 169, 175, 196, 207; peak democracy, 3, 169, 179, 185, 194, 196, 255, 303–5; religious opposition to, 266–67; technocratic governance and, 85, 148, 168–69, 173, 176, 207, 304–5. *See also* civil rights citizenship; conservatism and antistatism; environmental citizenship; neoconservatism; rustic rule; Talmadgism; voters and voting

Democratic Party, Georgia: "Great White Shift" and, 254–55, 268–76, 279, 284–85, 290–99; Jim Crow and, 14–15, 27–34, 42, 48, 108; neoconservatism and, 268–76; state politics and, 30, 166, 268, 275, 304, 308; successes of 1970s and 1980s, 254–55, 277; supporting democratization, 85–86, 108–12, 166–69, 170, 172–75, 185–96, 270. *See also* Carter, Jimmy; Jackson, Maynard; rustic rule; Talmadgism; Young, Andrew

Department of Energy, U.S., 198

Department of Justice, U.S., 296

Department of Natural Resources, Georgia, 219

Department of the Interior, U.S., 129, 285–86

Detroit, Mich., 21, 117, 213, 244

developing world, 6, 36, 38, 87, 89, 117, 211

Dickens, Andre, 308

Dickey, James, 164

Diggs, Charles, 283

Dillard, Morris, 80

direct action: 1950s–60s, 8, 78, 80–83, 137, 140, 143, 186; 1970s, 236, 240–41, 247

diseases: asthma, 314; cancer, 112, 199, 203, 240, 251, 277, 294; diarrhea and dysentery, 90, 93, 107; gastrointestinal, 107; as general concern, 22, 89, 93, 95, 107, 239–40; hepatitis, 107; malaria, 102, 126; polio, 95; prevention, 61; pulmonary, 24, 184; rabies, 63; tuberculosis, 24, 61–62, 102; typhoid, 26, 90, 93, 95, 107, 115–16. *See also* air pollution; microorganisms; water contamination and pollution

disenfranchisement. *See* voters and voting

Dixiecrat Party, 270

Dobbins Air Force, 112

Dobson, Andrew, 210

dogs, 63, 238

Doraville, Ga., 95, 114, 196, 213

Douglas County, 127, 278, 312

Douglass, Harlan, 26

Dow Chemical (company), 283

Drake, David, 287

Drinking Water Act (U.S.), 200

Druid Hills (neighborhood), 13, 23, 34–35, 43–44, 130, 231–32; Civic Association, 58, 72–73, 76, 147; environmental concerns, 72–73, 147–50, 153; High School, 127; North, 39; Presbyterian Church, 152. *See also* freeways and highways; Mackay, James Edward; *and specific parks*

Duany, Andres, 235

Dubois, W. E. B., 55

Duke University (N.C.), 42

Duluth, 206

Dumping in Dixie (Bullard), 240

Dundee, 213

Dundee Mills, 206

Dunwoody, Ga., 288

Earth Day, 119–20, 188, 259, 294

East Point, Ga., 35, 94, 99

East Point Klan, 31. *See also* Ku Klux Klan in Atlanta

Ebenezer Baptist Church, 13, 45, 47, 65, 80, 302; activism in, 31, 54, 80; *The River Jordan* painting, 83. *See also* King, Martin L., Jr.,; King, Martin L., Sr.

Echols County, 27–28

Eckerd (company), 233

ecology and ecologists. *See* environmental sciences; *and specific ecologists*

economic citizenship, 6, 51, 82; civil rights citizenship and, 51, 82, 137, 211; environmental citizenship and, 247; federal impacts, 185, 197

economic history (field of study), 3, 11

economic inequality, 114, 167, 170–71, 215; Black politicians and, 185–86, 190–92; civil rights movement and, 136, 141, 169, 236–39, 285; environmental movement and, 88, 123, 247; neoconservatism and, 265, 268, 282, 284–85; rural versus urban, 171, 209–10, 215, 305. *See also* cleavage capitalism; compressive capitalism; income and wealth distribution

Economic Opportunity Atlanta, 143–45, 191, 192

economy, southern colonial, 15, 16, 36. *See also* Atlanta, Ga.: economy; economic inequality; income and wealth distribution

edge cities, 10, 212, 225, 235, 305

Edgewood (neighborhood), 151

Edmund Pettus Bridge, 248

education and schools: Black communities and, 50, 58, 138, 144, 173; construction, 33, 144; education levels, 4, 32, 43, 173; privatization, 70, 307; religion in, 255–56, 260, 265–66, 306; Talmadgism and, 70, 75. *See also* buses and busing; racial inequality; segregation

Eggleston Hospital, 68

Eisenhower, Dwight D. (president), 272

elections. *See also* voters and voting

—abolition of all white-primary, 27

—congressional: 1964, 124, 186; 1966, 125, 129, 186; 1972, 189; 1974, 270, 273–74; 1984 and 1986, 288; 1990, 290; 1994, 292, 295, 298–99

—county-level: 1980, 288; 1986, 288

environmental state:

—federal: 1930s–50s, 89, 91, 93, 99, 101–2; 1960s, 106, 108, 125, 133, 144–45, 154–55; 1970s, 9, 159–60, 162–63, 167–68, 177–84, 197–207, 232; 1980s onward, 232, 234, 245, 261, 264, 284–91. *See also* air pollution; parks; water contamination and pollution

—Georgia: 1900–1960, 30–31, 98–106; 1960s, 108–17; 1970s, 163–65, 167–70, 179, 183, 194–96, 203, 208; 1980s, 208, 264, 266–70, 294, 306

Environmental Trust, 294

environmentalism. *See* environmental citizenship; environmental movement

Equal Opportunity Atlanta (EOA), 143–45

Equal Rights Amendment (ERA), 243–44, 261–62, 268, 272–73

Euclid Avenue, 152

Evangelical citizenship, 265–70, 276, 284–88, 291, 298, 305; Bircherism and, 272; business-first citizenship and, 276. *See also* churches and religion

Evangelicals, white, 254–57, 259–60, 263–68, 272–73, 277–79; gender and, 254, 260–65, 272–73; nature and, 258–64 passim; politicians and, 259, 279, 281, 284, 287–88; race and, 259, 262. *See also* churches and religion; Evangelical citizenship

Evans, John, 226

Evans, Walker, 63

exurbs, 224–25, 228, 305, 314

Faber, Daniel, 228

Facebook, 292

factories and manufacturing: aerospace, 36, 211, 213, 257; assembly, 36, 95, 213; auto, 26, 51, 213; capital-intensive, 17, 213; comparative wages, 37, 213; fertilizer, 23–24; foodstuffs, 36, 95, 106; forest products, 36; labor-intensive, 17, 36, 213; processing, 17; textile, 17, 23, 24, 36, 95, 133, 184, 205–6. *See also* jobs; workers; workplace environment and oversight; *and specific industries*

Fair Fight, 302

Fair Labor Standards Act of 1938, 37

Fairburn, Ga., 187

Fairhaven (subdivision), 57

Falk, William, 215

Fallows, James, 117

Falwell, Jerry, 267, 284

Farber, Daniel, 228

farms and farming. *See* agriculture and agrarianism

Faulkner, William, 2

Fayette County, 224, 289

Fayetteville, N.C., 215

Federal Act of 1954, section 221, 67

Federal Aid Highway Act of 1956, 66

Federal Housing Administration (FHA), 39

Federal Reserve Bank, 19, 211–12

Federal Water Pollution Control Act of 1948, 101–2, 110

Federal Water Pollution Control Administration, 160

Feldman, Roberta, 142

Fellowship for Christian Athletes, 263

Fenno, Richard, 270

Fernbank: Forest, 72–73, 131, 147, 150, 156–57; Science Center, 126, 147

financial industry: 1900–1940, 19; 1970, 212–13; 2008, 309; jobs in, 215

financialization, 212–13

First Baptist Church, 257, 278

First Methodist Church, 18

fish and fishing, 90, 127, 170, 219; licenses, 174; pollution and, 101–3, 104, 107; rods, 131

Fisher, Colin, 45

Five Points Pub, 233

Flint River, 16, 110, 176

Flynt, John (congressional representative), 270, 277–79, 280, 283

Forbes, 222, 229, 281

Ford (company), 36, 51

Ford, Gerald, 200, 203

Ford Factory Square, 233

Forrest Avenue, 64

Forsyth County, 157, 163, 220, 225

Fortune 500 list, 212

Forward Atlanta, 17

Foster, Charles, 130

Fowler, Wyche (congressional representative), 245, 249

Fox News, 292

Franklin, Shirley (mayor), 308–9

Freedom Park, 309

freeways and highways: Black communities and, 60, 66, 147; building, 30–33, 65–66, 109, 150, 154, 156, 211; New Deal and, 303; opposition to, 120, 147, 150, 153–56, 177, 188, 190, 192–93; planning of, 61, 70, 146–49, 156, 178. *See also* urban renewal

Freund, David, 35

Friends of the [Chattahoochee] River, 7, 157–58, 162, 179, 190, 243

Fulton County, 19–20, 33, 36, 38, 55; Black communities of, 48, 52, 67; Commission, 104; County Welfare Department, 63; environmental features and concerns, 85, 94, 99, 100, 114,

democracy and democratization; *and specific agencies, departments, politicians, and parties*
Governor's Conference on Transportation, 178
Grady, Henry, 16, 17
Grady-Willis, Winston, 81
Grant family, 19
Grass Roots Congress, 125
Great Compression. *See* compressive capitalism
Great Depression, 13, 33
Great Migration, 49
Great Museum Park, 245
Great Park, 192
Great Raft Race, 161
Great Recession, 311
Great Society, 124–25, 143, 167
Great Speckled Bird, 119, 152
Great White Shift (or "Switch"), 278, 284, 288–89, 291, 296, 308
Greenbriar Mall, 239
Greensboro, N.C., 80
Gregory, Jethro T., 184
Greider, William, 197
Griffin, Marvin (governor), 76–77, 108
Grove Park Civic League, 96
Growth Strategies Commission, Georgia, 252
Gulf of Mexico, 16, 88
guns, politics of control of, 263–64, 268, 272–73, 275, 279, 281
Gwinnett County, 222, 289, 291, 312

Habersham County, 88, 105, 126, 228
Hamilton, Grace Towns, 48–52, 55, 58–59, 66
Hancock County, 173
Hanie, Robert (Bob), 126–31, 133, 158, 175–76, 292
Hannity, Sean, 292
Hapeville, Ga., 40, 188
Harbin, Virginia, 155–56
Harkins, Catherine, 228–30
Harris, Joe (governor), 208
Harris Neck, 240
Harrisburg, Pa., 278
Hartsfield, William (mayor), 32, 51, 53, 56, 70, 80; administration, 52; on "Negro citizens," 59–60
Hartsfield-Jackson Airport, 211, 214, 234, 283, 289
Harvard School of Health, 110
Hastings, Don, 230
Hayden, Dolores, 130
Hays, Samuel, 8, 120, 222
hazardous and toxic wastes: occurrence and over-sight, 112, 203–4, 240–42; politics and activism, 203–4, 210–11, 236, 240–42, 247, 251
Head Start, 143

health departments, 93, 95–96, 100–101; Georgia, 85, 101–5, 109–10, 181
Helms, Charles, 152
Helms County, 164
Henry County, 13, 312
Heritage Foundation, 276
Hickel, Walter, 162
High Museum of Art, 233
Highpoint Apartments, 57
highways. *See* freeways and highways
Hill, C. W., 65
Hill, Gladwin, 85, 90
Hill, Lynn, 129
hinterland, Atlanta's, 17, 34, 36, 42, 230, 305
Hinton, Elizabeth, 143
Hitler, Adolf, 29
Hobson, Maurice, 196
Hogan, A. E., 25
Hohle, Randolph, 140–41, 321n18
Hollywood Road, 115–16
Holtzman, Frank, 232
Home Builders Association, 61
home building and development: 1900s–1930s, 22–25, 32, 35, 38, 60; 1940s–60s, 33, 38–41, 67–68, 72; 1970s–90s, 179, 190, 219, 226–27, 233, 235–36, 309–11; for Blacks, 25, 55, 57, 67. *See also* housing; public housing
homeowners and homeownership, 10, 20–22, 38, 121, 170, 221–26 passim, 303; Home Owners' Loan Corporation (HOLC) and lending, 35, 38, 221; racial comparisons, 19–20, 38, 52, 221–22, 226, 303–4. *See also* racial transition of neighborhoods; segregation
—Black: 1900–1960s, 38, 52; 1970s onward, 225–26, 257; 2008, 309; associations, 190, 238; Atlanta Urban League and 49, 54–56, 66; citizenship and civil rights, 54, 58–59, 78–79; political activism, 190, 192, 196, 238. *See also* Atlanta Urban League; segregation
—white: associations, 43, 58, 72–73, 76, 147–53, 190–92, 233; environmental consumption and, 22, 121, 210, 222–23; politics and activism, 121, 147, 150–53, 190, 192, 204, 288, 315; upper middle-class, 43, 72, 74, 214, 222–23, 289. *See also* segregation
Honeydew Baptist Church, 130
House of Representatives Ethics Committee, U.S., 279
housing: Black politicians and, 185, 187–88, 191–92; codes and enforcement, 25, 62, 64, 67; consumption, 22, 49, 57, 121, 210, 222–36; federal programs and, 35, 38, 60; New Urbanism and, 10, 233–34, 289; racial segregation and, 25, 28,

Marx, Karl, 315
Massell, Sam (mayor), 153–55, 158, 178, 186, 190
mass-transit system, 148, 154, 197. *See* Metropolitan Atlanta Rapid Transit Authority
Mattingly, Mack (senator), 282, 288
Mayo Chemical (company), 201
mayors. *See specific mayors*
Mays, Benjamin, 80
McCammack, Brian, 45
McCartin, Joe, 196
McDaniel Street, 66
McDonald, Larry (congressional representative), 254–55, 268, 270–76; compared with Gingrich, 280, 283–84, 286
McDonnell Aircraft (company), 157
McGill, Ralph, 26
McGirr, Lisa, 271
McGrady, Chuck, 247–48, 252
McKenzie, Kay, 158, 162, 190
McKinney, Cynthia (congressional representative), 295
Meadows, Jan, 192
Mechanicsville (neighborhood), 142
Medicaid, 124, 272, 307
Medicare, 124, 272
Mein Kampf (Hitler), 29
Methodists (Protestant denomination): Black, 27, 237; white, 13, 18, 42, 74, 130, 257
Metropolitan Atlanta Rapid Transit Authority (MARTA), 154–56, 192, 213, 234, 307, 309
Metropolitan Planning Commission (MPC), 55, 56, 58, 101
Mexico, 7, 17
Mexico City, 36, 41
Miami, Fla., 36, 62
microbiome: human, 87; rivers and streams, 87, 89–90, 96, 107, 115–16
microorganisms: *Bacteroides* (bacterial species), 86–87, 89–90; coliform (bacterial species), 311–12; *Salmonella typhi* (bacterial species), 90, 115; *Sphaerotilus* (algal species), 115. *See also* water contamination and pollution
middle class: 1900–1930s, 5, 15, 18–19, 21–22, 38, 303–4; 1940s–60s, 8, 34, 38, 41, 43, 170; 1970s–90s, 10, 209–15 passim, 221, 225, 310, 315; democratization and, 4, 8–9, 303; patrimonial or "new," 17, 19, 38, 43, 126, 310; politicians and, 125, 284–85, 287, 298. *See also* Atlanta, Ga.: economy; homeowners and homeownership; housing; income and wealth distribution; jobs; segregation; suburbs and suburbanization; wages and salaries
—Black, 19, 38, 46–47, 52, 54; 1900–1930s, 19; 1940s–60s, 38, 54, 57, 66, 78; 1970s–90s, 185,

191, 197, 209–15 passim, 221, 225–26, 237–38; civil rights movement and, 8, 50, 54–55, 57, 78, 81–83, 140, 197, 226, 237–38, 241; colleges and, 79–80; environmental movement and, 192, 236–42 passim; greenery and, 7, 54, 79–80, 210, 221–22, 225; neighborhoods of, 39, 54, 66–67, 78–79, 225–26, 237; new environmental regime and, 9, 109; urban renewal and, 65–66
—white: 1900–1930s, 5, 38, 123, 191; 1970s–90s, 209–15 passim, 230–31, 270; Black politicians and, 186, 191; environmental politics, 1960s, 7, 9, 121–26 passim, 135, 147, 157–59, 163, 202; environmental politics, 1970s–80s, 250–51; neighborhoods of, 39, 43–44, 111, 127, 152, 257, 260–61; neoconservative politics, 254, 271–72, 275, 279, 282, 289, 298; new environmental regime and, 9, 109, 111; proto-environmentalism and, 73–74; rustic rule and, 33, 43–44, 70–71, 121, 140, 163
Miller, Alexander, 43
Minneapolis, Minn., 6, 122
Mirex, 276–77. *See also* agriculture and agrarianism
Missouri School of Mines, 158
Mitchell, George, 42, 43
Mitchell, Walter, 223
Montgomery, Ala., 45, 78
Moral Majority, 267
Morecraft, Joseph, III, 267, 272, 288
Morehouse College, 18, 48, 79, 80
Morningside-Lenox Park Association, 148–54, 178, 192
mortality rates, 26, 93, 203
mortgages: federal programs, 34–35, 38; interest rates and, 224; racial barriers to, 34–35, 226
Mother Earth News, 228, 231
Mothers on the March (MOM), 262–63
Mozley Park, 53–54, 56, 72, 79–80
Mud Creek, 105
Mussolini, Benito, 60

Nabisco (company), 222
Nader's Raiders, 117
Nancy Creek, 96, 111, 188
Nash Washington (neighborhood), 144
Nash Washington Neighborhood Service Center, 144
Nashville, Tenn., 18
Nasibitt, John, 286
National Air Pollution Control Administration, 181
National Association for the Advancement of Colored People (NAACP), 31, 47–51 passim,

10, 173, 181; local oversight, 33, 93, 96, 100; microbial versus "microphysicochemical," 87, 95, 102–3, 117, 203; recast as "environmental," 4, 8, 22. *See also* air pollution; diseases; hazardous and toxic wastes; health departments; microorganisms; sanitation; water contamination and pollution

public housing: before 1960, 34, 59, 61, 68–69, 97; after 1960, 47, 138, 145, 191–92, 193, 235

public land, 47, 76, 125, 199, 232, 246, 252. *See also* parks

public transportation, 154–56, 190, 192, 213–15, 307, 309

Public Works Department (Atlanta), 110

R. M. Clayton facility, 91, 97, 120, 157, 161, 163, 182; pollution, to 1960s, 85, 88, 95, 97–98, 107, 116; pollution, 1970s onward, 180, 200–201. *See also* sewage and sewers; sewage treatment plants; water contamination and pollution

racial authoritarianism. *See* authoritarianism, racial

racial coding: Democratic, 268, 274–75; Evangelical, 262, 264; Republican, 254, 281, 286–95 passim, 299, 306

racial inequality: in disease, 26, 93, 240; in education, 79–80, 212, 323n14; in public spaces, 45, 71, 80–81, 123, 138; in wealth, 19–20, 37–39, 305. *See also* civil rights citizenship; civil rights movement; economic inequality; environmental inequality

—in housing: 1900s–1930s, 22–26, 35; 1940s–50s, 38–41, 46–47, 52–54, 57–58, 61–67, 78–79; 1960s, 136–40, 146, 149–53, 158–59; 1970s–80s, 211, 221–27, 233–34, 237–38, 240, 257, 289

—in jobs: 1900s–1950s, 17–18, 27, 37; 1970s onward, 213–15, 225, 289

—in voting: to 1960s, 27–29, 48–49, 53–54, 113, 153; 1970s–90s, 185–86, 248–50, 295–98

racial transition of neighborhoods, 52–54, 57, 225–26, 229, 237–38, 257

Radio Free Georgia, 233

railroads and railyards, 16, 23, 31, 114–15

Ramspeck, Robert, 48

rats. *See* wildlife

Rawls, John, 352n12

Reagan, Ronald (president), 209, 234, 267, 288; corporations and wealthy, 211, 284–85, 285–86; energy and environment, 243, 245–46, 253, 285

Realtors Political Action Fund, 292

Reconstruction: Christian, 266–67, 271, 272; democracy and, 28; downfall, 4, 28–29; as historical benchmark, 31, 49, 185, 207, 253, 298, 307

Reed, Kasim (mayor), 308

regional governance. *See* planning and zoning; *and specific agencies*

Regional Housing Clinic on Urban Renewal, 67–68

Renaissance Park, 47, 233–34

renters and rentals: 1970s onward, 226, 310–11; Atlanta as city of, 20, 226, 310; dispersion of, 20–24, 40; downtown, 61–64, 66, 136–40; white, 20–24, 122, 226, 309–11

—Black, 6, 20, 57, 226–27, 310; associations, 54, 140; geography, 6, 20–24, 61–64, 136–40; politics and activism, 58–59, 140–43, 145, 237, 315. *See also* poor and poverty: Black; slums and slumhood; working class: Black; *and specific neighborhoods*

Republican Party: as anti-environmental, 306–8, 314; in counties, 289; environmental reversal, 252–55, 276, 278–80, 285–86, 290–91, 298; in Georgia, 166, 253, 268, 277, 288; national, 251, 284–85, 289, 313; southern strategy, 253, 281, 298; sweeping South, 254, 291–92

Resource Conservation and Recovery Act, 203

Reynoldstown, 23, 311

Richards, Roy, 281

Rich's (company), 127, 193, 240

Riggins, Darryl, 229

right-to-work laws, 6, 32, 37, 172, 174, 315

River Jordan, The (painting), 83

Rivers, Eurith (governor), 30

Rockdale County, 132, 288, 312

Rockdale Park, 35

Rome, Adam, 94, 168

Roosevelt, Franklin, 14

Roswell, Ga., 220, 227

Roswell Street Baptist Church, 257–60, 263, 266

Rottenwood Creek, 112, 119, 158, 161–62

Royal Knights, 143–44

Ruckelshaus, William, 117, 180

rural in-migration and migrants: agricultural practices of, 25; minimal assets and education, 17; motivations, 37; to northern cities, 20, 50

Rushdoony, Rousas John, 266–67, 271

Russell, Charles, 105

Russell, Richard (senator), 30

rustic rule: in Atlanta area, 31–34, 47, 165; clientelism and, 100, 109, 174, 270; coinage, 4; courthouse elites and, 30, 32, 43, 100, 304; environmental concerns and, 99–100, 106, 128; fall of, 9, 174; Jim Crow citizenship and, 33, 99; New Deal and, 37; opposition to, 42–43, 47–48, 74–75, 165, 171–72, 302; rise of, 27–30, 303. *See also* authoritarianism, racial; county unit system; Jim Crow citizenship; Talmadgism

Rutledge, Allen, 272

Safe Drinking Water Act (U.S.), 200

Sanders, Carl (governor), 7, 86, 108–10, 113, 166–67, 171–72, 177

Sanders, James O'Hear, 70

Sanderson Farms, 240

Sandy Springs, Ga., 158, 267

Sanford, Carolyn, 266

sanitary engineers. *See* Howard, Ralph "Rock"; Owens, Patrick

sanitation: 1900s–1930s, 25–26; 1940s–mid-1960s, 39–41, 87, 91–98, 104, 115–17. *See also* bathrooms; sewage and sewers; water contamination and pollution

—in Black neighborhoods: 1940s–mid-1960s, 39–40, 58–59, 61–64, 93–94, 97–98, 115–17; mid-1960s onward, 136, 144–45, 191–92

—governing: to mid-1960s, 31–32, 64, 93–96, 98–107; mid-1960s onward, 108–18, 144–45, 191–92

Satter, Beryl, 62

Savannah, 215

Savannah River, 117–18

Save Atlanta's Fragile Environment, 294

Save Our Vital Environment (SAVE), 162, 243

Save the River, 159. *See also* Friends of the [Chattahoochee] River

Schiffman, Steve, 267

Schlafly, Phyllis, 262, 263

Schockley, Agnes and William, 39–40

schools. *See* education and schools

Schumacher, E. F., 232

Scientific Atlanta (company), 213

SCLC/Women, 238, 240

Scott, David, 264

Scott, James, 207

Scottdale (neighborhood), 23–24, 40–41, 58, 145; urban renewal and, 94

Scotts Crossing (neighborhood), 97, 145

Sea Island, 230

Seaside, Fla., 235. *See also* New Urbanism

segregation: economic, 225, 260–61; labor markets, 17, 36

—racial, 6, 10, 14–15, 28, 45, 123; Carter and, 171–73; in civil rights and environmentalist relations, 48; civil rights challenges to, 55–58, 80–84; comparisons, 45–46, 53; historical studies of, 6, 147; in housing, 24, 33–34, 52–53, 55, 62–63, 123; legacies and persistence, 123, 136, 211, 225, 235, 259, 310; of parks, 23, 45, 53–54, 56, 71–72, 75–78, 82, 123; in politics, 29, 125; of schools, 28, 53, 75; support for, 26, 33, 52, 66, 108–9, 113, 147, 255; white opposition to, 26, 75, 121, 152, 259; of workplaces, 17, 20. *See also* civil rights citizenship; civil rights movement; racial inequality

septic fringes, 87, 92–93. *See also* bathrooms; sewage and sewers; water contamination and pollution

Sevananda (food cooperative), 232–33

sewage and sewers: in Black neighborhoods, 40, 58, 91–98 passim, 114–16, 293–94, 309, 311; cesspools, 78, 213, 310; construction, 89–91, 95, 96, 100, 102; construction and environmentalism, 119, 158, 159–60; New Deal and, 89, 91; two Chattahoochees and, 96–97, 157, 189. *See also* bathrooms; Combined Sewer Overflows; water contamination and pollution

—problems: 1900–1930s, 26, 89; 1940s–early 1960s, 32, 58, 85–87, 89, 93–94, 96, 97–98; mid-1960s onward, 114–17, 201, 294, 309

sewage treatment plants: Imhoff, 91; primary, to 1960s, 85, 87–91, 94–95, 102, 106–7, 113–16; primary, 1970s onward, 200–201, 203, 294; secondary, 95, 180, 201. *See also* sewage and sewers; water contamination and pollution

Shady Side Park, 247

Shaffer, Joe, 142

shantytowns. *See* slums and slumhood

Shapard, Virginia, 281

Shelton, Kyle, 148, 155, 321n16

Sherman, William, 16, 192

Shermantown, 24

Shipp, Bill, 172

Shoal Creek, 94

Shropshire, Miriam and William, 39–40, 57

Sibley, Celestine, 227–30

Sierra Club: 1960s–early 1970s, 7, 9, 74, 120, 131, 160, 162; mid-1970s–80s, 205, 242–52; politicians and, 249, 283, 289–93, 298

Sierra Club Committee on Political Education (SCCOPE), 248–49, 252

Silent Spring (Carson), 229

Sixth District, 270, 278, 296, 299

slavery: in Georgia, 16; in United States, 5

slums and slumhood, 7, 8; 1900s–1930s, 20, 25, 26, 138–39; 1940s–50s, 40, 46–47, 57, 59–62, 64, 66; in 1960s, 138–39, 142, 144, 151, 153; activism in, 57–59, 66–69, 136–37, 140–46, 196; comparative geography of, 40–41, 68, 332n126; ecology of, 63, 138, 144–45; federal programs in, 143–45; press and, 61–65; redevelopment of, 193–94, 200, 233–34. *See also* civil rights citizenship; civil rights movement; poor and poverty: Black

Smethurst, Lucy Cabot, 123, 127–30

Smethurst, Wood, 127

Smith, Lofton, 206

Smyrna, Ga.: air pollution and, 182, 201; garden clubs, 73–74; housing, 1940s–50s, 39, 41; water pollution and, 95, 111–12

Venable, James, 85

Veterans Administration (VA), 39

Vine City (neighborhood): activism within, 140–43, 145–46, 153; federal programs and, 143–45; living and socioeconomic conditions, 24–25, 115, 136–40, 142–43, 145, 234; Martin Luther King Jr. and, 79, 136–37; rating for mortgage risks, 35; SNCC and, 141–43

Vine City Foundation, 143

Vine City Improvement Association, 140

Vine City Voice, 142

Vinings, Ga., 182

voters and voting: Black, 31, 48–49, 153, 186–90, 248, 295–96; citizenship and, 49; courts and, 70, 108; disenfranchisement, 14, 29, 124; early twenty-first-century challenges to, 4, 316; Jim Crow and, 28–29, 48; redistricting, 124, 186, 249, 291, 296; registration drives, 31, 48, 312; rural, 4, 29; Voting Rights Act of 1965, 124, 129, 238, 279, 285, 312; white, under rustic rule, 32, 41, 113; white conservative, after 1970, 254–55, 272–75, 280–82, 288–89, 296–98; white environmental, 186–90, 249–50; widening electorate, 9, 186, 303, 305. *See also* civil rights citizenship; democracy and democratization; Jim Crow citizenship; rustic rule

wages and salaries: income segregation after 1970, 225; low-wage work, 17, 36–37, 41, 153, 214; in manufacturing, 36, 213; median incomes, 41, 171, 211, 289, 374n9; minimum wage laws, 29, 34, 37, 174, 273; in service industries, 153, 214. *See also* income and wealth distribution; jobs; taxes

—Black: before 1960, 18, 31, 38, 41; after 1960, 171, 214, 237

—white: before 1960, 18, 31, 37, 43; after 1960, 171, 214

Wagner Act, 30, 37

Walden, A. T., 42, 50, 80

Wall Street Journal, 234

Wallace, George (Ala. governor), 113, 166, 172

War on Poverty (U.S.), 124

Ward, Bill, 33, 141

Warnock, Ralph (senator), 302, 316

Warrenton, N.C., 241

Washington Park, 23

waste: animal or fowl, 105; human and organic, 90–91, 95, 102, 201; microbial versus "microphysicochemical," 87; treatment, industrial, 102, 106, 180–81, 201, 203–4, 242. *See also* air pollution; hazardous and toxic waste; landfills and dumps; sewage and sewers; water contamination and pollution

water contamination and pollution: 1900–1960, 89–90, 95–96; 1960s, 85–86, 107, 112–18, 127, 138, 170; 1970s–80s, 121, 188; in Black Atlanta, 97–98, 114–17; environmental groups and, 121, 132; monitoring, 96, 110–12, 114–15, 181, 312; state versus federal control, 113–14, 307; water supply and, 99; wildlife and, 90, 114–15, 219. *See also* chemicals, industrial; microbiome; microorganisms; sewage and sewers

—government oversight of: 1940s–50s, 88, 93–94, 101–6; 1960s, 85–86, 109–13, 116–18; 1970s, 180–81, 200–201, 203–4

—industrial: before 1960, 95–96, 102, 106; 1960s–70s, 112–15, 117–18, 180–81, 203–4

Water Control Board, Georgia, 180

Water Department, Atlanta, 59

Water Lords, The (Fallows), 117–18

Water Pollution Control Administration, U.S., 113

Water Quality Act (Ga.), 125

Water Quality Control Board, Georgia, 110–11, 115, 160, 175–76

water supply, 22, 32–33, 39, 99–103 passim, 208, 314; in Black neighborhoods, 41, 93; in poorer white neighborhoods, 40, 93. *See also* bathrooms; housing; sanitation; water contamination and pollution

Watergate, 277, 282

Watson, Tom, 28

Watt, James, 276, 285–86

wealth: Black versus white, 19, 51, 57; corporate, 43, 103; middle class gaining, 34, 38; "patrimonial," 19–20; political change and, 3–5, 11; upper echelons gaining, 10, 15, 19, 211–15. *See also* income and wealth distribution

Weir, Walter, 102–3, 105

Welch, Robert, 271

welfare: Evangelical criticism, 265, 267; politician criticism, 262, 281, 286–87, 292, 298; programs, 4, 144, 173, 281; "welfare state," 287

welfare department (county), 63, 281

Weltner, Charles L., 129

West Georgia College, 253, 278

West Hunter Baptist, 237

West Nile virus, 220

West Paces Ferry Road, 222

West Side of Atlanta, 23, 53–54, 72, 196, 293; Beltline and, 311; environmental concerns in, 97–98, 114, 138, 181, 203, 242; environmentalism in, 293–94; federal programs and, 144; mass transit in, 154–55; public housing in, 97, 115, 138, 144; racial tensions in, 52–53

Western Lumber (company), 276

Western Pennsylvania Conservancy, 125–26, 129

Western States Legal Foundation, 276
Westside Mutual Development Committee, 53
Westview Cemetery, 181, 242
Weyrich, Paul, 274
WGST-AM, 292
Wharton, Charles, 179
White, Leon, 241
white Evangelicals. *See* Evangelicals, white
white flight: 1940s–60s, 33, 186; 1970s onward, 221–22, 229, 244, 255, 257, 305. *See also* racial transition of neighborhoods; segregation: racial
white homeowners and homeownership. *See* homeowners and homeownership: white
White House: Conference on Natural Beauty, 125; Rose Garden, 199
white housing. *See also* homeowners and home-ownership: white; housing; renters and rentals: white; suburbs and suburbanization: white
white nationalism, 2, 28; Confederacy and, 1–2, 28, 33, 76–77
white neighborhoods. *See* freeways and highways; homeowners and homeownership: white; poor and poverty: white; renters and rentals: white; suburbs and suburbanization: white
white renters and rentals. *See* renters and rentals: white
white suburbs. *See* suburbs and suburbanization: white
white supremacy: in Atlanta, 51, 70, 103; citizenship and, 52, 62, 66, 77; in Georgia, 30, 43, 47–48, 113, 167, 173; neoconservatism and, 268; in United States, 2, 315–16. *See also* Jim Crow citizenship; rustic rule; Talmadgism
white upper and upper middle classes. *See* upper and upper middle classes
white voters and voting. *See* voters and voting
whiteness of environmental movement, 3, 48; 1960s, 9, 71, 122–23, 130, 134–36, 157; 1960s freeway revolt, 147, 151; 1970s, 132, 169, 188, 202, 210, 240; 1980s, 243, 251–52, 293
Whole Earth Catalogue, 228, 231
Wiese, Andrew, 40
wildlife: amphibians, 219; chipmunks, 221; crawfish, 219–20; deer, 127, 220; eels, 170; fish, 90, 103, 104, 127, 170, 219; opossums, 127, 220; raccoons, 127, 220; rats, 63–64, 138, 144–45, 188, 191; skunks, 72; squirrels, 72, 127, 220; whales, 170. *See also* birds
Williams, Adam D., 13
Williams, Hosea, 190
Williams, Rhonda, 141
Williams, Willie, 142
Wilmington Ten, 238
Wilson, Robert, 314

Window of Opportunity (Gingrich and Drake), 287
Withers, John, 135
women in politics and activism: antipoverty programs, 144; civil rights, 140, 238–39; environmentalism, 129–30, 151, 158, 181, 247; neoconservatism, 262–63, 266; political exclusion, 43; as politicians, 48–49, 281; proto-environmentalism, 110. *See also* gender
Wood, Roy, 162
Woodhall Creek, 114
Woodward, C. Vann, 5, 329n88
workers: aerospace, 39, 119, 213, 257, 259, 265; factory, 23–24, 213; government, 155, 191, 214; hospitals, 186; New Deal, 36–37; sanitation, 120, 186, 190, 197; textiles, 17, 23, 31, 37, 184, 213. *See also* jobs; labor unions and movements; wages and salaries; working class
Workers Compensation Board, Georgia, 176
working class, 11, 17–21, 213–15, 265, 267–68; Black politicians and, 185–86, 188–89, 190, 249; economic citizenship, 51; white politicians and, 29, 133, 172, 267–68, 274. *See also* economic citizenship; jobs; labor unions and movements; wages and salaries
—Black, 24, 29, 37, 138, 171, 197; activism and politics, 82, 137, 196, 236–37, 239–40, 251–52; neighborhoods of, 23, 25, 82, 185, 207, 252, 304
—white, 28, 30–33, 37, 157–58; neighborhoods of, 23, 31, 39–40, 151–52, 158, 221, 223, 258–59; politics and, 29, 113, 133, 165, 172, 174, 268, 274; rural, 154–56, 170, 172
workplace environments and oversight, 24, 167–68, 175–76, 183–84, 199–200, 205–6; attacks on oversight, 273, 276, 281
Works Progress Administration, U.S., 91
World Congress Center, 250
Worley, David, 290
Wright, Gavin, 34
Wright, Jim, 283
Wyatt, Roy, 230

Yarn, Jane, 162
Young, Andrew (congressional representative and mayor), 169, 185–90, 234–37, 243–54, 274
Young, Evelyn, 237–38
Young, Katie, 144–45
Young, Whitney, 120
Young Men's Christian Association (YMCA), 51
Young Women's Christian Association (YWCA), 54

Zelizer, Julian, 176
zoning. *See* planning and zoning

ENVIRONMENTAL HISTORY AND
THE AMERICAN SOUTH

CPSIA information can be obtained
at www.ICGtesting.com
Printed in the USA
LVHW011202140723
752286LV00002B/306

9 780820 344089